Business Economics

Business Economics

Roger Perman and John Scouller

Department of Economics, University of Strathclyde

OXFORD
UNIVERSITY PRESS

OXFORD
UNIVERSITY PRESS
Great Clarendon Street, Oxford OX2 6DP
www.oup.co.uk

Oxford New York
Athens Auckland Bangkok Bogotá Buenos Aires Calcutta
Cape Town Chennai Dar es Salaam Delhi Florence Hong Kong Istanbul
Karachi Kuala Lumpur Madrid Melbourne Mexico City Mumbai
Nairobi Paris São Paulo Singapore Taipei Tokyo Toronto Warsaw
and associated companies in
Berlin Ibadan

Oxford is a registered trade mark of Oxford University Press

Published in the United States
by Oxford University Press Inc., New York

First published 1999

British Library Cataloguing in Publication Data
Data available

Library of Congress Cataloging in Publication Data
Perman, Roger, 1949–
Business economics/Roger Perman and John Scouller.
p. cm.
Includes bibliographical references and index.
1. Managerial economics. I. Scouller, John. II. Title.
HD30.22.P44 1998 338.5'024'658–dc21 98–37832
ISBN 0–19–877525–3
ISBN 0–19–877524–5 (pbk)

1 3 5 7 9 10 8 6 4 2

Typeset by J&L Composition Ltd, Filey, North Yorkshire
Printed in Great Britain
on acid-free paper by
The Bath Press Ltd, Bath, Somerset

Preface

You are about to embark on what we hope will be an interesting, stimulating, and informative course of study in business economics. Since you have chosen this book the authors have an obligation to give you a brief account of its genesis and its motivation. We will defer telling you what the book contains and how you can use the book to make the most of it until the Introduction below.

The authors have for several years been involved in teaching business economics to postgraduate business school students (chiefly taking the MBA degree programme). The brief given to us by the programme director has been to design a course in business economics that is integrated with, and provides the foundations for, a companion course in business policy. Together we call these General and Strategic Managment.

A conventional microeconomics principles course does not fit this bill, yet we believe strongly that the *analytical approach* taken by economists must remain at the core of any good strategic policy programme. To use some jargon that will be discussed later in the book, one of the core competencies of any good business strategy analyst is the analytical approach used in economics.

This belief has gained some credence in European and American business schools. In recent years the business policy/strategy literature has developed a more rigorous economic foundation but this is not yet apparent in most business economics texts. The text intends to fill this gap. In seeking to do this, the authors have adopted the following principles in writing this book.

- the text should not be unreasonably long, given the time constraints of MBA and similar courses;
- the book should not focus on analytical technique *per se*;
- material covered in business economics courses should be linked to business organization and policy issues studied elsewhere in business school programmes;
- the text should be amenable and attractive to students completely new to economics and to those already familiar with economics.

What makes this Text Distinctive?

Although you may have had little or no exposure to other texts, we believe you will be interested to know what (we hope) makes this text distinctive. First, there is the scope of the book. The text covers the basic analytical principles of economics of markets and business, supply and demand, costs, competition and monopoly, and public policy. But it also incorporates into this presentation of principles a wide-ranging discussion of non-standard issues: the nature and objectives of the enterprise, entrepreneurship, transactions costs, rents, sustainable competitive advantage, corporate architecture, corporate governance, the market for corporate control, diversification, and acquisition.

Secondly, the philosophy of the book is distinctive. Right from the outset we define economics as being about the search for value creation or added value. Thus we look at the market mechanism as a means of co-ordinating the search for value, and the firm as an organization created to search for, exploit, and protect opportunities to add value. Added value or rent generation is designated as the driving force of economic activity, in preference to the more usual idea of profit maximization. This accords well with the current business strategy and business policy literature which is now organized around these concepts.

Thirdly, our text offers a novel and useful outline of macroeconomic issues. At all times, our consideration of macroeconomics is constrained by what is thought to be useful to those interested in business policy. We avoid a convoluted theoretical presentation, using a supply and demand oriented approach which follows on from the techniques studied in the first part of the text. Our view is that managers may find it useful to have some acquaintance with economic forecasting using leading indicators, and so this is included in the text.

Acknowledgements

We thank our wives, Val Perman and Janice Scouller, for their patience during the writing of this book. Virginia Williams did a superb job copy-editing the manuscript, for which we are very grateful. Our thanks also go to Ruth Marshall and her colleagues at Oxford University Press for the efficiency with which they executed the conversion of the manuscript into book form.

Roger Perman
John Scouller

Contents

Introduction

This book is an introduction to the economic analysis of the market system, business organization, and business policy. It is conceived as a course text for business students who need a solid but not excessively theoretical introduction to economic principles and processes along with an introduction to more advanced business policy/strategy material such as competitive advantage and the resource-based theory of the firm.

It is useful to begin by explaining the way the text is structured. There are four parts to the book, corresponding to particular broad areas within business economics. These are:

Part I: The Search for Value, Markets, Consumers, and Firms;

Part II: The Search for Value, Prices, Profits, and the Firm's Competitive Environment;

Part III: The Search for Value, Value Creation, the Scope of the Firm and its Governance;

Part IV: The Search for Value and the Wider Environment of the Firm.

You may be intending to study all these sections, or just a subset of them. We describe below under 'Study Modes' a number of alternative permutations of these sections for the reader who is tightly constrained by time, and wishes to focus his or her studies in particular areas.

The first part, which incorporates Chapters 1 to 5, has the following objectives:

- it defines and explains some fundamental tools of economic analysis;
- it considers the objectives of those engaged in economic activity: that is, individuals as consumers, individuals as suppliers of resources, and individuals as members of firms;
- it analyses the determinants and characteristics of the individual's (and the market) demand for a product;
- it analyses the determinants and characteristics of the firm's (and the market) supply of a product;
- it analyses the way in which market demand and supply interact in the process of market exchange.

In many ways, this section is the most 'conventional' part of the book. However, we often treat conventional questions in relatively unconventional ways. Fundamental to the text is the principle that the fundamental purpose of all economic activity is value creation. Value creation is much written about in business policy, but often without any clear notion of what constitutes value. We establish a precise meaning for this concept right from the beginning, showing both how it is grounded in the standard economic notion of scarcity, but more importantly, also showing what it means for any one firm.

This emphasis on value allows us to define economic mechanisms in a particularly useful way. An economic mechanism is a set of institutions and processes by which choices are made. We can assess alternative types of economic mechanism in terms of the extent to which they facilitate the generation of value. Specialization and exchange turn out to be important because they are mechanisms which can contribute strongly to value creation. For any business, it is not value generation as such but the generation and appropriation of added value which really matters. We explain how added value can be measured at the firm level, and begin to examine how added value can be achieved.

As the dominant economic mechanism at the present time is the market economy, it is essential to begin with an examination of market behaviour. Supply and demand analysis is a principal tool in the economist's tool-box, allowing us to understand the determination of price and the quantity traded in a market, and to see how markets adjust when any of the underlying conditions of supply or demand alters. For the manager developing business strategy, supply and demand (or market) analysis will help to understand the environment in which the firm is operating, and to comprehend the changes that are taking place in that business environment.

The penultimate chapter in Part I investigates the nature, purpose, and the objectives of the firm. We argue that its purpose is to search for, exploit, and protect opportunities to add value. One component of this objective involves keeping down or minimizing costs. In order to provide a framework in which we can address cost minimization, we conclude the part by considering production decisions and the consequences these have for business costs.

Part II contains what many regard as the heart of economic analysis: the extent to which market structures constrain the ability of the firm to add value. What is possibly the key model in economics—the model of perfect competition—examines the nature and implications of a hypothetical state of extreme competition. This is a key economic model because

- from it economists derive their fundamental belief in the social efficiency of competitive markets, a theme we examine in Chapter 13;
- it provides a foundation for the study of the nature and sources of sustainable competitive advantage and for the study of business policy in general, which is the theme of Part III of this book.

At the opposite end of a continuum of possible market structures is the pure monopoly case. It seems reasonable to argue that a single-firm monopoly can only persist over time in the presence of effective barriers to entry. Our emphasis in discussing monopoly is placed, therefore, on the nature and significance of barriers to entry.

Many markets are best described as oligopolies. Here there is what may be called imperfect competition between a small number of rivals which collectively dominate the market. Whilst rivalry is the inevitable outcome of firms searching for a 'competitive advantage' over others, it can also damage the value-generating potential of firms. We shall investigate the nature and implications of oligopoly, putting particular emphasis on how firms may try to manage rivalry. To do this, we make use of some elementary game theory to shed light on strategic behaviour and corporate rivalry.

Part III consists of Chapter 9 to 12. We begin this part by recognizing that firms are intended to be ongoing entities, existing through many periods of time. A firm is an asset, and its owners will be interested in increasing the value of this asset over time—its net present value. Chapter 9 shows how the value of a firm can be thought of as the discounted value of its current and expected future earnings. The concept of present value is used to analyse the capital investment decision of the firm, providing insight into the optimal capital stock of a firm, and so linking back to our analysis of production and costs in Chapter 5. This analysis provides a solid foundation for later chapters in this part which make use of the concept of the value of a business organization.

Each of the remaining chapters in Part III examines how the value-generating potential of a firm is influenced by its *distinctive capabilities*, the *scope* of its activities, and its mode of *governance*. We shall consider extensions to the scope of the firm—that is, diversification, and the processes of mergers and acquisitions through which the scope or scale of the business is changed. The analysis of corporate governance takes us back once again to the issue of business objectives first raised in Chapter 4. We consider the nature and implications of several aspects of the modern business corporation, namely the separation of ownership from control, market power, and the increasing size and complexity of organizations. We examine in particular the nature and implications of managerial objectives, the ability of owners to detect and control managerial actions, incentives for managers, and organizational design. Public ownership and its problems are also examined.

Our ultimate goals in Part III are to see whether there are any generalizations that can be made about the roots of business success and the potential for value-driven growth, and to identify the nature and sources of sustainable competitive advantage.

Part IV contains the final four chapters of the text. In the first of these, Chapter 13, we shift the focus of the analysis from the study of the private search for value by individuals and organizations to consider the legislative, regulatory, and institutional environment in which businesses operate, and by which they are constrained. There are two main themes developed here.

First, the social consequences of the private search for value are not always those that are deemed acceptable to the public or its political institutions. The notion that the private search for value does not necessarily lead to socially desirable outcomes underpins competition policy and anti-trust legislation. We introduce the idea of social efficiency, use this to identify circumstances in which private business behaviour leads to market structures and practices that may be socially inefficient, show how competition policy may be understood in this manner, and then demonstrate the way in which competition policy impinges upon the firm's search for value.

A second way in which the private search for value does not necessarily lead to socially desirable outcomes concerns the environmental impacts of economic activity. We employ the concepts of externalities and public goods to show how wedges may be driven between privately and socially efficient outcomes, and trace the emergence of environmental protection policy—at national and international levels—in response to these environmental impacts. We examine how environmental regulations and controls are likely to evolve in the medium and longer terms, and how these will influence corporate behaviour.

Businesses search for value in the context of a domestic and world economy, the macroeconomic conditions of which are largely outside the control of individual firms. These conditions have important implications for business behaviour, however, and it is important for managers of the firm to have some understanding of the way in which the macroeconomy operates, and to be able to make reasonable predictions about its likely evolution in the near and longer-term future. Chapter 14 introduces the basic mechanisms of the macroeconomy, using a supply and demand framework. Short-term fluctuations in output over business cycles are examined, as are longer-term changes through the process of economic growth. We examine how 'demand-side' policy instruments are used by government to smooth cyclical fluctuations over a business cycle, and how 'supply-side' policies have been used to improve the overall economic efficiency and to pursue more rapid and sustainable economic growth.

Chapter 15 introduces the reader to some simple forecasting techniques. It is important that firms develop some ability to foresee changes in key variables of interest to them in the economic environment. Our goal is to provide managers with a road into and an introduction to this important but rather complex literature.

The final chapter of the book examines the international dimensions of business activity. It is a commonly made observation that we now live and work in a global economy. What does this mean and what implications does it have for business behaviour? It is questions such as these that we address in Chapter 16.

Mathematical Content and Prerequisites

Simple algebra will be the most that is expected of any reader. However, some topics are amenable to succinct exposition using simple calculus, and the technique permits more powerful and general understanding. Accordingly, in a few places, an optional section will present an alternative exposition of an argument using elementary differential calculus. These sections can be missed by those who feel uncomfortable with the technique, or who have no prior knowledge of it.

Studying with this Text

To help you find your way around this book, we have introduced each part with a brief overview of the material it contains, and the theme which unifies each of the chapters. Every chapter also commences with an (often extensive) introduction, setting the scene for what comes in that chapter, and showing you how it is built up. We finish each chapter with a conclusion which gives a very brief reprise of the main concepts covered, and which usually links forward to that which will follow.

Each chapter also contains two other learning devices:

A set of questions for review Some of these are in multiple-choice format, and are intended as a quick check on understanding. Others are discursive and open ended, and are designed to review what you have read and learned. They are best talked through with other people taking your course (although we recognize that this will not always be possible). Some of these questions might also be set for seminar or tutorial group discussion purposes on taught programmes. The answers to these questions are given on the internet (see below for details).

A list of references for further reading Our intention here has been to provide a small number of indicative readings; we recognize that your available study time is short. These recommendations are accompanied by brief comments which should help you in selecting what it is that you wish to pursue at more depth. We have avoided giving what might be called 'more of the same' type suggestions.

Our references are either to more advanced discussions, or to specific applications, as well as to some of the classics in the relevant fields.

Do not forget that many other sources are used throughout the book. Full references to all of these can be found in the bibliography at the end of the book.

What we have *not* done in this text is to provide two other features which are becoming increasingly common: lists of key concepts covered, and bullet-point summaries of central ideas. The text has been written to make these points stand out clearly as they are covered, and we believe they would offer little of added value to the discerning reader. Your time would be better spent in following up one or two recommended further readings.

Internet Support

A set of web pages has been written to support this book. This, we believe, is more useful and more accessible than an instructor's or reader's workbook. It also has the major advantage that it can be readily updated. The Internet address is: http://www.oup.co.uk/academic/Business/busecon.

The web site initially contains the following information:

1. contact addresses of the authors of the book;
2. the answers to the questions at the end of each chapter of the text—or where there is no 'correct answer', some suggestions for incorporation into an answer.

We intend to add to the site in the future, on an ongoing basis:

1. further questions and answers;
2. a complete list of errors in the text that have come to our notice. It is almost certain that in a book of this length, some errors will have crept in at writing and subsequent stages. These will be placed on the web site as and when they are spotted by us, or brought to our attention;
3. a set of useful internet links to other economics and business web sites. We will be pleased to receive readers' suggestions for other links to add to this list.

Study Modes

We have designed this text so that it can form the basis of a variety of different courses, depending on the availability of time and the areas of business economics that you or your course organizer has chosen to focus on. Five permutations are indicated below. With a little imagination, other sensible options can no doubt be found!

A forty-hour complete business economics course: all chapters of this book. You will not be surprised to learn that this is the one we most strongly recommend.

A thirty-hour core course on business economics: Chapters 1 to 12 inclusive but omitting Chapter 3.

A twenty-hour course on business economics: Chapters 1 to 11 omitting Chapters 3 and 9.

A short course on the economics of business policy/strategy: Chapters 1, 2, 4, 5, 6, 10, and 11.

A short course on the business environment: Chapters 1, 2, 13, 14, 15, and 16.

Part I

The Search for Value, Markets, Consumers, and Firms

The fundamental purpose of all economic activity is value creation. In the final analysis, the success of an economic system can be judged by the extent to which it generates value for its citizens. This raises the question of what value actually is; we answer this in the first chapter. Our explanation will show that value is related to resource scarcity. In any economy resources are limited. But the desires, wishes, or wants (you can choose the most appropriate) for goods and services are not limited. So these wishes will constantly outstrip the capacity of the economy to satisfy them. It is the conjunction of limited productive resources and unlimited wishes and wants that creates 'scarcity' in the economic sense.

Whenever a society is confronted by this form of scarcity (which seems to be always!), choices must be made about how the resources are to be used. An economic mechanisms is a set of institutions and processes by which these choices are made. The economic mechanisms of specialization and exchange play important roles in the generation of value.

As the central focus in this text is on the economics of business, it is also necessary to understand what value creation means at the level of the individual firm. More particularly, our attention is given to the *added* value generated by a firm's activities. What this is, how it is achieved, and how it can be measured, are questions we raise for the first time in Chapter 1. However, approaching a full answer to each of these questions will be our objective in the text as a whole, and so they are questions to which we continually return.

The dominant economic mechanism in the present day is that of the market economy. The second chapter provides a preliminary examination of market behaviour. A market consists of the interactions between all the potential buyers and potential sellers of a particular product. We introduce the concepts of the supply and demand for a product, show how the forces of supply and demand interact to determine equilibrium price and quantity traded, and show how markets adjust when one of the underlying conditions of supply or demand alters.

The usefulness of this kind of market analysis is twofold. First, the techniques of supply and demand analysis give us tools which are very powerful and very general. Just as in mathematics we require some general tools that can be used to solve a wide variety of particular problems, so problem-solving in economics requires such tools. Secondly, in the process of developing business strategy, managers need to understand the environment in which they are operating, and comprehend the changes that are taking place in that business environment. Supply and demand analysis can be of great value to managers in developing this understanding.

We have chosen to present our analysis of market behaviour in an intuitive way, avoiding proofs and derivations, and concentrating instead on applications of the ideas. Some readers, however, may wish to see a more careful derivation of the two foundation stones—demand and supply—that we use. Chapter 3 provides this for consumer demand. There we show how an assumption of rational consumer behaviour can be used to provide a very powerful concept of the market demand for a good or service. Note, however, that Chapter 3 is designed to be optional reading. If you are happy with the intuitive approach to demand we have taken in Chapter 2 (and if you are unhappy with technical arguments), you may omit reading Chapter 3 without any loss of continuity. Your lecturer will be able to give you advice on this.

But no such option exists for the 'supply' component. As this is a *business* economics text, it would clearly be inappropriate to omit an investigation of the concept of supply. Furthermore, no analysis of business strategy is possible without a knowledge of business costs. So in Chapters 4 and 5, we investigate business costs and product supply. Our first task is to analyse the nature, purpose, and the objectives of the firm or enterprise. Individuals search for value not only through individual production and exchange but also through joining together and co-operating with other individuals to create coalitions of specialized resource owners called firms or enterprises. In Chapter 4, we seek an understanding of the precise nature of these organizations and their objectives. Our conclusion from this will be that the purpose of the firm is to search for, exploit, and protect opportunities to add value; one might say that the rest of the text is concerned with exactly how firms go about this!

The last chapter in this first part of the book is concerned with the problem of keeping down or minimizing costs. We analyse the relationship between production and costs in both the short run—where the firm faces a capacity constraint arising from its previous capital investment choices—and the long run—where the firm is free to use whatever amounts it chooses of any productive input that maximizes its value-adding opportunities. We show how costs depend on the scale of output, the scope of the firm's activities, and the accumulated total of output of a good that it has produced at any particular point.

1 Economic Activity and Value Creation

Introduction

Section 1.1 of this chapter introduces some fundamental concepts of economics, and demonstrates their relevance to the operation of market economies. The concepts we consider are:

- limited resources and unlimited wants;
- scarcity;
- choice;
- resources and resource allocation;
- opportunity cost;
- value and added value.

We show that resources are *scarce* because any society's capacity to satisfy wants is less than total individual wants. Therefore, *choices* have to be made about the way resources are used. Any choice will incur an opportunity cost. When alternative ways of achieving a particular goal are available, rational behaviour implies selecting the option which minimises opportunity cost. This leads us to the idea of *value*. Economic activity can be thought of as driven by the search for value.

Having established the *objective* of economic activity, we turn in the second section of the chapter to consider some of the *means* by which value can be generated. Three concepts are explained and illustrated:

- specialization;
- comparative advantage;
- exchange and trade.

Our central thesis is that specialization according to comparative advantage and the process of exchange are means by which value is created.

Section 1.3 introduces the idea of *economic mechanisms*. An economic mechanism is a set of institutional arrangements through which the search for value is organized, co-ordinated, and regulated. A fundamental objective of mechanism design is the efficient allocation of available resources: that is, making the best possible use of available resources to create value.

The economic mechanism could in principle involve pure exchange among individuals through markets. However the economic mechanism we are all familiar with in modern industrial economies uses a mixture of markets and collective organizations, namely business firms and states. The discussion in this chapter thus serves as an introduction to the main themes of the book: the operation of markets, the firm's search for value, and the role of the state in a private enterprise, market-driven, economy.

1.1 Scarcity and Choice

Resource Scarcity

We begin by examining resource scarcity and its implications. Resources lie at the heart of all economic activity, making production possible and providing the means of satisfying consumer wants. These resources are in most cases scarce, which has implications for all forms of economic decision-making. Consider the household in its role as a consumer of goods and services. Each household has a limited budget which imposes a constraint on its feasible consumption behaviour. The household's resources are scarce, and so households must choose how to use these scarce resources so as to get the highest amount of satisfaction (or value) possible. Secondly, consider business management. A manager has access to a limited quantity of scarce resources. Good management involves using these scarce resources in the way which maximizes the returns to the firm, or in other words which maximizes the amount of value generated and appropriated by the firm. This basic principle also applies at the level of the whole economy.

Definitions of economics are often based on the role of scarcity in economic activity. For example, one conventional definition is that:

Economics is the study of how society decides what, how and for whom to produce.

This definition implies that three types of decision must be made in all economies.

- *What* goods and services (from here on collectively termed 'goods') should the economy produce?
- *Which* techniques should be used in the production of these goods?
- *How* should the economy's output be distributed among its members?

Implicit in this definition, and the three questions which follow from it, is the notion that resources are scarce. The 'what to produce' question would be irrelevant if scarcity of resources did not limit productive potential. Similarly, the 'choice of technique' and 'how to distribute' questions only become relevant in a situation of scarce resources.

A simple way of beginning to appreciate the nature of scarcity is to consider an economy's production possibility frontier (PPF). Consider an economy which has, at some point in time, a fixed amount of productive resources. These resources can be used to produce food (F) or another good that we shall call 'all else' (A). The PPF for this economy is illustrated in Figure 1.1.

The PPF is the locus of all combinations of F and A which can be produced if all the available resources are fully used and combined in efficient ways.[1] For example, resources could be entirely devoted to food production, in which case the point F_1 shows the maximum feasible amount of food. Alternatively, the maximum feasible amount of A is indicated by the point A_1. But people may prefer a mixed bundle of F and A. The points labelled C and D represent two different combinations of A and F, in each case ones which result from using all available resources efficiently.

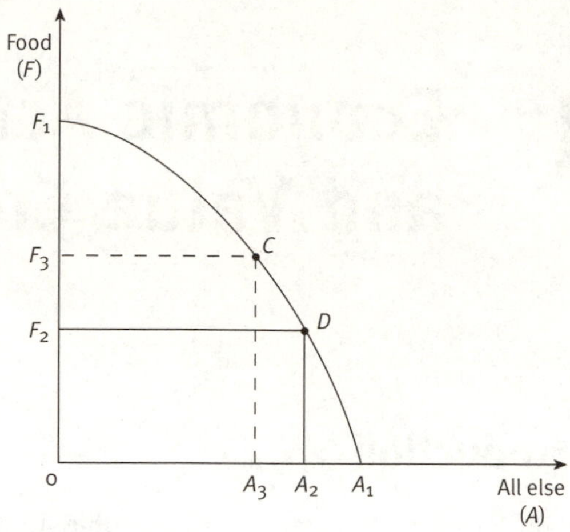

Figure 1.1 An economy's production possibility frontier

All points below and to the left of the PPF are feasible: they can be produced either by not using all resources, and/or if resources are used at less than full efficiency. Points above and to the right of the PPF are not feasible. Given available technology and present stocks of resources, they cannot be produced. Of course, with the passage of time, improving technology and rising stocks of resources will tend to move an economy's production possibility frontier outwards.

The first of our three questions—what goods to produce?—can be thought of in terms of choosing where the economy should be on its PPF. We can see from the PPF that this choice involves trade-offs: for example, moving from C to D the output of A is increased from A_3 to A_2, but at the expense of having less F.

Limited Resources

One of the reasons why resources are scarce is because they are limited or finite. Resources consist of all the primary inputs which are available for production. One simple classification places resources into the following groups:

- land;
- fuel and raw materials;
- labour time;

[1] Loosely speaking, a production technique is 'efficient' if it uses no more resources than necessary to produce some given quantity of output, so that no resources are used wastefully and therefore no opportunities are squandered. A more precise definition of this term is best left until we discuss production costs in Chapter 5.

- entrepreneurship and managerial skills;
- capital.

The fact that each of these resources is available only in finite quantities at any point in time has been true in the past and will remain the case for the foreseeable future. Let us look at land resources. Measured in spatial terms, land is clearly finite and therefore limited. Of course, measuring land resources solely in terms of area is too narrow; fertility, location, and quality also matter. Furthermore, even the area of useful land can be changed by reclamation measures, superior productive techniques, and so on. But, no matter how we choose to define land, its availability at any particular point in time is limited.

This is also true for fuel and raw materials. Stocks of non-renewable resources such as gold, crude oil, and bauxite are finite. What really matters, though, are the proportions of these stocks that are known and which can be extracted given reasonable forecasts about how technological know-how will evolve in the future. As techniques improve and exploration identifies additional sources of these minerals, the quantities available may actually increase (as they have with crude oil and natural gas stocks in European offshore areas, for example). But none of this alters the fact that ultimately there are ceilings on availability set by the finiteness of the resources, and that at any given point available stocks are finite).

Renewable resources (such as fisheries or aquifers) possess a natural growth or regeneration potential. However, because this natural growth is itself limited, it is still appropriate to regard renewable resources as limited in any time period. Moreover, extraction and use today often imply lower availability tomorrow, as is evident for many commercial fish stocks in marine fisheries. A particular class of renewable natural resources—natural energy flows such as solar, tidal, and wind power—warrants special attention. Clearly it is not meaningful to refer to finite stocks of these resources. However, they become useful only after other (limited) resources are applied in harnessing the energy flows.

What about capital, labour, and entrepreneurship? Whilst capital and technology typically accumulate over time, each country will have a finite stock of capital at any moment, imposing constraints on productive potential. Much the same is true of labour and entrepreneurship. Both the quantity and quality of workers and entrepreneurs may grow over time, but at any instant an economy has a more-or-less fixed potential force of workers and managers (subject of course to the qualification that migration may reallocate people between different economies).

Unbounded Wants

The fact that productive resources are limited does not, by itself, imply that they are scarce. We also need to consider the *claims* being made on resources. It is often argued that human wants are unbounded or limitless. This is by no means an uncontroversial view, and there are grounds for arguing that wants are generated, or reflect particular cultural values.

But for our purposes, it is only necessary that the reader accept as a working hypothesis that current human wants and material desires cannot be fully satisfied by available productive capacity, and that this will remain true for the foreseeable future. As even the most affluent economies show little sign of consumer wants having reached a point of satiation, this view seems highly plausible.

Scarcity, Choice and Opportunity Cost

In economics, the term scarcity is used in a special way. Scarcity arises from the conjunction of resource finiteness with unbounded wants. It exists whenever limited resources coexist with unlimited wants. We provide a schematic portrayal of the concept in Figure 1.2. Put another way, scarcity is a consequence of the condition that peoples' wants exceed the capacity to satisfy them. If the means to satisfy wants are scarce then choices must be made about how those resources are used. As we show in the final section of this chapter, a market system is one mechanism through which these choices can be made.

The production possibility frontier showed that choices involve trade-offs. For example, if some scarce resources are allocated to health care, then these resources are no longer available to satisfy other wants such as defence or education. These trade-offs are evident in many countries which in recent decades have enjoyed substantial welfare state provisions but which are now confronted with the consequences of ageing population structures. The shares of public expenditure needed to maintain state-provided welfare services are rising,

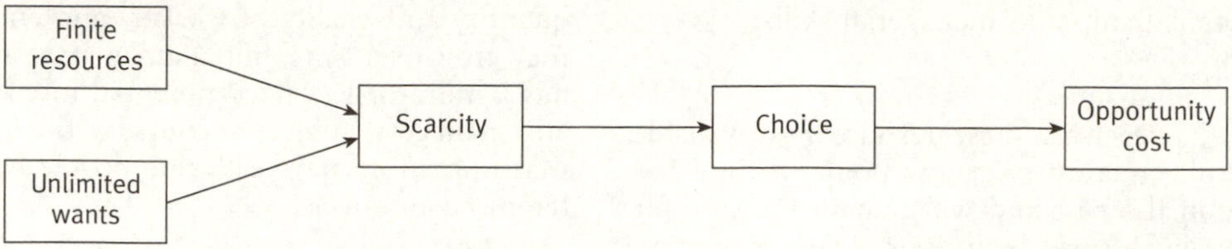

Figure 1.2 Scarcity, choice, and opportunity cost

thereby putting additional pressures on the budgets available for other government activities. Many governments have chosen to switch some parts of welfare provision from the public to the private sector. Note that if taxes are increased to fund additional public expenditures, the trade-offs are not avoided, as private expenditure would be driven down to make way for increased public expenditure.

You will see throughout this book that the concept of *opportunity cost* is fundamental to economic analysis. The opportunity cost of any choice is the most valuable alternative forgone by using resources in a particular way. To illustrate the idea of opportunity cost, and why it might be a useful aid to good decision-making, we consider an example of a woman with farm management skills. She can use these skills in only two ways, either as a self-employed farmer or as a salaried manager on another farm. Table 1.1 lists the various revenues and costs in a given period of time for the two options.

What choice should she make? The accounting profit of using her skills as a self-employed farmer is £1,260, this being the difference between total revenue and those costs given in the accounts shown for the first option. One might argue that as the farm generates positive accounting profits, the option of being a self-employed farmer is a sensible one. Nothing seems to indicate that she should not remain in that business.

But if maximizing the value obtained from using her skills is the woman's objective, then it would be better to be a salaried farm manager. If she does this, her net return would be £1,400 (the salary less travel costs), which exceeds the accounting surplus of the first option. Is there a way in which the information in Table 1.1 could be restructured so as to make her best choice more evident? The answer to this is: yes, costs should be expressed in terms of opportunity costs.

Note that the first option in Table 1.1 does *not* include a figure for the costs of the woman's own management of her farm. But an opportunity cost is incurred in using her time on her own farm. That cost is the income forgone by not working as a salaried farm manager, less the travel costs involved. So the opportunity cost of the woman's time in working on her own farm is £1,400. This cost should also be subtracted from farm revenue in calculating economic profit (as opposed to accounting profit). When this is done, the farm generates an economic *loss* of £140. It is then clear that the first option is not a good one.

Amending the information shown for the second option in an equivalent way, we find that working as a salaried manager on another farm yields an economic *profit* of £140 (that is, the £1,400

Table 1.1 The choice between two uses of farm management skills

First option: Self-employment as a farmer			
Revenue		Costs	
Revenue from sale of goods	£1,500	Seed and fertilizer	£90
		Capital costs	£80
		Hired labour	£70
Total revenue	£1,500	Total costs	£240
Second option: Employment as a farm manager			
Managerial salary	£1,600	Travel costs	£200

accounting net income less an opportunity cost of £1,260 by not working on her own farm). Expressed in this way, the nature of the choice facing the woman is more starkly posed, and it is clear how she should spend her time.

Now one should not try to make too much of this example. It is clearly unrealistic in a number of ways, and it begs a number of important questions (such as how the figure for capital costs was arrived at). Any choice of career is likely to involve far more considerations than our simple example dealt with. Nevertheless, it does illustrate a point of profound consequence: unless costs are properly identified and evaluated, it is all too easy to make poor decisions. We shall have many occasions to return to this principle throughout the book.

Other Applications of the Concept of Opportunity Cost

Economic activity is intrinsically bound up with making choices. Choices are made by individuals in their dual roles as consumers and as producers; by firms in the various facets of their productive activity; and by governments in their taxation and expenditure decisions. Our understanding of opportunity cost can be enhanced by examining the nature of some of these choices.

Individual Choice

Consider someone's choice of desired hours of paid work per week. The opportunity cost of time in work is the value to that person of the forgone leisure time. Similarly, leisure incurs an opportunity cost, as each additional hour of leisure implies a loss of money income. Lower income reduces the quantity of goods that the individual can purchase. The choice of desired hours of work will be shaped by the magnitudes of these two opportunity costs, as we demonstrate in detail in Chapter 3. Matters are of course more complicated when the individual is not *able* to find any paid employment or is not able to work for exactly the number of hours desired. For example, the opportunity cost of leisure time is not equal to the wage rate if no wage could be earned! But this merely reinforces the point that in calculating the true cost of any choice, one must be very careful about specifying exactly what the available alternatives are.

Once an individual's desired work time has been chosen, the wage rate will then determine the amount of earned income (provided the desired amount of work can be found). In any case, once an individual's income has been determined, a further choice has to be made: how to allocate this income between the various competing claims on it. We shall also investigate this area of consumer choice in Chapter 3.

These kinds of analyses can be made richer by more exactly classifying the ways in which time can be used. Suppose that the total time available (after sleep and other necessary biological activities) can be used for leisure, for paid employment, or for domestic production tasks, such as cooking, cleaning, and child rearing. Time spent on domestic production also incurs an opportunity cost, given by whichever of paid employment or leisure is of higher value to the individual.

The spread of higher education and training has meant that, for many individuals, real income from paid employment has increased significantly in recent years. This has been one factor contributing to the increased participation of females in the labour force. However, as people have attained higher real incomes and in many cases devoted more time to paid employment, the value which they attach to their time remaining for leisure has increased.

A consequence of this is that the opportunity cost of domestic production time has risen, inducing searches for ways of reducing the time spent on those tasks. One way is by using durable consumer goods, such as washing-machines and microwave ovens. Technological change has also been a contributory factor here. It is unlikely that the markets for such goods would have developed so rapidly if the opportunity cost of domestic production time had not risen sharply. There have, of course, been many other ways in which individuals have reduced the time which they commit to household production tasks, including the use of crèche and childcare facilities, and the hire of domestic servants.

Managerial Choice about the Development of New Products

The concept of opportunity cost can help us to understand decisions about the development of new products. For example, the motor vehicle manufacturers Volkswagen and Ford both took the decision to phase out an existing model from their product range (the VW Beetle and the Ford

Cortina) at a time when sales of the model were relatively high. The opportunity cost of continuing to devote corporate resources to producing existing models includes the forgone long-term profits expected from taking a lead in product innovation. The benefits of devoting existing resources to existing lines of production are sufficiently evident for us not to need to spell them out here. The decisions to replace the Beetle and the Cortina by new models appear to have been based upon judgements that the benefits from continuing with existing models were outweighed by their opportunity costs. The demise of the UK motor-cycle industry in the 1960s and 1970s might have been much less severe if it had identified these costs and benefits more quickly in the face of growing competition from Japanese firms with innovative and reliable products.

The Concept of Value

The term 'value' has been used several times in this chapter. It is now time to be precise about what it means. In the process, you will see that the term has a variety of meanings. We will demonstrate that one of these—added value—is particularly relevant to an assessment of business performance.

Until the mid-nineteenth century, it was common to assert that the value of a good was a reflection of the labour time embodied in it: the labour theory of value. More generally, one might argue that the value of a good is a weighted sum of the quantities of *all* inputs which are embodied in the good. This might be called a resource input theory of value; the greater is the quantity of embodied inputs, the greater is the value of the output.

At first sight, it seems reasonable to claim that a battle tank made of 20 tonnes of steel is more valuable than one made of 10 tonnes. But a little reflection shows this has serious drawbacks. The most important problem is that value is seen purely from the supply side—it takes no account of whether a big tank is more valuable to its users than a small one. It is most unlikely that a 20 tonne tank is exactly twice as useful as a 10 tonne tank. And one can envisage circumstances in which a small tank would be more useful.

Taking this argument a stage further, a resource input theory of value can lead to the unreasonable conclusion that a good can have value even when no one wants it. A well-known example of this concerns the chronic excess production of some goods that plagued the USSR planning system. In the absence of a price mechanism, output decisions were based upon production targets set by the planning apparatus. Large differences emerged between the patterns of actual and desired output of consumer goods. Under the Soviet materials accounting system, the output value was measured by the quantity of resource inputs employed. Measured output value increased even when the goods produced had no customers. Furthermore, if increased inefficiency led to more inputs being required for the production of some output quantity, this could be measured as an increase in the value of output!

This suggests that we might approach value from the demand side rather than the supply side. In this spirit, value would be measured in terms of the satisfaction that individuals derive from consuming or using a good. Let us call this the use theory of value. From this perspective, value is something which is subjective rather than objective. The value of something is determined by the individual who consumes it. If you purchase and play a music compact disc, its value is given by your subjective assessment of the extent to which it satisfies your wants. If I purchase and play the same disc, the value I attribute to it might be entirely different.

Students or practitioners of marketing and business policy will find such an approach to value both familiar and attractive. These disciplines think in terms of business strategy as a process in which the firm's offering is aligned as closely as possible with the value framework of potential consumers. However, by placing attention exclusively on the demand side and ignoring supply and cost conditions entirely, one might be concerned that 'the baby has been thrown out with the bath-water'.

As it happens, it is not necessary to make a choice between these two conceptualizations of value. The two are mutually consistent, this being brought about through the process of exchange. The way in which this is done will be explained more fully in subsequent chapters, but it will be instructive to briefly sketch out the argument. In a market economy, producers will offer goods at prices denominated in terms of money. Producers seek a price at least equal to the input costs of the commodity. On the other side of the market, consumers are seeking to acquire goods, and will be willing to purchase a good when their subjective valuations of it (expressed in money terms) exceed the good's asking price. A transaction will take place when both parties benefit.

An important property of this process is that when all mutually beneficial transactions have taken price, the equilibrium market price of the good will be equal to both

- consumers' subjective valuations of additional units of the good (expressed in money terms), *and*
- the costs of producing an additional unit of the good.

It is important to be clear that the equality we are referring to here applies to the *marginal* unit of the good, not to all the units bought and sold. For example, if the market is for cans of cola, and 3 million are traded each month, the additional or incremental unit we have in mind is the 3 millionth unit, not any of the previous 2,999,999. The market price—what could be called its exchange value—will thus reflect both types of value we have been discussing *at the margin*. Therefore, it is quite legitimate to think of value from any of the three perspectives. The value of one more or less of a good is the subjective valuation of those who consume it; it is the costs of the inputs embodied in it; and it is given by the rate at which it exchanges for money in markets. A well-functioning price mechanism will drive these measures into line with each other.

To help your understanding of this rather difficult idea, look at Figure 1.3. The curve labelled *D* in panel (*a*) shows a relationship between price and the quantity consumed of cola per period of time. It is a cola market demand curve. This curve shows consumers' willingness to pay for additional units of the good. For example, when 2 million cans have been bought already in one month, someone in the market is willing to pay \$0.5 for one more can. Note that as the quantity consumed rises, the price that consumers are willing to pay for another can falls. The reason why the demand curve is downward sloping will be explained in Chapter 3. At this point we ask you to take this on trust.

Now look at panel (*c*). Curve *S* represents a market supply curve, and it shows the cost of producing additional (or marginal) cans of cola at various rates of total output per period. You can see that it costs \$0.2 to make one more good when the output rate is 2 million units per month. For reasons that we shall explain in Chapter 5, we assume that the cost of producing additional cans of cola rises as the total rate of production gets higher. The equilibrium market price of cola is determined by the interaction of market demand and supply, and is shown in panel (*e*) as \$0.3, at which price 3 million units are traded each month. (A full explanation of what we mean by equilibrium price will be given in the next chapter.)

Now look at panel (*b*). The shaded area under the demand curve between zero and 3 million units of the good shows the total consumers' willingness to pay for 3 million cans per month. (You can think of this area as adding up or 'integrating' the willingness-to-pay (WTP) for each successive unit up to the total of 3 million). As an individual's WTP for a unit of a good is a reflection in money terms of the value he or she places on it, the shaded area can be interpreted as the total use value (or utility as economists sometimes call it) of the 3 million cans of cola. This area is one legitimate way of thinking about and measuring the total value of all the 3 million cans that are traded.

Now consider the area indicated by the upward-sloping hatch lines in panel (*d*). By similar reasoning, this shows the total cost of producing 3 million units of cola per month. It is the sum of the incremental costs of producing the first can, the second can, and so on up to the 3 millionth can. So from an embodied-resource-value perspective, this area denotes the resource value of the 3 million cans of cola.

Let's call the shaded area in (*b*) output value (V_Q) and the shaded area in (*d*) input value (V_I). It is clear that the value of the output of 3 million cans of cola (the value to consumers) is greater than the value of the inputs used in making it (the total cost of the cola). The surplus of output over input value is a measure of the *added value* (*AV*) generated by using resources to produce cola. This added value is represented in panel (*e*) by the horizontally hatched triangular area, *ace*. So we have

V_Q = Value of output = the total use value derived from all units purchased

V_I = Value of inputs = the total cost of producing all units purchased

Added value = value of output − value of inputs

or in symbols

$AV = V_Q - V_I$.

Added value is a gain to the economy as a whole: production is taking place that generates something that is more valuable than the resources used in

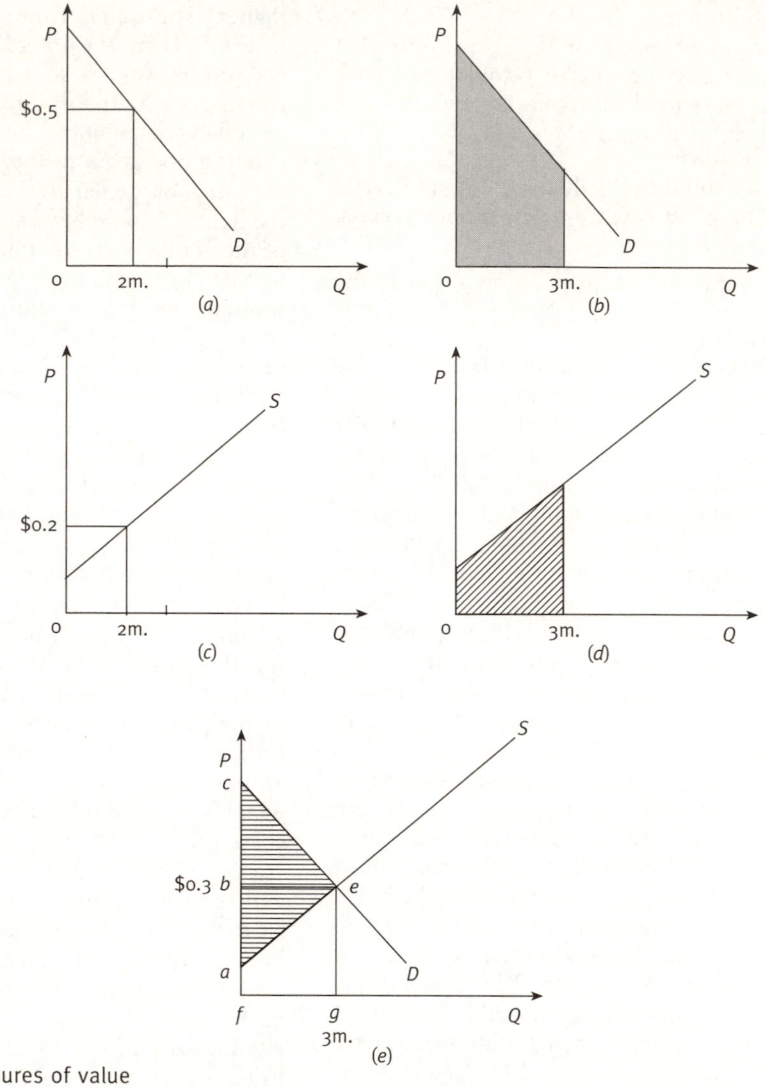

Figure 1.3 Alternative measures of value

making it. But who actually gets this added value—consumers or producers or both? The answer is that the total added value is shared between the two. Consumers obtain a portion given by the area *bce* (known as consumers' surplus). Producers obtain a portion given by the area *abe* (known as producers' surplus). To see why this is so, reason as follows.

Consumers pay a fixed market price of $0.3 for each unit. As they purchase 3 million cans, total expenditure is the area *begf*: price times the quantity bought. But total use value is the larger area, *cegf*. The difference—*cbe*—is consumers' surplus, the portion of added value obtained by consumers. Similarly, producers receive a revenue of *begf* (identical of course to consumers' expenditure). But the total cost of producing 3 million cans of cola is smaller than total revenue by the amount *abe*, the producers' surplus. This is the producers' share of the added value. Not surprisingly, both consumers and producers gain from productive activity and exchange: if they did not both benefit, exchange would not take place. Note that the portions going to each side of the market will depend on the positions and slopes of the *D* and *S* curves. We will have a lot more to say about this in later chapters.

Added Value Looked at from the Point of View of a Single Firm

Our central focus in this book is upon the business sector and its elements: firms. So let us now turn attention to that part of added value which firms receive, the part we have called producers' surplus. It has been argued in this chapter that the principal objective of business activity is to generate value. Now we are in a position to be more precise about this. The fundamental business objective is to add value: to produce output which is more valuable than the inputs it uses and to appropriate as much of that added value as possible.

Is it possible to *measure* the amount of value a single firm adds and appropriates for itself through its economic activities? It is, and we now show how. A firm's added value (or economic profit as we shall also call it) is found from the expression: added value appropriated by the firm (economic profit) = value appropriated by the firm as sales revenue (R) less costs of inputs employed (C):

$$AV\ (= \Pi) = R - C.$$

Before proceeding any further, let us repeat a warning we gave above. It is very important to understand that, in general, the amount of added value a firm can appropriate from its activities is less than the total amount of added value being generated. (We say 'in general' because sometimes it can be done, as in the case of perfect price discrimination: see Chapter 7.) But consumers also get added value. So in referring to a *firm's* added value, it is the area *abe* that we have in mind (that is, economic profit), *not* the total amount of added value *ace*.

C is the sum of the costs of each type of input the firm uses. Inputs can be classified as materials and intermediate (semi-produced) goods, labour inputs and capital inputs. So we can write

$$C = \text{cost of materials} + \text{cost of labour} + \text{capital costs}$$

to obtain

$$\Pi = AV = R - (\text{cost of materials} + \text{cost of labour} + \text{capital costs}).$$

Table 1.2 shows the revenues, costs, and amounts of added value, in millions of ECUs, obtained by two firms in 1990 (Glaxo and the Dutch electrical corporation, Philips) and in 1989 for two divisions of BAT (the tobacco division and the financial services division). The information has been taken from

Table 1.2 Added value for three companies (in million ecus)

	Glaxo	Philips	BAT tobacco	BAT financial services
Revenue	3,895	24,247	12,988	6,734
Material costs	1,528	15,716	8,844	5,647
Wages and salaries	901	7,666	2,354	842
Capital costs	437	2,932	1,065	469
Added value	1,120	−2,067	725	−225

Source: Kay (1993).

Kay (1993), who used data from company annual reports and accounts.

It is interesting to compare added value with some other often-used measures of business 'profitability'. To do so, let us look at Philips. It will be useful to do this in conjunction with Figure 1.4. This shows how various cost deductions from a firm's sales revenue yield different measures of profit. Going from left to right in Figure 1.4, the list of costs being deducted becomes increasingly comprehensive, and so the resulting profitability measure diminishes.

First, subtracting all materials costs from revenue gives a firm's *net output*. This cannot be regarded as a good profit measure as it is so restrictive in the costs which are being accounted for. On this criterion, a firm which uses virtually no material inputs (such as a writer of computer software) would call virtually all of its revenue profit![2]

Operating profit is a commonly used profit measure. It is obtained by subtracting not only materials costs but also wages and salaries from revenue.[3] Despite the popularity of this measure, it is also a flawed measure of profit as no deduction is made for capital costs. But productive activity is not possible without the use of capital, and the acquisition of capital incurs costs. A proper measure of economic profit will subtract all input costs (V_I) from revenue (V_Q). This measure, which we are calling *added value*, is the residual item in the final column on the right-hand side of Figure 1.4.

[2] Given the nature of the output, are these profits *virtual profits*?

[3] In practice, deductions for interest charges are also sometimes made from revenue in arriving at operating profit. But interest charges are more appropriately treated as part of capital costs, as you will see shortly.

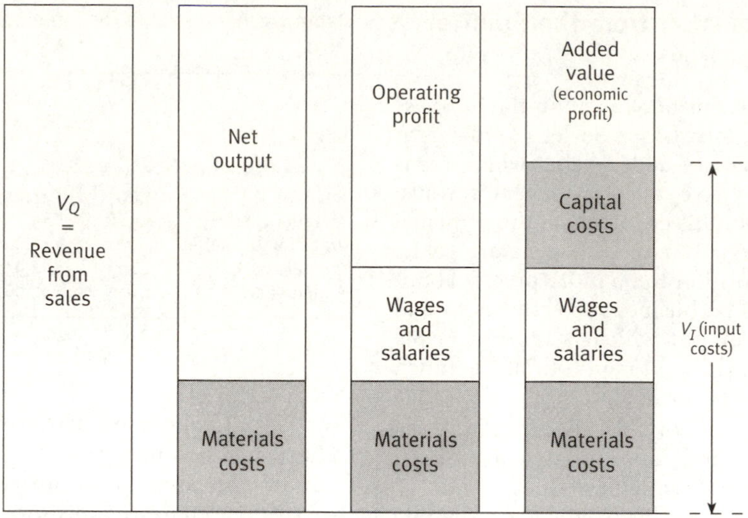

Figure 1.4 Various profitability measures

A potential source of error is confusion of the terms *added value* and *value added*. Readers may be familiar with value added as the principal basis of expenditure taxation in the European Union countries. Value added is not the same thing as added value. The former is the difference between the value of the material and semi-produced inputs which a firm buys in and the value of the output which it sells. It is therefore equal to the firm's net output. Added value is only a part of value added, as Figure 1.4 makes clear. In this book, we make no use of the concept of value added. Our interest is exclusively in added value: it is this latter concept of value which the firm searches for and tries to create and appropriate for itself.

Alternative Ways of Calculating Added Value

To calculate added value in the way we have just shown, a figure for capital costs is required. Capital costs consist of payments the firm makes (or imputes) on the debt and equity components of its capital. Some firms might be able to calculate these directly. Alternatively, capital costs can be thought of as the decrease in value of its capital over the accounting period in question (from wear and tear, depreciation, obsolescence, and other uses of its capital). In some circumstances, this might also be directly measurable.

But it is sometimes the case that capital costs cannot easily be arrived at directly by these routes. However, by using information about the total value of a firm's capital employed together with an average figure for the cost it has to pay in financing each unit of capital, capital costs can be obtained indirectly as:

capital costs = total value of capital employed × cost per unit of capital employed.

The reader must be careful about the meanings of some of the terms we are using. The 'cost of capital' refers to a percentage or proportionate rate the firm has to pay to suppliers of capital to the firm: it is the cost per unit of capital employed. The term 'capital costs' refers to the total amount of money a firm incurs in using its capital. To illustrate, suppose that the total value of capital employed by Philips is 35,102 (in millions of ecus), and that it has to pay on average to its creditors and shareholders a return of 8.353 per cent (0.08353 in proportionate terms) for each unit of capital. Then its capital costs can be calculated as:

capital costs = 35,102 × 0.08353 = 2,932

which is the same figure as shown in the capital costs for Philips in Table 1.2. You will have suspected by now that the accounting necessary to arrive at a measure of added value can be presented in several different yet equivalent ways. We show below two further equivalent ways, using the data for Philips.[4] We have selected these alternatives as they are currently being widely used (and even more widely advocated) as methods of calculating added value. You should work your way through them carefully to convince yourself that they are indeed equivalent to the information shown in Table 1.2.

ALTERNATIVE ONE

Capital employed (K)	35,102
Revenue (R)	24,217
Materials costs (C_M)	15,716
Wages and salaries (C_W)	7,666
Operating profit (OP) = $R-C_M-C_W$	865
Return on capital (r_1) = OP/K	865/35,102 = 0.0246 or 2.46%
Cost of capital employed (r_2)	= 0.0835 or 8.35%
Real return on capital employed $r = r_1 - r_2$	= −0.0589 or −5.89%

Added value (AV) = $K \times r$ = 35,102 × −0.05889 = −2,067

ALTERNATIVE TWO

Capital employed (K)	35,102
Revenue (R)	24,217
Materials costs (C_M)	15,716
Wages and salaries (C_W)	7,666
Operating profit (OP) = $R-C_M-C_W$	865
Cost of capital employed (r_2)	= 0.0835 or 8.35%

Added value (AV) = $OP - (K \times r_2)$ = 865 − (35,102 × 0.083528) = −2,067

Several useful pieces of information can be extracted from these two alternatives. First, although neither explicitly shows the firm's capital costs, these can be calculated from the information shown. For example, using the data in the first alternative, the implied capital costs are given by total value of capital employed × cost per unit of capital employed = $K \times r_2$ = 35,102 × 0.0833 = 2,932. This is the same number as shown in Table 1.2.

Secondly, the amount of a firm's added value can be found as the value of its capital employed (K) times a *real rate of return*; this real return is the rate of return it gets without deducting any charge for capital (r_1) minus the rate it pays in raising its capital (r_2). We show in Chapter 9 that the cost of raising capital will be a weighted average of the interest rate the firm pays on its debt and the return it has to pay holders of its equity.

Added Value and '*Economic Value Added*'

A measure which has become very prominent in the business management literature in the last few years is that of 'economic value added'. Leading consultancy firms are vying with one another in a struggle to get firms to use their own particular brand of business performance measure. The New York consultancy firm, Stern Stewart, which advocates the use of one particular performance measure—economic value added—has even registered *EVA* as a trademark, along with the term *EVAngelist*. Table 1.3 (adapted from *The Economist*, 2 August 1997) shows how Stern Stewart obtains the *EVA* of South African breweries for the year 1996.

By comparing the structure of this table with that

Table 1.3 Added value for South African Breweries

1996 (million rands)	
1. Economic capital = shareholders' equity	5,799
+ goodwill, written off	1,521
+ capitalized cumulative unusual loss	930
+ deferred tax	405
+ minority interests	2,352
+ total debt	4,415
= Economic capital	15,422
2. Net operating profit after tax (*NOPAT*) = operating profit	3,406
+ interest expense	689
− unusual gain	68
− taxes	978
= *NOPAT*	3,049
Weighted average cost of capital (*WACC*) =	17.5%
EVA = *NOPAT* − (Capital × *WACC*) = 3,049 − (15,422 × 17.5%) = 350	

Source: © *The Economist*, London 2 August 1997.

[4] To do these calculations, we also need to know either a value for K, the capital stock, or the 'cost of capital employed', r_2. In fact, the authors do not know either of these and assumed that K = 35,102. (It then follows that r_2 must be 0.083528, as capital costs are the product of the amount of capital employed and the cost per unit of capital employed.) Making this assumption about K does not invalidate the final figure for added value, as any value of K chosen would imply an associated cost per unit of capital employed such that the final AV figure is identical to that for any other value of K.

we presented as alternative two, you will see that *EVA* is, in all fundamentals, identical to added value. It is not a measure of value added at all but of added value! There are other terminology differences: for example, Stern Stewart denotes capital employed as 'economic capital'.

The Stern Stewart calculations of *EVA* show some additional detail. These relate to the precise ways in which Stern Stewart suggests that capital should be measured and 'operating profit' should be adjusted. The particular detailed procedures of obtaining the measures of capital and *NOPAT* required for the *EVA* measure need not detain us here. What is reassuring is that leading firms of business consultants are recommending that a firm's performance is best judged by how much economic profit or added value it generates (a proposition which economists have advocated for more than 100 years!).

Added Value and Scarcity

We began this chapter by introducing the idea of resource scarcity. How does this relate to the concept of added value? Whether or not resource scarcity exists, produced goods and services will often be useful to consumers—they will get utility from consuming them, and so the *goods* have value in that sense. But if a *resource* were not scarce, then no person would be willing to pay a positive price to acquire it, even if it helped to produce useful products. The absence of scarcity implies that it could be obtained at zero price. Presumably this is what people have in mind when they describe some plentiful (non-scarce) natural resources as 'free gifts of nature'. No market would exist for this resource, it would have no price, and the resource would not be valuable in any of the senses we have described. Scarcity is, then, a precondition for any resource to possess value.

The notion of opportunity cost is also helpful in understanding this point. Let us return to the so-called 'free gifts of nature', such as the amenity services provided by fresh air or the extensive forests found by the first 'pioneers' migrating into the American north-west. It would be appropriate to label these resources as free (i.e. not scarce) if the consumption of them by one person did not involve any opportunity cost. This was probably correct for both air and forests in the early years of the USA.

But it seems to be no longer true. One firm or one person's use of air for disposing of emissions does impose costs on others: opportunity costs are now not zero. The resource has become valuable! It may be sensible to place a price on the use of air (perhaps in the form of a pollution tax) to reflect this value.

1.2 Specialization and Exchange in the Search for Value

Economic activity is driven by an ultimate goal: maximization of the value obtained from using the resources available. How do individuals and groups organize their use of resources to achieve the most valuable outcome? By thinking through this problem we will discover the importance of the processes of specialization and exchange.

Imagine an economy consisting of one isolated individual: we shall call him Robinson Crusoe. Robinson has needs and wants, and would like to satisfy these as much as possible. Unless Robinson is so despondent that he wants to end things quickly, he will undertake a variety of production and consumption activities. Robinson's well-being is determined by the total amount of *use value* he gets from those activities. Exchange value is of no relevance here, as there is no other person with whom an exchange could occur. There is not much of interest to the business economist here so we shall consider the isolated Robinson no further.

But now assume that Robinson Crusoe is joined by Man Friday. Now that there is more than one person on the island, we have the rudiments of an economy. In contrast to an earlier version of this tale, suppose that the two are not related as master and servant. Robinson and Friday could choose to live in separate parts of the island, and produce and consume separately. Alternatively, they might co-operate whenever that is mutually beneficial. It is likely that each will realize that there are mutually beneficial gains to be had from collaboration. What is the source of these gains?

The first potential gain arises from *specialization* of their productive activities. We explain this by means of a simple example. Among the various things that Robinson and Friday want are food and clothing. Both are capable of producing food

Table 1.4 The individuals' productivities

	Clothing	Food
Friday	12	8
Robinson	6	20

and clothing, but they differ in their productive capacities. The amounts that Robinson and Friday could produce in one hour of work are given in Table 1.4. Within each row, the numbers shown in the table are mutually exclusive. So, for example, in one hour Friday could make 12 units of clothing *or* 8 units of food, but not both. (We do not, though, rule out the possibility that an hour of work could be shared between clothing and food production.)

It is useful to interpret these numbers in terms of opportunity costs. For example, the opportunity cost to Friday of 12 units of clothing is 8 units of food. Dividing each of these two numbers by 12, it follows that the opportunity cost (*OC*) of 1 unit of clothing is 8/12 units of food. By similar reasoning, we find that the *OC* of 1 unit of clothing is 20/6 units of food. To summarize:

For Friday: *OC* of 1 unit of clothing = 8/12 units of food;

For Robinson: *OC* of 1 unit of clothing = 20/6 units of food.

By reversing the direction of comparison, we also find that:

For Friday: *OC* of 1 unit of food = 12/8 units of clothing;

For Robinson: *OC* of 1 unit of food = 6/20 units of clothing.

The first pair of ratios shows that Friday is more productive than Robinson in clothing manufacture because Friday has a lower opportunity cost in the production of clothing than Robinson. Similarly, the second pair of ratios shows that Robinson is more productive than Friday in food manufacture because Robinson has a lower opportunity cost in the production of food than Friday.

Despite these productivity differences, the two individuals could elect to use their own labour time to produce goods purely for their own consumption. How much output would each obtain in ten hours of work per day if the ten hours of labour time were divided equally between the two products? The quantities that would be obtained are shown in Table 1.5. If the two were to operate in isolation from each other, what each produces will also, of course, be what each consumes.

Table 1.5 The self-sufficient (no specialization nor exchange) economy

	Clothing production	Food production
Friday	60	40
Robinson	30	100
Whole economy	90	140

Producing and consuming independently turns out to be a very poor choice. It is easy to show that co-operation between the two offers the prospect of each being better off. Table 1.6 describes the case in which each specializes by devoting all his time to producing the good in which he has an opportunity cost (productive) advantage over the other.

Specialization has increased the combined output of both goods. In the absence of exchange, it also means that Friday has all the clothes, and Robinson all the food. Nevertheless, the two could negotiate an exchange of food for clothing so that they are both better off in consumption terms than they were without specialization and trade. For example, if Friday exchanged 50 units of clothing for 50 units of food from Robinson, the outcome would be as shown in Table 1.7. Both individuals are better off after specialization and exchange than by acting non-co-operatively.

Although we chose one particular exchange rate for the numerical example (a rate of $1F = 1C$, with 50 units of each being exchanged in total) that rate

Table 1.6 The economy with complete specialization but no exchange

	Clothing production	Food production
Friday	120	0
Robinson	0	200
Whole economy	120	200

Table 1.7 The economy with complete specialization and exchange at the rate of $1F = 1C$

	Clothing production	Food production
Friday	70	50
Robinson	50	150
Whole economy	120	200

is not the only one that is mutually beneficial. There is a range of exchange rates within which both parties would benefit. The two rates at either end of this range are known as the limits to the terms of trade. By looking at the two individuals' clothing opportunity cost ratios, you should be able to deduce that any mutually beneficial rate must lie somewhere in the interval $1C = 2/3F$ to $1C = 10/3F$. The rate at which exchange actually occurs will determine how the gains from specialization and exchange are distributed between the individuals involved. This is also a proposition that you should try to verify from the numbers we have used in this example.

The Comparative Advantage Case

Our numerical example dealt with the case in which each individual was better, in terms of output per hour, at one good in comparison with the other person. This is called the 'absolute advantage' case. Friday had an absolute advantage in producing clothes, whilst Robinson had an absolute advantage in food. But do the conclusions we have drawn about the *mutual* benefits of specialization and exchange carry over to the case where one person is better, in absolute terms, at producing *both* goods?

The answer is that they do. Even where one person has an *absolute* productive advantage in both goods, it will be the case in general that he or she will only have a *comparative* advantage in one of the goods. Moreover, the other person will have a comparative advantage in the other good! The reasoning which lies behind this assertion is as follows. Consider the person who is absolutely better at producing both goods. Unless the opportunity cost ratios happen by chance to be identical, he will have a greater proportionate advantage in one good than the other good. For example, if Friday can produce 3 units of clothing or 2 units of food in one hour, while Robinson can produce 2 clothing or 1 food, then Friday's proportionate advantage is larger in food. It also follows that Robinson's proportionate disadvantage is lower in clothing.

We can describe this in more simple terms by saying that Friday has a comparative advantage in food and Robinson has a comparative advantage in clothing. We will not work our way through this numerical example, although this is done (for two countries rather than two individuals, and for a different pair of goods) in Chapter 16 where we discuss international trade. Unless you go through the arithmetic in Chapter 16 now, we ask you to take the following result on trust. If individuals specialize in the production of goods in which they have a *comparative advantage* and then exchange with others, mutually beneficial gains are attainable. These gains will be larger the greater are the opportunity cost differences between the individuals concerned.

Other Benefits of Specialization

Specialization may lead to benefits over and above those from comparative advantage. A second gain arises from learning effects; the benefits from learning tend to be more easily appropriated when activity is focused. Another potential advantage comes from scale effects. When activity is specialized, the scale at which it is undertaken in any one establishment will often be larger. Large-scale production can lead to technological, marketing, financial, and other benefits which lead to lower average costs. Whilst many of these will not be relevant in the simple two-person production and exchange story, they are relevant to the national and international economies which are the main focus of business economics. We will examine these effects in Chapter 5.

An Economy Consisting of Many Individuals

The principles we have just established carry over to more general circumstances. In any community there will be potential gains from co-operation. Production according to comparative advantage can increase total output, and processes of exchange will enable these gains to be realized by individuals in the way we have just indicated.

Moreover, the potential benefits from specialization and trade are likely to increase considerably as the numbers of people increase. It should also be obvious that there is no need for all the co-operating individuals and groups to live within single nation-states. Specialization and exchange take place within national economies and between national economies; in the latter case, we describe the phenomenon as international trade. Although we may choose to call production units in different countries (or even the various countries themselves) competitors, it remains the case that trade, national and international, is essentially a co-operative activity. Those countries which are currently seeking to become members of the European Union clearly recognize this point.

Market Exchange

One further fundamental insight remains to be established. It concerns the manner in which exchange takes place. In simple economies, such as Friday's and Robinson's desert island, the medium of exchange might well be barter—the direct exchange of goods by negotiation. Barter exchange is likely, however, to be an extremely cumbersome and inefficient affair in any economy beyond the most simple type. Economic history shows that as economies develop, direct exchange of goods and services tends to be replaced by two more organized processes of exchange. First of all, the direct exchange of goods is replaced by exchange through the medium of some recognized standard of value. Eventually, this standard of value takes the form of money.

Secondly (and usually later), exchange takes place through organized markets. These organized processes represent more complex forms of co-operation, and help to mediate and facilitate the processes of exchange. It is to these processes that we turn in the final part of this chapter.

1.3 The Nature and Functions of Economic Mechanisms

An economic mechanism is the means by which individuals and societies search for and generate value. In Section 1.2, we showed that the processes of specialization and exchange play central roles in the generation of value. This book is concerned with economic mechanisms and how they contribute to value generation. In the final part of this chapter we shall, for the purposes of setting the scene for later, consider briefly the nature and functions of economic mechanisms.

The main functions of an economic mechanism are as follows:

- *promoting* or motivating the search for an efficient allocation and utilization of resources;
- *co-ordinating* the action of individuals in their search for value;
- *regulating* the individual search for value when circumstances arise where this might conflict with wider social objectives such as consumer safety or a healthy environment.

A possible way of organizing economic activities, at least in theory, is called the pure market exchange mechanism. This would involve private property and the use of markets for all trade and exchange between individuals. There would be no collective organizations such as enterprises and only a minimalist state to ensure the existence of private property. This would be the ultimate in decentralized decision-making co-ordinated by market forces. The pure market system would obviously provide strong incentives for individuals to search out and exploit value opportunities and market prices would provide clear signals to people about the relative values of resources, goods, and services and so act to co-ordinate individual desires and actions. Ever since Adam Smith first clearly expressed the principle of the 'invisible hand' of market forces in *The Wealth of Nations*, economic analysis has established that the market mechanism has good efficiency-promoting properties. However there have also been many critics of the market mechanism in practice who point in particular to the problems of unemployment and inequality in many market-based economies.

Pure market economies do not exist in practice. The main reason for this is that firms and governments in some circumstances perform certain functions more effectively than pure exchange through markets. For example in Chapter 4 we will look at how economists rationalize the existence of firms in terms of what we call 'transactional difficulties and costs'.

But a pure market economy (or a market economy in which production is largely co-ordinated by firms) contains no mechanism through which individual actions are *regulated* when they might conflict with the wider social interest. It is in the performance of this function that government plays its most important economic role. We devote Chapter 13 of this book to an examination of this role, but a few preliminary remarks will be in order at this point. First, it may well be in the private interest of producers to behave in ways which restrict competition. This may conflict with society's overall interest, thereby implying potential social gains from governments restricting anti-competitive practices.

Secondly, individual or business consumption and production behaviour may impose external costs (or benefits) on others. A clear example of this can be found in the environmental pollution arising from some production processes. In these circumstances, government regulatory mechanisms can lead to substantial social benefits. Thirdly, there are situations in which markets cannot exist, and so cannot lead to socially beneficial outcomes. We shall explain this in Chapter 13.

The regulatory function of government is supplemented by the role it plays in co-ordinating economic behaviour. Among the more important are government's general management of the overall level of economic activity of the economy through monetary and fiscal policy (see Chapter 14), and the provision of important services such as education, training, and fundamental research which may be inadequately provided by private markets alone. More controversial is the co-ordination of business behaviour through industrial policy. Few would argue that managers should not co-ordinate the activities of their firm. If one regards the economy as a whole as a firm writ large, then one may argue that the government should manage (that is, co-ordinate) the activities of the 'national firm'. Whether this argument has any validity depends, of course, on the appropriateness of the analogy we have drawn. The fact that industrial policy has become less widely used in recent years even in Japan suggests that many people now think it is not appropriate.

A final role of government warrants attention. Societies may take the view that some resource allocation choices should be made through political choice mechanisms. Few of us, for example, would regard it as appropriate or desirable that national defence choices were made through markets. Similarly, the allocation of resources to public health programmes, to basic education, and to law and order institutions, are widely felt to be choice areas which cannot be left entirely to markets. Nevertheless, it is interesting to note that even where political choice has dictated that a service should be publicly provided, it is becoming increasingly common to find internal market mechanisms being employed to allocate resources within the service, the British National Health Service being a prominent example.

The pure market economy and the mixed market economy are not the only economic mechanisms available. At the other extreme from a pure market economy is the pure centrally planned economy. The intellectual proponents of central planning have typically argued that the promoting, co-ordinating, and regulating functions are better performed by central planning mechanisms. Evidence seems to cast considerable doubt on the validity of this claim. For example, it now seems clear that while the Soviet-type planned economies achieved rapid growth rates in the early phases of heavy industrialization, they became ossified and highly inefficient as these economies began the transition towards more diversified, modern economies. Central planning stifled the incentives that are necessary for innovation, and in the absence of markets, administered prices sent out wrong signals, leading to severely distorted industrial structures.

Whether better planning processes could have been developed that would have resolved these problems is something we shall probably never know. What is evident is that even before the demise of central planning, the Soviet-type economies were beginning to develop mixed structures, with markets flourishing alongside the planned sectors. This mix of market and centrally administered resource allocation can be seen in the Chinese economy. Casual inspection of Chinese evidence suggests that the introduction of markets can generate tremendous dynamism in economies that have stagnated under excessive central control.

Most economies are in fact mixed economies, based essentially on market mechanisms along with many collective organizations (corporations, firms, banks, unions, professional partnerships) and considerable government involvement (but stopping far short of centralized planning). Resource allocation is based therefore on a mixture of market and political or administrative mechanisms. The economic mechanisms we use are human constructs, and reflect the outcomes of people's search for efficient methods of dealing with scarcity. Our typical choice of mixed economies reflects a belief that no single pure mechanism is the best way of organizing all our economic activities.

Conclusions

The conjunction of limited resources and limitless wants or desires produces scarcity. Economists use the term scarcity, therefore, in a particular manner which should not be confused with the everyday use of the term. Scarcity results in the need to make choices; given available resources, society cannot produce everything that its members would like. Every choice involves a cost, known as the opportunity cost. This is the highest valued alternative forgone when resources are used in a particular way.

Value has several dimensions, but ones which are linked through the process of exchange. Production and exchange can generate added value. Some part of an economy's total added value can be extracted by businesses. It is the search for added value that is the firm's fundamental objective.

Production that takes place through *specialization* according to comparative advantage permits an increased value of output from a given quantity of resources. Trade permits these gains to be distributed among all co-operating individuals. Economics is the study of the nature, characteristics, operation, and performance of economic mechanisms. It is about better understanding these mechanisms in the hope of making better use of them. Economics emphasizes the role of the market mechanism, or the price system, in motivating and co-ordinating the individuals' search for value. Markets have the appealing features of simplicity and cheapness, and have attractive properties in terms of motivating and co-ordinating behaviour. The study of market mechanisms suggests that they have weaknesses as well as strengths. These weaknesses can at least partly help us to understand why other mechanisms—hierarchical organizations we call firms and government—complement markets in resource allocation. Business economics in particular is the study of the entrepreneurially guided collective search for value by firms/enterprises operating within a market environment and subject to government regulation.

Further reading

As the central theme of this chapter has been the concept of added value, an appropriate reference for further reading is John Kay's *Foundations of Corporate Success* (1993). Its analysis of value generation by the individual firm is a *tour de force* and the book has become a modern classic. The related concepts of added value, rent, and supernormal profit can be traced back to Ricardo (1817). Schumpeter (1943) developed the notion that rent-seeking is the driving force of business behaviour. An interesting collection of papers on the nature and origins of microeconomics is contained in W. Baumol (ed.), *Microeconomic Theory: Applications and Origins* (1986).

Questions

1.1. Propose a test for deciding whether or not a particular resource is scarce. Use this test to decide whether water is a scarce resource.

1.2. Explain how the concept of opportunity cost can be used to assist decision-making in:

(a) a business firm

(b) the British National Health Service (NHS).

(If you do not have any experience of the NHS, here are a few basic facts to help you understand the system. The service is provided free at the point of use, in doctors' surgeries or in hospitals. The national budget for the service is provided by the government. This budget is made available as limited annual resources to a large number of area health authorities which provide the finance for all operations, drugs, and other medical care including salaries and running costs of hospitals.)

1.3. How does added value differ from value added? Does the pursuit of value-added make sense as a business objective?

1.4. The opportunity cost of using a resource is:

(a) the present market price of that resource

(b) the highest valued alternative necessarily forgone

(c) the actual money payment made for the use of that resource

(d) the lowest valued alternative necessarily forgone?

1.5. How can the added value generated in different activities within a firm assist in its internal allocation of resources?

1.6. We have explained added value at the level of a single firm in the context of a commercial business. Does the concept of added value also apply to not-for-profit organizations such as charities, universities and public health organisations? If you think it does, how could one measure the added value of these organisations, and what difficulties would arise in doing this?

2 The Operation of the Market, Market Forces, and Market Equilibrium

Introduction

This chapter investigates the operation of markets, showing how demand and supply interact to determine market price and output. The concepts of a market, market supply, and market demand each have a specific meaning in economic analysis; we shall demonstrate that much confusion arises in formulating business policy because of failures to use these concepts properly.

The second section of the chapter investigates how supply and demand analysis can be used to understand price and quantity changes in a number of actual markets, including that for crude oil. We also show how this kind of analysis can shed light on decision-making in a publicly provided health service, and on the workings of markets for hard drugs.

Section 2.3 examines the concept of elasticity of demand, applies it in various ways, and shows how knowledge of elasticities can be useful to decision-makers in business and in the public sector.[1] This section ends with a discussion of some of the pitfalls that one can easily fall into when trying to estimate demand, supply, or elasticity from available data. As you may be asked to do this at some point, it is strongly recommended that you read this section carefully. The chapter concludes with some reflections on the workings of market mechanisms in general.

[1] Discussion of elasticity of supply will be left until Chapter 5.

2.1 The Nature of Market Behaviour and Equilibrium

Markets as the Interaction between Buyers and Sellers

A market is a process rather than a place. It is the process of interaction between those who wish to sell and those who wish to purchase a good.[2] Consumers have intentions about their desired purchases, shaped by prices, incomes, and tastes, among other things. Similarly, producers have intentions about how much they would like to supply, shaped by prices, costs, and so on. A market, therefore, always has both a supply and a demand side.

Our method of analysis begins by stripping away particular features of 'real world' markets which are of secondary importance in order to concentrate on what is essential. For simplicity, we ask you to think about a market for some well-defined single product, in which producers and consumers interact directly without the intervention of any intermediaries. By the end of this chapter, you should be able to analyse more complicated examples.

Markets, Voluntary Exchange, and Rationality

Market behaviour is voluntary behaviour: no one is compelled to buy or sell. Buyers and sellers have schedules of intentions to trade at particular prices. The amount actually exchanged will depend upon

[2] We use the word 'good' to mean both tangible products and intangible services.

the price which prevails in the market. This is the principle of voluntary exchange. However, this lack of compulsion does not mean that actors in the market will always be able to buy or sell their desired quantities, as we demonstrate in the second section of this chapter. Indeed, whenever a market is not in equilibrium (a term to be defined shortly) conditions of excess demand or excess supply will prevail, preventing some buyers or sellers from attaining their intended quantity of trades.

Economic analysis assumes that individual economic behaviour is rational. Each person has a set of objectives and seeks to attain these to the highest extent possible, subject to any constraints that exist. One of the most important constraints consists of the information that the individual possesses (or has access to). Rationality implies that individuals make the best use of available opportunities, given the information at hand. Using the concept of added value that was introduced in the first chapter, it is clear that value-maximizing behaviour is another way of defining rational behaviour.

Rationality does not, of course, imply that the *outcome* of choices will always be the best. The information available at the time a decision is made may be less than perfect. In these circumstances, it is quite possible that decisions will be made which, with the benefit of hindsight (that is, additional information accruing with the passage of time), are not the best ones. Rational behaviour implies that *ex-ante* choices are optimal, even though *ex post* they may turn out to be poor ones. Later (in Chapter 8) you will see that rational behaviour by individuals can lead to outcomes which are collectively suboptimal. For example, advertising expenditures by oligopolistic rivals acting without collusion may be individually sensible but could also lead to industry profits being lower than without advertising. Price-cutting exercises that spark off a price war among rivals can have similar consequences.

Objectives of Consumers

Individuals, in their role as consumers, seek to maximize value: the satisfaction of wishes, wants, needs, and desires. This satisfaction is obtained by consuming bundles of goods that confer various services. Economists use the term *utility* as a label for this satisfaction or well-being, and argue that the objective of consumers is maximization of utility.

Each individual will have a set of preferences, which determine how much utility he or she gets from the consumption of various bundles of goods. Furthermore, each person will face a budget constraint: given the prices of available goods, current and expected future income sets limits to the amounts of various bundles of goods that it is feasible to purchase. Utility maximization implies that an individual arranges his or her consumption pattern to obtain the greatest amount of satisfaction, subject to a budget constraint. The detailed implications of this individual behaviour are explored in Chapter 3. For the moment, however, we turn our attention to the *collection of all individuals* who intend to purchase some quantity of a particular product: what we shall call the market demand for that product.

Market Demand

The market demand for a good may be represented by a demand schedule. This expresses the quantity demanded of a good in the market as a whole in relation to a set of explanatory variables. The market demand for a particular good, x, can be expressed symbolically in the following way:

$$q_x^d = f(P_x, P_1, P_2, \ldots, P_n, Y)$$

where q_x^d refers to the quantity demanded of good x during some specified period of time, P_x is the price of that good, $P_1, P_2, \ldots, P_n$ are the prices of n other goods, and Y denotes aggregate consumers' income.

What does this expression tell us? If we knew the particular numerical values of all the explanatory variables (those listed in parentheses on the right-hand side of the equation), and we knew the exact form of the relationship between demand and these explanatory variables, then we could calculate exactly what the quantity demanded of good x would be in the market as a whole.

You will have noticed that it is necessary to know the nature of the relationship itself to make this calculation. The symbol f stands for that relationship. Writing the relationship simply as f in this way does not tell us what the relationship is, merely that there is one! However, roughly speaking, what the relationship actually is will depend upon consumers' tastes or preferences; if for any reason these change, so will the relationship itself.

Now, it would be useful if the demand schedule

for a good could be represented in a simple graphical or tabular form. But that is difficult as things stand. You can see that there are $n+2$ variables explaining demand—the good's price, consumers' income, and the price of n other goods. And n might be a large number. To see why, just ask yourself how many types of goods there are likely to be whose price affects the demand for cars!

So any table or graph would have to be multidimensional if it is to entirely describe demand. For each possible configuration of values of all these $n+2$ variables, there will be a particular quantity demanded. This is simply too much to handle without using complicated mathematical tools. But there is a simple way of making progress. We can ask:

How will the quantity demanded of the good in which we are interested alter as one explanatory variable changes, but with all other influences upon demand remaining constant?

This is the kind of analysis we are going to do here. This reduces the problem to one of two dimensions—quantity demanded and the explanatory variable we choose to focus on—thereby allowing us to use diagrams in the analysis of demand. But which explanatory variable should we choose? In a business economics course, the obvious candidate is the price of the good itself. This is, after all, the only one which firms in the industry in question have any direct control over. If I produce cars, it is natural for me to be interested in how the demand for cars will change as the price of cars change, because the price of cars is something over which I may have some influence.

Effects on the Quantity Demanded of a Good of Changes in the Market Price of that Good—the Market Demand Curve

In general as the price of a good changes, intuition suggests that the quantity demanded of that good will change in the opposite direction. A negative relationship between the price of a good and the quantity demanded per period of time is sometimes called *the law of demand.* We depict such a relationship in Figure 2.1. It turns out to be the case that this intuition is generally correct. If you wish to back up this intuition with some solid theoretical foundation, or you wish to see some empirical evidence to support it, you will have to turn to Chapter 3. Meanwhile, we ask you to accept, for the sake of argument, that there is an inverse relationship between price and quantity demanded for most types of goods and services. In Section 2.2 of this chapter, we will make some further conjectures about the shape of this relationship for particular products: after all, knowing that the relationship is an inverse one does not really tell us very much!

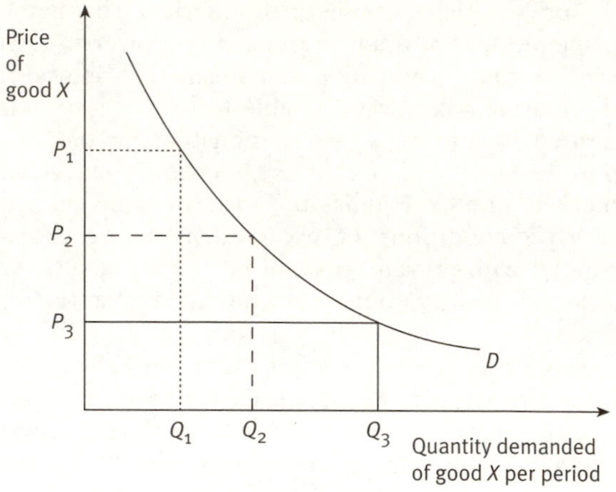

Figure 2.1 A market demand curve

It is important to remember that a demand curve shows the relationship between quantity demanded of a good and the price of that good for particular (and unchanging) levels of all the other variables that affect demand. So the demand curve in Figure 2.1 assumes particular (and unchanging) levels of money income, consumer preferences, and prices of other goods. It follows from this that if any of these other factors were to change, the position (and possibly the shape) of the demand curve would alter. There would be what is called an 'increase in demand' or a 'decrease in demand' depending on whether the change in income, other prices, or preferences is causing more or fewer of the goods to be demanded at each price. We shall return to this point shortly.

Two other features of demand curves should also be kept in mind.

- Demand curves describe demand *intentions*, that is, they describe the quantities that consumers intend to purchase at various prices. For example, in Figure 2.1 consumers desire to purchase Q_1 at price P_1.
- The demand for a good is the *flow* of units of a good demanded over a period of time. We may think of the demand for oil per year, the demand

for newspapers per day, and so on. The phrase 'the demand for a good' should always be thought of as the demand over a particular interval of time. Whenever you are referring to the demand for a good, it is up to you to make it clear what time period is relevant for the quantities you have in mind.

Increases and Decreases in Demand

For the reasons we have just explained, changes in income, preferences, or the prices of other goods may shift the position of a demand curve. By convention, it is usual to describe a shift in the position of the demand curve as a change in demand. The change is described as an increase in demand when more is demanded at each price, so the demand curve in Figure 2.1 shifts to the right. A change is described as a decrease in demand when less is demanded at each price, and so the demand curve shifts to the left. In contrast, a movement along a given demand curve, caused solely by a change in the price of the good itself, is known as a 'change in the quantity demanded'. The notation is tricky here, but it pays dividends to stick to it wherever possible. Let us briefly consider each of the possible causes of *changes* in demand. We recommend that you try to sketch out for each of these cases the direction in which the demand curve might shift.

Changes in the Prices of other Goods

If the price of another good changes, the effect will mainly depend upon the relationship between the two goods. If consumers feel that the two are *substitutes* for one another, then we expect a positive relationship between demand for one good and the price of another. For example, fuel users may consider oil and coal to be substitutes. Then a fall in oil prices induces customers to switch, wholly or partially, from coal to oil consumption, and so leads to an decrease in the demand for coal. We would expect, therefore, that the demand curve for coal would shift to the left if oil prices were to fall. Indeed, this is what has happened in recent years as oil prices have fallen relative to coal prices.

On the other hand, if two goods are complements—they are jointly consumed—there will tend to be a negative relationship between the demand for one and the price of the other. For example, large increases in crude oil prices in 1974–5 and again in 1979 were associated with a substantial decline in the sales of large cars. This reflects the complementary relationship between fuel (extracted from crude oil) and the use of cars.

Goods may not be related in any direct way for these kinds of price effects to take place. Consider, for example, energy prices and confectionery demand. Even if energy and confectionery are neither substitutes nor complements for one another (which seems likely), changes in energy prices can alter the demand for confectionery by altering the real purchasing power of consumers' money incomes. This leads us on to the next point.

Changes in Consumers' Income

Changes in the level of consumers' income are likely to affect the demand for goods. The direction and magnitude of this effect will depend upon the good in question and the size of the income change. For most goods, an increase in income results in an increase in demand; these are known *as normal goods*. Other goods—known as *inferior goods*—are those for which an increase in income results in a decrease in demand.

When goods are defined in broad classes, statistical evidence suggests that few goods are inferior in this sense. However, when product categories are defined more narrowly, the likelihood of finding inferior goods increases. For example, although cars as a whole appear to be normal goods, particular types of cars (such as small, low powered, low quality cars) might be inferior goods, particularly in an economy in which average income levels are relatively high.

Consumer Preferences

Changes in consumer tastes or preferences obviously affect the demand for goods. Suppose, for example, that people choose to drink more wine as a result of a new medical finding suggesting that moderate wine consumption may lead to improvements in health. This increase in the strength of consumer preferences for wine results in a greater quantity of the good being demanded, other things remaining equal, and the demand curve for wine shifts to the right.

Substitution Effects and Income Effects of Price Changes

In discussing the effects of a price change on quantity demanded of a good, it was said that the effect will *in general* be negative. Why was the caveat 'in general' adopted? The answer to this lies in the presence of so-called income effects of price changes. A change in the price of a good will in general have two distinct effects on demand. The first of these is known as the *substitution effect*. When the relative prices of goods change, rational consumers will substitute from the relatively more expensive to the relatively less expensive good. This effect is always 'negative' in the sense that if the price change were the only relevant effect, then a fall in the price of good x would always result in an increase in the quantity demanded of good x.

But there is a second effect at work too. A change in the price of a good, with money income unchanged, alters the real income of consumers. Real income refers to the purchasing power of money income. If the price of a good that a person buys increases then the real purchasing power of his or her income falls. (Think about the effect on the real income of a person with a house mortgage when there is a rise in mortgage interest rates.) Because a change in price changes real income, an *income effect* may induce further changes in the quantity demanded.

Now drawing together all these threads, we can reach the following conclusion. If a product is an inferior good, then a rise in its price will reduce real income and so increase the quantity of it demanded. If the magnitude of this effect is sufficiently large to dominate (or outweigh) the substitution effect, a positive relationship will exist between price and quantity demanded! Suffice to say that while this possibility exists, it is very unlikely to be realized in practice.

Market Supply

Objectives of Firms

For the purposes of this chapter, we will proceed on the assumption that the ultimate objective of firms is to maximize profits (or equivalently, to maximize their value). This assumption is far from being uncontroversial, and several writers would vehemently challenge its validity. Moreover, for many public sector and not-for-profit organizations, it seems to be clearly inappropriate. Nevertheless, for commercial businesses at least, it is a plausible working hypothesis and we will adopt it for the moment in this spirit. Subsequent chapters of the book (especially Chapters 4, 11, and 12) will examine that assumption critically and in some depth.

We will now briefly examine the supply side of markets in much the same way as we analysed demand. One point of caution is warranted here. Supply curves (in the sense that we use them below) only really exist in competitive markets. The logic of this assertion should be clear once you have read Chapter 6. So we proceed on the assumption that the markets we are referring to are 'competitive markets'. The precise meaning of this phrase will be explained in Chapter 6. For the moment, just take it to mean a market in which there is a large number of firms producing a single standardized product.

The Market Supply of a Good

We can represent market supply by a schedule relating the quantity supplied of a good over a period of time to the values taken by a set of explanatory variables. This can be written as

$$q_x^s = g\,(P_x, P_1, P_2, \ldots, P_n, F_1, F_2, \ldots, F_m, Z)$$

where q_x^s is the quantity supplied of good x in a given period, P_x is the price of good x, $P_1, \ldots, P_n$ are the prices of n other goods and $F_1, \ldots, F_m$ are the prices of m productive inputs. The relationship between supply and its determinants is denoted by the function symbol g. This will, in turn, depend on the state of technology. Technical progress will alter the relationship between supply and the determinants of supply listed on the right-hand side of the supply equation.

The Supply Curve

A market supply curve shows the relationship between a good's price and the intended quantity supplied of that good from all firms in the relevant market. This price–supply relationship is constructed conditional on all the other determinants of supply being at particular, unchanging levels.

Figure 2.2 illustrates the expected shape of a supply curve. Notice that we expect a positive relationship between willingness to supply a good and its own price. A full explanation for this will be given in Chapter 5 dealing with production. However, intuitively you can see that higher prices lead to more profitable production and so create an incentive for firms to increase their output or for other firms to enter the market. Furthermore, these higher prices compensate a firm for any increase in the costs of producing additional units of output.

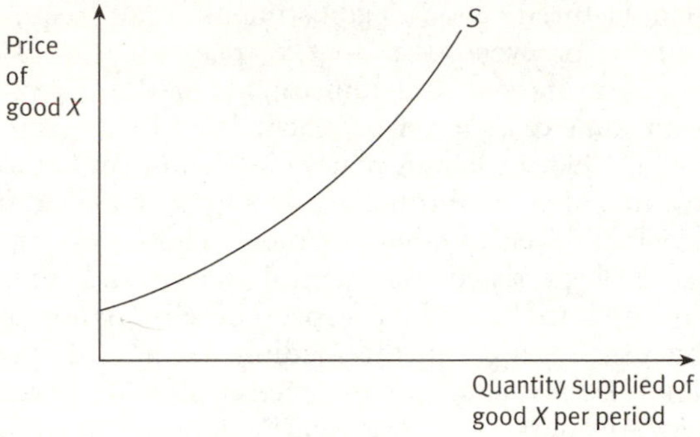

Figure 2.2 A market supply curve

Two important features of demand curves also apply to supply curves.

- The supply curve describes sellers' *intentions.*
- Supply, like demand, is a *flow.* It is the intended supply per period of time.

Because a supply curve is drawn for some particular set of values taken by the explanatory variables (other than the good's own price), it follows that a change in any of these variables would shift the position of the supply curve to the right (an increase in supply) or the left (a decrease in supply). Let us briefly examine each of these kinds of changes.

The Prices of Other Goods

If the price of another good rises, then its production becomes more profitable than before, relative to good *x*. Firms will therefore have an incentive to switch production towards this other good. If resources can be reallocated in this way, a negative relationship will exist between the supply of a good and the price of other goods. Consider a firm which is currently producing both large cars and small cars. Let 'good *x*' be large cars, whilst the 'other good' in question is small cars. If the price of small cars increases, the firm is likely to switch some of its production from large to small cars. This relationship is likely to be stronger in the long term than in the short term, because time lags may exist in the process of adjusting output from one good to another.

Input Prices

If an input price rises, a firm will find it more costly to produce a given output quantity than before, and so the price at which the firm is willing to supply that quantity of the good will increase. Looked at in another way, at any particular price, the quantity the firm is willing to sell will fall. This means that there is a negative relationship between input price and market supply. For example, if labour costs in car production increased then, other things remaining equal, we would expect the supply of cars to fall, represented by a shift to the left (or upwards if you like) of the supply curve for cars.

Technology

The state of technology determines the maximum volume of output that can be obtained from a given quantity of inputs. Improvements in technology will, other things being equal, improve profitability and so increase supply. The supply curve of the good in question will be displaced to the right. A striking example of this occurred in UK North Sea oil extraction. Remarkable technological improvements in oil search and extraction took place in the 1980s. The consequent fall in costs helped to offset the lower profits caused by falling oil prices between 1985 and 1989. But for this, the decline in North Sea production activity would have been far more severe.

Market Equilibrium

Equilibrium is a state in which the forces operating on a variable are in balance. A market is in equilibrium when the forces of supply and demand are balanced, so that the price has no tendency to change from its current level. To see how this works, place the demand and supply curves for some good together on one diagram, as we have done in Figure 2.3. When the price is at P_1 the

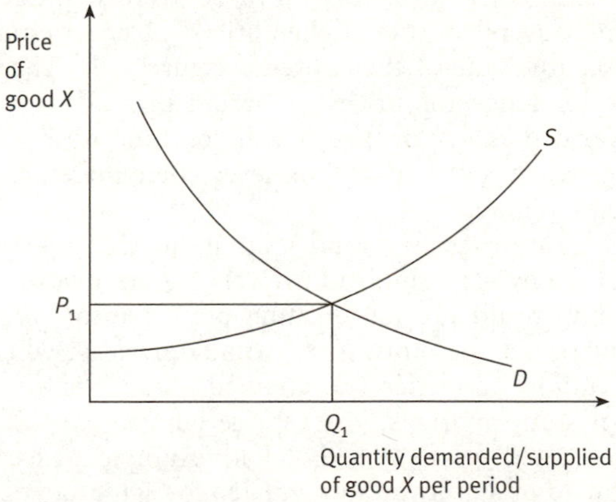

Figure 2.3 Equilibrium price and quantity traded in a market

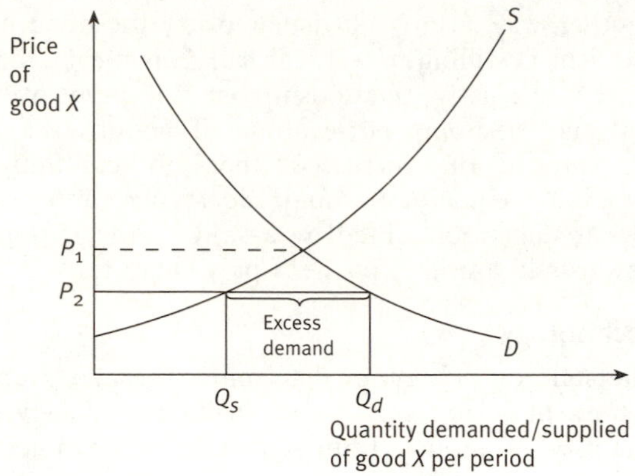

Figure 2.4 Excess demand in the market for good *X*

market is in equilibrium. At that price, both sides of the market wish to trade the quantity Q_1. The equilibrium price is one at which the intentions of buyers and sellers are mutually consistent. In this state, there will be no tendency for the price to change.

Figure 2.4 illustrates what happens when the price is below the equilibrium price. At price P_2, suppliers intend to sell Q_s but purchasers intend to buy Q_d, and so buyers' and sellers' intentions are inconsistent. As all exchange is voluntary, the amount actually traded will be Q_s: sellers cannot be forced to sell more than they wish. Sellers' intentions will have been satisfied, but not those of consumers. The market will be in a state of *excess demand*, indicated by the gap $Q_d - Q_s$.

What happens in a state of excess demand? Some consumers will be unable to secure all they wish to purchase, and the shortage of goods will induce some buyers to offer higher prices, in an attempt to secure some of their intended purchases. There is a tendency for prices to be bid upwards. This upward pressure on prices will continue until the price reaches its equilibrium level where there is no excess demand.

Similar processes would result if the market price were above its equilibrium level. A state of excess supply would prevail, creating pressures for price reductions. These pressures would only cease when an equilibrium price was attained.

In some markets, these price adjustments will take place very quickly. For example, excess demand or supply on unregulated foreign exchange markets or in the markets for stocks and shares would be eliminated within minutes or less. For manufactured goods, adjustments may require months, or even years, to take place. In the case of labour markets, full adjustments may take years, or in some cases never be reached at all. For example, in 1998 the labour market as a whole in France was in a state of chronic excess supply, reflected in very high levels of unemployment. This excess supply had persisted for several years, and there appeared to be little prospect of elimination of this excess supply in the medium term. A discussion of *why* adjustment speeds differ so much between markets is, however, beyond the scope of this book.

2.2 Market adjustment and the Market Mechanism

We have now seen how the demand and supply conditions for a good interact to determine the equilibrium market price. We will now use the tools developed in Section 2.1 to analyse how equilibrium prices and quantities are likely to change in response to changing business conditions. It is this kind of analysis that you may find useful when undertaking an 'environmental analysis' of changing business conditions in an industry of interest to you.

Changes in Demand

A Change in Consumers' Preferences

What happens to equilibrium price and quantity traded of a good when consumer preferences for that good increase? It is very easy to arrive at some qualitative conclusions. An increase in tastes implies that consumers as a whole intend to purchase more of the good in question at any particular price than previously. Market demand rises and so the demand curve shifts to the right. You should draw a diagram to convince yourself of the following. Assuming that the supply curve has a conventional upward slope, the rightward shift in demand implies that the demand/supply curve intersection is at a higher price and a higher quantity. Both the market equilibrium price and the quantity traded will rise.

An interesting example of this seems to have occurred in the market for very high quality violins. We examine this in Box 2.1. What makes this example particularly interesting (but also rather

Box 2.1 The Price of High Quality Violins

The principal tool of the trade for any professional orchestral violinist is a high quality violin. It is widely believed that the best instruments were made in the eighteenth century, mainly in Italy. Violin technology—unlike that associated with most other orchestral instruments—had reached its peak by that time, and ageing has imparted a mellowing and warmth of tone that gives these violins a superb sound.

One generation ago, a London rank and file orchestral player earning £1,000 a year would have had to spend around £500—half of one year's salary—to acquire a violin of this age and quality. In 1997, such a player earns around £27,000 but would need to spend over £50,000 for the equivalent instrument. Relative to musicians' salaries, eighteenth-century violins have increased in price fourfold (see The *Guardian*, Friday 7 November 1997).

Why has this occurred? The answer is to be found in the conditions of demand and supply. There is a fixed stock of violins of this age and quality. However, the demand for possession of such an instrument has been rising with the passage of time, as the musical industry worldwide has expanded, sponsorship has increased, and so market purchasing power has grown. We portray this schematically in Figure 2.5(*a*). The vertical line labelled S^* denotes the fixed stock of eighteenth-century violins. The demand for ownership of such instruments one generation ago is represented by the curve D_1^*; the current demand by D_2^*. An increase in demand can bring forth no additional stock, and simply bids the price of existing violins up. However, like all durable goods, violins do not only provide services to consumers (or producers) in just one period: they are long-lived assets, yielding flows of services over time. In this respect, they share a similarity with goods such as cars, houses, and precious-stone jewellery. For all such durable goods, we can think of two kinds of equilibrium: a stock equilibrium and a flow equilibrium. It is a *stock* equilibrium (or rather a change in such an equilibrium) that is being shown in Figure 2.5(*a*). The 'supply' curve is, properly speaking, merely a stock curve—one which is in this case fixed in quantity terms and so completely independent of price. The demand curve shows the total quantity of instruments that musicians as a whole would wish to hold at any particular price. It is the increase in this 'stock demand' that has caused the price rise.

However, we can also conceive of a second kind of equilibrium: a *flow* equilibrium. At any point in time, there will be some people wishing to sell and some wishing to buy. These supply and demand flows are the ones shown in Figure 2.5(*b*). Notice that the curves D and S are not the same as D^* and S^* in the left-hand-side diagram. Also note that the flow supply curve, S, does show some price sensitivity: as the price that can be obtained on the market rises, there will be more violins offered for sale.

The magnitudes of these flows will usually be much smaller than the stock level S^* shown in Figure 2.5(*a*). To convince yourself of this, it may be useful to think about the equivalent situation in the housing market. In any period of time, only a small proportion of the whole stock of houses are actually being supplied, demanded, and traded.

It would also be perfectly legitimate to argue that it is the flow equilibrium in the market portrayed in Figure 2.5(*b*) that determines the price of violins (and so the change in price whenever demand or supply conditions

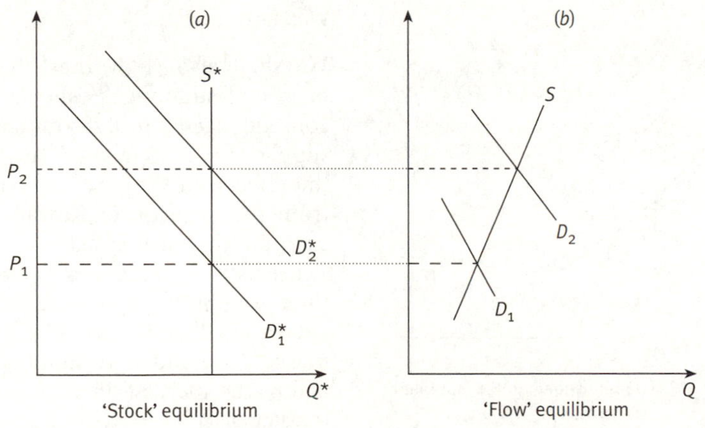

Figure 2.5 The market for very high quality Italian violins

Box 2.1 continued

change). But this appears to leave us in a quandary: it seems to be the case that the price is determined separately in two markets. But how can that be? The answer is, again, very simple. In a 'full' equilibrium with durable goods, the equilibrium price must be identical in both markets. If it were not, adjustments would take place until they were identical (and therefore the market could not have been in equilibrium in the first place)!

As a final check on your understanding, ask yourself what kinds of adjustments would bring about equality of price in the stock and flow markets. To do this, it may also be helpful to think about the housing case, where these processes are likely to be more evident. But note one big difference between the housing and violin cases. Unlike eighteenth-century violins, the stock of houses can (and obviously does) increase over time.

difficult!) is that, to all intents and purposes, there is a fixed stock of these types of violins. Equilibrium also involves stock and flow considerations, as you will see from the discussion.

A Change in Consumers' Income

Let us next consider the effect of a change in consumers' income. To illustrate, we go through the case of a fall in income; you should be able to work out the consequences of the opposite case. The first question to consider is whether a fall in income increases or decreases demand for the good in question. If the good is *normal*, demand will fall when income falls; if it is *inferior*, demand increases when income falls.

Figure 2.6 gives a schematic representation of the case where the good being considered is normal. The initial (prior to the income fall) demand curve is labelled D_1. The income fall implies (in this case) that less of the good is demanded at each price, and

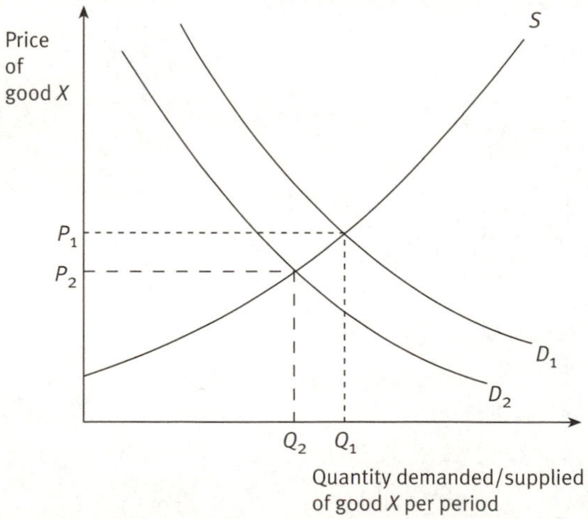

Figure 2.6 A decrease in demand for good *X* and its effect on the market equilibrium

so the demand curve shifts to the left, to D_2. There has been a decrease in demand.

The consequences of this change are the reverse of those we saw arising from an increase in consumers' preferences, with both the equilibrium price and the equilibrium quantity traded falling. Box 2.2 examines a practical example of how this line of reasoning might be used to form an assessment of future price changes for copper.

The Effects of Changes in Supply on Equilibrium Price and Quantity Traded

Changes in supply are depicted in an essentially equivalent way to changes in demand. (Indeed, if you have read through Box 2.2, you will already have seen how this is done.) The supply curve can be changed in position (that is, there can be an increase or decrease in supply) as a result of changes in:

- prices of other goods;
- input prices;
- technology.

We shall also show that changes in expenditure taxes and supply-side 'shocks' can have important consequences through induced shifts in market supply curves. A good illustration of the latter is the effects on the price of crude oil that followed from the invasion of Kuwait by Iraq in 1990. We examine this in Box 2.3.

Let us now examine what would happen if wage rates for all firms in one industry increase. The curves labelled D and S_1 in Figure 2.8 depict the market demand and supply curves for the good before the increase in wage rates. The equilibrium market price is P_1.

After wage rates have risen, firms find it more costly to produce a given output quantity than

Box 2.2 The Asian Economic Crisis and the Price of Copper

The skills of a business economist may sometimes be used to make quick assessments of short- and medium-term price movements for some good of interest to a business. Suppose you were asked, at the start of 1998, to predict what will happen to copper prices during the following twelve months.

There are, of course, many methods of making economic forecasts; we shall look at some of these methods later, in Chapter 15. What we show here is that supply and demand analysis can be helpful in marshalling available information to make predictions of a qualitative type: do we expect the price to rise or fall? Do we expect price changes to be large or small?

In the early part of 1998, the following information is available, or can be gleaned by a little industry analysis:

- among the things which strongly affect the demand for copper are the production levels of motor vehicles, electrical motors, piping for fluids, and other electrical components;
- the economic crisis in Asia which began in 1997 seems likely to substantially reduce the short- and medium-term growth rates of many Asian economies, including Japan; this will reduce the demand for all the items listed above;
- copper production capacity will increase for several years at least (after 1997); producing firms, acting in expectation of continuing demand growth, have opened up additional mines, and technological progress in the refining of copper has significantly reduced the costs of copper.

We can put these ideas together in a schematic form as shown in Figure 2.7. The curves labelled D_{1997} and S_{1997} represent demand and supply curves for copper before the Asian downturn become apparent. Copper producers, anticipating continuing growth in demand, had installed sufficient extra capacity for the supply in 1998 to be that shown by the curve S_{1998}. This level of supply intentions will be the one that is the outturn in 1998. If producer forecasts about demand had been correct, demand would have shifted to D_{1998}. Given this, the 1998 market equilibrium price would have been at the level indicated by point *b*, a higher price than in 1997. This is also what most copper market analysts predicted before the onset of the Asian crisis.

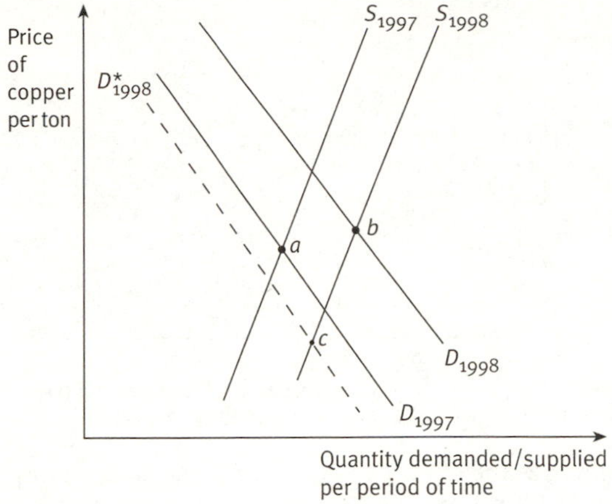

Figure 2.7 Copper prices: the effects of the Asian economic crisis

But demand for copper will fall rather than rise, with the demand curve shifting leftwards to D^*_{1998}. Given this demand and supply intentions remaining as S_{1998}, price will fall, not rise, to the price indicated by point *c* in Figure 2.7. This price fall could be rather large for two reasons:

1. the copper supply curves are very steep: large price falls will be required to reduce the quantity being supplied by even modest amounts;
2. the fall in demand (and so the magnitude of the shift from D_{1997} to D^*_{1998} may well prove to be severe.

Clearly, this kind of analysis—like any forecasting—may turn out to be wrong. Only the passage of time will tell us if that is the case. But decision-making is inextricably linked with forming assessments about future conditions. This item shows that supply and demand analysis may be a useful part of one's tool-kit in arriving at such assessments.

before. The price at which firms are willing to supply that quantity of the good will, therefore, increase. The position of the supply curves shifts upwards from S_1 to S_2, as illustrated in Figure 2.8. The vertical amount of this shift (for example, the distance *ab* in the diagram) will be equal to the increase in the incremental cost of producing a unit of output that arises from the higher wage rate. An increase in input prices results in a *decrease in supply* therefore.

The reader may find this a little confusing on first reading: how can an upward shift of a supply curve be described as a 'decrease in supply'? It is easy to resolve this paradox by looking at the diagram in a different way. Take any price, for example the price P_1. Now compare the supply intentions

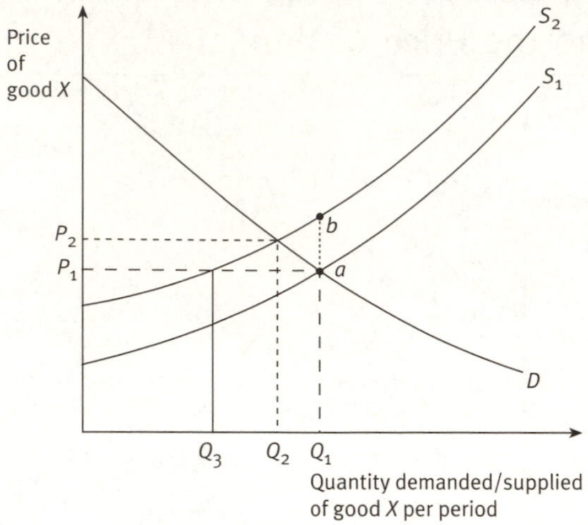

Figure 2.8 The effect of an increase in the industry wage rate on market equilibrium price and quantity traded

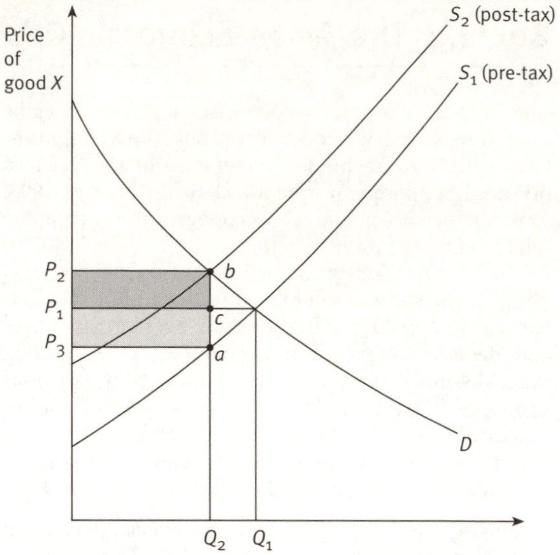

Figure 2.9 The incidence of a sales tax

before and after the wage rate increase. Before, firms intended to sell Q_1 at price P_1; afterwards, they intend to sell Q_3 at that price. The amount they intend to sell has fallen at this price, or indeed at any other price. In this sense, you can see that it is appropriate to describe this as a decrease in supply.

What is the effect of this fall in supply on the equilibrium market price? Returning to Figure 2.8, it is clear that a new equilibrium will be achieved when the market price reaches P_2. At this price, the quantity being exchanged in the market will be Q_2, lower than its level prior to the wage rate increase. A decrease in supply raises equilibrium price but lowers the equilibrium quantity traded on the market.

The Effects of a Change in a Sales Tax

Suppose that government imposes a fixed value sales tax on some good. As the tax will be collected from the seller, the supply curve moves upwards (that is, there is a decrease in supply). The amount of the vertical shift in the supply curve will be equal to the value of the sales tax per unit of the good; this is shown as the distance *ab* in Figure 2.9. You will note the similarity between the effect of a sales tax and an increase in wage rates: they both impose extra costs on firms, which they try to pass on to the consumer by shifting the supply curve upwards.

However Figure 2.9 illustrates something that was not highlighted in Figure 2.8. Firms will not, in general, succeed in passing on *all* of a cost increase in higher prices—whatever the origin of that cost increase. So let us examine the incidence of the sales tax, that is, who actually bears it.

The sales tax increases the equilibrium price from P_1 to P_2. But this increase is clearly less than the amount of sales tax firms have to pay to the government on each unit sold, *ab*. Clearly, our earlier contention is true in this case: the firms in this market do not succeed in passing on the sales tax to buyers, each of whom only pays *bc* more in price after the tax has been introduced. It is also clear after a little inspection that the distance *ac* (or equivalently $P_1 - P_3$) is the share of the tax paid by firms.

Put another way, the government collects in tax revenue an amount equal to the sum of the areas of the two shaded rectangles: the sales tax per good *ab* multiplied by the total number of units sold. Of this tax revenue, consumers collectively pay a share indicated by the upper, more heavily-shaded rectangle. Firms pay an amount indicated by the lighter shaded area. Notice that firms suffer in two ways from the tax. First, they pay some proportion of the tax themselves, thus having lower margins; secondly, they sell a smaller quantity after the sales tax has been introduced.

Finally, under what conditions would the firm not suffer in either of these ways from a sales tax? Only where the market demand curve is vertical—an unlikely case—would this be true. We suggest that you sketch out this special case to convince

Box 2.3 The Effects of a Supply-Side Shock: The Case of Iraq's Invasion of Kuwait

The invasion of Kuwait by Iraq in 1990 led to a substantial fall in the flow of oil onto world markets. Iraq and Kuwait oil had, prior to the Gulf war, supplied about 9 per cent of world oil output. The conflict led, therefore, to a decrease in oil supply, shown by the leftward shift in the supply curve in Figure 2.10. The oil supply curves show two interesting features. At prices below $7 per barrel, the supply curve is more or less horizontal; oil suppliers will not supply any oil when price falls below marginal (incremental) cost. We can infer that when spare capacity was available, marginal costs of oil supply in 1990 were in the neighbourhood of $6. However, the supply curve becomes almost vertical when oil output reached over 50 million barrels per day. This arises because of capacity constraints. For a given number of wells and associated production infrastructure, there will be some physical constraint on how much oil can be delivered in any period of time. When this capacity is reached, the marginal costs of oil become immense, as extra oil can only be supplied by installing additional capacity.

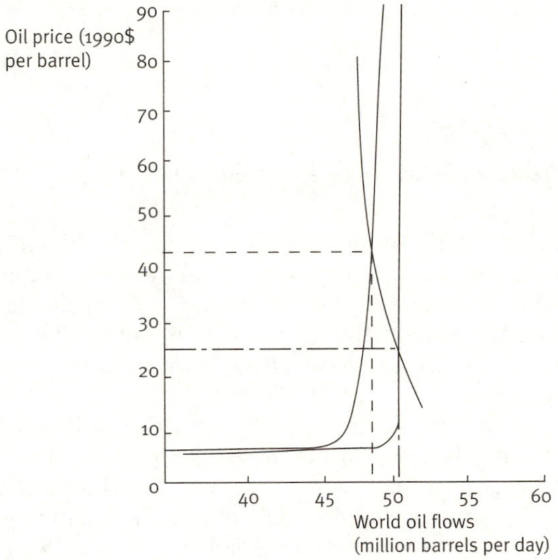

Figure 2.10 The Gulf war and its effect on the price of crude oil

The demand curve shows that the quantity of oil demanded is relatively unresponsive to price changes. This is particularly true when the oil price is already quite high. What we are portraying in Figure 2.10 is what you might call a short-run demand curve for oil. In the long run—when consumers of oil have had sufficient time to make full adjustments to oil price changes—we would expect oil demand to be far more sensitive to price. But it is not a long-run oil demand curve that we are showing here.

Notice the effect that the fall in oil supply had on crude oil prices. The price increased by approximately 80 per cent. A fall of about 4 per cent in the quantity traded (from 52 million barrels at the original price to about 48 million barrels at the new price) was associated with a price rise from $25 to $44. The sharpness of this price rise is due largely to the fact that the demand curve shows little sensitivity of quantity demanded to price changes.

yourself that the contention is true. As an additional exercise, you might also like to consider the incidence of a sales tax in the (also very unlikely) case where the market demand curve is horizontal.

Two Other Applications of Market Analysis

We conclude our examination of market price determination by considering two other examples. The first is the market for heroin. This demonstrates that even where markets are illegal, the fundamental forces of supply and demand still operate in the ways we have already seen. Our second example is the 'market' for publicly provided health services in the UK. It will be shown that some of the problems that beset the British National Health Service (and others like it elsewhere) can be attributed to the *absence* of normally functioning markets.

The Market for Hard Drugs

Even where a product is illegal, and so trading in it is prohibited by law, a market for that product may still exist. Moreover, behaviour in that market will still be subject to the forces of the price mechanism. In this section, we analyse the market for hard drugs. In doing so, it is hoped that you will see the power of supply and demand analysis, and will appreciate how it can be used to shed some light on this very important area of social policy.

To simplify, let us use the name heroin as a shorthand for the set of highly addictive, dangerous, and prohibited drugs. Even though no legal market for heroin exists, it is clear that illegal (or unofficial, or black) markets do exist.[3] We represent the UK market for heroin in Figure 2.11. The demand for heroin is shown by the curve labelled *D*. In drawing this curve, we have tried to depict the idea that the demand for heroin is, in the short run at least, extremely unresponsive to changes in price. As a first approximation, a heroin addict will want his daily supply and be prepared to pay whatever price is necessary to secure that supply. To employ a concept that will be explained at length in section 2.3, the demand for heroin in the short run is very price-inelastic.

What about the supply curve? Making some informed guesses, we conjecture that the heroin supply curve will resemble that labelled as S_1. This has a rather strange shape, which comes from the following assumptions. Heroin is supplied by criminal organizations (this is, of course, true by definition!). Criminal organizations carry out criminal activity. But that is not a single homogeneous thing. It encompasses drug supply, the control of prostitution, protection rackets, car theft, and many other activities. Crime bosses wish to appropriate profits, just like any other commercial organization. They allocate their crime efforts among these forms of activity depending on the relative rates of return offered by each. For example, when returns from prostitution are high (as they are now in many parts of Eastern and Central Europe after the collapse of communism), that will attract much of their resources and efforts. When bootlegged alcohol offers very high returns (as it did in Prohibitionist America) that is what criminals will tend to concentrate upon.

The supply curve shown in Figure 2.11 becomes nearly horizontal at some relatively low price. What is going on here is simple: when the returns from heroin supply fall to a level significantly below that obtainable in other activities, drug supply will be abandoned in favour of one or more of those other activities. The supply curve is roughly vertical over most of the rest of its range: criminal organizations, having once decided to be active in this field, will set up a set of supply chains, bringing in a more or less fixed quantity of the drug. This will be sold at whatever the price market will bear. We simplify matters by assuming that higher prices will not bring forth more supply in the short term (although new entry will occur, and so supply will increase, in the long run; we shall have more to say on this in Chapter 6, where the role of new entry in illegal drugs markets is examined further).

[3] This is not quite correct. Heroin can be legally prescribed for particular medical reasons, but this is not relevant for our analysis.

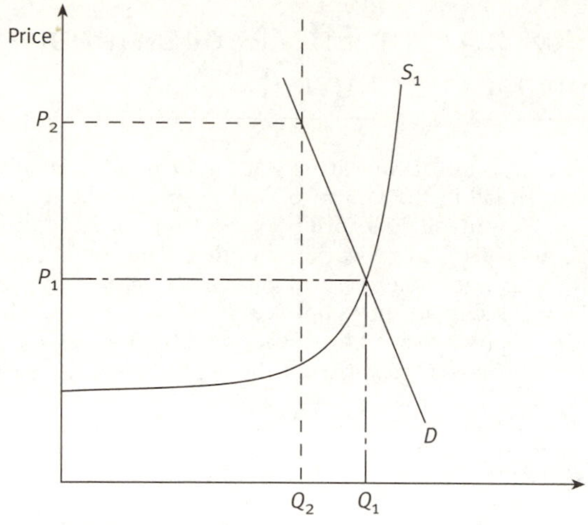

Figure 2.11 The market for heroin

Given all this, the equilibrium price of heroin is P_1, and the amount purchased is Q_1. Now suppose that government finds this outcome intolerable, and pursues a 'supply-side' policy of trying to intercept drugs through more policing and surveillance. This is likely to be effective for a while. For the sake of argument, assume drugs busts reduce actual supply to Q_2. We draw a vertical line at this quantity to portray the 'constrained supply'.

What happens to the price of heroin? With unchanged demand but reduced supply, prices are driven up to P_2. The drugs policy has been effective in so far as less heroin is consumed, but the rise in price is worrying for several reasons. Two of these are particularly important.

- Given the need to feed the habit, higher prices may lead to more petty criminal activity on the part of heroin users.
- The higher market price of the drug will stimulate an increased amount of activity being allocated to drug supplying by organized criminals. Like any rational business, in the long run they will allocate more resources to activities from which a higher value can be appropriated. The supply curve thus shifts to S_3 (see Figure 2.12).

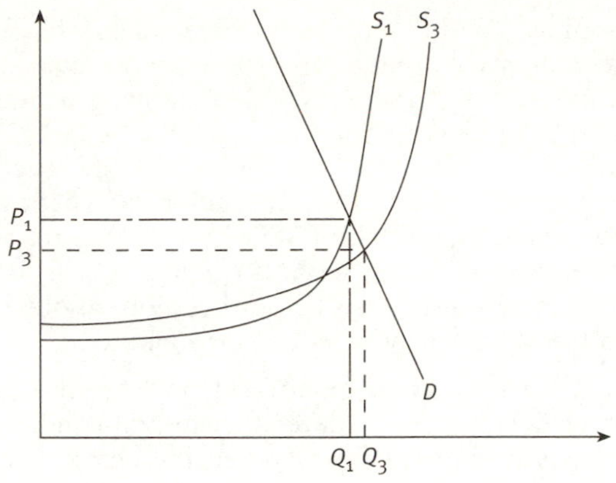

Figure 2.12 The market for heroin after new entry of suppliers

It is also safe to predict that, with the passage of time, the earlier policing efforts will weaken in effectiveness. Alternative supply routes will be found. For simplicity, we assume that all effectiveness is lost. So where do we finish up? The new equilibrium price is P_3, and Q_3 of heroin is traded, as shown in Figure 2.12.

One might further speculate that the demand for drugs might also increase during the processes we have described. Criminalization of heroin, combined with a stronger policing effort, may lead to a drugs subculture being developed that outsiders find very hard to influence. But that is clearly a moot point. What seems to be more clear as far as social policy is concerned is that supply-side controls probably do not work, and may even intensify the extent of drug use. It would be better to focus efforts to a greater extent on the demand side, using measures designed to reduce the demand for drugs. How exactly this can be done is a question that social policy analysts have, unfortunately, found very hard to answer. We examine this issue a little further in Chapter 6.

A Publicly Provided Health Service

We have seen how price changes operate, through the market mechanism, to reallocate resources in response to changes in underlying economic conditions. What kinds of resource allocation problems arise when there is no market mechanism operating to carry out this function?

We can get some interesting insights into this question by using the techniques of supply and demand analysis to examine the operation of the UK National Health Service (NHS). Treatment in the NHS is free at the point of use, being funded from general taxation. As the NHS services have no market price, no market demand curve can be observed. Nevertheless, there is an underlying (or implicit) demand curve for health-care services, which describes the community's willingness-to-pay for various levels of health-care provision. It is this implicit demand curve that is labelled *D* in Figure 2.13(*a*).

The provision of health-care services is determined by the quantity of funds that government chooses to allocate to the NHS at any point in time. We represent the current level of health-care provision by the vertical line labelled $\bar{S}$. Note that this is not, strictly speaking, a supply curve, as there is no price for this activity. Instead, $\bar{S}$ is a politically determined quantity of resources made available for health care.

An explanation for 'queuing' for hospital treatment in the NHS can be found in Figure 2.13(*a*). With no charges made at the time of use, the effective price of health services is zero. The quantity demanded of health care is, therefore, Q_2.[4] But the amount of health-care services provided is limited to $\bar{S}$. As a result, there is excess demand for health care, which will be manifested in a variety of forms: lengthy waiting lists for operations, choices by health-care managers about which forms of treatment they will and will not offer, restrictions on drugs available on prescription, and so forth. There are at least three kinds of response to the 'problem' of waiting lists and other forms of health-care rationing.

Charge a fee at the point of use for health services (instead of funding the service from general taxation). It is clear from our diagram that if the price $\bar{P}$ were charged, then demand would equal the politically determined supply $\bar{S}$. There would be no excess demand. Note that this does not increase the quantity of health care provided, it merely chokes off some of the quantity demanded. In some parts of the NHS, fees at the point of use are now being employed, one example being charges for prescription drugs.

Abolish a publicly provided health service, and replace it by a private health service. Suppose that the supply curve of a private health service

[4] We have drawn the demand curve as touching the horizontal axis at a finite quantity. Another possibility is that the demand curve approaches the horizontal axis without reaching it at any finite quantity. In that case, the demand for health care at a zero price would be infinite.

were that shown by S in Figure 13(a). Then, assuming the market demand curve remained at D, a market equilibrium price of P_1 would result. In this case, no excess demand for health care would exist (although there might still be people who would wish to receive additional health care, of course). Indeed, as we have drawn the diagram, there would be less health care provided in total under this regime.

Increase the quantity of resources allocated to the NHS We examine this option in Figure 13(b). The supply of health-care resources is increased to $\bar{S}'$, thereby reducing the extent of health-care rationing. To the extent that demand for health care remains constant, this succeeds in reducing waiting lists. But there is a dilemma lying in wait here. In the longer term, increasing the quantity of heath-care resources is likely to increase life expectancy, and also add to our expectations of what can reasonably be expected of a health-care system. So the demand for health services will increase. Trying to eliminate waiting lists by putting more resources into the system may be doomed to failure.

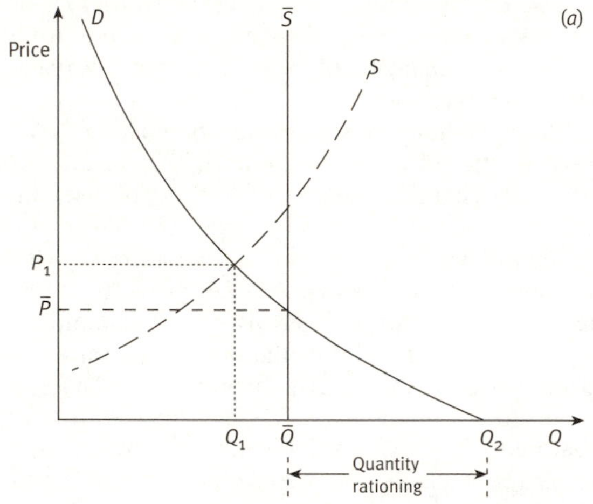

Figure 2.13a The effect of quantity rationing

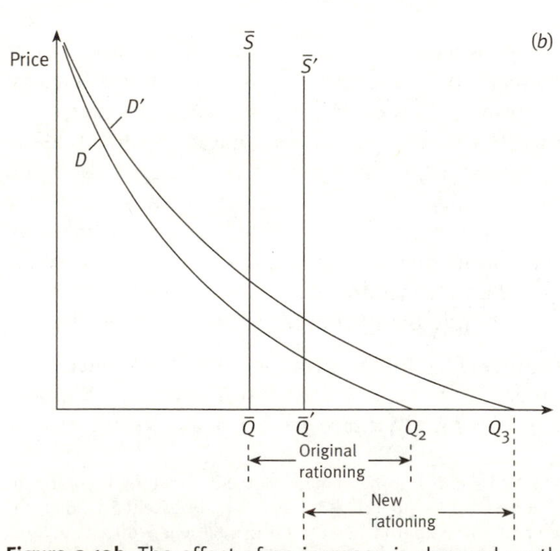

Figure 2.13b The effect of an increase in demand on the amount of rationing

The challenge facing politicians and health-care managers is how to achieve efficient and equitable health provisions in an era when the demand for costly health services is rising, in an environment where conventional market-based pricing is widely regarded as politically and morally unacceptable. Management within the health service is now increasingly using internal pricing as a tool to assist in resource allocation decisions. Thus while it is still uncommon for actual patient charges to be invoked, use is being made of accounting or shadow prices to assist decisions about how limited health-care resources are to be deployed over the many claims on them.

2.3 The Elasticity of Demand

The Concept of Elasticity

Elasticity of demand is a measure of the extent to which demand responds to changes in any of its underlying determinants. Knowledge of elasticities is useful for many purposes. In the private sector, sensible decisions on pricing depend on information about the likely magnitude of demand response to price changes. This will also be true for public sector organizations producing marketed products (such as the railways or electricity supply industries in many countries). Government policy-making can also be improved by such information. For example, the net effect on tax revenues of changes in VAT can only be calculated if elasticity estimates are available.

Three kinds of demand elasticity are of particular importance:

- price elasticity of demand;
- cross-price elasticity of demand;
- income elasticity of demand.

Price Elasticity of Demand

We shall deal with price elasticity in depth, the other two very briefly. There are two reasons for this. First, the principles and calculations underlying income and cross-price elasticities are the same as for price elasticity. What you learn in this section can easily be adapted to the other two. Secondly, price elasticity is the one that impinges directly on business policy as a firm can change the price of its own product, but not the prices of other goods nor consumers' income.

The price elasticity of demand (*PED*) for a good *x* is defined as:

$$PED \equiv \frac{\text{proportionate change in quantity demand of good } x \text{ per period}}{\text{proportionate change in price of good } x}.$$

Since demand curves are typically negatively sloped, *PED* will usually be negative. It will be useful to express this definition in mathematical notation. Let *P* and *Q* denote the price and quantity demanded of good *x* respectively, and let ΔP and ΔQ be small changes in price and quantity demanded of the good. Then we can write the expression for *PED* as

$$PED = \frac{\frac{\Delta Q}{Q}}{\frac{\Delta P}{P}} = \frac{\Delta Q}{\Delta P} \times \frac{P}{Q}.$$

So if, for example, a 2 per cent rise in price (a change of 0.02 in proportionate terms) is associated with a 2 per cent fall in quantity demanded (a change of −0.02 in proportionate terms), the *PED* is −1. This is known as *unitary elasticity.* If a 2 per cent rise in price was associated with a 5 per cent fall in quantity demanded, PED would be −2.5; this is a case of *elastic demand.* A word of caution is warranted here. Measuring percentage (or proportionate changes) can sometimes be a source of ambiguity; the reason for this ambiguity and a way of avoiding it are explained in Box 2.4. You should read this now.

Two extreme cases of elasticity are

1. *perfectly inelastic demand*: this describes the case where a change in price leaves quantity demanded unchanged; *PED* is zero in this case;
2. *perfectly elastic demand*: this describes the case where a change in price, no matter how small that change is, results in quantity demanded falling to zero (if the price rises) or quantity demanded increasing ad infinitum (if the price falls). The numerical value of *PED* is minus infinity in this case.

Table 2.1 sets out the terminology which is commonly used to describe alternative values, or ranges of values, of *PED.*

Because elasticity of demand expresses, in numerical form, the responsiveness of quantity

Table 2.1 Price elasticity of demand

Price elasticity	Verbal description
$PED = 0$	perfectly inelastic demand
$-1 < PED < 0$	relatively inelastic demand
$PED = -1$	unitary elasticity of demand
$-\infty < PED \; -1$	relatively elastic demand
$PED = -\infty$	perfectly elastic demand

Box 2.4 The Arithmetic of Calculating the Price Elasticity of Demand

The arithmetic of elasticity measures is often a source of confusion. This confusion arises because of ambiguity in the meaning of 'proportionate change'. A change of price from £2 to £3 can be thought of as proportionate increase of either 0.5 or 0.33, depending on whether we relate the change of £1 to the base of £2 or the base of £3.

One way of dealing with this difficulty is to express the price change relative to an *average* base price; that is we take the average of the initial and final price, and express the price change as a proportion of that. Similarly, we should calculate the quantity change as a proportion of the average of the initial and final quantities.

Thus if $\{P_1, Q_1\}$ and $\{P_2, Q_2\}$ represent the initial and final pairs of price and quantity respectively, the formula for calculating *PED* is:

$$PED = \frac{\Delta Q / \frac{[Q_1 + Q_2]}{2}}{\Delta P / \frac{[P_1 + P_2]}{2}}$$

where ΔP and ΔQ represent the change in price and quantity, repectively. Note that this expression simplifies to

$$PED = \frac{\Delta Q / \, [Q_1 + Q_2]}{\Delta P / \, [P_1 + P_2]}.$$

demanded to changes in price, it is related to the slope of the market demand curve. The slope of the demand curve at any point is given by the rate of change of price with respect to quantity, that is $\Delta P/\Delta Q$, but if you look back to the formula for elasticity of demand, you will see that elasticity is not equal to the slope of the demand curve. Instead, elasticity of demand is the inverse of this slope (that is, $\Delta Q/\Delta P$], multiplied by P/Q, the ratio of price to quantity at the point on the demand curve at which elasticity is being measured. So the slope of a market demand curve provides some information about the price elasticity of demand, but it does not provide all the information necessary to calculate elasticity. However, in two special cases, illustrated in Figure 2.14, the inverse value of the slope of the demand curve and the numerical value of elasticity are equal.

The relationship in Figure 2.14(*a*) illustrates a demand curve for which demand is perfectly inelastic. *PED* is zero, as quantity is completely unresponsive to price changes. If you imagine the axes being rotated so that Q is on the vertical axis and P on the horizontal axis, it will be clear that $\Delta Q/\Delta P$ is zero at each point on the curve. Figure 2.14(*b*) shows a completely elastic demand, for which at each point *PED* is minus infinity.

Elasticity and the Shape of Demand Curves

In general, there is no reason to believe that a demand curve will have the same price elasticity at every point along its length. This should be clear from the formula for *PED*. Even if the slope of a demand curve is constant, the ratio of P/Q will vary at different prices. Therefore, at different price and quantity combinations on a demand curve, *PED* will be different.

Therefore it is not appropriate to ask what 'the elasticity of demand' is for a particular good. We need to qualify any such question by making clear at what price (or quantity) we wish to calculate the value of *PED*. It also follows from the maths of *PED* that, contrary to what you might expect, a straight line, negatively sloped demand curve will exhibit a *PED* which goes from perfectly elastic to perfectly inelastic as the price falls from its highest to its lowest levels.

Elasticity and Total Revenue

Now consider the relationship between price elasticity of demand and total revenue. Total revenue (R) is the value of sales, which is price times quantity sold:

$R = P \times Q.$

Since quantity sold will normally change in the opposite direction to price, it is not immediately clear how total revenue will be affected by price changes. The concept of elasticity, however, allows us to deduce the *direction* of the revenue change.

The upper panel of Figure 2.15 shows a linear demand curve, and divides it into two regions: one in which *PED* is elastic, the other in which it is inelastic. In the lower panel we show the revenue at each quantity. Note that revenue is maximized where *PED* is -1 in value (that is, where demand has unit elasticity). In the region where demand is elastic, a price decrease increases total revenue; in the region where demand is inelastic, a price decrease reduces total revenue. We shall return to

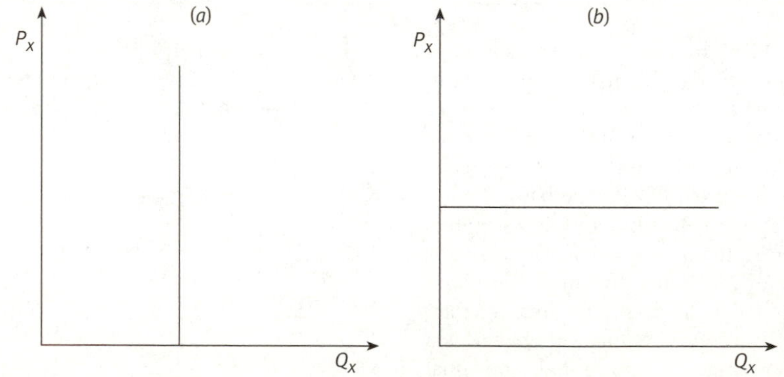

Figure 2.14 Perfectly inelastic and perfectly elastic demand curves

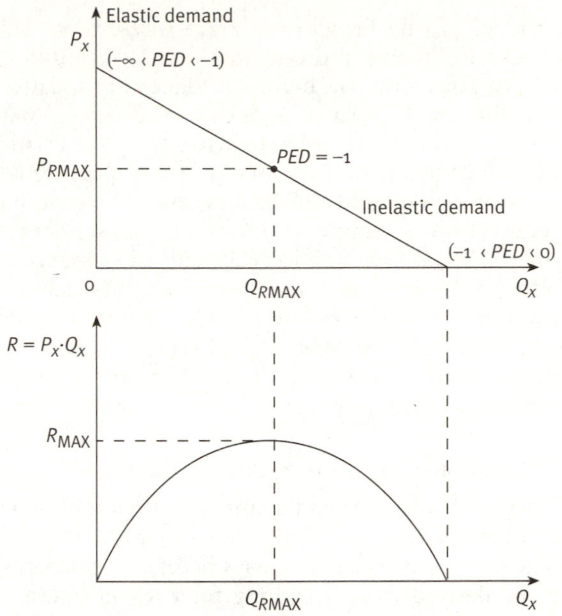

Figure 2.15 A demand curve, elasticity, and total revenue

examine this relationship in Chapter 7 in our discussion of monopolistic markets.

The direction of change in total revenue depends solely on the price elasticity of demand. If, for example, *PED* is elastic, a fall in price will always increase total revenue. If, on the other hand, *PED* is inelastic, a fall in price will always decrease total revenue. Table 2.2 shows the relationships between price changes, *PED* and the direction of change in total revenue. It would be a good idea to check for yourself that you can verify each of the results shown in the table.

Table 2.2 gives us information about the *direction* of revenue changes. But it does not tell us by *how much* revenue changes for any particular price change when demand is either 'relatively elastic' or 'relatively inelastic'. We can answer questions about the magnitude of revenue changes (and not only about their direction), but only if some additional information is available. Specifically, we need to know what the price is prior to its change, and what quantity was demanded at that price.

With this information, knowledge of the numerical value of *PED* allows us to calculate the magnitude of the change in quantity demanded for the good and the price change in question. Knowing the amounts of demand and the prices before and after the price change, one can then calculate the amount of the change in total revenue.

For example, suppose that at a price of £20, 100 units of the good are demanded. Now suppose that the price of this good is reduced from £20 to £19. Calculating the proportionate price change (expressed relative to its original level), this constitutes a proportionate fall in price of one-twentieth (that is, a proportionate change of 0.05 or 5 per cent). If the average price elasticity of demand between these two prices on this good's demand curve is −2, then quantity demanded will rise by twice that amount, in proportionate terms: that is, demand will rise by a proportion of 0.1 or 10 per cent. As quantity demanded was initially 100 units, an increase in demand of 10 per cent takes this figure to 110. So the new total revenue is $P_2Q_2 =$ £19 × 110 = £2,090. Total revenue has risen from £2,000 (£20 × 100) to £2,090, a proportionate increase of 90/2000 = 0.045, or, in percentage terms, an increase of 4.5 per cent.

Effective decision-making is considerably enhanced if information on price elasticity of demand is available. Consider a monopolist railway operator that seeks to maximize its fare revenue from its existing level of services. (Note that maximizing sales revenue is not the same thing as maximizing profits; whether it would be sensible to maximize *revenue* from ticket sales is a matter that we do not discuss here.) Should the operator increase or decrease ticket prices?

If demand for rail transport is relatively elastic,

Table 2.2 The relationship between total revenue and price elasticity of demand

Price elasticity of demand	Direction of change in total revenue when price increases	Direction of change in total revenue when price decreases
Completely elastic	Decrease (to zero)	Increase (of an infinite amount)
Relatively elastic	Decrease	Increase
Unitary elastic	No change	No change
Relatively inelastic	Increase	Decrease
Completely inelastic	Increase (in same proportion as ΔP)	Decrease (in same proportion as ΔP)

reducing fares would lead to a more than proportionate increase in the quantity of tickets sold, thereby increasing total revenue (assuming that spare capacity exists). In contrast, if demand for rail transport is relatively inelastic, increasing fares would lead to a less than proportionate decrease in the quantity of tickets sold, thereby increasing total revenue. So the decision as to whether to raise or lower fares depends upon whether demand is elastic or inelastic at the existing price. We also know, from Figure 2.15, that total revenue is maximized by setting price at the point where the demand curve has unitary elasticity. Knowledge of price elasticity at different points along a demand curve would clearly be very useful to a revenue-maximizing firm!

Determinants of Price Elasticity of Demand

What are the factors which influence the magnitude of price elasticity of demand? Three are likely to be particularly important.

The Closeness of Substitutes

If there are very close substitutes for a particular kind of good, the demand for that good is expected to be relatively elastic. This is so because consumers can switch easily between substitutes as the relative price changes. In terms of our earlier analysis of the effects of price changes, we would say that the substitution effect of a price change will be large in this case. Returning to our railways example, long distance rail, bus, and air travel seem to be reasonably close substitutes, and there is good reason to believe that they are becoming even closer substitutes. Certainly, air and rail travel between London and Paris are now close substitutes, and so we would expect the elasticity of demand of each of these services to be high.

Another example relates to cigarettes. For those who smoke, cigarettes have no close substitutes; demand is strongly inelastic. However, different brands are often perceived as close substitutes; the demand for a particular brand is thus highly elastic. This explains why cigarette producers are willing to incur great expenses to create strong brand loyalty; if this can be done, the degree of substitutability of its brand will fall, allowing the seller to raise prices without large proportionate falls in sales.

There is one very important consequence of all of this. It is very important to distinguish between market elasticity of demand (for example, elasticity for hatchback cars) and elasticity of demand for the product of one firm in a market where there are rivals producing more-or-less close substitutes. Clearly, elasticity will be much higher in the latter case than in the former. Suppose, for example, that a study has reliably estimated that the price elasticity of demand for transatlantic scheduled flights between Britain and the USA is -0.5. It would be foolish for one airline operating on that service to infer that its own-service elasticity of demand is also -0.5. If it were the sole operator, such an assumption would be reasonable. But if at least one other operator offers a rival service that customers regard as being a perfect substitute, its own-service elasticity of demand would be infinite!

Proportion of Income Spent on the Good

When individuals spend a large proportion of their income on a given good, demand for that good tends to be price elastic. This is because the benefits to be derived from searching for cheaper alternatives are large in absolute terms; consumers will be 'cost conscious'. When the goods being purchased are expensive relative to one's income, the absolute benefit to be gained by finding prices lower by some given proportionate amount may well be large enough to justify incurring additional search costs.

Period under Consideration

Elasticity of demand tends to be higher in the long run than the short run. Several reasons explain this.

- Some consumption may be habitual. Habits can be broken, but not always easily. They may also decay gradually, but the persistence of habits limits the short-run effects of price changes at least.
- It takes time for individuals to become aware of price changes and adjust demand accordingly. This is particularly true for those goods bought relatively infrequently. Thus for many consumer durable goods, elasticity of demand may rise considerably when measurements are made over a longer horizon so that adjustments will have had time to occur, or when consumer perceptions have adjusted to changes in prices and qualities.
- For technological or other reasons, consumers may be 'locked into' particular patterns of purchases in the short run. For example, the demand for oil is more elastic in the long run

than the short run. This is partly a reflection of the fact that the demand for oil as a source of primary energy for electricity production cannot easily be adjusted in the short run, as electricity producers will have capital equipment dedicated to oil energy use. If high prices persist, the capital stock will adjust, and as it does so, the measured demand change will become greater. Similar arguments apply to the use of (refined) oil in transport uses.

Cross-Price Elasticity of Demand

Cross-price elasticity is concerned with the relationship between the demand for one good, say good *a* and the price of another, say good *b*. The cross-elasticity of demand between goods *a* and *b*, CED_{ab}, is defined as:

$$CED_{ab} = \frac{\text{proportionate change in quantity demand of good } a \text{ per period}}{\text{proportionate change in price of good } b}.$$

The sign taken by the cross-price elasticity depends upon the nature of the relationship between the two goods in question. First of all, the goods may be complementary to one another; they are jointly consumed to some degree. If the pair are *complements*, *CED* will usually be negative. For example, for some people bread and butter are complements. Cars and petrol (or cars and diesel fuel) are also examples of complementary goods. Another example is the pair, computers and computer software. As the price of computer hardware has fallen, so the demand for software has increased dramatically.

Other goods may be substitutes for one another. For example, different brands of cigarettes are mutual *substitutes*. Apple Macintosh computers are substitutes for IBM-compatible personal computers (although they are not perfect substitutes). If two goods are substitutes, *CED* will usually be positive.

These expectations are summarized in Table 2.3.

Table 2.3 The effects of a price change on the demands for substitutes and complements

	Change in demand for good *a* where *a* and *b* are:	Change in demand for good *a* where *a* and *b* are:
	Substitutes	Complements
Price of *b*:		
Rises	Increase	Decrease
Falls	Decrease	Increase

The reason for the qualification 'usually' is to do, once again, with the income effects of price changes. For example, suppose that oil prices were to rise. One would expect that since coal is a substitute for oil, the *CED* between coal and oil would be positive. This would imply that a rise in oil prices would lead to a rise in the demand for coal. However, the income effect will tend to offset this somewhat: higher oil prices reduce real income, and this will reduce the demand for any good which is a normal good. If coal is a normal good, the income effect in this situation works in the opposite direction to the substitution effect. In exceptional cases, the income effect could be so strong that the actual *CED* between coal and oil has the opposite sign to what one might initially expect.

We invite the reader to consider how knowledge of cross-price elasticities may be useful in developing strategic policy. What is clear is that if one could reliably estimate the cross-price elasticity at the level of firms' rival products—if, for example, the cross-price elasticity of Coca-Cola for Pepsi-Cola could be estimated—this would be of great benefit to a firm in setting its price. Unfortunately, such information is not likely to be available, and even where it is, there is no reason to believe that what was true in the past will also be true in the future, particularly when the number of rival firms is relatively small. You might also like to consider the complications which arise when all rival producers of a certain product simultaneously try to make use of cross-price elasticity information in setting prices. It is too early in this book to enter into a discussion of these matters; however, we will shed a little light on them in discussing the operation of oligopolistic markets in Chapter 8.

Income Elasticity of Demand

The income elasticity of demand for good *x*, *YED*, is defined as:

$$YED = \frac{\text{proportionate change in quantity demanded of good } x \text{ per period}}{\text{proportionate change in consumers' income}}.$$

Knowledge of income elasticity of demand may be useful to firms considering their future product offerings. Other things being equal, it would be desirable to produce goods for which demand rises strongly as income grows: goods with a high positive income elasticity of demand. In the period of post-Second World War reconstruction, the

Japanese planning ministry seems to have given preferential support to several industries—including electrical consumer goods and automobiles—that it judged would have a high income elasticity. Hindsight shows this to have been a very good assessment.

Calculating Demand: Pitfalls to be Avoided

A common—and potentially very costly—mistake is the attempt to calculate demand curves directly from consumption and price data. In this section, we will explain this process, show why it is incorrect, and explain why the mistake can be costly.

Roughly speaking, what is sometimes done is this. A set of recent years is chosen, and data are collected on the level of consumption and the price of the good in each of these periods. The data are then plotted on a scatter diagram, with price on the vertical axis and consumption on the horizontal axis. A trendline—or some other line that best represents the price–quantity relationship—is then fitted on the scatter diagram. The resulting trendline is then described as the demand curve for the good in question.

However, except in very special circumstances, it is no such thing. To see this we will go through one such exercise ourselves. Table 2.4 contains data on the market price, and the world consumption and world production, of crude oil for each year from 1965 to 1993.

Table 2.4 World oil prices, consumption and production, 1965–1993

Year	Production (m. tonnes)	Consumption (m tonnes)	Price ($ 1990)
1965	1564.4	1535.7	8.24
1966	1696.4	1649.3	8.01
1967	1822.4	1767.6	7.79
1968	1989.5	1912.7	7.48
1969	2143.9	2081.9	7.10
1970	2361.9	2252.0	6.70
1971	2494.0	2379.5	7.99
1972	2633.3	2555.3	8.57
1973	2870.5	2755.6	8.94
1974	2877.4	2714.8	31.76
1975	2731.7	2680.2	28.08
1976	2952.5	2854.4	29.22
1977	3063.7	2949.1	29.55
1978	3089.0	3055.1	28.10
1979	3221.3	3103.4	31.15
1980	3077.7	2980.1	47.29
1981	2905.9	2876.7	50.77
1982	2788.3	2784.4	50.85
1983	2776.9	2764.9	45.64
1984	2841.7	2812.7	40.29
1985	2809.0	2809.2	38.26
1986	2934.4	2897.7	18.92
1987	2941.1	2949.1	23.63
1988	3050.0	3039.1	18.25
1989	3112.4	3090.1	21.10
1990	3153.9	3140.1	26.34
1991	3139.2	3119.7	21.27
1992	3168.5	3145.6	19.95
1993	3164.8	3121.4	17.07

Source: BP Statistical Review of World Energy, June 1994.

Now let us plot oil consumption against price; in doing so we obtain the scatter diagram shown in Figure 2.16(*a*). Using the package EXCEL to fit a trendline, we obtain the 'demand curve' shown in Figure 2.16(*b*).

The fact that the trendline is upward sloping should warn you that this is not a demand curve. But even leaving this to one side, what makes us think that this is a demand curve at all? Look at the data for consumption and production in Table 2.4; you will see that they are very similar for each year, and they move together very closely. (You can confirm this by plotting the two series together against time). This is of course what one would expect. Apart from changes in stocks, oil production and oil consumption are just different ways of measuring the same thing: the amount traded on the market!

Now suppose that another researcher plots a scatter diagram of production against price, obtains a trendline, and then calls this a 'supply curve'. Evidently, the results would be almost exactly the same as those shown in Figure 2.16. The supply and demand curves seem to be the same thing.

But neither of these exercises produces a supply curve or a demand curve, because consumption is not the same thing as 'demand' and production is not the same thing as 'supply'. Look back to the first part of this chapter to see how supply and demand are defined. Demand, for example, is a schedule of intentions: how much people would choose to buy at different prices. And most importantly, a demand curve is drawn on the assumption that all the other things that affect demand (such as income, prices of other goods, and so on) remain constant.

But all these other things did not remain constant. Indeed, over the period 1965 to 1993, there were substantial changes in both demand and supply. Looking at the price series, you can see that it

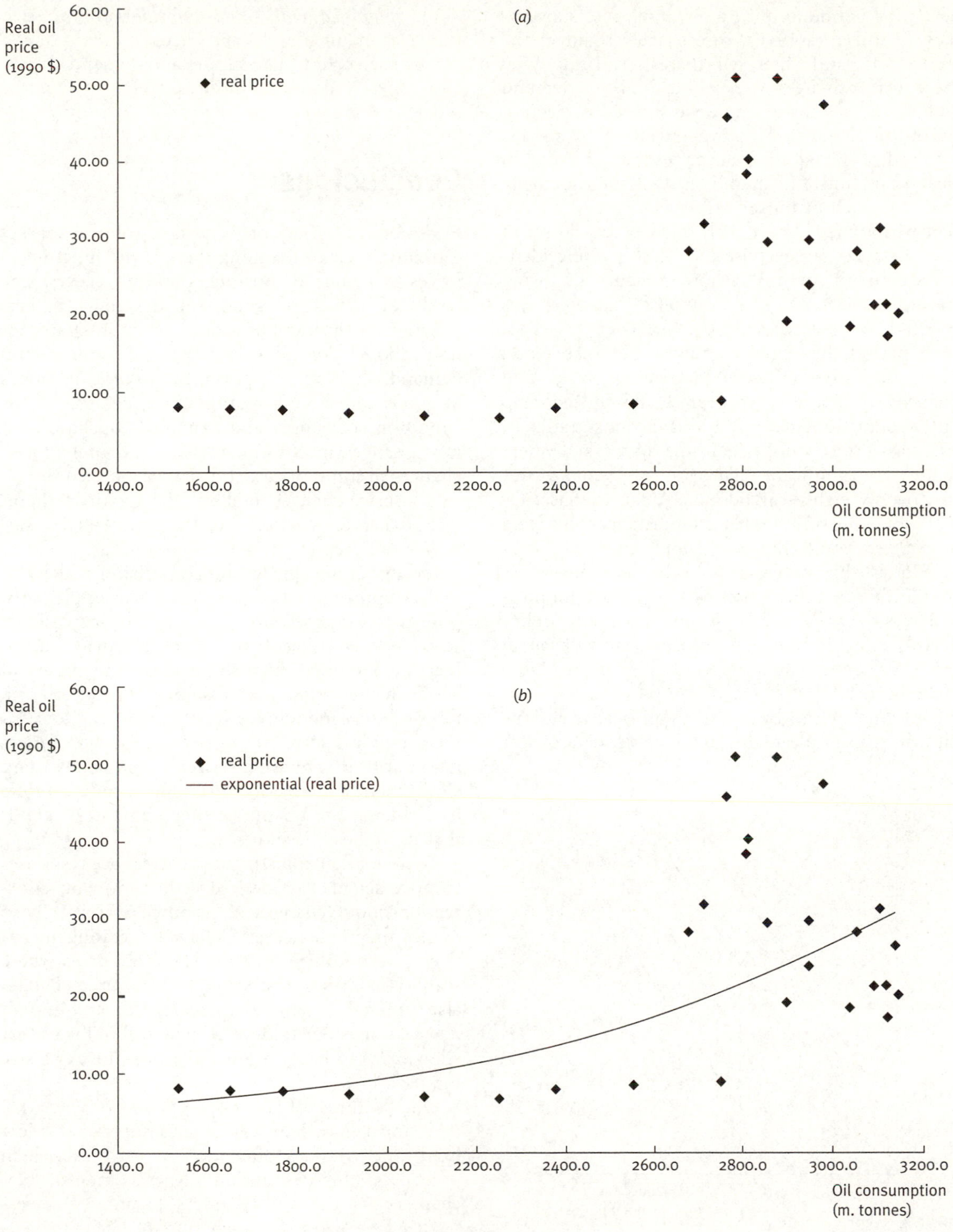

Figure 2.16 Oil consumption plotted against the real oil price

began the period at quite a low level, rose substantially in the mid-1970s, rose sharply again in the late 1970s, and then fell thereafter. Underlying these price changes were shifts in both demand and supply (as for example we showed in Section 2.2 of this chapter). All our graphs have captured is a record of the equilibrium prices that prevailed in each year, and the quantities that were actually traded in each of those years.

It was argued earlier that, under a special set of circumstances, an exercise such as this would identify a demand curve. We show in Figure 2.17 what circumstance is necessary. Suppose that there was no increase or decrease in demand over the whole time period, but supply changes did take place. Then the observed combinations of price and quantity traded in each year would indeed map out a demand curve. But this is most unlikely, and was certainly not true in the oil market, where there were significant changes in oil demand over this twenty-eight-year period. (As an exercise, try and work out under what circumstances this kind of exercise would identify a supply curve.)

Why is this potentially costly? The answer is simple. If you believe that what you have found is a demand curve, but it is not, then any policy decisions based on that information will be at best misleading, and at worst disastrous. Little more need be said.

One final point: by using a statistical technique known as multiple regression analysis, data of this kind, *combined with other information* (on such things as income levels and prices of other goods), can be used to estimate supply and demand curves. How this is done is, unfortunately, outside the scope of this book.

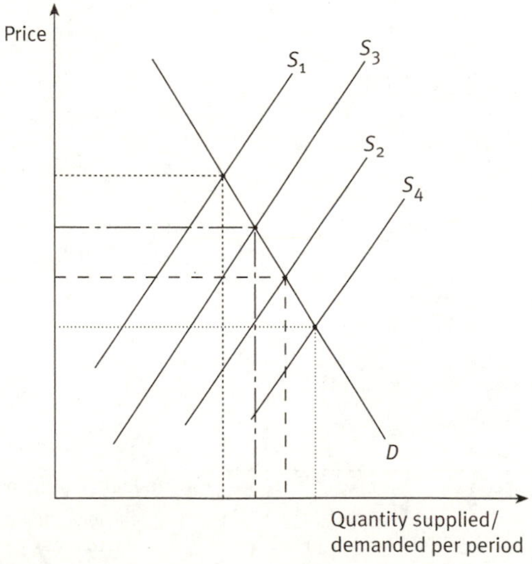

Figure 2.17 Shifts in supply identifying a demand curve

Conclusions

Prices play a variety of important roles in market economies. Central among these is the function of prices as *signals* to consumers and producers. The levels of prices of goods in different markets (together with prices of productive inputs) are signals about prevailing patterns of supply and demand. But more importantly, *changes* in prices of goods convey information about changes in the conditions of supply and demand. You have seen how changes in consumer tastes and preferences, changes in input prices, and changes in income can lead to price changes. It should be apparent, therefore, that price changes can transmit valuable signals about changes in market conditions.

Ideally, these signals induce decision-makers to make appropriate adjustments. For example, suppose that some resource is becoming increasingly scarce. Other things being equal, this will tend to increase its price, and so increase the prices of goods made using that resource. Producers will respond to rising input prices by switching towards the use of less scarce resources—ones whose prices have not risen, or have not risen to the same extent. Consumers will respond to higher product prices by reducing the quantities they demand of goods that make heavy use of scarce inputs.

These market adjustment processes are responses to price signals that are correctly conveying information about changes in resource scarcity. In so doing, they enhance efficiency by creating incentives to economize on the use of resources where scarcity is biting most strongly. The price changes also generate incentives to search for and exploit new resources, or to develop new technologies that allow firms to become less reliant on the expensive inputs.

Our outline of the operation of a market mechanism has, however, been a somewhat 'idealized' one. Markets often do not work as well in practice as this description suggests. Indeed, later chapters (particularly Chapters 13 and 14) investigate some ways in which markets 'fail' to generate efficient allocations of resources. We saw in

Chapter 1 that market mechanisms are not the only way in which resources can be allocated, and Chapter 4 will demonstrate that even in so-called 'market economies' other mechanisms are widely used, particularly within those organizations that we call firms.

Further reading

The best way of developing your skills in applied supply and demand analysis is to read one or two business journals or newspapers as often as you can. Good examples are *The Economist* magazine and the *Financial Times* newspaper, both of which often carry articles or lengthy surveys of particular markets. When you are reading matter of this kind, try to use the conceptual frameworks we have been through in this chapter to organise and structure the information presented.

Market or industry analyses placed in a more explicit economics framework can also be found in several of the commercial bank reviews (such as the *Barclays Economic Review* and the *Lloyds Bank Economic Bulletin*) and in some periodic journals which are posed at the border between academic papers and pieces for the intelligent layman. Good examples include the *Business Strategy Review* (Oxford University Press), the *National Institute Economic Review*, the *Oxford Review of Economic Policy* (Oxford University Press), and *The Economic Review* (Philip Alan Publishers Ltd, Deddington, Oxford).

Questions

2.1. Analyse how the price of large family saloon cars is likely to be affected by a substantial increase in the price of crude oil.

2.2. A rise in consumers' income will increase the demand for cars. Is this statement correct?

2.3. Construct a diagram to show the effects on the equilibrium price of cars and the equilibrium quantity traded of cars as a result of a decrease in the price of capital equipment in the manufacture of cars.

2.4. Show diagrammatically a situation of excess supply in a market. What would be the consequence of this in a free market? Show how excess supply may arise in the labour market if a statutory minimum wage were to be introduced or increased.

2.5. How do changes in resource allocation occur in planned economies? Are the appropriate changes likely to be made quickly and smoothly?

2.6. Will the following shift the demand curve or the supply curve, and in which direction:

(a) a rise in the good's own price;

(b) an increase in the price of a competing (substitute) good;

(c) a decrease in consumers' income;

(d) an increase in the price of energy?

2.7. Why may some goods be inferior? What types of goods are these likely to be?

2.8. If, as a result of an increase in price from £13 to £14 a bottle, the consumption of gin fell from 10,000 to 8,000 bottles a week (with other things remaining unchanged), what is the value of the arc elasticity of demand between these two points?

2.9. Consider the following information on the demand for coffee:

	1996	1997	1998
Price (£) per lb	1.21	2.10	3.40
Quantity (lbs) per person per year	16.8	13.6	12.0

Is it possible to calculate the price elasticity of demand for coffee from this information? If it is possible, what is the elasticity? If it is not possible, explain why it is not.

3 Individual Choices, the Supply of Work, and the Demand for Goods

Introduction

In Chapter 2 a market was defined as the process of interactions between consumers and producers of a good. In discussing supply and demand, the concepts we had in mind were *market* supply—the schedule of intentions to sell a good at different prices, aggregated over all potential suppliers—and market demand—the schedule of intentions to buy the good at different prices, aggregated over all potential purchasers. In this and the following two chapters we turn our attention to *individual* consumers and producers. By looking at individual behaviour, we can give a solid foundation for market supply and demand.

This chapter considers the behaviour of an individual in his or her role as a consumer of goods. However, we begin our analysis one step earlier. Each individual has a certain amount of time available to allocate between work time and leisure time. We begin by looking at the individual's choice of hours of work.

A choice of hours of work influences the budget that the individual has for consumption purposes. How does the consumer allocate that budget between available goods? This is the question we address in the second section of the chapter, making use of *utility theory*. In the process, a solid theoretical underpinning to the notion of a demand function is generated. Furthermore, the analysis of the income and substitution effects of price changes gives valuable insights into the relationship between demand and prices.

3.1 The Individual's Choice of Hours of Work

In our investigation of the way a typical individual makes choices, a variety of simplifying assumptions will be made. This leads to some very powerful insights into the nature of an individual's economic behaviour. We do pay a price, however, in making simplifying assumptions. In particular, the analysis will be unable to capture all the important features of the work–leisure choice. But it is not our intention to be able to explain everything. The objective is to introduce the reader to a way of thinking which makes use of a small number of fundamental principles. These principles can be used to analyse more 'realistic' cases as the need arises.

Each individual has available each day a certain amount of time which, after performing various necessary biological functions such as sleeping and resting, can be used for either paid employment or leisure. How will he or she choose to allocate that time? The key to answering this question follows from the premise that individuals seek to use their resources to maximize value. Put in an equivalent way, individuals seek to maximize their *utility*.

Individuals generally obtain utility from their leisure time. Do they also obtain utility from work? For some people work is enjoyed in itself, for others it is not enjoyed or it is disliked. Work in itself, therefore, may confer zero, positive, or negative utility. For simplicity, we shall assume that work has no effect in itself on an individual's utility, although our analysis could easily be amended to cover other cases.

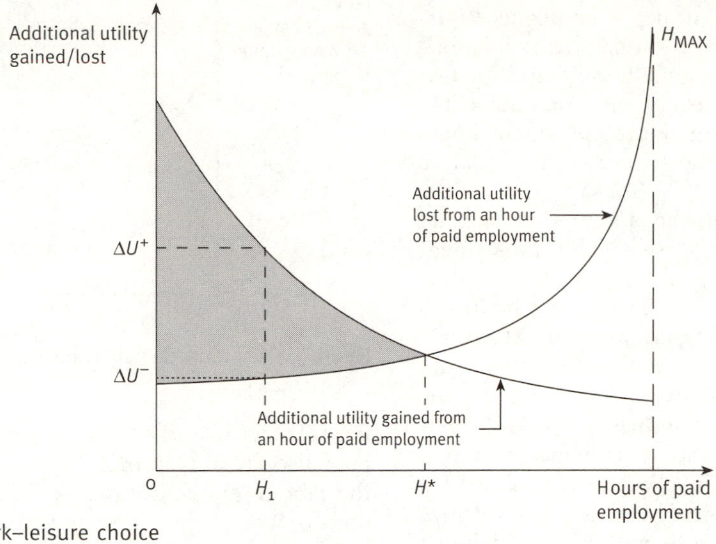

Figure 3.1 The work–leisure choice

But even if work does not *in itself* generate utility, it does provide the means by which an individual obtains utility. Paid employment generates income for the worker, and this income gives command over goods which are satisfying. Leisure and paid employment each, therefore, involve an opportunity cost. If an additional hour of work is chosen, the gross benefit to the individual is the utility that derives from consuming those goods and services which can be purchased from the additional money income. The opportunity cost of working an additional hour is the utility lost from forgone leisure.[1]

A rational person will choose to apportion available time between leisure and paid employment in such a way that the total utility obtained is at a maximum. How is this be done? Consider Figure 3.1, in which two schedules are represented. One is the additional utility gained from one extra hour of paid employment. The other is the additional utility lost in forgone leisure time as an extra hour is worked.

One schedule shows that the additional utility obtained from an extra hour of paid employment falls as the total number of hours worked in a given period of time rises. This is not because the individual is paid less for additional hours of work, but rather that the additional utility gained from extra income tends to fall as income rises. The other schedule shows that the additional utility lost in forgone leisure time as an extra hour is worked tends to increase as the total hours of work become higher. A justification for this might be that as leisure becomes more scarce to the individual, its value will tend to rise.

The choice of hours of work that maximizes total utility is shown as H^*, the number at which the additional utility lost in forgone leisure time as an extra hour is worked just equals the additional utility gained from one hour of extra paid employment. The amount of total utility that the individual enjoys by working H^* hours is shown by the shaded area between the two schedules, up to H^* hours of work. To convince yourself of this, look at the hours choice H_1. At this level of hours the additional utility gained from one more hour exceeds the additional utility lost: the individual would gain more than he or she loses if this hour were worked. But this argument is true for any choice of total hours up to H^*. Summing up all these incremental differences between gains and losses, we arrive at the shaded area in Figure 3.1 which represents total utility to the individual.

Figure 3.1 has been drawn in terms of utility losses and gains from *additional paid employment.* We could, of course, have done the analysis in

[1] We have just assumed that work confers zero utility in itself. However, if paid employment is intrinsically unenjoyable (or more precisely confers negative utility) that utility would be an additional cost of devoting some available time to paid employment. If, on the other hand, paid employment is intrinsically enjoyable, yielding positive utility, that utility would be an additional benefit from devoting the time to paid employment.

terms of utility losses and gains from *additional leisure*. In that case, a utility-maximizing *leisure* level would be deduced by a similar form of reasoning. Both approaches are equally valid and the two 'stories' are entirely consistent with each other: the sum of the utility-maximizing employment hours and the utility-maximizing leisure hours would be the total available time.

One may object that the assumption that an individual can choose hours of paid employment is often unrealistic. After all, even if an individual has paid employment, he or she may not be free to choose the number of hours worked. Moreover, some individuals may be unable to obtain paid employment at all. These two features are certainly characteristic of many economies in the 1990s. But a moment's reflection should convince you that they do not necessarily invalidate our analysis. We have described the individual's choice of *desired* hours of work and leisure, not the actual hours obtained.

Policy Implications

In the introductory remarks to this chapter, we claimed that our analysis would be useful; let us put this to the test. One application of the analysis is that it enables us to draw implications about government policy. Suppose that government wished to encourage individuals to work for longer hours. How might this be done? One method operates by shifting upwards the schedule of additional utility gained from extra hours of paid employment. Suppose that workers currently pay tax on additional labour income. If the tax rate were to be reduced with other things remaining constant, this would have the effect of shifting this function upwards, as illustrated in Figure 3.2. Note also that if high income levels are taxed at high marginal rates, reductions of these marginal rates will shift the curve upwards *and* tend to make it fall less steeply from left to right. In either case, the individual will choose to work more hours. The reason for this is that the terms of the trade-off between utility from work-income and utility from leisure have altered; a lower tax rate has increased the attractiveness of work relative to leisure.

This analysis can only be suggestive of the possible effects of changing tax rates. There are very many other effects that would need to be considered before placing any confidence in any resulting predictions. In addition to inducing existing workers to work longer hours, lower tax rates may also encourage more people to participate in the labour market. Some individuals may choose not to work when tax rates are high, but may choose to do so when tax rates are lower. The effect of tax rates on the incentive to work, and on the choice of hours, has been at the heart of tax reform programmes in the 1980s and 1990s, and has been an important factor contributing to reductions of marginal tax rates in a large number of countries.

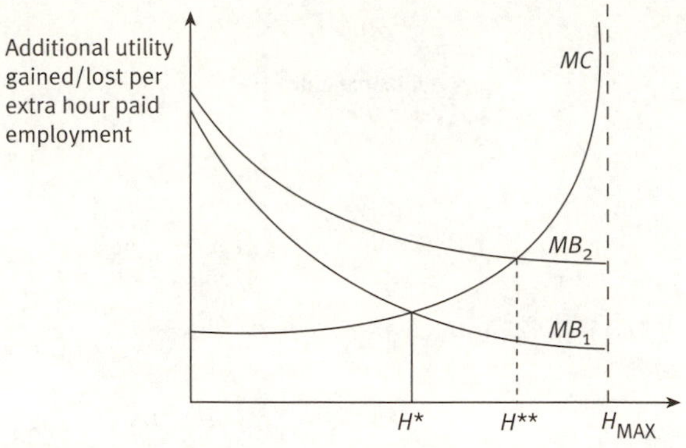

Figure 3.2 The work–leisure choice and a tax-rate reduction

3.2 Utility Analysis and Consumer Demand

The first section of this chapter introduced the 'marginal' way of thinking. Once the work–leisure choice is made, money income is determined. The individual will now face a budget constraint that limits consumption expenditure.[2] Our next task is to investigate how the individual allocates this budget between different goods. To do this, we shall make use of the principle of utility maximization subject to a budget constraint.

Utility and Consumer Preferences

Utility refers to the satisfaction or enjoyment which comes from the consumption of goods over some interval of time. For simplicity, suppose that only two goods are available for consumption. It does

[2] Consumption choices are often made by a family rather than an individual. We shall stick with the individual as the decision-maker, but note that *the individual* could be taken to mean one person, or we could extend its meaning to that of one decision-making unit, in which case it could refer to a family unit.

not really matter what these are: we simply label the two goods x and y. An individual gets utility from consuming particular bundles of the two goods. The amount of utility obtained is described by the individual's utility function, which can be written as

$$U = U(Q_x, Q_y)$$

where U denotes the individual's *total utility*, and Q_x and Q_y denote the quantities of goods x and y consumed per period of time. The qualification 'per period of time' is an important one here; we are building a theory of demand, and demand is a flow concept. Different individuals will, of course, obtain utility from various bundles of goods in different ways and to different extents. However, irrespective of what any individual's preferences might be, we assume that each person has a utility function which incorporates those preferences. We now introduce the idea of an individual's indifference curve for the goods x and y.

An indifference curve shows all combinations of the two goods which yield a particular level of utility.

The shape of an indifference curve will depend upon the utility function of the individual concerned. One likely shape for an indifference curve is shown in Figure 3.3. By definition, as the two points labelled 1 and 2 both lie on one indifference curve, they yield an equal utility level, $\bar{U}$. Indeed, *all* points along the indifference curve yield that amount of utility. The reason why the term 'indifference curve' is used is as follows: since each combination yields the same amount of utility, a rational consumer will be indifferent between alternative bundles along any one such curve.

An indifference curve demonstrates that the individual is confronted with trade-offs in consumption. In moving from point 1 to point 2, for example, the consumer can give up some of good y in return for more of good x, without changing the amount of utility he or she attains. If an indifference curve were linear—that is, it could be drawn as a straight line—the terms of this trade-off would not alter as the individual changes the proportions in which the two goods are consumed. However, the indifference curve shown in Figure 3.3 is not linear, and so the terms of this trade-off are not constant. As we have drawn it, an individual has to

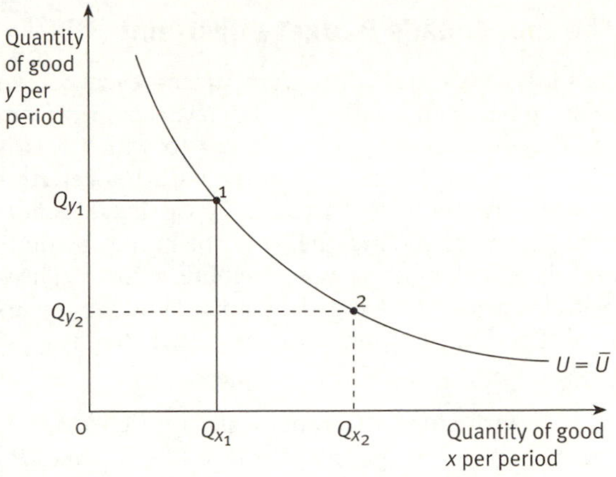

Figure 3.3 An indifference curve for the goods x and y

give up increasingly small amounts of y in return for additional units of x if utility is to remain unchanged.

For any utility function, there will be an indifference curve for each feasible utility level. We show three indifference curves in Figure 3.4. These correspond to the different utility levels, $\bar{U}$, $\tilde{U}$, and, such that $\tilde{U} > \bar{U}$ and $\breve{U} < \bar{U}$. The individual is indifferent between the combinations at points 1 and 2 as they confer the same utility level ($\bar{U}$). Similarly, the individual is indifferent between the combinations at points 3 and 4 as they confer equal utility ($\tilde{U}$). However, the combinations shown by points 3 and 4 are preferred to those at 1 and 2. Any combination on the indifference curve for utility level $\bar{U}$ is preferred to any combination on that for $\breve{U}$.

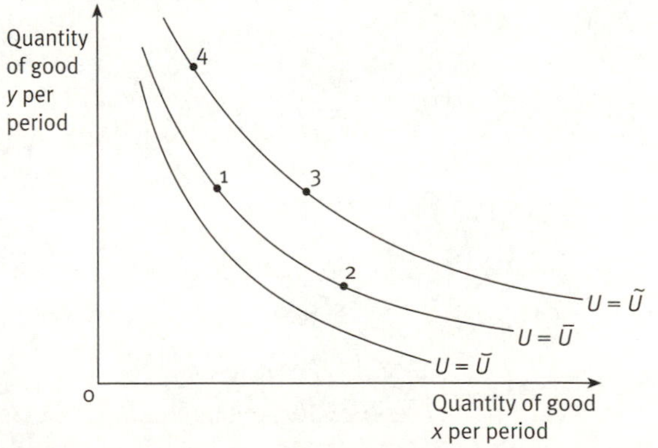

Figure 3.4 A family of indifference curves for the goods x and y

The Individual's Budget Constraint

As individuals are utility maximizers, each person seeks to be on an indifference curve as far away from the origin as possible. The extent to which this is possible is limited by the individual's budget constraint. The budget constraint states that expenditure cannot exceed income. Let m be money income, and P_x and P_y be the prices of goods x and y. These prices cannot be changed by an individual consumer. The budget constraint can be written as

$$P_xQ_x + P_yQ_y \leq m$$

and is represented diagramatically in Figure 3.5. If the prices of the goods x and y are P_{x_1} and P_{y_1} respectively, and available money income is m_1, the individual's budget constraint is given by the shaded area. Given this set of prices and money income, it shows all combinations of the two goods that it is feasible for the consumer to purchase. For reasons that will be clear shortly, the individual will choose a combination of goods on the outer diagonal boundary of the budget constraint (the line denoted M_1). From now on it is this line that we shall call 'the budget constraint'.

The slope and position of the budget constraint depend on two factors:

- the relative prices of the two goods: that is, the ratio P_x: P_y. Relative prices determine the slope of the budget constraint;
- the level of money income. This determines, for any given set of prices, how far the budget constraint is located away from the origin.

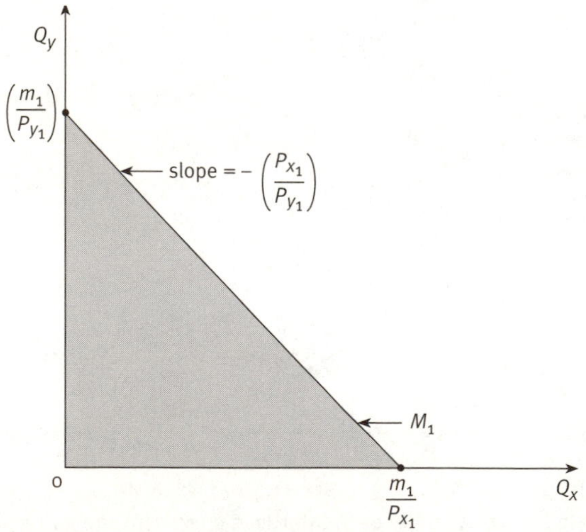

Figure 3.5 An individual's budget constraint

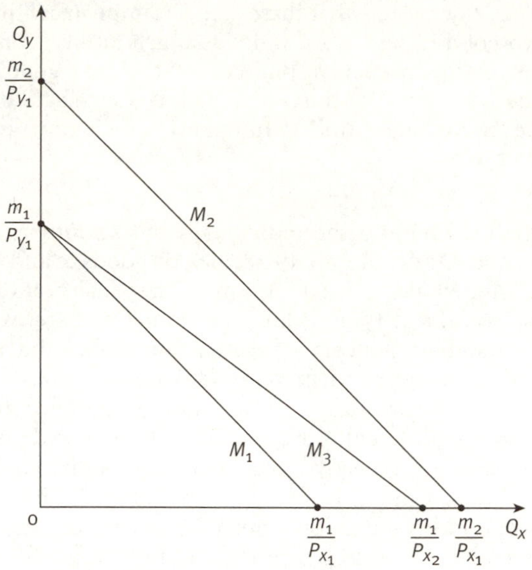

Figure 3.6 A set of budget constraints

An individual's budget constraint will change whenever there is a change in prices or money income. For example, the budget constraint shift from M_1 to M_2 in Figure 3.6 occurs when money income is increased from m_1 to m_2 but with prices remaining unchanged. On the other hand, the budget constraint shifts from M_1 to M_3 if the price of good x falls to P_{x_2} but money income and the price of y remain unchanged.

Utility Maximization Subject to a Budget Constraint

For a consumer with a limited income (and that is all of us once our work–leisure choices have been made), the best or efficient allocation of spending is the one which gives the greatest total utility. From all combinations of goods that are feasible to purchase given the budget constraint, the individual seeks that combination which will give the highest level of utility. We illustrate a solution to this problem in Figure 3.7. At the point Ω, utility is maximized at the level $U=\bar{U}$. To confirm that this is true, consider any point other than Ω which also satisfies the budget constraint. An indifference curve passing through such a point must lie below the highest attainable one, and so would yield lower utility. Note that the individual would prefer to be at a point on a higher indifference curve (such as

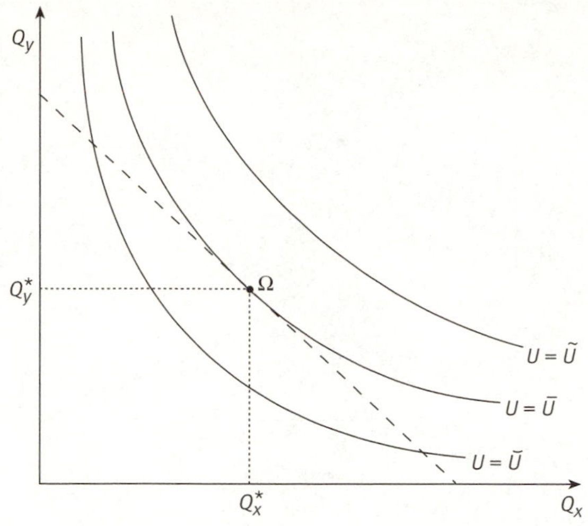

Figure 3.7 Utility maximization subject to a budget constraint

$U = \tilde{U}$) but that is not possible as it would require that spending exceed available income.

One characteristic of this solution is of particular interest. Provided that indifference curves are smooth and continuous, and are bowed inwards in the way we have illustrated them (that is, they are convex from below), then the utility-maximizing combination of x and y purchased will lie at a point of tangency between the budget constraint and an indifference curve.

The Efficient Allocation of a Consumer's Budget

We have just seen how a utility-maximizing consumer allocates a budget between two goods. It is possible to generate a simple rule from this analysis that enables us to get a good intuitive understanding of consumer behaviour. Before we derive this result, another concept is needed—the concept of marginal utility.

Let us return to the notion of an individual's utility function; we wrote this earlier as

$$U = U(Q_x, Q_y).$$

Suppose that, in some period of time, an additional unit of good x is consumed without any change taking place in the amount of y which is consumed. This additional consumption of good x will lead to an increase in the consumer's total utility. The *marginal utility* of good x is the change in total utility resulting from the consumption of an additional unit of that good. This can be represented by:

$$MU_x = \frac{\Delta U}{\Delta Q_x}$$

where the symbol Δ (read as 'delta') means 'a small change in' some variable of interest, Q_x is the quantity of x consumed per period, and MU_x is the marginal utility derived from good x. In a similar fashion, $MU_y = \Delta U/\Delta Q_y$, is the change in total utility resulting from the consumption of an additional unit of good y (with consumption of x unchanged).

Now let us return to the tangency condition we noted above. When the consumer is maximizing utility, the slopes of the budget line and the indifference curve are equal. The slope of the budget line is given by (the negative of) the price of x divided by the price of y. That is

$$\text{slope of budget constraint} = -\frac{P_x}{P_y}.$$

On the other hand, the slope of an indifference curve at any point along it is given by (the negative of) the marginal utility of x divided by the marginal utility of y. That is

$$\text{slope of indifference curve} = -\frac{MU_x}{MU_y}.$$

The derivation of these two results about the slopes is given separately in Box 3.1. If you would prefer to avoid the maths, you will have to take the results on trust.

Finally, as these two slopes are equal at a point of utility maximization, the following must be true when an individual is optimizing his or her expenditure pattern:

$$-\frac{P_x}{P_y} = -\frac{MU_x}{MU_y}$$

which after multiplying through by −1 and then rearranging gives

$$\frac{MU_x}{P_x} = \frac{MU_y}{P_y}.$$

What does this result tell us? It shows that maximum utility is achieved by allocating total income between different goods in such a way that the marginal utility derived from each good consumed per unit of money spent is equal over all goods. If we interpret MU_x and MUy as the 'values' derived at the margin from small, additional amounts of x

Box 3.1 Derivation of the Slopes of an Indifference Curve and a Budget Constraint

Consider one indifference curve. Let the individual consume a small additional amount of x. The effect of this on total utility is given by the rate of change of utility with respect to a change in x, $\Delta U/\Delta Q_x$, mutiplied by the amount of the change in x, ΔQ_x. Next suppose that the individual reduces his or her consumption of y in such a way that the loss of utility caused by having less y exactly compensates for the gain in utility from having more x. The loss in utility from having less y is given by the rate of change of utility with respect to a change in y, $\Delta U/\Delta Q_y$, multiplied by the amount of the change in y, ΔQ_y.

If we constrain the changes in x and y to be along one indifference curve, as illustrated in Figure 3.8(a), then the overall change in utility must be zero. Therefore we have

$$\Delta U = 0 = \left(\frac{\Delta U}{\Delta Q_x}\right)\Delta Q_x + \left(\frac{\Delta U}{\Delta Q_y}\right) DQ_y.$$

Rearranging this we obtain

$$\left(\frac{\Delta U}{\Delta Q_x}\right)\Delta Q_x = -\left(\frac{\Delta U}{\Delta Q_y}\right)\Delta Q_y.$$

and so

$$\frac{\Delta Q_y}{\Delta Q_x} = \text{slope of indifference curve} = -\frac{\Delta U/\Delta Q_x}{\Delta U/\Delta Q_y}$$

But the final term in this expression is the negative of the ratio of the marginal utility of x to the marginal utility of y (see Figure 3.8 (b)). So we conclude that

$$\text{slope of indifference curve} = -\frac{MU_x}{MU_y}.$$

The Slope of the Budget Constraint

The equation of a budget constraint is

$$P_xQ_x + P_yQ_y = m.$$

Rearrange this to give an equation for Q_y in terms of Q_x as follows:

$$P_yQ_y = m - P_xQ_x$$

$$Q_y = \frac{m}{P_y} - \frac{P_x}{P_y} Q_x$$

Therefore, the slope of the budget line is given by $-(P_x/P_y)$, as shown in Figure 3.8(c).

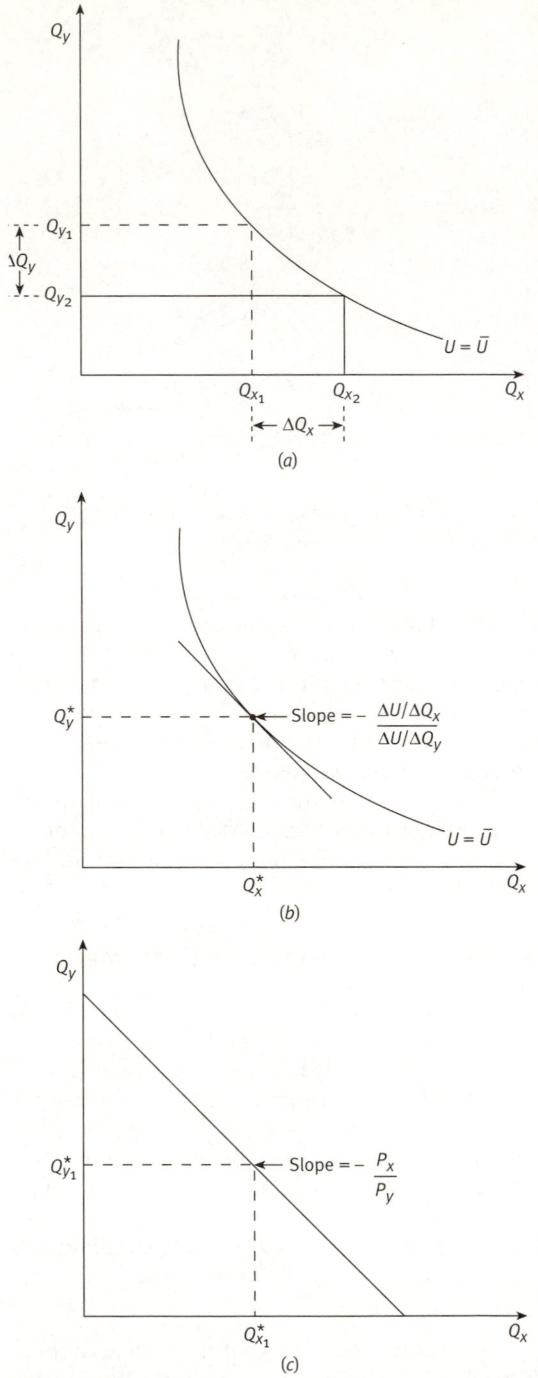

Figure 3.8 The slopes of an indifference curve and of a budget constraint

and y respectively, then we can say the following. A utility maximizing individual purchases goods in quantities such that the 'value-for-money' derived from each good at the margin is equalized.

To obtain an intuitive understanding of the condition, it may be helpful to ask what would happen if the consumer's pattern of purchases did not equalize 'value for money' at the margin for each good purchased. If these values for money ratios are not equal, then some goods must offer more value for money than others. A rational individual would switch expenditure between goods, away from those with low value for money and into those giving high value for money. This reallocation would enable the individual to get more total utility from the same income level, demonstrating that the original allocation was not an efficient one.

Price Changes and an Individual's Demand Curve

We now demonstrate that if a good rises in price, the quantity demanded of it is likely to fall. A geometric analysis of maximizing utility subject to a budget constraint is used. Begin with a situation in which a consumer is currently in a utility-maximizing position, at the point indicated by 'a' in Figure 3.9. Money income is m, prices are P_{y_1} and P_{x_1}, and maximized utility is u_1.

Now suppose that the price of good x falls from P_{x_1} to P_{x_2}, but money income and the price of good y remain unchanged. This rotates the individual's budget constraint anti-clockwise; its position changes from the line connecting the points (m/P_{y_1}) and (m/P_{x_1}) to the line (m/P_{y_1}) to (m/P_{x_2}). The set of feasible consumption choices is now enlarged, and the consumer attains a new utility maximum at the point 'b' on the indifference curve u_2.

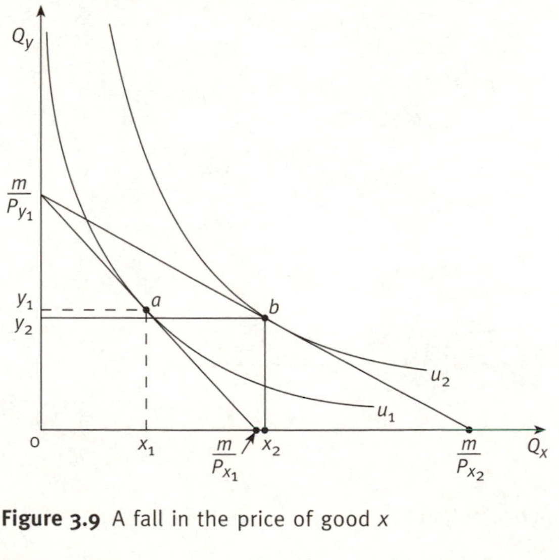

Figure 3.9 A fall in the price of good x

What has happened to the quantity of good x that the consumer demands as the price of good x falls? It has increased, from x_1 to x_2. The individual's demand curve for x is, therefore, negatively sloped (at least in this region) as a lower price has resulted in a greater quantity demanded.

The Substitution and Income Effects of a Price Change

Although a consumer's demand curve for any good x is likely to be downward sloping we cannot be certain of this because of the presence of the income effect of a price change. Whenever a price changes, that change will affect the demand for the good in two ways:

1. The price of this good, relative to others, has changed. This induces a substitution effect. The change in relative prices will lead to a reallocation of spending between goods. Less of the good which has become relatively more expensive will be purchased and more of the good which has become relatively less expensive will be bought. The substitution effect will *always* be negative: a change in the price of a good will lead to a change in the opposite direction in the quantity demanded of it.
2. A price change (with a fixed level of money income) will change the consumer's *real income* (the purchasing power of the money income). As the consumer's real income is changed, there will be a change in the amount of this good (and others) purchased. However, the direction of this change is uncertain, for the reasons we explained in Chapter 2. If the good in question is a normal good, higher real income will increase the quantity demanded. Conversely, if the good is an inferior good, higher real income will decrease the quantity demanded.

The demand curve for a good describes the overall relationship between price and quantity demanded, and so incorporates both the substitution effect and the real income effect of a price change.

We can obtain a graphical representation of the decomposition of a price change into substitution and income effects in the following way. First, the substitution effect of the price change is identified. The income effect is then obtained as the difference between the total effect and the substitution effect of the price change.

The substitution effect can be identified by asking how much demand for the good would change if

1. its price changes, and
2. the consumer is compensated for a price increase (or financially penalized for a price fall) by just the amount required to prevent the consumer from gaining more utility than he or she had prior to the price change.

Refer to Figure 3.10 which illustrates the reasoning. Suppose the consumer initially allocates his or her money income of m by purchasing y_1 units of good y (at the price P_{y_1}) and x_1 units of good x (at the price P_{x_1}). This utility-maximizing expenditure pattern obtains utility level u_1. We next suppose that the price of good x falls, with money income and the price of good y remaining constant. This causes the individual's budget constraint to rotate anticlockwise. The consumer now switches expenditure to the allocation shown by point b, at which utility is maximzed at the higher level, u_2.

The consumption of x increases from x_1 to x_2. This is the total effect of the price change. Let us now conduct the following hypothetical experiment. Starting from the new (post-price-change) budget constraint, we take away from the consumer the maximum amount of income that is just compatible with him or her being able to attain the *original* utility level u_1 at the *new* set of prices. This results in the consumer's budget constraint moving to the line *de*. With this budget constraint (and at the new set of prices, P_{y_1} and P_{x_2}), the highest level of utility level attainable is u_1, its original level. This is achieved by purchasing x_3 units of x and y_3 units of y.

This has removed the income effect of the price change. Any change in the demand for good x can, therefore, be attributed to the substitution effect alone. For good x, the substitution effect (SE) of the price fall consists of the change from x_1 to x_3.

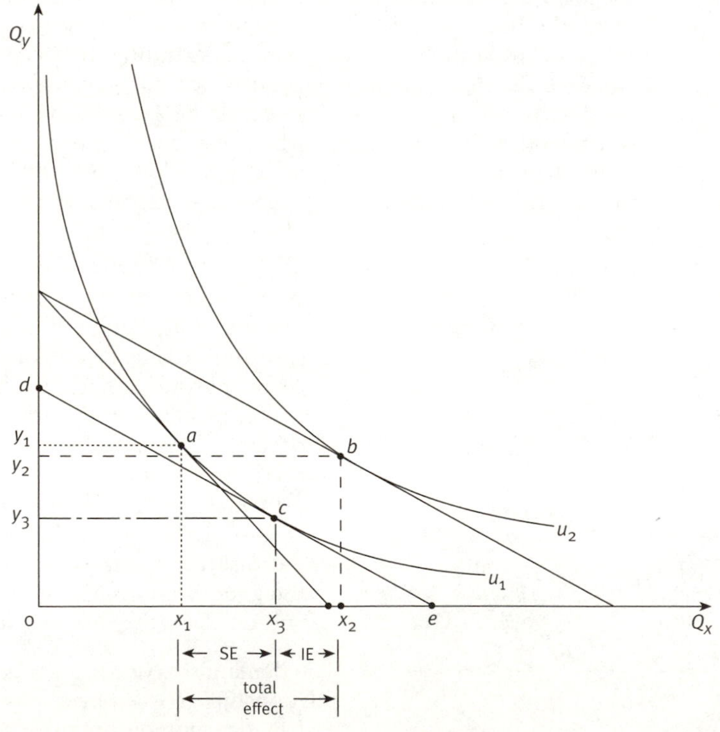

Figure 3.10 The substitution and income effects of a fall in the price of good x

The income effect (IE) of the price change consists of the change in quantity from x_3 to x_2. To see why this is so, note that if we were to begin at the point *c* and, without changing relative prices, return to the consumer the money income previously taken away, the individual would move from *c* to *b*, thereby raising consumption of *x* from x_3 to x_2.

The following can be said by way of conclusion:

Total effect of a price change	= substitution effect	+ income effect
(x_1 to x_2)	(x_1 to x_3)	(x_3 to x_2)

The case we investigated in Figure 3.10 was one in which the two component parts of the overall effect work in the same direction, so reinforcing one another. It can be deduced from this that *x* is a normal good, as an increase in real income has resulted in an increase in the quantity demanded of the good.

But as some goods are inferior, there are other possibilities. These are illustrated in Figures 3.11 and 3.12. In these two cases, *x* is an inferior good, and so the income effect of a price change works in the reverse direction to the substitution effect, thereby *reducing* the size of the overall effect. Figure 3.11 shows the case where the income effect only partially offsets the substitution effect. Overall, a fall in the price of good *x* results in a greater quantity being demanded, even though the size of the overall change has been reduced by the income effect.

Figure 3.12 illustrates a theoretically plausible, but very unlikely, situation. The extent of the income effect is so great that it not only reduces the overall effect, it actually reverses it. Here, a fall in the price of good *x* results in a fall in the quantity demanded of that good. The demand curve has a positive slope!

Empirical evidence shows that there are few, if any, Giffen goods in practice. Theory also suggests that the probability of Giffen goods is extremely small. Most goods are normal goods. But even where a good is inferior, the income effect is likely to be small in magnitude in comparison with the substitution effect. Unless a very large proportion of income is spent on one good, the income effect will be small for moderately sized price changes. Only in very exceptional circumstances would an income effect dominate the substitution effect in the way required for Giffen goods.

From Individual Demands to the Market Demand for a Good

Up until this point in this chapter, our focus has rested entirely upon the individual consumer. For economic and business analysis, though, it is market demand that matters. How does market demand relate to the demands of individual consumers? The answer is very simple. The market

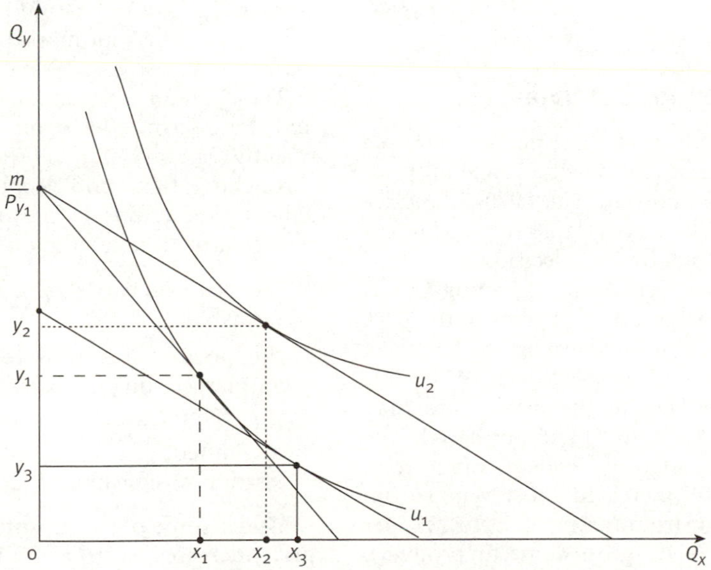

Figure 3.11 A fall in the price of good *x*, where good *x* is an inferior good

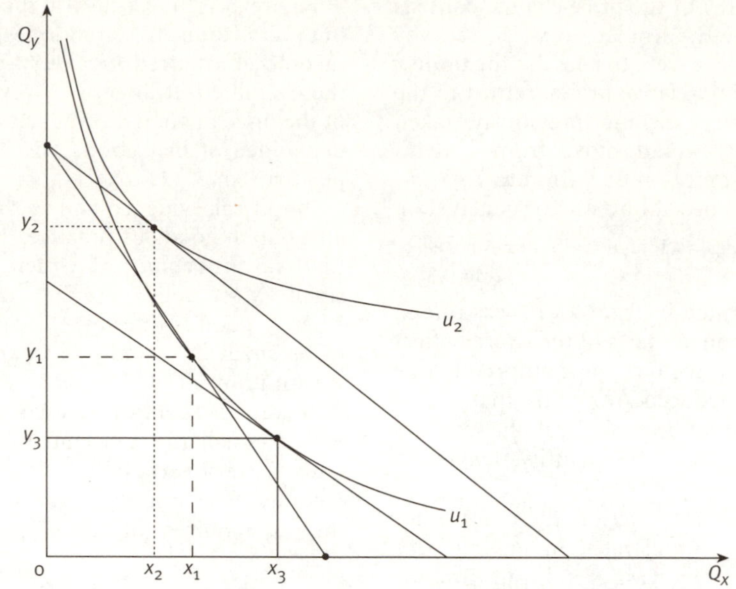

Figure 3.12 A fall in the price of good *x*, where *x* is a Giffen good

demand for a good is simply the sum of all individual consumer demands for that good. To obtain this sum, take one price and find the quantity demanded by each individual at that price. Then sum these quantities to find the market demand at that price. Repeating this analysis for all possible prices, we obtain the market demand schedule.

Demand Analysis: An Example

To illustrate the effects of a price change, we investigate some consequences of a crude oil price change. During the mid- and late 1970s, the price increased substantially in two large steps. The first episode was triggered by the decision of OPEC (The Organization of Petroleum Exporting Countries) to use an embargo on oil exports to the USA and Europe as an economic weapon in the attack on Israel by Egypt and Syria in late 1973. Cutbacks in production led to the price more than quadrupling, from \$2.59 to \$11.65 per barrel. The importance of this step is evident when it is understood that this increased the revenue from one year's oil output from 0.5 per cent to 2½ per cent of the world's GDP (gross domestic product). In so doing, it had a major impact on the distribution of income and wealth between countries. The price increase diverted about 2 per cent of all the world's income away from the purchasing power of net oil importing states into the pockets of the oil exporters.

After a period in which the real price of oil slowly declined, the revolution in Iran paralysed oil production, and initiated a second episode of sharp price rises. The official OPEC price rose to \$34 a barrel, with the spot market price rising as high as \$40.

These oil price changes had major short-term and long-term effects on demand (and subsequently supply) for a wide variety of goods throughout the world economy. The income and substitution effects of the oil price changes were particularly large for three reasons:

1. the price increases were large in proportionate terms;
2. the price increases were nearly instantaneous and largely unanticipated;
3. the good whose price had risen—crude oil—accounted, directly or indirectly, for a large proportion of consumer budgets.

Consider some of the substitution effects. Crude oil price increases led to a rise in the cost of production of many goods and services that used energy inputs. These cost increases were particularly important in the case of petroleum refining, electricity production, transport and distribution, and the industrial materials and chemicals sectors. Cost increases in these sectors led to subsequent price increases, as producers attempted to pass on costs to purchasers. Secondly, many consumer goods are complements to goods whose price had risen because of the crude oil price increases. For example, cars are complements to petroleum, a derivative of crude oil. So oil price rises led to an increase in the cost of car transport.

To some extent, the substitution effect operated by reducing the demand for car transport as a whole. Car sales dropped, fewer miles were driven, and the average speed of traffic fell, increasing the mileage driven per unit of petrol. Within car transport itself, other substitutions took place. Large-engined, fuel-inefficient cars became relatively more expensive to operate in comparison with smaller vehicles. Consumers chose to buy smaller, more fuel-efficient cars. These substitution effects were greater in the long term than in the short term.

Price increases also had major impacts on real incomes. In the oil importing countries, reduced real incomes reduced the demand for oil and for a wide range of other goods. Although real incomes rose in oil exporting states, much of the export revenue was used to acquire financial assets, and so did not generate additional demand for manufactured goods exports which would have compensated oil importing economies. As a large proportion of oil export revenue was saved, the price increases precipitated a depression in the level of world demand at the same time as price-inflation accelerated. The conjunction of price-inflation and demand-stagnation became known as 'stagflation'.

Oil price increases had important supply-side effects too. The incentive to search for new sources of oil increased rapidly, and higher prices meant that high-cost oil fields (such as those in deep offshore waters) became profitable to exploit. It is one of the ironies of this whole process that the adjustments set into motion by the oil price rises—increased supply from new sources and decreased demand from users—were so great that OPEC lost its dominance of the oil industry. Just prior to the Iraq invasion of Kuwait, the real price of oil (the price in purchasing power terms) had fallen to its 1973 level.

Conclusions

In this chapter, we have used fundamental principles of economic theory to do two things. First, we analysed the work–leisure choice of a rational (utility-maximizing) individual. From this, we have been able to show how desired labour supply can be affected by fiscal policy. This can be of great benefit in assessing the likely impacts on the labour market of changes in the government's tax and welfare benefits programmes.

Secondly, we have constructed a theory of consumer demand, and used this to infer what properties demand curves can be expected to possess. In most circumstances, one would expect there to be a negative relationship between the price of a good and the quantity of that good demanded, when all other determinants of demand remain constant. However, the presence of income effects means that this negative relationship—what is sometimes called the law of demand—is not necessarily the case.

Further reading

There are very many excellent texts that explore demand theory more fully than we have done in this chapter. Unless you are particularly interested in studying some refinements in the theory of consumer demand, however, we do not suggest you delve into this area any further. For the adventurer, though, an outstanding, and reasonably accessible, text is Hal Varian's *Intermediate Microeconomics* (1990). You could do no better than explore this to master consumer demand theory.

Chrystal and Lipsey (1997, chapter 10), give a fine presentation of the economics of employment, including a discussion of contracts and performance monitoring (something we also study in Chapter 12 of our text). An excellent, and reasonably accessible, presentation of labour supply theory—including a large amount of empirical evidence, and a good discussion of labour market behaviour and unemployment theory (which will be discussed later in Chapter 14 of this text) is given in Robert F. Elliott (1991) *Labour Economics*.

Questions

3.1. What effects on desired labour supply would you expect from

(*a*) an increase in the marginal rate of income tax;

(*b*) an increase in the rate of value added tax on expenditure?

3.2. Suppose we regard consumption today and saving today (leading to extra consumption tomorrow) as two 'goods', and that they are the only goods available. Moreover, any income saved will earn an interest rate of 10 per cent per period. Assuming a fixed amount of earned money income in both periods, and that prices remain constant, what does the consumer's budget line look like for these two goods? Use indifference curve analysis to illustrate the consumer's optimum saving–consumption choice.

3.3. Which of the following statements must hold when an individual is maximizing her utility?

(*a*) The marginal utility of all goods equals unity.

(*b*) The marginal utility from the last £1 spent on each good must be the same.

(*c*) The ratio of the marginal utilities of the goods consumed equals the ratio of their prices.

(*d*) The marginal utility of all goods consumed is the same.

3.4. Are all Giffen goods inferior goods? Are all inferior goods Giffen goods?

3.5. Which of the following is always true?

(*a*) As a good's own price falls, the quantity demanded of the good will increase.

(*b*) The substitution effect of a fall in a good's own price will lead to an increase in the quantity demanded.

(*c*) As an individual's income rises, the quantity demanded of a good will rise.

3.6. 'If an increase in the price of oil reduces the demand for cars, an increase in the price of cars must reduce the demand for oil.'

Is this statement true? Explain your answer.

3.7. If all prices rose by 15 per cent and an individual's income rose by 10 per cent, the individual's real income:

(*a*) Would rise, because the increase in money income offsets any increase in prices.

(*b*) Would fall, because the increase in money income does not fully compensate for the increasing prices.

(*c*) Would fall, because real incomes always fall during inflation.

(*d*) Might rise or fall. It is not possible to tell with these data.

4 The Nature, Purpose, and Objectives of Firms

Introduction

In this chapter we connect the individual's pursuit of value through exchange with the pursuit of value by groups of individuals, or coalitions, co-operating together in organizations called firms or enterprises. A great deal of value creation, of production and innovation, in modern industrial economies takes place inside firms rather than through immediate market exchange. To understand the operation of the economy we have to understand the nature of the business firm, its purpose, and its objectives.

It is conventional in economics to make a working assumption that firms exist to maximize their profits. Profit maximization can be described in other ways too: maximizing the value of the firm to its owner(s), generating and appropriating as large a quantity of added value as possible, or maximization of shareholders' wealth. In Chapter 1 we described the objective of the firm as the pursuit of maximum added value. These are not unreasonable assumptions for analytical purposes. Indeed in many chapters of this text we shall be using this assumption. However the question of what it is firms seek to do is so fundamental to business economics that it is worth while considering this issue more closely. For example, what do we mean when we talk about the objectives of a firm? Firms as such cannot have objectives. Only individuals have objectives. So the question is what determines the extent to which individual objectives get effectively harnessed to produce an overall collective or coalition objective?

Our goal in this chapter is to analyse the firm—its nature and its objectives—from first principles. This will shed light on what we mean by business objectives, and how firms pursue those objectives. We begin by considering the nature of the entity called the firm.

4.1 The Nature of the Firm

Economics is the study of value creation, or how people go about making the best use of scarce resources to satisfy their needs. We have seen how trade and exchange between individuals can increase the well-being of those involved; market exchange is value creating. As we explained at the end of Chapter 1, it is possible to envisage an economy in which *all* economic activity takes place between individuals using market exchanges. The label used there for such an economy was a *pure exchange economy*.

One might object that a pure exchange economy would make it impossible for individuals to obtain goods of great complexity as the production of such goods requires bringing together and co-ordinating the use of many productive inputs, possibly over a considerable period of time. This objection is misplaced. It might be *difficult* to produce complex goods by individual exchange alone, but it is not *impossible* in principle. For example, suppose you wish to acquire a newly built house. You could obtain it by dealing only with other individuals through a carefully designed and mutually consistent set of contracts. These would include contracts with other individuals to acquire land and raw materials, have the foundations built and the bricks laid, roof constructed, walls plastered, the electrical wiring installed, and so on. Of course, if we are talking strictly about a pure exchange economy, all those with whom you make contracts must be individuals as well. These other people will have to establish their own system of contracts to acquire the inputs for the things they are supplying to you.

No matter how sophisticated the goods and services are that people desire to consume, an economy *can* in principle operate on the basis of pure exchange between individuals alone, without the

Box 4.1 On the Importance of Large Firms in the Modern Economy

The percentage share of the 100 largest manufacturing firms in net output[1] in the manufacturing sector in the UK and the US for various years has been as shown in Table 4.1.

Table 4.1 The percentage share of 100 largest manufacturing firms in net output

Year	UK	US
1909	16	–
1949	22	23
1958	32	30
1970	41	33
1980	41	33
1989	39	33
1992	39	–

Sources: Prais (1976), *Business Monitor*, PA 1002, and the OECD.

It may help you to appreciate the significance of these figures to know that the total number of firms in the UK manufacturing sector in 1989 was around 130,000! Of these, 96 per cent were small firms (those with fewer than 100 employees) and these accounted for only 20 per cent of net output. Medium-sized firms, employing between 100 and 5,000 people accounted for just over 40 per cent of net output.

The *Financial Times* provides periodic listings of the 100 largest companies in Europe. Among the many interesting pieces of information that can be gleaned from this publication is the number of people employed in these giant companies. In one case over 400,000 people were employed in one organization. This is more than the total workforce of several members of the United Nations.

need for any ongoing complex hierarchical organizations, except perhaps a government to provide and uphold a necessary framework of law and order. But in practice this is not at all what we observe! The economic landscape does indeed consist of lots of individuals making market exchanges. But production activity is largely undertaken by collections of labour and capital co-operating on an ongoing basis in organizations called firms. Indeed, a relatively small number of giant firms *dominate* production in most developed economies. Some evidence on this is given in Box 4.1.

Firms operate within a market environment but their organization and internal operations are not characterized solely by market-based exchange: one might say that they operate 'beyond' or 'alongside' markets. For example, what the average employee in a firm does on a particular day is not dictated directly by market forces but by administrative decisions. And what the average employee is paid is not determined on a continuous basis by market forces but by negotiation and bargaining, often by groups of employees, at relatively long intervals. In short, the economies we actually observe are populated by business organizations whose internal mechanisms are different from those that characterize pure market exchange.[2]

Why should this be so? Why should the economic landscape be dominated by organized groups of individuals co-operating with one another in firms on a basis different from that found in markets? Since this co-operation is voluntary, those involved must presumably benefit, in terms of their ability to create and appropriate value for themselves, from trading and contracting with others on a basis different from that found in simple market exchange.

The source of these advantages is not immediately obvious. Our task now is to identify some of the potential advantages that firms have over pure market exchange in the process of value creation. It is worth previewing our argument. We return to a previous example. Call C_1 the total cost you would incur if you chose to obtain a new house through a set of market contracts with other individuals. Let C_2 be the price you would have to pay to obtain the

[1] Net output was defined in Chapter 1.

[2] Nor are business firms the only ongoing organizations in market economies. The economic landscape is also marked by the presence of another large collective unit called the government which operates to an even greater extent 'beyond' markets. We earlier gave one reason why government exists: to provide the framework of law and order that is required to sustain any market economy. This is not, of course, the only role for states.

same house from a firm which produces houses. Your choice will depend on the relative cost of the two options.

If C_1 is less than C_2, no rational person will buy the house from a firm. If this is true for all those who wish to get a new house, there will be no house-building firms, as no one would buy from them. More generally, if C_1 is less than C_2 not just for new houses but for every conceivable good anyone might want, then there would be no firms at all in the economy! It would be a pure exchange economy.

But what if C_1 is greater than C_2 for a new house? Then every rational person who wants a new house would get it from a house-building firm. For any good, whenever C_1 is greater than C_2, it would be purchased from a firm rather than obtained by pure market exchange.

The existence of firms depends, therefore, on firms having cost advantages over market-based exchange.[3] This cost advantage cannot come from differences in the resources used in building the house itself: we are comparing like with like, and the resources used are the same in both cases. Any difference must arise from the difficulties and costs involved in organizing the provision of goods by firms as compared with through pure market exchange. We will explore the source of these cost differences in the following section. Let us consider first the costs involved in pure market exchange.

Costs and Market Transactions

It is clear that firms exist. It might therefore seem to be irrelevant to consider why firms exist. However this is not necessarily the case. Whilst it is clear that firms exist, it is not obvious why so many firms of different shapes and sizes exist, or why each industry is not run by a single completely integrated enterprise as in the old Soviet model. What determines which activities are carried out inside firms and which are left to markets? Some firms for example internalize transport services, or produce some of their own input requirements. For example, many car assemblers also make their own engines and car bodies but they do not produce tyres or paint or glass. What determines what is done inside a particular firm by employees and what is left to independent outside contractors? Is this simply the result of historical accidents or is there an economic logic involved?

If all trade and exchange could be arranged at zero cost to the parties involved, then market-based exchange would in principle suffice for all transactions. Complicated (and so expensive) organizational structures would not be necessary. But of course the process of exchange generally does involve costs.[4] For the simplest kinds of transaction (such as having your windows cleaned), these costs are likely to be negligible. For others, such as buying a house or hiring the services of an advertising agency, they may be large. For very complex transactions involving contracting with many separate parties, such as arranging the supply of complex components or contracting with others to have a house built, these costs can be very large. When transactions are costly, those costs will deter people from making them. Transactions costs act as a sort of tax on transactions. As a result, valuable exchanges are missed.

This seemingly innocuous fact, that the process of trade and exchange, of transacting, involves costs, turns out to have great significance. It was first pointed out in a pioneering article by the economist Ronald Coase in 1937. What Coase showed, and what others later developed, was this. There are various costs involved in using markets:

- the costs involved in searching for information about prices and suppliers;
- the costs involved in negotiating, drawing up, monitoring, renegotiating, and enforcing contracts.

These kinds of costs are now described as 'transactions costs'. Transactions costs have been defined as follows:

A spectrum of institutional costs including those of information, of negotiation, of drawing up and enforcing contracts, of delineating and policing property rights, of monitoring performance, and of changing institutional arrangements. In short, they comprise all those costs not directly incurred in the physical process of production. (*Palgrave Dictionary of Economics*)

[3] The existence of firms also requires that those who co-operate *within* them must do better than they could do on their own. For if they did not, they would not co-operate in this way. We shall also explain below where this benefit can come from.

[4] It is important to be clear that the costs we have in mind here do *not include* the purchase price of the good itself.

What factors give rise to transactional costs? They arise from the interaction of certain aspects of human nature and the conditions surrounding particular transactions. Some of the factors involved are now briefly outlined.

Opportunism

This refers to the propensity of individuals not only to pursue their own interests but to do so in deceitful or guileful ways. That is, we sometimes lie and cheat and can be counted on generally to look after ourselves. Opportunism means that individuals are not completely trustworthy and that we are likely to misrepresent situations and intentions to our advantage. Thus we normally assume that a person selling us a car or a house is unlikely to be telling us the whole truth about its qualities and we normally make allowances for this. If people were not opportunistic, life would be much simpler and contracting less problematic and less costly. People could contract with one another without recourse to writing and monitoring complex contracts. Your word would be your bond.

Bounded Rationality

Economic theory often makes strong assumptions about the capacity of people to recognize and solve the complex computational problems necessary for optimal decision-making. In reality our capacity for wholly rational decision-making is limited or bounded by our capacity to acquire, store, and process the relevant information. This is significant to the contractual basis of transactions between individuals. It seriously limits our ability to develop fully specified, or complete, contracts. The future is too unpredictable and too complex for us to anticipate and compute all possible events affecting a contract over its lifetime. We cannot even imagine all the possible contingencies that might arise during, say, an employment contract, so many contracts will be necessarily incomplete. This implies a possible need to continually negotiate the terms of the contract as circumstances change in an uncertain environment.

Asset Specificity

If productive assets were generally very good substitutes for one another they could move from one use to another in response to price signals without losing any of their market value. In reality this is not always the case. Some assets are highly specialized and specific to a particular use or transaction. For example, a newspaper printing press can not easily be used to print books and a car assembly plant can not easily turn to assembling computers. Specific assets are those which have low value in alternative uses so that moving from one use to another causes losses to the owner. These assets have been developed with a specific use in mind and once developed or put in place have a value in that use which is much higher than in any alternative use. This is a problem because it creates a 'lock-in' effect. The parties to a transaction involving the creation of specialized specific assets are mutually dependent on one another. In this situation each party may try to take advantage of the other by attempting to obtain more favourable terms than had been agreed before the asset was created. In other words, there is scope for trying to appropriate more of the value of the asset than was previously agreed. We get what is called nowadays 'opportunistic recontracting'. An example of asset specificity in the production of cars is given in Box 4.2.

Asymmetric Information

This refers to the fact that one of the parties to a transaction is often better informed about certain aspects of the transaction than the other. The former cannot be relied upon to disclose information honestly and the latter cannot find it except at high cost. This asymmetry leaves one of the parties vulnerable to exploitation by the other. Someone who has bought a second-hand car may know the feeling. The seller is unlikely to tell you about its failings and you cannot determine them precisely without paying for a full assessment. Asymmetric information takes two forms which give rise to two separate problems for transactors.

Hidden information This is common in labour markets. Employees know more about their real abilities and capacity for hard work than potential employers. It is also a problem for the insurance business. The sort of people who buy health insurance, for example, will not be a random sample of the population but the people who judge themselves most likely to need the insurance. What happens when an employer sets a wage reflecting the average abilities and capacities of individuals or an insurance company sets terms reflecting average propensity to ill health? Individuals who know they are above average workers or below average health risks refuse the offer. Individuals who are below

Box 4.2 Asset Specifity in the Car Industry

Asset specificity is pronounced in the car industry. Car assemblers typically purchase components, such as tyres, batteries, and instruments from specialist suppliers. Very often, an assembler requires components (such as car seats) to be manufactured to precise specifications for a particular model in its range. Both sides make investments which can only be justified if the relationship is likely to be a continuing one and involves a scale of throughput sufficient to recover the large initial development costs. Clearly, pure market exchange could be a very costly means of dealing with such transactional relationships, and the risks involved from opportunistic recontracting by either side could actively discourage valuable transactions.

Two of the ways in which the car industry has attempted to deal with the potential problems of asset specificity warrant attention. One has been through greater vertical integration. Large-scale assemblers often produce their own components rather than purchasing them from independent specialist suppliers. By having all parties concerned under the single authority structure of the firm, opportunistic recontracting can be virtually eliminated. However, vertical integration can also be costly. Part of the firm's resource base is being directed towards activities for which it may not have special capabilities, and the advantages of specialization are being missed.

In the last decade (as we describe in more detail in Chapter 16) car assemblers have been increasingly divesting their non-core activities following the lead of Japanese companies in particular. To avoid the possible adverse consequences that asset specificity brings about, major assemblers have developed very close and long-term collaborative relationships with components suppliers. These relationships try to obtain the benefits of vertical integration but at a lower cost. Economists such as John Kay of the Oxford University Business School suggest that patterns of close co-operation stopping short of being internalized entirely within the firm have become critical pathways in the process of value creation in modern business.

At the same time, however, it is reported by *The Economist* magazine that some component manufacturers are moving into final assembly of cars. The Finnish component maker Valmet assembles cars for Porsche, Lada, and Saab, and the Austrian company Steyr has been assembling for Chrysler and Mercedes. This is seen as a the outcome of a policy of outsourcing even final assembly work by the major car producers. In Japan it is said that only one-fifth of the added value in a car is added by the assemblers. Will we perhaps one day have a car maker that makes no cars?

average workers or above average health risks find the offer acceptable. The employer or the insurance company faces an '*adverse selection*' problem. Poor workers and bad risks drive out better workers and good risks.

Hidden actions Another common contractual problem is this. It is sometimes difficult or impossible to be sure when the other party has fulfilled her contractual obligations. For example, when a worker's productivity is below expectations, can you tell what is causing this? Was the worker slacking, or was his machinery faulty, or was the material being worked of poor quality, or was the factory too warm that week? Often it will be difficult to tell, and the worker is unlikely to admit that the problem was his effort level. Similarly, if you take out an insurance policy on your car, it is difficult for the insurance company to be sure that you will always drive carefully and keep it locked when parked. Indeed the very fact that you are insured makes you somewhat less careful than you might otherwise be. This general problem of verifying the reasonableness of actions taken within a contract is known as the *moral hazard* problem. Moral hazard is of course a form of opportunism that arises when the actions desired or required under a contract cannot be easily observed or measured. The result is to discourage trade.

Team Production

When many individuals are involved in a particular joint activity but their separate contributions to total output cannot easily be evaluated, we have what is called a team situation. This creates a measurement problem because if it is not clear who is contributing what, then two issues arise. First, how do you reward the individuals on the basis of their individual efforts? Secondly, if you cannot reward individuals on the basis of their own efforts what is to stop individuals from free-riding on the efforts of others? Even agreeing to split the outcome of the team's efforts equally does not overcome the problem. Indeed individuals who are promised the same share as everyone else have the same incentive as everyone else—which is to do as little as possible! How then do these individuals transact with one another to get the job done?

Imperfect Commitment

This refers to the fact that the parties to a contract are often unable to give totally credible commitments about their future behaviour. Thus all drivers will promise their insurers to drive carefully and so on. But insurers know that these promises are not credible and cannot be relied upon. Individual drivers would gain if they could make credible binding commitments, but achieving such commitment is likely to be difficult and costly.

Costs and Firms

Let us now turn our attention to the organization of economic activity within firms. It is clear that this process *also* involves costs. We shall label these as *organization costs.* However, it is clear from looking at the definition of transactions costs quoted above that organization costs could also be called transactions costs incurred within firms. Moreover, the factors giving rise to organization costs are more or less the same as those we listed above. Firms need to search, make contracts with their members, and monitor performance. They also face the problems of opportunism, bounded rationality, asset specificity, asymmetric information, team production, and imperfect commitment.

However, the nature of the firm as an organizational unit means that it may be able to deal with these problems more effectively than is possible for individuals undertaking market-based contracting. For example, its 'permanence' and its internal authority structure means that the firm may be less exposed to some types of opportunistic behaviour. Also, a firm should be able to benefit from economies of scale in contracting, thereby lowering overall costs. More generally, firms are likely to build superior abilities in organizing and managing multiple contracts than is possible via pure market exchange. The food and clothing retailer Marks and Spencer, for example, has developed organizational skills in order to achieve tighter quality control over the food and clothing it purchases than would be possible at the same cost for more fragmented contractors. This creates value for both Marks and Spencer and its customers.

However, the creation of a firm does not eliminate opportunism, it does not make the problems associated with bounded rationality and asset specificity disappear, nor can it eliminate the costs of organizing and managing transactions entirely. It can at best mitigate the extent of these problems and reduce the magnitude of their costs. The firm is essentially a relatively cost-efficient mechanism for organizing and co-ordinating economic activity.

As Coase argued, the firm is a device for reducing the net costs of transactions, co-operation and exchange in a complex and uncertain world. The aim of the firm is to encourage exchange and co-operation by reducing the difficulties and costs involved. The firm is a mechanism, or governance structure to use Williamson's phrase, for organizing and managing the exchange process when transactional difficulties make it impossible to conceive complete contracts (Williamson, 1985). The firm is an organized network of incomplete contracts with the following aims:

- promoting effective co-operation among the owners of specialized inputs;
- building trust and co-operation through continued association which allows for learning and the development of reputations;
- promoting the creation of firm-specific skills and procedures;
- allocating rights and responsibilities in a clear and routine way;
- economizing on the costs of search, bargaining, negotiation, measurement, monitoring, and enforcement;
- regulating the exercise of opportunism;
- allowing for change and adjustment to changing circumstances without continuous and lengthy renegotiation of individual contracts.

Our discussion of the nature of the firm seems to imply a simple outcome:

- firms *develop* whenever the costs of transactions through markets exceed the costs of organizing and co-ordinating production within firms.

There is no reason, however, to expect the relative cost of market and firm-based transactions to be constant over time. When these relative costs change, the proportion of transactions taking place through these two mechanisms will change. One example of this seems to be taking place in the UK insurance industry at present. It has been common for individuals seeking insurance (especially car insurance) to use the services of brokers. The specialist knowledge acquired by brokers, and economies of scale in search activities, meant that the costs of searching for the lowest premiums available were lower than individuals would face when searching for themselves. Overall, organized brokerage activity offered a cheaper means of arranging insurance than direct market exchange.

But this situation has been changing in recent years. Several factors have contributed to the change. First, increased competition in the telecommunications market has lowered the real price of telephone services. Secondly, developments in electronic information storage and processing have allowed insurance companies to offer prices closely linked to the riskiness of individual customers, and to quote prices virtually instantaneously. Insurance companies and individual customers both have much less to gain from the intermediation of a broker. So here is a case where one kind of firm—the insurance broker—is finding it increasingly difficult to survive, as the relative cost of market exchange has fallen.

The growth in outsourcing by industrial firms in the 1980s and 1990s also owes much to such changes in relative costs. Many firms are finding it increasingly more cost-effective to contract with outside specialists for particular goods and services than to provide them in-house. A study in 1996 by the consultants PA of hundreds of businesses in the UK found that a quarter of what they defined as 'key business processes', hitherto carried on within firms, had already been outsourced. Over this same period of time another significant trend within some organizations has been the increasing use of 'internal markets' as ways of allocating resources within the organization. This trend has been particularly evident in public sector organizations such as the NHS in Britain and in large multidivisional businesses.

So what we find is that economies do not depend entirely on markets or on firms to organize productive activity, but on a combination of the two. The particular mix involved changes over time and varies between different kinds of activities. For example the IT (information technology) revolution has had an important effect on the mix with what appears to be a strong shift to greater outsourcing taking place during the last decade. Markets and firms therefore are not mutually exclusive alternatives but coexist happily as means of co-ordinating the exchange process.

4.2 Entrepreneurs, Firms, and the Search for Value

Our analysis has shown how a firm, by dealing more effectively than markets with transactional problems, might create value. In this part of the chapter we investigate the value-creation process more closely. Our treatment here is introductory. Later chapters of the book (particularly Chapter 12) will consider the issues involved in more depth.

As we have seen, a firm can only exist if it provides a good or service to individuals at a lower cost than the individuals would have to incur were they to seek to acquire the good through pure market exchange. Once in existence, the source of a firm's added value lies in its ability to supply goods for which individuals are willing to pay in excess of all the costs incurred by the firm in supplying the goods.

It is worth illustrating this with a hypothetical example as set out in Figure 4.1. Suppose that I was willing to pay up to £2,000 for a P300 computer. Were I to try and obtain such a computer by market contracts with other individuals, buying the components separately and paying someone to assemble them, it would cost me £1,500. So if I did select this route, I would generate £500 of added value, and appropriate it for myself.

However, suppose a firm can produce and supply a computer of this specification for £800, and is willing to sell it to me for £1200. Clearly that would be the value-maximizing option for me. By buying from the firm, I get £800 of added value for myself and the firm gets £400 for its efforts.

The total added value in this case is £1,200 (my £800 plus the firm's £400). The fact that total added value has risen by £700 is not a result of the product being different, but arises from the fact that the firm can produce the good more cheaply than is possible for me to achieve by pure market exchange, because the firm is able to economize on what we earlier called transactions costs.

The fact that both the firm and the individual who acquires the computer gain value is important for what follows later. If the firm realizes that I am willing to pay up to £2,000, it might try to appropriate rather more of the total £1,200 added value by selling at a price closer to that level. But here the ability of other firms to produce computers comes into play. If there are no barriers stopping others producing a P300 computer of the specification I

A P300 COMPUTER

Willingness to pay	£2,000

Case A: Obtain via pure market exchange	
Cost to individual	£1,500
Added value	£ 500

Case B: Obtain via a firm	
Price at which firm sells	£1,200
Cost to firm	£ 800
Added value	
(*a*) to individual	£ 800
(*b*) to firm	£ 400
Total added value	£1,200

Increase in added value: £1,200 – £500 = £700

Source of this increase:
Cost of pure market exchange – cost of firm provision:

£1,500 – £800 = £700

Figure 4.1 The source of added value

want, then competition is likely to drive the market price down towards the firm's cost level (£800), leaving all the added value to be appropriated by me! But this is getting ahead of ourselves: we will examine the role of competition in determining the appropriation of added value in Chapters 6 and 7.

Who then creates the firm and why? These collections of people and money do not arise spontaneously. Someone has to recognize the opportunities available for organizing and managing the exchange process and take the necessary steps to create the collective to realize these opportunities. Such a person is called the entrepreneur, literally the intermediary or organizer. The entrepreneur is the person who spots an opportunity to encourage exchange and co-operation by reducing the difficulties and costs involved, of economizing on transaction costs by organizing and managing the process of negotiation, development, monitoring, and enforcement of contracts which define the firm. The entrepreneur's function is to make judgements about what is possible, organize the necessary collection of resources, co-ordinate its activities, assume responsibility for the ultimate performance of the collective, negotiate and bargain with members of the collective, monitor the activities of the collective, judge how best to achieve the whole-hearted co-operation of members of the collective, judge how best to keep the collective adaptable in the face of changing circumstances, and so on.

The entrepreneur's job is complicated and valuable because creating a firm can only be an attempt to reduce the impact of transactional difficulties, not to eliminate them altogether. Therefore considerable effort is needed to deal with the problems caused by opportunism, bounded rationality, and asymmetric information. The entrepreneur's job is one of designing and operating appropriate mechanisms for dealing with the reality of transactional problems.

Note therefore that a firm can only exist if someone with the necessary entrepreneurial skills finds it personally worthwhile to create it and if other people find it personally worthwhile to join the entrepreneur in a collective relationship. Thus a firm by definition is likely to be value enhancing for society as a whole because it encourages exchange between individuals beyond what would otherwise take place. The creation of firms thus helps individuals and society as a whole to pursue efficiency and the creation of wealth. That is their point.

The Entrepreneur's Reward: Profits, Rents, and Added Value

What is the reward for the entrepreneur? What determines whether or not it is worthwhile for an entrepreneur to go to all the trouble involved in creating the collective? The prospect of personal gain would seem to rank highly in the motives of entrepreneurs. No doubt you can think of examples where the entrepreneur claimed her motive was to help humanity or to promote international understanding but it seems reasonable to assume that these are special cases. Entrepreneurs who are not in it for the money are probably exceptions although one should perhaps not underrate empire-building as a motive.

What is the source of the personal gain? Assuming enforceable property rights are established, the entrepreneur will have a strong incentive to organize and manage the firm in such a way as to produce a residual value available to her once all the other contracts have been fulfilled, that is, once employees, financial backers, and suppliers are paid in accordance with their contracts with the entrepreneur. Note also that the entrepreneur should take into account the need to produce a residual large enough to cover the opportunity costs of her time as an entrepreneur, and the going rate for any personal capital she contributes to the firm. If she was not spending her time as an entrepreneur herself, she could be earning money doing something else and this sets a lower limit to her entrepreneurial earnings. If she cannot earn at least this amount she has no incentive to become involved with entrepreneurship.

This is the so-called capitalist or free enterprise model of the firm. This model has very attractive properties for the pursuit of value creation because it attracts individuals with the right skills to use these skills to organize and manage others in the pursuit of value creation. Of course, like everything else the value of entrepreneurial skills will depend on their scarcity. If entrepreneurship was easy and needed few special qualities, it would be in plentiful supply and the rewards to entrepreneurs would be low. But given the requirements of entrepreneurship in terms of perception, organizing ability, negotiation skills, and reputation, the skill is likely to be scarce and the rewards attractive. You may note in passing that 'free enterprise' can only exist in a situation where property rights are enforceable. That is where the rule of law applies. Hence the state must precede the existence of enterprise.

The entrepreneur's prospective residual value is of great significance because it animates the whole process of value creation beyond the market. For this reason it has a special name. Indeed, just to confuse things, it has several special names (not counting the pejorative names used in some circles). These are *profits*, *added value*, and *rents*. These concepts are of great importance to economics in general and business economics in particular. They are also widely used in the field of business policy, which is nowadays described by many writers as the study of the firm's search for rents. It is therefore important to understand these terms properly because they are central to the study of business and you will come across them often in the business literature.

The economics textbook generally refers to the entrepreneur's surplus as profit, or more precisely economic profit, to avoid confusing it with accounting profit. It is defined as the difference between the firm's total revenue and total costs where the latter include not only the usual costs of material purchases, depreciation, and labour but also the cost of the finance employed by the firm, including any from the entrepreneur herself, and including an allowance for the opportunity cost of the entrepreneur's time and efforts. Economic profit then is a genuine surplus left after the opportunity costs of *all resources* used by the collective have been properly accounted for. Note that if the firm produces just enough income to keep the collective together but no more, that is, there is no economic profit as defined here, then the economics textbook refers to the firm as earning 'normal profit'. As will be explained later (Chapter 6) this 'normal profit' is treated as a cost in economic analysis and is thus incorporated in the cost functions used in later units. It is therefore important to recall that when economists talk about profit they mean economic profit or true entrepreneurial profit as we have defined it here.

It is apparent from the above definition that when a firm is generating economic profit, it is adding value. In other words, the value of its sales are more than sufficient to cover the economic costs, that is, the value of all the resources used by the collective. The owners of these resources must be getting at least the opportunity cost of these resources otherwise they would not continue to make them available to the collective. So any surplus produced represents an addition to the value of all the resources tied up in the coalition of resources which we call the firm. Note that to the extent that some members of the coalition are able in some way to achieve rewards in excess of what is necessary to keep them in the coalition, then they are appropriating some of the coalition's potential added value for themselves. Circumstances under which this might arise will be discussed later.

So far we have been (implicitly) discussing a firm in which there is a single entrepreneur who creates and 'owns' the firm. Strictly speaking, what the entrepreneur owns is the right to acquire the surplus generated by the collective: that is, its added value. Do any of our conclusions alter when the ownership of the firm is extended to many people through the issuing of equity shares? Although the story becomes a little more complicated, nothing of substance changes. The right to share in the surplus created by the firm has been sold by the entrepreneur to other shareholders for a price. The shareholders, including the entrepreneur if she or her family retain a proportion of the shares, are now the collective 'owners' of the business. Of course this could have implications for the search for value and the appropriation of added value, as we discuss briefly later in this chapter, but a full analysis of this issue is best left until later. We shall examine this issue under the heading of corporate governance in Chapter 12.

Now let us consider the term rent which is used, especially in the modern business policy literature, as a synonym for economic profit. We need to be especially careful here. The term *rent* is used in different ways, with somewhat different meanings, reflecting its historical origins and its developing usage. An appreciation of the origins of this term and its modern usage in economics and business policy is important for students of business in general and business policy in particular. We have attempted to provide an outline of the developing usage of this term in Box 4.3.

The Appropriation of Added Value and the Owners of Productive Resources

Will all the added value generated by the firm be appropriated by the entrepreneur? Not necessarily. To the extent that some members of the firm are able to achieve rewards in excess of what is sufficient to keep them in the coalition, then they are appropriating some of the coalition's added value for themselves.

Suppose that a commercial football club attempts to improve its playing (and so its financial) performance by recruiting Alan Shearer, currently Britain's most expensive player. Will this be successful? If Alan Shearer really is a player of outstanding ability then there is a good chance that the team's results will improve. But, contrary to what you might imagine, brilliant football players are not necessarily good at producing added value for the clubs that recruit them. The owners of resources of exceptional talent will seek to appropriate the full value of their productive services in their salaries and fees. These salaries and fees will tend to be very high because exceptional talents are rare and their supply inelastic. The added value generated by successful football teams tends, therefore, to be appropriated by the star players and coaches rather than by the clubs themselves as profit-seeking businesses.

It follows that in a successful enterprise—one which *does* generate economic profits for the owner/entrepreneur—the special qualities must reside in the skills of the owner/entrepreneur or in the collective nature of the organization he or she has created—rather than in the quality of the individual resources used by the firm. An interesting example of this is discussed by John Kay in his book *The Foundations of Corporate Success.* Kay gives a convincing account of how Liverpool Football Club for long periods achieved better than expected performance from the collection of player resources at its disposal by encouraging a culture based on teamwork. This is one example of what Kay calls the distinctive capability of architecture about which more later.

The Sustainability of Added Value

When a firm is generating economic profit, it is creating and appropriating some added value for itself and its owner(s). The value of its sales is more than sufficient to cover the cost of all the resources used by the collective. This surplus represents an addition to the value of all the resources tied up in the coalition of resources which we call the firm. What determines whether these economic profits can be sustained over time? First, the economic profit that a firm generates depends on the supply of other entrepreneurs who, spotting the success of the pioneer, are willing and able to copy her. To put it another way, if the entrepreneur's initial success is easy for others to reproduce, any success in generating profit cannot be sustained. To the extent that a particular entrepreneur creates a firm which generates profits over a longish period then the enterprise itself must have something special. Like Alan Shearer, the enterprise must possess an attribute which others, no matter how hard they try, cannot replicate. If what an entrepreneur does is easy to identify and copy, then other people will do it also and compete away her profit. We shall analyse the competitive model which demonstrates this result formally in Chapter 6. Secondly, the economic profit generated by a particular firm depends on the ability of supplier firms to extract some of this value for themselves.

Box 4.3 Concepts of Rent

A Rent as a return to owners of land

A1 Ricardian Rent

The rent concept goes back to one of the founding fathers of economics, David Ricardo, and its use arose as follows. A fierce debate was taking place in Britain in the early nineteenth century about the price of food. One view held that landowners were charging too high a price for their land, the supply of which was more or less fixed. As a result, the price of food was high because it reflected this high price for land.

Ricardo believed that this view was erroneous. He argued that the reasoning involved was back to front. Landowners could not determine the price of their land; it was the demand for land in relation to its supply which determined its price. The demand for land was determined ultimately by the demand for food. The steep rise in the price of land was a consequence of a rapidly rising demand for food against a backdrop of a relatively fixed (that is, inelastic) supply of suitable farm land. In Ricardo's view, landlords unwittingly benefited from these greater returns to land—what he called rents. You should be able to replicate Ricardo's analysis using the tools of supply and demand introduced in Chapter 2.

Notice that the ultimate source of the rent is the difficulty of increasing the supply of appropriate land. If more land could easily be made available (if land could be 'produced' to order) whenever the demand for it increased, then these land rents could not persist. Competition from new suppliers of land would drive the price of suitable land down and eliminate the rents. In fact what happened in Britain was that the opening up of new farm land in Canada and New Zealand, and the ending of import controls, eventually increased the supply of food grains available for British consumers and caused the decline of British land rents.

A2 Differential Rent

In practice the availability of land used for a particular purpose in a particular country *can* be increased when the demand for it increases. However, the additional land will tend to be of lower quality, in terms of location and fertility, than land already in use because farmers will already be using the most suitable land. Ricardo recognized this and in doing so introduced the idea of differential rent. The price of land is determined, said Ricardo, at the margin. As food prices rise, more land is brought into cultivation. The marginal unit of land—the last unit of land to have been brought into cultivation—will be of lower quality than all others; it is only cultivated once food prices have risen far enough to make it worthwhile using it for food production. So the rent on marginal land will approach zero.

However, all parcels of land which are of better quality than the marginal unit will earn positive returns: the higher the quality of the land, the higher these returns. Ricardo called these earnings differential rents. It is clear that these arise from qualitative differences between different parcels of land within the overall fixity of land available.

B Rent as a Return to any Productive Input

Ricardo was concerned with the rent that could be appropriated by one particular resource: land. However, land is not the only resource that can earn rents. The concept of rent subsequently came to be applied to a portion of the earnings of *any* productive resource; specifically, that part of the earnings of a resource which exceeds the level of its opportunity cost, or what it could earn in its next best use. For example, the opportunity cost of land used for grain production in Britain was what the land could earn by grazing sheep.

The earnings of many talented sports-persons, and entertainers, have a high rent element because what these people could earn in their next most suitable occupation is likely to be much lower than their current earnings and these high earnings tend to persist over time because the supply of exceptional talent is highly inelastic. You cannot easily increase the supply of top class footballers or actresses just as you cannot easily increase the supply of first-rate farm land: unless, of course, you follow the British example with land in the nineteenth century and look abroad for a new source of supply (although, of course, the worldwide pool of talented footballers is itself limited)!

Like Ricardian rents, therefore, these high earnings derive essentially from barriers to increasing the supply of the resource in question. Where the supply of a resource can easily be increased, it cannot earn significantly above its opportunity cost for very long. Why? Because if its earnings were to rise above its opportunity cost, supply would increase and the earnings would fall back to normal levels. For example, a sudden increase in the demand for taxi services in a big city can lead temporarily to increased earnings for cab drivers. But not for long because it is not difficult to increase the supply of taxi services. So why do some people command prices well above their opportunity costs? And why do these prices persist over lengthy periods of time? The answer is that for some reason, such as the possession of special talent, people who *would* happily

Box 4.3 continued

do the job for a lot less than the incumbent (e.g. play for Manchester United, or sing at the Met) *cannot* effectively compete with them to bid the price down. A special quality of the resource in question means it cannot be easily reproduced by others and this limits competition. If talent could easily be reproduced it would soon cease to be regarded as such.

C Rent as a Return to a Firm

C1 Rent as a Return to the Special Qualities of the Firm as a Collection of Resources.

It has become common in business policy literature, especially in the USA, to refer to the economic profits or added value of a firm as its rents and to describe the objectives of firms as searching for rents. But of course a firm is a collection of resources. Competitive markets will ensure that individual factors are valued correctly and rewarded appropriately. Especially talented individuals may therefore earn rents as a member of a collective (for example, a scientist working for Glaxo), but these are individual rents not collective rents. So what might be the source of rents to the collective, or the firm? Collective or firm rents must come from something special or unique that the *firm as a collective entity* possesses over and above the special qualities of the individual resources involved. We have in mind a kind of synergy whereby the whole is more valuable than the sum of the parts.

These special qualities that the firm possesses could come in different forms. One of these is superior cost performance compared with rival firms; somehow or other, the organization is able to produce things at a lower cost than the competition, even though everyone can bid for the individual resource components. Another is the ability of a particular organization to make superior product offerings to those of its rivals, without incurring commensurably higher costs.

Note that this view of rents bears some similarity to differential rent, as it arises from heterogeneity or qualitative differences. Where it differs from Ricardian differential rent, however, is that the special quality involved lies in the way the resources are organized and utilized in a particular business rather than in any of the individual resources themselves.

C2 Rent as Sustainable Economic Profits

Some writers use the term rent to describe economic profits which can be sustained over time. It is this feature of sustainability that they wish to emphasize. However, in essence this view of rent is not different from the kind discussed in the previous paragraph. To see this, ask how this *sustainability* may arise. In the final instance, it must come from particularly fruitful and valuable ways in which the firm organizes its resources, or from the firm's superior ability to align what it offers with what customers want. We are back to the previous case. The importance of this view lies in what it invites entrepreneurs and managers to think about: it invites them to consider how their firm can marshal the available resources to achieve a competitive edge over its rivals in such a way that its rivals find it difficult to copy them and compete away their economic profits.

C3 Rents based on the Exercise of Market (or Monopoly) Power

A somewhat older tradition also uses rent as a label for monopoly profits. As we shall see in Chapter 7, monopoly profits also have their source in a kind of scarcity, but one engendered by the firm's exercise of its monopoly power based perhaps on a patent or a government licence.

Monopoly profits may also come from price discrimination. In most circumstances, firms sell a product at a single price to all customers. But sometimes firms sell goods at different prices to different customers, even though the products are identical and there are no differences in the costs of making them. This is known as price discrimination. As we show in Chapter 7, this practice requires that the seller has some monopoly power, that resale between customers can be prevented, and that different parts of the market for the product have different 'willingness to pay' for the product.

However, some care is required in perceiving the surplus earnings arising from monopoly power as a distinct form of rent. A firm may acquire monopoly power as a result of being much better than its rivals at what it does. If so, the monopoly power is a consequence of the firm's special abilities, and so it would be inappropriate to describe monopoly rents as being different in kind from those in categories C1 and C2. For example, Microsoft clearly enjoys something close to a monopoly in personal computer (PC) operating-system software. But Bill Gates would argue that the firm's strength and its market position derives from a massive competitive advantage conferred by the special qualities developed over time by Gates and his colleagues. Microsoft's profits, he would argue, are a return on its unique qualities and the difficulties rivals have in building similar qualities, not a result of its monopoly power. This is not just an esoteric argument. Microsoft and the US Department of Justice are currently engaged in an expensive anti-trust battle which hinges on this point.

C4 Schumpeterian Rent

The Austrian economist Joseph Schumpeter discussed the returns that come from innovation. These returns are inherently transitory, occurring in the time between the initial innovation and the rise of imitators. Although they are ultimately transitory, they may nevertheless generate high returns to the innovators for considerable periods of time. A part of the earnings of companies such as Sony and Glaxo might therefore be seen as Schumpeterian rents.

The special qualities or attributes created by firms are important in two ways. First, they make the firm 'profitable'—that is, they put it in a more favourable position than its rivals. So even if other firms in the same market are struggling to add value, only the firm with special qualities is able to do so successfully. Secondly, if they are hard to replicate, they create barriers to imitation which sustain these profits. Some discussion of the sustainability of profits in the information technology sector, stressing the importance of replicability and distinctiveness, and the role of supplier firms, is given in Box 4.4.

Box 4.4 Sustainable Profits in Computing: Hardware versus Software

By looking at firms such as IBM, Intel, and Microsoft, we can find some interesting lessons about the sustainability of profits. In 1981 IBM introduced what has become known as the personal computer (PC). This major innovation launched a dramatic growth in business and (subsequently) personal computing. The early success of the PC was made possible and supported by IBM's technological and organizational strengths, its brand-name, and its reputation as a computer hardware supplier. For some time, IBM was earning substantial rents from its sale of PCs.

However, its adoption of an open standard left IBM exposed to imitation, and the market soon became flooded by rivals such as Compaq selling PC clones. The qualities which had generated IBM's initial profits in the PC market became increasingly less special. As the diffusion spread and the industry matured and became more competitive, the ability to produce at low cost, to be innovative in design, and to respond rapidly to customer wants, became of increasing importance. In effect, the value of IBM's capabilities declined.

As the PC market became more competitive, it also became evident that a large share of the added value was being appropriated by two other firms which controlled the supply of two key components of the standard PC package: Intel, which supplied the microprocessors, and Microsoft which supplied the software-operating interface Windows. In fact what used to be called IBM clones are now referred to as Wintels reflecting the shift in power in this particular industry.

Intel's profitability from microprocessor sales has remained very high, because of its huge economies of scale in the production of computer chips, its very rapid rate of technical progress in processor design, manufacture, and performance, and its marketing and legal skills which have made it difficult for others to follow. However, at the end of the 1990s signs emerged that even Intel's position could be threatened.

Microsoft has also been a major winner in this market. This cannot be explained in technical terms alone. The standard mid-level operating system, DOS, was not first developed by Microsoft, and the lower-level Windows user interface was pioneered by Apple (although not under that name). Indeed Apple found that despite being a brilliant innovator it lost the 'value-added race', principally because it was unable to prevent others from finding and successfully deploying substitute products.

Microsoft did just that. By forming a network of organizational and product linkages with other hardware and software firms, and by clever marketing, it was able to become the dominant player in the computing industry, and sustain its profits in a way that almost no others have done in such a rapidly changing technological environment.

The prospects for sustainable profits seem to be much stronger in computing software than in hardware. IBM's recent 'Business Solutions' marketing slogan, emphasizing the services that computer providers can offer (rather than the capabilities of the machines themselves) is a reflection of this, and in some ways represents an attempt to add value once again by exploiting one of its long-standing distinctive capabilities.

4.3 The Objectives of the Enterprise

It is reasonable to say that as far as the entrepreneur is concerned, the objective of the enterprise is to create the maximum residual value achievable after allowing for the opportunity costs of her own time and effort. Or that the objective of the enterprise is to search for value by organizing the co-operation of others. But does this mean that all firms, at all times, are in fact oriented towards maximizing the entrepreneur's added value? Clearly this is unlikely. The firm is a collection or coalition of many individuals. These individuals have objectives of their own which they pursue by joining a coalition and co-operating with others. So individuals are co-operating first and foremost in pursuit of their own objectives not the objectives of the collective or those of the entrepreneur. A perfectly constructed machine can no doubt be programmed to do exactly what its maker bids, but this cannot be true of a human organization. Whilst there must be some collective interest in 'the firm' doing well, this is by no means the same thing as everyone being personally dedicated to maximizing the entrepreneur's added value.

What an organization actually does, and how it performs, depends ultimately on the objectives and behaviour of all its members, on the extent to which any conflict between individual aims can be resolved, and on the extent to which personal aims can be harnessed to an overriding collective aim consistent with that of the owner/entrepreneur. In other words, it depends on the degree to which individuals are prepared to co-operate with one another in pursuit of a particular collective goal or the extent to which they can be induced to co-operate towards achieving such a goal by external threats such as competition or by the design of appropriate internal arrangements.

Achieving the wholehearted co-operation of many individuals in pursuit of a single goal can be very difficult. Why should this be so? Why, if co-operation towards a particular goal is desirable and valuable, might it be hard to achieve? Why, if each individual is at least as well off in a coalition as out of it, might they not co-operate wholeheartedly in pursuit of maximizing the coalition's residual value?

In calculating the personal net gains (benefits less costs) to be achieved through particular levels of co-operation with other individuals, each person will take into account the likely degree of co-operation (effort and honesty) of other members of the collective, and the extent to which they will 'play fair' in what they put in and what they take out of the collective. Each individual has reason to be concerned that, other things equal, for some of the time, other individuals will not be co-operating as fully as they could or should. This is because of the evident propensity of individuals to put their own interests first, to take advantage of the efforts of others if they can, to behave opportunistically towards others, to 'free ride' on the efforts of others, to get something for nothing. Economists might be thought unduly cynical about the capacity of individuals for pursuing their own interests by fair means or foul, but anyone who considers the effort some people put into avoiding paying taxes for public goods, such as defence and the roads network, will appreciate the point.

The Prisoner's Dilemma

The problem of achieving valuable co-operation in the face of individual self-interest can be clearly demonstrated using the analysis of a situation called the Prisoner's Dilemma. In this hypothetical situation two people, Ms Smith and Mr Jones, have been arrested as suspects in a serious crime. The evidence available to the police is, however, not sufficient to confirm their guilt, and, in the absence of a confession, the two prisoners are likely to be charged with only a minor crime (loitering with intent) as opposed to the major crime the police are convinced they committed. So the prosecutor presents each prisoner separately with the following deal: 'If you confess, you will get off lightly with a one-year sentence whilst your partner will get ten years. If neither of you confesses, you will be charged with the lesser crime and face a two-year sentence each. If both of you end up confessing you each face a seven-year stretch.' The pay-offs for the various possible combinations of choices by the prisoners are given in Figure 4.2. For each choice combination, the number above the diagonal line denotes the pay-off to Mr Jones and the number below the diagonal line denotes the pay-off to Ms Smith. Note that the way this situation is structured means that co-operation between the prisoners is valuable to both of them. If neither confesses, they each face only a two-year stretch which is better

		Mr Jones	
		Confess	Don't confess
Ms Smith	Confess	7 / 7	1 / 10
	Don't confess	10 / 1	2 / 2

Figure 4.2 The Prisoner's Dilemma

than failing to co-operate and facing seven years. But will they co-operate?

Not necessarily. Prisoner Smith figures it this way: 'If I confess the worst that can happen is a seven-year stretch, and I just might get away with a year! If I don't confess, I might get ten years or at best I will get two years, depending on what my mate does. So the way I see it *no matter* what Jones does (confess/not confess), I am better off confessing. Because if he confesses and I don't, I get ten years rather than seven. And if he doesn't confess and neither do I, then I get two years instead of just one. So either way it is in my best interest to go along with the police and confess.' Of course Prisoner Jones is sitting in his cell making exactly the same calculation. And Prisoner Smith knows that!

So what will they each do in their own best interests? Will they co-operate, refuse to confess, and receive a lighter sentence? That is not likely in this case. They will each act in their own self-interest even when they both know categorically that co-operation would produce the best result for the collective. Why? Because the pursuit of what is best for the individual dominates the pursuit of co-operation in favour of the collective. But wait a minute, you might argue. What if the two prisoners realize before they set up in business together that they will sooner or later face exactly this situation. Surely they will talk it over, realize that co-operation is best for the firm, swear an oath to silence, and shake on it? Of course they will. And they might even mean it at the time. But faced with the offer in a prison cell, with the wily police telling each of them that the other is weakening, the result is a forgone conclusion. They both confess and they each get a seven-year sentence. The prisoner's dilemma is only a parable of course but a cursory examination of the newspapers each week suggests that it is not necessarily 'unrealistic'.

So much then for the idea that the individual's pursuit of his own self-interest will necessarily lead to a good outcome for everyone. Under the circumstances of the Prisoner's Dilemma, the individual's pursuit of his own self-interest leads to an outcome which is not at all optimal for the individuals concerned. Co-operation would in fact be better than the pursuit of self-interest both for individuals and the collective but it does not happen, and the fact that it does not happen leads to a perverse result. By pursuing their own best interests, by looking after number one, the individuals concerned actually come off worse than if they had co-operated! This suggests that anything that helps to encourage co-operation, or allows individuals to commit themselves credibly to the collective will, will be valuable.

The Prisoner's Dilemma is a ubiquitous phenomenon with important and costly consequences for any collection of individuals, be it a firm, a club, or a state. For example, we all know that it would be socially valuable if we did not drop litter or drive too fast in built-up areas. But self-interest leads us to do so just the same. We all know that honesty is the best policy, and that we should do an honest day's work for an honest day's pay, but if we reckon we could do better ignoring these nostrums then of course most of us, most of the time, will. Nations with a common fishery ground know about the dangers of overfishing but will all tend to overfish. We shall see in Chapter 8 that co-operation is valuable for oligopolistic firms but that it is hard to achieve sustainable co-operation, as the history of OPEC, the oil cartel, makes clear. Such then is human nature, and the human dilemma, as the economist sees it.

The potential conflict between the individual and collective interest is likely to affect the large firms which dominate the modern industrial landscape. These firms are complex organizations consisting of shareholders and other suppliers of capital, the bankers who lend the firms money, component and service suppliers, managers, and other workers. Not all of these will necessarily see it as in their best interests to co-operate wholeheartedly towards the maximization of the profits of the enterprise, even though wholehearted co-operation may in fact ultimately be good for them and for the collective. Workers have an inclination to shirk, managers a tendency to feather their own nests, suppliers a tendency to cut corners on quality. In general we all have a tendency to see our own interests as paramount.

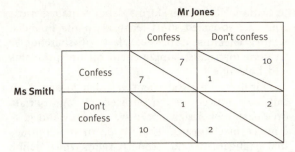

Achieving more Effective Co-operation

What factors determine the objectives of firms in practice? What determines the extent to which the individual desire to create and appropriate value is harnessed effectively to an overriding collective or organizational goal such as maximizing profit or shareholder value? The following factors would seem to be relevant.

First, the extent to which individuals are prepared to *trust* one another to co-operate in collective situations is of great importance. In view of what we have just said it is clear that trust is a scarce (and so a valuable) commodity. However, it may be that cultural values and social conditioning make trust less scarce in some places than in others, or at least cheaper to build and maintain. It might, for example, be the case that trust is scarcer in the USA (hence all those lawyers) than it is in Japan (which has proportionately very few lawyers) with Britain somewhere in the middle. The scarcity of trust makes the USA a poorer country than it might be because it means that lots of opportunities for valuable co-operation are lost, and a lot of scarce resources are used in dealing with the problems caused by lack of trust. Conversely, if the Japanese are more inclined to trust one another until proven wrong by events, this would help them to create co-operation more cheaply and so take advantage of more opportunities for valuable co-operation. Could this be the secret of Japan's competitive advantage?

Secondly, the extent to which it is possible to induce co-operation by external forces and threats, in particular the threat of competition from other collectives, is of importance. This is the main reason why economists believe that firms will ultimately pursue value-maximizing behaviour. Under competitive conditions, which we will analyse formally in Chapter 6, firms which can achieve a relatively high degree of co-operation will eliminate those that cannot. Therefore at any given time, the successful firms in a particular competitive environment will be those which are solving the problems highlighted by the Prisoner's Dilemma better than the others. Not completely, of course, just better. This fact is seen clearly when a hitherto relatively closed economy faces greater foreign competition from countries with a more co-operative spirit. Suitable examples are not hard to find. Inadequate co-operation takes many forms: labour–management conflicts; so-called short-termism in the financial sector reflecting a possible lack of shareholder trust in managers; supply-chain quality problems and hold-ups.

Thirdly, there is the extent to which co-operation can be induced or encouraged by appropriate organizational design, incentive systems, and governance mechanisms. These concern the contractual arrangements and property rights which define the business organization, the reward mechanisms in operation, the choice of organizational design, the extent of investments made in building trust and co-operation, and the extent to which each of these is successful in creating a focus on value creation for the collective. Note also that since the firm can be seen as a coalition of individuals with voting powers of different types (shareholders, workers, and so on), it is reasonable to view it as a political entity so that the political skills and leadership qualities of the coalition leaders will be very important.

The extent to which firms actively pursue the maximization of the coalition's added value thus depends ultimately on the nature and organization of the firm itself. It depends on governance mechanisms, incentive mechanisms, and organizational design. Getting these things right is the fundamental problem of business organization, and thus a fundamental determinant of business performance. We shall return to this issue in Chapter 10 where we shall refer to these matters under the heading of organizational architecture. In the meantime we shall now follow, over the next five chapters, the conventional economic approach to the question of *how* firms go about adding value, which means focusing on the determinants of costs and prices, or the problems involved in getting costs down and keeping revenues up.

It is worth noting at this point that many people, particularly in the field of business strategy, argue that the value or profit-maximizing view of the purpose of enterprise is too narrow, too economics- and finance-oriented, for the analysis of business policy. Some people seem to believe that organizations have a more transcendent purpose than simply 'adding value'. Our view is that they are wrong. For a well-argued defence of this view, we recommend Rappaport (1992) whose argument we summarize briefly in Box 4.5.

Box 4.5 Shareholder Value and Competitive Advantage

Rappaport, writing in 1992, argues that company managers are becoming polarized into two camps: those who consider shareholder value to be the key to managing companies, and others who see the manager's job as attaining 'competitive advantage' which they believe is not consonant with pursuing shareholder value. He observes that this is a new form of an old debate between going for outstanding short-term results and investment for long term prosperity.

Rappaport argues that this dichotomy is not valid, and that the debate it engenders is rather barren. In his view, there is a common link between shareholder value and competitive advantage; that link is productivity. A company has a competitive advantage when it adds value—when the value of its output is greater than its total costs (including capital costs). This advantage can be obtained by providing superior value to customers, by lower costs, or both.

But it is also productivity to which the stock market reacts in determining a company's share value. A firm's share price reflects the market's view about its future profit-generating potential. So when the market builds expectations of high future productivity growth into its valuation, that is equivalent to a belief that the firm has a sustainable competitive advantage.

Why then do managers believe that there is a conflict between the two? One reason is that earnings per share—the rate of return to a shareholder—are not well correlated with managers' expectations of future profitability.

Rappaport points out two things here. First, if the market already expects a firm to do well, its share price will be bid up to reflect these expectations. Thus investors buying shares in a well-performing company may get high dividends but they will also have to pay a high price for the shares. So 'earnings per share' will not be high at current stock prices and dividends. Indeed, as Rappaport shows, if all profits were fully anticipated by the market, expected market rates of return would be equalized over all firms, irrespective of how well they performed! The only way in which above-average rates of return can be obtained by shareholders is by chance, or where high returns are not anticipated by the market (for example, by using insider information). So the fact that earnings per share do not correspond well to competitive advantage is not, nor should it be, a reason to distrust the objective of maximizing shareholder wealth. Shareholder wealth depends on the level of share prices, not the rate of return on shares.

Secondly, many managers (claims Rappaport) believe that share prices are poor indicators of a firm's competitive advantage. Typically, managers value their firms more highly than the market. And this is most likely in the case of firms which show no evidence of having obtained a competitive advantage, and which are regarded by the market as poor performers. Rappaport shows that the market puts a finite horizon on the time over which it sums up future expected profits in determining the value of a firm's shares. Firms with a good performance record, such as Pepsi-Cola and Coca-Cola, may have expected profits over the next twenty years built into share prices. Poorly positioned firms may have valuations based on as little as one or two years' expected profits.

Rappaport argues that this is exactly as it should be. Stock market valuations are ways of allocating scarce resources; they send out signals as to where investors have and should put their funds. The outcome of all this for corporate strategy is clear, says Rappaport. Managers who wish for corporate growth will find no conflict between maximizing shareholder value and gaining competitive advantage. These are merely different reflections of the same thing: the ability of a firm to add value.

Rappaport's conclusion is this. A firm achieves a competitive advantage when:

- it generates profits and increases the value of the firm;
- it achieves competitive success *vis-a-vis* other firms.

There is no conflict at all between these two things.

Source: Adapted from Alfred Rappaport, 'CEOs and Strategists: Forging a Common Framework', *Harvard Business Review*, May–June 1992, pp. 84–91.

A Note on the Objectives of Organizations Operating 'Beyond' the Profit Motive

Many readers of this text who work in local government, or the National Health Service, or for co-operatives or charities, may be wondering what our discussion so far has to do with them. We have taught economics to many groups over the years and this question generally arises at this stage. Many students, and many readers, do not come from a conventional enterprise background, where conventional is taken to mean the private profit-seeking business sector. These students/readers come from organizations which appear not to conform to the model of capitalist enterprise which is assumed here and which is generally assumed in business policy texts. They work in the public sector or in the not-for-profit sector covering organizations such as charities. Is the economic approach to the world relevant to such organizations or is it of relevance only to the capitalist profit-seeking enterprise? The answer is yes, it is relevant, and no, economics is categorically not just for capitalist profit-seeking firms.

The fact that local government authorities, the National Health Service, the Co-operative Insurance Society, and Oxfam are not capitalist-type business organizations seeking to make profits does not mean that they do not exist in order to create added value in the economic sense. Remember the creation of value and its appropriation are two separate issues. The fact is that a health service or a charity or even a university uses scarce resources in order, at least in principle, to provide valuable services for its customers or clients. In each case, there is a demand for services, and in most cases payment, albeit indirect, for these services. In addition, there are resource costs in supplying these services. In each case the organization has to compete for resources with lots of other organizations (Oxfam competes for resources with Save The Children and The Salvation Army; universities compete with one another as do hospitals). In each case, the organizational purpose in principle is to maximize the value created for and appropriated by its customers and clients, by supplying the services demanded in the most cost-effective way possible. Each organization has to decide the nature and quantity of services to be provided, how to acquire the necessary resources to finance provision, and how to use these resources most effectively. Anyone who works in a charity or a school or a hospital must be familiar with these questions even though they do not think of themselves as being 'in business' in the conventional sense.

The idea that not-for-profit organizations do and should live beyond the imperatives of economics and value creation is the product of woolly thinking which sees services such as health, education, and charity as somehow too important to be run as businesses following the normal rules of value creation. These services are important, however, exactly because they are potentially so valuable to society, and as a result should be produced and delivered as efficiently as possible. Unfortunately, however, this is often not the case. It seems to be that as a result of confusing 'not for profit' with 'not for adding value', many not-for-profit organizations are not in fact very good at delivering value to the clients they claim to serve. This is possibly the result of the fact that often the resources involved are obtained through general taxation, or donations, and allocated by employees without due regard to the priorities of their clients. There is, in fact, often no mechanism for adequately measuring the priorities of clients or for allocating scarce resources to their most valuable, highest priority, use. Hospitals and universities do surprisingly little market research and until recently had a very poor understanding of their costs of production. Not-for-profit organizations which do see themselves as being in the value-creating business will, we suggest, be far more valuable to their clients than those which see their function as somehow transcending such mundane requirements.

A good question therefore for people who do work in not-for-profit organizations is: are we creating and delivering added value for our clients? Is the value of our services to our clients in excess of the economic value of the resources we use to produce and deliver those services? If it is not, the next question should be: what exactly are we in business to do if not to create value for our clients and might it not be the case that someone else could use the scarce resources we employ better than us?

Conclusions

In this chapter, we have set out to connect the individual search for value to the search for value through groups of individuals in organizations called firms. We have considered fundamental questions such as why we need firms at all, the nature of entrepreneurship, and the rewards of entrepreneurship. We have argued that firms come about essentially because they provide a superior way of achieving the co-operation and co-ordination of individuals in their search for value: superior to pure market-based exchange and co-ordination that is. The reasons we gave for this came under the general heading of transactional problems and costs. We have argued that the creation of the firm is motivated by the entrepreneur's desire for personal gain in the form of residual value generated by the firm. We called this residual value economic profit, added value, or rent and gave these terms precise definitions.

We then considered the distinctions between the entrepreneur's objective, the objectives of other members of the firm, and what the organization actually does. We concluded by outlining the factors which seem likely to determine the extent to which the individual desire to search for value is harnessed to an overriding collective or organizational goal such as maximizing the residual value of the collective.

What then can we reasonably assume to be the objective of the enterprise? It is reasonable to say that the *purpose* of the firm is to search for and exploit opportunities to add value but that just how assiduously a particular firm tries to add value depends on the firm's environment and the extent to which it is able to create an organizational focus on value-adding activity.

With this assumption in mind, we can now leave the issue of *what* firms are seeking to do in order to concentrate on *how* they do it. The following chapters are concerned with different but related aspects of the firm's search for value, the problems the firm faces in its search for value, and the ultimate determinants of the firm's success at adding value. The firm's search for value creates a number of distinct but related problems which are outlined below. The people in charge of the enterprise have to develop a strategy which addresses the following interlinked problems:

- keeping down or minimizing costs (Chapter 5);
- determining the best or optimal price (Chapters 6, 7, and 8);
- managing challenges from new entrants (Chapters 7);
- managing rivalry within the industry (Chapter 8);
- managing investment in quality and innovation (Chapter 9);
- finding a source of sustainable competitive advantage (Chapter 10);
- adding value through extending the scope of the firm (diversifying) or by making acquisitions (Chapter 11);
- business motivation and corporate governance (Chapter 12).

Further reading

Kay (1993) is a superb, thought-provoking presentation of the economics and business strategy of the firm. Chapters 3 and 4, in particular, deal with the issues we have examined in this chapter. Miller (1994), though not an easy read, is a brilliant analysis of the economics of organizations and organizational objectives. Reading in full Rappaport's (1992) article (summarized in the text) will richly reward the effort. Ricketts (1994) is also highly recommended for a deeper analysis of the economics of business enterprise.

Questions

4.1. What are transactional difficulties and costs and why do we need to be concerned with them?

4.2. What factors give rise to transactional difficulties and costs?

4.3. According to the transactional view of the world, what exactly are firms for?

4.4. According to the transactional view of the world, what exactly is the function of entrepreneurship?

4.5. Think of a famous entrepreneur, for example Bill Gates of Microsoft or Richard Branson of Virgin. In which ways and to what extent, do this person's qualities and activities match the description of entrepreneurship given in this chapter?

4.6. Explain the nature and the significance of the terms added value, economic profits, and rent. How does the added value approach suggest we judge business performance? Does this seem sensible to you?

4.7. Evaluate the view that successful high street retailers such as Marks and Spencer are successful because they were lucky enough to have acquired the best high street locations before their value was really appreciated.

4.8 Is it appropriate to assume that the objective of the enterprise is generally the same as the objective of the entrepreneur, or the owner of the enterprise surplus?

4.9. 'The Prisoner's Dilemma is an interesting story but it isn't very realistic.' Discuss.

4.10. What factors ultimately determine the objectives of the enterprise?

4.11. Is the value or profit-maximizing view of the purpose of enterprise too narrow, too finance-oriented, for the analysis of business policy?

5 The Search for Added Value and the Costs of Production

Introduction

Our study of business behaviour and the firm's search to create value begins in this chapter with an examination of

- the production process—the conversion of productive inputs into outputs of goods and services;
- the relationships between the firm's level of output and its costs of production.

The study of business costs is important because these costs have a major effect on the amount of value which a firm generates. For any choice of output, the value-seeking firm will seek to minimize costs. In order to understand business costs, it is helpful to look in a general way at the production process.

In this chapter, we take you through the way economists analyse the production process, in the process explaining the ideas of the short-run and the long-run production periods. The concept of the production function is used to identify the relationships between the firm's inputs and outputs in the short-run and the long-run. Several cost measures—specifically total, average, and marginal costs—are constructed to examine the variation of costs with output.

In a major study of the determinants of costs, Michael Porter (1985) analysed a number of structural factors which he called 'cost drivers'. Four of these cost drivers are of particular importance, and are examined in this chapter:

- patterns of capacity utilization associated with variations in the intensity of utilization of a firm's resources;
- economies and/or diseconomies of scale associated with variations in the scale of output which might be chosen by a firm;
- learning and/or experience effects associated with the accumulated volume of production of a product by a firm over time;
- economies and/or diseconomies of scope associated with linkages and interrelationships among different products made by the one firm.

The first of these cost drivers will be examined in Section 5.1 in our analysis of production and costs in the short run. This is followed in Section 5.2 by a discussion of economies and diseconomies of scale. In our presentation of these two cost drivers, our analysis will proceed on the assumption that firms operate at all times on their production frontiers. Production is assumed to incorporate best technical practice and best combinations of inputs (subject, in the short run, to constraints imposed by the presence of fixed factors). By implication, the relationships implied the lowest feasible costs.

But in a world in which new products and new processes are being continuously developed, firms will typically go through learning processes in which costs are only gradually lowered towards lowest possible levels. We briefly examine this accumulation of relevant experience by considering learning effects, the third of the cost drivers we discuss in this chapter.

In the final part of this chapter, potential cost savings which arise from the joint production of two or more distinct products—scope economies—are investigated.

5.1 The Production Function

The production process is a technical relationship in which inputs are transformed into outputs. This relationship can be represented by the *production function*, which may be written as:

$Q = f(X_1, X_2, \ldots, X_n)$.

The quantity of output Q is determined by the quantities used of n different inputs, X_1 through to X_n. More precisely, the production function describes the *maximum* amount of output which can be obtained by using particular amounts of inputs. For simplicity, we consider a special case in which output is produced using only two inputs, physical capital (K) and labour (L). The production function can then be written as

$Q = f(K, L)$.

We suggest that you now read Box 5.1. That explains more fully what is meant by a production function, and discusses three forms that a production function might take.

Production Time Periods

Production decisions take place within a framework of *constraints*. One type of constraint concerns the inputs a firm uses. An input is said to be *fixed* if it does not vary with the quantity of output. An input is *variable* if the quantity employed varies with the firm's output. For example, a firm using a blast furnace to convert iron into steel has iron as one of its variable inputs. The blast furnace itself, though, is a fixed input.

Fixity of an input is not a physical property. We can see this by considering a football club. Suppose that we regard the club's league points total as the measure of its output. The club manager is a fixed input as its points total can vary without altering the quantity of its managerial input. It is clear that this fixity is not a consequence of any physical immobility of the manager.

This example suggests another way of thinking about fixity or variability of inputs. An input might be fixed because of contract conditions. The manager of a commercial football club will have a contract specifying a particular period of time over which he will receive guaranteed remuneration. Of course, contracts may be renegotiated, or new managers found, even if payments are still made to a previous manager. But until these changes can be implemented, the manager constitutes a fixed input (and so imposes on his club a fixed cost).

Fixity of inputs may also arise from transactions or adjustment costs. Imagine that a firm wishes to expand output, and would like to acquire additional quantities of all inputs to do so. Some inputs may be obtainable immediately through market transactions at going market rates. In other cases, obtaining inputs quickly may involve incurring high search and negotiation costs. For some specialized inputs, quantities may not be available for immediate delivery without substantial premia payments to persuade scarce inputs to be moved from other uses. In such circumstances, the inputs in question are, to some degree, fixed.

So the notion of a fixed input has two meanings. The first concerns the fact that the use of a fixed input does not vary with output: we shall tend to stress this view when looking at the input–output relationships in production. The second is a consequence of the type of contract that the firm has entered into with the owner of the input, or the magnitude of the costs that will be incurred if the firm tries to adjust the use of the input quickly; we shall tend to adopt this interpretation when analysing the costs of production.

Economists use the notions of fixed and variable inputs to define two production time periods:

> *the short run* is that period during which at least one input is fixed;
>
> *the long run* is that period during which all factors are considered to be variable.

It is hard to think of any circumstances in which a firm will not have some fixed inputs. As a result, we could say that all production takes place within the short run. However, firms can and do plan for the future. These plans include intentions about the quantities of inputs to be used in the future. In this process of planning, managers are treating all factors as if they were variable, and so are adopting a long-run perspective.

This suggests that it is useful to think about the short run and the long run as different types of planning periods. The long run refers to a hypothetical state in which managerial decisions are not hemmed in by any input quantity constraints. In contrast, managerial choices are constrained in the short run by legacies of past choices, in the form of fixed inputs (and so fixed costs).

5.2 Production and Costs in the Short Run

We now consider production in the short run. Here the firm has one or more fixed inputs, the levels of which depend upon past decisions. Suppose that

Box 5.1 The Production Function

The production function

$$Q = f(K, L) \tag{5.1}$$

states that the quantity of a firm's output, Q, depends upon the amounts of capital K and labour L employed. The symbol $f(.)$ denotes that a functional relationship exists between Q, K, and L. In general form, the function $f(K, L)$ tells us that *some* relationship exists but not what the actual relationship is.

Consider some possible particular forms that the production function might take. One very simple form occurs where output is a linear function of the productive inputs. An example of this is given by equation (5.2):

$$Q = 2K + 3L. \tag{5.2}$$

Once the particular form of the input–output relationship is specified, the output that could be obtained from certain quantities of inputs can be calculated. In this case, 10 units of capital and 10 units of labour could yield 50 units of output. It is also possible to produce 50 units of output using other input combinations. For example, 16 capital and 6 labour also produce 50 units of output, as does the combination 4 capital and 14 labour. Figure 5.1 shows all the combinations of (positive amounts of) K and L that allow an output of 50 units to be produced. The line drawn in the figure is known as an isoquant—it shows all input combinations that yield a given quantity of output. As an exercise, you should now ask yourself where the isoquant for 100 rather than 50 units of output would be drawn in Figure 5.1.

It is most unlikely that actual production functions are linear, not least because a linear function implies perfect input substitutability: output can be kept at an unchanged level by replacing one input by another at a constant rate, irrespective of how much of either input is already being used.

A second possible form of production function is the fixed-proportion or Leontief type:

$$Q = \min \{aK, bL\} \tag{5.3}$$

where a and b are constant numbers. The Leontief production function applies in cases where inputs must be combined in a fixed proportion. The parameters a and b determine what that proportion is. If a and b were each 5, the Leontief production function would be:

$$Q = \min \{5K, 5L\}.$$

The isoquant for $Q = 50$ for this production function is shown in Figure 5.2. An output of 50 is obtained using $10K$ and $10L$. However, more than $10K$ without any additional L will not produce any extra output; similarly more than $10L$ without any extra K will not produce any extra output. Output can only be increased by increasing both K and L simultaneously and in the appropriate fixed proportion. For a Leontief function no substitution is possible between the two inputs.

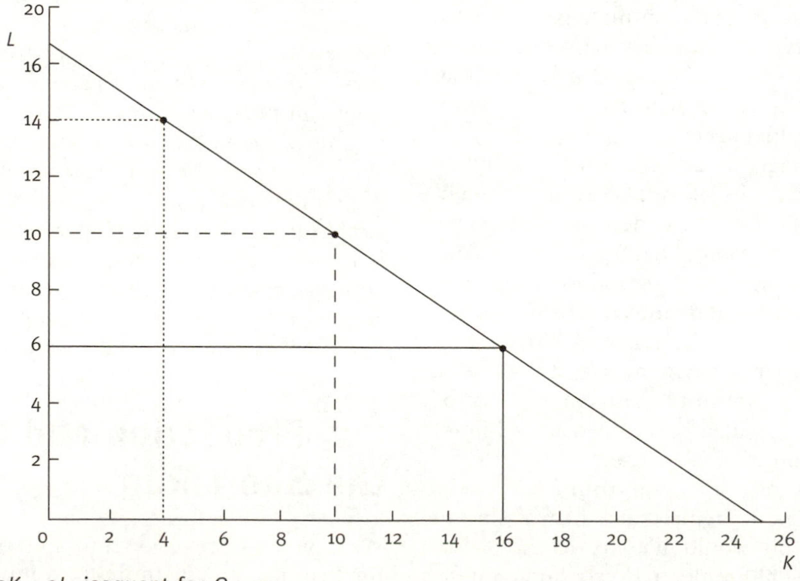

Figure 5.1 $Q = 2K + 3L$; isoquant for $Q = 50$

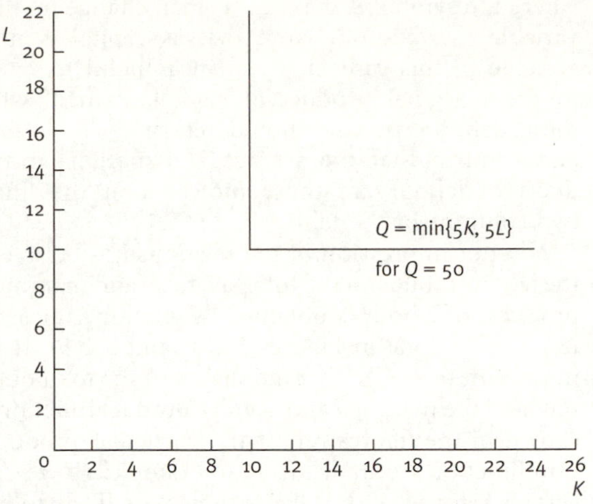

Figure 5.2 $Q = \min\{5K, 5L\}$; isoquant for $Q = 50$

Both economic theory and empirical evidence suggest that production functions will rarely, if ever, exhibit perfect input substitutability or zero input substitutability. In contrast, in the Cobb–Douglas production function inputs are substitutes for one another, but they are less than perfect substitutes. The form of the Cobb–Douglas function is given by equation (5.4)

$$Q = AK^{\alpha}L^{\beta}. \tag{5.4}$$

In this expression the parameters A, α, and β are constant numbers. The parameter A represents the efficiency with which inputs are converted into output; the parameters α and β determine the impact on output of changes in capital alone and labour alone respectively. Figure 5.3 shows the isoquant for $Q = 50$ which is derived from the Cobb–Douglas production function in the case where $A = 5$, $\alpha = 0.5$, and $\beta = 0.5$, that is:

$$Q = 5K^{0.5}L^{0.5}.$$

For purposes of comparison, we have also included in Figure 5.3 the $Q = 50$ isoquants for the linear and Leontief production functions. Note that one can interpret the Cobb–Douglas production function as a case intermediate between the perfect substitution of the linear function and the zero substitution of the Leontief function.

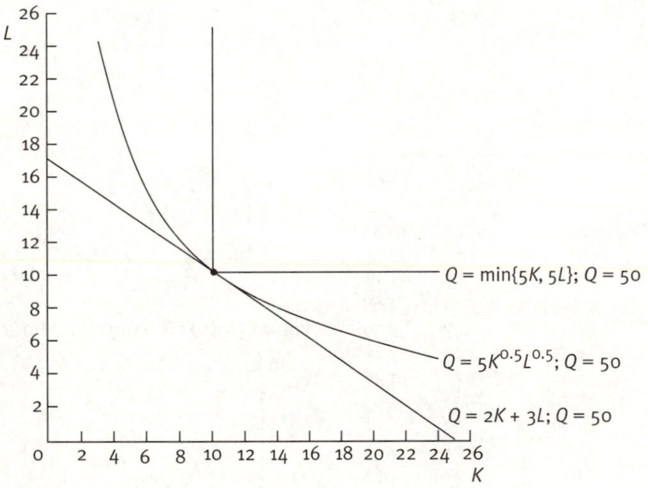

Figure 5.3 Substitution possibilities for three production functions

the firm uses just two inputs, capital and labour. Moreover, capital is a fixed input and labour is variable, as the firm is able to use whatever quantity of labour it likes at any point in time.

In these circumstances:

1. how does output change as the firm varies the amount of labour it uses in conjunction with a fixed level of capital;
2. how do production costs vary with the level of output?

To answer the first question, we will investigate the input–output relationship for the particular case where the firm has the following Cobb–Douglas production function:

$$Q = \bar{K}^{0.5}L^{0.5}$$

The bar over the letter K indicates that capital is a fixed quantity, which we suppose is 100 units. With this information, the output quantity corresponding to any amount of labour input can be calculated. The third column of Table 5.1 shows the output quantities corresponding to labour inputs of between 1 and 15 units.

Average and Marginal Product

Average Product (*AP*)

The average product of an input is the output per unit of that input employed. A separate average product measure can be constructed for each type of input used. Therefore in our example we have:

Average Product of Labour (AP_L) = Q/L

Average Product of Capital (AP_K) = Q/K.

Marginal Product (*MP*)

The marginal product of labour (MP_L) is the change in output that arises from a small change in the amount of labour employed, when all other inputs remain constant. So we have

$$MP_L = \Delta Q/\Delta L$$

Table 5.1 A schedule of output measures for the illustrative short-run production function

Labour input (L)	Capital input (K)	Output (Q)	AP_L	MP_L
1	100	10.00	10.00	10.00
2	100	14.14	7.07	4.14
3	100	17.32	5.77	3.18
4	100	20.00	5.00	2.68
5	100	22.36	4.47	2.36
6	100	24.49	4.08	2.13
7	100	26.46	3.78	1.96
8	100	28.28	3.53	1.83
9	100	30.00	3.33	1.72
10	100	31.62	3.16	1.62
11	100	33.17	3.02	1.54
12	100	34.64	2.89	1.47
13	100	36.06	2.77	1.41
14	100	37.42	2.67	1.36
15	100	38.73	2.58	1.31

Notes:

- All figures shown in Table 5.1 have been rounded to two decimal places.
- The variables were calculated in the following ways:

  $AP_L = Q/L$ = column 3 / column 1

  $MP_L = \Delta Q/\Delta L$ (This is derived from the output levels in column 3, by subtracting from each output the output at one less unit of labour input.)

where the symbol Δ denotes 'a small change in' the variable in question. Note that as capital is not variable in this case, it is not meaningful to refer to the marginal product of capital. Armed with these definitions, you should return to Table 5.1 and confirm that the average and marginal products of labour are those indicated in the final two columns of the table.

A better impression of the relationships between the labour input and the total, average, and marginal products of labour is obtained by graphing the series. This is done in Figures 5.4(a) and 5.4(b). It is important to realize that the shapes of the total output, and the marginal and average product functions shown in the figures reflect the particular production function we are using as an example. However, certain features of the curves shown are likely to be characteristic of most production functions.

In particular, the negative slope of the marginal product curve reflects what economists call the *law of diminishing returns*, which states that:

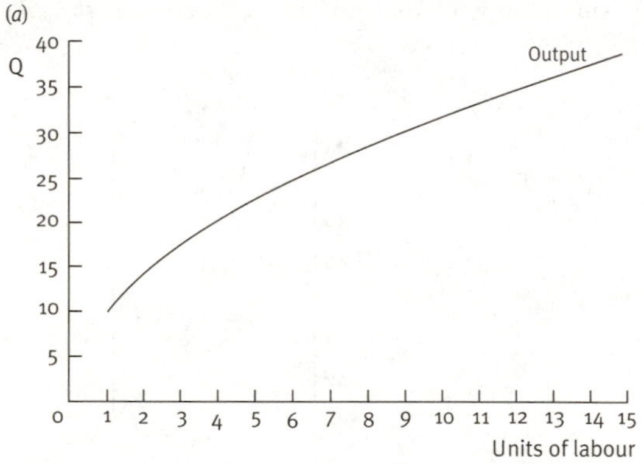

Figure 5.4(*a*) The output–labour relationship when $K = 100$

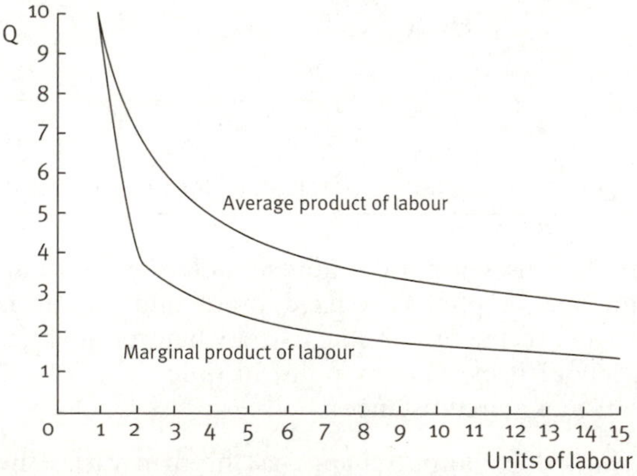

Figure 5.4(*b*) Average and marginal products of labour at $K = 100$

As additional units of a variable factor are combined with a given level of a fixed factor, there will come a point after which the marginal product of the variable factor continuously declines.

In our example, the marginal product of labour falls immediately and continuously, although for other production functions, there may well be a range of labour inputs over which the marginal product of labour is initially increasing. The important point here is that beyond *some* level of employment of the variable factor, its marginal productivity will fall continuously.

Short-Run Costs of Production

We now establish how costs vary with output in the short run. This requires information about *input prices.* Let input prices be given by price of capital (P_K) = £10 per unit and price of labour (P_L) = £10 per unit.

The capital price we have in mind here is the rental or hire price of capital, not the price paid to purchase the capital asset outright. Where the firm has purchased the capital outright, the rental or hire price will have to be imputed somehow or other. Box 5.2 outlines how this might be done.

It is now time to define a set of cost measures for use in subsequent analysis. The *total cost* (C) of producing a level of output (Q) needs no further definition. *Average cost* (sometimes called unit cost) and *marginal cost* (also known as incremental cost) are defined in the following ways:

Average cost (AC) = C/Q

Marginal cost (MC) = $\Delta C/\Delta Q$.

We can illustrate how these various cost measures are calculated by using the production data in Table 5.1. Remember that this hypothetical data derives from a particular case of the Cobb–Douglas production function. The calculations which follow

Box 5.2 The Cost of Capital

How can the cost of capital be calculated? First consider the case in which the firm hires or leases K units of capital at a rental price of r per unit capital. Capital costs are then given by $r \times K$. There are no difficulties in measuring capital costs in this case.

Now consider a second (and more common) case in which the firm purchases rather than rents its capital. Matters are less straightforward now, as the firm uses its own capital assets rather than paying a rental price for that capital. The firm's capital costs can still be thought of as being given by $r \times K$, but in this case, calculation of capital costs will require *either* applying an *imputed* capital rental price to the amount of capital used *or* getting a measure of total capital costs by some other route.

How can an imputed rental price of capital be obtained? The answer is found by recalling the concept of opportunity cost. The cost of using a resource in one way is the benefit forgone by not using it in its next best alternative use. For capital, this alternative benefit forgone will be approximately equal to the rate of return obtained in well-run firms elsewhere in the economy. This in turn can be approximated by the nominal rate of return on long-term, corporate bonds on the stock market. Suppose that this rate of return is 10 per cent. Then if the firm's capital stock is valued at £10 million, the imputed cost of capital is £10 million multiplied by 10 per cent, that is £1 million.

This begs one further question. How is the value of the firm's capital obtained? One way is to value capital at historic cost—the actual price that was paid for it. But for long-lived assets historic costs may bear little similarity to their present value. The proper measure uses current costs—the amount that would have to be paid today to acquire the asset.

One final matter remains to be discussed. Nothing has been said so far about depreciation in capital values, whether through wear and tear or through obsolescence. If capital assets were leased, the rental price would include a charge for expected depreciation. If the firm purchases its own assets, then the cost of capital should include an additional component to take account of depreciation.

It will be useful to summarize this with a numerical example. Suppose the following information is known:

current value of capital: £100,000,000;

depreciation in each period: 8 per cent of the current value at the start of the period;

long-term bond rate: 10 per cent.

Using this information, we can deduce the following:

capital costs =
imputed capital charge + depreciation charge
£100,000,000 × (0.1) + £100,000,000 × (0.08)
= £18,000,000.

embody our assumptions that capital and labour are each priced at £10 per unit. The costs are presented in Table 5.2. Total costs (shown in the fourth column) consist of two components: the *fixed cost* of capital (100 units at £10 per unit = £1,000) and the *variable cost* (given here by the amount of labour used multiplied by the unit price of labour, £10).

The average cost data, shown in the penultimate column, can be obtained in two ways. First, the total cost figures (column 4) can be divided by the associated levels of output (column 3). This calculates average cost directly from the formula $AC = C/Q$. Secondly, we can use the decomposition of total costs into fixed costs (FC) and variable costs (VC). Then by calculating average fixed costs ($AFC = FC/Q$) and average variable costs ($AVC = VC/Q$) and summing the two, we obtain average costs as

$$AC = AFC + AVC.$$

Finally, how are marginal costs calculated? Marginal cost is the change in cost arising from a small change in output. When output is changed from one level to another level, the marginal cost is the difference in total cost between the original and the new level of output. Thus marginal cost, $\Delta C/\Delta Q$, can be obtained by finding the increase in total costs (ΔC) between two successive rows, finding the associated increase in output (ΔQ) between the same two rows, and then dividing the former by the latter. Before proceeding, you should verify that the calculations in Table 5.2 are correct.

Table 5.2 A variety of measures of short-run cost

L	*K*	*Q*	*C*	*AFC*	*AVC*	*AC*	*MC*
1	100	10.00	1,010	100.00	1.00	101.00	n/a
2	100	14.14	1,020	70.71	1.41	72.12	2.41
3	100	17.32	1,030	57.74	1.73	59.47	3.15
4	100	20.00	1,040	50.00	2.00	52.00	3.73
5	100	22.36	1,050	44.72	2.24	46.96	4.24
6	100	24.49	1,060	40.82	2.45	43.27	4.69
7	100	26.46	1,070	37.80	2.64	40.44	5.10
8	100	28.28	1,080	35.35	2.83	38.18	5.47
9	100	30.00	1,090	33.33	3.00	36.33	5.83
10	100	31.62	1,100	31.62	3.16	34.78	6.16
11	100	33.17	1,110	30.15	3.32	33.47	6.48
12	100	34.64	1,120	28.87	3.46	32.33	6.78
13	100	36.06	1,130	27.73	3.61	31.34	7.07
14	100	37.42	1,140	26.73	3.74	30.47	7.35
15	100	38.73	1,150	25.82	3.87	29.69	7.61

We are now in a position to deduce the relationship between output and average costs in the short run. Recall that by definition

$$C = FC + VC.$$

Dividing both sides of this equation by Q, we obtain

$$C/Q = FC/Q + VC/Q$$

or

$$AC = AFC + AVC.$$

In Figure 5.5, we show graphically how *AFC* and *AVC* vary with output. The figure shows that average fixed costs decline geometrically towards zero as output rises, because a fixed cost is being spread

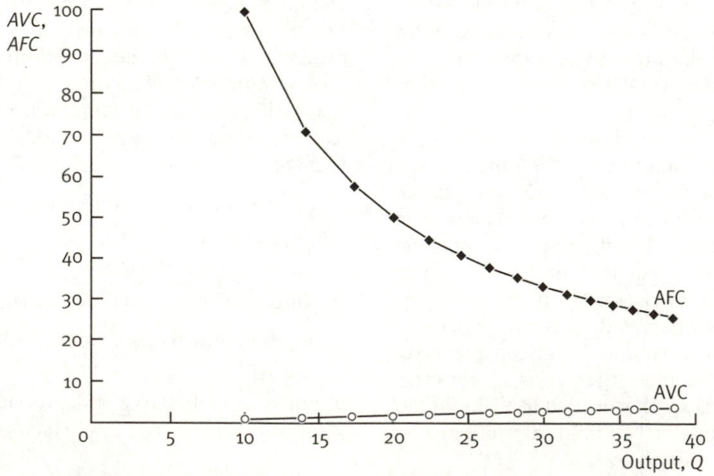

Figure 5.5 Average fixed and variable costs

over an increasingly large output. Average variable costs, on the other hand, rise continuously, reflecting the impact of the law of diminishing returns: the falling marginal productivity of the labour input implies (given a constant wage rate) that average variable costs are increasing.

The conjunction of falling *AFC* and rising *AVC* implies that the average cost curve will be U-shaped, falling at first, reaching a minimum point, and then eventually rising. For our illustrative data, the falling *AFC* curve completely dominates the rising *AVC* curve. But eventually the rising AVC curve will become dominant, resulting in rising short-run average costs.

The characteristic U-shape of average cost curves can be seen in Figure 5.6, in which *MC* and *AC* are plotted against output. We have extended the calculations up to an output level of 235 to allow the shapes to be clearly manifested. Note that the marginal cost curve intersects the average cost curve at its lowest point. It follows from this that

MC is less than *AC* whenever *AC* is falling;

MC is more than *AC* whenever *AC* is rising.

Although the average and marginal cost curves in Figure 5.6 are derived from our particular numerical example, there are good grounds for believing that they are indicative of the general shapes found in short-run cost curves. In particular, the spreading of fixed costs will lead to rapidly falling average costs as output is increased from very low levels, and the law of diminishing returns implies that the average cost curve will eventually be upward sloping.

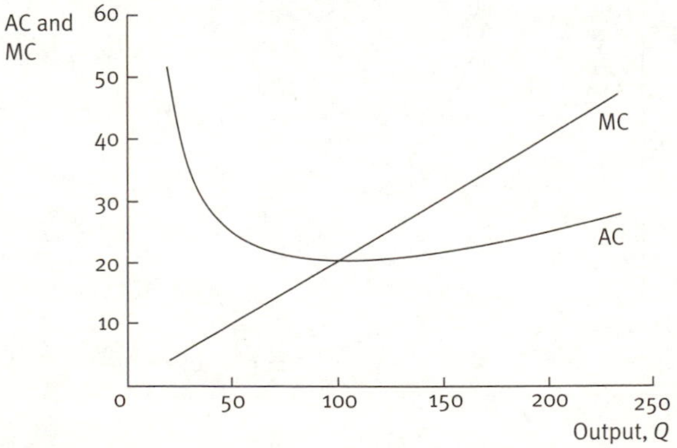

Figure 5.6 Marginal and average costs

5.3 Production and Costs in the Long Run

In the long run, the firm is in a position where it can make strategic choices about

- its scale of output;
- its output mix (its scope of output);
- the length of its production runs;
- the locations of its production units.

Our main focus will be on the first three of these choice areas. We examine the ways in which choices about scale, scope, and length of production run have important implications for business costs, and present some relevant empirical evidence. The choice of business location is dealt with only cursorily, as it involves complexities that would take us beyond the scope of this book.

We begin by investigating the relationship between the scale of production and costs in the long run. In the long run all productive inputs are variable, and so the firm can employ any quantity of any input that it wishes. As managers *plan* for the expansion (or contraction) of the scale at which the firm is to operate, they seek the optimal combination of inputs along what we shall call an expansion path.

How do costs vary with the scale of output where managers are free to choose any mixture of productive inputs? To answer this, we proceed in two steps:

- find the way in which output varies with changes in the quantities of inputs;
- using this information, together with information about the prices of productive inputs, deduce how costs vary with the scale of output.

Step 1: How does Output Vary with Changes in the Quantities of Inputs used by the Firm?

The answer to this question will depend upon the nature of the firm's production function. Let us continue to suppose that the firm's production function is the Cobb–Douglas function:

$Q = K^{0.5}L^{0.5}$

However, in this case K is not a fixed quantity. We can investigate how output varies with changes in input quantities by substituting various values of K and L into this function and calculating the corresponding levels of output.

Figure 5.7 gives a graphical representation of the data from this production function. Levels of capital and labour input are shown on the axes labelled K and L respectively. For any pair of K and L co-ordinates, the vertical height of the production surface above the base plane shows the resulting level of output.

One feature of this figure warrants particular attention. If we superimpose a line on the production surface for all input levels at which $K = L$, this would show how output varies as capital and labour inputs are changed in equal proportions. It is evident that output rises in a linear manner as the scale of inputs is increased. In particular, a doubling of inputs always leads to a doubling of output. We shall return to this characteristic in detail below. At this point just note that this particular relationship between inputs and outputs will not always occur. It is simply a consequence of the particular production function that has been chosen for illustration.

Step 2: How do Costs Vary with the Scale of Output in the Long Run?

This is difficult to answer in general terms. Capital and labour—indeed any two inputs—will usually be substitutes for one another to some degree. Therefore many input combinations exist with which it is feasible to produce any target level of output. Which of these combinations should be chosen? If the firm wishes to maximize the amount of value it adds, it should choose that combination which minimizes the cost of producing the target output.

The cost-minimizing mix of inputs has two major determinants:

- the *production techniques* available to the firm: the technologies underlying welding, for example, might imply that advantages are conferred by moving to more capital-intensive production methods as the scale of production expands;
- the *relative prices* of the inputs that the firm employs: other things being equal, cost minimization implies that a firm will substitute towards using more of an input if it becomes relatively cheaper.

Let us now demonstrate these two propositions. To do so, we shall use two concepts. The first is the notion of an isoquant, which we explained earlier when introducing the production function. An isoquant shows all the combinations of K and L which, when used in a technically efficient way, produce a particular level of output. The isoquants for outputs of 50, 75, 100, and 125 from our Cobb–Douglas production function are shown in Figure 5.8.

The second concept we need is an isocost line. This shows all the combinations of inputs that can be hired for a particular level of expenditure. With rental prices per unit of capital (P_K) and per unit of labour (P_L) each £10, and an expenditure of £2,000, the combinations of K and L that the firm can hire are shown in Figure 5.9 by the isocost line labelled

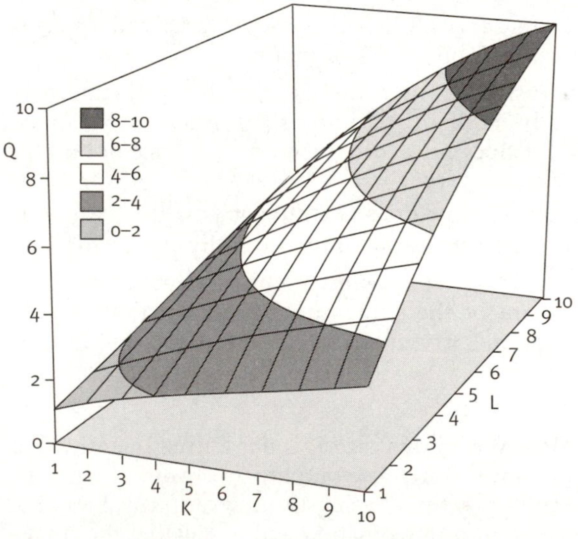

Figure 5.7 A representation of the production function

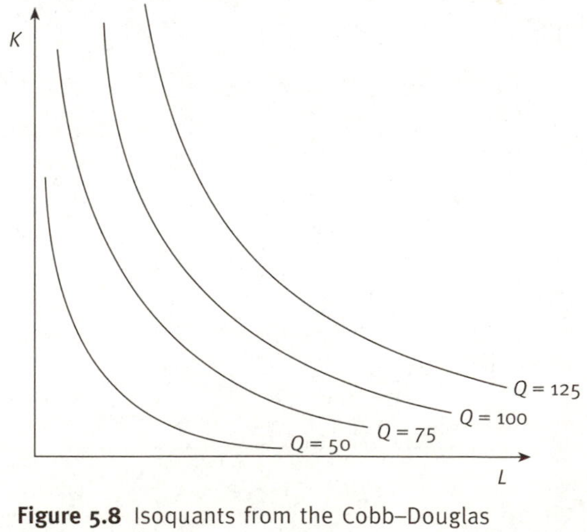

Figure 5.8 Isoquants from the Cobb–Douglas production function

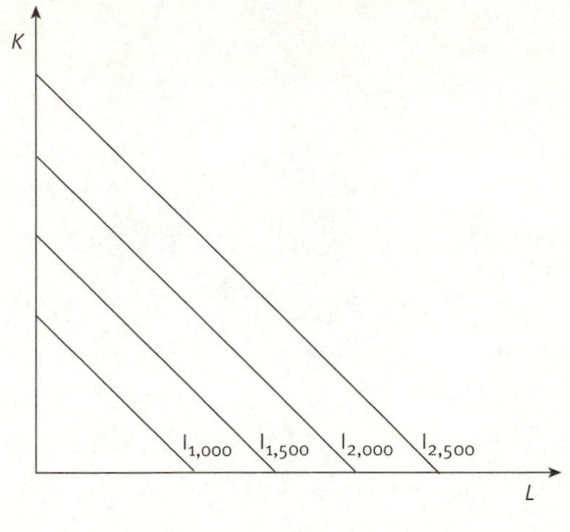

Figure 5.9 Isocost lines

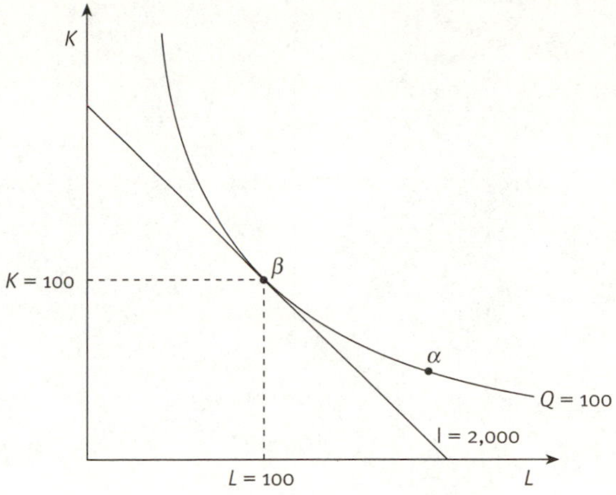

Figure 5.10 A cost-minimizing input choice

$I_{2,000}$. Also shown are isocost lines for £1,000, £1,500 and £2,500.

The firm wishes to produce its target output at least cost. Each isocost line shows a particular level of total input costs. Isocost lines close to the origin show lower total costs than those distant from the origin. On the other hand, any particular isoquant shows a particular output level. So in selecting a target level of output, we can think of this as the firm selecting a particular isoquant that it wishes to reach. The optimal point on that particular isoquant is the one which incurs the lowest total input cost.

The cost-minimizing point on a particular isoquant will be that point at which it meets the lowest possible isoquant. Given the smooth convex shapes of the isoquants drawn in Figure 5.9, such a point will be one at which there is a tangency between the isoquant and an isocost line. A cost-minimizing input combination is shown in Figure 5.10. Suppose the goal is to make 100 units of output at minimum cost. With capital and labour input prices each £10, the minimum cost is £2,000 using 100 units of labour and 100 units of capital.

One way of convincing yourself that the cost-minimizing input choice must be one at which an isocost curve is tangential to the relevant isoquant is as follows. Consider what is implied if the firm chooses an input combination at some other point. Take the point labelled α in Figure 5.10. The isocost line which passes though the point α must involve a cost greater than £2,000 as it lies to the right of the I = 2,000 isocost line. But as α lies on the same isoquant as β, it corresponds to the same output level. Thus α cannot be cost-minimizing as there is another input combination that can produce the same output level at a lower cost. By elimination, we can deduce that only tangency points can be cost-minimizing ones.

The Firm's Expansion Path

Suppose we ask what is the cost-minimizing input choice for $Q = 50$, $Q = 75$, $Q = 100$, $Q = 125$, and so on. By repeating the analysis explained above for each feasible output level, we can identify all cost-minimizing combinations of inputs. The locus of all such points is known as the firm's expansion path. This concept is illustrated in Figure 5.11.

In our example, the expansion path shows that

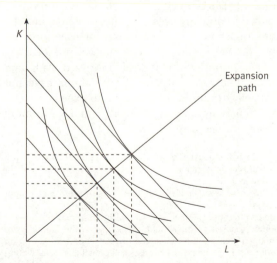

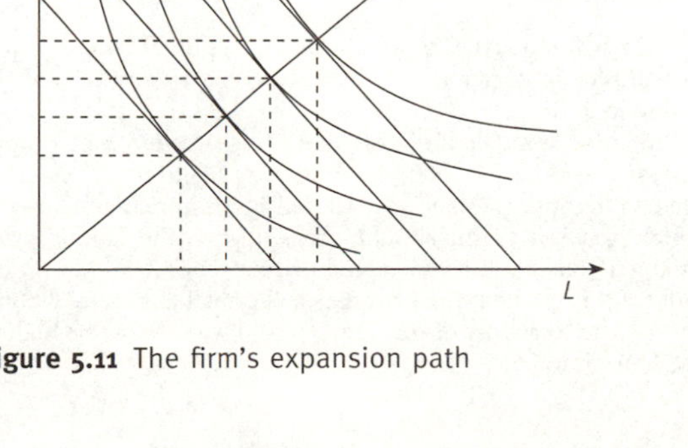

Figure 5.11 The firm's expansion path

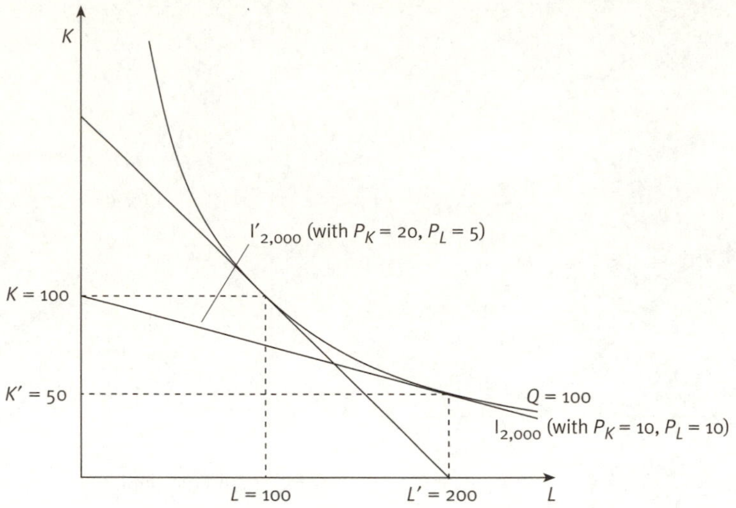

Figure 5.12 The consequences of a change in input prices

the cost-minimizing mix of inputs always involves equal amounts of labour and capital. This follows from two assumptions we have made. First, K and L enter the production function in a symmetrical way: capital and labour have equal productivity properties. Secondly, the prices of capital and labour are taken to be identical.

But in general the cost-minimizing mix of inputs will not necessarily use equal amounts of labour and capital.[1] For example, Figure 5.12 shows the cost-minimizing input choice for $Q = 100$, but this time with the rental price of capital being £20 and the rental price of labour being £5. The cost-minimizing input mix now involves 50 units of capital and 200 units of labour.[2] A more labour-intensive production mix has become the cost-minimizing one.

The reason for this is straightforward. Although the productivities of capital and labour have not changed, capital has become more expensive relative to labour and so it is efficient to use more labour and less capital.

[1] Nor will it be true in general that the optimal ratio of input use will remain constant (let alone always be 1:1) as the scale of production alters.

[2] In this example, the cost of making 100 units of output remains the same (£2,000) for both sets of input prices. This happens because the labour price fall just compensates for the capital price rise. You should check that if the labour price remained constant but the capital price rose, cost-minimization would still imply that the firm uses less capital and more labour, but that the total cost of making $Q = 100$ would now be higher. (See Question 5.5.)

Long-Run Costs of Production

We now investigate how costs of production are related to output in the long run. Once again, three cost measures—total, average, and marginal cost—are analysed. In our example, total costs are given by $C = wL + rK$, where w and r are the wage rate and the rental price of capital respectively. Average and marginal costs are defined in the same way as they were in our analysis of the short run, that is:

Average cost (AC) = C/Q

Marginal cost (MC) = $\Delta C/\Delta Q$.

It will not be true in general that the numerical values of long-run average costs (or marginal costs) are the same as those of short-run average costs (or marginal costs). In the long run, the firm can produce its target output using the cost-minimizing combination of inputs: it can select whatever amounts of capital and labour it wishes. In the short run, the firm has less freedom of movement in producing output—it can choose the amount of any variable input, but it cannot vary its use of a fixed input. Unless the fixed input quantity happens to be equal to what it would have freely chosen, the firm will be using a more costly input combination than is possible in the long run. Short-run average and marginal costs will in general be greater than their long-run counterparts.

Figure 5.13 plots the *long-run* total cost, average cost, and marginal cost curves for output levels up to 130 units per period using the Cobb–Douglas

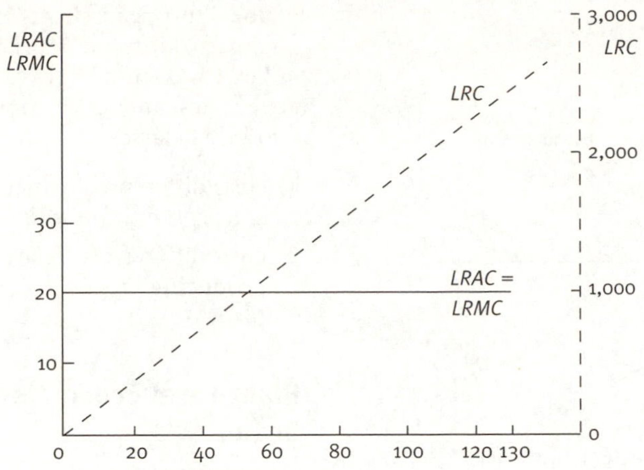

Figure 5.13 Long-run costs

production function example with capital and labour rental prices each being £10.

Long-run total costs rise proportionately with output, and so average costs are constant. The term, *no economies or diseconomies of scale*, is used to describe this case. Intuition suggests why we might expect this outcome. A firm could expand its scale by replication—in other words, it could construct as many plants identical to its initial one as are necessary for whatever scale it selects. One would expect each plant to have the same average cost as any other. Therefore long-run average costs would remain constant over different scales of output.

Despite the plausibility of this story, there are reasons why long-run average costs might not be constant. It is to these reasons we now turn.

Economies and Diseconomies of Scale

Some production functions (including the one we have used in our numerical examples, $Q = K^{0.5}L^{0.5}$) possess the property that an x per cent change in both inputs will always lead to an x per cent change in output. In this case, the production function exhibits *constant returns to scale*. Moreover, if the prices of K and L do not change as the scale of production of the firm alters (as we have assumed in this chapter until now), then it will also be true that the long-run average cost curve is constant, and so the long-run average cost curve exhibits *no economies or diseconomies of scale*.

The concept of *constant returns to scale* reflects a purely technical relationship—the conversion of inputs into outputs. The concept of *no economies or diseconomies of scale* is broader, as it also incorporates price information. Even if a firm experienced constant returns to scale, the property of no economies or diseconomies of scale would not hold if input prices changed as the scale of output altered.

This distinction is useful as it suggests two main reasons why long-run average costs may not be constant:

- the production function may not be characterized by constant returns to scale;
- one or more input prices may alter as the scale of production changes.

For the moment, we shall focus on the first of these two possibilities. To do so, we continue to imagine for the moment that input prices do not vary with the scale of output. Figure 5.14 shows three possible shapes that might be taken by a firm's long-run average cost curve. Curve (*a*) shows again the case you have seen previously, where the firm experiences constant returns to scale. It was generated from the Cobb–Douglas production function that we have been using in our numerical examples.[3] Curve (*b*) shows the case of *economies of scale*, in which long-run average costs decline with output.

[3] Many production functions exhibit constant returns to scale, and so would generate a horizontal long-run average cost curve. For example, all Cobb–Douglas functions have constant returns to scale, provided that α and β sum to unity. Many other types of production function also exhibit constant returns to scale.

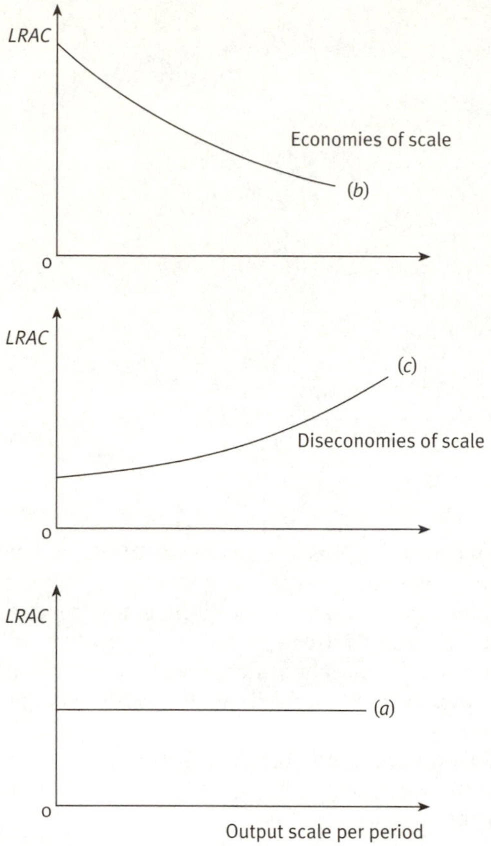

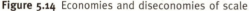

Figure 5.14 Economies and diseconomies of scale

As we are here assuming that prices are constant, this also implies that the production function is one in which output rises at an increasing rate as the scale of input use is increased. In other words, there are increasing returns to scale. Curve (*c*) exhibits *diseconomies of scale*, in which average costs rise as the scale of output increases. With input prices constant, this implies decreasing returns to scale.

Economies of Scale and Diseconomies of Scale in Practice

Considerable interest surrounds the possible causes of economies of scale and their significance in practice. Justifications for proposed mergers and acquisitions, for example, are often given in terms of the presumed long-run efficiency advantages of large scale. A major benefit, some argued, from completing the process of creating a single European market, would be cost savings arising from giving European firms free access to a much enlarged 'domestic' market.

Let us examine the various possible sources of economies and diseconomies of scale. There are two basic classes of scale effect:

1. cost differences which relate to the size of a *single production unit* (a plant or establishment);
2. cost differences related to the size of a *firm* producing a good in one or more than one plant.

Plant-Level Economies and Diseconomies of Scale

Let X_1 and X_2 denote two different quantities of the same product. $C(X_1)$ and $C(X_2)$ denote the total costs of producing these two amounts separately in different plants. $C(X_1, X_2)$ denotes the total cost of producing the amount $X_1 + X_2$ jointly in a single plant. Then:

- plant-level economies of scale occur if $C(X_1, X_2) < \{C(X_1) + C(X_2)\}$;
- plant-level diseconomies of scale occur if $C(X_1, X_2) > \{C(X_1) + C(X_2)\}$.

The sources of scale economies at the plant level include the following.

Economies of Large Dimension

For some items of capital equipment the unit cost of manufacture and maintenance tends to fall with increasing dimension. This is best seen using a simple example known as the two-thirds rule. Imagine the construction of a cubical storage tank. The area of material used in the tank increases as the square of the tank perimeter, but the volume of the tank increases as the cube of the perimeter. A doubling of the tank's capacity can be achieved with a two-thirds increase in materials. Since productive capacity will depend upon volume, while costs depend upon area, unit costs fall with the increase in scale.

Indivisibilities

Some production processes or items of equipment can only be operated efficiently at large output volumes. For technical reasons, the process or capital item is not capable of being scaled to a size that is appropriate for each possible scale of output. Computer hardware systems exemplify this property. The existence of indivisibilities gives rise to threshold effects. Expansion of the scale of output is initially associated with duplication of items of capital or small-scale processes. However, when planned output per period reaches a threshold level, it becomes cost-effective to switch to using a larger-scale process.

Consider the following simple case. Two processes are available, labelled small scale and large scale. The input levels required to operate each process and the associated outputs are shown in Table 5.3.

Assume that any unwanted output can be disposed of at zero cost to the firm. For any target output up to 50 units per period, least-cost production implies that the small-scale process is used, replicated as many times as is necessary. At an output of 50 units, the two processes imply equal costs; 50 units could be made by replicating the small-scale process 50 times, using 50 capital and 50 labour inputs. The large-scale process can utilize the same amount of inputs to make 100 units, 50 of which are superfluous to requirements.

It is from this last point that the scale economy arises. Suppose the target output is greater than 50 units. The large-scale process will be used, and as the scale of output increases towards 100 per period, the cost per unit output (that is, average cost) will fall. Over some range of output, therefore, average costs will be diminishing. As the number of distinct and indivisible processes increases, the long-run average cost curve will tend to approximate more closely one exhibiting continuous economies of scale.

Economies of Specialization

Recognition that the 'division of labour' can improve labour productivity dates back to the writings of Adam Smith. Labour and capital can be used more efficiently if they perform specialized tasks. The extent to which specialization can happen depends on the size of the plant; large output scale implies large input use, and this in turn permits the intensity of input specialization to increase. Specialization economies will cause the long-run average cost curve to fall quickly as scale is initially expanded. Beyond some scale at which specialization of tasks has been taken to its furthest limit, no further average cost savings are possible. Economies of specialization can thus account for the L-shaped long-run average cost curve that we discuss in Box 5.3.

Table 5.3 Indivisibilities and scale economies

Type of process	Labour input	Capital input	Units of output
Small scale	1	1	1
Large scale	50	50	100

Plant-Level Diseconomies of Scale

The possible sources of diseconomies of scale at the plant level include the following.

Transport Diseconomies

Suppose that the markets that could be served by a plant's output are geographically widely dispersed and that there are substantial transport costs borne by the supplier in delivering its product to those markets. As the plant's scale of output increases and it delivers goods to increasingly more distant markets, unit or average transport costs rise with output, although less than proportionately so. Large plants supplying output over large distances will therefore experience average cost penalties compared with a number of smaller plants, located close to particular regional markets.

Upward Pressure on Labour Input Prices

As a plant size increases, it will tend to increase its demand for labour. Where labour is relatively immobile geographically, increased demand for labour in local markets will tend to increase wage rates. Higher wage costs increase average production costs.

Industrial Relations Problems

It has sometimes been suggested that large plant size is correlated with poor industrial relations. If this is true, then increasing the plant size may give rise to an increase in average costs. However, it is unclear both whether such a relationship actually exists and, if it does, why it occurs. Possible explanations include the tendency for larger plants to be more highly unionized, to contain workforces with less loyalty to the firm, to suffer from greater alienation effects, and to have less flexible workforces leading to more demarcation disputes.

Managerial Diseconomies

Plant-level diseconomies may arise in the organization and management of the production unit, particularly when plant expansion is associated with

Box 5.3 The Minimum Efficient Technical Scale (METS) and the L-shaped Average Cost Curve

The first three explanations of plant-level economies of scale that we have discussed can, individually or collectively, give rise to long-run average cost curves of the form shown as curve (*b*) in Figure 5.14. Alternatively, they could produce what is called (somewhat inaccurately) the L-shaped average cost curve, shown in Figure 5.15.

The L-shaped average cost curve can be thought of as consisting of two distinct parts.

- Between output levels of zero and Q^*, long-run average costs fall continuously. Of particular interest is the rate at which average costs fall over this output range. One measure of this is the cost gradient, defined as the percentage fall in long-run average cost as output scale rises from one-half of Q^* to Q^*. Using the notation in Figure 5.15:

  Cost gradient $\dfrac{C_1 - C_0}{C_0} \times 100.$

- At Q^* the curve reaches a minimum value—average costs remain constant for any scale of output beyond Q^*.

Q^* is known as the *minimum efficient technical scale* (METS) of production. It is the smallest scale at which all available economies of scale are fully exploited. The qualifying word 'technical' refers to the fact that the economies which have been fully exploited at Q^* are technical ones. As we shall see shortly, there are other possible scale economies that are not technical in nature.

Considerable empirical evidence exists to suggest that long-run average cost curves are approximately L-shaped in many industries, particularly in the extractive and manufacturing sectors. We shall present some of this evidence a little later. At this point, we consider an example discussed by Rhys (1993). Table 5.4 presents estimates by Rhys of average costs in the European car industry for a variety of output scales.

Rhys found that almost no additional scale economies existed for output levels above 2 million units per year. If the cost index of 66 is taken as the minimum value of the average cost curve and Q^* is taken to be 2 million units, then at half Q^* the unit cost of 70 is 6 per cent higher than at Q^*. The cost gradient at half METS—the fall in average costs as output is increased from one-half of METS to METS—is 6 per cent.

The process of making a car consists of a number of distinct processes. One could ask what the METS is of each of these distinct processes. There is, of course, no reason why these should be identical for each process. In Table 5.5, we present the estimates made by Rhys of the METS for six sub-processes in car manufacturing.

The differences in 'optimal size' of these activities provide some clues as to the organization of car

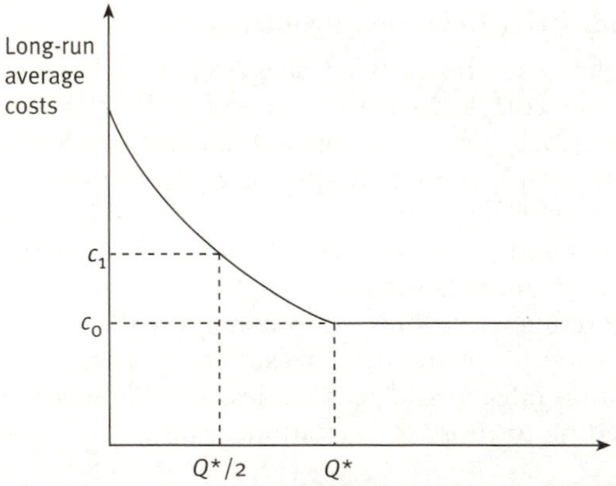

Figure 5.15 The L-shaped long-run average cost curve and the minimum efficient technical scale

Table 5.4 Long-run average costs in European car production

Output per year	Index of unit average costs (cars)
100,000	100
250,000	83
500,000	74
1,000,000	70
2,000,000	66

Source: Garel Rhys, 'Competition in the car industry' in *Developments in Economics* vol 9, 1993, edited by GBJ Atkinson, Causeway Press.

Table 5.5 The METS for processes within car making

Activity	METS (Output per year)
Casting of engine block	1,000,000
Casting of various other parts	100,000–750,000
Power-train machining and assembly	600,000
Pressing of various panels	1,000,000–2,000,000
Paint shop	250,000
Final assembly	250,000

Source: Garel Rhys, 'Competition in the car industry' in *Developments in Economics* vol 9, 1993, edited by GBJ Atkinson, Causeway Press.

manufacturing. In order to fully exploit scale economies in the pressing of car-body panels, up to 2 million units should be produced per year. Engine block casting also requires very large throughputs to exploit scale advantages. If distinct models can be defined in terms of the way in which they are painted and assembled, much smaller volumes are necessary. There are clear advantages to manufacturers in using common engine blocks and body panels over several models of cars so that each activity can be operated at its METS.

Where large differences exist between the METS of different activities, it may be advantageous for several firms to use a common external supplier of some component that is ideally produced on a very large scale. This practice has been adopted by some car producers, such as Toyota and Nissan since 1992.

more complicated organizational structure. Information can become distorted as it flows through the organization, or more costly to acquire. The ability to monitor and administer performance may become more difficult. However, as plant-level expansion does not usually have significant effects upon organizational structure, one would expect these diseconomies to be relatively unimportant. They are likely to be far more important at the level of the *firm*, as we explain below.

Economies and Diseconomies of Scale at the Firm Level

Now we turn attention to scale effects operating at the level of the *firm as a whole.* We begin with a firm producing a single product. This may be made in one plant or in more than one plant. The economies of scale referred to under this heading are *additional* to any plant-level economies that may exist.

Let X_1 and X_2 denote two quantities of the same product produced in different firms. $C(X_1)$ and $C(X_2)$ denote the total costs of producing these two amounts separately in different firms. $C(X_1, X_2)$ denotes the total cost of producing the amount $X_1 + X_2$ jointly by a single firm. Then:

- firm-level economies of scale occur if $C(X_1, X_2) < \{C(X_1) + C(X_2)\}$;
- firm-level diseconomies of scale occur if $C(X_1, X_2) > \{C(X_1) + C(X_2)\}$.

The sources of firm-level *economies of scale* include the following.

Economies of Massed Resources

Individual plants are likely to need stocks of inputs, semi-finished outputs, and components to ensure the smooth running of the production process. When a firm is composed of a number of separate plants it is often possible to economize on such stocks. These and similar effects are often referred to as 'multi-plant economies'.

Managerial Specialization

Large firm size may allow managerial specialization, and by implication higher efficiency; this is particularly likely in the management of finance, marketing, and innovation. Underlying this explanation (and the previous one) is the notion of indivisibility that we met earlier.

Purchasing and financial economies

Large firms are likely to be able to negotiate preferential bulk-purchasing terms. Ford buys many tyres and IBM many microprocessors. The purchasing power they bring to bear in components markets will allow these firms to negotiate lower prices than are available to small purchasers. This effect is well known in the retail food and groceries sector, with chains of large supermarkets able to enjoy very favourable terms for inputs. Another case concerns access to credit and the cost of financial capital. Largeness often confers a variety of financial advantages, implying a lower cost of capital.

Firm-Level Diseconomies of Scale

There are also reasons why diseconomies of scale exist at the firm level. The most important is *managerial diseconomies.* We noted earlier that complexity of organization at the plant level can impede managerial efficiency. Organizational complexity is more likely to be a significant source of cost disadvantages at the firm level. As shown in Chapter 10, the ultimate source of firm diseconomies rests in organization and management—the firm's organizational architecture. Expansion of the firm may be associated with the development of an organizational structure in which information flows become distorted, or more costly to acquire, and the ability to monitor and administer performance may become more difficult. Many large firms or corporations have adopted decentralized or divisional structures to minimize managerial diseconomies. Examples include firms in the private sector such as ICI and IBM, and public sector organizations such as the British National Health Service. This is discussed more fully in Chapter 12.

Economies of Scale in European Industry: Some Recent Evidence

In the period during which preparations were being made for the intended completion of the single European market in 1992, the European Community commissioned a variety of studies into the possible scale advantages of market integration. Box 5.4 provides some evidence on the extent of scale economies in European industry during the late 1980s. You should now turn to Box 5.4 for a review of that evidence.

Economies of Scope

The scale effects described so far concern possible differences in the average cost of producing units of a *single good* as its scale of production is altered. We now consider cost differences which are related to the mix of different goods produced by a firm. Simple observation shows that many firms produce a variety of goods, which suggests that there may be cost advantages available to firms which do this. One source of this advantage is economies of scope.

We define an economy of scope in the following way. Let x and y denote the output of two distinct goods. $C(x, 0)$ is the total cost of producing good x alone (that is, with zero production of y) and $C(0, y)$ is the total cost of producing good y alone. Let $C(x, y)$ denote the total cost of producing x and y jointly by one firm. An economy of scope exists if $C(x, y) < \{C(x, 0) + C(0, y)\}$.

Figure 5.16 uses the idea of a production possibility curve to represent the concept of economies of scope. Consider a fixed stock of resources which can be used to produce cars, lorries, or both. The straight line connecting the points A and B describes the various combinations of cars and lorries that can be produced with the available resources where there are no economies of scope. The negative slope arises because more lorries can be produced only by switching resources from car to lorry production. Along the line connecting A and B the opportunity cost of lorries—the number of cars that have to be given up to produce an additional lorry—remains constant. The outward-bowed curve ending at points A and B describes the production possibilities where there are economies

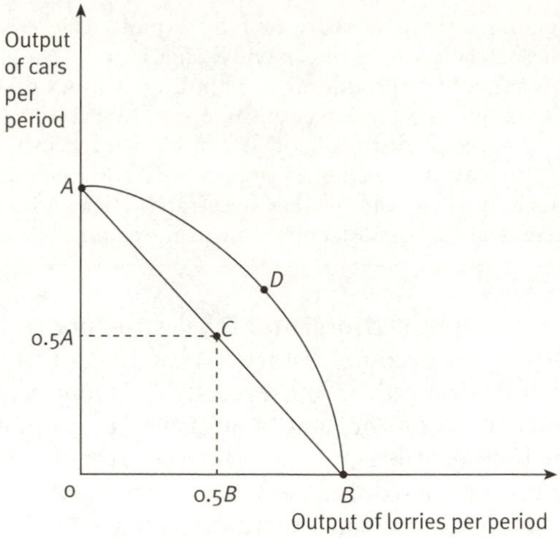

Figure 5.16 Economies of scope

of scope. Points towards the centre of the curve represent outcomes where the resources are used in the joint production of both goods.

Imagine that the resources are divided equally between two firms. One firm uses its share to produce cars only, obtaining an output of $0.5A$; the other uses its share to produce $0.5B$ lorries. The sum of the two outputs is shown by point C. However, if all resources are given to one firm which can obtain scope economies by producing cars and lorries jointly, a point such as D is obtainable, giving more of each good. What are the *sources* of these economies? There are two main circumstances in which the mix of goods produced by a firm can alter the average costs of making the goods in the mix first, where cost complementarity occurs in the production of two or more goods so that the average cost of making one falls as the scale of production of another is increased.

A well-known case of cost complementarity occurs in the petro-chemicals industry. Crude oil is a necessary source from which a number of individual products are derived. If the production of the set of products of crude oil is undertaken by one firm, this will economize on the use of inputs compared with the case where individual products are produced separately. Many examples of technical complementarity of this kind exist, and the cost reductions associated with exploiting these scope economies are often substantial. The organization of some industries—for example, chemicals and oil processing—can largely be explained by the responses of firms to this type of economy of scope.

Box 5.4 Economies of Scale in European Industry

Table 5.6 gives some results from a 1987 survey by Cliff Pratten of existing studies of scale economies in European industries. Branches of industry are classified according to the importance of the economies of scale which can be achieved, irrespective of the level at which they can be made (that is, product, plant, or firm).

The column labelled Cost gradient at half METS indicates the percentage reduction which can be expected in long-run average costs as the scale of output is raised from one-half of METS to METS. It should be remembered that the branches are highly aggregated, and may therefore contain a wide range of cost gradients. For example, in the Other transport sector, the cost gradient

Table 5.6 Economies of scale in European industries

Branch	Cost gradient at half METS (%)	Remarks
Motor vehicles	6–9	Very substantial EOS in production and in development costs.
Other transport	8–20	Variable EOS: small for cycles and shipbuilding (although economies are possible through series production level), very substantial in aircraft (development costs).
Chemical industry	2.5–15	Substantial EOS in production processes. In some segments (pharmaceutical products), R&D is an important source of EOS.
Man-made fibres	5–10	Substantial EOS in general.
Metals	>6	Substantial EOS in general for production processes. Also possible in production and series production.
Office machinery	3–6	Substantial EOS at product level.
Mechanical engineering	3–10	Limited EOS at firm level but substantial for production.
Electrical engineering	5–15	Substantial EOS at product level and for development costs.
Instrument engineering	5–15	Substantial EOS at product level, via development costs.
Paper, printing, and publishing	8–36	Substantial EOS in paper mills and, in particular, printing (books).
Non-metallic mineral products	>6	Substantial EOS in cement and flat glass production processes. In other branches, optimum plant size is small compared with the optimum size for the industry.
Metal articles	5–10 (castings)	EOS are lower at plant level but possible at production and series production level.
Rubber and plastics	3–6	Moderate EOS in tyre manufacture. Small EOS in factories making rubber and moulded plastic articles but potential for EOS at product and series production level.
Drink and tobacco	1–6	Moderate EOS in breweries. Small EOS in cigarette factories. In marketing, EOS are considerable.
Food	3.5–21	Principal source of EOS is the individual plant. EOS at marketing and distribution level.
Other manufacturing	n/a	Plant size is small in these branches. Possible EOS from specialization and length of production runs.
Textile industry	10 (carpets)	EOS are more limited than in the other sectors, but possible EOS from specialization and length of production runs.
Timber and wood	n/a	No EOS for plants in these sectors. Possible EOS from specialization and longer production runs.
Footwear and clothing	1 (footwear)	Small EOS at plant level but possible EOS from specialization and longer production runs.
Leather and leather goods	n/a	Small EOS.

Source: *European Economy* (1988), p. 109.

Box 5.4 continued

is 8 per cent for shipbuilding and 20 per cent for aircraft. More detailed cost gradients for more dissaggregated sectors can be found in Pratten (1987).

The extra costs that arise from operating a plant at only 50 per cent of the technically optimal size can be very substantial, varying between 1 and 36 per cent. In one-quarter of cases, the cost penalty exceeds 10 per cent. Economies of scale are largest in the transport equipment, chemicals, machinery and instrument manufacture, and paper and printing sectors. These account for about 55 per cent of industrial production in the European Community (when it consisted of twelve countries) and tend to be those sectors using the most advanced technology and with the most rapid growth rates.

Table 5.7 lists subsectors in which the cost increase at 50 per cent of METS is 10 per cent or more, and also tabulates the METS as a percentage of total production in the UK market and in the twelve EC countries as a whole. The additional information in this table allows us to see how many firms could exist in the subsector in question with scale economies being fully exploited. Consider dyes and aircraft. Both industries can experience large average cost reductions by operating at a scale equal to their respective METS. But in each case, the METS exceeds the current size of the UK market. There is not room in either industry (in the UK) for more than one firm if scale economies are to be fully exploited. In contrast, whilst substantial scale economies are also available in brick production (the cost gradient is 25 per cent), there is 'room for' 100 firms in the UK or 500 firms in the European Community.

Table 5.7 Products for which the cost slope at half minimum efficient technical scale is greater than or equal to 10 per cent

Product	METS as percentage of production: UK	EU	Cost gradient at half METS
Books	n/a	n/a	20–36
Bricks	1	0.2	25
Dyes	>100	n/a	17–22
Aircraft	>100	n/a	20
Titanium oxide	63	50	8–16
Cement	10	1	6–16
Synthetic rubber	24	3.5	15
Electric motors	60	6	15
Kraft paper	11	1.4	13
Petrochemicals	23	3	12
Nylon	4	1	12
Cylinder block castings	3	0.3	10
Small cast-iron castings	0.7	0.1	10
Carpets	0.3	0.04	10
Diesel engines	>100	n/a	10

Source: European Economy (1988), p. 112.

The second major source economies of scope occurs where a number of related goods are produced using a common process or a common input, resulting in a reduction of the total cost of the set of goods by virtue of spreading the cost of some 'overhead' activities over a variety of products. The manufacture of cars illustrates this scope effect well. Car companies typically produce a sizeable range of different models using common components, capital equipment, assembly structures, and routines. Very often, distinctive skills acquired by firms can be applied to other technically related areas, such as the production by single firms of various types of metering equipment or electronic components.

The common process in question need not be tangible. For example, research and development teams may generate knowledge that can be applied in innovations over a range of different products. Some car and motorcycle manufacturers, for example, maintain factory racing teams; materials innovations and design knowledge developed in racing can be applied in mass-market vehicle production. The back-up of a large vehicle manufacturing base can clearly offer considerable reciprocal benefits to racing teams.

Many assets have the possibility of being deployed for scope economy purposes. Suppose that in one production activity, a forecaster is employed to enable predictions to be made of future market trends. A second activity may also benefit from those forecasts. One firm undertaking both activities need only employ one forecaster, whereas if the activities are undertaken by separate firms, each may find it necessary to employ a forecaster. What is interesting about this example is that the forecaster's product is a 'public good'—the consumption of it by one user does not reduce its availability to others. Scope economies are common in the presence of public goods.

Another example of an asset that can generate scope economies is managerial resources. Managerial skills can sometimes be effectively used over different products, particularly in the case where the skills in question are public goods. On the other hand, if using management time in one activity is at the expense of its use in another activity (that is, management time is a private good), comparative advantage arguments suggest that there may be disadvantages in departing too far from managerial specialization.

As a final example, consider the asset a firm might have by virtue of its good reputation. This may be capable of being exploited to generate customer demand in other lines of business, so conferring scope economies. For example, Marks and Spencer and the Virgin group have both diversified into the provision of financial services, presumably in the expectation that reputations developed in their core areas will benefit the newer ventures.

It is difficult to measure the magnitudes of scope economies. However, some indication of the potential importance of scope economies can be found in Table 5.8. This gives estimates of the potential cost benefits from scope economies in some European Union manufacturing industries. The economy of scope figures refer to the percentage increase in average costs expected if each producer in the industry in question halved the number of its models.

Product-Specific Economies: Costs and the Cumulative Scale of Output over the Life of a Product

In this section, we switch our focus to investigate the behaviour of average costs with the passage of time. First, so-called product-specific economies are considered.

Table 5.8 Scope economies in European Industry

Type of activity	Economy of scope
Motor vehicles	8
Pharmaceutical products	5
Electrical machinery	5
Office machinery	5
Domestic-type appliances	5
Man-made fibres	3
Carpets	3
Machine tools	1
Cement, lime, and plaster	0

Source: Pratten (1987).

The production of many types of goods necessitates incurring one-off expenditures. Of major importance are the costs of developing new products. These costs bear some similarities to fixed costs, but they are not identical. Fixed factors (and so fixed costs) exist only in the short run. But the one-off expenditures we have in mind in this section are not choice variables even in the long run. Irrespective of the scale at which the firm chooses to operate, development costs and the like will involve more or less fixed initial expenditures.

Let X_1 denote the quantity of good X produced in time period 1, whilst X_2 denotes the quantity of the same product made in period 2. Suppose that $C(X_1)$ is the total cost of making the amount X_1 in period 1. Let $C(X_2)$ be the total cost of making the quantity X_2 in period 2 under the assumption that no production had already taken place in period 1. Finally let $C(X_1 + X_2)$ be the total cost of producing X_1 in period 1 followed by X_2 in period 2. Product-specific economies (otherwise known as cumulative scale economies) occur if $C(X_1 + X_2) < \{C(X_1) + C(X_2)\}$. All that is necessary for this to be true is that some one-off expenditures are necessary before any output is made.

It may be easier to appreciate the idea of cumulative scale economies by means of a simple example, the production through time of one type of jet aircraft. The development of a jet aircraft requires considerable up-front expenditure irrespective of the quantity that is subsequently sold. Consider what happens to the average cost per unit produced as the cumulative total of units produced rises over time.

A numerical example is provided in Table 5.9, adapted from HMSO (1978). The example assumes that average production costs (excluding development expenditures) remain constant at £1 million. Each row of the table refers to a different assumption about the magnitude of the initial development costs. The figures in the cells of the matrix show the cumulative average cost, including development expenditures at different levels of total output.

Note that when development costs are low relative to production costs (as in the upper rows of the table), cumulative average costs fall as the volume of sales rises, but the effect is relatively small. When development costs are large relative to unit production costs (as in the lower rows of the table), the cumulative scale effect is much greater.

Table 5.9 Development costs and production volume

Total development costs for product (£m.)	Production costs per unit (constant) (£m.)	Cumulative average cost, including production and development costs (£m.) on total sales of: 25	50	100	200	500
1	1	1.04	1.02	1.01	1.005	1.002
5	1	1.24	1.10	1.05	1.025	1.010
25	1	2.00	1.50	1.25	1.125	1.05
50	1	3.00	2.00	1.50	1.25	1.10
100	1	5.00	3.00	2.00	1.50	1.20

Source: HMSO (1978).

For example, if development costs are £100 million, average costs fall to just 24 per cent of their original level (1.20/5.00 × 100) as cumulative output rises from 25 to 500.

Development costs may also give rise to economies of scope. In the car industry, for example, a firm may invest in general development research covering aerodynamics or safety. To the extent that research findings can be applied to a variety of different cars in the company's range, we are observing economies of scope. There are advantages in producing a variety of different models, and having a bigger share of the market, in situations where such costs arise. In Table 5.10 we give some empirical estimates of the magnitude of cumulative scale economies.

Learning or Experience Effects

Product-specific economies—the relationship between unit costs and cumulative output—can also arise because of learning or experience effects. Think about aircraft once again. Assume the company has successfully developed a new model and puts it into production in a new plant. Many of the people at the plant may have assembled aircraft before but not this particular model. To begin with therefore, production is likely to be quite slow as people get used to the new assembly requirements. But as production builds up, individual managers, supervisors, and line workers undergo a learning process such that the total time taken to assemble a complete aircraft falls. Supply and assembly problems are gradually ironed out. Short cuts are developed. Fewer mistakes are made so there is less waste and less need for expensive rectification. The variable cost of the tenth unit produced will be less than for the first unit, and the variable cost of the hundredth unit will be less than for the tenth.

Table 5.10 The estimated size of total cost reductions as a result of doubling cumulative production for a variety of activities in the US economy

Industry or service sector	Fall in unit costs as a result of cumulative production being doubled
Electrical components	30
Microcomputing	30
Ball-bearings	27
Industrial plastics	25
Equipment maintenance	24
Life insurance	23
Aerospace	20
Electricity	20
Starters for motor vehicles	15
Oil refining	10

Sources: Boston Consulting Group (1972) and (1981); Hirschman (1964).

This is a very common phenomenon in a wide variety of industries. So much so, indeed, that there is even a mathematical formula for the expected shape of the learning relationship. Figure 5.17 shows the average costs of B-29 bombers produced by Boeing at its Wichita plant. Figures such as this are sometimes labelled as illustrating the 'learning curve'. This is not correct however. Whilst some of the dramatic fall in average costs as the cumulative output rose can be attributed to learning effects, a part is also played by the spreading of development costs over larger output.

Learning effects on costs can also help to explain cost differences between suppliers of the same product. In any particular industry, there will exist differences in the length of time over which the product has been made. New information is not always absorbed immediately, and we tend to find gradual learning over time as experience is acquired. Firms which have only travelled part of

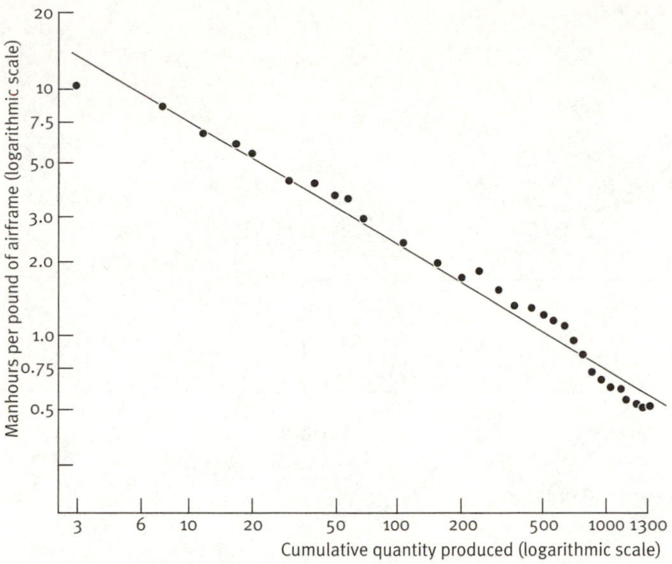

Figure 5.17 Learning curve for B-29 bombers produced at Boeing's Wichita plant

Source: Kay (1993), adapted from F.M. Scherer and David Ross (1990). *Industrial Market Structure and Economic Performance*. Third Edition. Copyright © 1990 by Houghton Mifflin Company. Used with permission.

the way down the learning curve will tend to have higher costs than their more experienced rivals.

Costs Differences between Firms

We began this chapter by mentioning Michael Porter's idea of 'cost drivers'. Subsequent sections examined four of these determinants of costs in some detail. For Porter, understanding a firm's cost drivers is the first step towards controlling and reducing costs, and so maximizing the amount of value a firm is able to generate.

If costs are the consequences of the quality of managerial decisions and the effectiveness of a firm's organizational architecture (see Chapter 10), this implies that in any particular industry there could be variation in cost performance between firms, depending on the qualities of those decisions and organizational structures. The industry would consist of firms located at different points along a spectrum of cost performance. It will be useful to look a little more closely at the reasons why different firms in the same industry might have varying costs. These can be classified into three groups.

Class A Costs differ between firms due to learning and/or experience effects. Consider the case where *X* has been making a good for longer than *Y*. As a result, *X* should be further down its learning curve. Also, where production has involved significant up-front development costs, *X* will have spread these over a greater amount of cumulative output, and so is further down its experience curve. Notice that whilst there can be observed cost differences for these reasons, the differences do not reflect *avoidable* inefficiencies (unless learning is not taking place as quickly as it could be).

In contrast, the following two classes *do* consist of avoidable cost inefficiencies.

Class B Managers are minimizing costs for the existing organization of production and installed capacity, but the organization and/or capacity chosen is not optimal. In other words, the firms are 'cost-efficient' in what they are doing but they are not doing the right things. A wrong choice of capacity is illustrated in Figure 5.18. Firm *X* is producing 100 million units in one plant at the lowest attainable point on the long-run average cost curve. In contrast, firm *Y* uses four plants each producing 25 million units. Although each plant is fully cost efficient for 25 million units, *Y* is not long-run cost efficient, as it is not choosing the least cost plant size for an output of 100 million units.

Alternatively, efficiency differences might arise not from capacity choices but from the degree to

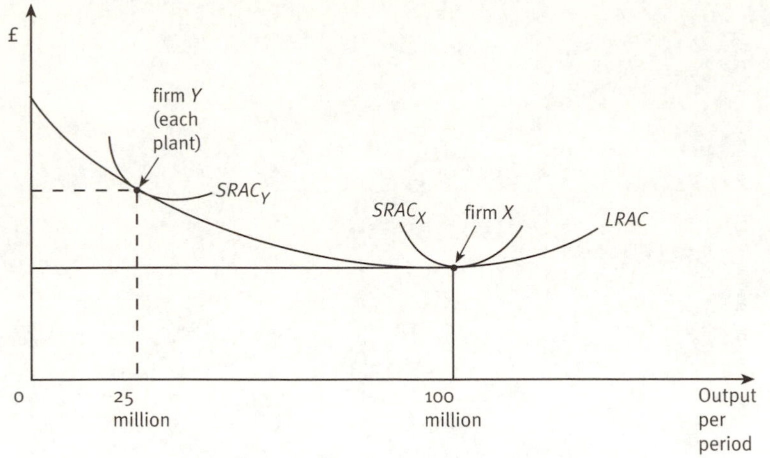

Figure 5.18 Long-run and short-run average costs

which firms exploit available economies of scope. Many car manufacturers, for example, have come to recognize the significance of scope economies arising from the joint production of different car models. Volkswagen has plans to build all its models from each of its four brands (Audi, Seat, Skoda, and VW) on just four platforms. The high throughput of common components this generates will allow it to achieve very favourable input costs through bulk purchase (Haig Simonian, *Financial Times*, 8 September 1997).

Class C Cost inefficiency might also arise because the firm *fails* to extract the highest level of output from available resources or because managers *choose* to run the firm in a suboptimal way (measured in terms of maximum value added for the firm). In both cases, resource use is wasteful, implying excessive unit costs. This is sometimes described as *X*-inefficiency. Failure to minimize costs can arise for many reasons, including ignorance, incompetence, laziness, internal conflict, incomplete learning from experience, and poor staff motivation.

Another factor influencing costs is the formal and informal structure of the firm—its organizational architecture. Cost differences might reflect differences in choices of architecture. We examined the ways in which the structure of a firm can affect costs in Chapter 4, and we shall return to this later in Chapter 10 in discussing distinctive capabilities.

The notion that managers may choose to run firms in suboptimal ways is mainly associated with managerial theories of the firm (Marris, Baumol, Williamson: see Chapter 12). Managerial goals such as sales revenue or growth maximization can sometimes conflict with maximization of the value of the firm. Moreover, in the face of limited information, bounded rationality, and diverse interests among different stakeholders in the firm, managers may replace optimizing objectives with the goal of satisfactory performance.

Cost Control Mechanisms

Although there are many reasons why cost differences might emerge between firms producing similar products, there are also several economic mechanisms operating to limit the size of these differences. Three of these mechanisms are of particular importance:

1. incentives within firms to control costs;
2. competitive forces in product markets;
3. external cost control mechanisms.

The incentives to control costs that operate within firms are relatively straightforward. For any given output choice, cost minimization implies profit maximization. Whenever any incentive structure is in place that rewards members of the firm for the profits generated, there will be cost reduction incentives. However, the efficacy of this mechanism may be limited in practice. It is often difficult to design reward (or penalty) systems that give incentives at the level of small groups or individuals. Moreover, some incentive structures may work to increase costs rather than decrease them. For example, where managerial salaries are related to the size of the responsible division or unit, increased staff expenditures may be encouraged.

A second mechanism reducing cost inefficiencies arises from competition in the markets in which the firm operates. Low cost makes possible low product prices, and the possibility that in times when price competition is particularly intense, high cost firms may be unable to survive. For example, the world car industry presently exhibits considerable excess capacity. World output of cars in 1996 was only 75 per cent of the total capacity of 70 million vehicles a year. (Haig Simonian, *Financial Times*, 8 September 1997). The situation is even worse in Europe; the European Commission estimates that manufacturers are operating at just 42 per cent of full capacity. This is expected to get worse in the early years of the twenty-first century as capacity expands faster than demand. For car manufacturers, cost reduction is perceived as being a condition for long-run survival. Volkswagen, the leading European manufacturer in the family hatchback market segment, has devised a platform technique which promises to cut assembly times for its new Golf model from thirty to twenty-three hours.

A corollary of this is that cost minimization pressures may be relatively weak in markets in which competition between rivals is low. The movements to dismantle statutory monopolies and to privatize state-owned businesses that have been so prevalent in the past decade are largely concerned with cost reduction goals.

But even in the absence of rivalry between firms in product markets and powerful internal cost reduction pressures, there remains a third force controlling costs. What we have in mind here is the market for corporate control. A firm is a collection of resources with value-generating potential. It is this which determines the true worth of the firm. If the firm fails to operate to its full potential (perhaps by not minimizing costs), the current market value of the firm will fall below its true worth. If this gap becomes large enough, acquisition by an outside party becomes a possibility. Given that incumbent managers would be likely to suffer in this process, this mechanism can be seen as a special case of the first cost-control mechanism we have discussed. This portrayal of the workings of the market for corporate control is rather simplistic, and we shall examine it more fully in Chapter 12. Finally note that other stakeholders in the firm—its creditors, suppliers, and so on—also have interests in the prosperity of the firm, and so may constitute additional external cost-minimizing pressures. Of note here is the way in which major car component suppliers have been forced to rationalize their operations to reduce component costs by their principal customers, the large car manufacturers.

Conclusions

In this chapter, we have provided an extensive analysis of the major determinants of business costs. As costs (together with revenue) determine a firm's profitability, this puts in place one of the major foundations stones of our subsequent analyses of business decision-making.

We have developed an analysis of business costs built upon the idea of a firm's production function. This led us to draw a distinction between short-run and long-run costs. In the short run, a firm has at least one input (often some element of its physical capital) that is fixed in the sense that it cannot freely choose how much of the input it wishes to employ and pay for. Some costs are, therefore, fixed. The variation of costs with output is significantly affected by the presence of such fixed costs. However, a second factor is also important. The marginal product of variable inputs is likely to fall (and so the marginal cost of output is likely to rise) as employment of the variable input is pushed towards higher levels. All of this suggests that average costs are likely to be U-shaped with respect to output in the short run.

In the long run, it is more difficult to draw general conclusions about the cost–output relationship. The nature of the production function itself can lead to either economies or diseconomies of scale. But even where there are no technical reasons for average costs to change with output, average costs may vary with changes in the scale of a plant or the scale of a firm for marketing, financial, and other reasons.

We also demonstrated that the scope of what the firm does can have important implications for its costs, and showed how dynamic effects—in particularly learning by firms—affects cost structures. Finally, we recognized that firms may differ in cost performance even where there are no technical differences between them (such as technology used or scale of operation). The reasons why some firms may have superior cost performances to others is a matter to which we return at several points later in this book.

In the immediately following chapters, armed with an understanding of business costs, we turn our attention to the profit-maximizing choices of firms in various market structures.

Further reading

A more advanced treatment of business costs, looking at some complications we have ignored, and surveying empirical evidence on cost functions can be found in Hay and Morris (1991), *Industrial Economics and Organization.* Another extensive theoretical and empirical review is given in John Panzar's article *Determinants of Firm and Industry Structure* in Schmalensee and Willig (1989). Pratten (1987), *A Survey of the Economies of Scale*, is a good empirical account of scale economies; more on this topic can be found in Emerson *et al.* (1988). W. Brian Arthur (1996) provides a stimulating analysis of the prevalence of increasing returns in the high technology knowledge-based sectors of the economy.

Discussions of learning and experience effects are found in Boston Consulting Group (1972), Henderson (1973), Lieberman (1984) for the chemicals processing industry, and Alberts (1989). Michael Porter's book *Competitive Advantage: Creating and Sustaining Superior Performance* (1985) is a classic reference for the practice of minimizing costs, and contains an extensive analysis of what he calls cost drivers. A more extensive analysis of costs and their implications for competitive strategy can be found in Besanko *et al.* (1996). Implications of the ideas of costs for accounting systems—particularly in activity-based costing and modern managerial accounting—are examined by Shank and Govindarajan (1989).

An important class of costs—those which are not recoverable—are sunk costs. These have important implications for business policy. However, we leave our discussion of sunk costs until Part II of the text.

Questions

5.1. Consider a producer (extractor) of crude oil. What kinds of input are likely to be fixed in the short run and the long run for such a firm? Now answer the same question for (*a*) a crude oil refiner and (*b*) a commercial football club.

5.2. Draw the isoquant for an output level of 100 for the linear production function:

$Q = 2K + 3L.$

If input rental prices were P_K = £1 and P_L = £1, use isocost lines to deduce what would be the cost-minimizing input choice in the long run.

5.3. Diseconomies of scale in the production of a good exist if:

A an extra worker taken on with existing equipment would reduce the average amount produced per worker;

B a doubling of output requires more than doubling of all inputs;

C output can be increased by using all inputs in a more technically efficient way at the same scale.

(a) B only;

(b) A and C only;

(c) B and C only;

(d) A and B and C.

5.4. Which of the following statements concerning the long-run average cost curve are correct?

(a) If there are economies of scale, one would expect the long-run average cost curve to be downward sloping.

(b) The minimum efficient scale of production is the level of output where long-run average costs are minimized.

(c) The long-run average cost curve is U-shaped because of the law of diminishing returns.

5.5. Look again at Figure 5.9, in particular at the isocost line corresponding to total costs of £2000. Use isoquant and isocost analysis to verify the following assertions. If the rental price of labour were to remain at £10 per unit, but the rental price of capital rose from £10 to £20:

(*a*) the cost-minimizing input mix would comprise a smaller quantity of capital than labour, and (*b*) the total cost of producing 100 units of output would exceed £2,000.

5.6 The relative costs of oil pipelines fall rapidly as the diameter of the pipeline increases. More specifically, a quadrupling of pipeline volume (and so maximum throughput) can be obtained with just a doubling of pipeline costs. Using the formulae for the area and circumference of a circle, demonstrate why this saving in average costs will take place.

5.7. The term 'long run' as applied to a firm's decision-making refers to:

(a) the number of years over which a firm can expect to produce with unaltered factors of production;

(b) any period of time between three and five years in which a firm can increase or decrease all the factors of production it employs;

(c) any period of time over five years in which a firm can increase or decrease all the factors of production it employs;

(d) the time period in which a firm can increase or decrease all the factors of production which it employs.

5.8. How do the concepts of the short run and the long run apply to a publicly funded hospital operating under borrowing limits imposed by central government?

5.9. Consider the long-run average cost function of a business school institution specializing entirely in the provision of taught postgraduate degree courses in business economics.

(i) Would you expect this cost function to exhibit economies of scale, diseconomies of scale, or neither?

(ii) What kinds of scope economies might be available if this institution broadened the range of courses it provided?

(iii) Show how the concepts of development costs and learning effects can be used to explain what will happen to average costs of the provision of a new course by this institution.

Part II

The Search for Value, Prices, Profits, and the Firm's Competitive Environment

Our study of business behaviour and the firm's search for value continues in the next three chapters with an examination of the problem of maximizing the difference between the firm's revenues and its costs.

Business economics is about the firm's search for profits or added value and the problems involved in creating and sustaining profits or added value. Since added value is the difference between the sales revenues generated and the economic costs incurred, the value-seeking firm seeks to achieve the best possible combination of costs and sales revenues (that is, maximum profits) by pursuing policies aimed at keeping costs down and revenues up. Note, however, the firm is *not* viewed as seeking to maximize sales revenue *per se* but to maximize the difference between revenue and cost, that is profit.

As with minimizing costs, this search for maximum profits is a complex, ongoing, process for the firm and its managers, which involves the juggling of many variables, and economics does not seek to describe how managers do this or indeed to tell them how to do it. The problem is so complex and the circumstances of different industries are so varied, from banking to water to telecoms, that this would be impossible. What economics seeks to do is to develop an understanding of what Porter (1980) calls the 'competitive drivers' of an industry and their significance for prices and the firm's search for profits, that is, to consider the relationship between the competitive environment of the firm, its ability to set prices, and its ability to create and sustain profits.

In the following three chapters, therefore, we shall be concerned with understanding exactly how the firm's competitive environment influences its ability to create and sustain value and how firms might seek to influence their competitive environment. Michael Porter, in his best-selling textbook *Competitive Strategy* argues that a fundamental determinant of the firm's ability to create and sustain profits is the firm's competitive environment and buyer/supplier power. Intuitively, the ability of any firm to squeeze value out of a particular piece of territory will depend *inter alia* on how many other firms are operating there, how easy it is for more firms to invade that territory, and on the bargaining power of suppliers and buyers. Porter formalized this intuition into what he called the five-forces framework for analysing the forces of competition in any industry and showed how this could be used for developing an appropriate competitive strategy for managing these forces. The five forces identified by Porter as the determinants of what he called 'industry attractiveness' are as follows.

Rivalry among sellers already in the industry or market This will depend on factors such as the number of firms in the industry, the relative size of these firms, how and how hard they fight one another for market share. If there is only one firm in an industry, that is, a monopoly exists, then there is by definition no rivalry. With two or more firms we get the emergence of rivalry which can constrain the ability of firms to set prices and generate profits. With a very large number of firms competing over a particular market we get a much higher degree of rivalry which can be unattractive for the firms involved.

The threat of new entry into the market or industry Under normal circumstances it is expected that if an industry is generating above-normal profits it will attract the attention of firms outside the industry. The higher the current profits, the more the attractions there will be to outsiders. If new entry takes place, the prices and profits of the industry are likely to fall. However, if for some reason it is difficult for new firms to enter what appears to be an attractive industry, that is, if there are 'barriers to entry', then the profits of existing firms will be easier to sustain.

The threat from substitute products If there are close substitutes for the products of a particular industry, then the ability of firms in this industry to generate above-normal profits will be lessened. The existence of substitute products affects demand conditions for the industry and this works to constrain the ability of firms to set prices which generate profits. For example, the manufacturers of glass bottles would have much more market power, and the industry would be more attractive, were it not for the existence of plastic bottles and aluminium cans.

Buyer power This refers to the ability of buyers to negotiate and bargain over purchase prices. If buyers are powerful, then they can squeeze the prices and profits of suppliers. If buyers are weak, then suppliers are relatively unconstrained.

Supplier power This refers analogously to the ability of suppliers to an industry to negotiate and bargain over supply prices. If suppliers are powerful, they can squeeze the profits of the buying industry, and if suppliers are weak, then buyers can sustain higher profits, other things being equal.

Industries with many rivals, easy entry, several close substitutes, powerful buyers and suppliers are therefore unlikely to be 'attractive', whereas industries with a monopoly seller, with high barriers to entry, no close substitutes, and weak buyers and suppliers are very likely to be 'attractive'. Competitive strategy, according to Porter, is thus about understanding what makes industries attractive so that you can avoid unattractive industries and endeavour to keep your own industry attractive.

You will have noticed that we have used the term 'attractiveness' in two different senses in our discussion. It is important to be clear about the two uses of this term and the relation between them.

First of all we used 'attractive' in the everyday sense to mean a currently profitable market which attracts the attention of firms and entrepreneurs outside the market. If these outsiders enter the industry or offer substitute products, then ultimately the market will lose its attractions as profits are squeezed down. This is a short-term performance view of attractiveness. Secondly we used the term 'attractive' in the Porter sense to mean a situation where incumbent firm profitability is sustainable because it is difficult for outsiders to enter or offer substitutes. This is a longer-term structural view of attractiveness. In the short term attractiveness is a function of profitability. In the long term profitability is a function of attractiveness.

The development of a market or an industry over time involves the interaction of these two relationships. Think of the personal computer industry. In the early years, a few innovators created what was essentially a new industry with high profits. These high profits attracted lots of new entrants (the so-called clones). In structural terms the industry became less attractive despite very high sales growth rates. Rivalry was intense even with small numbers, entry was relatively easy, suppliers of crucial parts were powerful, and many customers were powerful. Profits were therefore hard to sustain. Look at the experience of the innovators, Apple and IBM.

Porter's framework is based firmly on the long-standing ideas developed by the Harvard school of industrial economics whose fundamental premise is that:

> Industry performance (economic profitability) is determined by firm conduct which in turn is determined by industry structure.

In other words, structure determines conduct determines performance. Hence the shorthand name for this school, which is the 'SCP' school. Exponents of this school see industry structure as determined by exogenous factors such as technology and demand conditions but they recognize the possibility of firm conduct, such as mergers, being aimed at changing structure. Harvard is not the only approach to industrial economics, for example there is a Chicago school, but it is very much the dominant school of thought. Porter's five-forces framework has become a standard part of business strategy analysis and for this reason it is important for students of business to appreciate some of the economic analysis which underlies the Porter framework. It is this that the following three chapters will seek to achieve.

Understanding the nature and significance of the competitive process and the drivers of competition is not easy. Porter's framework, and everyday observation, suggest that competition is a complex process involving a number of different factors: the number and size distribution of firms, entry conditions, cost conditions, product differentiation and substitution possibilities, and the degree to which rivals compete or co-operate with one another. How are we to approach an understanding of this complex process?

One strategy would be to work through a series of case studies of competition in a variety of markets or industries with a view to building up a store of useful observations and generalizations. However, given the sheer variety of industries and markets available, you might have to read a lot of case studies to develop a good understanding of the relationship between the firm's competitive environment and its ability to add value. How many case studies would be sufficient to develop rigorous general conclusions? Two or twenty-two?

Economists are naturally inclined to look for a less costly and a more rigorous approach. The economics approach to understanding the nature of the 'competitive drivers' is to develop and analyse simple, somewhat abstract, models of industry, or market, structure, and conduct which focus on the key aspects of the drivers and their significance for prices and profits. Economists have developed a variety of models along a spectrum from the intensely competitive to the monopolistic as pictured in Figures II.1 and II.2.

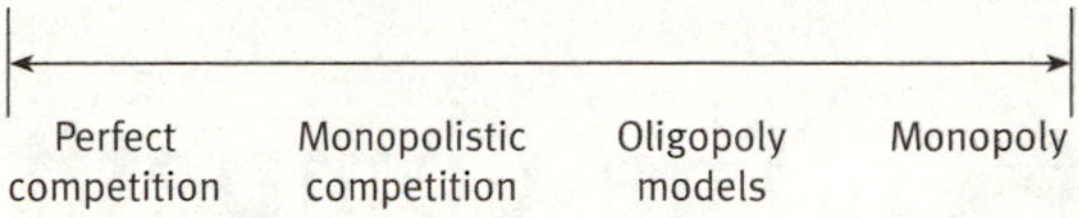

Figure II.1 The spectrum of models of market structure

Chapter 6 will develop the model of perfect competition to examine the implications of a hypothetical state of extreme competition caused by a combination of large numbers and easy entry. This is a key model in economics for several reasons. First because from this model economists derive their fundamental belief in the social efficiency of competitive markets, a theme we return to in Chapter 12. Second because it provides a foundation for the study of the nature and sources of sustainable competitive advantage in business policy, a theme we return to in Chapter 10. This chapter will also briefly consider the model of monopolistic competition which is essentially the competitive model with a twist of monopoly added.

Chapter 7 moves to the other end of the above spectrum to study the implications of the complete absence of competition in a model of a monopolistic producer with no close substitutes and protected by barriers to entry. This chapter will also discuss the nature and significance of barriers to entry and the potential for managing the threat of new entry.

Chapter 8 examines the nature and implications of oligopolistic rivalry, in particular the problems caused by strategic interdependence among a small number of rivals, and the incentives for and implications of collusion. This chapter will introduce some ideas from game theory for understanding strategic interactions among rivals.

Characteristics of market structure

Market structure	**Number of firms**	**Entry conditions**	**Substitutes**
Perfect competition	Large number	Easy entry	Perfect
Monopolistic competition	Large number	Easy entry	Imperfect
Oligopoly models	Small	Difficult	Either
Monopoly	One	Blocked	Distant

Figure II.2 Models of market structure

6 The Competitive Market Model

Introduction

This chapter develops the model of perfect competition in order to examine the implications of a hypothetical state of extreme competition in a market. As we explained above, the competitive process and the search for profits involves two interacting relationships: industry attractiveness as a function of short-term profits and long-term profits as a function of industry attractiveness. Both of these relationships are seen at work in this model.

It is important to understand that perfect competition is a model, not an attempt to describe the real world. An economic model is an intellectual construct built in order to derive rigorous conclusions from simple premises. These models are useful to the extent that they provide insights into the real world, help us to understand complex processes, and allow us to generate predictions about the real world. The model of perfect competition is useful in all of these senses. It provides insights into the competitive process, helps us to understand the nature and significance of competitive forces, and allows us to make some predictions about the way a competitive industry will respond to changing circumstances.

This model is central to economics because it creates the yardstick for judging the economic efficiency of differing market structures and it is a basis for public policy towards industry. This is the subject of Chapter 13. However, whilst competition may be good for society in general, it is not necessarily good for the firms involved. The forces of competition make the search for profits hard work. The aim of 'competitive strategy' is to endeavour to escape to some extent from the rigours of intense competition analysed in this chapter.

The chapter is structured as follows. First, we define a perfectly competitive market. We then analyse the profit-maximizing output choice of the firm in a competitive market in the short run, that is, where the level of one or more inputs is fixed. Section 6.2 considers the behaviour of a typical firm, and the industry as a whole, in the long run, where all inputs are variable. We then demonstrate how changes in market demand result in expansion or contraction of the number of firms in the industry. Next, we give some examples and applications. Finally, we discuss the model of monopolistic competition: markets which possess all the characteristics of perfect competition *except* that rival firms produce differentiated (rather than homogeneous) goods.

6.1 Revenue, Pricing, and Output in the Short Run

The Characteristics of a Perfectly Competitive Market

A market is perfectly competitive market if all the following characteristics are present:

- there is a large number of buyers and a large number of sellers, none of whom is large enough individually to influence the market price;
- the products being traded in the market are homogeneous; that is, they are perceived by consumers as being perfect substitutes;
- all buyers and sellers have complete information about market prices;
- individuals have no preferences concerning those with whom they trade;
- there are no barriers to entry into or out of the industry in the long run (the notion of barriers to entry or exit will be discussed more fully in Chapter 7);
- all sellers have equal access to the resources required for production at prevailing prices.

These characteristics determine the two key properties of perfectly competitive markets. The existence of large numbers of buyers and sellers means that any individual market participant has an insignificant effect on the market as a whole. The quantity of sales of any one firm is like a drop of water in an ocean: even if its sales were to halve or double, the effect on total market output and the market price would be negligible. In determining output, sellers act independently. Each seller believes that what it chooses to do is of no importance to the others and what the others do is not important to it. Buyers and sellers in a competitive market are therefore said to be *price takers.* The price which prevails in the market at any point is determined by the aggregate behaviour of all buyers and sellers. No individual can influence the market price.

The second property is that only one price prevails in a market at any point. This property is known as the *law of one price.* This follows from the characteristics of *homogenous goods, buyers indifferent to sellers,* and *complete and equal information about prices.* Taken together these conditions exclude the possibility of any seller being able to sell at a price above the market price. Moreover, as we shall see shortly, there is no incentive for a firm to try to sell at a price below the market price.

The Firm in a Perfectly Competitive Market in the Short Run: Revenues and Costs

We begin our analysis by considering the firm's output decision in the short run. You will recall that the short run has been defined as that period of time during which at least one of the inputs which the firm employs is in fixed supply. How would a profit-maximizing firm select its output level in the short run?

We now have in place nearly all of the tools necessary to analyse the profit-maximizing output choice. By definition, profit is the difference between sales revenues and costs. The relationship between demand and sales revenue was explained in Chapter 2. The way in which costs of production vary with output was explained in Chapter 5. Bringing together these two basic 'building blocks' allows us to find out how profits vary with output. But there is one more step necessary before this can be done. Our analysis of demand in Chapter 2 was concerned with market demand. In this section what matters is the demand facing a single firm in a competitive market. How are market demand and the firm's demand related? And how do average and marginal revenue relate to the firm's demand? Let us consider these questions.

Total, Average, and Marginal Revenue

A firm's total revenue (R) is the income received from the sale of its output. By definition

$$R \equiv q \times P$$

where q denotes the quantity of output sold by the firm in a particular period of time, and P denotes the price at which each unit is sold. Notice that for this expression to be meaningful, each unit of the good must sell at the same price—the firm cannot sell at different prices to different customers in the same time period. You will see shortly why this condition must hold in a perfectly competitive market.

Average revenue (AR) is the revenue received by the firm for each good sold. Clearly, average revenue must equal price, as can be seen from the following definition and its rearrangement:

$$AR \equiv R/q = (q \times P)/q = P.$$

Marginal revenue (MR) is the increase in a firm's total revenue arising from the sale of an additional unit of the good. Algebraically it is expressed as:

$$MR \equiv \Delta R/\Delta q$$

where the symbol Δ (the Greek letter delta) means 'a small change in' the variable concerned.

Market Demand and the Individual Firm's Demand

The left-hand panel in Figure 6.1 shows how the equilibrium market price and quantity traded are determined in a competitive market. You can check your understanding of market equilibrium in Chapter 2. The fundamental point to grasp here is that market price is set by the interaction between the two forces of market supply and market demand.

The right-hand panel in Figure 6.1 shows the demand curve facing one individual firm. Recall that each firm is a price taker; it sells any output it produces at the going market price over which it has no control. Suppose the firm were to change its own output level, with the output levels of other

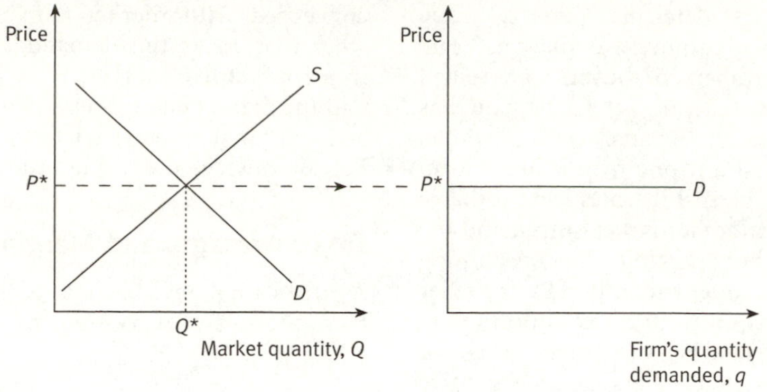

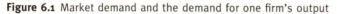

Figure 6.1 Market demand and the demand for one firm's output

firms remaining unchanged. The large numbers assumption means that total market output is not significantly changed, and so the individual firm's decision has no effect on market price. The firm can, therefore, sell as little or as much as it likes at the given market price. It has a horizontal (that is perfectly elastic) demand curve, set at the level of the market price.

Two points should be noted about the manner in which we have drawn Figure 6.1. First, we use different notation for market output and an individual firm's output. Upper-case Q is used to denote market quantities, whereas lower-case q denotes one firm's output. Secondly, the scale of measurement on the horizontal axis of each panel in Figure 6.1 is different. Recall that the market consists of a very large number of firms. One inch along the market quantity axis consists of a much greater amount of output than one inch along a firm's quantity axis. It also follows that if we were to sum the individual levels of q over all firms in the market, the resulting total is Q. That is, if q_i is the output of the ith firm and there are N firms in the market (with N a large number) then: $Q = \sum_{i=1}^{i=N} q_i$

Readers coming to Figure 6.1 for the first time may find it paradoxical. How can the market demand curve be downward sloping while each firm's demand is horizontal? This paradox can be resolved by recognizing that the *individual firm's* demand curve is constructed on the assumption that each firm acts independently. It describes what will happen to the quantity demanded of any one firm if that firm alone were to attempt to set a price above or below the market price. If the firm tries to set a price above the market level, it can sell nothing because the product is widely available at a lower price. If the firm tries to set a price below the market level it can not sell any more than it can at the going market price. The market will take all the firm wants to produce at the market price. Note, however, that if all firms in the market simultaneously increased output then market prices would change because the market will only accept significantly more output at a lower price. This is exactly what is shown by the *market* demand curve.

Readers may find it difficult to accept that the individual firm can sell whatever quantity it likes at the prevailing market price; that is, it does not experience any effective demand constraint. This seems to be in conflict with 'common sense'. But note we are only claiming this to be true in principle for the firm acting individually in a perfectly competitive market. This emphatically does not mean that the typical firm in perfect competition actually chooses to produce as much output as the market will take. Remember the firm is seeking to maximize its profits not the total quantity of its sales and it is necessary to bring costs into the picture to determine the firm's output choice.

The Firm's Demand, Average Revenue and Marginal Revenue

Looking again at the right-hand panel in Figure 6.1 you can see that the individual firm's demand is such that:

- the price it receives for each good is constant irrespective of the number of goods it offers for sale. The firm's average revenue is thus equal to price (as we explained above) and so we label the firm's demand curve as its average revenue;

- if the firm were to sell an additional good, its additional (or marginal) revenue would be equal to the price of the good. It is therefore the case that the firm's demand curve is also its marginal revenue.

To summarize, we have for any individual firm acting in isolation:

$P = \text{AR} = \text{MR},$

each element of which is represented by the individual firm's demand curve. Finally, note that as the law of one price operates in a perfectly competitive market all firms must face identical demand conditions and so have identical marginal and average revenue functions.

The Individual Firm's Costs

We know from our analysis in Chapter 5 how the firm's costs vary with output in the short run. In that chapter, we focused on the behaviour of average and marginal costs. For convenience, we reproduce in Figure 6.2 our assumptions about the variation of short-run average and marginal costs with output for a typical firm.

The Relationship between Profit and Output for an Individual Firm

We now have available the required building blocks: the relationships between costs and output, and the relationships between revenue and output. The profit–output relationship can now be derived.

First, note that, by definition, total profit equals total revenue minus total costs. Algebraically we can write this as:

$\Pi = R - C,$

where Π denotes total profits, R denotes total revenue, and C denotes total costs.

What level of output per period maximizes total profits? There are several ways of answering this question. Let us begin by looking at how total revenue and total cost vary as the firm's output changes. This is illustrated in Figure 6.3.

The total revenue curve (labelled *R*) rises as a straight line through the origin: at zero output revenue is zero—thereafter, as output rises, total revenue increases in proportion to output, as the individual firm can sell all it likes at a constant market price. The total cost curve (labelled *C*) also shows costs rising with output, but is characterized by the following features:

- total costs are positive even when output is zero: this follows because the diagram shows the firm's short-run costs, one element of which will be fixed costs, f;
- costs rise with output in a non-linear manner: this comes from the assumption that the law of diminishing returns applies in the short run (see Chapter 5).

Now as profit is the difference between revenue and costs, the profit-maximizing output is the one where *R* exceeds *C* by the largest amount. This

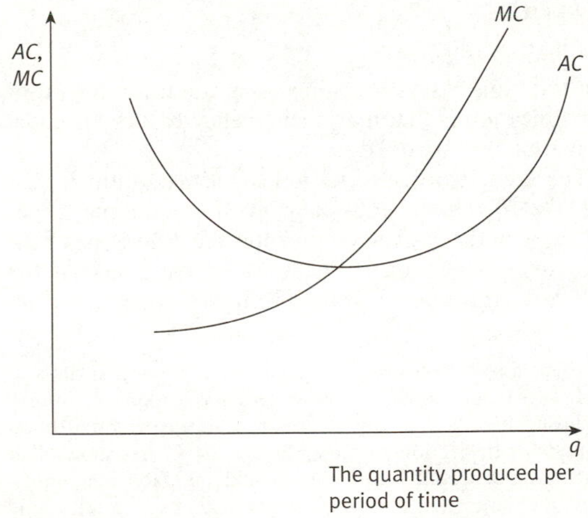

Figure 6.2 A typical firm's short-run average and marginal cost curves

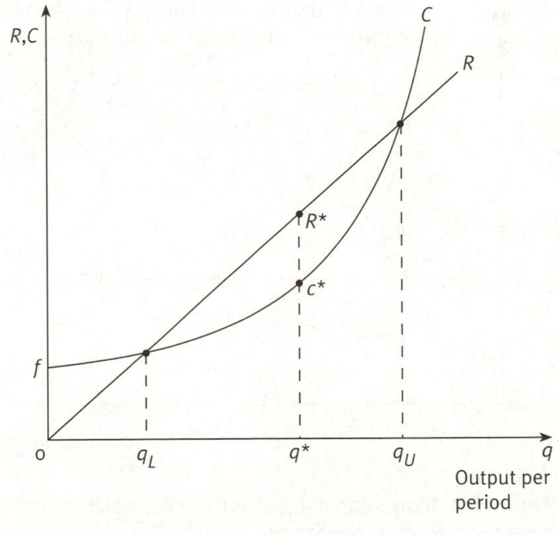

Figure 6.3 Revenue, cost, and profit

Box 6.1 The Marginal Principle of Profit Maximization

Why should it be the case that selecting an output level at which marginal revenue equals marginal cost is required for a profit-maximizing level output? To answer this, look at the marginal revenue and marginal cost curves in Figure 6.4

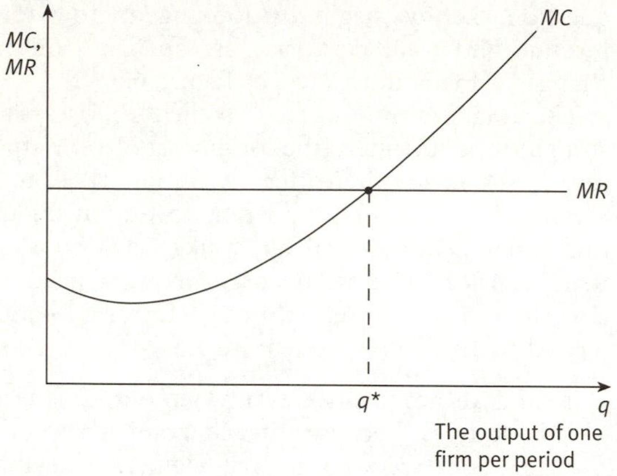

Figure 6.4 The marginal principle of profit maximization

Whenever *MR* exceeds *MC* (which is true everywhere to the left of output q^*), the revenue gained from producing one more unit exceeds the cost incurred in making that additional unit. So producing this marginal unit will increase total profit by an amount equal to $MR - MC$. This suggests profits will increase continually as output is raised to the level q^* from any lower level. Similarly, above the output level q^*, *MR* is less than *MC* and so total profit would be reduced if marginal units of output were produced in that region. Thus the output level q^* must be the profit-maximizing level of output.

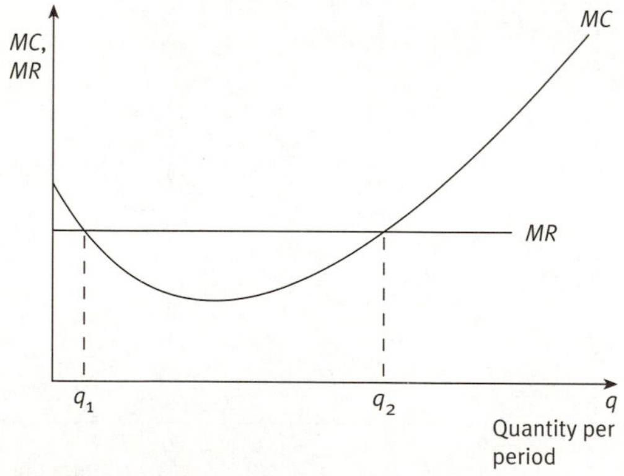

Figure 6.5 More than one output level at which marginal revenue equals marginal cost

The condition that marginal cost equals marginal revenue is, however, only a necessary condition for profits to be maximized. It is not a sufficient condition. An additional condition is required to guarantee that an output level at which *MC* equals *MR* is a profit maximizing output. The additional condition is that *MC* must cut *MR* from below at the point where the two are equal. In the case of Figure 6.4, the marginal cost curve inersects the marginal revenue curve only at one level of output.

In contrast, Figure 6.5 shows two outputs at which $MC = MR$. The intersections at $q = q_1$ is characterized by *MC* intersecting *MR* from above. At this point, profits are in fact at a miminum level.[1] Only by producing more can the firm begin to generate more profits. Only by producing at q_2 can the firm maximize its profits.

Using the marginal analysis with which we commenced our arguments in this Box, you should convince yourself of these results before moving on.

For readers who prefer mathematical reasoning and know some elementary calculus, here is an alternative demonstration of the result that profit maximization requires that an output level be chosen such that MC equal MR.

Let profits be denoted by Π. Then we have:

$\Pi = R - C.$

Now as *R* and *C* are both functions of output, *q*, we have:

$\Pi(q) = R(q) - C(q).$

The first-order condition for maximization of Π requires that $d\Pi/dq = 0$. Thus we obtain

$d\Pi/dq = dR/dq - dC/dq = 0$

and hence

$dR/dq = dC/dq.$

But this simply says that a necessay condition for profit maximization is that marginal revenue (dR/dq) is equal to marginal cost (dC/dq).

The second-order condition for a maximum is that $d^2\Pi/dq^2<0$. This is equivalent to the requirement that the slope of the *MC* curve is greater than the slope of the *MR* curve, which is true if the *MC* curve intersects the *MR* curve from below at the profit-maximizing output.

[1] This assertion is not quite accurate. At a point such as q_1 profits are in fact at what is known as a 'local minimum'—they are lower there than at any other output in the neighbourhood around q_1. Inspection of either Figure 6.4 or 6.5 shows that much worse profit outcomes would in fact happen at extremely large outputs because marginal costs are climbing ever higher above marginal costs, and so large losses must be being incurred on incremental units.

occurs in Figure 6.3 at the output level q^*. Note that profits are shown by the vertical distance $R^* - C^*$. You might like to confirm for yourself that at the profit-maximizing output, the slopes of the R and C curves must be equal; they are parallel at that output level.

Before we move on, another piece of useful information can be obtained from this diagram. Only output levels in the range q_L to q_U are profitable. These two end-points are break-even points where revenue equals cost. It is clear from the diagram that, although the individual firm *can* sell all it wishes at the going price, it will not be profitable to do so. Producing outputs greater than q^* would lead to falling profits; producing outputs greater than q_U would lead to negative profits (that is, losses) which become larger the more is sold!

A second approach to the selection of the profit-maximizing output is also widely used by economists, and provides valuable insight. This approach is based on *marginal* revenues and *marginal* costs. Profit maximization is attained by selecting an output level at which marginal cost is equal to marginal revenue and selling this output at the going market price. An explanation and a proof of this vital result is given in Box 6.1 which you should now read through.

Figure 6.6 brings together the short-run average and marginal cost curves and the demand curve for a single firm in a competitive market. In drawing this diagram, we are using the equilibrium price of P^* established in the market as a whole. Note that we have added the labels *AR* and *MR* to the firm's demand curve.

We know that profit maximization requires that an output is chosen at which $MC = MR$. The only output level that meets this condition is q^*. Moreover, as *MC* intersects *MR* from below at this point, the output level q^* is indeed the profit-maximizing output level. How much profit does the firm make by producing q* and selling that output at price P^*? To answer this question, we can make use of the average cost and average revenue curves. Note first that as total profit equals total revenue less total costs:

$$\Pi = R \quad C,$$

then dividing each side of this equation by output we obtain an expression for the average profit per unit of output:

$$\Pi/q = R/q - C/q = AR - AC$$

Average profit per unit is simply the difference between average revenue and average cost. At any given output level, *total* profit is simply the difference between average revenue and average cost multiplied by output. From an inspection of Figure 6.6, we can see that the firm's total profit is represented by the area of the rectangle described by the points *A*, *B*, *C*, and P^*. The distance *CB* indicates average profit margin. Multiplying this by output, *AB*, the total amount of profit, is obtained.

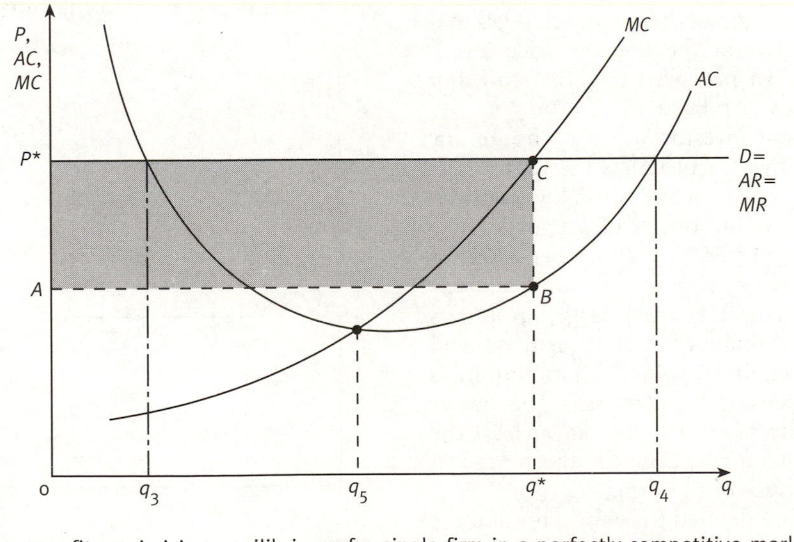

Figure 6.6 Short-run profit-maximizing equilibrium of a single firm in a perfectly competitive market

We can also deduce the following from Figure 6.6:

- output levels q_3 and q_4 each satisfy $AC = AR$. These are break-even (that is, zero profit) output levels for the firm;
- all output levels lower than q_3 and higher than q_4 lead to negative profits, since AC is greater than AR;
- the maximum level of average profit (the maximum profit margin) is obtained at the output level q_5. But this is *not* the output which maximizes total profits. Choosing an output at which the firm maximizes its margin of price over average costs will not maximize its profits.

Normal Profits and Supernormal Profits

The profits shown by the shaded rectangle in Figure 6.6 are described by economists as *supernormal* profits. To understand what this expression means it is necessary first to understand the associated concept of *normal* profit. Normal profit denotes the minimum return required to induce an individual or a firm to invest in a particular productive activity.

To explain this idea, consider the following scenario. An individual has at his or her disposal some monetary assets. These assets could be invested at some rate of return at negligible risk. For example, many governments offer index-linked government securities that guarantee a fixed yield and certain repayment of the principal at an agreed date in the future (adjusted to compensate for any changes that might have occurred in the average price level). Such a rate of return may well be rather low, but the asset is virtually risk free.

Clearly, a rational investor will not choose any other more risky investment unless the return is at least as great as this risk-free return. Now consider an individual who is the owner of a firm, or is a shareholder in the firm. Using his or her assets in this way will carry some risk. In some circumstances that risk could be very large, in others somewhat smaller. But any such investment will only be undertaken if an additional premium is available to compensate for this risk. The owner must expect to earn a return equal to at least the risk-free return plus a premium for the perceived risk in order to invest in the firm.

Normal profits are defined to be the sum of these two components. Moreover, as normal profits are in effect the minimum required return to capital in risky ventures, they are treated by economists as being essentially costs of production and are therefore included in the cost functions of the firm. In our equation

$$\Pi = R - C,$$

normal profits are therefore included in the term C. The symbol Π denotes any profit the firm earns over this 'normal' amount, and so is called supernormal profit.

Profit Maximization: Profits and Losses

Figure 6.6 illustrates a case where production is 'profitable' in the short run. The firm, at its profit-maximizing output level, earns a return greater than the minimum amount required to induce owners or shareholders to invest in the business. In other words, it earns supernormal profits. But this outcome simply reflects the way the figure has been drawn.

There is no reason why this must be the case: competitive markets are not necessarily profitable. If the market price had been significantly lower than the one shown in Figure 6.6, or if the firm's costs had been significantly higher, the firm might be in a loss-making position. Such a situation is shown in Figure 6.7. Even at its 'profit-maximizing' (or, if you prefer, loss-minimizing) output, total revenue is lower than total cost. The amount of the loss is shown by the shaded rectangle. What would a firm do if it expected this situation to continue indefinitely into the future?

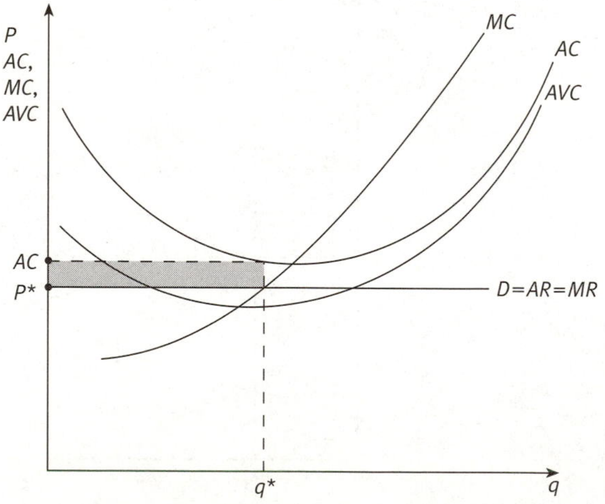

Figure 6.7 A loss-making firm in the short run

The only rational decision would be to leave the market, looking for some other activity in which its resources could be employed at a better return. But this still leaves open the question of *when* the firm should shut down. A loss-making firm has two choices in the short run:

1. cease production immediately;
2. continue production at the output level at which $MC = MR$, and so at which losses are at their minimum level for any positive output level.

Would the firm close down immediately or would it continue in operation in the short run? Both choices result in a loss. The better choice is the one with the lower level of loss. Which choice leads to the lower level of loss depends on whether the firm's total revenue at the loss-minimizing output level exceeds its variable costs (the costs of the variable inputs that it must employ if it continues to produce any output).

What is the loss for the first option? It is just the firm's fixed costs. Remember that in the short run, the firm incurs some fixed costs. These must be met irrespective of its output level (and so will have to be paid even if it shuts down). As these would be the firm's total costs if it shut down immediately, and because its total revenue would be zero, the firm's loss in this case is equal to its fixed costs.

What is the loss for the second option? The loss is given by:

Loss = total revenue − total costs
= total revenue − total fixed costs − total variable costs

Option 2 will result in a smaller loss than option 1 if total revenue exceeds total variable costs. Total revenue will exceed total variable cost if price exceeds average variable cost. So we reach the following conclusion: a loss-making firm will continue in production in the short run provided price exceeds average variable costs at the loss-minimizing output level. In essence, by continuing in production in this situation, the excess of price over average variable costs on each unit sold goes some way towards covering the firm's fixed costs and so reduces the size of its loss. This is the situation portrayed in Figure 6.7. Although the firm does make a loss at output q^* (the loss-minimizing output level), note that $AR>AVC$ at that output level. This margin of revenue over variable costs on each good produced serves to lower the firm's total losses below what would be incurred if closure were immediate. In the language of accounting, a 'contribution' is being made to recovering some of its fixed costs. In contrast, if price is below average variable cost, the firm will cease production immediately.

There is an important caveat to the conclusions we have just reached. Our argument has assumed that fixed costs are also sunk costs. If fixed costs are not sunk costs, then the costs involved can be recovered. If a firm shuts down its operations, the items which give rise to fixed costs may be redeployed elsewhere, sold, or rented out. The monetary costs could thus be avoided. In this case, the shut-down decision is altered: a firm will shut down its operations immediately if average revenue is less than average total cost, and redeploy the fixed assets in another use. Sunk costs are defined and explained more fully in Box 6.2.

Changes in Demand, the Firm's (Short-Run) Supply, and the Industry (Short-Run) Supply

You now know how a profit-maximizing competitive firm selects its output given a particular market equilibrium price. Clearly, if market demand shifts for any reason, the market equilibrium price will change, and this will cause each firm in the market to alter its output level. Let us now see how this works. In so doing, we shall explain how the firm's short-run supply curve is obtained, and from this, how the market supply curve is determined. This will tie up a loose end left in Chapter 2, where we asked you to take the shape of the market supply curve on trust until you reached this chapter.

In Figure 6.8, we show the consequence of a sequence of shifts in market demand. The left-hand portion of the diagram shows market equilibrium price rising from P_1 through to P_4 as a result of the market demand increasing from D_1 through to D_4. In the right-hand side of the diagram, the implications for the firm of the sequence of changes in market price are shown. Specifically, the firm's demand curve rises from d_1 through to d_4. As a consequence of these changes, the firm's profit-maximizing output rises from q_1 through to q_4.

By definition, a firm's supply curve shows how planned output varies in response to changes in the price on offer. It is now easy to deduce the shape of supply curves in the short run. As price rises from P_1 through to P_4, the firm's profit-maximizing

Box 6.2 Fixed Costs and Sunk Costs

Fixed costs and sunk costs are not identical. An understanding of sunk costs provides some valuable insights into business behaviour. A sunk cost is a non-recoverable cost. Suppose that a firm plans to enter the passenger ferry business. At the planning stage no costs are actually incurred, so there are no fixed costs or sunk costs (other than the cost of planning, of course, which is a sunk cost). But once the plan is implemented, expenditures have to be made. Let us think about one particular item, the costs of the ferry boats themselves. A ferry boat's capital costs are certainly fixed costs but are they also sunk costs? The answer depends on whether or not the capital costs can be recovered easily. If there are other ferry operators who would be willing to purchase or lease the boats involved, or if they could be used for some other purpose, the capital costs will not be sunk. It seems likely that ferry boats will have a good second-hand market and so these costs are not sunk.

Now consider the cost of advertising the new ferry service and trying to establish its presence. If the plan to enter this market fails, and the firm has to exit, these costs can never be recovered. A failed advertising campaign has no resale or second-hand value. It is decidedly a sunk cost.

Now take another example. A category of costs which are fixed and also sunk consists of single-purpose, customized, machine tools such as machine presses used to stamp out body panels for a particular model of car. In the absence of alternative uses, these costs are difficult to recover except when the machines are used as intended. We are led to the conclusion that fixed costs may be, but are not necessarily, sunk costs. Note also that some costs may be partially recoverable, so yielding a category of cost which is a mixture of sunk and non-sunk components.

The significance of the nature of costs is seen by returning to our example of the ferry operator. Suppose that expectations turn out to be over-optimistic and that insufficient revenues are generated to cover the firm's outlays, as the following flows indicate:

revenues = \$1000
labour and fuel costs (variable) = \$700
capital costs (fixed) = \$400.

Note that the capital costs in this example are amortized capital costs, not the total cost of capital charged to one period only. Should the ferry operator continue in business? In the text, we argue that the firm should not shut down immediately if average revenue is greater than average variable cost, but should exit only in the long run when it can cease making any contractual payments on its ferry boats. The condition that average revenue exceeds average variable costs is clearly satisfied here. By staying in business in the short run, losses can be reduced from \$400 to \$100. But as we noted above, this conclusion is conditional on the fixed capital costs being sunk (and so not recoverable). In these circumstances, capital expenditures once made and non-recoverable are of no further relevance. Only variable costs are relevant here to the decision about leaving or staying in the business.

But what if the fixed costs are not sunk because the firm can hire out (or sublet) the boats at \$400 per period. Clearly, the optimum choice for the firm in this case is to close its own ferry operation immediately, rent out its unwanted vessels at \$400, and so avoid the loss of \$100 completely. You should be able to work out how the firm can choose its best course of action when costs are partially (but not wholly) sunk.

To make a sensible shut-down decision requires that the firm compares the relative size of losses from all the opportunities open to it. This means paying attention to the opportunity costs involved in the decision. The degree to which costs are sunk can have an important bearing on these opportunity costs, and so on the optimal choice.

---

supply increases from q_1 through to q_4. Thus the firm's short-run supply curve is simply its marginal cost curve! There is one minor qualification we need to add to this statement. The firm will shut down immediately (and so produce no output) if price falls below average variable cost. This determines the minimum price at which the firm will make any supply available to the market. The firm's supply curve does not exist at prices lower than this (shown by price P_1 in the figure).

The market (or industry) supply curve is just the sum of the supply curves of all firms making up the market. This is the basis for the upward-sloping market supply curve which was first introduced in Chapter 2.[2] Now that the idea of a market supply curve has been explained, we can move on to the associated concept of elasticity of supply. In Box 6.3, we define the concept of elasticity of supply.

[2] It turns out to be the case (as we explain in the next chapter) that the concept of a supply curve representing a one to one relationship between the industry price and the willingness to supply is only really meaningful in the context of the perfectly competitive model. It is not possible to derive a meaningful supply function under monopoly or oligopoly as we shall see. This is because the question, 'what is the individual firm willing to supply at a particular market price?', is more difficult to answer when we leave the simplified world of perfect competition.

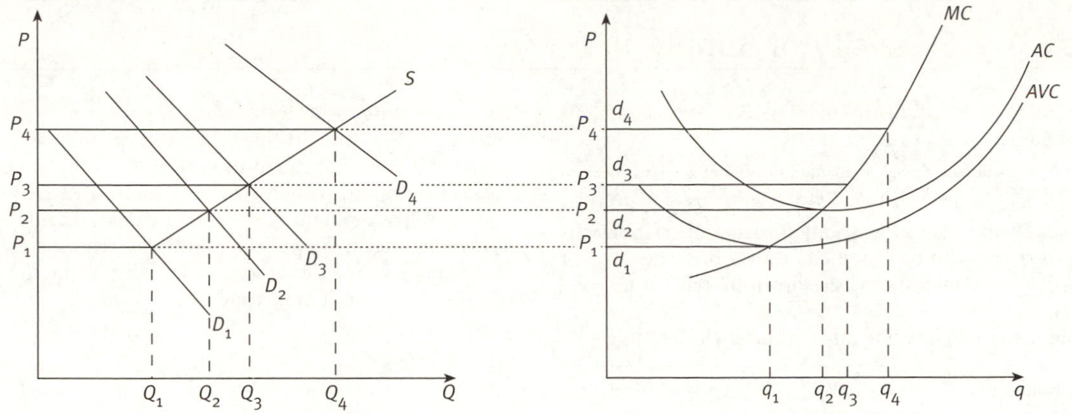

Figure 6.8 The firm's supply curve and the industry (market) supply curve

Supply elasticity is closely related to the concept of price elasticity of demand which we examined in Chapter 2. The difference between the two, of course, is that whereas demand elasticity is a measure of the proportional responsiveness of consumer demand to price changes, supply elasticity measures the responsiveness of market supply to price changes.

Supply elasticity is of great importance when one tries to predict movements in market prices and quantities as economic conditions change. Suppose that demand for gas rises as a consequence of pressure to use more environmentally friendly primary fuels in power production rather than coal. This will necessarily bid up the price of gas. The magnitude of the gas price increase (and of the extra amount of gas that will be forthcoming as its price rises) will depend on the elasticity of supply of gas. If more gas can easily be brought to market, then prices will not rise by much. But if increasing the supply of gas is complicated, then prices will rise more steeply.

Short-Run and Long-Run Supply Curves

Supply curves, and so elasticity of supply, can refer to either the short run or the long run. In the previous section, the supply curve being discussed was the short-run supply curve (of the firm or the industry). Assuming that capital is the fixed factor, a short-run supply curve shows how market supply varies as market price changes in that time frame in which the industry capacity is fixed. Output can be changed, but only by using that capacity more or less intensively.

A long-run market supply curve shows how total market supply responds in the long run to price changes, taking *all* adjustment mechanisms into account. These long-run adjustments will include any capacity changes made by existing firms in the industry and any new entry into or exit from the industry that price changes induce. It is very likely that price changes will induce greater changes in the long run than in the short run. So we would expect long-run elasticity of supply to exceed short-run elasticity of supply.

Whether short-run or long-run supply curves are more appropriate for market analysis depends very much on the time frame that we wish to consider. If, for example, one is trying to forecast long-term price movements, the appropriate supply concept to use is long-run market supply (in conjunction, of course, with long-run market demand). It is important, therefore, when talking about price elasticity of supply, to be clear about whether it is short-run or long-run elasticity of supply that we have in mind.

So far in this chapter, we have shown what determines the shape and elasticity of short-run supply curves. You now know that the short-run market supply is determined by the shapes of the firms' marginal cost curves. Unfortunately, it is beyond the scope of this book to explain the determination of the shape of long-run market supply curves: to do so would require quantifying the magnitude of long-run changes in industry size as prices alter and we do not have the space to develop this issue.

Box 6.3 Elasticity of Supply

The price elasticity of supply (*PES*) for some good *X* is defined as:

$$PES = \frac{\text{proportionate change in quantity supplied of good } X \text{ per period}}{\text{proportionate change in price of good } X}.$$

Just as in the case of elasticity of demand, price elasticity of supply can be classified into various categories of 'elasticity' or 'inelasticity', as shown in Table 6.1.

Table 6.1 Some special cases of elasticity of supply

Description of elasticity	Numerical magnitude of PES	Shape of supply curve
Perfectly elastic	Infinity	Horizontal
Elastic	Between 1 and infinity	Upward sloping
Unit elasticity	1	Upward sloping
Inelastic	Between 0 and 1	Upward sloping
Perfectly inelastic	0	Vertical

One interesting result is that if the supply curve is linear (that is, it is a straight line when drawn on a diagram showing price and quantity) *and* the supply curve passes through the origin (that is, the point where price and quantity are both zero), elasticity of supply will always be one in numerical value. The reason for this is contained in the definition of elasticity, as the following simple proof demonstrates.

By definition:

$$PES = \frac{\Delta Q/Q}{\Delta P/P}$$

$$= \frac{P}{Q} \times \frac{\Delta Q}{\Delta P} = \frac{\frac{\Delta Q}{\Delta P}}{\frac{Q}{P}}.$$

But for a straight-line supply curve going through the origin $Q/P = \Delta Q/\Delta P$, and so PES = 1

6.2 The Firm and the Industry in Long-Run Equilibrium

It is not possible, without substantially increasing the complexity of our arguments, to derive any general results about the shapes and elasticities of long-run market supply curves. But we can easily obtain *some* results which relate to what economists call the 'long-run equilibrium' in a perfectly competitive market. A long-run market equilibrium refers to the price and quantity conditions which one would expect to prevail in that market for given demand and supply conditions, when all existing firms have been allowed to choose their capacity levels and when all firms that wish to enter or leave the market have done so.

Begin by going back to the 'short-run equilibrium' of an individual firm that we illustrated in Figure 6.6. In that figure, the firm portrayed is earning supernormal profits. But given the characteristics of perfectly competitive markets, the outcome described there can only be an ephemeral state. It cannot persist for two reasons:

- existing firms may choose to alter the scale at which they operate. As firms move along their long-run average cost curves in search of the optimal scale of production so the output of the representative firm will alter;
- new firms may decide to enter the industry, or existing firms may leave. In either case, as we shall see, this will affect industry supply, which affects the industry price, and thus the position of the demand function of the individual firm.

To keep our analysis brief, we shall concentrate here on the second of these processes. You will recall from our definition at the start of this chapter that competitive markets are characterized by complete freedom of entry and exit. The profitability of existing firms drives this process of entry and exit.

What happens when a typical firm in the industry is earning supernormal profits? These profits create an attraction for entrepreneurs to pull resources into this industry. The entry of new firms disturbs the short-run equilibrium of the industry. Conversely, if the typical firm is making losses (more precisely, if it is not attaining even normal profit levels), some firms will leave this industry in search of higher returns elsewhere.

This movement of firms into or out of the industry can only take place in the long run. However, when it does occur, a process of adjustment will take place until an equilibrium is achieved in which there is no remaining incentive for any firm to enter or leave the industry. This is known as the long-run equilibrium of the industry (and the firms that make up the industry).

No incentive to enter or leave the market will exist when the typical firm earns just normal profits. This outcome is illustrated in Figure 6.9. At the market equilibrium price P^{**}, industry output Q^{**}, and firm output q^{**}, the following conditions are satisfied:

- each firm already in the industry is doing as well as it can. There is no incentive for any firm to leave the industry;
- there is no incentive operating to attract new firms into the industry.

You should be aware that we have hidden a few technical complications to keep our presentation simple. One of these is important, however, and is worth noting. A true long-run industry equilibrium can only exist when each firm in the industry has adjusted its output level (and its use of inputs) so as to fully exploit any available economies of scale, that is, it has reached the minimum point of its long-run average cost curve. Suppose the long-run cost curve facing the firms in this industry is of the shape shown in Figure 6.10. A firm can only be at its long-run optimum output level when it produces an output level of q^{***}. This in turn requires that the firm has chosen a size of plant exactly appropriate to minimize costs at output level q^{***}. The firm's short-run average and marginal costs will then be those labelled as *SRAC* and *SRMC* in Figure 6.10. In terms of Figure 6.9, this means that the curves labelled *SRMC* and *SRAC* must be those shown in Figure 6.10.

A full long-run equilibrium is, therefore, characterized by the following:

- each firm already in the industry is doing as well as it can. There is no incentive for firms to leave the industry;

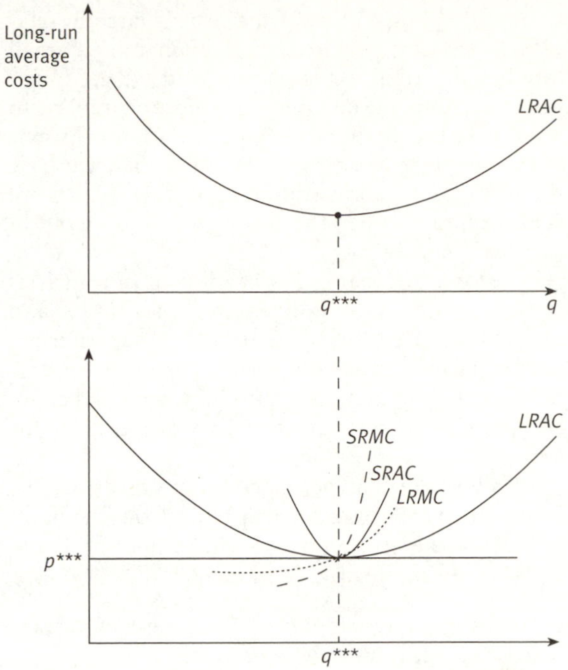

Figure 6.10 A firm's optimum long-run level of output

- there is no incentive for new firms to enter the industry;
- each firm has achieved its optimum long-run level of output.

One important and interesting implication of these conditions for long-run equilibrium is that if continuous economies of scale can be gained by continuous expansion of the size of the firm, market equilibrium is not compatible with competition! Only if the optimal output of the typical firm is very small in relation to the size of the market can we have enough firms for perfect competition. If

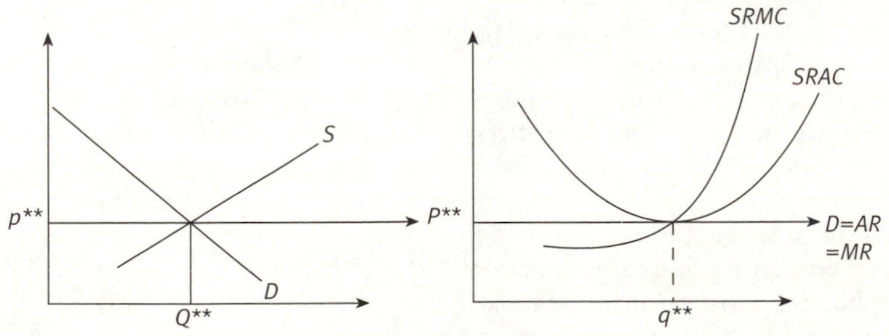

Figure 6.9 Long-run equilibrium of the firm and industry

the optimal output size of the firm is large in relation to the size of the market, then only a small number of producers is feasible and we get oligopolistic competition which is more complex to model. If the optimal output size of the firm is such that only one firm is feasible, then we have the absence of competition altogether which we shall examine under the heading of monopoly in the next chapter.

A second interesting implication of our analysis is this: competition is hard work for firms and ultimately unrewarding in terms of supernormal profits. Firms compete to earn supernormal profits but end up with none. In other words, perfect competition is not an attractive proposition for firms.

Finally, note that perfectly competitive markets have some very attractive properties from the point of view of the economy as a whole. Specifically, in equilibrium the firm is producing:

- at the minimum point of the long-run average cost curve, thus scale is optimal;
- at the minimum point of the short-run average cost curve, so plant utilization is optimal;
- at the point where price equals marginal cost ($P = MC$) in both the short and the long run.

We shall discuss later how economists use these results to define the social desirability of competitive markets and the socially undesirable features of monopoly power.

6.3 Examples and Applications

We explained in our introduction to this chapter that perfect competition is an analytical model which has been developed in order to gain some insight into the competitive process. As such it is not meant to be a description of any particular industry and it is not meant to be 'realistic'. Nevertheless you might ask whether there are industries which at least approximate to the model we have outlined.

One could begin to answer this question by looking for industries consisting of a large number of firms. This could be done, for example, by looking at official Census of Production data such as that available in the UK and USA. Among other things, this will show the total number of firms operating in various industry categories. For example in the USA, one would find that in 1987 there were over 5,000 sawmills operating, 1,406 producers of women's dresses, 557 aluminium foundries, and 950 producers of printed circuit boards. Similarly in the UK there are hundreds of building firms, brewers, and bakers.

But a market or an industry with several hundred firms is not necessarily competitive in the carefully specified sense used in this chapter. Even if there is a large number of firms operating in a particular market, the industry may well be dominated by a small number of firms, four or five say, in which case it would be appropriate to describe it as an oligopoly. Moreover, even where there are no relatively large players dominating an industry with hundreds of firms, products may be differentiated in some way, for example, by location or by brand. It might not matter too much to someone in downtown Boston that there are 5,000 sawmills in the USA, or 50 in Boston alone, because some will be a lot nearer than others and this serves to differentiate the firms in the eyes of consumers. Such a market may be described as monopolistically competitive rather than perfectly competitive because the products are no longer perfect substitutes for one another. We discuss monopolistic competition briefly below and oligopoly is the subject of Chapter 8.

A more fundamental problem with this approach is that perfect competition is a model of markets, not of industries, and the two terms are not synonymous. The model involves important assumptions about consumers as well as producers. For a market to be perfectly competitive, remember, all of the following conditions must be satisfied:

- there is a large number of buyers and a large number of sellers, none of whom is large enough individually to influence the market price;
- the products being traded in the market are homogeneous; that is, they are perceived by consumers as being perfect substitutes;
- all buyers and sellers have complete information about market prices;
- individuals have no preferences concerning those with whom they trade;
- there are no barriers to entry into or out of the industry in the long run;

- all sellers have equal access to the resources required for production at prevailing prices.

Some economics texts suggest that the market for foreign currencies is close to satisfying the conditions for perfect competition and quote it as an example. However, the required conditions may not hold exactly even in this case. Recent events suggest that some individual speculators can and do trade in sufficient quantities to affect market prices. For example, according to press reports, the Hungarian-born currency speculator George Soros controls $18 billion of funds and his transactions have been credited with helping to force the devaluation of the pound sterling in 1992. At the time of writing, the super-wealthy Sultan of Brunei is reported to be intervening in exchange markets in an attempt to stabilize the currencies of a number of South East Asian 'Tiger' economies. It is also probable that some governments have sufficient financial assets to influence currency prices and that they try to use these resources to this end. Finally, the currency markets are trading markets only: markets in which fixed stocks of paper claims—national currencies—are exchanged. There is no production taking place, there is no output decision to make, and there is ultimately no freedom of entry into the 'market'. If the yen is proving to be popular, new producers can't very well enter the yen production industry.

Other examples commonly suggested by textbooks include markets for agricultural products such as wheat, rice, and coffee and markets for some primary commodities such as aluminium and copper. It is true that some agricultural and commodity markets do approximate to some of the required conditions, particularly at the world level. However, in practice, agricultural markets are often distorted by producer co-operatives and cartels and by government agricultural policies so that the outcome is not always that predicted by the competitive model. But the very fact that agricultural and commodity markets are often the subject of expensive private and public efforts to cartelize them or to 'stabilize' prices does tend to support our understanding of the effects of highly competitive markets as seen in this chapter. Such markets put producers under a lot of pressure and make it difficult for anyone to earn above-normal profits. Prices tend to be unstable, reflecting shifts in demand and supply conditions, with agricultural markets particularly prone to supply shocks. Cartelization and price support efforts may be seen as attempts by producers to gain some control over the pitiless logic of competitive forces.

The difficulty of identifying a realistic example of perfect competition does not mean that the model is not useful. The usefulness of the model becomes more apparent if we switch from thinking of perfect competition as a static description of a market to thinking of it as telling us something about the *process* of competition. Competition is a process which is fundamental to all market-based economies. Whenever profit opportunities are identified, there will be a tendency to create firms to seek to grab a slice of these profits. Good ideas and new products will eventually be copied or imitated, innovative products will go through life cycles in which ultimately they tend to become standardized commodities, early rents will be dissipated by new entry, and the forces of national and international competition will eventually challenge monopolistic bastions wherever they exist. Who would ever have thought the personal computer would come to be regarded as just another commodity? It is all these things that we mean by the process of competition. The competitive model suggests what tends to happen if these competitive forces are allowed to operate unhindered in market economies.

It has been argued by economists such as William Baumol of Princeton that the most fundamental feature of competitive markets is not, in fact, the large numbers property central to the model of competition described in this chapter, but rather the freedom of entry and exit to and from the market. Indeed the so-called theory of contestable markets suggests that contestability alone—defined as the ability to enter and leave markets rapidly without losing your initial investment (also called 'hit and run' entry)—is sufficient to bring about the long-run equilibrium outcomes we have described in this chapter. A little reflection makes it clear how this might come about. Even if a market currently consists of only a few firms, the possibility of 'hit and run' entry can be sufficient by itself to stop industry profits rising much above the normal level. A fundamental requirement for contestability turns out to be the absence of sunk costs which we discussed earlier in Box 6.2.

Many commentators argue that world markets have become more competitive in recent decades. To the extent that this has happened, it is largely the consequence of the freeing-up of market entry conditions. The fundamental driving forces have been the liberalization of world trade: reductions of tariff and non-tariff barriers to trade between countries, deregulation of markets and the breaking-up of statutory monopolies created by governments. Let us consider a few examples. First, the rates of return in personal banking services in many countries have been driven down by financial deregulation and the penetration of domestic banking markets by foreign financial institutions. Profitability in the motor vehicle industry throughout the world, but especially in Europe, has been under pressure as capacity grows and new car-producing countries establish a market position. The car industry in the established vehicle-producing countries is responding to these pressures with major structural reorganization that is often described under the heading of globalization. Finally, think about the personal hi-fi or Walkman, first produced by Sony. The phenomenal market success of this product quickly brought about imitation and replication; in any high-street electrical goods retail shop today we can see a wide range of more or less identical products, each earning relatively small margins for the producers as a result of the play of competitive forces. Electrical goods producers are engaged in a constant search to be first in the market with new, innovative products in order to maintain their profits.

The competitive model also helps us to understand what the consequences of government intervention in competitive markets will be, even if the market does not meet all the criteria for perfect competition. Consider the hugely expensive attempts to interdict drugs like heroin coming into the USA and elsewhere. These efforts, we would argue on the basis of economic analysis, are almost certainly a waste of time and valuable resources. Illicit drugs now represent 8 per cent of world exports (according to the *UN World Drug Report* (1997)) despite all the efforts being made to control this trade. To the extent that interdiction is successful at stopping a small proportion of supply getting to the market, this reduction in supply will drive prices up beyond the market equilibrium level without interdiction, especially given the relative inelasticity of demand for the product. But there are many possible suppliers keen to supply the product and the higher prices resulting from interdiction tend to encourage even more production, new entrants, and so an even greater willingness to supply. Interdiction efforts cannot overcome the laws of the market and so are unlikely to achieve their goal; such efforts act like a tax on the supply of the product, raising the final price to the consumer but not effectively stopping demand, nor even reducing supply significantly in the long run.

Consider also the taxi cab business in big cities such as London and New York. Here is a promising example of a competitive industry, with large numbers of driver owners, it is easy to enter with low sunk costs, hard to differentiate the product, while consumers have no preferences concerning producers. Competition should mean that cab prices are at a level where only normal returns are earned. And so they would be in a totally unregulated market. However, the taxi business in most big cities is regulated by local authorities keen to set minimum standards and thus requiring taxi owners to be properly qualified and licensed. Often the number of licences issued is kept below the desirable level and this acts as a barrier to the entry of new firms into the industry and so tends to raise the profits of those who have an operating licence. In fact, this results in such licences themselves becoming valuable commodities which trade for large sums of money in cities such as New York. The same effect can be expected in any market where licensing arrangements can operate to restrict new entry, an example being the medical profession in many countries.

Perfect competition, then, is an analytical model developed in order to gain some insight into the competitive process and to provide a benchmark for understanding the implications of different market structures. It is best to view the model we have looked at in this chapter in this light. If the competitive process described by this model were the only process taking place in market economies, one would expect that the kinds of results we have obtained in this chapter would become increasingly prevalent. But of course there are other forces at work too: products are being differentiated, new products are being developed, barriers to entry are being built, alliances, mergers, and acquisitions are leading towards increased market 'concentration' and various forms of preferential treatment are given by governments to 'their' firms.

Furthermore, the struggle for profitability will see firms searching for, and sometimes acquiring, competitive advantages over others. Players in markets will be successful in these quests to different degrees, leading to another form of heterogeneity in markets as these forces play their way out. We discuss these matters—the search for competitive advantage—in detail in Chapter 10. What we observe, therefore, is the consequence of a continuous dynamic interplay between forces promoting and restricting competition, and between forces acting to make markets more homogeneous and more heterogeneous. The markets and industries we observe in reality are the realizations, at particular points in time, of the pushes and pulls of these opposing sets of forces.

6.4 The Search for Value: Differentiation and Monopolistic Competition

As we have seen, the prospects for individual firms achieving sustained added value in competitive markets look very bleak. Although perfect competition is consistent with supernormal profits being earned in the short run, these rewards are ephemeral. Freedom of entry into the market implies that profits greater than normal will disappear in the long run, as new entry drives prices down to firms' minimum average costs.

The student of business policy or strategic analysis may be inclined to think that individual firms do have ways of sustaining above-normal profits even when other firms in the market fail to do so. Two commonly suggested ways of gaining a 'competitive advantage' over others are *superior cost performance* and *product differentiation.* Let us briefly examine the scope of these in the context of markets which are, in other respects, perfectly competitive.

Intuition suggests that in competitive markets there is little scope for individual firms to earn supernormal profits through superior cost performance. In the long run, entry into the industry will continue as long as any prospect of profit for well-run firms remains. Firms whose costs are above those which are attained by cost-minimizing firms will be driven out of the market in the face of this relentless competition. It is as if an evolutionary process is taking place in which only efficient (low-cost) firms will be successful in the struggle to survive. The population of firms in the industry will *not*, in the long run, contain a marked spread of cost performances in which one can do particularly well by being in the low cost tail of the distribution. Of course, if one can gain an advantage by some new technique or the like, transitory supernormal profits can be earned. However, unless the source of the cost advantage cannot be replicated by others—perhaps because of the ownership or control of some scarce strategic asset—the effective management of costs is a prerequisite for survival in this type of market, not a recipe for excess profits. The conclusion to which we are led is that cost-cutting *per se*, in the sense of simply keeping costs at a minimum level, is not likely to be a fruitful means of achieving and sustaining supernormal profits (at least, not in the context of perfectly competitive markets).

Does product differentiation offer a more promising path to above average returns? There is a large number of ways in which product differentiation has been incorporated into economic analysis. Here we shall consider just one of these, the model of monopolistic competition first proposed by Chamberlin (1933).

Monopolistic competition is a market in which the following conditions are satisfied:

- there are a large number of buyers and a large number of sellers;
- the products being traded in the market are differentiated; that is, they are perceived by consumers as being less-than-perfect substitutes;
- all buyers and sellers have complete information about prevailing market prices;
- there are no barriers to entry into or out of the industry in the long run;
- all sellers have equal access to the resources required for production at prevailing prices.

In two important respects, monopolistic competition is no different from perfect competition. In both cases, the *large numbers* and the *freedom of entry* conditions prevail. Another similarity concerns the condition that all sellers have equal access to productive resources.[3] But the markets differ in one fundamental way: firms in a monopolistically competitive market sell differentiated products. As

[3] It is worth noting that by making this a condition of monopolistic competition, we are excluding the possibility that some firms can have a cost advantage over others through the ownership of strategic assets. One may feel that this assumption is unduly restrictive. Clearly there are many cases in practice where some firms do earn rents by virtue of ownership or control of strategic assets. But the key point is that these rents are derived from that strategic asset, and do not arise from the structure of monopolistic competition itself.

a consequence of this, it will be the case that individuals may have preferences concerning those with whom they trade. Moreover, although no firm is individually large enough to affect the 'market' price, a firm is no longer simply a price taker as in perfect competition. The firm will be able to increase its price a little without losing all its sales, and a price reduction will not win it the whole market. If the extent of perceived differentiation is large, the firm's ability to determine its own price may be substantial. This does not mean, of course, that a firm with a differentiated profit can increase its price without limit. Increasing price still involves a trade-off in terms of lower sales; but the terms of that trade-off will no longer be catastrophic.

What does product differentiation mean for the shape of an individual firm's demand curve? The answer is simple: it will be downward sloping, not horizontal as in a perfectly competitive market. This follows because of the degree of substitutability of products. In perfect competition, product homogeneity means that goods are perfect substitutes, and so the firm's demand curve is perfectly elastic (that is, horizontal) at the market price. With differentiated goods, products are less-than-perfect substitutes, and so the individual firm's demand is less than perfectly elastic. In other words, it will be downward sloping.

A full analysis of the consequences of a downward-sloping demand curve is best left to the following chapter, where we examine *pure* monopoly markets. At this point, we content ourselves with an intuitive account of the outcomes one would expect in a monopolistically *competitive* market. Not surprisingly, a typical firm—and so the industry as a whole—may be able to make supernormal profits in the short run when the capacity of incumbent firms are fixed and new firms do not enter the market. Of course, positive profits are only possible where market demand is sufficiently strong and costs are sufficiently low, but these will often be satisfied in the short run for many categories of goods.

But the long-run outcome will, once again, be characterized by firms earning only normal profits. The reason for this is exactly the same as that encountered in the case of perfect competition. Freedom of entry brings new firms into the market in the long run whenever profits are supernormal (and existing firms adjust to the optimum size).

We can think of this in the following way. In monopolistic competition, although products are differentiated, the offerings of rival firms are nevertheless regarded by consumers as being sufficiently close to one another to constitute a distinct 'product type' in a distinct 'market'. It is meaningful, therefore, for us to refer to a 'market' demand curve for the product, even though the boundaries and composition of any market will be harder to pin down than has been the case in any of our previous discussions.

It will be helpful to an understanding of monopolistic competition to have an example in mind. Restaurants in London, Paris, or any large town or city exemplify monopolistic competition. There is a large number of restaurants in Paris, and entry into the market seems to be easy and regular. Restaurant meals—or more accurately the package of services that a restaurant supplies—are certainly differentiated products. Restaurants are close substitutes but not perfect substitutes. Our analysis suggests that in the long run firms in this industry should be able to make only normal profits, and this does seem to be borne out by the available evidence. Restaurants located at prime sites, of course, such as those adjacent to the Eiffel Tower or inside Disneyland Paris, may seem to do better than average but this is likely to be an illusion. The high returns generated by good business at these sites are returns to the ownership of the prime sites, not returns to the restaurant business *per se*. Once the opportunity costs of these sites are properly accounted for, the returns to the restaurants using them will appear to be about average.

Let us return to the notion of the 'market' demand curve in monopolistic competition. At any given point, we can regard this demand as fixed in a position which depends on such things as consumers' income and tastes. Its position also depends on the amount of effort that firms collectively have put into promoting and differentiating their products. When a firm promotes its product, that effort will not only have a specific effect on that firm's demand but it may also have spillover effects, increasing the demand for the product-type in the market. Imagine, for example, the effect on the demand for motorcycles when Honda, BMW, and Ducati all promote the sales of their own models.

Individual firms are competing for shares of the market demand curve. As new entry takes place, more firms must share in a given market demand. Each firm's share of total demand decreases (moves to the left) in this process, which squeezes the firm's profitability. New entry will only cease when the typical firm makes no more than normal profits. The long-run equilibrium will, once again, be characterized by zero supernormal profits.

In this story, product differentiation does not offer the prospect of sustainable excess profits. Freedom of entry prevents that! However, some caution is warranted before concluding that this is the end of the matter. First, differentiation may well increase the magnitude of short-run profits significantly (although, note, it will involve additional costs too: differentiation cannot be had for nothing). Secondly, it may also make new entry a slower process, increasing the duration of time over which profits may be available. Differentiation tends to be associated with product variety, branding, and changing product characteristics. Given that successful entry will also require the newcomer to offer a differentiated (rather than a standardized) product, the time needed for market penetration may tend to increase. Finally, if a firm is so successful in differentiating its product that the good comes to be seen by consumers as wholly distinct from others, the firm has effectively redefined the market. The firm effectively becomes the sole producer of a product for which there are no close substitutes: it becomes a monopoly! Certain types of designer clothing seem to have achieved this at various times: parents will be aware of children arguing that *only* the latest variety of Nike Air training shoes will do! Adults are not immune to such perceptions either: there are some who believe that only a Rolex will convey the signal they wish to send to their fellows. Clearly, sustainable profits are possible in this context even when, to a dispassionate observer, close substitutes are readily available. It is to the analysis of monopoly that we turn in the next chapter.

Conclusions

Firms in perfectly competitive markets may temporarily enjoy above-normal profitability, but the competitive process itself, principally the process of searching for profit opportunities leading to new entry into attractive markets, is continuously eliminating these profits. This, of course, is the paradox of competitive markets. The search for supernormal profits, or rents, by entrepreneurs leads to an equilibrium in which only normal profits, the absence of rents, are possible.

The characteristics of the long-run position of the firm in a perfectly competitive market makes competition attractive to the consumer and to society as a whole. Competition promotes efforts to be cost-efficient and it forces prices down to these cost efficient levels. The social attractions of competitive markets will be considered further in a later chapter. It is evident, however, that competitive markets are hard work for firms seeking to earn supernormal profits and that competition is not something which is attractive to the firms struggling to deal with its pressures. In the next chapter we shall look at a situation at the other end of the market spectrum from perfect competition: a situation where a single firm supplies the whole market and is not threatened by the possibility of entry. We shall see that from the point of view of the firm this is a decidedly better situation than the one analysed in this chapter. It is indeed for this reason that firms pursue policies aimed at escaping the rigours of extreme competition by, for example,

- searching for new products or new markets which the firm can dominate;
- producing differentiated goods and reducing substitution possibilities;
- building a reputation in an attempt to develop buyer loyalties and make switching less likely.

The paradox therefore is that competition might well be described as the search for monopoly or the search for market power!

Further reading

The competitive model is the mainstay of economics textbooks. Some good, alternative presentations of the theory of competitive markets may be found in Parkin and King (1995, chapter 11), Baumol and Blinder (1991, chapter 2) and Lipsey and Chrystal (1999, chapter 9).

William Baumol—in his theory of contestable markets—argues that potential entry into a market is, in some circumstances, sufficient to bring about the perfectly competitive market price/output outcome. This argument is developed in Baumol *et al.* (1982). It is also explained in Tirole (1989), which also contains an excellent (but technically quite advanced) analysis of competitive markets. You should note that these last two references are considerably more difficult than the previous three we have given.

Questions

6.1. Can it ever be rational to stay in business in

(*a*) the short run, and

(*b*) the long run

if the firm runs at a loss?

6.2. Which markets, if any, in practice conform closely to the 'ideal' competitive market? For those which you believe fit this description, which properties of these markets prevent them from being *perfectly* competitive?

6.3. In many markets we observe 'price spread': firms sell their versions of a particular product type at slightly different prices. Look back to the assumptions of perfect markets which were listed earlier in this chapter. Which of these are important in preventing price spread, and why?

6.4. How does the economist's concept of a 'competitive firm' differ from the notion of a competitive firm in the business policy sense?

6.5. If the long-run average cost curve for some product exhibits continuous economies of scale, is it possible for there to be a competitive market in that product in the long run?

6.6 What role does international trade play in shaping the degree of competition in the market for some product?

6.7. Is it possible for firms operating in a perfectly competitive market to generate sustained supernormal profits?

7 The Monopoly Model and Barriers to Entry

Introduction

In this chapter we are concerned with the behaviour and performance of firms in markets in which producers have market power. We thus move the analysis to the opposite end of the structure spectrum from perfect competition to look at what happens to prices and profits when competition is absent. Once again we see how industry attractiveness is a function of short-term profits whilst long-term profits are a function of industry attractiveness defined in structural terms. The pure monopoly model discussed in this chapter helps to define what we mean by structural attractiveness.

It must be remembered, however, that when we say that monopoly is 'attractive' we mean that it is attractive to those who own and operate the monopoly. Whilst monopoly is attractive to firms, and business strategy might be defined as a search for market power, it is not necessarily good for society as a whole and this raises the question of public policy towards monopoly power. We do not examine the social implications of monopoly or public policy towards monopoly in this chapter but we shall come back to these important aspects of the economics of monopoly in Chapter 13.

The chapter proceeds as follows. In Section 7.1 we begin by defining the characteristics of monopolistic markets and briefly discuss the causes of monopoly. Section 7.2 then develops a formal model of monopoly in order to analyse the consequences of monopoly for prices, output, and profits and to show why monopoly is considered to be 'attractive'. In Section 7.3 we examine some ways in which the monopolist can increase the level of profits, in particular the use of price discrimination, and some factors which might operate to reduce the expected level of monopoly profits. We then consider in Section 7.4 the crucial question of the sustainability of monopoly profits by examining the nature and significance of barriers to entry.

Note that some of the analysis in this chapter makes use of results derived in the previous chapter on the competitive model, such as the marginal conditions for profit maximization, and the derivation of these results is therefore not repeated in this chapter.

7.1 The Characteristics and Causes of Monopoly

A pure monopoly is defined as follows.

1. There is only one firm in the industry. The firm and the industry are therefore synonymous. There are no rivals for the firm to worry about. The demand curve facing the firm is thus the downward-sloping market demand curve for the firm's product. The term monopoly means single seller.
2. There are no close substitutes available for the monopolist's product. There are, of course, ultimately substitutes for most things so we are not saying that there are no substitutes but that the substitutes available are not close. For example, electricity and gas are substitutes but not perfect ones and, in some uses, not very close. Therefore a single producer of electricity (or gas) would be a monopolist. By comparison only one firm produces Ford cars which means that Ford has an element of monopoly but other firms produce very close substitutes and so Ford does not meet this particular criterion for monopoly. Substitution can be measured in principle by the cross-elasticity of demand (Chapter 2) and what we are saying here is

that, for a monopolist, the cross-elasticity of demand is positive but small. This means that the monopolist does not consider the reactions of any rivals when it sets its price. If it did this, it would be an oligopolist as we explain in the next chapter.

3. Entry into the industry is very difficult. The monopolist does not have to worry about potential competition appearing over the horizon when it decides how much to produce. If entry is not difficult, a monopoly situation is not sustainable because the profits associated with market power would attract other firms and market structure would change.

Together these characteristics define a situation where a firm has complete discretion in choosing its output or its price. The firm is described as a price maker rather than a price taker as in the previous chapter. Note, however, we say choosing output *or* price. Not even a monopolist can choose both independently as we shall see, at least not if it seeks to maximize its profits. The firm has complete discretion because it does not have to bother much with customers switching to substitutes or with the possibility of new entrants.

In practice, of course, pure monopoly as defined here may be rare but firms with substantial monopoly power or market power are more common. For example, a firm with a very substantial share of a particular market, say over 80 per cent, has a great deal of market power but is not a monopolist in the pure sense defined here. An economist would refer to this as a dominant firm rather than a pure monopolist. To confuse the issue even more, the legal definition of monopoly in most countries involves market shares which are far less than 100 per cent. In the UK, for example, a firm with over 25 per cent of a defined market is considered to have potential monopoly power and might be investigated by the Monopolies and Mergers Commission.

In the following analysis we make an additional assumption:

4. The monopolist is not selling to another monopolist which is the sole buyer of its output, that is, the buyer is not a monopsonist (a single buyer). Buyers must be price takers. If this is not the case, we have a situation of bilateral market power which is more difficult to resolve than the case we deal with here.

Causes

Why might a situation arise where there is only one firm operating in an industry? Three distinct possibilities exist. First, the firm might be an innovator producing a product no one had thought of before, such as a desk-top computer, in the process creating a new market that no one had perceived before. Secondly, the firm might come about as the result of all the existing producers in an industry deliberately merging together in order to create a single firm. (A variant of this would be the state merging all the firms in an industry together to create a public monopoly, or nationalized industry, as happened to many British industries in the late 1940s). Thirdly, the competitive process might lead over time to the emergence of a monopolist which is able to drive other firms out through superior competitive capabilities. However, none of these situations would persist for very long if the monopoly was generating economic profits and other firms could enter the industry to challenge the incumbent firm. Therefore the crucial determinant of monopoly is that something prevents other firms from challenging the incumbent. There are many reasons why this might happen. We shall consider these only briefly here because a fuller discussion of barriers to entry comes later.

First, the incumbent firm might be able to get legal protection of some sort. For example, our innovative computer maker might be able to obtain patents which prevent other firms from copying his product. Patents are a common legal device for encouraging innovators by giving them a period of monopoly power. Another possibility is that the government gives a firm the sole licence or an exclusive right to produce a particular good or service. For example, until recently most countries had a single telecoms provider because the state would not license other operators. In the UK the national lottery organizer Camelot has an exclusive right to run a national lottery. In the past Britain had many 'statutory' publicly owned monopolies called nationalized industries whose monopoly position could not be challenged by law. Finally, the state might act to protect what it sees as a 'national champion' by placing high tariffs on imports in order to prevent foreign competitors from entering the local market. For example, many countries see the local airline as a 'national' airline or flag carrier and so prevent foreign companies from competing.

Secondly, the incumbent firm might have some advantage over outsiders which makes it difficult for outsiders to challenge it. For example, our innovative computer maker might be able to achieve first-mover advantages as a result of its foresight. This means simply that setting up and establishing itself first gives the first mover a sufficient cost advantage over a challenger to discourage any challenge. This advantage might come from moving down the learning curve quickly or establishing a scale of operations which provides substantial economies of scale. Alternatively, entry might involve substantial sunk costs which would increase the risks associated with failure. Note, however, that there is nothing inevitable about first movers gaining an advantage. Often first movers simply establish the existence of a promising market opportunity but can not exploit it properly and get swept aside by late movers.

Another possibility is that the incumbent might control a key aspect of the production process which it is not prepared to license to challengers. For example, challenging ICI's position in the UK salt market has been made difficult by the fact that ICI controlled the only approved pumping technology for salt mining in Britain, not to mention the mineral rights to many of the promising sites. Similarly, until the gas regulator (OFGAS) acted in 1996, British Gas controlled the UK gas pipeline distribution network and would not let potential suppliers of gas use its pipelines. Of course, in principle, a potential supplier could have built its own pipeline network but the cost of doing this would have meant that the average cost of provision for both suppliers was now much higher than the average cost achieved by one firm on its own. This is what economists refer to as a 'natural' monopoly situation because the advantages of large-scale production make it possible for a single producer or provider to supply the entire market at a lower average cost per unit than two or more producers each producing a smaller level of output.

7.2 The Short-Run Behaviour of the Monopolist

The analysis of monopoly behaviour requires three building blocks:

1. an understanding of the firm's revenue;
2. an understanding of the firm's costs;
3. an assumption that the firm is seeking to maximize its profits.

We shall look at each of these in turn.

Total, Average and Marginal Revenue for a Monopolist

On the revenue side the monopolist faces a situation quite different from that faced by the competitive firm in the previous chapter. So total revenue, average revenue, and marginal revenue all look different. To demonstrate this, let us begin with the demand function facing the firm. Because the firm is a monopolist it faces the downward-sloping market demand function for its output as shown in Figure 7.1 below. The firm is not a price taker now, it has to decide the price to charge by itself. However, if it wishes to maximise profits, it cannot simply choose the highest possible price available and wait for the money to roll in. The reason for this is evident from Figure 7.1. The higher the price set by the monopolist, the lower will be the quantity of output sold. The monopolist therefore faces a trade-off because of the downward-sloping demand condition it faces. High price means low sales. Lower prices mean higher sales. What price–output combination will the monopolist choose to maximise profits? This will depend on what happens to total and marginal revenue as price changes, so we shall now examine this.

As before, the total revenue (R) for the firm is the total value of the firm's sales. Thus, using P to

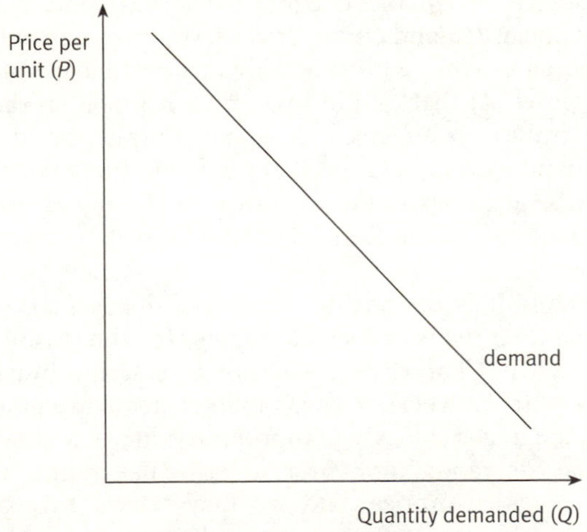

Figure 7.1 The demand function of the monopolist

denote the unit selling price of output and Q the quantity sold, we have as usual:

$R = PQ$.

Because the monopolist's price P will depend on its output level Q, that is, P is a function of Q, and because the quantity of output also enters directly into the expression for sales revenue (PQ), we know that revenue may be expressed solely as a function of output (Q).

What will this total revenue function look like? This will depend on the shape of the demand function. For simplicity, we shall assume a simple linear demand function rather than anything more complicated, that is, a demand function of the form:

$P = a - bQ$

as shown in Figure 7.2. The letters a and (-b) are fixed parameters representing respectively the point where the demand line cuts the price axis, that is, the price at which sales are zero, and the downward slope of the demand function.

Total revenue is P times Q so if we multiply both sides of the demand equation by Q we get:

$R = PQ = (a - bQ)Q = aQ - bQ^2$.

Thus, whenever the demand function is linear, the total revenue curve will be quadratic with respect to output. That is, it has an inverted U-shape as illustrated in Figure 7.2. One of the important results shown in Figure 7.2 can be understood by using a result we obtained in Chapter 2. There we demonstrated that if a firm wishes to maximize total sales revenue (note, not maximize profit), it should select an output level at which the price elasticity of demand is equal to (minus) one. For any linear demand curve, price elasticity of demand is equal to (minus) one at only one particular output level. At that output (assuming it is sold at the maximum price given for that output by the demand curve), the sales revenue in the market will be at a maximum, as shown in the figure. An explanation of the line labelled MR will be given below.

While it is reasonable to assume that a market demand curve is *downward sloping* (for the reasons we gave in Chapter 3), it will not necessarily always be linear. However, a linear market demand curve can be regarded as an approximation to a non-linear demand curve over a particular range of prices or quantities, and we may regard this as one justification for using linear demand functions as the basis for our presentation. Moreover, none of the important results derived in this chapter requires that the demand curve is actually linear and our reason for making this assumption is arithmetical simplicity.

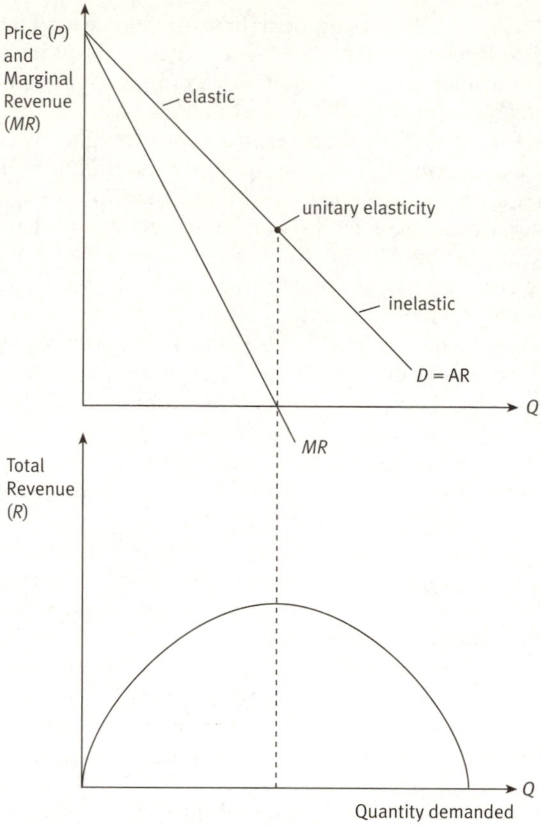

Figure 7.2 The relationship of demand to total revenue and marginal revenue for the monopolist

We have seen that total revenue (R) is the income received from the sale of a firm's output where Q = output quantity sold by the firm, and P = price per unit sold. Now let us consider two related revenue functions, the average and the marginal revenue.

Average revenue (AR) is the mean revenue received on each good sold:

$AR = R/Q$.

Notice that, from the definition of total revenue, R, average revenue is identically equal to price. So we can also write:

$AR = R/Q = PQ/Q = P$.

The average revenue function is therefore just another name for the firm's demand function.

Marginal revenue (MR) is the increase in a firm's total revenue arising from the sale of an additional unit of output or more generally the rate of change of revenue with respect to output:

$MR = \Delta R/\Delta Q$ (where 'Δ' means 'a small change in').

Let us explore the monopolist's marginal revenue function more closely.

Marginal revenue is affected in *two distinct ways* when output is increased. First, because additional output is sold, revenue will increase and this will make marginal revenue *positive*. But there is a second factor, working in the opposite direction. Because the monopolist faces a downward-sloping demand curve, the firm will only be able to sell a higher level of output if the market price is lower than before. This is shown in Figure 7.3: in order to increase the quantity sold from Q_1 to Q_2 per period, the firm's price must be reduced from P_1 to P_2. Notice, however, that this price reduction must take place on all units sold, not just the additional unit sold. Therefore, because quantity sold can only be increased if the market price is reduced, the firm will receive a lower price than that obtained at the output Q_1. It was previously selling this output at price P_1, now it must sell it at the lower price P_2. This will *reduce* marginal revenue.

We therefore have an important result. For a monopolist, marginal revenue must be less than price: that is, $MR < P$. The marginal revenue must be less than price, or average revenue, because each extra unit sold brings in an amount equal to

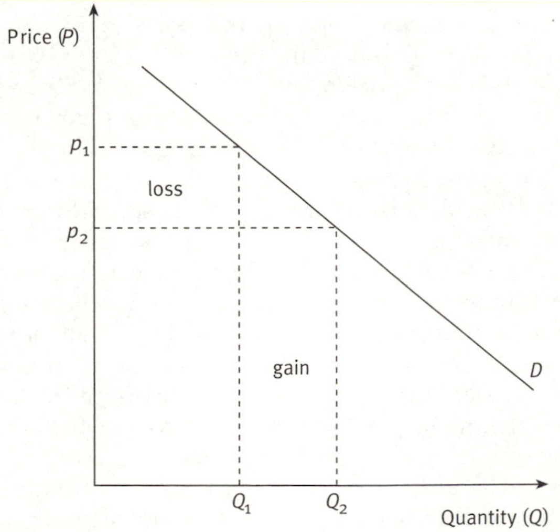

Figure 7.3 The derivation of the marginal revenue of the monopolist

the new (lower) price *minus* the fall in revenue resulting from selling the original output level at the now lower price.

The overall change in total revenue (that is, the marginal revenue) is the sum of these two effects, and is illustrated in Figure 7.3. The rectangle marked 'gain' represents the additional revenue gained by selling more (ΔQ) at the new price P_2. The rectangle 'loss' shows the revenue lost by selling the original level of output, Q_1, at the lower price P_2. Therefore, marginal revenue is given by the gain rectangle minus the loss rectangle. This means of course that marginal revenue might be negative. This will happen if the loss of revenue resulting from a reduction in price is greater than the gain in revenue resulting from an increase in sales: that is, if area 'loss' exceeds area 'gain'. Note, of course, that average revenue will never be negative because this would imply a negative price.

For a downward-sloping demand curve, marginal revenue will always be less than price, for the reasons just indicated. Hence, the marginal revenue curve will lie below the demand curve. For the case of a linear demand curve, the associated marginal revenue curve was illustrated in Figure 7.2.

Four points should be noted although we will not formally demonstrate these points.

1. If the demand curve is downward sloping, the marginal revenue curve will also be downward sloping. However, the gradient of the MR curve will be greater (in absolute terms) than the gradient of the demand curve. That is, it will slope downwards more steeply than the demand curve.
2. In the case of a linear demand curve, the MR curve will always have a negative slope twice as great as that of the demand curve. Hence, in the linear case, the MR curve intersects the quantity axis at a point half-way from the origin to the point where the demand curve touches the quantity axis.
3. Marginal revenue is zero at the point where the demand curve has unitary point elasticity of demand. At this point, total revenue will be at its maximum level. Note that where marginal revenue is zero, a small change in output will leave total revenue unchanged (in this case at its maximum value). However, as you will see in a moment, total *profit* is not (usually) at its maximum at the output which maximizes revenue.

4. Marginal revenue and its relation to elasticity can be expressed precisely as follows: $MR = P - P/e$. As we have seen above when $e = 1$, MR is zero. When $e>1$, MR is positive, and when $e<1$, MR is negative. Note that in this expression we take the 'absolute' numerical value of e and ignore the fact that the elasticity of demand has a negative sign.

To confirm your understanding of these revenue concepts try the following exercise.

The Colorado ski resort has only one ski lift. The local economist has estimated the demand function for the ski lift as: $P = 20 - 2Q$. Complete Table 7.1 using the information provided for quantity demanded. Examine the shape of total revenue and the relation between average (P) and marginal revenue (MR). Confirm that marginal revenue might be negative.

The second building block concerns the monopolist's costs. In this case we assume that costs are typical short-run costs for a firm, that is U-shaped as in Figure 7.4. The difference between the monopolist and the competitive firm in this case has to do with the position of the cost functions in relation to demand rather than the shape of the cost functions themselves. For the monopolist, the cost functions show the firm's output as large relative to the size of the market, whereas in perfect competition the firm's output is small relative to the market. This, of course, is the essential difference assumed between competition and monopoly.

The final building block for our analysis of monopoly is the assumption of profit maximization. We have explained in the previous chapter (see Box 6.1) what this involves. To summarize,

Table 7.1 Measures of revenue for the illustrative demand function

Demand (Q)	Price (P)	Total revenue (R)	Marginal revenue (MR)
0	20	0	—
1	18	18	18
2	?	?	?
3			
4			
5			
6			
7			
8			
9			
10			

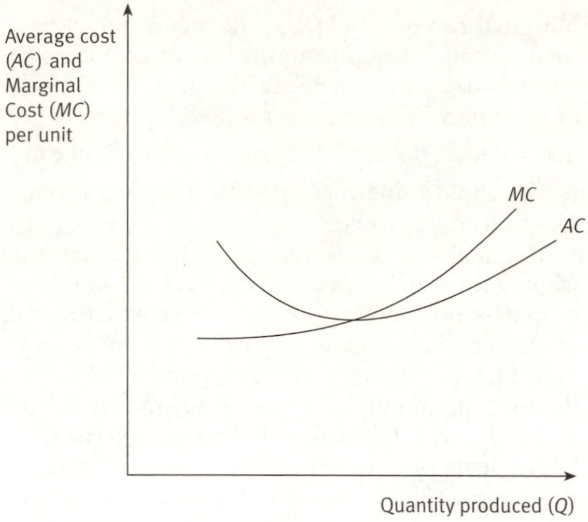

Figure 7.4 The average and marginal cost of the monopolist

we wish to maximize the difference between total revenue and total cost ($R - C$). This will happen only at the point of production where the marginal revenue earned by the firm equals the marginal cost of production ($MR = MC$) and where marginal cost intersects marginal revenue from below. The intuition involved is this. If marginal revenue exceeds marginal cost, then the firm can increase profits by producing and selling more. However, if marginal revenue is less than marginal cost, the firm can do better by reducing output and sales. Only when the two are in balance is profit maximized.

It is important to note at this point that we are not purporting to describe here how exactly a firm determines its price/output in practice. We know that in practice firms may not calculate their marginal costs and revenues for this purpose, although some firms undoubtedly do make very sophisticated calculations for pricing purposes. However, economics is not about describing the actual process by which firms determine their price/output. Economics is about trying to work out where the process of searching for profits might logically lead and deriving a suitable rule for analytical purposes. In practice, the firm's search to maximize profits may involve a search process over time in which the firm can learn from experience what increases profits and what does not. If the firm increases output/sales and this increases profits, then it will continue in this way until it reaches a point where it finds that profits are no longer increasing. At this point, although the firm may not know it, marginal revenue will be equal to marginal cost.

The same distinction can be found for example in psychology. Most of us cross a busy road every day without being aware of the precise mathematical calculations we are making in order to maximize our chances of staying alive. A psychologist, however, might wish to model exactly how we do this in order to derive the precise rules involved which might help, for example, in improving road safety. If a psychologist then told us what these rules were, we would not be very likely to recognize them as such because we are not usually aware of them. But the fact that we manage to cross roads successfully means that we must have learned from experience what improves our chances of success and what worsens them. We are optimizing without being aware of the fact. This is the thinking behind our profit-maximizing rule.

Short-Run Profit-Maximizing Equilibrium of the Monopolist: Properties and Significance

To find the profit-maximizing equilibrium of a monopolist, we combine the information about its revenue and its costs in Figure 7.5. We then use the profit-maximizing rule ($MR = MC$) to find the monopolist's price–output choice. In Figure 7.5 we see that the condition for maximizing profits is true only for output Q*. The profit-maximizing price is then found by determining the price at which this output would sell, which we find from the demand function to be P^*. So $\{Q^*P^*\}$ is the profit-maximizing output–price combination. Note again the point that the monopolist cannot choose what output to produce and what price to set independently. Choosing the profit-maximizing output determines the profit-maximizing price, and vice versa. The monopolist cannot, for example, set a high price and decide to sell a high quantity at that price. The demand curve determines what is an acceptable price–output combination and only one of these combinations will maximize profits.

How much profit is earned by the monopoly firm in this case? The shaded rectangle in Figure 7.5 represents the supernormal or economic profits generated by the firm. The firm's normal profits are included in the average cost curve, as explained previously. The distinction between normal and supernormal profits is explained more fully in Chapter 6. This rectangle is also called monopoly rent because it represents earnings in excess of the opportunity costs of the resources employed to produce the output. From the firm's point of view this is its added value.

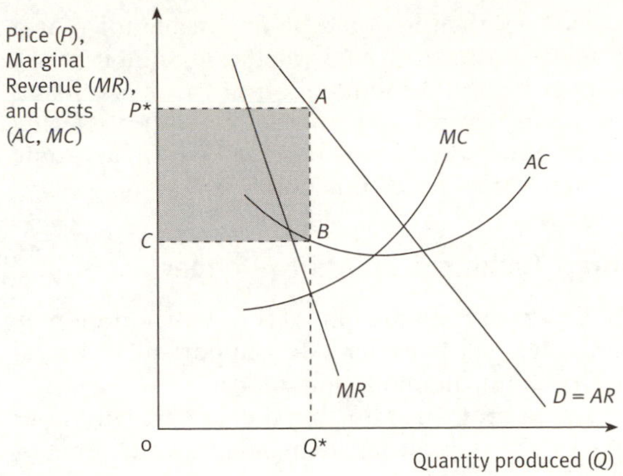

Figure 7.5 The monopolist's profit-maximizing output and price

Examining Figure 7.5 again you can check that the shaded area does indeed correspond to profits by noting:

total profit = total revenue minus total cost

which is

$P^*ABC = P^*AQ^*O$ minus CBQ^*O.

Alternatively, the supernormal profit per unit is given by AB; since total units sold equal CB, total profits must be P^*ACB.

Note, finally, that the price chosen by the monopolist exceeds the marginal cost of production ($P>MC$) and thus it exceeds the price that would be determined by competitive conditions in the long run. Furthermore, the output chosen by the monopolist does not correspond to the output which would minimize average cost as happens under perfect competition. Monopoly works basically by restricting output below the competitive industry level and raising prices above the competitive industry level. This is what enables the monopolist to generate positive economic profits.

Before we go any further, let us make a crucial point about monopoly profit. There is no guarantee that a monopolistic firm can make positive profits just because it is a monopolist. We have shown a representative case but whether profits are possible depends on the relative positions of the cost and revenue curves. Clearly, if at all output levels, AC

exceeds *AR* then it would be impossible for a firm to make positive profits, whether or not it was a monopolist. So a monopoly firm can make losses despite its control over price and even if it is being run as efficiently as possible. See Box 7.1 for some further discussion of this point.

Three Technical Points to Ponder

To finish our discussion of the basic monopoly model we will consider a few important technical points about the monopoly model.

First, a profit-maximizing monopolist will never operate at a point where demand is inelastic, that is, where elasticity is less than one. The monopoly price must always be at a point on the demand function where demand is elastic. Why is this? The reason is that profit maximization requires that marginal revenue equals marginal costs. Since marginal cost must be positive the marginal revenue must be positive, when the firm is maximizing profits. If marginal revenue is positive, then demand must be elastic. Refer back to Figure 7.2 to see the relationship between elasticity and marginal revenue. This suggests that if we observe a monopolist operating at a price where demand is inelastic, either the firm is not a monopolist at all or it is not a profit maximizer. There is good evidence, for example, that the demand for oil products in the USA is inelastic at current prices. It is further claimed that US oil companies act together, or collude, to set a monopoly price (we explain collu-

Box 7.1 Monopoly Losses

A common error concerning monopoly is the belief that a monopoly position guarantees profits, as the firm can charge any price it wishes. It is true that a monopolist can set the price at any level it wishes (unless of course there is state regulation of prices). However, as we have explained, the firm cannot sell as much output as it likes at this price. What it can sell will be determined by the demand function. Profits will then be determined by the relationship between demand conditions and costs conditions.

It is quite possible, therefore, for a monopoly to incur losses even if it is trying to maximize its profits (that is, setting *MC* to equal *MR*), if costs are 'too high' or demand is 'too low' or some combination of these. This is illustrated in Figure 7.6.

Railway companies in many parts of the world are monopolies but this does not guarantee any profits, still less supernormal profits. Demand is generally lower than the system was created to serve and this means costs exceed revenues. Note, however, that if a loss-making rail company was able to apply perfect price discrimination (this concept is explained later) it might be able to make a profit despite the unpromising relation between its costs and revenues.

Another example is the Anglo-French Channel Tunnel. Because of the very high fixed costs involved in building the tunnel, average costs are very high in relation to demand and the operating company finds it difficult, despite its monopoly and despite making great efforts, to make any profit. Note, however, that this only applies as long as the enterprise which built the Channel Tunnel stays in control of it. If the enterprise were to be made bankrupt, its main asset, the tunnel, could be sold to another business which would not be saddled

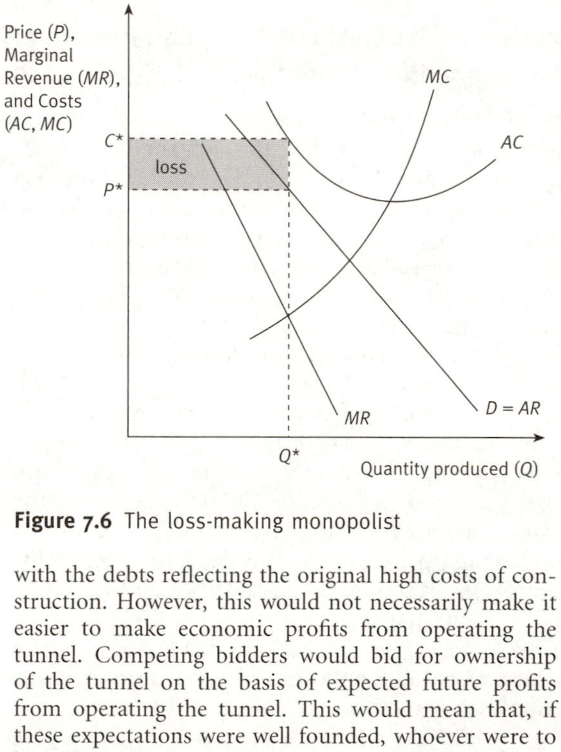

Figure 7.6 The loss-making monopolist

with the debts reflecting the original high costs of construction. However, this would not necessarily make it easier to make economic profits from operating the tunnel. Competing bidders would bid for ownership of the tunnel on the basis of expected future profits from operating the tunnel. This would mean that, if these expectations were well founded, whoever were to buy the tunnel would pay a price which properly reflected the discounted value of these future profits. And if someone was over-optimistic about potential future profits, they might even pay too much for the tunnel and find that the monopoly did not pay. We discuss this again later.

sion in the next chapter). Therefore it looks as if either the estimates of demand elasticity are wrong or that the collusion is unsuccessful or that the colluders are not very good at arithmetic.

Secondly, the extent to which price diverges from cost in the monopoly model will depend on the value of elasticity of demand at the monopoly price. As you might expect intuitively if the demand is very elastic at the monopoly price, for example it equals 4, the price–cost margin will be thin. If, however, demand is much less elastic, say it equals 1.5, then price will diverge more from costs. In fact it is possible to derive the following result (note again we refer to the numerical value of e and ignore the negative sign):

$$(P - MC)/P = 1/e.$$

Thirdly, there is no supply curve under monopoly, that is, there is no function which tells you exactly how much will be supplied at each price. The concept of supply in economics, concerning an unambiguous relationship between the price and the quantity offered for supply, is well defined only in the case of perfect competition where the individual firm is a price taker and the firm's marginal cost function indicates its willingness to supply at a particular market price. Under monopoly, the firm decides how much to produce and the demand function decides the price at which this may be sold, or the firm chooses its price and the demand function decides the quantity to be sold at this price. The firm is no longer a price taker, it is now a price maker. It is therefore no longer possible to derive a precise one-to-one relationship which tells us how much will be supplied at a particular price.

The everyday meaning of 'supply', as opposed to the economic concept of supply, refers to the industry's capacity to produce (its supply potential). But to an economist, supply is not about the capacity to produce, it is about the willingness to produce as the market price varies. Firms may have the capacity to produce but choose not to because prices are 'too soft' and they cannot make any profit. The capacity to produce and the willingness to produce are thus two different things. The firm's existing capacity to produce is the result of past decisions, based on expected costs and revenues, but its current decision about how much to produce depends on its current marginal cost and marginal revenue. These might dictate an output which is near to current capacity or less than current capacity.

7.3 Looking at the Level of Monopoly Profits

Our analysis so far has suggested that it is potentially profitable to be a monopolist. However, any particular monopolist can in fact be even more profitable than the basic analysis suggests, or indeed less profitable, depending on a number of factors which we shall now consider. First, we shall look at how a monopolist might increase the level of profits being generated through policies such as price discrimination and advertising, and then we shall examine factors which might reduce the level of monopoly profits below the supernormal level predicted by the basic model.

Price Discrimination

It is possible for a monopolist to increase its profits by using a technique known as price discrimination. Price discrimination is formally defined as a situation where different customers are charged different prices for the same good or service for reasons which are not related to the cost of provision. The definition is important because it tells us that not all instances of firms charging different prices for the same commodity are instances of price discrimination. Thus it often happens that companies charge different prices to different customers for reasons which are in fact related to the cost of provision and this would therefore not be what we have in mind as price discrimination. For example, electricity companies often charge more for electricity at peak consumption times of the day to reflect the fact that the marginal cost of producing for peak loads is higher than normal. This is because older, less efficient generators are usually brought on stream at peak times and so the marginal cost of production increases.

However, if electricity companies had a policy of charging householders in middle-class areas a higher price than householders in other areas at the same time of the day, then this would be an attempt at price discrimination. I say an attempt because, as we shall see, whilst price discrimination is generally good for profits and therefore worth trying it is not always easy to achieve and so it does not always happen. Let us see first what the attractions might be for a firm in using price discrimination.

If we simplify and redraw the monopoly model as in Figure 7.7, we can explain the attractions of price discrimination. (Note we simplify by assuming constant long-run costs for the monopolist so that average costs and marginal costs merge.)

Note first that the consumer's willingness to pay for a particular unit of product is given by the demand function whilst the producer's costs are given by the cost function. Note that for any particular unit of output up to the point where the demand function intersects the cost function, the consumer's willingness to pay exceeds the costs of production for that unit. In other words, the consumer values that unit of output more highly than the cost of producing it. Therefore, if we added up the difference between the consumer's willingness to pay and the firm's cost of production for each unit of output, we would get an area given by the triangle *xyz* in Figure 7.7. Economists call this area consumer surplus because if price was set at the level of costs in this market (*P*=*AC*), then consumers would appropriate a considerable surplus because they would be getting the output involved for far less than they would be willing to pay for it.

We have shown in Chapter 6 how competition drives prices down to cost levels. Another way of saying this is that, under competitive conditions, consumers benefit from the appropriability of available consumer surplus. Now look at what happens to consumer surplus under monopoly conditions. We explained above how the monopolist is able to earn positive profits by restricting output and keeping prices above costs. The source of these monopoly profits is now evident. Monopoly allows the firm to capture, or appropriate, a significant proportion of the available consumer surplus as represented by the shaded monopoly profits rectangle in Figure 7.7.

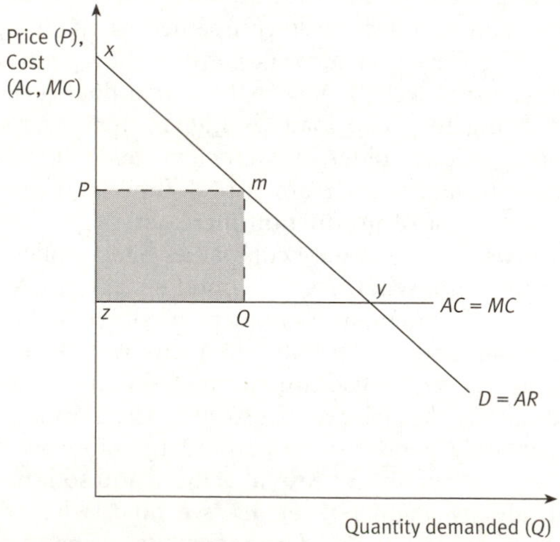

Figure 7.7 Perfect price discrimination and consumer surplus

Now note a crucial point: monopoly captures some of the available consumer surplus but not all of it. There is still a lot of consumer surplus left uncaptured by the monopolist, and the question thus arises for the monopolist: how can we capture even more of the available surplus? The answer is, it is possible to capture more surplus if it is possible to use the technique called price discrimination. That is, if the monopolist can charge different consumers different prices instead of charging all consumers exactly the same price.

Consider first the most extreme case conceivable which economists call perfect price discrimination. Let us say that a monopolist is able to sell each individual unit produced at the maximum price a consumer is willing to pay for that unit. Imagine, for example, that you had all the tickets for the soccer World Cup final and that to maximize your profits you intend to sell them one by one according to the maximum willingness to pay of each supporter who comes along. If this were possible, you would make a great deal of money, far more than could be made by selling the tickets at a single monopoly price level. You would be able to capture all the available consumer surplus rather than just some of it. Of course this would be difficult to achieve, for reasons we shall explore below, but the attractions of such price discrimination are evident.

Now consider a less extreme scenario: less than perfect price discrimination. Let us be realistic and say that the monopolist is unable to find out the maximum price each consumer is willing to pay for a ticket. However, the monopolist is aware that Italian supporters have a much higher willingness to pay than Brazilian supporters and that Brazilians are prepared to pay more than neutral supporters. There are thus three distinct markets for tickets rather than just one in which to try to maximize profits. So the monopolist charges a high price for a blue ticket, a medium price for a gold ticket, and a low price for a white ticket to reflect different demand conditions in each sub-market. This is less profitable than perfect price discrimination but more profitable than no price discrimination at all.

Think of the possibilities: pay-as-you-view television programmes where each viewer pays a price which reflects her maximum willingness to pay; paying for electricity to reflect your individual willingness to pay; telephone call charges which are higher for women than for men; train fares which are high for non-car owners and low for car owners; the price of a pint of Guinness set according to the accent of the customer.

The attractions of price discrimination are evident. So shall we always observe price discrimination in practice? No, for reasons which readers should be starting to identify already. First, it is not always easy to separate markets into distinct sub-markets according to differences in the willingness to pay. It may be possible to do this in principle but it will not necessarily be cheap to do so. The knowledge required is unlikely to be free or easy to obtain. You would need good information about the level of demand and demand elasticity in each sub-market which would require some research, and the costs would increase depending on the number of sub-markets to be considered. A crucial point to recognize here is that it is not going to be in the interests of consumers to reveal the necessary information about their willingness to pay for individual units of output. It would evidently not be in the interests of women to reveal that they are willing to pay more for a telephone call than men or for Italians to reveal how keen they are to buy a ticket for the World Cup final. People are able to work out that revealing exactly how much they would pay for a particular unit of output is an invitation to be charged that amount. Auction markets work in a way which forces people to gradually reveal their true valuations, but of course it is not easy to sell train tickets or telephone calls by auction.

The second reason why successful price discrimination is difficult in practice is arbitrage. Successful price discrimination requires that it is not possible to trade between the different sub-markets. That is, it is not possible for those who purchase in the low-price segment to resell to those in the high-price segment of the market. If it is possible, people will observe the potential for making a profit by buying units in the cheap segment and reselling them in the expensive one. For example, to continue our earlier example, neutral supporters could buy tickets at a low price and resell them to Italian supporters at a higher price. This, of course, would lead to a change in demand for tickets by neutrals and a change in supply of tickets to Italians and would tend to bring prices into line. (You might correctly observe that an even more likely outcome in this case would be for Italians to pretend that they were neutrals.) Similarly men could buy lots of telephone lines and resell them to women. To prevent arbitrage from spoiling the advantages of price discrimination, producers have to monitor and enforce the separation of markets which will raise their costs and reduce the net benefits of discrimination.

Overall, therefore, we can say that price discrimination is an attractive proposition for firms with market power in principle, but that there are important factors which significantly limit its success in practice. In particular, it might be too costly to identify separate groups of customers according to their willingness to pay and it might be costly to prevent arbitrage between the groups. Overall, we can say that when the benefits involved exceed the costs then firms will exercise price discrimination.

Advertising and Product Variety

It is possible for a monopolist to increase its profits by advertising and/or increasing product variety although there will be limits to this. We look first at advertising. You might consider, if a firm is a monopolist, that it will not be worth while advertising because it already has the whole market at its mercy and there are no rivals to worry about. This, however, is not the case. A monopolist may find it worthwhile to advertise if advertising can increase its revenues by more than it increases its costs. Advertising will certainly increase the firm's costs: first, because of the cost of advertising itself; secondly because if advertising leads to extra sales, it will need to produce extra units of output. The question is by how much can the firm increase its revenues. It can do this by shifting the demand curve outwards and possibly by making it less elastic.

Recall that the demand curve we normally draw is a relationship between price and output, holding other things constant. One of these other things is advertising. Advertising therefore is a shift variable, that is, something which if it changes will shift the demand curve from one position to another. A shift in demand will enable the monopolist to increase its sales revenue. What a profit-maximizing monopolist will wish to achieve is a level of advertising where the marginal revenue from additional advertising equals the marginal cost involved (including the increasing production costs, of course). For any particular monopolist, this might involve a low or a high level of advertising. There is no single answer that will apply to all markets. A producer of electricity might not find advertising very useful but a lottery company might find it very worthwhile. It depends on the responsiveness of demand to advertising inputs.

The same is true of increasing product variety. A monopolist may well find it profitable to produce a range of products rather than a single version of its product. Thus a cigarette producer may find it worthwhile to produce several different blends, for example, a strong and a weak blend, in order to appeal to different types of consumers rather than producing a single blend which appeals to the average consumer but not to those with a strong preference for strong or weak blends. Similarly, a soap powder producer might find it worthwhile to produce a machine-wash blend and a hand-wash blend. Of course, increasing variety will involve increasing production and marketing costs, so once again it is a matter of ensuring that what the firm does increases its revenues more than it adds to its costs. In other words, the firm should increase outlays on increasing variety until the marginal revenue generated equals the marginal costs involved, or at least it should approach such a position. Therefore it might prove profitable for our cigarette producer to have three blends but not profitable to have four. Rational profit-maximizing producers will generally not supply a demand for variety unless this can be done economically.

There may be other attractions for the monopolist related to advertising and/or increased product variety. These activities may help the monopolist to build barriers to entry and thus to sustain profits over a longer period of time. For example, advertising can be used to build brand-names which newcomers find difficult to overcome and product variety can also create difficulties for potential entrants. We shall discuss these possibilities more fully below.

Problems for the Monopolist which might Reduce Monopoly Profits

There are several reasons why monopoly profits might be lower than the level predicted by the standard model of monopoly. Let us consider some of these.

First, consider regulation by the state. It is common in many countries such as the UK for the state to take action to control the behaviour of monopolists. The state might wish to control the exercise of monopoly power because, whilst monopoly is good for the monopolist, it is not so good for the consumer and society in general. The reasoning behind this is discussed more fully in Chapter 13. In the UK each of the privatized public utilities, such as telecoms and electricity, are regulated by state bodies in an effort to ensure that they do not exploit their market power to the full or act so as to make entry difficult. Bodies such as OFTEL (Telecoms), OFFER (Electricity), and OFGAS can limit the prices of the privatized companies and can act to encourage new competition in the industry, for example, by forcing incumbents such as British Gas to allow entrants access to the gas pipeline supply network at a reasonable price. It may be said fairly categorically that, in the absence of regulation, companies such as British Gas and British Telecom would be significantly more profitable than they are.

Secondly, consider the cost of 'buying' the monopoly. In some cases, the right to operate a monopoly is sold by the state to a private firm. The private firm is granted a franchise to operate as a monopoly in a particular activity for a particular period of time. A good example of this is Britain's national lottery company, Camelot, and Britain's commercial television companies such as Thames and Granada. These franchises are potentially very profitable, a licence to print money, as the late Lord Thomson admitted. However, this need not be the case. If the state is sensible, it will open such franchises to a competitive bidding process in order to appropriate as much as possible of the potential profit for itself. Private companies such as Camelot bid for a franchise against one another and so bid the price up to a realistic level. If the potential profitability of the monopoly is well known in advance, then the winning bid is likely to be such that the state appropriates all the available supernormal profits and the operator is left to earn only normal profits. However, if there is uncertainty about the profit potential of the franchise, things are more difficult. One possibility is that the winning company bids too much for the franchise and cannot operate at a profit. Economists call this the winner's curse. In practice, we would observe a monopoly losing money. We observed such an example earlier: the company which won the right to build and operate the Channel Tunnel. Another possibility is that the winning company bids too little and is then able to earn monopoly profits for the period of the franchise. Since bidders generally underestimated the potential profits of the lottery franchise, Camelot acquired its monopoly relatively cheaply and will earn supernormal profits until its franchise comes up for renewal. The cost of 'buying' a monopoly is a good example of what we shall refer to later, in Chapter 10, as '*ex ante* competition' for the monopoly position and how, in general, competition to achieve a monopoly position can reduce the profits of the business that achieves the monopoly.

Thirdly, a lack of competition can take the edge off incentives in a business and reduce the desire to search for profits. A monopolist by definition does not have to worry about being pushed out of a market if it fails to minimize its costs. Costs could increase substantially and cut into profits without worrying the monopolist too much. The monopolist has a big cushion of profits to fall back on. As a result, it is unlikely that a monopolist will seek to control costs as hard as it might or to innovate as often as it should. If managers take life a bit easier and workers indulge in extra tea breaks, if salaries and wages are a bit higher than the going rates, this might be seen as just spreading the monopoly jam a little more widely. And given that profits are often highly taxed, the company may feel even less inclined to act. Therefore the published level of profits for a monopolist might be significantly less than the actual level because some of the profits are being appropriated by other members of the organization.

Fourthly, there is the question of managerial control and objectives. As we shall discuss fully in Chapter 12, the modern business corporation is characterized by a separation between ownership and control. The owners no longer control the business on a day-to-day basis and the managers who do control the business no longer have a significant ownership stake. It is argued that managers might wish to pursue objectives which differ from maximizing profits; objectives such as growth. If pursuing growth conflicts with the search for profits (and it can, as we explain in Chapter 12), then managerial control of monopolies will cause them to earn lower profits. Once again, the observed profits of monopoly will be lower than the potential level.

Fifthly, there is the countervailing power of suppliers and customers. In our analysis of monopoly we implicitly assumed that the monopolist bought its inputs in competitive markets and sold to many customers. But what if the monopoly bought inputs from a monopoly supplier or sold its output to a single customer? This would make life very complicated both for the monopoly and for economic theory. Economists examine such situations under the heading of bilateral monopoly, but the analysis is rather too complex to go into here. However, we can state the conclusion of the analysis. When there is a situation of bilateral monopoly, the outcome is indeterminate. The selling monopoly wants to charge its profit-maximizing price but the buying monopoly (or monopsonist) wants to buy at the lowest possible price, which is the competitive price. We cannot say a priori which monopoly, the seller or the buyer, will capture the potential profits involved. It depends essentially on the distribution of bargaining power. However, in general, if a monopolist faces a powerful supplier of a key input or a powerful buyer of its output, it is unlikely to be able to ensure that it earns maximum monopoly profits. Some of its profits will be appropriated by the buyers and/or the sellers involved.

Finally, consider the durability problem. If we examine the basic monopoly model, we see that the monopolist has a dilemma. Its profit-maximizing output choice allows it to earn positive profits but not to capture all the available consumer surplus. The fact is that, once the monopolist has sold the profit-maximizing output, it has an incentive to reduce its prices and sell extra units to those consumers who will not pay the monopoly price. In a sense, the monopolist has an incentive to renege on its own monopoly price. Now this will not matter to a monopolist who sells a product where demand renews itself each period. For example, it will not matter much to a baker or a burger seller. But if the monopolist sells a durable product which lasts for several periods, then a problem arises.

Let us assume the monopolist produces tractors. In the first period the situation is given by Figure 7.8. The monopolist in the first period sets price and output to maximize profits as usual. But the people who buy these tractors in the first period are now out of the market because the product lasts for more than a period and in the next period demand for tractors shifts to the left. You should be able to demonstrate then that prices must fall in the second period. (The demand function shifts to the left,

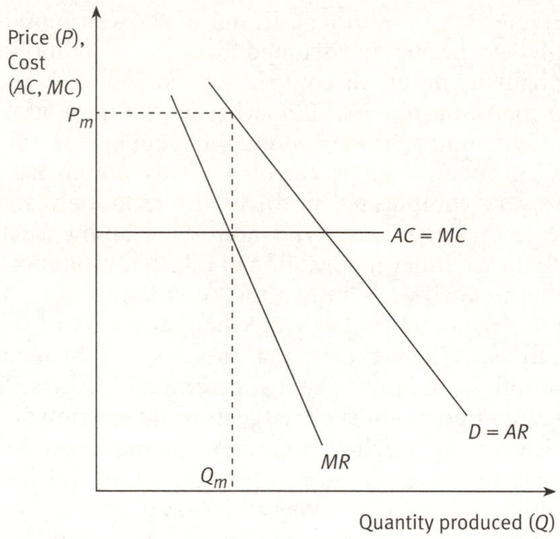

Figure 7.8 The case of durability

so does marginal revenue, and the new profit-maximizing equilibrium is at a lower price.) Now consider this question. If you are a potential buyer and you know that prices will be lower next period than they are today, will you buy a tractor in the first period? Possibly not. The knowledge that prices will fall over time will affect consumer behaviour and make life more difficult for the monopolist who sells a durable product. The monopoly price may be said to lack credibility. This, in fact, is said to be the reason why companies like Xerox and IBM preferred to lease their durable products in the 1970s rather than selling them outright. There was no incentive to reduce lease prices once set at the monopoly level because to do so would have meant reducing lease prices for existing as well as new leases. So the lease price had greater credibility than the price of selling outright and customers had no reason to postpone leasing in the hope of lease prices falling.

7.4 Sustaining Monopoly Power and Profits

The Nature and Significance of Barriers to Entry

The profits generated by a successful monopoly present an attractive target for outsiders keen to shift resources to areas promising above-normal returns. If this happens, if new firms are able to enter the industry, then monopoly profits are reduced and industry profits will be driven lower, perhaps even to zero (we discussed this case in the previous chapter). The crucial determinant of monopoly power and profit is therefore whatever prevents outsiders from challenging this situation. For obvious reasons, we refer to what stops outsiders from entering the monopolized industry as barriers to entry. It is time to take a closer look at these.

Consider the point of view of someone outside the monopolized industry. The outsider has to consider not just the current attractive level of industry profits but the profit potential of an actual entrant. That is, the outsider has to consider this question: what are the chances that I can earn supernormal profits if I set up a new business to compete with the incumbent business? We can say that barriers to entry exist if a potential entrant calculates that it cannot in fact expect to capture a share of the supernormal profits available, or that it might do so but only at an unacceptable level of risk, and so stays out.

Of course, this means that it is very likely to be in the interest of incumbents to actively invest in building barriers to entry as a strategic response to the possibility of entry and we would therefore expect to see monopolists behaving in this way. However, not all barriers to entry are the result of strategic actions by incumbents. Some are more fortuitous in nature, the result of structural factors rather than deliberate actions. Other barriers are a mixture of both structural and strategic factors. We shall consider some of the possibilities.

Scale as a Barrier to Entry

A potential entrant often faces a dilemma concerning the scale at which to enter. It might calculate as follows: if I enter on a large scale I risk 'spoiling the market' by increasing supply substantially, causing prices to fall and squeezing industry profits to unattractive levels, thus making entry unprofitable. In addition, entry on a large scale is likely to be more difficult to finance because it is riskier. Therefore it might be better to enter on a small scale and avoid these problems. This would indeed be a reasonable calculation except where economies of scale are important. In an industry characterized by strong scale economies, a firm producing on a small scale suffers a major cost disadvantage

Box 7.2 Some examples and evidence on monopoly profits

The founder of the Thomson Organisation, the Canadian Roy Thomson, was one of the first people to buy a commercial television franchise in the UK in the 1950s. This franchise gave the owner the sole right to broadcast commercial television programmes and advertising in a defined area, in Thomson's case Scotland. Owing to good luck, a good understanding of the value of market power, or exemplary foresight these franchises were bought at a relatively low price and as a consequence generated very high profits for their owners. Thomson became famous for describing his franchise as a 'government licence to print money'. Subsequently, of course, once the value of these franchises had been established, there was greater competition for the franchises when they came up for renewal and lower profits for the franchise owners.

Another licence to print money would appear to be the licence purchased by the Rank Organisation in Britain in 1956 which gave it the exclusive rights to make and sell a product recently developed after many years research in the USA. The product was called 'indirect electrostatic reprographic equipment', or photocopying, which was developed and patented by Xerox. The licence gave the British company, renamed Rank Xerox, the rights to make and sell Xerox equipment outside the USA. Rank Xerox subsequently became extremely profitable, as of course did Xerox itself in the USA, and it was the subject of an investigation by the UK Monopolies and Mergers Commission (MMC) in 1976.

Rank Xerox certainly was a firm with monopoly power: at one time it had held 100 per cent of the market although this had fallen to 90 per cent by the time of the investigation as other companies began to work around Xerox patents. There were substitute products but these were judged by the commission to be 'not very close'. And there were barriers to entry in the form of patents (Xerox had 677 patents registered in the UK), first-mover advantages, and the established Xerox brand which had become synonymous with photocopying. The MMC investigated Rank Xerox's profits and produced a comparison between these and the average level of profitability in UK manufacturing industry. This is reproduced in Figure 7.9. Note how the average level of profits for Rank Xerox was almost three times the UK average during the period considered, when the monopoly was most secure. Of course the Rank Xerox monopoly did not last for ever. Patents expired, other manufacturers appeared, and Rank Xerox lost market share gradually into the 1980s and its profits declined substantially. The high profits of the good years had also made Rank Xerox less assiduous than it should have been about controlling its cost base and this also caused profits to decline. But for a time, Rank Xerox was a very profitable company indeed.

There are many other examples in the cases of dominant firms (although not quite strictly defined monopolies) studied by the MMC over the years of what might be construed as monopoly profits or the profits

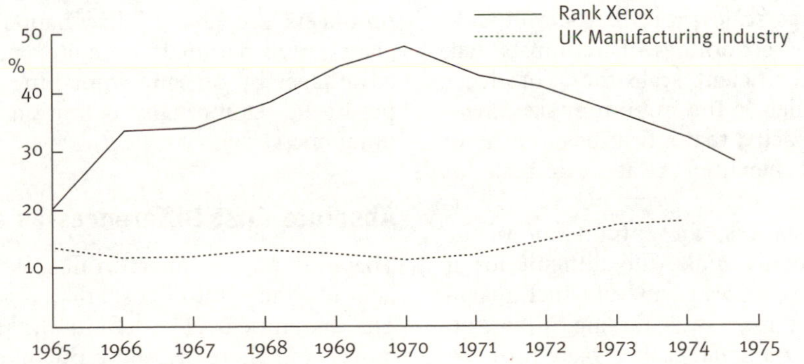

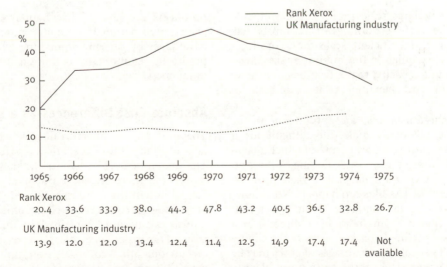

	1965	1966	1967	1968	1969	1970	1971	1972	1973	1974	1975
Rank Xerox	20.4	33.6	33.9	38.0	44.3	47.8	43.2	40.5	36.5	32.8	26.7
UK Manufacturing industry	13.9	12.0	12.0	13.4	12.4	11.4	12.5	14.9	17.4	17.4	Not available

Figure 7.9 Comparison of Rank Xerox's return on capital employed in its UK reference business with the return on capital employed in UK manufacturing industry

Source: Monopolies and Mergers Commission, (1976).

Box 7.2 continued

of market power. Examples of cases where profits were over twice the average level for large industrial companies were as follows: colour film (Kodak), household detergents (Proctor and Gamble), breakfast cereals (Kellogg), salt (British Salt), tampons (Tambrands), cat and dog food (Pedigree), anti-depressants (Hoffman La Roche), roofing tiles (Marley), contraceptives (London Rubber), and electrical equipment for vehicles (Champion).

There are also signs of companies seeking to use price discrimination and advertising/product variety as ways of boosting profits: Rank Xerox, Proctor and Gamble, Hoffman La Roche, Birds Eye, Rank Xerox, British Plasterboard, London Brick, London Rubber, Metal Box, and British Oxygen. However it has to be said that in the majority of dominant firm investigations excess profits were not found and this may reflect one or more of the factors discussed above which can make life harder for a monopolist in practice than in theory. For example, the countervailing power of buyers, durability, the disincentive effects of monopoly leading to cost escalation, and managerial choices. Alternatively, it could reflect an absence of serious barriers to entry of the type discussed in the section 7.4. Finally, it could reflect the presence of significant rivals and oligopolistic competition as examined in the next chapter.

It is also evident in the history of public monopolies in the UK that firms with what appears to be substantial monopoly power may fail to generate any economic profits. Whether this was a product of bad luck (declining industry case such as railways or coal) or bad management (electricity, telecoms, airlines) or a result of government failure to set clear objectives is arguable. It is certainly the case in some of these industries that, since privatization, profit rates have increased substantially and this appears to have had a lot to do with decreasing costs rather than increasing prices. This suggests that some of these industries did behave like monopolies when it came to pricing but that they lost control of their costs because of a lack of competitive pressure and a lack of pressure from owners for good dividends.

In the USA, studies of firms with substantial market power, such as IBM and Boeing and AT&T, show these firms to be earning good profits but at perhaps a lower level than their market power would suggest is possible. According to Shepherd (1990), the reasons for this lie in the tendency of monopoly firms to lose the incentive to control costs and to innovate. In addition he also suggests that these firms may have used some of the profits earned in areas which they monopolized to diversify into areas where they were relatively unsuccessful. This is something we come back to in our discussion of diversification in Chapter 11. It might also be the case, although Shepherd does not suggest this, that countervailing power and durability have been problems for some of these firms.

compared with large-scale producers simply as a result of the scale economies. Economists talk about a minimum efficient scale for a producer (see Chapter 5) which is the minimum size, measured in output capacity, that a firm has to achieve to avoid any cost penalties related to scale of operations.

In these circumstances, the entrant knows the incumbent could easily make life difficult for it after entry by cutting prices to a level which makes the entrant unprofitable, thus forcing it to exit. This makes entry on a small scale a risky proposition and therefore less likely to happen. Note, however, that we are talking here about an entrant wishing to challenge an incumbent directly in a particular well-defined market such as the family car market. The scale disadvantages of entry may be overcome to some extent if the entrant can identify a niche market within the mass market where consumers are prepared to pay a higher price for something specialized. Thus many small-scale car producers are able to live happily alongside the giant multinationals despite huge scale disadvantages by offering something which the mass producers cannot by definition offer: product uniqueness.

Absolute Cost Differences as a Barrier

There are reasons apart from scale why an incumbent may have lower costs than a potential entrant. The incumbent, by definition, has been a first mover and there are some potential advantages in this, although there are risks as well. The existence of an experience effect is well documented in many industries and was explained in our chapter on costs. The experience effect means basically that certain operating costs fall over time as workers, managers, and engineers learn more about the product and the production process and as a result become more efficient. For example, an incumbent firm involved in the production of computer chips will have come across and solved a myriad of problems involved in this complex process. To the extent that the knowledge so acquired is difficult to acquire other than by direct experience, a potential entrant has no option but to go through this learning process for itself. It can not buy learning off the shelf or obtain it from a manual. This means that the incumbent has a built-in cost advantage over an entrant until the entrant has time to catch up on this learning process, by which time, of course, the incumbent will have moved further down the experience curve. Once again the entrant has to take into account the possibility that, whilst it is trying to get established, the incumbent could cut prices to a level at which the entrant is unable to make any money. Of course, the incumbent might not necessarily do this in practice, but the possibility might be enough to discourage entry. There is case-study evidence of this effect in many industries: titanium oxide, disposable nappies, commercial aircraft, and synthetic fibres.

Note, however, that not all first movers gain in this way. It is not unknown for pioneers to demonstrate the existence of a new market and to bear the risks involved only to fail to capitalize on these efforts, or else to make strategic errors, and be swept aside by more timid followers. The case of Apple springs to mind here but the most quoted example of this phenomenon is the successful development of the body scanner by the British company EMI. In these cases, first-mover advantage proved to be no advantage at all.

Patent Protection

Learning is not the only advantage in moving first. First movers are often able to obtain patents for a product or production process which potential entrants have to find a way around. This is not always impossible, as is evident in the pharmaceutical industry where it is sometimes possible to design a copy-cat drug without infringing existing patents. However, the need to find a way around existing patents raises entry costs, and risks, and thus must affect the entrant's calculations. Incumbents can of course be more or less aggressive when it comes to protecting their patents. Some firms appear to deliberately develop a reputation for the aggressive pursuit of patent infringement, even when the infringement is minor or arguable, simply to discourage potential entrants by tying them up in lengthy court battles. For example, Intel has been accused of pursuing such a strategy to defend its dominance in the microchip market (see Jackson (1997) for a detailed account). Other firms pursue a strategy of licensing patents, although they might take care to build into the licensing agreement a clause which keeps competitors away from what they regard as their home market. Thus Pilkington licensed its float glass technology around the world but, it is said, only on the understanding that the British market was not invaded.

Buyer Switching Costs

Entrants by definition have to win customers from the incumbent, and incumbent firms may obtain an advantage if customers face significant switching costs in moving to a rival. For example, many PC users are now so used to Microsoft products that switching to an alternative product would create significant costs for them. An entrant in this case would have to offer something, not only comparable to or slightly cheaper than the incumbent product, but significantly superior to make the switch worthwhile. Some firms deliberately try to raise switching costs for consumers by offering schemes such as frequent flier programmes and loyalty cards.

Licenses and Exclusive Franchises

A potential entrant will find it difficult to enter a market where the incumbent has been given sole licence to operate or an exclusive franchise. For some activities, such as running a national lottery or commercial broadcasting, operators need a state licence. The licence generally confers monopoly power upon the operator for a fixed period, say ten years, and excludes new entrants. Private companies sometimes offer exclusive franchises also. A car producer, for example, may offer an exclusive right to sell and repair its products in a defined area to a single company. An airport may offer the right to run a taxi service from its property to a single operator.

Of course, you may well have noticed that in such cases the potential monopoly profits do not necessarily accrue to the licence holder. They will at least partly, and perhaps fully, be appropriated by those with the power to sell the licence. The British government, for example, appropriates a sizeable proportion of the profits of the lottery operator Camelot and the commercial television providers in Britain because the licences are now the subject of a competitive bidding process. This raises the possibility that the franchisee can bid too much for its exclusive rights and, despite its monopoly, end up losing money. Economists even have a name for this: the winner's curse. It should also be noted that a franchisee in this position cannot just raise its prices to make even more monopoly profits. The maximum profits available to a monopolist are determined by the relevant cost and demand conditions and these are not changed by the need to meet the cost of its exclusive licence to operate.

You may also have noticed that the franchise holder is likely to build up important advantages during the franchise period, such as learning, which makes the next round of the bidding process more difficult for newcomers. It should therefore in principle be able to offer more than a newcomer to win the licence again. In other words, it builds barriers to entry against competitive bidders for its franchise which enables it to appropriate more of the available profits.

Control of Key Inputs or Technologies

Airlines need airports and ferry companies need berthing facilities. There is, however, a limited capacity at airports and seaports especially at peak times of the day or the year and these are generally taken up by existing companies with long-term contracts. New companies wishing to enter this market are thus at a disadvantage if they have to land their passengers at less popular or less convenient ports or airports. For example, the 1989 Monopolies Commission report argued that a new entrant was finding it difficult to challenge the dominance of P&O and Sealink in the cross-channel market because these companies operated from the most popular port, Dover, which did not have room for another operator. The entrant had to operate from Ramsgate and as a consequence found it difficult to become established. Note again, however, that if the owners of Dover port were aware of their market power they should have been able to appropriate a significant share of the ferry operator's profits for themselves in this case and therefore the Monopolies Commission should probably have been investigating Dover's market power rather than that of the ferry companies.

Another example of this type of barrier arises in vertically integrated industries, such as gas, when there is only one transmission or distribution network in existence which is owned and operated by the dominant supplier. Independent gas suppliers might wish to enter the market but cannot do so because the dominant company owns the road to the customer and even if it cannot prevent other companies from using the road, it can set prices for using it at uneconomic levels for the independents. The Monopolies Commission was of the view that British Gas had acted in this way. British Gas has now been forced by the gas industry regulator (OFGAS) to allow gas suppliers to use its pipelines at an economic rate.

Finally, as we observed above, patents give companies certain control over the use of their own innovations. If companies choose not to license a successful new production process to entrants, then these entrants are going to find it hard to compete with the innovator on equal terms unless they can come up with something better. In some circumstances, of course, licensing might be the shrewd decision because this reduces the number of people looking for something even better. Imagine where Apple would be today if it had chosen to license its innovative graphical interface technology rather than giving Microsoft the incentive to develop Windows.

Making the Industry Less Attractive

An incumbent will appreciate that it can act deliberately to discourage entry by making entry seem less attractive to outsiders whilst keeping the industry attractive to the incumbent. An obvious way of doing this, although not necessarily a sensible one, would be to cut prices below the profit-maximizing level and thus reduce the level of profits available to an entrant. This is not necessarily sensible for the following reason.

What is the point of deliberately reducing your profits before entry happens just in case that might happen? The time to think about cutting your prices is probably after entry happens when you can calculate an optimal strategy for dealing with the entrant. You might cut prices at this point and try to force the entrant out with big losses to bear which will make other entrants think even harder about entry. Alternatively, you might decide that you can live with the entrant as long as you can reach an agreement not to compete too hard and squeeze one another's profits. As we shall see in the next chapter, oligopolists can co-operate to keep industry price at a profitable level, assuming there is no further entry. They do not necessarily have to cut each other's throat.

Making Entry even More Risky

Of course, an even better (that is, more profitable) strategy for the incumbent than either pre-emptive price cutting or post-entry price cutting might simply be to advertise the strong likelihood that an entrant will be met with aggressive price cuts and squeezed out. This has the advantage of being considerably cheaper than actually having to cut your prices to discourage entry. Note, however, that such a strategy would be illegal under the anti-trust rules in certain countries. All this strategy requires is a reputation for aggressive behaviour towards entrants. How might an incumbent achieve this effectively?

The secret is credibility. Obviously an incumbent could threaten to blow up an entrant's new plant, but in most countries this threat would lack credibility. The fact is that most incumbents are unlikely to go this far to discourage entry. However, an incumbent with a cost advantage, or deep pockets, can sustain prices at a low enough level to squeeze the entrant without bankrupting itself. Therefore an incumbent with a cost advantage, or deep pockets, has more credibility than one that does not. Another factor which might lend credibility to an incumbent is the existence of excess capacity which would allow it to supply the extra demand generated by its lower prices.

It also helps credibility if the industry has a high level of sunk costs. Sunk costs are costs of acquiring assets that cannot be easily recovered simply by selling the asset or using it for a different purpose if the initial purpose proves unprofitable. Why should this matter to a potential entrant? The reason is, because it signals to a potential entrant that there is a stronger likelihood that an incumbent will fight harder to protect its investment. If costs are not sunk, the incumbent may be easier to push against because it can more easily recover some of its set-up costs by selling or redeploying assets. Sunk costs are the equivalent of 'burning your bridges' behind you. They tell people you are here to stay and prepared to fight newcomers.

Sunk costs have added advantages for an incumbent because they can act to discourage potential entrants as well as signalling incumbent willingness to fight. For a potential entrant making the pre-entry calculation, an important consideration is this: what will it cost me if I enter this market, fail to become established, and have to exit again? If there are no sunk costs involved in entry then there is no problem. If you can resell the assets you had to acquire in order to enter at the original price of purchase, less wear and tear of course, then your potential losses are limited. Attempting entry will not be financially disastrous. If, however, it is impossible to resell the acquired assets for anything near the original price, then the potential risk is significant. Exit will be very expensive. If exit is a possibility, then the incidence of sunk costs will make it an expensive experience and this is bound to influence your decision.

For example, consider the difference between the following two cases. First, consider entry to the market to carry holiday passengers from Britain to Spain. You could do this by leasing a few aircraft with the required staff, renting an office, and offering your services to one of the big holiday companies. If after a year you find the industry is less attractive than you thought, what does it cost you to exit? Very little. You return the leased aircraft and give up the office. Now consider entering the electricity generation business. Building a power station is expensive but this is not the real issue. The real issue is whether you can easily recover some of your money if generating electricity turns out to be unprofitable. The answer is no. You cannot easily get your money back. There is not much of a second-hand market for power stations because they tend to be rather immobile, although in fact it is not unknown in Britain for one to be dismantled and sold abroad. Therefore a lot of the costs incurred are likely to be sunk ones. Knowing this before you start, is likely to affect your view, or that of your bankers, of the riskiness of entering this industry.

Given that sunk costs may influence the calculations of potential entrants, it is possible for incumbents to try deliberately to raise the level of sunk costs an entrant has to bear. This may be one of the purposes of brand-names. The cost of getting established in an industry with strong brand-names is greater than it would be without the brand-names because the entrant has to spend heavily to establish a new brand. The costs involved in doing this are sunk costs. So the costs of failure are raised.

Finally, consider the use of brand proliferation as a strategy for making entry more risky. Take a situation where an incumbent monopolist in the tobacco industry sells only one brand of cigarettes, brand *X*. A potential entrant has to encourage some of those who are prepared to try a new brand in order to win a foothold and this is made easier by the fact that there will only be two brands fighting for shelf space at the supermarket. People who do not mind trying a different brand do not have to think a lot about the available options. Now consider what happens if the incumbent sells five brands, each in distinctive packaging and with minor variations in taste and strength. The supermarket shelf now has several options already for those consumers who like a change now and again and do not identify too closely with any single brand. The entrant now faces a bigger problem in establishing a presence on the shelf and in getting a reasonable proportion of brand swappers to try its new brand. The costs involved in establishing a presence and encouraging brand swappers to try your new brand, such as offering heavy discounts, are sunk costs. If you fail, these costs cannot be recovered. This makes entry more risky than before.

Finally, it is important to note that high investment costs *per se* do not act as a barrier to entry. The fact that it is expensive to build a power station does not act to deter people from entering the power-generating industry. If an investment has a demonstrably positive return after accounting for risk, then it will in principle be able to secure financing. The fact that setting up oil wells in the North Sea was expensive and risky did not prevent a large amount of investment taking place. What acts as a barrier to entry is not the amount of money involved but the prospects of earning a decent return on the money. Microsoft's earnings represent an attractive target for potential entrants and entering the software industry looks a lot easier than entering the oil industry. However, Microsoft is protected by barriers to entry and the chances of an entrant being able to overcome Microsoft's advantages and capturing some of its profits are not high. Of course this does not mean this is impossible. At this moment you may be sure there are lots of people thinking up ways to do this and someone someday may be able to challenge Microsoft's dominance. After all IBM was once dominant, and so was the British shipbuilding industry.

Some Evidence on Barriers to Entry

Research by Myers (1993) provides some evidence about barriers to entry in Britain. Myers examined thirty-seven reports of the Monopolies and Mergers Commission concerning dominant-firm markets covering products such as concrete, beer, and petrol. He found that strategic barriers were identified more often than structural barriers; in fact around 75 per cent of the barriers identified were thought to be strategic in nature. Important barriers were exclusive agreements and ties such as long-term contracts (eighteen cases), control of inputs (twelve), brand-names (ten), government regulations (nine), switching costs (seven), excess capacity (three), incumbent pricing behaviour such as credible threats to cut prices and squeeze entrants (ten), economies of scale (four), and sunk costs (seven).

Conclusions

A pure monopolist is a single seller of a good. Unlike competitive firms, the monopolist faces a downward-sloping demand curve, that is, the market demand curve.

For a monopoly to exist, there must be significant barriers to entry into the industry.

Because of the downward-sloping demand curve, the monopolist's marginal revenue will be less than price at any output level. The monopolist can usually earn supernormal profits in the long run because of industry entry barriers.

We have explored the nature and consequences of monopoly. We have formally analysed the consequences of monopoly for price, output, and profits. We have seen that monopoly is potentially very profitable and that one could describe the competitive process as the search for market power and monopoly. Monopoly is very attractive for profit-seeking firms. We have then considered some factors which increase and decrease potential monopoly profits. For example, price discrimination might increase them and regulation or cost escalation might decrease these. We have considered the sustainability of monopoly profits and the nature and significance of barriers to entry. We have seen that firms have an incentive to seek to create barriers to entry and how they might go about this.

The essential point is therefore that compared with the competitive firm, the monopolist is able to generate sustainable economic profits.

Further reading

Two introductory texts which give a very good account of monopoly theory, although like most introductory texts they do not pay enough attention to entry barriers, are Chrystal and Lipsey (1997), *Economics for Business and Management*, chapter 7, and Parkin *et al.* (1997), *Economics*, chapter 12.

For an outstanding, but more advanced, introduction to entry barriers, see Office of Fair Trading (1994), *Barriers to Entry and Exit in UK Competition Policy* and Myers (1993), *Barriers to Entry.*

For an account of Intel's use of legal challenges to make life hard for entrants, see Jackson (1997), *Inside Intel.* For the details of the Rank Xerox story in its monopoly phase, see Monopolies and Mergers Commission (1976), *Indirect Eletrostatic Reprographic Equipment.* For case studies of IBM, AT&T, and Boeing, see Shepherd (1990), *The Economics of Industrial Organisation.*

Questions

7.1. How might an incumbent act to make a threat of retaliation credible?

7.2. What is a monopoly and why might a monopolist firm arise? Is it the case that a monopoly will always be very profitable?

7.3. Explain how an already profitable monopoly might make itself more profitable by employing price discrimination.

7.4. Since price discrimination can increase a firm's profits, why is it not practised by all monopolies?

7.5. What factors determine the sustainability of monopoly positions?

7.6. 'Monopolies appropriate value not by generating new value but by obtaining existing value from consumers.' Discuss.

7.7. Does the monopolist need to take into account the possible reactions of other firms when making its price/output choice?

7.8. A monopolist is defined as the sole supplier of a particular product. How can one define a single product?

7.9. Why is marginal revenue less than price in a monopolistic market, but not for an individual firm in a competitive market?

8 Oligopoly and Strategic Competition

Strategic thinking is the art of outdoing an adversary knowing that the adversary is trying to outdo you

(Dixit and Nalebuff, 1991)

Introduction

In this chapter, we consider the behaviour of firms in markets which are dominated by a small number of sellers of a particular type of good or service. The number of firms is said to be 'small' when the actions of any one firm have significant impacts on the market (or industry) as a whole. Such markets are called oligopolistic markets. Compare this with our definition of perfect competition in Chapter 6 to appreciate the vital distinction being made here.

In some oligopolistic markets, firms produce identical (undifferentiated, homogeneous) products which are perfect substitutes. Where this is the case, firms face a common market demand curve. The law of one price (see Chapter 6) implies that these products must sell at a single market price. This is also true, of course, in perfectly competitive markets. But in contrast to that case, the small numbers in oligopolistic markets mean that each firm's output choices influence the market price and thus the choices of other firms. This implies a special kind of interdependence between firms in the market.

In other oligopolistic markets, rivals produce and sell differentiated products. Differentiation is fundamentally a property of consumer perceptions. Two technically similar products (for example, colas) are differentiated if consumers regard them as being different from one another in some significant way, yet still belonging to one common product group. It is this which enables us to refer to goods as being traded within one market even though the goods are not quite perfect substitutes. In these circumstances, the notion of a single market demand curve becomes rather tenuous, as we discussed in Chapter 6. Each firm will face its own downward-sloping demand curve, but one in which the quantity demanded is a function of the prices set by itself and all the other firms in the market, not only the price set by the firm itself.

The key feature of any oligopolistic market is strategic interdependence. Strategic interdependence exists whenever the pay-offs of a firm's choices depend on the choices of other firms. Interdependence arises from the existence of a small number of rival firms in the market. Consider pricing decisions in the market for Internet browser software. When Netscape changes the price of its browser, this is likely to have a significant impact upon the demand for its competitor's software packages. Moreover, the extent to which sales of Netscape will change following any such price change will depend on the reactions of Microsoft and other rivals. Clearly, the smaller the number of players in any given market, the greater will be the degree of this form of interdependence.

As a result of strategic interdependence, oligopoly differs fundamentally from pure monopoly and perfect competition. In the former case (pure monopoly), one firm supplies a product for which there are no close substitutes. Having no rivals in the market, the firm does not operate in a state of interdependence (although it will have to take account of substitution possibilities from products in other markets, and, of course, the threat of entry from potential rivals). In the latter (perfect competition) case, each firm operates in a market with a large number of others selling identical goods. But precisely because there is a large number of competitors, the behaviour of any one firm has negligible effects on all others and so they ignore it. It is entirely reasonable for each firm to assume that its actions will bring about a negligible response from others; there is therefore no strategic interdependence in such cases. Only in oligopolies do we find what the Harvard economist Michael Porter calls 'rivalry' and what most people think of simply as competition.

How might firms behave in markets where behaviour is interdependent? Three possibilities suggest themselves.

- Firms may simply ignore the existence of this interdependence, behaving *as if* other firms did not exist or do not matter.
- Firms recognize their interdependence and recognize that acting together—colluding—offers an opportunity to maximize the combined profits of the group. We call this *the co-operative*-behaviour approach to oligopoly.
- Firms recognize mutual interdependence exists, but for some reason are unable to co-operate or they choose to act independently. However, in making its commercial decisions, each firm will attempt to anticipate its rivals' decisions and responses, and take these into account. Since firms cannot or choose not to co-operate, we call this the *non-co-operative*-behaviour approach to oligopoly.

The first possibility—simply ignoring interdependence—almost inevitably leads to a very poor outcome for any group of firms which behave in this way. If all firms ignore their mutual interdependence, that is, behave as if their independent profit-maximizing output choices do not matter to the group, market outcomes will in general approach those you will expect in perfect competition. This is because each firm would set its output on the assumption that its demand is highly elastic at the going industry price. This being the case, profits will be hard to come by. However, such behaviour seems implausible and irrational in a small group setting, although plausible and rational in very large groups such as were described in the perfect competition model.

The second possible behavioural option suggested is co-operative (or collusive) behaviour. Intuition suggests that where a small number of firms are in a situation of strategic interdependence, they will seek to invest in efforts to collude with one another for mutual protection and benefit. Competition and rivalry are made worse by the costs and risks of failure. Collusion, that is, agreeing not to compete, looks a lot more attractive. The idea is to achieve an informal monopoly outcome for the industry and to share the resulting monopoly profits. Collusion could take many forms. It might be open and explicit; or it could be covert or tacit. Moreover, firms may co-operate over some things but not over others. For example, it is often argued that airlines collude over prices and compete through image advertising. As we shall see, the idea of collusion is to allow firms to 'manage' rivalry, perhaps steering it into forms which do not have large potentially damaging downside consequences for profits.

It is not difficult to find examples of co-operative business behaviour. Possibly the best known case of overt and, at least for a time, successful collusion is OPEC, the oil producing and exporting countries cartel. Another well-known example is to be found in the international diamond market. Up until the 1950s, when laws were introduced to control collusion and increase competition, the *norm* in most British industries was collusion. Some people think of trade unions as labour cartels set up to raise wages above the competitive labour market level. Partnerships, joint ventures, alliances, and the like are similarly forms of co-operative behaviour.

However, whilst co-operation is likely to be beneficial to all parties involved, this in itself does not guarantee that it will happen, or that if it does happen it will be easily sustained. Section 8.3 of this chapter demonstrates that there can be even greater benefits to a particular firm from persuading others that co-operation is beneficial but subsequently cheating and reneging on the deal. Oligopolistic firms therefore continuously face this fundamental dilemma: co-operation is good, but cheating is potentially better.

Furthermore, there can be circumstances in which co-operation is very difficult to achieve and sustain even when the parties involved are not opportunistic! These considerations suggest that co-operation will often be attempted but may be more or less unstable so that industries tend to oscillate between periods of calm co-operation and more intense rivalry.

The third possibility, that firms recognize their interdependence but behave non co-operatively, must therefore be taken seriously. This scenario has been widely studied by economists and we examine some of these efforts in the second section of the chapter. Here each firm is assumed to act independently, doing the best it can given its expectations and beliefs about the nature and behaviour of its rivals. Firms may send out signals, issue threats or warnings and so on, in attempts to turn the situation to their own advantage, but ultimately behaviour is rivalrous and non-collusive. It is evident that in many oligopolistic markets, competitive or rivalrous (rather than co-operative) behaviour is the norm. This seems to be true, for example, at least at times, in the grocery supermarket industry, personal banking, national newspaper, and insurance markets in many economies.

In Section 8.2 we consider some of the basic dimensions of oligopolistic interdependence and go on to consider some efforts to model the consequences of non-co-operative behaviour. This will allow us to make some direct comparisons between oligopolistic outcomes and the results we have derived for price and output under perfect competition, pure monopoly, and monopolistic competition. Of particular interest is the extent to which oligopolistic structures allow industry prices to diverge from costs. We shall see how difficult this is to predict given the complex nature of oligopoly.

Before we do this, however, we shall briefly consider the causes of oligopoly and the many different types of oligopoly.

8.1 The Nature and Causes of Oligopoly

Causes of Oligopolies

What determines the structure of an industry? Why are some industries monopolies, some duopolies, some dominated by a small number of large firms, others characterized by a large number of small firms? A detailed answer to this question is beyond the scope of this chapter, but some of the basic determinants of industry organization can be outlined.

Industry structure is, of course, a dynamic entity. Structures evolve over time, sometimes going from highly competitive situations to tight oligopolies, sometimes moving from monopolies to multi-firm oligopolies. For example, the US car industry contained dozens of firms in the early part of this century but developed gradually into a tight oligopoly dominated by General Motors and Ford. The arrival of Japanese producers in the 1980s, of course, has loosened this oligopoly considerably. On the other hand, the US telecoms industry was monopolized from the beginning by AT&T (Ma Bell), the biggest private corporation in the world, until the 1970s when US government actions forced its breakup and the creation of a number of independent 'Baby Bells' which now run the industry. The British electricity industry was similarly transformed from a public monopoly into a privatized oligopoly in the 1990s.

Underlying industry structure is the relationship between demand and cost conditions. More precisely, the relationship between the size of the market and the optimal size of the firm supplying that market, its minimum efficient scale, as determined by cost factors (see Chapter 5 on costs). For example, if the market size for cement is one million tons per year and the optimal firm size for cement production is around 200,000 tons per year, then the industry has 'room' for only five firms. If technological change shifts optimal firm size to around 300,000 tons per year, then the number of firms operating in the industry must eventually fall. Changes like this are happening all the time in all industrial economies. Business newspapers are full of stories about how changing technology or changing market boundaries are forcing industries to restructure and firms to 'get bigger (or smaller) or get out'. Many European industries have been undergoing a process of structural change in the 1990s brought on by increasing competition from the Asian tigers, technological change, and the completion of the European market area in 1992. Examples include bulk chemicals, steel products, passenger aircraft, banking and insurance, brewing, pharmaceuticals, defence equipment, and automobiles. American industry has been restructuring and 'downsizing'. Many Japanese industries are currently undergoing a painful restructuring to deal with the era of slower growth and increasing international competition.

Of course, structural change can also be the result of deliberate strategic efforts by firms to create a more favourable, that is, less competitive, environment. The most obvious example of this is a merger between two or more firms in the same industry. A series of mergers in the 1960s transformed the British electrical engineering industry and created the giant GEC. The US car giant, General Motors, was built initially on a series of merger deals. The same process transformed the French luxury goods industry creating LVMH, and more recently, the European power engineering industry creating ABB.

Firm strategies affect industry structures in less obvious, more subtle, ways also. For example, monopolistic and oligopolistic firms often endeavour to discourage new entrants into an industry by deliberately raising the costs and/or risks of entry. Thus heavy advertising and product proliferation act to make entry either more expensive or more risky. Entrants have to incur higher sunk costs to enter the industry and persuade consumers to switch suppliers or to find shelf space for their products. Firms may also deliberately create excess capacity in the industry as a way of signalling to potential entrants that they could easily boost production and squeeze prices if they entered the industry. Finally, firms naturally seek patent protection for their innovative ideas to prevent imitators taking advantage of their R&D efforts.

Governments, of course, are often heavily involved in one way or another in the process of structural change. (Why governments get involved in the process of industrial change is examined in a later chapter.) The privatization of previously nationalized monopolies has transformed the structure of many British industries such as electricity and gas. Governments also attempt to influence structural changes through controls on merger activity or, in other cases, actually encouraging mergers to create 'national champions', a policy much favoured in Britain at one time, and in France until quite recently, and still apparently favoured by the European Union. (Chapter 13 has more to say about the nature and significance of merger controls.) Governments also grant patent protection to innovators and sometimes take action to prevent incumbent firms from discouraging new competition too actively. In recent years, for example, the US government has accused Microsoft of deliberately acting to discourage potential competitors, although of course Microsoft denies this.

Types of Oligopoly

Oligopolies are pervasive phenomena in most modern economies, but there are several different types. In some cases, oligopolists produce homogeneous, or non-differentiated, products. Examples are to be found in standardized commodity markets, such as oil, aluminium, cement, and steel production. In other cases, rival products are not homogeneous, but differentiated to some extent. This second case encompasses three subdivisions.

- Oligopolies characterized by product differentiation and branding: rival products are technically very similar but as a result of successful branding efforts are not perceived by consumers as perfect substitutes, just close ones (examples include colas, cigarette and tobacco products, petrol, instant coffees, soap powders and detergents, telecommunications, sunglasses, and banks).
- Oligopolies characterized by significant ongoing product development efforts: in these markets, developing the quality and features of a particular product over time is vital, as is the scale of accumulated output to amortize these development costs. Again technically, the products are very similar but are not perceived as perfect substitutes by consumers, although in this case with perhaps more justification than the brand-names alone. The market boundary is inherently more dynamic, as qualitative changes continually shift meanings and definitions of markets (examples include automobiles, civil aircraft, consumer electronics, personal computers, and office computer software packages).
- Innovation-based oligopolies: markets in which incumbent firms compete predominantly by the introduction of qualitatively different new products not just improved versions of existing products. Firms are typically multi-product firms, introducing new product innovations as products reach maturity or the end of their life cycle (examples include military aircraft and defence equipment, pharmaceuticals, consumer electronics, and computer chips).

Another way we might classify oligopolies relates to geographical scope. Some oligopolistic markets are international in scope (for example, crude oil or diamonds), others (such as brewing and retail banking) are national in scope, or at least were until quite recently, some are regional (such as electricity distribution), whilst others are essentially local (such as cinemas and restaurants).

The importance of this lies not so much in the matter of geographical scope *per se*, but in what it tells us about the nature and meaning of markets. In discussing perfect competition and monopoly, the ways in which we defined them made the notion of a market an unambiguous concept.

Even in monopolistic competition, by restricting attention to differentiation within narrowly defined product areas, there is little difficulty in visualizing the notion of the relevant market. But matters are much less simple in oligopolies. A market is a process of interaction between buyers and sellers in trading a product or a class of products that are regarded by the buyers as being reasonable substitutes for each other, but much less substitutable with products in other markets.

Market boundaries change, therefore, as the opportunities open to consumers change, as technological changes alter substitution possibilities, and as consumer preferences and perceptions of products change. Consider the case of retail banking. Until a few years ago, personal banking services were only readily available to individuals from banks in the country where the individual lived: retail banking was national in scope. Structural changes have altered this significantly. Telephone banking, for example, has meant that personal banking is increasingly an international market. Similarly, whilst product innovation and development sometimes alter circumstances *within* one market, they may also change markets themselves, sometimes resulting in the formation of entirely new markets, as in the case of personal computers in the 1980s and more recently the case of Internet communications.

8.2 Non-Co-operative Behaviour in Oligopoly

It is clear from our introductory discussion that oligopolistic competition is a complex multidimensional phenomenon. Competitive strategies will therefore vary across industries and interdependence in practice will often involve more than just price and output decisions. Indeed, the intensity and unpredictability of price competition might cause firms to seek ways of competing for market share, such as product differentiation, in an attempt to reduce price competition. However, price and output choices have been the focus of our analysis of monopoly and competition models and it is natural to ask how oligopoly might affect these variables. It is, however, difficult to provide a simple answer to this question and it is necessary to stress that what follows is simply an introduction to this complex topic.

Price and Quantity Behaviour in Oliogopolistic Markets

In terms of the number of firms in the market, an oligopoly lies somewhere between a perfectly competitive market (with a very large number of firms) and a pure monopoly (with just one firm). Intuition suggests that the price, quantity, and the price–cost margin outcome of an oligopolistic market will lie somewhere between the two extremes set by perfect competition and monopoly. This intuition turns out to be more or less correct, if somewhat imprecise. What economic analysis suggests is that 'anything is possible', between these two extremes under oligopoly, given the number of possible scenarios that can be imagined describing oligopolistic competition, including collusion which we examine later in the chapter.

Here we confine attention to the two basic forms of oligopolistic competition: quantity competition and price competition. Recall a fundamental fact of life for any firm, even for the monopolist of the previous chapter: you can set the price you charge or the output you sell but not both simultaneously. If you set output, the market tells you what price you can get for it and if you set price, the market will tell you how much you can sell at that price. In quantity competition, firms focus their attention on deciding how much to produce, their capacity to produce if you like, and price is determined consequentially by the demand for the product. For example, hotel groups have to decide how much capacity to build in a particular city given their understanding of demand factors and knowing that other groups are planning to build as well. Similarly, for supermarket companies, cement manufacturers, aluminum smelters, and steel makers. Capacity decisions have to be made well in advance and in the light of market factors and the possible choices of rivals. Once built, capacity or planned output cannot easily be altered.

In contrast, firms in some industries focus their attention on the pricing decision and stand ready to supply what is required at that price so that output is determined consequentially by demand factors. For example, holiday tour companies set prices annually in their brochures, companies bidding for construction work compete on price, and so do companies bidding to be suppliers to big assembly companies like Toyota. In such cases, price decisions are made in advance in the light of market factors and what is known about rivals. Once made, these pricing decisions cannot easily be altered.

The distinction between price and quantity competition sounds rather innocuous but the analysis below will suggest that, at least in theory, it can make a big difference to the outcome of oligopolistic competition.

The ability of oligopolistic firms to extract value from a market is also influenced by whether the firms sell homogeneous or differentiated products. This is particularly important where price competition prevails. Price competition among producers of homogeneous goods, as we shall see, is likely to push profits towards zero. But where goods are differentiated, margins and profits will tend to be higher provided, of course, that barriers to entry make it difficult for new firms to enter the market, so pushing it towards conditions of monopolistic competition.

Finally, it is vital to remember that oligopolistic firms are strategically interdependent. The behaviour of any one firm is likely to have significant effects on others in the market and vice versa. Business strategies will also be shaped, therefore, by the beliefs which firms have about how rival firms will behave. In particular, strategies will depend on expectations about how rivals might react to particular output or price choices. These beliefs (or 'conjectures' as economists call them) are another factor which influence the outcome of oligopolistic competition.

In summary, the analysis below suggests that profits in oligopoly depend on various factors including:

- whether competition is quantity or price based;
- whether products are homogeneous or differentiated;
- what kinds of conjectures firms make about the actions and reactions of their rivals.

Game Theory

How might we go about trying to identify the outcome of oligopolistic competition? One of the most fruitful approaches to understanding the workings of oligopoly has come from the theory of games. A *game* refers to a situation of strategic interdependence. Any game contains three elements:

- a set of players;
- a set of specific choices (or strategies) available to each player;
- a set of rules that determine the outcomes (pay-offs) for each player for each possible configuration of strategies.

In the discussion of oligopoly, the players are of course firms. The choices we shall be examining here concern the outputs or prices set by each firm. Pay-offs consist of the profits achieved from the various choices. Interdependence is shown by the property that the pay-offs available to each firm from its own strategic choices depend on the choices made by the other firms. For example, the pay-off to Toyota from a particular price depends on the price Nissan is likely to set.

Quantity Competition in Homogeneous Goods Oligopolistic Markets

Suppose that oligopolistic rivals regard the quantity of output they sell as their primary decision variable, leaving price to be determined residually by whatever the market will bear. This form of competitive behaviour—what we call quantity competition—was first studied by the French economist Cournot, and so is usually described as Cournot competition. We deal first with the standard case where rivals sell homogeneous products.

So that we can get some numerical results for purposes of illustration and comparison, we shall investigate a simple case in some detail. In this case, there are just two firms in the market: it is a duopoly. The market demand curve for the product is assumed to be linear and is given by:

$$P = 190 - Q \tag{8.1}$$

where P is the market price and Q is the combined output of the two firms. Denote the outputs of firms one and two as q_1 and q_2 respectively, so that,

$$Q = q_1 + q_2. \tag{8.2}$$

Note that, because the two firms produce identical goods, they must sell at a single market price. By combining the two equations above, you can see clearly that the market price depends on the combined output of the two firms. This of course is what we mean by interdependence. The price received by each firm depends on the output choices of both firms. Finally, to complete our assumptions, let both firms have identical costs with each producing the good at a constant average and marginal cost (c) of £10 per unit.

Now suppose that each firm can choose to produce either 45 or 60 or 90 units. From the demand

		q_2		
		45	60	90
q_1	45	4,050 / 4,050	4,500 / 3,375	4,050 / 2,025
	60	3,375 / 4,500	3,600 / 3,600	2,700 / 1,800
	90	2,025 / 4,050	1,800 / 2,700	0 / 0

Figure 8.1 The profitability of available output combinations

and cost information provided, the profits each firm would make from the available choices can be calculated. These are shown in Figure 8.1. With each firm having three available choices, there are nine possible combinations of outputs. In each cell in Figure 8.1 the number below the diagonal line shows the profit obtained by firm one, and the number above the line indicates firm two's profit. For example, if firm one produced 60 units and firm 2 produced 90 units, firm one would receive profits of £1,800 and firm two would receive £2,700. You should to try to verify the numbers shown in the pay-off matrix. The calculations needed to find the profits are shown in Box 8.1 if you are stuck.

Which output might we expect each firm to choose? To answer this question we look for an equilibrium outcome. The reason for focusing on equilibrium outcomes is simple. If an outcome of a set of strategic choices is not an equilibrium, there will be pressures leading to change, just as when supply and demand are out of equilibrium, there are forces leading to changes until the two are back in equilibrium. Only in equilibrium will there be no forces for change. The definition of equilibrium that we use here was first proposed by the American economist John Nash.

A Nash equilibrium is a state in which each player is doing the best it possibly can *given* the choices of all other players.

In a Nash equilibrium no firm will wish to change its strategy. A mutually consistent set of individually optimizing choices is being made. It may be that no firm is doing as well as it wishes to or as well as it could do if the other firms would leave the industry or stop pursuing their own best interests; but each firm is doing as well as it possibly can *given the choices made by the other firms.*

It is worth setting out our assumptions about how the game is played. It is a single-period game. Each firm must simultaneously select its output choice and so neither can wait until the other has revealed its choice. (If a player is able to wait for another player to reveal its hand before making its own choice, then we have a sequential game which is a different type of game leading to different outcomes.) Both firms are assumed to be profit maximizers.

Box 8.1 Calculating the Firms' Profits

In this box we go through two output combinations, explaining in each case how the profits shown in Figure 8.1 are derived. You may verify all the other profit outcomes using this method.

Outputs: q_1 = 60 and q_2 = 60

Step 1: calculate market price

$P = 190 - Q = 190 - (q_1 + q_2) = 190 - 120 = £70$

Step 2: calculate firm one's profit (Π_1)

$\Pi_1 = R_1 - C_1 \quad = Pq_1 - cq_1$
$\quad = 70 \times 60 - 10 \times 60 = £3,600$

Step 3: calculate firm two's profit (Π_2)

$\Pi_2 = R_2 - C_2 \quad = Pq_2 - cq_2$
$\quad = 70 \times 60 - 10 \times 60 = £3,600$

Conclusion: Π_1 = £3,600, Π_2 = £3,600

Outputs: q_1 = 60 and q_2 = 45

Step 1: calculate market price

$P = 190 - Q = 190 - (q_1 + q_2) = 190 - 105 = £85$

Step 2: calculate firm one's profit (Π_1)

$\Pi_1 = R_1 - C_1 \quad = Pq_1 - cq_1$
$\quad = 85 \times 6- - 10 \times 60 = £4,500$

Step 3: calculate form two's profit (Π_2)

$\Pi_2 = R_2 - C_2 \quad = Pq_2 - cq_2$
$\quad = 85 \times 45 - 10 \times 45 = £3,375$

Conclusion: Π_1 = £4,500, Π_2 = £3,375

Inspection of the pay-off matrix in Figure 8.1 shows that there is only one Nash equilibrium for our game: both firms produce 60 units and obtain profits of £3,600. Why is this particular combination of output choices an *equilibrium* whilst the others are not? It is because 60 units is the profit-maximizing output for each firm, given that the other produces 60. To see that the choice $\{q_1: q_2\} = \{60: 60\}$ is a *unique equilibrium* consider any other combination of outputs in the matrix. For example, consider the top left-hand-corner combination corresponding to the output pair {45: 45}. Would firm one be content to produce 45 units if firm two were to choose to produce 45 units? No, it would not. If firm two produced 45 units it would be better, that is, profit maximizing, for firm one to produce 60 units, so increasing its profits from £4,050 to £4,500. Exactly similar reasoning applies if we reverse the labels of firms one and two. Firm two would not be content to produce 45 units if firm one were to choose to produce 45 units. The combination {45: 45} is not an equilibrium of this game. Inspection of all other boxes will reveal that no output pair except {60: 60} is an equilibrium. We advise you to confirm for yourself the validity of this statement before going any further. Note, of course, that the combination {60: 60} is not the best combined outcome for the firms concerned. The best combination would in fact be {45: 45} but this could only be achieved by co-operative behaviour as discussed later. This best combination is not a non-co-operative equilibrium, however, since neither firm would maximize its own profit by producing this output if the other firm chose it also.

Generalizing the Cournot Model

Our analysis so far has been artificial in restricting available output choices to one of just three numbers. Let us now generalize the analysis by assuming that each firm can produce any level of output it wishes. However, we still assume that the market demand curve is given by $P = 190 - Q$, there are only two firms involved, and that each firm has constant average and marginal costs of £10.

In order to proceed, a little more mathematics is required. The first thing we do is to obtain an expression which shows how each firm selects its profit-maximizing output given the possible output choices of the other. Remember that as we explained in Chapter 6, a necessary condition for profits to be maximized is that marginal cost equals marginal revenue ($MC = MR$). This condition for maximizing profits applies to all situations: it does not matter whether the market is competitive, monopolistic, or oligopolistic.

In our example we have assumed that MC is £10. How can we find MR? Each firm's marginal revenue in our example will be given by the expression $P - q_i$ where q_i refers to the firm's output as usual. A proof of this is provided in Box 8.2, but you will need some basic knowledge of calculus to follow this.

If you cannot follow this proof some intuition may help you to see why $P - q_1$ is firm one's marginal revenue and $P - q_2$ is firm two's marginal revenue in our example. The term P appears in the expression because if firm one sells an additional unit, it will obtain an additional revenue equal to the price at which the unit is sold, that is, P. But there is a second component to take into account. When firm one sells an additional unit of output, this drives the market price down somewhat, which has a negative effect on the firm's revenue. The size of this negative effect is given by the amount by which price falls (ΔP) multiplied by the quantity of output firm one is currently producing, q_1. Now, because the market demand equation in our example has a slope of minus one, one more unit of output will reduce price by one unit. So ΔP is in this case one. Thus the negative effect has a magnitude of one times q_1, or simply q_1. Adding together these two components, we find that firm one's marginal revenue is $P - q_1$. By similar reasoning, it is apparent that the second firm's marginal revenue is $P - q_2$.

One aspect of the Cournot analysis warrants careful note because it influences the outcome and because some presentations fail to point it out. We are here supposing that when one firm calculates its profit-maximizing output for any particular level of output from the other firm, it assumes that the other firm does not react to this choice and alter the level of output it used as the basis of its calculations. Both firms are assumed, for the purposes of the Cournot analysis, to make this special kind of conjecture about the reaction of its rival, the conjecture being that there will be no reaction. You can see that this is essentially a simplifying assumption in order to avoid feedback effects from one firm to the other. However, as we explain below, this so-called Cournot conjecture is not the only kind of conjecture that firms might make and this is important because it turns out that the predictions of the Cournot analysis are sensitive to this particular assumption.

We are now in a position to calculate the profit-maximizing output choices of each firm. An equilibrium for this game—more specifically, a Nash equilibrium as we explained earlier—consists of a pair of outputs, q_1^* and q_2^*, such that q_1^* maximizes firm one's profits when firm two chooses q_2^* *and* q_2^* maximizes firm two's profits when firm one chooses q_1^*. At this pair of outputs, and only at this pair, each firm is doing the best it can given what the other is doing. In addition, in equilibrium, each firm's assumption about what the other might produce is correct.

The output of both firms must satisfy the condition $MC = MR$. So for firm one and firm two, we have $P - q_1 = c$ and $P - q_2 = c$ respectively. But these two equations can only be satisfied together if $q_1 = q_2$: in our example, the Nash equilibrium must have both firms producing identical outputs. This is not surprising given that we are assuming that the two firms produce an identical good and have identical costs.

Now let us look at the output choice of firm one. The market demand equation tells us that $P = 190 - Q$, and we assume that $c = 10$. Substituting these into the $MC = MR$ condition we obtain:

$$190 - (q_1 + q_2) - q_1 = 10.$$

But as $q_1 = q_2$ we can write this as:

$$190 - 3q_1 = 10, \text{ so that } q_1 = 60, \text{ and so } q_2 = 60 \text{ also.}$$

It turns out that the profit-maximizing output choices of the two firms are the same as those we had in the case where output choices were restricted to 45, 60, or 90. The profits shown in the pay-off matrix in Figure 8.1 show, therefore, the maximized profits under quantity competition when there is no co-operation.

Box 8.2 The Mathematical Derivation of the Profit-Maximizing Output Choice in a Duopoly

Let Π_i denote the profit of the ith firm. By definition:

$$\Pi_i = Pq_i - cq_i$$

where q_i is the output of the ith firm and c is (by assumption) the firm's average and marginal cost.

Optimization theory tells us that the necessary condition for profit maximization is that:

$$\frac{d\Pi_1}{dq_i} = \frac{d}{dq_i}(Pq_i) \frac{d}{dq_i}(cq_1) = 0 \qquad \text{for } i = 1, 2, \ldots$$

The second term in the middle part of this expression is easy to compute:

$$\frac{d}{dq_i}(cq_i) = c.$$

This is simply the ith firm's marginal cost. The derivative of the first term in the middle part of this expression is less easy to obtain because P is itself a function of Q which is a function of q_i. Therefore, we have to make use of the product rule for differentiation. Writing $P = f(Q)$, the derivative is as follows,

$$\frac{d}{dq_i}(Pq_i) = \frac{d}{dq_i}([f(Q)]q_i) = f(Q)\frac{dq_i}{dq_i} + q_i\frac{df(Q)}{dq_i}$$

$$= f(Q) + q_i\left[\frac{df(Q)}{dQ} \cdot \frac{dQ}{dq_i}\right].$$

Now given that $P = f(Q) = 190 - Q$, $df(Q)/dQ = dP/dQ = -1$. We also assume, as explained above, that each firm conjectures that the other firm will not change its output in reaction to its own calculations of its profit-maximizing output. In this case, dQ/dq_i must be equal to 1. So the term in square brackets in the equation above must be 1 times -1, which is equal to -1.

Therefore we have:

$$= f(Q) + q_i\left[\frac{df(Q)}{dQ} \cdot \frac{dQ}{dq_i}\right] = P - q_i.$$

$P - q_i$ is what firm i *perceives* to be its marginal revenue, given its conjecture about the zero reactions of the other firm.

Gathering all this together, we have:

$$\frac{d\Pi_i}{dq_i} = P - q_i - c = 0 \tag{8.3}$$

But as this is true for both firms we have

$$P - q_1 - c = P - q_2 - c \tag{8.4}$$

and hence $q_1 = q_2$.

Therefore in the Cournot version of duopoly, when firms are symmetric, they will produce the same quantity. However, if costs differ between the firms, this result is altered.

Note that equation (8.3) can also be written as

$$P - q_i = c \tag{8.5}$$

which is the familiar condition that profit maximization requires marginal revenue ($P - q_i$ in this case) to be equal to marginal cost (c).

You may well find this result strange given that if both firms had produced 45 units rather than 60 units, they would both get higher profits (check this from Figure 8.1). But there is not really any paradox about this. If the two firms were to co-operate, then the best they could do would be to produce 45 units each. We shall discuss collusive behaviour later in this chapter, but at the moment we are assuming that the firms do not collude. The output combination {45: 45}, however, is not an equilibrium when the firms make decisions non-co-operatively for reasons explained earlier.

Comparison of the Oligopoly Outcome with that of Monopoly and Perfect Competition

One of our objectives has been to compare the outcomes—in terms of price, output, and price–cost margins—in oligopolistic markets compared with those that would prevail under the two 'extreme' conditions of perfect competition and monopoly. Under the assumptions we have been making so far—profit-maximizing firms, constant average and marginal costs, linear demand curves, and the conjecture that the other firm's responses will be zero—it turns out to be possible to make a precise comparison. The results are summarized in Figure 8.2 and in Table 8.1. Other things being equal, a two-firm oligopoly market producing homogeneous goods and engaging in quantity competition will produce an industry output Q_{nc} that is larger than that under monopoly conditions by a factor of four to three, and smaller than a perfectly competitive industry by a factor of two to three. Price P_{nc} will be higher than in a perfectly competitive market but less than in monopoly (but the precise relative magnitudes will depend upon the nature of the market demand curve). The points labelled *a* and *b* on the market demand curve in Figure 8.2 therefore define upper and lower limits to price and output under oligopoly. Finally, the price-cost margin will be greater than its long-run perfectly competitive level of zero, but less than it is under a pure monopoly.

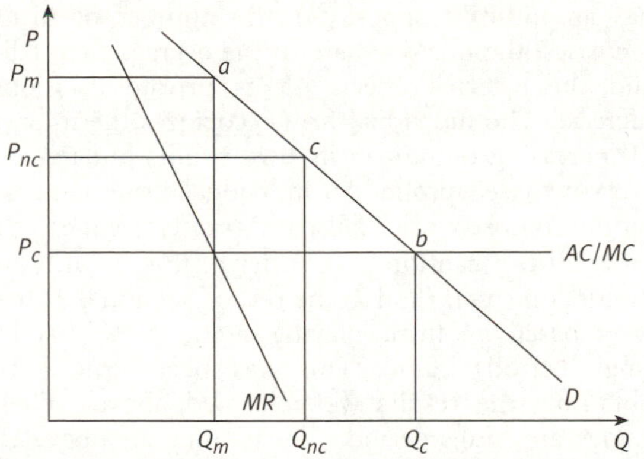

Figure 8.2 Comparing monopoly, perfect competition, and oligopoly

Notes: *m* = monopoly.
nc = non-co-operative oligopoly.
c = perfect competition.

Table 8.1 Prices, output, and profits under alternative market structures

	P	Q	q_i	Π	Π_i
Monopoly	100	90	na	8100	na
Two-firm oligopoly	70	120	60	7200	3600
Perfect competition	10	180	180/*n*	0	0

Notes:
These comparisons assume:

- market demand curve: $P = 190 - Q$
- $AC = MC = 10$ for all firms;
- the two-firm oligopoly produces undifferentiated goods, with each firm holding zero reaction conjectures.

For the mathematics behind these results turn to Box 8.3, where the outcomes under monopoly and perfect competition are derived using the same conditions we assumed for the oligopoly case.

It is important to understand that the results shown in Figures 8.1 and 8.2 and Tables 8.1 follow from the particular assumptions we have been making. However, under quite general conditions, it can be shown that the following will be true:

1. the aggregate output of an oligopoly industry engaged in quantity competition will be higher than under monopoly, but less than under perfect competition;
2. market price will be lower than monopoly price but higher than the competitive price. Price cost margins are positive;
3. aggregate industry profits will be lower than under monopoly, but will not be zero as would be the case under perfect competition in the long run.

Why are profits lower in the Cournot case than under monopoly? Think about what happens when firm one considers whether or not to raise its own output. It knows that this output increase will decrease market price. It must weigh up the

Box 8.3 The Derivation of the Monopoly and Perfect Competition Outcomes for our Example

The Monopoly Case

Using the profit-maximization condition that $MC - MR$ we obtain:

$MC = 10$ (by assumption);

$MR = dR/dQ$ (by definition).

We know that $R - PQ$ (by definition) and $P = 190 - Q$ (by assumption). Therefore:

$R = (190 - Q)Q = 190Q - Q^2$.

Then we make use of a result about marginal revenue given in Chapter 7: where the market demand curve is linear, the marginal revenue curve for a monopolist has the same intercept on the price axis (190 in this case), but a slope twice as great (-2 rather than -1). Therfore, $MR = 190 - 2Q$, and so equating MR, and MC we obtain:

$190 - 2Q = 10$

$2Q = 180$

$Q = 90$.

Market price is then found by sustituting $Q = 90$ in the demand curve, yielding the monopoly price $P = 100$.

The Perfect Competition Case

Using the profit-maximization condition that $MC = MR$ we obtain:

$MC = 10$ (by assumption);

$MR = dR/dQ$ (by definition).

Now we use a result from Chapter 6: in a perfectly competitive market, the marginal revenue of each firm is equal to the market price:

$MR = P$.

Equating MR and MC we obtain, $P = 10$. Industry output is then found by substituting $P = 10$ in the demand curve and solving for Q, yielding $Q = 180$.

relative advantages of higher output (which raises its profits) against lower price (which depresses its profits). In the Cournot quantity competition model, firm one does take proper account of this trade-off in so far as it affects itself.

But that is not the end of the story. The market price fall caused by firm one expanding output would also affect firm two adversely. However, because behaviour is non co-operative and self-interested, this 'external' effect is ignored in firm ones calculations. Exactly the same applies to firm two of course: its self-seeking behaviour leads it to ignore the adverse effects of any quantity increase on firm one. The incentive to organize the industry as a profit-maximizing cartel, in which firms co-operate to promote the monopoly output and price, is to ensure that these external effects taken into consideration so that combined profits are increased. We shall look at the co-operative approach later.

Cournot Quantity Competition with Many Firms

What happens in the Cournot model as the number of firms involved increases beyond two? As the number of firms in the oligopoly increases, it can be shown that the following results hold:

- the market price falls;
- the market output rises;
- for each firm, the margin of price over cost falls;
- total industry profits fall.

In the extreme, as the number of firms in the oligopoly becomes larger, the outcome—in terms of price, output, and profits—becomes identical to that generated under perfect competition. This result has an intuitive appeal. As the number of firms increases, the market share of the average firm falls and the external effects of its private decisions increase. The individual firm recognizes the impact of increasing output on its own profits but not on everyone else's profits. So individual firms increase output, industry price falls, and profits decline.

A word of caution is in order at this point. Our discussion so far (and in the rest of Section 8.2) has been based on firms playing a one-shot (that is, single-period) game. This has been crucial in obtaining the results we presented above. When games are multi-period, that is, they are repeated again and again over time, outcomes may be different, partly because of learning effects but also because the best strategies may be different when action today has effects upon future possibilities. We shall discuss this complication more fully in our analysis of co-operative oligopoly later on in this chapter.

Alternative Conjectures

The results obtained are based on the case where each firm assumes, when it makes its own profit-maximizing calculations, that its rivals outputs are fixed, and so will not change in response to its output choice. This amounts to an assumption that dQ/dq_i equals one in the expression for the firm's marginal revenue derived in Box 8.2. What this means is that the firm assumes that changes in its output do not cause other firms to change their output. But it is clearly possible for firms to make alternative conjectures and build these into the mathematics of the model.

For example, each firm might believe that if it changed its own output others would follow and change their output also. In the two-firm case, if this matching is expected to be exact (so that dQ/dq_i equals two), then it can be shown mathematically that the oligopoly equilibrium outcome is identical to that under monopoly: the monopoly price is charged, and each firm produces half the monopoly output. The intuition behind the mathematics is plain. If firms expect their rivals to react positively to their output choices, what should they do to maximize their own profits? Think about this and you should come up with the answer: if you believe that your rivals will choose a high level of output if you do and a low level of output if you do, what should you do? You should, in order to maximize your profits, choose to produce half the monopoly level of output for the industry and so maximize industry profits and your own profits simultaneously.

On the other hand, consider what might happen if firms conjecture that rivals will change output in the opposite direction to themselves? This is where dQ/dq_i equals zero, because any change in the output of one firm is assumed to be offset by changes in other firms such that total output is constant. The market equilibrium outcome in this case is identical to that under perfect competition! The intuition again is straightforward, even if the mathematics are not: each firm believes it can increase output with no effect on market price—it acts as if it has a perfectly elastic demand curve. This demonstrates the sensitivity of the standard Cournot model to variations in firm conjectures and this is one of the features of oligopoly which makes the outcome difficult to predict. Given the variety of conjectures that rivals can make about one another, oligopolistic competition can lead to a variety of outcomes.

Quantity Competition: Differentiated Goods

How important is the product homogeneity assumption to the Cournot outcome? In this case not very important. If the rival firms in Cournot-type competition are making differentiated products such as different brands of personal computers or different brands of soap powder we can think as follows.

Each firm is now producing a product, the market for which it monopolizes. Only Compaq produces Compaqs and only Dell produces Dells. So strictly speaking, there is now no well-defined industry demand function and there is no single industry price for a personal computer although it is still convenient and permissible to talk about the 'demand for PCs' in the non-strict sense. The law of one price does not apply when products are differentiated. Each firm faces its own downward-sloping demand function. Furthermore, each firm is now likely to have slightly different costs reflecting varying differentiation efforts. However, each firm still has to choose what level of output it wants to produce given its demand and this choice will still be influenced by what it thinks its rivals might produce because the price it achieves is determined by both its own output and the output of its rivals. In the case of differentiated products, it seems likely that each firm will believe that its rivals' decisions have somewhat less impact on its own prices and profits than in the homogeneous case. This is so because the rival products are no longer perfect substitutes. It seems likely therefore that, other things being equal, each firm will choose a profit-maximizing level of output which is higher than before because it regards its rivals as more 'distant' than before and therefore regards their output as being less important to its profits than before. However, what this means precisely for prices and profits is hard to say except that profits will be higher than under monopolistic competition (see Chapter 6) but lower than under a monopoly selling two or more differentiated products. You might reasonably ask, would a monopolist sell differentiated products? The answer is yes, it might, if the marginal benefit of variety exceeded the marginal cost of variety. A firm that monopolized the tobacco industry or soap powder industry, for example, could find it worthwhile, up to a point, to produce more than one brand.

Price Competition with Homogeneous Goods

Suppose now that the oligopolistic rivals regard prices as the choice variable leaving output to be determined by market forces, namely, market demand and the prices set by rivals. As with the Cournot analysis we are dealing here with simultaneous decision-making. This form of competitive behaviour was first studied by a critic of Cournot called Bertrand and so we describe this as Bertrand competition. As we shall see, in this case, differentiation becomes more important than before but to begin with we consider the case where the rivals sell a homogeneous product.

We imagine that price setting is done in the following way. Each firm forms an expectation about the prices its rivals will charge. Given this expectation the firm selects the price that will maximize its own profit. We also suppose that each firm believes that the price it chooses will not cause its rivals to reappraise the expected price. As before, therefore, the model implies a special form of conjecture about rival's reactions, namely, that there aren't any reactions! This again amounts to assuming that there are no feedback effects at work.

As before, consider an oligopoly consisting of just two firms: a duopoly. We retain the assumption of constant average and marginal costs. This time, call the two firms *X* and *Y*. Suppose that *X* expects *Y* to set its price at £50 per unit. What price should *X* set to maximize profits? Given that the goods are homogeneous, any price above £50 means that *X* could expect to sell nothing at all. Its profit-maximizing price therefore must be a shade lower than *Y*'s expected price of £50; by selling at £49, for example, *X* would expect to capture all the market.

But, of course, this thought process applies to both firms. Each expects (correctly) that it could capture all the market by undercutting any price its competitor might charge. No equilibrium is possible, therefore, unless both firms charge the same price and share the market. But at what level will this equilibrium price be set? Note that any price greater than average cost is not sustainable in price competition with homogeneous goods because each firm believes it can do better by undercutting such a market price and winning the whole market. Only when price has fallen to the level of average costs will there be no further incentive to cut price. The Nash equilibrium for price competition will therefore be one at which price equals average costs. Only then can both firms be doing the best they can given what their rivals are doing.

This is perhaps a surprising result. Price competition in a two-firm, homogeneous-product oligopoly yields an identical outcome to the one that would prevail in the very different circumstances of perfect competition. In terms of Figure 8.2 above, the outcome corresponds to point *b*. Indeed, it turns out to be the case that this is true irrespective of how many firms there are in the oligopoly. The logic of price competition itself leads to the price–cost margin being driven to zero. Therefore whilst it is often thought that a large number of firms is the essence of competition, product homogeneity itself appears to be sufficient to bring about the perfectly competitive outcome in the Bertrand case.

Alternative Conjectures

As with the Cournot case, the Bertrand result is based on a game where each firm assumes, in making its own decision, that its rival's prices are fixed and so will not change in reaction to its decision. For comparison with the Cournot case, this amounts to an assumption that dp_i/dp_j equals zero, where p stands for the prices of the firms concerned. This, however, is a much more heroic assumption than the equivalent Cournot assumption. Believing that your rivals will not react to your price choice is altogether less credible than believing your rivals won't react to your output choice. Setting a price a little below that of your rival threatens its existence, setting an output a little higher than your rival does not. Therefore firms that compete on price will, one expects, be less prone to hold the conjectures implied by the Bertrand analysis, making the analysis suspect. It seems altogether more likely that such firms would formulate conjectures of the type that involved positive reactions from rivals, that is formally dp_i/dp_j would be positive. In this case the Bertrand conclusions would be altered because firms would then be aware that efforts to win market share through undercutting rivals would not work. Rivals would be expected to follow these cuts and everyone would be worse off as a result. Once again this demonstrates the difficulties of modelling behaviour involving interdependent decision-making and making robust predictions. This, of course, is disappointing for business economists but it has to be said by way of defence of economics that no one else has anything more precise to say about what happens in such complex situations.

Price Competition with Differentiated Goods

There is another way around the stark conclusions of the Bertrand analysis. Firms can make efforts to differentiate their products. In some cases, of course, this will not be an option. A producer of standard grade mercury will find it difficult to convince buyers that its mercury is better than that of a rival's. But in many cases it might be an option. Producers of bottled water seem to have no trouble in convincing some consumers that one type of water is distinguishable from another. The same goes for soap powders, colas, batteries, and many other familiar products. In many oligopolistic markets, rivals sell differentiated goods, that is, different brands of a generic good. The demand for the distinctive product of each firm is now a function not only of its own price but also of the prices set by other firms. Because goods are imperfect substitutes, a degree of price spread is conceivable. A firm will not find its demand falling to zero if it charges a slightly higher price than its rivals, and it will not expect to win all the customers if it chooses a price below its rivals.

It is difficult to derive general results which hold when products are differentiated. However, we may say that the prices charged will depend upon a number of specifics, such as costs, how differentiation affects the size of the market, and the way in which consumers perceive the differences between products. Mathematical models of the Bertrand case with differentiated products suggest that a Nash equilibrium will be characterized by firms setting prices above average costs, and so achieving supernormal profits. We shall not pursue the mathematics here but will attempt an intuitive account. Remember that our approach is to assume each firm seeks to do the best it can given what it believes its rivals will do. In principle each firm can work out its optimal price given the expected price of its rivals. With differentiated products, each firm realizes that the higher the price chosen by its rivals, the higher it can set its own price. Setting a price slightly above your rivals, is no longer terminal. What is more, product differentiation implies that the benefits of setting a low price are lower than in a homogeneous goods market because it is now more difficult to attract customers from rivals. Therefore in this case, firms tend to choose prices which exceed cost levels and which produce some positive profits. Note, however, the result does not mean that the firms make as much profits as would a monopolist selling different brands or several firms colluding to maximize their joint profits. The non-co-operative outcome is profitable but less so than successful co-operation.

Non-Co-operative Behaviour: Some Concluding Comments

To sum up, our discussion of non-co-operative behaviour has shown the complex nature of oligopolistic interdependence and the difficulties of predicting the outcome of oligopolistic competition. We have seen that it is possible to generate a number of simple models of oligopoly by varying the assumptions involved and that these models lead to different predictions for prices and profits. It is possible for oligopoly to generate positive profits but it is conceivable that it could lead to very low or zero profits depending on the precise details of the scenario being analysed. The Cournot model with many firms and the Bertrand model with just two firms are pessimistic about the profitability of non-co-operative behaviour. However, Cournot with small numbers and Bertrand with differentiation are more positive. In addition both Cournot and Bertrand depend on a very simple view of what firms conjecture about the reaction of other firms to their actions and in the Bertrand case the conjecture assumed is particularly heroic. Introduce different, arguably more realistic conjectures, and you obtain more positive outcomes. In general, therefore, and aware of the dangers of prediction in this area, it is likely that oligopolistic structures do produce positive outcomes even when behaviour is non-co-operative. This is particularly the case if numbers are small, products are effectively differentiated, firms believe that other firms are responsive to their own choices, and where of course, barriers to entry exist. Let us now move on to co-operative behaviour to see if we can produce any stronger predictions.

8.3 Co-operative Behaviour in Oligopoly

Up to this point we have restricted our attention to non-co-operative behaviour. That is, we have treated firms as acting independently from one another and have thus ignored the possibility of co-operation. We have seen that the outcome of oligopolistic interdependence can lead to a variety of outcomes, many of which are likely to be unsatisfactory from the point of view of the firm. If nothing else, it is clear that non-co-operative oligopoly behaviour creates uncertainty because so many outcomes are conceivable. This uncertainty in itself will harm the firm's search for value but in addition to this our analysis suggests that the independent search for profits will often lead to an outcome in which industry profits are below the maximum possible. It is now time to consider if *co-operative* behaviour is the answer to this problem.

Intuitively it seems obvious that co-operation will lead to a better outcome for the firms involved in oligopolistic rivalry. By co-operating, or colluding, in the creation of a cartel, firms can act, in principle, as if the industry was a monopoly and so ensure that industry profits are at the maximum possible level. But if co-operation is valuable, why doesn't every oligopolistic industry operate on co-operative principles? We shall see that whilst co-operation is valuable for oligopolistic firms, it is not necessarily easy to organize and maintain. Like everything else, there are costs involved in producing the desired benefits. This will lead us to consider the chances of organizing a collusive industry successfully.

Co-operation and the Profit-Maximizing Cartel

A likely form of collusion among independent firms is the explicit profit-maximizing cartel. We have mentioned earlier some well-known examples of this such as OPEC and the world diamond market, dominated allegedly by the De Beers Central Selling Organisation. There are, however, many less prominent cases. For example, hundreds of cartel-like arrangements have been registered with the British Restrictive Practices Court whose job is to examine the practices and judge their impact on the public interest. From time to time unregistered agreements also come to light in industries as far apart as cement and bread.

The incentives for co-operation among oligopolistic firms are not hard to understand. First, co-operation enables firms to set prices at a high, possibly even at the monopolistic, level and avoid poorer outcomes such as those predicted by the Cournot and Bertrand models we outlined earlier. Secondly, it can help to avoid price wars breaking out. Price wars are, of course, bad news for most firms. Just look at what happened to profits in the grocery supermarket sector when a price war (or more precisely a loyalty card war) broke out in 1995. Sainsbury suffered its first profit decline in over twenty years. Or what happened to profits in the newspaper industry when a price war was started by News International in 1993 after a long period of stability. Market share was shuffled slightly, total sales stagnated, and everyone lost money (except the consumer, of course). Thirdly, co-operation promises a period of stability and allows for better planning of investment and employment, not to mention an easier life for management. Co-operation takes some of the guesswork out of oligopoly.

How exactly does it work? Look back to Figure 8.2. Imagine an oligopolistic industry with several firms and no co-operation. The industry price has settled at a low level such as that shown at point *c* because firms have been using the type of conjectures we described under Cournot quantity competition. Industry output is at Q_{nc}, and the industry price is P_{nc}. Industry profits are not being maximized at this level of prices, although each firm is doing the best it can to maximize its own profits given what the others are doing.

How will co-operation help in this situation? Assuming the firms can negotiate an acceptable cartel agreement among themselves which allows for the cartel executive committee to order each firm to produce less output than before, then industry supply can be reduced and prices pushed up. Ultimately if the cartel committee had good information about industry demand conditions and industry marginal costs, it could determine the precise industry profit-maximizing level of output, divide this up among the firms involved according to some negotiated formula, and achieve the industry maximum profits. Each firm would share in these profits according to its allocated output quota. The profit-maximizing level of output for the industry is of course the monopoly level as shown in Figure 8.2 as Q_m. The industry price is then the monopoly price P_m.

Of course, the precise gap between non-co-operative profits and co-operative profits will depend on many things such as the number of firms in the industry, the nature of the competition involved, and the quality of information available to the cartel executive. But the basic principle is this: successful co-operation among rivals will generally produce a more profitable industry than will non-co-operation. All the cartel has to do, which we shall soon see is not as easy as it sounds, is to determine the output quotas for each firm and to encourage each firm to stick to this quota. A licence to print money or so it would seem!

A cartel arrangement is even consistent with the appearance of considerable rivalry. Until recently, the world air transport system was regulated by the International Air Transport Association. Despite this, there was evidence of rivalry among the firms involved, in the form of advertising and other efforts to differentiate products, or more correctly services. It might even be argued that the unpredictable nature of price competition causes firms to seek to avoid this by price collusion and to channel their efforts to build market share into other areas such as product differentiation and product development.

If Co-operation is so Good Why Doesn't Everyone Do It?

The question now arises, if co-operation is so good why doesn't everyone do it and take the guesswork and uncertainty out of oligopoly? The fact is that not every oligopolistic industry is effectively cartelized. Why not? Let us consider why, despite its apparent attractions co-operation is not always attempted, and if attempted, why it is not always successful.

First, it may be that some or all of the owners or managers in a particular industry believe they are good enough to win the competitive battle and create a profitable dominant firm on their own. A cartel might be seen by aggressive firms therefore as an attempt to stop the best firms from pushing out the weaker firms. Few managers believe they are below average and many may think they are good enough to sustain high profits without the help of a cartel. Hubris may even be a qualification for the job. Of course in some cases and in certain circumstances, such a belief might be well justified by the results. Intel, for example, presumably felt little need for price co-operation in the computer chip industry, nor did Microsoft in software. In others, however, it might simply lead to temporary shuffling of market shares and permanently low profits, an example being the newspaper price wars in the UK mentioned above.

Secondly, co-operation may be against the law. To the extent that co-operative behaviour is successful, it is so at the expense of the consumer. If cartels keep up the price of diamonds or air fares, then consumers pay higher prices than otherwise and fewer consumers enjoy the product or service. Governments in many countries, such as the USA and the UK, have therefore seen it as necessary to regulate co-operative efforts among firms in the interests of consumers. The precise theoretical rationale for these actions is discussed in a later chapter. In Britain, for example, cartels are not themselves illegal, although the new Labour government is considering making them illegal. At present, cartel arrangements must be registered with the Registrar of Restrictive Practices and if they wish to continue to operate within the law, they must be able to demonstrate that they work in the public interest. This is not an impossible thing to do but, on the basis of experience, it is extremely difficult so that cartels are effectively forbidden in the UK. This, it must be said, does not necessarily mean that they no longer exist in Britain because they do and from time to time such unregistered agreements come to light. It is strongly suspected by some, for example, that retailers of electrical goods in the UK operate in a way consistent with a cartel. See Box 8.4 for some information on this.

Thirdly, a cartel has to meet a basic economic condition: the benefits involved have to exceed the costs. We analysed the benefits of co-operation above and they are clearly positive but we did not consider the costs involved in creating and maintaining a cartel. They include negotiating costs, contracting costs, monitoring costs, and enforcement costs. These can be considerable especially in the light of the fact that cartel arrangements are often strictly regulated by the state and so cannot be negotiated publicly and cannot be enforced by members through the courts. Consider OPEC for example. Member countries have to create an organization which is regularly renegotiating quotas, monitoring oil shipments and contract prices, and enforcing agreed quotas. None of this is easy or cheap. Think of what you would need to do to monitor all oil shipments How exactly would OPEC force Nigeria or Saudi Arabia to stick to its quota? Two factors in particular influence the cost-benefit calculation: the threat of new entry and cheating.

Box 8.4 How Shoppers Pay High Prices

In a recent article in the *Sunday Times* newspaper, the prices of widely available electrical goods were compared across different retail store groups in the UK. The article argued that British shoppers were paying inflated prices for electrical goods such as televisions and videos. The evidence given for this was the very close similarity of the prices quoted by different stores, some of which are shown in Table 8.2, and the fact that prices in the USA were significantly lower for exactly the same products (not shown here).

Table 8.2 Price spreads for a variety of products (£)

Product	Dixons	Argos	John Lewis	Comet	Currys
Sony Play Station	197	196.5	197	197	197
Sega Saturn	197	197	196	197	196
Sony TV	699.99	n a	699	699.99	699.99
Psion Organizer	329.99	329.99	329	n a	329.99
Aiwa CD/tape	130	129.99	n a	129.99	129.99

Source: Stephen McGinty, *Sunday Times*, 17 November 1996.

Of course, it might well be the case that there is a perfectly innocent explanation for such price similarities and we have already suggested earlier what this might be. For example it is possible, although perhaps unlikely, that retailers are making Bertrand-style conjectures (see above) and ending up at the competitive price level which is the same for everyone. It is certainly difficult to differentiate one store from another because most of these stores are located close to one another, so you have a homogeneous product situation here where it is hard to see how a price spread could develop. The Office of Fair Trading, however, takes the view that what is happening is that manufacturers are trying to prevent price competition between the stores and thus are enforcing their prices on the hapless retailers. Retailers which step out of line may be refused supplies and this keeps prices at the levels desired by the producers.

Fourthly, the cartel has to be able to discourage new entrants if it is to remain successful. If a cartel successfully achieves a position where firms are earning economic profits, these will act to encourage new entry into the industry. If the cartel cannot discourage new entry, market supply will increase and squeeze prices down. For example, the rise in oil prices engineered by OPEC in the 1970s led to a surge in investment in oil exploration outside (and indeed inside) OPEC which eventually increased supply and caused prices to fall back again. OPEC had no control over the actions of non-OPEC countries, nor as it turned out enough control over its members, and so could not prevent new entry attracted by the prospective profits available at the price set by the cartel. Of course, the new entrants might enter and join the cartel but this would make it somewhat more expensive to operate and somewhat less profitable because more firms then share the available industry profits. The cartel would eventually become pointless if any positive economic profits resulted in more entry. Professional organizations for doctors and lawyers provide an example of how entry might be controlled by controlling the supply of licences to new entrants.

Finally, all cartels face a serious internal problem as a result of cheating. The problem is that whilst co-operation is good for the individual firms in the industry, pretending to co-operate and then reneging can be even better. In a successful cartel, as we saw above, the industry price is kept well above the level of costs. This means that for any individual firm the marginal revenue from selling units of output above its quota exceeds the marginal cost of production because at the industry price each individual firm faces an elastic demand function. This means the cartel quota allocated to the firm is not its Nash equilibrium output. At the cartel price, the firm is doing nicely but it is not doing as well as it could do given what the others are doing. This is why the cartel organizers must set each firm a quota and try to ensure that it sticks. Each profit-seeking firm would like to sell a lot more than its quota at the industry price because selling at the cartel price is so profitable for a firm. But it is only profitable for a particular firm if all the other firms stick to their quotas and support the industry price. And this is the fundamental problem the cartel faces. Why should any firm stick to the industry price when it is so profitable to renege and when there is a good chance that if you do not renege the others will do so and your good behaviour will simply make it easy for them?

The threat and reality of cheating is a major problem for those seeking to create or maintain a successful cartel. This is because it raises the costs of cartel organization. The cartel members have to meet the costs of an executive body charged with monitoring the cartel agreement to ensure individual members stick to their quotas and to enforce these quotas when some members cheat. In some cases, these costs may be manageable but in others they may be prohibitive and make the cartel non-viable. Thus if monitoring individual member output is simple and if enforcing agreements is relatively easy, then a cartel can work to produce a net benefit for the firms involved. But if monitoring is difficult and enforcement is hard, then the costs involved in maintaining the cartel rise rapidly and overtake the benefits. We shall consider in more detail below what determines the chances of success for collusive oligopolists.

However, before we do so, we can examine the problem of cheating more rigorously by considering a famous game called the Prisoner's Dilemma. This game and its significance is described in Box 8.5.

The Chances of Successful Co-operation?

What determines the chances of successful collusion? Our discussion so far suggests that the chances of success depend on:

- the temptation to cheat, which depends on the size of the rewards available;
- the chances of detection;
- the chances of effective punishment.

We can get some insight into the likelihood of successful co-operation by considering each of these factors in a little more detail.

The Temptation to Cheat

First consider the temptations to cheat and the rewards available. In some industries the temptations will be greater than in others. For example, when customers make orders which are large in relation to the market size, cheating will be tempting. Also in industries with high fixed costs and cyclical demand patterns, such as steel, the pressures to keep capacity filled during downturns can be very severe and this creates a temptation to start cheating on quotas. Similarly, when production involves a high level of specific capital, that is, capital which has little use outside a particular industry, then firms will be reluctant to exit during a downturn. Their assets have little resale value and so any sales which cover variable costs are desirable. Squeezing capacity down to realistic levels becomes very difficult and price wars can break out. Finally, if there are cost differences among firms, the low-cost firms may be more tempted to cheat in the hope of squeezing the higher-cost firms out of business altogether.

However, if there are cost differences between firms, another form of oligopolist behaviour could emerge. In conditions where one firm has significantly lower costs than the others, and this cost advantage makes it the dominant supplier, it is possible that this firm may be recognized and accepted as a price leader in the market. The low-cost firm then chooses a price which maximizes its own profits; this becomes accepted as the market price for the other higher-cost firms following the price leader. Where a powerful leader exists to set and sustain the industry price, this could help to overcome cheating. The leader has no incentive to cheat, because it already has a profit-maximizing position, and the followers can supply what they want at the leader's price given their higher costs.

Price leadership is a form of tacit collusion. In addition to the conditions we have just described, it is most likely to emerge when formal co-operation is either prohibited or excessively costly, and where the consequences of cheating by one or more members of a formal cartel would be large.

Before we move on, let us consider the temptation to cheat a little further. Our discussion to this point has been confined for simplicity to what are called single-period (or one-shot) games. But it is often more useful, although more complicated, to look at oligopolistic competition as a repeated game where the players interact continuously over a period of time. This can make significant differences to the results of oligopolistic competition. Repetition raises new strategic possibilities for the players involved and this can make cheating less attractive, and co-operation more attractive, than in the single-period game. However, this is in itself not sufficient to ensure successful co-operation when the game is repeated. Let us explain the problem.

In a repeated game setting, the possibility of punishing cheaters and trying to make them less anti-social arises. In particular, the other players can play what is called a tit-for-tat strategy whereby if one firm cheats in period one, the others will break the agreement in period two, and possibly period three, four, and so on. The cheater then has to make a difficult calculation. He has to compare the short-term benefits of cheating with the long-term costs.

Box 8.5 The Prisoner's Dilemma

An often-discussed game—the so-called Prisoner's Dilemma—illustrates the potential advantages and disadvantages of co-operative behaviour. More generally, it shows the limitations of what we might call 'rational self-interested behaviour'. An example of this game is shown in Figure 8.3.

Two suspects are arrested for a serious crime and kept in separate cells unable to communicate with one another. The evidence available to the prosecution is not sufficient to ensure conviction on the serious crime in the absence of a confession. If there are no confessions the charge will be reduced to a lesser crime with a much lower sentence. The prosecutor therefore tells each prisoner that if neither confesses they will be prosecuted on the minor charge carrying a two-year sentence. However if one confesses and incriminates the other (who does not confess), he will get only one year whilst his partner will be given a hefty ten-year sentence for his stubbornness. Finally, if both confess, then each will get a seven-year sentence. The pay-offs to the two prisoners are shown in Figure 8.3, with negative signs indicating that the pay-offs are bads rather than goods.

As the prisoners are unable to communicate, they have no choice but to behave non-co-operatively. What should these prisoners do? The choice of confess is the best strategy for both players and so we expect both prisoners to confess. This is also a Nash equilibrium for this game. Given that the other person is likely to confess, confessing is the best thing you can do. You can work this out as follows if you are ever a prisoner:

If I confess, what is the worst that can happen (seven years) and what is the best (one year)? If I keep quiet, what is the worst that can happen (ten years) and what is the best (two years)? Therefore *no matter* what my partner does, it is always better for me to confess. Seven years is better than ten, and one year is better than two. QED.

		Prisoner two	
		Confess	Don't confess
Prisoner one	Confess	−7 \ −7	−1 \ −10
	Don't confess	−10 \ −1	−2 \ −2

Figure 8.3 The Prisoner's Dilemma

It is clear, however, that even though both players think like this, and that the subsequent outcome is an equilibrium one, it is suboptimal for both players. If neither had confessed each would have received a jail sentence of only two years as opposed to seven years. One might think that as each would realize this, neither would choose to confess. But not confessing is very risky for the players in this game. If one does not confess but the other does, the non-confessor will receive the maximum sentence of ten years.

How could the best outcome for both be achieved? Suppose the two prisoners are allowed to communicate and so to seek a co-operative outcome. They could then agree not to confess and minimize the likely sentences. Co-operation seems to be preferable for both compared with behaving non-co-operatively. Or so it might seem.

Unfortunately for prisoners everywhere, the structure of pay-offs in our game suggests that co-operation is not necessarily a rational strategy even in these circumstances. It may be better to offer to co-operate and then to renege in the hope of getting the minimum sentence of one year. If prisoner one agrees with his partner to refuse to confess, but then breaks the agreement and confesses, he receives the minimum punishment and his partner get the maximum. Of course, given the symmetry of the game, the other player is likely to reason in the same way too. So even when co-operation is possible, not confessing is a dangerous choice and a risk-averse person is likely to avoid it because of the probability of being 'cheated against'.

Why is this game called the Prisoner's Dilemma? The dilemma is not a consequence of irrational behaviour or of a misunderstanding of the game by the players. It is also not a consequence of a failure to recognize the consequences of your own choices. Rather, the dilemma arises from the structure and pay-offs of the game: the benefits of co-operation are recognized by both players but they choose not to co-operate in practice because they both also recognize the advantages of cheating and the disadvantages of being cheated against.

The Prisoner's Dilemma is best seen as a parable. Its relevance to us is that many business problems have a structure and pattern of pay-offs similar to those of the Prisoner's Dilemma. It is easy to see, for example, how it might apply to a cartel arrangement such as OPEC. Replace the confess/don't confess choice with a cheat/don't cheat on my quota choice. Can you see why cheating is a likely outcome for the cartel in the absence of an effective means of enforcing quotas? Cheating is always likely to appeal to cartel members because *no matter* what the others do, they can do better by cheating.

		Player two	
		Co-operate	Cheat
Player one	Co-operate	7 (player one) / 7 (player two)	1 (player one) / 10 (player two)
	Cheat	10 (player one) / 1 (player two)	2 (player one) / 2 (player two)

Figure 8.4 The co-operation game

To illustrate, consider the matrix of pay-offs shown in Figure 8.4. You will note that the numbers are the same as we used in the Prisoner's Dilemma example with the minus signs removed. The numbers show the positive rewards to each player from co-operating and cheating (after agreeing to co-operate). Now envisage that the game is played several times over a number of periods. We can reason as follows.

Co-operation gives each player a nice steady profit of seven per period. Cheating by one player gives him ten, at the expense of the other player who gets one. Let us say a player decides to cheat once and then revert to being co-operative. If the other player now retaliates and plays tit for tat in the next period, then the cheater becomes the cheated. The cheater therefore has to take into account: will the other play tit for tat? And if he does, will he play it for one period and revert to co-operation or will he, once I have cheated, refuse to co-operate with me ever again?

In general, it appears that the potential for retaliation should ensure incentives for collusion. The losses for the cheater, even if the others retaliate for only one period, are significant. The cheater stands to lose when the other player retaliates and the loss is six, the difference between the seven from joint co-operation and the one from being on the wrong side of the cheating this time round. The cheater must realize that, in these circumstances, reneging on an agreement just is not worth it because short-term gains are outweighed by long-term losses. Unless the future is very heavily discounted by the cheater, cheating is simply not worthwhile. So this surely means that co-operation will tend to be the norm in small group competition over many periods because cheating just does not pay in the long run.

But does it? Here is the problem. If the number of periods over which the game is played is finite, let us say the game is to last for ten periods, and all the players know this, then co-operation can still be difficult to achieve. The reason for this is as follows. In the final period of the game, cheating becomes the best strategy because at the end of the game the threat of retaliation is gone. But if there is a likelihood of defection in period ten would anyone willingly co-operate in period nine? This is unlikely because they would be tempted to get their reneging in first, and so on back to period one. Repetition does not guarantee good behaviour. Players co-operate when it seems likely that co-operation will promote reciprocal co-operation into the future, but if there is a final play in sight, the temptation to cheat before someone else does is too strong. So co-operation breaks down. Therefore it is only when the game looks as if it will be one with either an *infinite* or an *unknown* number of repetitions that it is likely that purely rational calculation will lead to co-operation.

Here is an example of the application of the tit for tat strategy from OPEC's ongoing attempts to keep cheaters in line. In the June 1997 meeting of OPEC in Vienna, there was much discussion about quotas and quota cheating. Chronic cheating by Nigeria and Venezuela was felt to be responsible for driving prices down from \$25 a barrel to \$17 a barrel over a few months. According to reports in the financial press, the world's most important producer, Saudi Arabia, made it clear at the meeting that it would increase production itself if the cheating was not stopped. This was certainly a credible threat because Saudi Arabia had the capacity available to increase production and it had in the past followed this strategy to keep cheats in line. Subsequently oil prices hardened a little, but not by much, at around \$19 a barrel in October 1997. The Saudi threat has perhaps served to curtail the cheating but obviously not to end it completely. Perhaps in this case, the cheaters calculated that whilst Saudi Arabia had the ability to play tit for tat, it ultimately lacked the will to do so because it feared the total collapse of OPEC.

The Chances of Cheating being Detected

It is clear that cheating is more likely to happen when it is more difficult for the cartel members to detect and the greater the period of time that cheating might go undetected and thus unpunished. What determines the chances of cheating being detected? Essentially the costs of detection. If the cost of detection is low, then cheating is likely to be detected. But as these costs rise, the chances of detection fall and so cheating becomes more and more likely. The question is, what factors determine the costs of detection. It is difficult to catalogue all the factors which might be involved but the following are likely to be prominent.

1. **Product homogeneity** If the products from each producer are exactly the same, the law of one price will operate and price cutters should be apparent. However, if products are differentiated in important ways, then prices are likely to be different also and so price cuts by 'cheaters' can be rationalized as changes in the quality or dimensions of the product. Thus it would be more difficult for a producer of aluminum ingots to cheat on an agreement than it would be for a producer of personal computers.

2. **Number of customers and their propensity to switch suppliers** If the industry sells the bulk of its output to a few large customers with a low propensity to switch suppliers, then sudden switching of orders from one supplier to another becomes apparent very quickly. On the other hand, if the industry sells to thousands of small buyers with a high propensity to shop around, then the effects of cheating are harder to pinpoint. Thus it would be more difficult for a producer of car batteries, which are sold largely to vehicle producers, to cheat on an agreement than it would be for a producer of batteries for household use.

3. **Visibility and transparency of prices and contract terms** If industry prices are highly visible, then cheating should quickly become apparent, but if prices are negotiated and settled in private the opportunities to sweeten a deal with special discounts multiply. Thus it is hard to see how a newspaper publisher could cut the cover price undetected, but easy to see how a shipyard could negotiate a price for a standard bulk carrier below an agreed level.

4. **Number of suppliers** If there are few large suppliers, sudden shifts in market share should be easier to detect than when there are many suppliers. Thus if there were only two oil exporting countries in the world, cheating would be much easier to detect than if there were a dozen.

5. **Demand variability** If demand varies little from period to period, then sudden changes in market share will be apparent. When demand is highly cyclical, however, it might be possible to pass off changes in market share as the inevitable results of random shifts in demand. Thus it might be easier for firms producing steel to cheat than it would be for firms producing bread.

The Chances of Effective Punishment

Finally consider the chances of effective punishment for cheaters. Clearly, if effective punishment is possible, cheating will be less likely to happen than if no effective sanctions exist. What determines the likelihood of effective punishment? The following factors are likely to be crucial.

1. **The legality of collusion** If collusion is legal, then binding legal contracts are possible and cheaters can be punished through the legal process. For example professional associations of lawyers and doctors with state-granted licensing powers are legal and people operating without a licence can be punished though the courts. Similarly, in France, the 'Comité Interprofessionel du Vin de Champagne' (CIVC) controlled the champagne industry for many years and had the power itself to impose fines, withdraw licences, and close down capacity. However, it is increasingly the case at the national level that collusion is not legal and thus cannot be the subject of legally binding contracts. Therefore generally, the law will not be of much help to colluders.

2. **The nature of the colluders** Collusion among drug suppliers in New York is likely to be quite effective given the nature and reputation of the people involved. Collusion among car manufacturers is more difficult to sustain because it is unlikely that cheaters will be the subject of a proverbial 'offer you cannot refuse'. Collusion among nations, such as oil exporting countries or coffee producers, is even more difficult. It is not clear how OPEC could punish Nigeria for cheating other than by implementing a tit for tat strategy. OPEC has no warships to send to Lagos to demonstrate its displeasure about price cutting and no international law court in which to enforce its agreements.

3. **The sociology of the industry** An industry with a strong social environment is likely to be easier to cartelize because you are somewhat less likely to cheat your neighbours than those more distant. Thus industries such as Scotch whisky and champagne, which are confined geographically, consist of producers with strong social ties, where the threat of ostracism or ejection from the club is

likely to be meaningful. The Arab countries within OPEC tend to be more disciplined than the non-Arab countries. Industries such as the European bulk chemical industry have no such social environment and cheaters have fewer social qualms about cheating.

To sum up our discussion of co-operation, therefore, we can say that co-operation has evident attractions for oligopolistic producers but that for various reasons, not all industries will be able to achieve co-operation all of the time. Indeed there are reasons for believing that many industries find collusion difficult to sustain much of the time. Particularly important reasons for this are that co-operation may run into legal restraints and that co-operative agreements suffer from incentives to cheat as exemplified by the Prisoner's Dilemma. Finally, the chances of successful co-operation depend on a variety of related factors which influence the temptation to cheat and the chances of detection.

Conclusions

The key feature of oligopoly is strategic interdependence and this makes oligopoly harder to understand and analyse. We have examined two basic approaches to analysing oligopoly: the non-co-operative approach and the co-operative approach. Game theory provided a common analytical link between these two approaches. The non-co-operative approach involves efforts to model oligopoly by varying the basic assumptions such as product homogeneity. The result of these modelling efforts suggests strongly that the outcome of oligopolistic competition is sensitive to changes in the underlying characteristics involved. For example, the Cournot and Bertrand models contrast price competition and quantity competition and lead to very different outcomes. Similarly, price competition with differentiated products contrasts strongly with price competition with a homogeneous product. Some models suggest that oligopoly is potentially profitable for the firms involved, others suggest that profits will approach the perfectly competitive level. It all depends on assumptions employed in building the model. Since it is possible to conceive of a large number of different combinations of assumptions, it is possible to obtain a number of different predictions. Arguably, however, the more realistic scenarios suggest that oligopolistic structures can produce positive profits for the firms concerned with non-co-operative behaviour.

The co-operative approach involves examining the attractions of co-operation for oligopolistic rivals and how these are offset by the difficulties involved in negotiating and maintaining co-operation. This suggests that some oligopolistic industries will move between periods of co-operation and periods when co-operation breaks down and rivalry breaks out. The key factors making co-operation difficult are legal constraints and the fact that co-operative agreements are susceptible to cheating. We considered the circumstances for successful co-operation and discussed the factors which influence the temptation to cheat, the chances of cheats being detected, and the possibility of effective sanctions against cheats.

Oligopoly, as we have observed many times, is a complex phenomenon. It covers a wide variety of market structures from near monopoly to near perfect competition. It involves strategic interactions, where firms have to take the actions of other firms into account when making decisions. It is therefore not surprising that no simple predictions can be made about the outcome of oligopoly comparable with the predictions of monopoly. As Tolstoy might have put it, monopolies are all the same but oligopolies are all different.

Further reading

A superb introduction to game theory, easy to read, and of direct business relevance, is Dixit and Nalebuff (1991), *Thinking Strategically: The Competitive Edge in Business, Politics, and Everyday Life.* John Kay (1993), *Foundations of Corporate Success*, provides a fascinating analysis of business strategy in which oligopoly and game theory play a central role.

For a more formal analysis of oligopoly theory, see Varian (1990), *Intermediate Microeconomics*, chapters 25 and 26, or Katz and Rosen (1991), *Microeconomics*, chapter 14.

Questions

8.1. What is or are the essential difference or differences between a monopolistically competitive and an oligopolistic market?

8.2. It is often said that firms in an oligopolistic market do not have a unique, or well-defined demand curve. Explain what is meant by this and why it is the case.

8.3. A cartel such as OPEC will maximize profits through collusion only if it operates at an output level where:

(*a*) average cost equals average revenue;

(*b*) price equals both average cost and marginal revenue;

(*c*) price equals both marginal cost and marginal revenue;

(*d*) marginal cost equals marginal revenue, as under both competitive conditions and monopoly.

8.4. Why do petrol companies tend to charge more or less the same price for their products? How would you describe the nature of competition between petrol companies?

8.5. Consider the case of Cournot competition between two firms described in Figure 8.1. Suppose, however, that the market demand curve had been $P = 300 - Q$ and that both firms had constant marginal costs of £15.

(*a*) Calculate the Cournot non-co-operative equilibrium in this case.

(*b*) What would be the co-operative equilibrium?

8.6. What is the Prisoner's Dilemma? How might it be avoided?

8.7. Two luxury hotels in Hong Kong face a problem due to the decline in custom resulting from the Asian crisis. Each hotel has to decide whether to cut price or leave price at the present level. Construct a pay-off matrix showing that whilst one outcome would be jointly beneficial, rational non-co-operative behaviour is likely to lead to a different outcome.

Part III

The Search for Value, Value Creation, the Scope of the Firm, and its Governance

Business economics is about the firm's search to create and sustain profits/added value. We continue our analysis of this search for value with an examination of several vital and related issues involved in the ongoing search for value. In their search for value, firms have to make decisions about their investment priorities. Firms have to consider questions of strategy such as whether or not to diversify or acquire another firm. Firms, to be successful, have to try to develop a source of sustainable competitive advantage. Finally, as successful firms grow and become more complex, ownership and management become separated and the implications of this for owners, managers, business motivation, and the governance of the business, have to be considered.

In Chapter 9 we consider the relationship between the value of the firm and its capital investment decisions. In the search for value firms are looking for ways of increasing revenues whilst keeping costs under control. Firms have to devote resources to actions which will increase revenues, such as advertising, the development of new products, and product improvements, and to actions which will reduce costs such as employee training, organizational improvements, and new plant and equipment. The general name for actions taken by firms to promote their search for value is investment. The problem every firm faces is that there are many possible investment opportunities to consider: building a new factory, spending on R&D, increasing advertising outlays, buying a new computer system, acquiring a competitor, retraining the workforce, improving the supply chain. The question is, which of these investments should actually be made and when? How can you compare an investment in R&D with an investment in a new factory or an acquisition? Are all of them really necessary? Will all of them be worthwhile? Are some of them more risky than others? How are these risks taken into account?

To an economist the fundamental question to be considered is: will this investment make the firm more valuable? We show that it is in principle possible to answer this question using the techniques of investment appraisal developed by economists. We introduce you to the concept of the present value of an investment and the idea of discounted cash flow. We explain how it is possible to calculate the value added by any particular investment and compare it with other possible investment opportunities. We explain the nature and significance of the opportunity cost of capital which the firm uses to finance its investment programme. And we explain briefly how risk might be taken into account.

In Chapter 10 we examine the fundamental determinants of the firm's long-run capacity to generate real added value. Firms, to be valuable, have to be successful at creating and sustaining added value. This will not be easy for most firms most of the time because there will be competition for resources and for customers, and competition for successful, value-adding, territories. To be successful a firm needs to develop a source of competitive advantage which will be sustainable over a reasonable period of time. This means being able to protect its territory against the actions of actual and potential rivals. Some firms manage to do this successfully but most do not. Is it possible to identify the ultimate sources of sustainable competitive advantage and the foundations of business success? Are there any useful generalizations to be made about this or is the nature of business success too elusive to generalize about? In recent years, some writers have attempted to construct a general theory of business performance based on the development of what they call distinctive capabilities. We shall examine the nature and significance of these capabilities and the ongoing development of a resource-based theory of the firm by business economists.

In Chapter 11 we consider the relationship between the value of the firm and some key aspects of its development strategy. In their search for value many firms extend the scope of their activities through diversification and many firms extend their size or scope through mergers and acquisitions. Indeed the concept of business strategy is treated by some as synonymous with diversification and acquisition. However, to an economist, these actions are just another type of investment opportunity which firms might consider and whose contribution to value needs to be and can be examined logically. We consider a number of questions about these policies. Why do firms diversify and acquire? Should firms diversify and acquire? What is the potential for adding value through diversification and acquisition? Do diversification and acquisition always make sense in practice? Why don't all firms diversify and acquire?

In Chapter 12 we consider the relationship between the value of the firm and its governance. In this chapter we consider the implications for business motivation of the changing relationship between management and owners in the modern business corporation. As firms have grown in size and complexity, their ownership and their management have become separated. Owners (that is, shareholders) are by and large no longer involved in the management of the business, and managers by and large no longer own a significant proportion of the shares in the companies they manage. Owners are 'outsiders' and managerial insiders are in effective control of the business. The question arises: what are the implications of this for business motivation? Will managers necessarily be wholly focused on maximizing the value of the business for the owners? If not, what can owners do about it? What rights do owners have and how do owners exercise these rights? These are questions about the governance and organization of the modern business corporation which, as we shall see, have been the subject of considerable debate and controversy in many countries in recent years.

9 The Search for Value and the Firm's Investment Decisions

Introduction

In this chapter, we consider the firm's investment decisions. Investment is of fundamental importance as it determines the firm's resource base. This consists of the firm's physical capital assets and the firm's intangible assets, such as the quality and skills of its management team and workforce, and its reputation. The resource base not only determines the firm's present productive potential, but also plays a key part in determining its future possibilities. It is in the determination of the firm's present and future value-adding potential that the importance of investment lies.

The size and make-up of a firm's resource base is the outcome of managerial decisions made throughout the history of the firm. Changes in the firm's resource base come about through investment expenditures on new items of tangible or intangible capital. From time to time firms will need to make decisions about whether or not to *replace* parts of the capital resource base that have deteriorated in value over time. This deterioration may be the consequence of physical wear and tear. It may also result from a resource becoming technologically obsolete, putting the firm at a cost disadvantage relative to other firms with capital of more recent vintage. Finally, the stocks of some intangible assets may deteriorate in the sense that their impact diminishes with the passage of time, as is often true for the impact of advertising expenditures.

Capital replacement expenditure can have profound implications for the firm. When capital expenditures arise because of the need to replace parts of its resource base, it is likely that the replacement capital will embody new technology. This may reduce production costs, and perhaps broaden the range of goods the firm can produce. So even replacement capital expenditure can open up new business opportunities.

But investment expenditure is not only about the replacement of capital. Net investment *expands the firm's resource base*, increasing scale and growth. You will recall from Chapter 5 (in which we examined costs of production) that scale has implications for average costs of production. In the long run, the size of the firm's capital stock is a choice variable. The firm *chooses* its scale of operations, and selects a resource base of an appropriate size. Capital investment is the means by which the firm adjusts its resource base to its target level. This investment can take several forms. Direct purchase and installation of new capital lead to the 'internal growth' of the firm. Investment may also change the firm's scale and scope of operations through the vehicle of mergers and acquisitions, as we shall see in Chapter 11.

Finally, note that investment is not merely a vehicle for changing scale by doing more or less of the same thing. It is also one of the important means through which the firm can redirect its focus, or alter the range and make-up of the activities it undertakes. This brings us into the domain of strategic choice. Choices about the markets in which a firm operates, how diversified its activities should be (examined in Chapter 11), and the extent to which it should be vertically integrated are at the heart of business policy: whenever choices involve changes in direction or changes in scale, they will require investment expenditures for their implementation. In summary, we may say that capital expenditures—or investments, if you prefer that term—are the means by which the future value-adding possibilities of the firm are maintained, developed, and redirected.

9.1 The Firm and its Investment Decision

How do Firms Generate Investment Opportunities?

Much of the literature on investment is concerned with the appraisal of opportunities known to the firm. But it is important to begin our analysis one stage further back, by asking where investment opportunities come from, and how they are generated.

Sometimes investment opportunities are generated by processes external to the firm, such as the general progress of science and technology. In these cases, managers do not generate opportunities as such, but respond to those that are thrown up by the relevant external process. A problem with this view of investment, however, is that it confuses technical possibilities with business innovations. For example, in the so-called space race between the USA and the Soviet Union, it is easy to list major technical possibilities that were the (intended or unintended) consequences of the space-race activities. One oft-remarked item is the development of heat-resistant and low-friction materials that created the possibility of kitchen utensils with 'non-stick' properties.

But a moment's reflection shows the inadequacy of this as a general way of characterizing the process of creating investment opportunities. Scientific advance does open up new technical possibilities, but this is very different from what we have in mind by investment opportunities. An investment opportunity involves the (potential) application of some idea in a particular set of circumstances. For the new product of non-stick kitchenware to be made available, it was first necessary that the link between the properties of the new materials and their use in kitchen hardware was made, that a feasible engineering plan was devised, preliminary market research and costings carried out, and that the generators of the idea convinced senior managers of the potential profits to be had. Moreover, once this process has begun, a whole sequence of commercial applications follow, that no longer depend on further scientific advance.

It is clear that investment opportunities have to be searched for and developed, and so are costly. Managerial resources must be employed in the production of these opportunities, as well as in their appraisal and implementation. In this process there are likely to be large advantages obtained through experience and learning. Firms become better at generating new investment opportunities the more they do. The process of generating and implementing investment opportunities will develop a knowledge base that facilitates the effectiveness with which these activities can be done in the future. We expect to find that some firms are able to develop a cycle in which new investment opportunities are being generated on a regular basis, whilst others become caught in a passive state in which opportunities are awaited but rarely materialize.

There are, of course, many other reasons why firms differ in their ability to generate investment opportunities. Firms may develop particular competencies or distinctive capabilities in generating investment possibilities. We shall have much to say about the concepts of competencies and distinctive capabilities in Chapter 10.

Appraising Investment Opportunities: The Concept of Present Value and the Capital-Budgeting Process

Capital budgeting refers to the processes involved in appraising investment opportunities and arriving at decisions about which should be implemented. We use simple conceptual models to present a number of capital-budgeting techniques. The objective is to provide analytical insights that can be useful to managers in making investment decisions.

A characteristic of any capital expenditure is that outlays are made at one point in time in the expectation of later returns. To appraise a project—to decide whether or not it is worth doing—a common unit is needed to compare these outlays and returns. The unit we need for this is *present value.*

Suppose a firm can choose between two certain offers: receiving £1 today, or receiving £1 one year from today. Which option will it choose? The answer depends on which of the two is regarded as being the more valuable. One might suppose that as each offers a certain payment of £1, the two are of equal value. But they are not identical, as the offers have different dates. One way of ascertaining which is the more valuable is to compare their values at a single point in time. For example, how much are the two options worth one year from today? Clearly the monetary value of £1 received twelve months from now will be £1 at that time. But how valuable will £1 received today be in one year's time?

This depends on the rate of return the firm can get by lending or investing money. We restrict attention here to the return available *outside* the firm. Suppose that there is one rate at which money can be borrowed or loaned outside the firm. We call this the firm's *cost of capital.* If the cost of capital were 10 per cent, the firm could convert an income of £1 today into £1.10 (that is, £1 plus 10 per cent of £1) in one year. Given a cost of capital of 10 per cent, the option of £1 today will be preferred to the option of £1 one year later. By having the income today, it can be converted into £1.10 in one year, which is preferable to receiving £1 one year from now. There is an opportunity cost of receiving income later rather than sooner; it is the return forgone by deferral of that income.

Our comparison was based upon a reference point one year in the future. Alternatively, we might use the present as reference point. The *present value* of an income received with certainty at some future date is the amount that someone would be willing to pay today to obtain entitlement to that future income. It should be clear from the forgoing that £1.10 receivable after one year has a present value of £1. A firm, able to lend at an annual rate of 10 per cent, would be indifferent between receiving £1 now and receiving £1.10 one year later.

The present value of an income received in one year's time can be calculated by dividing the income by a discount factor, given by one plus the cost of capital (expressed in proportionate terms). The present value of £1.10 after one year, at a cost of capital of 10 per cent (or 0.1 in proportionate terms), is calculated as

$$\frac{£1.10}{(1+0.1)} = £1$$

This process of discounting is the reverse of the more familiar process of compounding. If £1 is lent at an annual interest rate of 10 per cent, then the compounded amount of principal plus interest is £1.10 after one year. By reversing this compounding process, we find that the present value of £1.10 in one year is £1 (provided the rate of interest is 10 per cent).

With a positive cost of capital, discounting implies that the *present* value of a future income is less than its *nominal* value. The economic logic which lies behind this divergence is that an opportunity cost, equal to the return forgone, is incurred when the receipt of an income is deferred. The present value is less than the future nominal value by the amount of this opportunity cost.

Exactly the same procedure is used when the choice concerns outlays at different points in time rather than receipts at different points in time. Inflows and outflows of cash are treated in a symmetrical way when converting future values into their present value equivalents. Given a cost of capital of 10 per cent, the present value of £1.10 to be paid in one year is £1. The firm would be indifferent between making a payment of £1 today or £1.10 in one year's time.

A General Expression for the Present Value of a Cash Flow

The example we have just considered was a special case in which:

- the rate of return was 10 per cent;
- we were seeking the present value of a future income of £1.10;
- the choice involved receipt now or receipt one year in the future.

A general expression for obtaining the present value (PV) of a cash flow of £A received or disbursed n years in the future, and where the cost of capital is r, is given by:

$$PV = \frac{A}{(1+r)^n}$$

If you are not familiar with this expression, you may find it useful to follow its derivation in Box 9.1.

The present value of an income declines as the time at which it is received (or paid) recedes further into the future. Table 9.1 lists the present values of an income of £1,000 received after a delay of between one and twenty years, at an annual cost of capital of 10 per cent. The *PV* numbers are given to one decimal place of accuracy.

These figures are plotted in Figure 9.1. Note how the present value falls exponentially over time. After seven years, the present value has fallen by nearly one-half, and after twenty years the present

Box 9.1 A General Expression for the Present Value of a Future Cash Flow

We begin by obtaining an expression for the present value of £1.10 in one year's time for any cost of capital, not just a rate of 10 per cent. Let the cost of capital be r, where r is expressed as a proportion. For a cost of capital r, the present value of £1.10 received at the end of one year is given by:

$$\frac{£1.10}{(1+r)}.$$

So if the cost of capital were 20 per cent ($r = 0.2$) the present value of £1.10 in one year would be £0.92 (to two decimal places of accuracy). By generalizing one step further, we find that the present value of £A received in one year is:

$$\frac{£A}{(1+r)}.$$

Thus, at a 20 per cent cost of capital, the present value of £110 in one year is £91.67. Finally, we need an expression for the present value of a cash flow at any specified time in the future, not just one year ahead. As a first step, note that the present value of £1 received in *two* years time at a cost of capital of 10 per cent is £0.8265. This can be verified as follows. If £0.8265 were lent today at an annual rate of 10 per cent, after one year the combined value of principal and interest would be £0.9091. If this latter figure were invested for one further year, then at the end of the second year, a value of £1 would be obtained. That is, £0.8265 is the present value of £1 received in two years' time at an annual rate of 10 per cent (with interest added discretely at the end of each year). Algebraically we can write this as follows:

$$£0.8265(1+0.1)(1+0.1) = £0.8265(1+0.1)^2 = £1.$$

Then by dividing each side by $(1+0.1)^2$ we obtain the following expression:

$$£0.8265 = \frac{£1}{(1+0.1)^2}.$$

More generally, the present value of £1 received at the end of n years in the future with an annual cost of capital of r is given by the value PV which solves the equation:

$$PV = \frac{£1}{(1+r)^n}.$$

Finally, putting all these pieces together, we obtain the following expression: the present value (PV) of a £A received after n years at an annual cost of capital of r is given by:

$$PV = \frac{A}{(1+r)^n}.$$

where the £ sign has been omitted.

Table 9.1. The present value of £1,000 with a 10 per cent cost of capital

Number of years after which £1,000 is received	Present value of £1,000
1	909.1
2	826.4
3	751.3
4	683.0
5	620.9
6	564.5
7	513.2
8	466.5
9	424.1
10	385.5
11	350.5
12	318.6
13	289.7
14	263.3
15	239.4
16	217.6
17	197.8
18	179.9
19	163.5
20	148.6

value of £1,000 is £148.6, merely 15 per cent of its nominal value. The data can also be interpreted as showing that if £148.6 were invested at an annual rate of 10 per cent for twenty years, the accumulated sum of initial capital plus interest would amount to £1,000.[1]

[1] Note that in doing present value calculations, our discounting technique has used discrete rather than continuous compounding, and has assumed a once-per-year application of the annual cost of capital. Slightly different figures would have been obtained from an exercise in which discounting were done discretely but at a greater frequency than once-per-year, or if continuous discounting were applied. For example, after twenty years of continuous discounting at an (instantaneous) rate of 10 per cent, the present value of £1,000 would be £135.3, rather than £148.6 as given in Table 9.1. Continuous rather than discrete discounting leads to a modified expression for obtaining present values. However, as this adds to the technical complexity of the arguments, but make little difference to the underlying logic, we will only consider the discrete case.

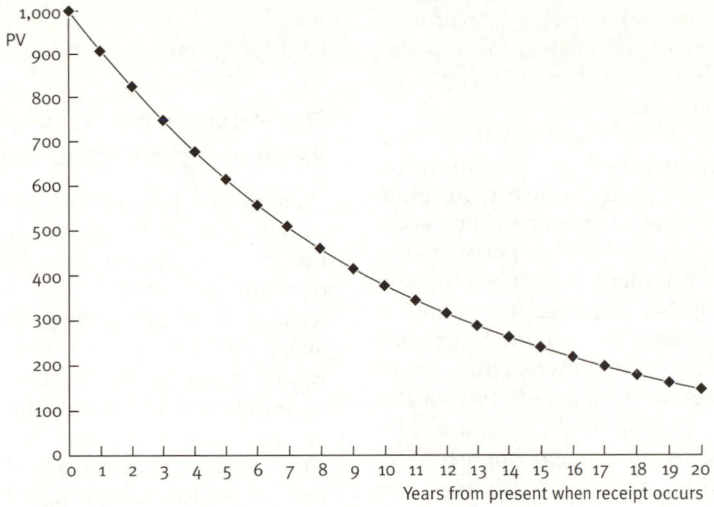

Figure 9.1 The present value of £1,000 with a 10 per cent cost of capital

A Single Investment Project and its Evaluation

How should a firm decide whether a single capital project is undertaken? We begin by posing the problem in its simplest form, and assume that the following conditions are satisfied.

1. The project is independent. Doing it (or not doing it) has no implications whatsoever for any other project that the firm could conceivably undertake, now or in the future. It is therefore legitimate to appraise the project in isolation from any other.
2. The firm has access to funds for financing the necessary capital expenditure as long as it can demonstrate the potential of the project.
3. Managers have perfect foresight. All costs and revenues associated with the project, now and in the future, are known with certainty.

The basic principle underlying investment appraisal is that a project should be undertaken if the value of the firm is increased by doing so, but not otherwise. The total value of a firm is the present value of the stream of net income over its whole future. A project should be undertaken if its incremental value is positive, thereby adding to the total value of the firm.

The incremental value of a project is known as its *net present value*. So a project should be undertaken if its net present value (NPV) is positive. We shall use the following notation:

- V_t is the net cash flow (inflows less outflows) that results from the project in year t;
- r is the annual cost of capital
- $t = 0$ defines the start of the present time period (one period is taken to be one year)
- $t = n$ defines the project horizon; n is the number of years after which no cash flow will accrue from the project;
- Σ indicates that a sum is being taken of a sequence of terms. This sequence consists of the expression following Σ, evaluated first at $t = 0$, then at $t = 1$, and so on up to $t = n$.

The net present value of a project is given by.

$$\text{NPV} = \sum_{t=0}^{t=n} \frac{V_t}{(1+r)^t}.$$

NPV is the sum of the present values of the net cash flows arising over the whole life of the project. The net cash flow in any period is the *difference* between the cash inflows accruing to the firm and the cash outflows met by the firm during that period. The relevant inflows and outflows include only those attributable to implementing the project; in other words, they should be measured as the amounts by which inflows and outflows *change* as a result of going ahead with the project. Finally, the relevant costs should *not* include any capital depreciation charge, as depreciation is accounted for in another way: if the capital has any residual value at the end of the project's life, that value enters as a positive cash flow in whichever period the firm realizes that value by selling it to another firm or using it on some other project in its own business.

Let us illustrate an *NPV* calculation with the help of a simple example. Suppose that a manufacturer of radios is appraising a project which requires an initial outlay of £2 million. Revenues from additional sales of radios are £1.9 million per year. The life of the capital equipment is five years, after which it will be incapable of producing output of any form. The equipment has no resale (or any other) value after five years. Incremental costs, consisting of materials and fuel, labour, transportation, and increases in overhead costs are £1.4 million per year. Finally, investment opportunities exist elsewhere yielding a return of 7 per cent, and so the cost of capital is 7 per cent.

Table 9.2 lists the cash outflows and inflows associated with the project.

Using the formula for the net present value of a project, we obtain

$$\text{NPV} = \sum_{t=0}^{t=5} \frac{\text{NV}_t}{(1.07)^t} = \frac{-2{,}000{,}000}{(1.07)^0} + \frac{500{,}000}{(1.07)^1} + \frac{500{,}000}{(1.07)^2} + \frac{500{,}000}{(1.07)^3} + \frac{500{,}000}{(1.07)^4} + \frac{500{,}000}{(1.07)^5}$$

$$= -2{,}000{,}000 + 467{,}290 + 436{,}719 + 408{,}149 + 381{,}448 + 356{,}493$$

$$= 50{,}099$$

The project yields a net present value of £50,099. This is the amount by which the value of the firm would increase if the project were undertaken. Clearly a value-seeking firm would accept this project.

Thus we have a very simple decision rule in project appraisal:

If a project has a NPV > 0, that project should be undertaken;

Table 9.2 Cash flows for the illustrative project

Year	Cash inflow	Cash outflow	Net cash flow (NV)
0		−2,000,000	−2,000,000
1	1,900,000	−1,400,000	500,000
2	1,900,000	−1,400,000	500,000
3	1,900,000	−1,400,000	500,000
4	1,900,000	−1,400,000	500,000
5	1,900,000	−1,400,000	500,000

If a project has a NPV < 0, that project should not be undertaken.

The Relationship between Net Present Value and the Cost of Capital

Changes in the cost of capital will change NPV. This is evident from the previous calculations. If the cost of capital had been 8 per cent, the denominator would have been larger in each term and so the sum of those terms would be lower. At an 8 per cent cost of capital, the project would in fact have a negative NPV (−£ 3,645) and so should not be undertaken. As the cost of capital rises above 8 per cent, becomes an increasingly large negative number. On the other hand, as the cost of capital falls below 7 per cent, the NPV becomes an increasingly large positive number. For our example, the relationship between the NPV of the project and the cost of capital is shown in Figure 9.2.

The Internal Rate of Return (IRR) of an Investment Project

We have seen that the NPV of our project was negative at a cost of capital of 8 per cent or greater, and positive at a cost of capital of 7 per cent or lower. This information is shown in Figure 9.2, from which it can be seen that at a cost of capital of 7.9 per cent the NPV of the project is exactly equal to zero. This rate is known as the *internal rate of return* (IRR) of the project, which we denote by the symbol r^*.

The IRR of a project can be obtained from the NPV formula. To do so, we solve the expression for NPV for the cost of capital that would result in a net present value of zero. That cost of capital is the project's IRR. Algebraically, IRR is the rate r^* that satisfies the equation:

$$0 = \sum_{t=0}^{t=n} \frac{\text{NV}_t}{(1 + r^*)^t}.$$

So by definition, if the firm's actual cost of capital (r) is equal to the project's internal rate of return (r^*), the project's NPV equals zero. That is exactly what you would expect. If the rate of return on each £1 invested in the project is identical to the cost of each £1 of capital used to finance the project, then doing the project will have no impact on the value of the firm, and hence the project's NPV must be

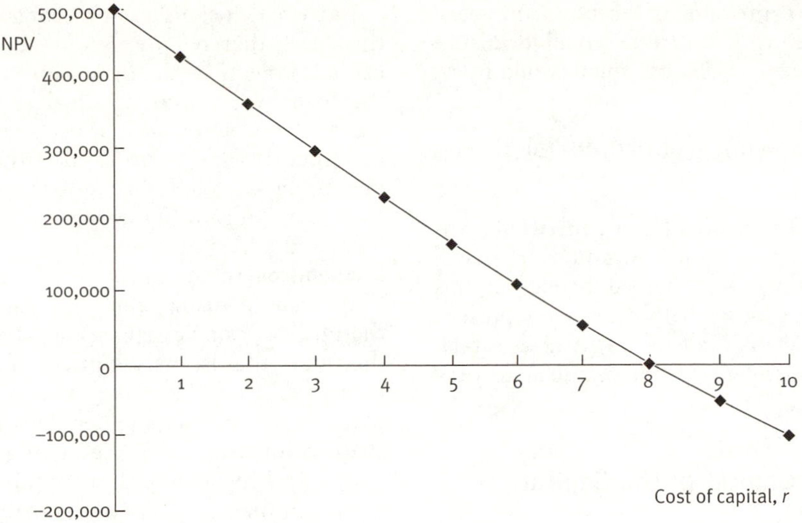

Figure 9.2 The relationship between NPV and the cost of capital

zero. We can now state the internal rate of return criterion for project appraisal:

If the internal rate of return (r^*) is greater than the cost of capital (r), then do the project;

If the internal rate of return (r^*) is less than the cost of capital (r), then do not do the project.

Under the assumptions we made, the NPV criterion and the IRR criterion will, in most cases, lead to exactly the same decision, and so it does not matter which is used for investment appraisal. Appendix 9.1 demonstrates that the IRR criterion can, in exceptional cases, lead to an incorrect decision. This is not true for the NPV rule, and so this is the safer one to follow.

The Cost of Capital Revisited

In practice investment funds are drawn from a variety of sources, and there may be differences in the rates of return required by the different providers. The firm's cost of capital will be a weighted average, with the weights reflecting the relative shares of each source of funds in the package. Moreover, even though there may be no limit to the *total* amount of funds the firm can obtain, there are likely to be limits on funds from particular sources. So as the firm's demand for funds rises, the funding structure, and so its overall cost of capital, might change.

Capital expenditures may be funded in the following ways:

1. bond issues;
2. long-term borrowing from financial institutions;
3. new equity capital raised in the capital markets;
4. retained profits.

Bond Issues

Firms obtain funds by selling bonds to investors. These typically guarantee a sum to be repaid (the principal) to the bond owner at a specified time. Fixed payments of interest are made until maturity. To induce investors to purchase newly issued bonds, the firm will have to offer a return on bonds at least equal to the investors' required rate of return, r_B. For some principal repayment (B) at maturity and interest payments made annually to the bondholder (I_t) over the years from bond issue until maturity (n), the investors' required rate of return will determine the price at which the firm can sell its bonds at issue (P_B.). Specifically, this relationship is given by

$$P_B = \sum_{t=1}^{t=n} \frac{I_t}{(1 + r_B)^t} + \frac{B}{(1 + r_B)^n}.$$

So the bond issue price is equal to the sum of the present values of the interest payments until maturity and the principal repayment. Note that the discount rate used in this expression is the bond investors' required rate of return. If a firm raised all its finance through bond issues, its cost of capital would be r_B.

Long-Term Borrowing from Financial Institutions

A second source of borrowed funds consists of loans made by financial institutions. Although there will be a spread of lending rates charged throughout this sector, we use the symbol r_F to denote a 'representative' rate. Once again, if a firm raised all its capital funds through borrowing from financial institutions, its cost of capital will be r_F.

Raising Equity Capital in the Capital Markets

The next two sources of investment funds do not involve the firm in borrowing but rather in persuading individuals or institutions to provide new capital for the firm. The first consists of selling new shares (stock) to investors. Suppose that r_C is the overall rate of return on stock required by an external investor. This return comprises two components. The first is the dividend payments made periodically by the firm to its stockholders. The second is the capital gain or loss arising from changes in the market price of stock. We shall explain how these are related to the overall return on stock in the following paragraphs where retained profits are examined. If a firm raised all its capital funds through the issue of new shares, its cost of capital would be r_C.

Retained Profits

A firm can also obtain funds by retaining profits. This can be viewed in terms of the new stock issue framework we have just examined. However with retained profits it is *existing* shareholders who are being asked to supply funds. The retention of profits means that current dividend payments to the firm's owners are less than the maximum possible. Suppose that the return which owners require in compensation for deferral of dividends is r_{SE}. The firm will have to offer its shareholders a return on retained profits at least equal to r_{SE} in order to persuade them to accept that deferral of dividends. If a firm raised all its capital funds through retained profits, its cost of capital will be r_{SE}.

But what does this return consist of? To answer this, note that retentions can be invested in new capital projects by the firm. This raises the value of the firm by an amount equal to the net present value of the additional projects undertaken. This increment to the value of the firm can be appropriated by a shareholder either in the form of a future capital gain (by selling his or her shares at an increased price) or in the form of increased future dividend payments.

We can formalize this idea algebraically, using the idea of a single representative share. Let V_0 be the value (that is, market price) of one share at the present time and V_n be the value of the share after n years. Suppose a shareholder plans to hold onto the share from now until n periods in the future, at which time he or she will sell it for a price of V_n. In the meantime, a stream of dividend payments (D_t, for $t = 1, 2, \ldots, n$) will be received. Given a required rate of return on retained profits, r_{SE}, the net incomes obtained by the firm must be sufficiently high that the expected future dividends and the expected share value after n years satisfy the following equation:

$$V_0 = \sum_{t=1}^{t=n} \frac{D_t}{(1 + r_{SE})^t} + \frac{V_n}{(1 + r_{SE})^n}.$$

Notice the very close equivalence between this expression and the one we used earlier for bond financing. To raise capital through retained profits, the firm must be able to achieve a net present value from its capital projects which is sufficiently high for the present value of future dividends and future share value to be at least equal to the present share value. Putting this another way, a shareholder will be willing to forgo current dividend payments if this is at least compensated by increased future dividends and/or capital gains.

The expression we have just used assumed that the shareholder intends to 'cash in' the shares at some point in time. But suppose the shareholder intends to keep the shares in perpetuity. In this case, the second term in the expression above will be zero—there is no point in time at which the shares will be sold for a price V_n. On the other hand, the shares will earn a stream of dividends in perpetuity. It is easy to see that the previous expression will in this case become:

$$V_0 = \sum_{t=1}^{t=\infty} \frac{D_t}{(1 + r_{SE})^t}.$$

Box 9.2 The Value of an Annuity Received in Perpetuity

Suppose that a perpetual annuity of a fixed rate of D per year is available. At a discount rate (or cost of capital) of r compounded annually, the capital value of this annuity—the amount someone is willing to pay to acquire that annuity—is given by its present value. If we denote its capital value by V_0 we have:

$$V_0 = \sum_{t=1}^{t=\infty} \frac{D}{(1+r)^t}.$$

From the arithmetic of geometrical progressions, this can be written in the simpler form

$$V_0 = \frac{D}{r}.$$

Now suppose that the annual payment on the annuity is not fixed at D, but instead is D in the present year and is expected to grow at a fixed rate of g per year.[2] The previous expressions then become

$$V_0 = \sum_{t=1}^{t=\infty} \frac{D(1+g)^t}{(1+r)^t} = \frac{D}{r-g}.$$

What is interesting about this expression is that it can be used to estimate what the investor's rate of return is revealed to be. Consider the case where we observe that £5 is the current size of the dividend payment on one share to a stock holder (so $D = 5$), and that the current price of the share is observed to be £100. Suppose we know that a typical investor expects dividend payments to rise on average over time at a rate of 3 per cent per year (so $g = 0.03$). It then follows from the previous expression that

$$100 = \frac{5}{r - 0.03}.$$

Solving this equation for r, we find that $r = 0.08$, or in percentage terms, the shareholder's required rate of return is 8 per cent.

You may at this point find it useful to read Box 9.2, which discusses the concept of the capital value of an annuity received in perpetuity. It also shows how we might use stock market prices to estimate the rate of return that investors on stock markets seem to require.

The Weighted Cost of Capital

Firms obtain project finance from a variety of sources: bond issues, long-term borrowing from financial institutions, new equity capital raised in the capital markets, and retained profits. In some circumstances the costs of capital from each of these sources—r_B, r_F, r_{SE} and r_C—would be equal to one another. For this to happen, all markets would need to be competitive, transactions costs in arranging funding would have to be identical in each case, and each type of funding would need to be a perfect substitute for any other. In this case the 'law of one price' would hold and the cost of capital would be the same from each source.

These conditions are unlikely to prevail in practice. The various sources of finance are not perfect substitutes. They vary in terms of repayment flexibility, and may also differ in the extent to which the creditor or investor will expect to have a say in how the funds are used. The sources of funds are best regarded as very different packages of attributes, and so in general the costs of capital from different sources will not be equal.

For each firm, there will be some optimum portfolio of sources of finance. The proportions of each type of funding in this portfolio will depend on the relative costs of capital, and on the particular needs and circumstances of the firm. The firm's cost of capital will be a weighted average of the relevant individual costs of capital. Suppose that α_1, α_2, α_3, and α_4 denote the proportions of total capital project funding coming from bond issues, financial institutions, new share issues, and retained profits respectively. The firm's cost of capital can be written as:

$$r = \alpha_1 r_B + \alpha_2 r_F + \alpha_3 r_C + \alpha_4 r_{SE}.$$

One final point remains to be considered in this section. The cost of capital might vary as the amount of investment undertaken changes. There are two main reasons why this might happen. First, the firm may choose to raise new capital from sources in different proportions to those in its existing capital structure. As the weights in the firm's overall cost of capital change, so its weighted

[2] No investor is really likely to believe that a dividend will actually grow at a fixed rate per year. But it may be reasonable to assume that an investor will have some expectation of the average underlying rate of growth. If he or she believes this long-term trend growth rate is g, then the expression used in the text can be interpreted in this way.

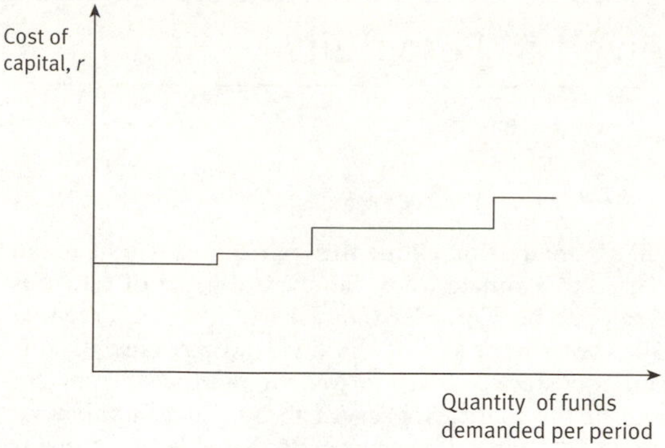

Figure 9.3 An increasing marginal cost of capital

cost of capital changes. Secondly, as the firm increases its demand for funds, it may be forced to pay an increasing rate of return to lenders or investors at the margin. The marginal cost of capital will not be constant but will increase in a step-wise manner, thereby pulling up its average cost of capital, as illustrated in Figure 9.3.

Investment Decisions when there are Many Projects Available

Previous paragraphs considered the appraisal of a single project. It is now time to consider investment appraisal where there is more than one feasible investment project, and the firm must decide which of these projects to undertake. We continue to assume that each project is independent of any other, and that the firm is not credit constrained. It turns out to be the case that the previous decision rules carry over to this case more or less unchanged. There are two criteria the firm could use.

The Positive NPV Criterion

The firm calculates the NPV of each feasible project. All projects with a positive NPV are selected. All projects with a negative NPV are rejected. Implementing all projects which offer a positive NPV will increase the firm's value to the greatest possible extent. The two assumptions we made were important in reaching this conclusion. As the firm is not credit constrained, it does not have to choose between projects each of which would be individually desirable. Secondly, because the projects are independent of one another, there is no need to look at any spillover or external effects of any project; each can be appraised in isolation from all others.

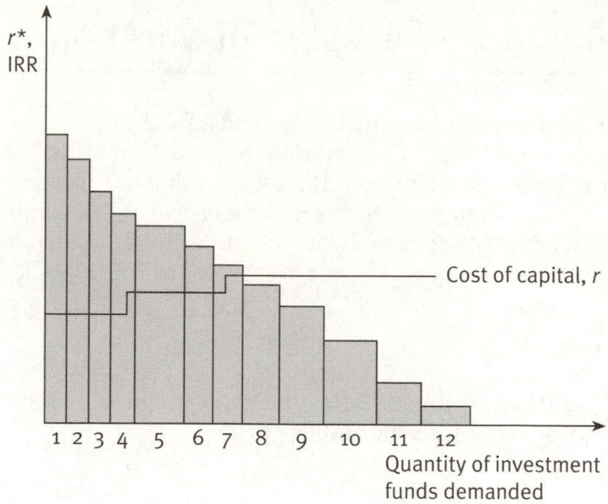

Figure 9.4 The Internal Rate of Return criterion

The IRR Criterion

For each feasible project, its IRR is calculated. All projects for which the IRR is greater than the cost of capital should be implemented.[3] This rule is illustrated in Figure 9.4, where the projects have been ranked in decreasing order of IRR.

Investment Decisions when there are Many Projects Available: Some Complications

What happens to the investment rules where we drop one or both of the assumptions we have been making? Where the firm is credit constrained—it faces a constraint on the amount of finance it can obtain—the rule of doing all projects for which NPV is greater than zero may not be applicable, as it might lead to a demand for funds which exceeds the funds available. The same kind of limitation applies to the IRR rule.[4] The firm must settle for doing the best it can with the limited resources for investment that are available.

This is not as easy to do in practice as one might at first think. Projects are likely to differ in scale, for example, having different NPVs but also having different funds requirements. A firm could use a search procedure to see:

[3] Once again, this rule can break down in exceptional cases. See Appendix 9.1.

[4] See Appendix 9.1 again for a more serious limitation of the IRR rule when the firm is credit constrained.

1. which combinations of projects can be done with the funding available, and
2. which of these combinations is the one that yields the largest amount of total NPV.

In other words, the search procedure should identify that particular set of projects which can be done with available funds and which will maximize added value. Typically, the projects selected will be those generating the greatest NPV per unit of investment funding.

A second complication arises where projects are mutually exclusive: that is, if one is done, others cannot be. In a simple case, two projects are *mutually exclusive*—if one is undertaken, the other is not possible. For example, suppose a new art gallery is to be built. One project envisages the gallery being housed in a newly constructed building, whilst another entails that it will be housed in a converted, disused power station. Often mutual exclusiveness arises in conjunction with a funds limitation. Further complications arise where projects are dependent (that is, they are not independent of one another). There are many forms of such dependency, including the case where a project cannot be done without another already having been implemented.

The complications we have mentioned in this section can usually be handled within the confines of the NPV or IRR approach, although most will require the use of some kind of search procedure in which the objective is to maximize total NPV subject to the constraints which operate. The techniques of doing this are beyond the scope of this text. Several of the references at the end of the chapter take you through such special cases in detail.

9.2 Investment in the Presence of Risk and Uncertainty

Imperfect Foresight, Risk, Uncertainty

Where decision-makers have perfect foresight, any course of action taken by the firm will have one certain outcome. Not only will capital expenditures be known, but so will all future costs and revenues arising from the project. This assumption is in practice untenable. Firms undertake capital budgeting in conditions of risk and uncertainty. The meanings of these terms have their origins in a monograph by the economist Frank Knight (*Risk, Uncertainty and Profit*, 1921). An action is *risky* if probabilities can be attached to each possible outcome, but it is not known at the time of the action which of the possible outcomes will occur. There is a more profound departure from perfect foresight when the outcomes of actions are uncertain. *Uncertainty* exists whenever probabilities cannot be meaningfully attached to possible outcomes, or when the decision-maker cannot even describe all the possible outcomes.

Let us deal first with the situation where the implementation of a capital project involves risks, and so the net present value of a project is not known with certainty. How do firms respond to risk, and do the two capital budgeting rules we have considered previously (the NPV and the IRR criteria) still apply when firms perceive projects as being risky?

The Payback Criterion for Capital Projects

One way in which firms are observed to respond to risk is by using a payback rule. A terminal date is chosen, beyond which any subsequent financial implications of the project are treated as irrelevant. The firm makes its best guess about the costs and revenues from project implementation until the threshold or payback date. If the present value of the predicted revenues exceeds the present value of the initial capital and operating costs, the project satisfies the payback criterion and is accepted.

The length of the payback period is entirely up to the firm. Projects felt to be extremely risky will usually be required to pay back within a relatively short time, whilst less risky projects will be given longer payback periods. Where this criterion is used in practice, the payback period varies greatly. For example, USA federal water projects have sometimes required that the scheme covers costs within fifty years. Studies in the UK suggests that many firms work to payback periods of between three and five years.

The rule is simple (which is always an advantage), but there is little or no economic justification for the use of the payback criterion. It should be easy to see why this is so. By treating all costs and revenues obtained after some arbitrarily chosen date as being irrelevant, decisions might be made which conflict with common sense. One simple

Table 9.3 Present value flows for a project

Period	Costs (in £ pv terms)	Revenues (in £ pv terms)
0	−700	
1		100
2		200
3		300
4		400
5		500

example should suffice to illustrate this point. Suppose a firm adopts a three-year payback period. Also suppose that its capital costs, operating costs, and revenues are as shown in Table 9.3.

At the end of three years, accumulated revenues are £600, less than is required to pay back the initial investment cost of £700. The project fails to meet the payback acceptance criterion. But this conclusion seems to contradict common sense, given the fact that the revenue stream is increasing over time, and after five years generates revenues which are more than twice the initial cost.

Probabilistic (Actuarial) Approach

In situations of risk, the NPV of a project is not known, but one can calculate its *expected* net present value (ENPV). To illustrate what this means, suppose that implementation of a project leads to the following possible cash-flow outcomes and associated probabilities:

outcome *A*: cash flow = £200 with a probability of 0.4;

outcome *B*: cash flow = £500 with a probability of 0.4;

outcome *C*: cash flow = £800 with a probability of 0.2.

As outcomes *A*, *B*, and *C* are the only ones possible, the probabilities sum to unity. With this information, an *expected value* of the cash flow can be calculated. This is given by

$$EV(\text{cash flow}) = (£200 \times 0.4) + (£500 \times 0.4) + (£800 \times 0.2) = £440.$$

If the firm is neutral in its attitude towards risk (that is, it is indifferent between a certain cash flow of £440 and a risky cash flow with an expected value of £440), then nothing we have said about investment appraisal so far need be amended. All that is necessary is that expected cash flows replace actual (but unknown) cash flows in the NPV or IRR calculations. The resulting NPV (or IRR) should now be called an *expected net present value* (or expected IRR).

Using a Cost of Capital Adjusted for Risk

In discussing how a firm could calculate expected values of cash flows and then use these in obtaining the expected net present value of a project, we assumed that the firm (or its owners) have a neutral attitude towards risk. But individuals may not be neutral towards risk. If individuals are risk averse (that is, a certain cash flow of £*X* is preferred to a risky cash flow with an expected value of £*X*), then the NPV and IRR criteria should be revised to take account of this.

One method of doing so involves adding a *risk premium* to the cost of capital (when using the NPV criterion) or adding a risk premium onto the target rate of return that a project is required to attain (when using the IRR criterion). The size of the risk premium should be equal to the additional return that the owners of the firm require in compensation for being exposed to that risk. Clearly, this risk premium will tend to vary according to time, place, and degree of risk, as each of these can affect the owners' views about the required size of compensation for risk.

This implies that the risk-adjusted cost of capital will be higher than the risk-free cost of capital. Other things being equal, fewer projects will be undertaken in the presence of risk. This approach has an attractive property. The projects that will not take place when the cost of capital is adjusted upwards will be those whose NPV is closest to zero. These are the ones which are most likely to be unprofitable if conditions turn out to be less favourable than expected. Owners of financial resources who dislike risk exposure might do well to shelve projects whose NPV under 'expected' conditions is only marginally greater than zero.

Sensitivity Analysis

Sensitivity analysis is not an alternative to other forms of investment appraisal. Rather, it is an additional element in the capital appraisal process for use where outcomes are risky. Put very simply, it is an exercise in appraising the robustness of a firm's NPV calculations to changes in the assumptions of forecasts used in arriving at expected NPV.

Suppose a project has a positive expected net

present value. The firm may ask the following question: how much less favourable, in percentage terms, can an assumption be before the NPV of the project becomes zero? The firm could ask this question of each of the major assumptions it made in arriving at the ENPV of the project. For example, suppose a firm assumed that the cost of capital was 5 per cent. Given this, the NPV is expected to be £110. If the cost of capital were 10 per cent, though, the ENPV would be zero. In this case, the assumptions could be made less favourable by 100 per cent (the cost of capital doubles) before the project becomes zero value-adding.

There are several ways in which this information might be used. In one approach, the firm chooses in advance a minimum tolerable sensitivity factor. For example, it may decide that a project should not go ahead if a worsening by any amount below 10 per cent on any of its forecasts were to lead to the project having a negative NPV. Once this criterion is adopted, the sensitivities can then be calculated, and compared with the minimum tolerable sensitivity factor. it. For example, if a revenue flow of just 8 per cent less than expected would lead to a negative NPV, the project would not then take place. More generally, the firm might not use any formal rule, but rather just take information generated in this way into consideration before making its final decision about whether or not to go ahead with the project.

The Option Theory of Investment Decisions

Dixit and Pindyck (1994) have recently developed what has been called the option approach to investment. This deals with investment choices in a business world where project returns are risky, where investment decisions have irreversible consequences, and where the timing of the investment is a matter of choice for the firm.

We argued in the previous section that investment decisions take place within a risky business environment. There is uncertainty about the returns from (and sometimes the costs of) capital projects. However, most investment decisions also possess two other important characteristics:

1. the investment is partially or completely *irreversible*;
2. the investor usually has some leeway about the *timing* of the investment.

Let us explore these two properties a little more closely. The issue of irreversibility is concerned with whether or not a capital expenditure can in some sense be 'undone' and so the costs fully recovered. Some capital expenditures are reversible, but this is rarely the case. In particular, when an expenditure is firm specific, it will usually be a sunk (and so wholly or largely unrecoverable) cost. The advertising expenditures made by a firm are one example of such firm-specific capital expenditures. The same is also true for many industry-specific expenditures. Suppose, for example, that the installation of a blast furnace turns out, with the benefit of hindsight, to have been unwise. One might think that the capital could be sold to other firms in the industry. But it is likely that the conditions which rendered the decision unwise will be true for any firm in the industry, and so it will be unsaleable (at anything near its full cost). The investment is again irreversible. Even where capital expenditures are not firm or industry specific, there may be many other reasons why an investment is irreversible.

Next consider the degree of flexibility a firm has concerning the date at which an investment opportunity is implemented. Firms may not have the opportunity to delay undertaking an investment; a winner-takes-all situation may make it imperative that a project be undertaken immediately. More generally, strategic advantages may accrue from early behaviour. In most circumstances, however, the firm is not confronted by a now-or-never choice, and it has some flexibility about the timing of the investment. Investing now may confer advantages, but there can also be benefits in delaying investment until later when more information becomes available. Indeed, the value of delaying capital projects and so gaining additional information can be extremely valuable.

In some ways, a capital investment opportunity is similar to a financial call option. With a call option, the holder of that option has the right (but not the obligation) to buy an asset at a previously agreed price at any date it chooses within some specified period of time into the future. The option holder may decide to exercise that option to buy if conditions turn out to be favourable for the purchase. The parallel with capital projects is clear: when a firm identifies a capital project, it has the option to undertake the project now or at some point in the future.

When an option to do something exists, that

option is in itself valuable. When an option is exercised (in this case where the capital project is implemented), it kills that option, and so the value of the option is lost. The firm gives up the opportunity of waiting for new information to arrive that might affect the desirability or timing of the investment opportunity. In other words, there is an opportunity cost in exercising the investment option. This cost should be included as part of the cost of the investment. Note that this option is only valuable if the investment is irreversible; if it were reversible then the firm could simply change its choices as new information arrived, without suffering any costs.

The standard (NPV) theory suggests that if the expected net present value of the investment exceeds zero, it should be undertaken. Dixit and Pindyck show that this rule is correct provided that

- the investment is reversible (so that if the future turns out to be less good than expected, the investment can be undone and the expenditures recovered—that is, there are no sunk costs), *or*
- the project's cash flows are known with certainty, *or*
- the investment is a now or never proposition—if the firm does not undertake the investment now, it will never be able to do so.

The NPV rule should, however, be modified when any one of these conditions does not prevail. The second of these conditions will never be true in practice, and the third is extremely unlikely. Interest centres, therefore, on whether a proposed investment expenditure is reversible or not. When it is irreversible, the NPV rule should be modified in the following way:

An irreversible investment opportunity that need not be implemented immediately should only be undertaken now if the NPV of the project exceeds the opportunity cost of keeping the investment option alive.

The value of these options can be estimated using standard techniques for the valuation of call options developed in the financial markets literature. A description of these techniques is beyond our scope, but the interested reader can find the necessary details in Dixit and Pindyck (1994). It is worth noting that recent studies have demonstrated that these opportunity costs may be very large. Investment decisions which ignore these costs can, therefore, be grossly in error. Dixit and Pindyck report that where firms build the opportunity costs of options into target rates of return, these are often found to be three or four times the cost of capital.

Decision Theory: Choices under Uncertainty

It is useful to separate investment projects into two categories: those which have modest implications for the scope, scale, or direction of the business, and those which imply significant *qualitative* changes for the business. In this latter category, we have in mind projects which change what the business produces, which markets it operates in, how diversified it is, and the like. For the first category, the conventional tools of capital budgeting that we have outlined so far may well be entirely appropriate, particularly when augmented by adjustments for risk. But where capital projects involve, or open up the potential for, fundamental reshaping of the firm, those techniques leave much to be desired.

To a large extent this is because the second class of investment expenditures involve the firm in making choices in conditions of pervasive uncertainty. Once it is not possible to put probabilities on each possible outcome, and so to calculate expected net present values, much of what we have discussed so far becomes inoperative.

One approach which provides valuable insights in these circumstances is *decision theory*, a branch of the general theory of games.[5] In the examples of game theory we have used in our discussions of oligopolistic behaviour, the players in the game were clearly specified. One player is the firm of interest—your firm, if you like—whilst the other player is another firm, typically a competitor of the first, and with similar goals.[6]

Decision theory also analyses games. One of the players of this game—what we shall call 'the firm'—is the object of our interest: it is the choices of this player that we wish to analyse. The other 'player' is not clearly specified. We follow the convention of calling this other player 'nature'. In the so-called *complete-ignorance* version of decision

[5] The presentation of decision theory in this section owes a large debt to an exposition of this material given by William Baumol (1977).

[6] Game theory need not have only two players. But this is the simplest case to analyse.

theory, the firm must select a move in complete uncertainty about what alternative will be selected by nature (or in other words, about which state of nature will occur). However, it is presumed that the firm knows (or can make estimates of) its pay-off matrix. The pay-off matrix is a statement of the strategic alternatives open to the firm, the possible states of nature, and the pay-offs associated with each configuration of choices.

The firm's attitude towards taking chances and possibly also its present financial position will, in conjunction with the structure of pay-offs, determine which of the strategic alternatives it will select. It will be useful to have an example in mind, shown by the pay-off matrix given in Table 9.4.

The firm is a personal computer producer. It has the following alternatives available. Option *A* can be interpreted as a conservative or 'steady-as-she-goes' choice. The choice of *A* commits the firm to do more of what it already does, by refining and developing its products and attempting to increase the volume sold. Option *B* involves the firm in a substantial change of orientation, switching its focus to the development and subsequent production of a new type of computer, with little in-built processing capacity or permanent data storage facilities, but making use of computer network resources to deal with many of these tasks. In so doing, computer hardware costs could fall dramatically.

The possible states of nature are *C*, *D*, and *E*. State C is one in which the personal computer market continues to grow, but there is almost no take-up of the new networking products. In state *D* the market for PCs and the market for the new product each have slow growth. In state *E*, the PC market collapses and the networked computer market booms.

If *C* turns out to be the state of nature, the firm is richly rewarded by playing strategy *A*, receiving a pay-off of 120. In contrast, its returns from selecting B are very poor, obtaining a pay-off of just 5. The remaining four cells in the matrix show the firm's pay-offs from *A* or *B* when the state of nature is either *D* or *E*. Note that the best of all possible outcomes is that given by the lower right cell, in which the firm switches to the new product and where the market for that product booms.

Table 9.4 The pay-off matrix for two investment alternatives

	C	*D*	*E*
A: refine and develop existing personal computer line	120	50	10
B: develop new networked computer system	5	30	140

A few words about terminology are in order. It is legitimate to regard the firm as playing a game against nature, but it would not be appropriate to think of nature as playing a game against the firm. For this reason, this branch of game theory is very different from the kind we looked at in our earlier analysis of oligopolistic markets (where two or more firms were playing games against each other). We could think about nature's 'choice' as emerging from a myriad of economic and other processes taking place in the firm's business environment. The net effect of these forces determines which of *C*, *D*, or *E* actually happens.

How does the firm decide which alternative strategy, *A* or *B*, to take? Many decision rules have been proposed and analysed. Let us examine four of these.

1. The Firm Adopts a Maximin Rule

The firm identifies the worst outcome that could occur for each of its available strategies. It selects the strategy with the least bad possible outcome. The label *maximin* signifies that the firm goes for the alternative that maximizes its minimum possible outcome. Inspection of the pay-off matrix reveals *A* to be the firm's maximin strategy. If *B* were selected, the worst possible outcome is 5, whilst if *A* is selected the worst outcome is 10. As *A* involves a less bad worst outcome, it is maximin.

Whilst avoiding worst possible outcomes has some attraction, a maximin rule can easily lead to choices which seem to contradict good commercial sense. This arises because the maximin rule ignores most of the information in the pay-off matrix. In particular, the pay-offs in best possible cases are ignored. Moreover, a maximin approach loads decisions entirely on the basis of most adverse possibilities. If one strategy was only marginally better than a second in terms of its worst outcome, the first would be preferred no matter how much more preferable the second may be under all other states of nature.

2. The Firm Adopts a Maximax Rule

In contrast to what may be regarded as the very cautious maximin strategy, a maximax decision rule is very adventurous. The firm examines each of its available strategies to identify the best outcome that could happen, and then selects the strategy with the best possible outcome. This rule implies that the firm should play *B* as it contains the best of all possible outcomes (a pay-off of 140 when the state of nature is *E*).

A maximax rule suffers from a similar weakness to a maximin rule, as it ignores most of the information in the pay-off matrix. In this case, all payoffs other than the best possible ones are ignored. Once again, the choices implied by this rule can in many cases fly in the face of common sense.

3. Bayes Criterion

Suppose that the firm has no information about the relative probabilities of the various states of nature. In considering this problem, the French mathematician Bayes suggested the following criterion. In the absence of any better information, the firm should set each of these probabilities equal to one another, and then adopt the strategy whose pay-off has the greatest expected value. For our example, the Bayes criterion leads to selection of strategy *A*. A variant of the Bayes criterion is obtained when the firm assigns its own (subjective) probabilities to various states of nature, rather than setting these equal to one another. Where a firm possesses useful information which enables it to assign probabilities in this way, this variant of the Bayes rule is likely to be preferable to presuming that the probabilities are equal.

Unlike the two previous decision rules, the Bayes criterion does consider all alternatives in the payoff matrix. However, it has a fundamental weakness too. This arises because it is not always clear how one should classify the various alternative states of nature. By specifying some states in a more narrowly defined way, it is quite possible that the strategy which maximizes the firm's expected value of pay-off will vary. A decision rule whose choice is sensitive to the definitions of states of nature is unsatisfactory.

4. The Firm Adopts a Minimax Regret Rule

Fundamental to this rule is the notion that the firm considers the opportunity cost of each choice. The essence of the minimax regret rule is to protect the firm against the excessive cost of mistakes. To implement this rule, the firm uses the pay-off matrix information to identify the cost of missed opportunities (its 'regrets'). These can be listed in the form of a regret matrix. The regrets for our illustrative example are shown in Table 9.5.

Table 9.5 The regret matrix

	C	*D*	*E*
A	0	0	130
B	115	20	0

Once the regret matrix has been calculated, the firm plays a minimax game using these regrets. Each row of the regret matrix is examined to identify the largest possible regret. The firm's strategy with the lowest possible regret is chosen. Clearly, the minimax regret rule leads the firm to select *B* in this example.

What are we to make of this brief exposition of decision theory? Unlike the NPV and IRR criteria, and the variants of these we looked at in discussing risk, decision theory is not intended to be prescriptive—it does not attempt to lay down any criterion of optimizing behaviour. Decision theory can provide insights into how firms might behave in the face of uncertainty, and it can tell us something about the advantages and disadvantages of behaving in ways that have some apparent attractiveness. Decision theory cannot tell us which is the *best* way to make choices in an uncertain world. Sensible behaviour will vary from firm to firm depending on the way in which it feels about taking chances, and upon the opportunities and threats it faces.

Conclusions

The use of the net present value of a capital project is the most fundamental component of any investment choice process. We have explained how NPV can be used to make investment decisions in a wide variety of different contexts. In addition, the internal rate of return of a project can also be a useful measure of the attractiveness of projects, but it should be used with caution.

When risk in introduced into our analysis, the NPV approach to investment can still be used, provided the existence of risk is explicitly recognized in the appraisal process. Uncertainty *per se* poses greater problems, and it is not easy to obtain any clear rules about how capital decisions should be undertaken. All depends on the firm's attitude towards acting in the face of uncertainty.

As we said at the beginning of this chapter, we have only been able to touch the tip of an iceberg in our analysis of the investment decision. A large number of extensions to the basic net present value model are discussed in the economic, finance, and business policy literature. One very important issue that we have only mentioned in this chapter is how a firm should make investment decisions where choices made in the past affect what can be done in the future and how profitable later projects will be. The literature in this area is only now being developed.

Similarly, we were only able to pay cursory attention to the process of generating investment opportunities. It seems likely that the process of generating good opportunities is more difficult than the appraisal of those projects. It is certainly more important in the final analysis.

Further reading

Excellent accounts of the firm's capital investment decision are given in Mankiw (1992) and Chrystal and Lipsey (1997), chapter 11. Mankiw's treatment tends to focus on the macroeconomics of investment, whereas Chrystal and Lipsey use an *NPV* approach similar to that used in the text. Further refinements of the techniques covered by us are presented and analysed at length in Lumby (1988), which is probably the most comprehensive text on investment appraisal that is available.

For discussions of the investment decision within a corporate finance framework, see Ross *et al.* (1992) and Pike and Neale (1994). A completely different approach to investment decisions—using game theory—is taken by Dixit and Nalebuff (1991). This is very easy to read, and is a superb introduction to decision-making in situations of strategic interdependence.

A more formal theory of investment under conditions of uncertainty is given in Dixit and Pindyck (1994), which systematically develops the option theory of investment. The way in which taxes influence investment is discussed in Hall and Jorgenson (1967). A survey of current investment appraisal techniques as used in practice is given in Sangster (1993).

Questions

9.1. Discuss the relative merits of the IRR, NPV, and payback investment appraisal criteria. Are there any circumstances under which it might be appropriate to use the payback criterion?

9.2. A computer costs £7,500 and has an effective life of three years, with a residual value of £1,000 at the end of that period. Annual incremental net cash flows from using the computer are £3,500.

(a) Calculate the net present value of the investment at a discount rate of 5 per cent.

(b) What is the IRR of the project?

(c) Does the project satisfy a two-year payback criterion?

9.3. Suppose Trackrail, a private business responsible for the provision and upkeep of a country's railway line and signalling infrastructure, is about to decide on whether to install a new nationwide signalling system. You are asked, as an economic consultant, to make a recommendation on the approach Trackrail should take in making that decision. What would be your recommendation, and why?

9.4. How should a firm choose its discount rate for net present value calculations of possible capital projects?

9.5. Do the techniques of capital project appraisal discussed in this chapter have any relevance to public sector organizations, such as hospitals, which are not selling their output through conventional markets? If you believe they do, how can they be implemented in these sectors?

9.6. How might the payback criterion be set by a firm?

Appendix 9.1 Limitations of the IRR Rule in Investment Appraisal

Many good expositions of the limitations of the IRR approach to investment appraisal exist. The brief summary given here is based on that given in Baumol (1977).

Let us first deal with the case where the firm is not credit constrained. Projects typically involve large initial expenditures, followed by a series of revenue flows that build up and later tail off. The relationship between the NPV of the project and the cost of capital is, in these cases, usually of the form shown in Figure 9.2. That is, the project's NPV continuously declines as the cost of capital rises. Where this is true, the NPV > 0 and the IRR > *r* rule will always lead to the same decision in project appraisal.

However, for some patterns of costs and revenues, the NPV of a project is not a continuously declining function of *r*. Where costs are high at the beginning *and* end of a project (as in nuclear power generation projects, where decommissioning costs can be very large), the NPV curve can have a shape similar to that shown in Figure 9.5. The problem with the IRR rule is easily seen here; there are not one but two costs of capital for which NPV is zero. Which of these two (if either) should be the IRR of the project? In fact, neither has got a stronger claim than the other, and so the use of IRR is problematic. This problem does not arise with NPV. For any particular cost of capital there is a unique NPV. Whether that is positive or negative will determine the decision.

Where projects are mutually exclusive, the NPV and IRR criteria can sometimes rank the projects differentially. This can arise because whilst NPV uses the actual cost of capital in its discounting of future costs and revenues, the IRR does not use that cost of capital (but uses r^*, the internal rate of

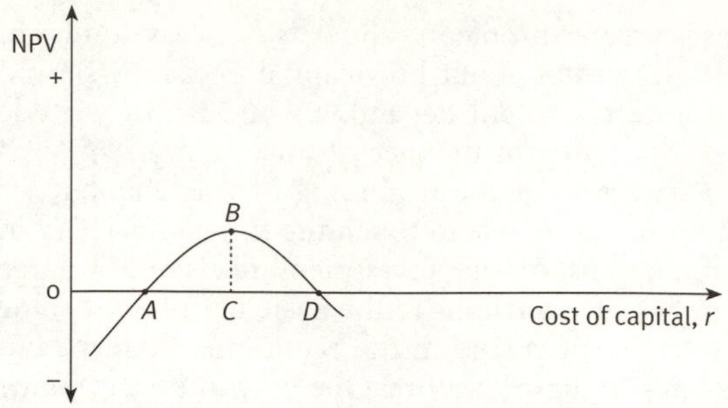

Figure 9.5 Multiple internal rates of return

return, instead). As the NPV ranking will always be correct, it is the preferred criterion.

In circumstances where the firm is credit constrained, use of the IRR criterion is beset by additional problems, and the NPV criterion cannot be applied without amendment, as explained in the text of the chapter. The underlying problem is that when the firm is credit constrained, the rate of return it actually pays on investment funds bears little or no relationship to the true cost of capital (the opportunity cost of the firm funds). Projects that could be done offer a higher rate of return than the rates the firm is charged for its use of funds, and it is the former (higher rate) that should be used in investment appraisal.

10 Value Creation and Sustainable Competitive Advantage

Introduction

This chapter continues our analysis of the firm's search for value with an examination of the ultimate determinants of firm success and failure. We have seen that success in adding value depends on the firm's capacity to protect its 'territory' against the actions of rivals and new entrants. But how do firms manage to do this? Some firms do seem able to generate added value on a sustained basis, sometimes for twenty or thirty years, and thus might be said to have exercised market power. But how did they achieve this position and what exactly is it that prevents actual and potential rivals from competing their profits away? How do these firms sustain their profits in the face of actual and potential rivalry? Can we identify the ultimate sources of sustained profitability? Are there any useful generalizations we can make about the fundamental nature of business performance which can help business strategists or is the nature of success so elusive as to make generalizations impossible?

We have argued (Chapter 4) that the objective of the firm is to search for, exploit, and protect opportunities to add value. We have subsequently examined how firms go about this by seeking to minimize their costs and by searching for ways to keep their prices from being competed down to average cost levels. From this we can reasonably conclude that the ability of the firm to add value depends on its ability to keep its costs as low as possible and its ability to limit actual and potential competition. And indeed this is exactly the advice we find emanating from the best business schools, and in dozens of textbooks on corporate strategy, reflecting the work of the most influential modern writer on business strategy, Harvard economist Michael Porter.

In his two best-selling and widely quoted texts on corporate strategy, *Competitive Strategy* (1980) and *Competitive Advantage* (1985), Porter argues that the fundamental determinants of the firm's performance are first, what he refers to as industry attractiveness, as determined by the forces of competition, and secondly, the firm's ability to manage its costs (or cost drivers as Porter calls them). Porter's books purport to provide detailed management programmes for achieving business success, based on a proper understanding of the principles of industry attractiveness and industry cost drivers.

However, the notion that successful firms belong to 'attractive' industries and have a good understanding of cost drivers seems to be at best an incomplete explanation of the relative performance of firms. We can see why a more complete explanation is required by thinking about the limitations of Porter's explanation of firm performance.

- First, it amounts to saying that business success is due largely to market power arising from the structure of the industry or market. The possibility that the firm's market power may be the product of superior competitive ability is not given a proper place in this analysis.
- Secondly, the empirical evidence on the relationship between industry structure and performance is in fact not very strong. Economists have conducted a huge number of empirical studies of the relationship, some of which suggest it exists, whilst some suggest it does not. If a relationship does exist between industry structure and performance, it is not very strong and a lot of the variation in industry performance remains to be explained.
- Thirdly, whilst it is clear that inter-industry profits do differ substantially (see Table 10.1),

Table 10.1 The after-tax rate of return on invested capital in US manufacturing industries, 1960–1985

Industry	1960–85 %	1981–85 %
Scientific instruments	9.1	4.2
Printing	8.6	7.3
Tobacco	8.1	9.5
Miscellaneous manufacture	6.1	5.6
Apparel	7.0	7.4
Electrical machinery	7.0	4.5
Chemicals	6.9	3.8
Transportation equipment	6.6	5.4
Paper	6.6	3.8
Leather	6.4	4.3
Non-electrical machinery	6.1	2.1
Food	6.0	6.1
Fabricated metals	5.7	3.7
Rubber	5.4	2.1
Petroleum	5.3	2.8
Lumber	5.0	0.9
Furniture	4.3	4.3
Stone, glass, clay	4.3	1.1
Textiles	4.2	1.8
Primary metals	2.8	−2.2

Note: After-tax return on invested capital is measured as inflation-adjusted, after-tax net income divided by the inflation-adjusted capital stock (net plant and equipment plus investments and intangibles).

Source: R. M. Grant, Contemporary Strategy Analysis, 2e (1995) based on Lawrence F. Katz and Lawrence H. Summers, 'Industry Rents: Evidence and Implications', *Brookings Papers: Microeconomics*, 1989, part 3, p. 214.

it is also the case that the profits of firms within a given industry differ substantially. Thus in the oil industry some firms consistently perform better than others. The same is true in the car industry, the computer industry, and most other industries. It would be useful, particularly for those involved in business policy, to understand the causes of these differences.

- Fourthly, the implicit advice that a manager should locate his businesses in an 'attractive industry' where the winds of competition are not too harsh seems at best vacuous and at worst misleading. There are presumably limits to what a particular firm is suited to doing, and simply aiming for the areas currently offering greatest rewards, irrespective of whether the firm's resources are suitable, is not particularly helpful. Furthermore, if several firms did take this advice, would a currently attractive industry continue to be attractive after the new entry had occurred? Our analysis in Chapter 6 of the consequences on industry profits of new entry suggests that this situation might not continue for long.
- Fifthly, the approach is not particularly useful. The structural conditions, or attractiveness, of an industry at any given point in time are largely 'given' and not subject to managerial control. Of course, managers can and do act to *influence* structural conditions, most visibly through mergers and acquisitions and building entry barriers, but generally managers cannot *determine* structural conditions to suit themselves, otherwise there would be no 'unattractive' industries. Industry attractiveness is not, therefore, a variable that managers can easily affect by the instruments available to them.
- Sixthly, there is what we might call the Porter paradox. Porter defines an attractive industry as one where a firm's profits or rents are sustainable. But the sustainability of a firm's performance depends on the capacity of other firms to copy or imitate or find a substitute for the sources of its profits or rents which by definition are firm attributes not industry attributes. In other words, it is not the industry that is attractive; it is the performance of particular firms in the industry that is attractive.

For these and other reasons, economists have recently tried to go beyond Porter's formulation of the conventional wisdom in order to identify the sources of individual firm success and failure at adding value and so develop a theory of individual firm performance as a basis for business policy. These efforts are by and large not motivated by the desire to provide a detailed management programme for corporate strategists, but simply to investigate and attempt to generalize about the fundamental sources of firm success and failure at adding value. It is the work of these economists that has come to be called the resource-based theory of the firm. We consider this work in this chapter, beginning with Porter's concept of sustainable competitive advantage.

10.1 Porter's Approach to Business Success

We begin by looking a little more closely at Porter's account of the sources of firm success in his 1985 text *Competitive Advantage* (sub-titled *Creating and Sustaining Superior Performance*). Porter begins by identifying superior performance with competitive advantage. The firm's search for sustainable profits is the search for sustainable competitive advantage. Given the structural conditions of an industry, which Porter says determine average performance or 'attractiveness', what is it that determines the relative competitive position and performance of a particular firm in that industry? Porter argues that there are only two types of competitive advantage. These are *low costs* and *differentiation.* Cost advantage arises when a firm can produce the same product (which commands a given price) as its competitors, at a lower cost. Differentiation advantage arises when a firm can command a premium price for a product which, although recognizably similar to other products on offer, is in some way recognizably different (or unique to use Porter's term). For example, an Apple is recognizably a personal computer (PC) but is also believed to differ in certain respects from other PCs and (at one time) it commanded a premium price.

The key to success according to Porter is cost analysis and understanding the cost drivers in an industry. This is because even when competition is based on differentiation, costs are still crucial. Differentiation raises costs because it involves better design or quality or features or reputation which have to be paid for, and there is no point in incurring these costs unless you can recover them through a price premium. That is, unless the customer actually perceives and values the differences between one product and another, differentiation is a wasteful activity from the firm's point of view. A famous case of this is the American engineering company which won the prestigious Baldridge award for quality one year and went out of business the next. Quality is valuable only if your customers are prepared to pay for it.

Competitive advantage requires understanding costs and what drives them. Note that it is cost *differences* between firms in the same industry which are important here. Porter argues that it is important to understand the nature of costs and the factors which drive them because understanding cost drivers can help firms to formulate an appropriate strategy for achieving competitive advantage. Porter implies that the search for minimum costs is not a straightforward optimization problem which any firm with the available information can solve. It is a complex and difficult exercise which can be done well or badly and which can thus provide a source of competitive advantage and superior performance. Those who understand these matters best and can exploit this understanding can win a competitive edge. His book purports to describe how exactly firms can go about understanding cost drivers and take advantage of them in formulating a strategy for competitive advantage. The best-seller status of Porter's book and his status as a consultant suggests that many managers agreed with him and sought competitive advantage according to the Porter recipe.

But many economists find this approach to an explanation of performance differences within an industry problematic. They ask the following questions. Why does the successful firm not buy the unsuccessful and teach it how to minimize costs? Why does the successful firm not sell its expertise in cost reducing to less successful firms? Why does the successful firm not cut its prices and drive its competitors out of business? Why does the unsuccessful firm not hire the executive in charge of cost drivers from the successful firm? (Which of course sometimes happens. Recall the battle between General Motors and Volkswagen for the services of cost guru Mr Lopez.) But most of all economists would ask the following question. If it is possible for Michael Porter to describe in detail precisely how to create and sustain competitive advantage, then surely all firms have equal access to this knowledge once Porter has conveniently codified it and every graduate business school teaches it? How then can this information by itself provide the basis for sustainable competitive advantage and superior performance? Economists might argue that what Porter has provided is really just an elaborate description of the nature of competitive advantage with some useful insights and programmes rather than a proper account of what differentiates successful firms from their less successful competitors. So whatever else Porter does, he fails to give us a robust explanation of the ultimate determinants of a firm's ability to create value on a sustainable basis. For this we need to move on to the emerging capabilities approach to the firm and the development of a distinctive resource-based theory of the firm.

10.2. The Capabilities Approach to Firm Performance

In recent years, several leading management thinkers have suggested what could be called a capabilities approach to understanding business performance. The essence of this approach is to try to pin down more carefully what exactly could give a particular firm an edge over its rivals. What could allow a firm to generate lower costs, charge higher prices, achieve better quality at the same cost, introduce new or improved products faster, than its rivals. Understanding these things will not necessarily provide a recipe for achieving them, but it should make for a better focus for the strategic management process.

First, Prahalad and Hamel (1990), referring to the core competence of the corporation, argue that the fundamental source of competitive advantage is to be found in management's ability to consolidate technology and production skills into competencies which empower the business to adapt quickly to changing opportunities. Core competencies are defined as the collective learning of the organization concerning the co-ordination of production skills and technology streams, a prominent example being Sony's miniaturization skills. Core competencies are described as the soil from which the firm's products are nourished and sustained.

Competencies, they argue, cannot be bought overnight; they have to be built over a long period. A crucial aspect of competencies is that because of the way they develop, they are difficult to identify precisely and thus hard to imitate. Indeed, Prahalad and Hamel suggest that firms often suffer because they fail to identify their own core competencies and so fail to nurture them or exploit them properly.

Next, Stalk *et al.* (1992), referring to competing on capabilities, argue that competitive advantage is based on the ability to respond to evolving opportunities which depends on business processes or *capabilities*. The essence of business success is choosing the right capabilities to build, managing them carefully, and exploiting them fully. The Japanese company Honda is used as an example.

Finally, Chandler (1990), summarizing his monumental study of the rise of big business in the West, identifies the building of capabilities as the basis of the development of successful companies and countries. Successful companies such as IBM and Bayer were those which made the initial heavy and risky investments in developing capabilities which allowed them to exploit the opportunities available for scale and scope economies.

The Nature and Significance of Capabilities

A major landmark in the development of the capabilities approach to the firm is John Kay's 1993 book, *Foundations of Corporate Success.* In this text, Kay explores the nature and significance of what he calls 'distinctive capabilities' more rigorously than previous writers, and goes on to discuss what determines the long-run value of a firm's capabilities. Kay's ideas are outlined below.

Kay points to three types of distinctive capability. He calls these *architecture, innovation*, and *reputation*. He also discusses the ownership of strategic assets as a source of competitive advantage for some firms, that is, success based purely on incumbency rather than on any detectable capability, although there is obviously a big element of judgement involved in telling the difference. For example, is British Telecom successful in generating value simply because it owns a strategic asset, the telephone line network, which no one would wish to duplicate, or does it also have capabilities which would make it hard to challenge in the absence of its strategic asset? It may be possible to judge this as British Telecom seeks to add more value by diversifying out of the UK and so competing with foreign telecom providers.

Architecture as a Distinctive Capability

Architecture is the name Kay gives to the network of contractual relationships which defines the firm. (Refer to Chapter 4 and our discussion of the nature of the enterprise and the role of the entrepreneur to remind yourself of what is meant by the contractual nature of the firm.) The value of architecture lies in the capacity of organizations which establish it to create and store organizational knowledge and routines, to promote more effective co-operation between the members of the firm, to achieve an open and easy flow of information between members of the firm, including supplier firms and indeed in some cases customers as members of the firm, and to respond flexibly to changing circumstances. Architecture depends on the ability of the firm to build and sustain long-term relationships and to establish an environment which encourages co-operation and discourages opportunism. Kay's examples of superior architecture include IBM in its heyday, Marks and Spencer, Liverpool Football Club, and many Japanese firms. He points in particular to the much-discussed Japanese employment system, its supplier networks, the close relations between industry and finance, the great emphasis on co-operation and collaboration, the development of long-term commercial relationships, and the generally higher level of trust which encourages co-operation.

Reputation as a Distinctive Capability

Reputation is identified by Kay as a second potential distinctive competence. Reputation is an important commercial mechanism for conveying information to consumers about product quality, but it is not equally important in all markets. Its significance depends crucially on how consumers learn about products and product quality: by search activity, by immediate experience, or by long-term experience in use.

Thus, if we want to buy a PC, we can find out a lot by searching through magazines which specialize in describing and evaluating what is available, going round the specialist shops, and talking to friends. Advertising for such products will tend to be informative and factual. Claims about quality are easily checked. You can learn from immediate experience and at low cost how you rate the quality of a particular beer or soft drink or instant coffee. Advertising in this case will tend to try improve the experience by association with image and personality so that you become a repeat customer, rather than make dubious claims about quality.

However, there is a category of goods for which product quality is all important but which consumers cannot learn about easily through search activity or immediate experience. Kay mentions such things as pension plans, funeral services, car-hire, accountancy services, medicines, and some consumer durables. The present authors would suggest roofing services and vitamin pills as prime examples. All students will also be familiar with the problem because choosing a university is a perfect example of a long-term experience good. Such goods are also called credence goods.

The fundamental problem with such goods is that whilst all firms will 'guarantee satisfaction', poor quality will take time to manifest itself. Consumers are prepared to pay for quality but they need some means of distinguishing the competing claims of sellers. If they cannot, they will assume low quality and offer to pay only low prices.

Reputation, therefore, is believed to be a potential source of advantage and success in certain industries because it allows firms to attract customers willing to pay a premium for quality assurance. Investing in and selling on reputation is saying in effect: we have a lot to lose if we fail to satisfy. It does not take many negative reports to damage an expensively created reputation. However, so called 'hit and run' producers do not worry about investment in reputation. They can try to sell on price alone and not be around later to deal with the problems and the complaints.

How might firms endeavour to establish a reputation in this sense? Possibly by advertising more heavily than hit and run producers. Interestingly, long-term experience-type goods have on average the highest level of advertising to sales ratio at 5 per cent compared say to search goods where the ratio is 0.4 per cent or short-term experience goods where the ratio is 3.6 per cent. Why should the producers of such products spend so much on advertising? Advertising is an example of a sunk cost as defined in our chapter on costs. So heavy advertising may be seen as a way of demonstrating a commitment to quality in a market for long-term experience goods, of telling consumers that you plan to be around for some time and that you stand to lose something from failing to deliver on quality. You stand to lose because if you do not deliver on quality, this will eventually become apparent and your heavy investment in advertising lost.

Innovation as a Distinctive Capability

The firm's capacity for innovation is seen by Kay as a possible distinctive capability. If a firm can build a capacity for lowering costs or improving its products or introducing new products ahead of its competitors, it can achieve a competitive advantage. But Kay argues that innovation by itself as a source of competitive advantage is actually quite rare, or at least less common than might be imagined. The reason why innovation can be a distinctive capability, but rarely is, is the same.

Innovation is very difficult. Anything that is easy to do is unlikely to give you a sustainable edge. But innovation is very difficult and many firms which seek competitive advantage by this route fail.

There is more to innovation than simply investing in R&D. Innovation is uncertain, it is hard to manage properly, and it can be difficult for firms which invest in R&D to secure or appropriate all the returns for themselves. Thus for firms which invest in R&D, there is uncertainty about what will emerge, uncertainty about the commercial viability of what might emerge, and uncertainty about what their competitors are up to and how they will react to what emerges. Further, the management and successful exploitation of innovation is hard and requires special skills. Many firms have proved able to generate good new ideas but unable to exploit them satisfactorily. Finally, it can be difficult for firms which invest in R&D to secure the rewards for themselves. There is what economists call an '*appropriability*' problem. R&D, when successful, leads to valuable new ideas for products or processes but it is in the nature of ideas that it is difficult to keep them to yourself. (Ideas are by nature a public good, as defined in Chapter 13.) If one firm discovers that people have a great desire to listen to music on the move, and comes up with a product which allows this, then other firms quickly get the message and imitate the idea. The first firm finds it difficult to appropriate fully the value of its good work. Much of the value of its efforts is appropriated by its competitors. This is good news for them, of course, and for customers but not exactly a strong incentive to look for new ideas in the first place.

For these reasons, Kay argues that what appears to be competitive advantage based on a capability for innovation is actually based on architecture. Successful innovators such as Sony or Glaxo have developed an architecture, and built the necessary complementary assets, which enables them to generate a flow of innovations which they can exploit commercially. Companies with a flair for innovation are often, in fact, marshalling three capabilities: innovation, architecture, and reputation. Note that this is also implicit in the work of Prahalad and Hamel, and Stalk *et al.* outlined earlier.

Corporate Objectives Once Again

Now recall our discussion of corporate objectives in Chapter 4. In that chapter we argued that whilst the entrepreneur, or those with rights to acquire the residual value generated by the enterprise, may be assumed to wish to maximize the firm's residual value, it is not appropriate to assume that everyone involved with the firm will necessarily work wholeheartedly to this end. Making such an assumption causes you to ignore the fact that the fundamental problem of those who organize and manage firms is in fact to try to ensure that as far as possible the firm is focused on the search for value. We pointed out earlier that the strength of the firm's desire to search for the maximum level of the firm's residual value depended greatly on the nature and organization of the firm itself; on the extent to which the various members of the organization could be induced or encouraged to co-operate, to focus their efforts on the search to maximize the firm's value, by appropriate incentive systems and contractual arrangements; on the extent of investments made in building trust and co-operation; on the leadership qualities of the coalition leaders; in other words, on architecture.

The significance of architecture, then, is that it is concerned with focusing the actions of the individual members of the coalition towards creating value for the collective and diminishing the impact of the 'Prisoner's Dilemma' which, you may remember, was explained in Chapter 4 and again in Chapter 8. The strength of the firm's desire to search for value is therefore something which has to be actively organized for and managed. And this is precisely why organizational architecture is so significant. The strength of the firm's desire to add value is a fundamental determinant of its likely success. A firm in which all the individual members are clearly focused on creating value for the coalition has a better chance of succeeding than a firm of equally talented people where such focus is lacking. It is a bit like any competitive sport. A team of individuals clearly focused on the quality of their team's product and its performance will generally beat a team of similarly talented individuals who are less well organized and more interested in their own performance and rewards than in that of the team's.

Organizing and managing the firm's human resources to focus on team objectives rather than personal objectives are thus necessary conditions for business success. These are the fundamental managerial tasks. They are what Japanese manufacturing firms have proved to be very good at. But it is not easy to do and not easy to codify in textbooks. If it could be, then anyone could do it and it would not be a source of advantage for any single firm. Recruiting, team building, motivating, and organizing are difficult, because they depend on such things as leadership and trust and 'creating the right chemistry'. And this is precisely why they are such a valuable capabilities, such a key source of competitive advantage. They are difficult to get right, they have to be worked at and invested in continuously, they are hard to build and cannot be bought 'off the shelf'. These qualities mean that those firms which get it right, by accident or design, have a valuable asset which potential competitors find difficult to 'buy in'. For example, it has been accepted for many years that the considerable success of Marks and Spencer in retailing has been due to its careful approach to organizing and managing its human resources and its supply chain. But knowing this and duplicating it are different matters, as competitors of Marks and Spencer have discovered. Similarly with the Sony approach to innovation, or the Liverpool approach to football. We shall now look more closely at precisely this issue, at what determines the value of a firm's capabilities.

The Value of Capabilities

The value of the firm's capabilities depends on a number of things. To be valuable, the firm's capabilities have to be reasonably *sustainable* and *appropriable.* A capability is something which makes a particular firm successful, but this success is going to attract competition from other firms looking for a piece of the action. If the capability is to be of long-run value to the firm, it has to be sustainable in the face of this challenge. It must be such that these other firms cannot easily identify it precisely or imitate it quickly and so catch up with the first firm. Further, the value of the capability to the firm will depend on how the total added value created by the capability is divided between the firm and the owners of the underlying resources.

In Chapter 4 we discussed the case of football clubs and the fact that even successful teams do not necessarily give rise to profitable businesses. This, we argued, was because the value generated by a successful team tended to be appropriated by the individual star players and coaches whose scarce services are much in demand. Only if the club can find a way of organizing and managing itself in such a way that it creates capabilities above and beyond that of the individual talents employed can it generate rents as a business entity. To the extent that a firm's capabilities depend greatly on the qualities of individual resources, then it is the resource owners themselves who will capture the value, not the firm. Thus the capability of a successful advertising agency must be based on more than the creative genius of a few individuals whose talents can be valued in the open market and who are thus able to appropriate the value of these talents. This is why the type of capabilities associated with above-average firm performance needs to be something quite complex, hard to define, and not associated with any particular individual (except the entrepreneur herself). Capabilities such as firm architecture or reputation or corporate culture or collective learning are essentially intangible assets. They are undoubtedly valuable but difficult to value. And although they are valuable, they are difficult to buy and sell.

Sustainability and appropriability depend on a variety of factors related to the nature of the capabilities involved, including *tradability, replicability, transparency, and substitutability.*

Tradability or Transferability

This refers to the extent to which capabilities are marketable rather than immobile or firm specific. If the source of a firm's advantage is a marketable resource then the resource's market value will reflect its worth and the resource will capture this value, or appropriates it, as we said above. The services of a brilliant scientist or soccer player are marketable, so a firm which simply hires the best available resources will not necessarily be successful at adding value. To be successful at adding value, or generating economic profits, the firm has to take generally available, market-valued, resources and over time build these into firm-specific capabilities, or if you prefer specialized assets, which are more valuable than the cost of the individual resources involved but which are immobile. Other firms could bid for the individual resources involved at the going rate but not for the capabilities, unless of course they bid for the firm itself. You cannot easily buy a bit of a firm's reputation or its committed workforce or its supply-chain organization. These things take time to build and are specific to the firm that builds them. The resources behind the capabilities are now more valuable in their present use than in any alternative use but this extra value, or rent, is captured by the firm not by the individual resources. Because this added value, or profit, is not the result of resource scarcity *per se (the capability is scarce but not the underlying resources of capital and labour)*, it is sometimes referred to in the business strategy literature as a quasi-rent to differentiate it from Ricardian, or scarcity, rent.

A simple example might help to make the point. The value of a team of eleven players is the market value of the players plus any value arising from this particular combination rather than another. If the players have played together for a long time, if they have developed a deep understanding of one another, if they work hard for one another, if they have a special commitment to one another, then the team is worth more than the sum of its parts. The team has a competitive edge which it is possible to build over time but which cannot be bought. The individual players can be transferred but the team's 'capability' cannot, unless of course you buy the team.

Replicability

This has to do with the ease with which potential rivals can copy or imitate the capabilities involved. A capability which is relatively easy to imitate is obviously not sustainable and therefore less valuable than a capability which is hard to imitate. Thus no football team is going to succeed for long purely on the basis of 'inventing' a new formation such as 4–4–2. Because, if such a formation proves successful, other teams will have no problem in adopting it. You cannot patent a formation, you cannot keep it a secret, and any team can try it. So it cannot provide a long-run advantage. On the other hand, the famed 'team spirit' of the great Brazilian teams has proved a little harder for other teams to replicate. This is why organizational 'software' can be crucial.

Transparency

This refers to the ease with which potential competitors can actually identify what it is that makes a particular firm successful. Identifying the capability involved is a prerequisite for copying it. Of course, this is not sufficient, but it would be a good start. But if the precise basis on which a firm is successful is hard to pin down, then competitors cannot even begin to think about replicating it or trying to acquire it. It used to be thought, for example, that the basis of the success of some Japanese firms was impossible to pin down and somehow the result of some 'cultural' conditions that Westerners could not understand and could not hope to copy. Now we know better. Western managers and academics have studied Japanese firms like Toyota closely and the basis of their success is better understood. Some of these things have now been imitated in the West and to this extent Toyota's capabilities have been made less valuable.

Substitutability

If a potential competitor cannot easily replicate the foundation of a successful firm, it might be able to find a way round it by developing a suitable substitute. Thus, the more difficult it is to find a substitute for a capability, the more valuable it will be to a firm. Therefore access to lots of cheap labour, or prime high-street sites, is unlikely to give a firm a sustainable advantage because other firms can find substitutes for these factors. Finding a substitute for Sony's collective knowledge of miniaturization technology, or Volvo's commitment to building safe cars, is harder.

Isolating Mechanisms

Economists working in this field have developed the concept of *isolating mechanisms* to describe those factors which act as natural barriers protecting and sustaining the value of a successful firm's capabilities. In the absence of isolating mechanisms, capabilities would be replicable or transferable and thus would not be sustainable as sources of added value. This indeed is the basis of the perfect competition model analysed earlier in Chapter 6. If all firms have access to the same information and the same resources, and if these resources are perfectly mobile, there is no scope for sustainable profits or rents. Anything one firm can do another firm can replicate. Therefore the identification of potential isolating mechanisms involves challenging these assumptions.

Thus, lack of transparency, or causal ambiguity as some authors call it, implies that not all firms have access to the same information. If potential competitors cannot understand what it is that the successful firm is doing right, they cannot easily challenge it. The lack of transparency acts to protect the successful firm. Similarly, the lack of transferability and replicability implies that not all firms can have access to precisely the same resources. If potential competitors cannot 'buy in' or replicate exactly what the successful firm has, then they cannot challenge the incumbent. Impediments to resource acquisition and replication thus act to protect the successful firm. Other isolating mechanisms have been identified. Some authors refer to 'time compression diseconomies' as a problem for imitators. This means basically that even when capabilities can be properly identified and replicated in principle, it is still difficult to do so in practice because of the extra costs associated with accumulating the required resources and building capabilities under time pressure.

10.3. A Resource-Based Theory of the Firm?

What has emerged from the growing efforts to explain the nature and sources of competitive advantage is a distinctive resource-based view of the firm, which complements the standard economics textbook model of the firm under perfect competition (see Chapter 6). The difference between the two approaches, the traditional textbook model and the new model, is this. The new approach sees firms as fundamentally heterogeneous and tries to explain the nature, sources, and implications of this heterogeneity. The new approach is concerned with how differences in the nature and performance of firms arise, how they persist, and what lessons can be learned from studying these differences. The new approach believes that a firm's capacity for adding value is a result of more than the exercise of market power (see Chapters 7 and 8). The new approach accepts that the standard competitive model is a powerful model which tells us why it is *difficult* for firms to achieve sustainable competitive advantage, but believes that it fails to consider adequately why it might be *possible* for some firms to do just that. The new approach is interested in examining the *process* of competition over time under realistic circumstances, whereas the standard approach is interested in examining the *result* of competition under somewhat extreme circumstances. The new approach is an attempt to explain why some firms are able to create added value on a sustained basis, whilst the old approach purports to explain why this is impossible.

Why do we use the term 'resource-based' approach? Because the new approach is concerned with the nature of the firm's resources; with the competition for these resources; with the mobility of these resources; with the way in which these resources are combined into capabilities; with what determines the value of these resources and capabilities; with the difference between general resources and firm-specific resources and capabilities; and with relating the firm's performance, its ability to add value or generate rents, to its resource base. Some authors talk about a new resource-based theory of the firm but most are reluctant to go this far until the approach is better developed.

An important contribution to the development of a resource-based theory of competitive advantage is that of Peteraf (1993) which is summarized in Box 10.1. In her article, Peteraf sets out to develop a general model of resources and performance which integrates various recent strands of thought about business policy and performance. The article is concerned primarily with the factors which determine the value of resources and capabilities rather than with identifying the nature of these capabilities. The article is concerned with isolating mechanisms and the appropriability of value produced by co-operating resource owners. Peteraf's article sums up the present state of the debate on resource-based theory which promises to become the basis of strategy analysis.

Conclusions

We set out in this chapter to further our understanding of the firm's search for value. In particular, we wanted to see what could be said about the ultimate determinants of firm performance, the ability of a firm to add value, to earn above-normal profits or rents. We have examined the concept of competitive advantage, the capabilities approach to firm performance, and the emergence of a distinctive resource-based approach to firm performance. We have discussed the nature and significance of capabilities, and what determines their value. We have discussed the issue of sustainability and appropriability of firm value and the concept of isolating mechanisms. This approach does seem to offer a realistic explanation of the ultimate sources of competitive advantage and firm performance, and it uses an explanation that does not simply attribute superior performance to the existence of market power. That is, it seems to explain why some firms can generate superior performance even when they have several rivals and even when there are no insuperable barriers to entering the industry. The problem for rivals and potential competitors is identifying and replicating the basis of the successful firm's success. To the

Box 10.1 Peteraf's Resource-Based View of Competitive Advantage

Margaret Peteraf's paper 'The Cornerstones of Competitive Advantage: A Resource-Based View', first published in volume 14 of the *Strategic Management Journal* in 1993, aims to bring out the economics underlying the resource-based theory of competitive advantage, and to integrate various existing perspectives into a parsimonious model of resources and firm performance. In this summary, we focus on the architecture of her model, paying rather less attention to its components. Concepts which are explained elsewhere in this chapter (or in other chapters of the book) are italicized.

Peteraf's model of competitive advantage is schematically represented in Figure 10.1.

As you can see from Figure 10.1, there are four key components to Peteraf's theory of competitive advantage. A firm is said to have a competitive advantage when it is able to

- achieve *rents*: which requires *heterogeneity* between firms;
- *sustain* those rents: which requires *ex-post* limits to competition;
- keep those rents within the firm: which requires *imperfect resource mobility*;
- enjoy rents that are not offset by the costs of achieving a superior set of resources: which requires *ex-ante* limits to competition for those resources.

Peteraf examines each of these elements in turn.

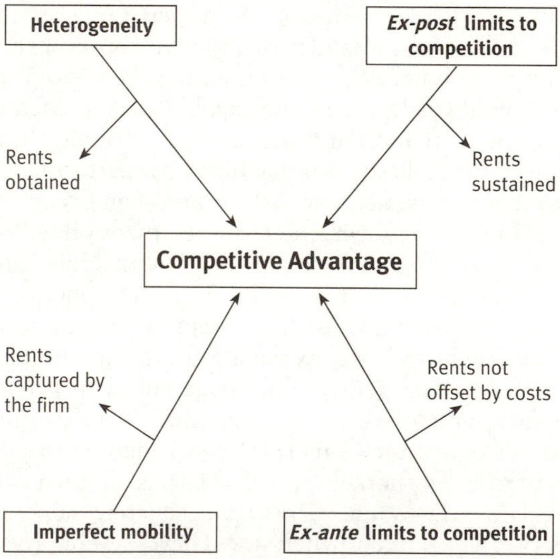

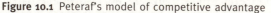

Figure 10.1 Peteraf's model of competitive advantage

Source: Adapted from Peteraf (1993). Copyright John Wiley & Sons Limited. Reproduced with permission.

Heterogeneity

Bundles of *resources* and *capabilities* are heterogeneous across firms. Heterogeneity implies that firms with varying capabilities will earn different levels of return. Those with only average resources will break even; those with superior resources will earn rents.

Sources of Heterogeneity

Heterogeneity may reflect the presence of *superior resources* or *capabilities* which are either fixed in supply or are 'quasi-fixed': their supply cannot be quickly increased. Owners of these resources/capabilities gain *Ricardian rents* or quasi-rents (see Chapter 4). These rents are only sustainable if the resource/capability is fixed or quasi-fixed. An important class of resources are those which are limited in the short run but may be renewed and expanded within firms that use them. Prahalad and Hamel (1990) argue that *core competencies*—particularly knowledge-based resources—are enhanced as they are applied.

Ex-Post Limits to Competition

Whatever the source of the rents, sustainable competitive advantage requires that the condition of heterogeneity be preserved. This will only be the case if there are *ex-post* limits to competition: there must be forces which limit competition for those rents from imitators. *Ex-post* limits to competition may arise from two kinds of factors we have examined in the text of this chapter:

- *imperfect imitability/replicability*, maintained by *isolating mechanisms*;
- *imperfect substitutability.*

Imperfect Mobility of Resources

This refers to the marketability of resources/capabilities. If the factors which make a firm different are tradable, then the factors themselves capture the rents involved rather than the firm. Thus a good high-street location is believed to be very important for firms in the retail business. But good locations are expensive because there is competition among retailers for these locations. The locations are tradable. Therefore having a good location will not necessarily make you a profitable retailer because the benefit of the location is capitalized in the cost of acquiring the location. Similarly, high quality players are important to football teams but players are tradable and competition means that the players rather than the business capture the rewards of success.

To ensure that the business captures the rents available, the resources which make the firm different, which are the source of its heterogeneity, must be relatively immobile or hard to trade. This means they cannot simply be bid away from the firm. They must be something fundamental to the firm and hard to conceive of separately from the firm. For example, the firm's reputation or its architecture.

Ex-Ante Limits to Competition

A final requirement for a firm to have a competitive advantage is that there are *ex-ante* limits to competition. What does Peteraf mean here? The source of a firm's rents is said to be a superior resource position. But imagine the situation before any firm has adopted that position. If many firms recognized its potential, a competitive struggle would ensue to occupy that position. This process would compete away all rents that could be obtained from occupying the position.

For example, suppose that many oil companies had known exactly how much oil was available to be extracted from North Sea oil fields, what price the extracted oil would command, and what costs would need to be incurred in extracting that oil. Using this information, calculations would have led these firms to identify a maximum price they would have been willing to pay in bidding for extraction licences. But competition between firms to obtain the licences would have pushed bid prices up to this maximum level, so firms would have been able to obtain no more than normal profits from owning the extraction licences.

Except by reason of good luck, above-normal returns—rents—can only be obtained by occupying a superior resource position if some firm had the foresight to acquire it or build it in the absence of such competition. This requires either the presence of uncertainty or incomplete information (so that there is scope for one firm to spot opportunities when others do not) or that there are differences in the costs that firms will have to incur in implementing strategic choices.

This argument can be put another way: there must be some difference between the *ex-post* value of a venture and the *ex-ante* costs of acquiring the resources necessary for implementing the venture if rents are to be positive.

Applications of the Resource-Based Theory

Peteraf concludes her article by discussing some of the potential applications of the theory. She argues that whilst the model is available to all, its strategic implications depend on a firm's particular resource endowment. Therefore her model does not produce a recipe for success à la Porter's approach to competitive advantage with which we began the chapter, but an approach to the strategy-making process itself.

She suggests the following uses of the model:

- to help managers identify resources which might support a competitive advantage;
- to help in deciding whether to license a new technology or develop it internally;
- to analyse issues regarding the scope of the firm's activities;
- to analyse whether a firm can add value through a merger or acquisition.

We shall have much more to say about the last two of these issues in the next chapter.

extent that this is difficult, it suggests that rivals and potential competitors have trouble either in identifying the sources of success or replicating them or finding a substitute for them. This is likely to be because the sources of success, the capabilities, are quite complex, take time to develop, and cannot be bought 'off the shelf'. Thus, a company's approach to human resource management or its relationship with its suppliers or its reputation for quality is very valuable, but it cannot be traded. Other retailers cannot buy a bottle of the 'Essence of Marks and Spencer'. They can try to duplicate it, of course, or find a substitute for it, and no doubt they try, but they cannot buy it ready made.

The resource and capabilities approach to the firm thus suggests the possibility of developing a solid analytical foundation for the study of business policy in the same way that many years ago the efficient markets approach provided a solid foundation for the study of financial policy.

Further reading

All of the following repay careful reading. Chandler (1990), 'The Enduring Logic of Industrial Success', Peteraf (1993), *The Cornerstone of Competitive Advantage: A Resource Based View*, Peters and Waterman (1982), *In Search of Excellence*, Prahalad and Hamel (1990), *The Core Competence of the Corporation*, and Stalk *et al.* (1992), *Competing on Capabilities: The New Rules of Corporate Strategy.*

As Michael Porter is so widely referred to, it would be a good idea to read Porter (1985), *Competitive Advantage.*

Excellent texts that include a coverage of the areas looked at in this chapter are Grant (1991), *Contemporary Strategy Analysis,* and Kay (1993) *Foundations of Corporate Success.*

Questions

10.1. Think of a successful firm with which you are familiar, and try to account for its success in terms of core competencies and/or capabilities.

10.2. What factors determine the value of a firm's capabilities?

10.3. Porter appears to argue that there are only two types of competitive advantage: low costs and differentiation. Critically assess this view.

10.4. Is it possible for one country to have a competitive advantage relative to another country?

10.5. Are a firm's strategic assets also part of its distinctive capabilities?

10.6. Why is it often difficult to transfer capabilities from one organization to another?

11 Value Creation, the Scope of the Firm, and Acquisitions

Introduction

This chapter continues our analysis of the firm's search for value with an examination of the potential for adding value through corporate diversification and acquisition. Many modern business corporations have extended the scope of their activities through diversification, for example, from cigarettes to financial services in the case of BAT Industries, and many have extended their size and/or scope through mergers and acquisitions, for example, Hanson or Saatchi and Saatchi. Not surprisingly, given the prominence of these activities in the business press, texts on business policy give a lot of attention to these two activities. Indeed, the concept of business strategy is treated by some as synonymous with diversification and acquisition. But does diversification or acquisition always make sense? For some it appears to have worked (Hanson), whilst for others it appeared not to (Saatchi and Saatchi), with other cases disputed (BAT Industries). Why should diversification or acquisition work for some firms but not others? Are there any useful generalizations to be made about the potential of these two approaches to growing the business which can help the business strategy process?

In this chapter we look at the economics of two prominent and much-discussed aspects of business strategy and corporate growth:

- extending the scope of the firm's activities through diversification;
- extending the size and/or scope of the firm through mergers and acquisition.

These two aspects of business strategy overlap but are not synonymous. Firms can diversify without acquisition, and acquisitions need not involve diversification. The development of large, complex, multi-plant and multi-product enterprises is one of the defining features of modern business development. Such enterprises have come about through business strategies involving diversification and acquisition. The questions we wish to consider here are:

1. How can complex firms, which consist in principle of a number of separable simple firms, add value over and above that already created by simple firms?
2. What is the potential for adding value through diversification and acquisition?

These questions are particularly relevant to business strategists in view of the evidence that complex firms, and acquisition-intensive firms, often fail to add value and are often reckoned to be more valuable broken up into their constituent parts, or unbundled as the business press puts it. For example, a recent book by Sadtler *et al.* (1998) has listed a number of prominent firms in need of breaking up, including giants such as General Motors and Ford. A prominent example of an acquisitive diversifier, Hanson, is discussed in Box 11.1 which introduces you to many of the issues discussed in this chapter.

11.1 Diversification

Diversification is a crucial aspect of the development of firms as you can see by examining the development options available to any firm:

- Possible directions of growth: horizontal integration, vertical integration, or diversification;
- possible locations for growth: home or abroad;

Box 11.1 Hanson's Future

The origins of Hanson's acquisitive activities began in 1950 when James Hanson took over his father's haulage business. Hanson was joined in 1954 by Gordon White. In those early years, the company grew through printing greetings cards, making fertilizers, and processing fish. By 1989, Hanson had become one of the ten biggest companies in Britain, and its relative—Hanson Industries—was in the top sixty industrial companies in the USA. Its scope covered activities as diverse as typewriters (Smith Corona), bricks (London Brick), and whirlpool baths (Jacuzzi).

Its acquisition criteria are very simple: each investment must be able to contribute to group profits in one year, and pay for itself in cash returns within four years (without taking account of profits from disposals). Its prowess has lain in its ability to spot businesses that meet these criteria. Given the uncertainty inherent in valuing potential victims, to minimize risks Hanson concentrates on mature, asset-backed organizations (such as brick companies) and buying firms with strong brand names (such as Imperial, maker of Embassy cigarettes).

Although Hanson claims to treat all firms as if it were going to keep them, Hanson does not aim to hold businesses in its portfolio indefinitely: it will sell them if the price is right. In the year to 30 September 1988, it was a net seller, selling more than £1 billion of businesses whose book cost was £370 million. It operates by being a highly efficient central manager, imposing tight financial controls and using powerful incentive structures to boost performance in its business units. However, there is almost no corporate Hanson culture and little loyalty to the parent itself is expected. Little attempt is made to add value by synergy between units.

In the early 1990s, Hanson's fortunes changed. Its share price, having risen dramatically in the 1980s, stagnated, and then fell precipitously. Acquisitions continued in the 1990s—particularly in the energy sector—but failed to generate quick profit gains for the conglomerate. Concern began to spread that the company had lost its way. After Derek Bonham became chief executive officer (CEO) in 1992, Hanson's strategy gradually switched from growth by acquisition to growth through internal investment, promoted by incentives to managers linked to the growth of individual businesses.

In 1995, Hanson decided to demerge. The group is to be divided into four coherent businesses: tobacco, chemicals, energy, and building materials (the rump of Hanson's earlier interests, and still to be known by the Hanson name).

Sources: 'Hanson's Future: The Conglomerate as an Antique Dealer', *The Economist*, 11 March 1989; 'Centrifugal Forces that Pulled Hanson Apart', *Financial Times*, 31 January 1996.

- possible means of achieving growth: internal or external (that is, mergers and acquisitions).

Firms can grow either by integration (horizontally or vertically), or by diversification, or internationally. Vertical integration along the firm's supply chain is a special type of diversification since it involves the firm in activities beyond its core activity (for example, a car assembler getting involved in producing sheet steel), whilst international growth can be seen as geographical diversification. So diversification, or extending the scope of the firm, is a crucial consideration for business policy.

Diversification takes two main forms (three if you include vertical integration). These are *related* (by customer type or technology used) and *unrelated* diversification. Diversification can be achieved by different routes. Internally, by the firm developing a new activity or externally, by the firm acquiring another firm whose activities are distinctive from its existing activities. Internal diversification may involve the firm using its technological expertise to develop products which take it into new areas of activity, such as ICI in chemicals and plastics. Alternatively, it could involve a firm exploiting its 'brand-name' to enter new activities as when Marks and Spencer moved into financial services. Diversification may also involve internationalization, so many diversified firms are also international in scope (for example, Hanson, Philips).

Studies of big business in many countries suggest that there was an increasing trend towards diversified firms from the 1950s onwards. The typical large firm nowadays is therefore diversified, although some are a lot more diversified than others. However, during the 1980s, the fashion for diversification slowed down somewhat and some diversified firms went into reverse and began to divest themselves of some of their activities. This trend was called 'getting back to basics', concentrating on the core, and more graphically, 'sticking to the knitting'. (This latter phrase comes from the best-selling book by Peters and Waterman, *In*

Search of Excellence, which gave this as one of the rules for creating business excellence!) These trends, first to greater diversity, and later away from diversification, were closely related to changes in acquisition activity in the USA and the UK which we discuss later.

Economists, in looking at the issue of firm scope, or diversification, seek to understand why such complex firms exist. In other words, they are interested in what they refer to as the *efficient boundaries of firms.* Production activity could in principle be organized in either of two extreme ways: a highly specialized world consisting of lots of simple specialized producers involved in a single activity such as car assembly, or a highly organized world where all activities are integrated into a single giant enterprise. In practice, we have neither of these extremes but a world in which there is a great variety of firms: many specialized producers, some vertically integrated firms, some moderately diversified firms, and some highly diversified firms commonly called conglomerates. Is the organization of production the product of purely random forces or is there an economic efficiency logic involved? Do diversified firms make sense economically? Why are some firms diversified whilst others remain resolutely specialized? Why are the firms in some industries more likely to diversify than in others? Why do some firms diversify and then go into reverse and 'return to basics'? Should firms diversify?

Causes, Determinants, and Motives for Diversification

There is no shortage of reasons available for firm diversification. Many books give long lists of 'reasons' which purport to 'explain' diversification. Figure 11.2, adapted from Reed and Luffman (1986), illustrates a good example of the genre. It rounds up and describes all the usual suspects for diversification. These include risk reduction, earnings stability, synergy, growth, adapting to customer needs, and the use of 'spare' resources. But such lists do not really *explain* anything. What such lists do is demonstrate that it is possible to think of lots of plausible reasons why firms might consider diversifying. But these lists do not explain why some firms do and others do not, or why some firms do and then go into reverse, or whether firms should diversify or not.

The logic of many of these so-called explanations for diversification is doubtful, however. For example, it is argued that there is no need for firms to diversify to stabilize earnings or reduce shareholder risks. Shareholders can easily build a private portfolio of shares in specialized firms with different risk/return characteristics, or invest through managed funds, to achieve their individual desired risk/return objectives. They do not really need to pay someone a lot of money to build and manage complex diversified firms to achieve their risk/return objectives.

The problem with these lists is that they ask the wrong question. They deal with the issue of the desire to diversify, and not with the issue of the ability to diversify successfully. The question we need to consider is not why firms might want to diversify but whether and to what extent firms can create value through diversifying? Of course, if the people who run firms have objectives other than seeking to add value, then firms may diversify to satisfy these objectives and in the process harm value creation, a possibility we take up in the next chapter. But our focus in this chapter will remain the firm's search for added value and we shall examine diversification solely from this perspective.

From the perspective of the firm's search for value, the question we need to ask is, in what way will diversifying add value? In what way will a complex firm, made up of a number of distinctive simple firms, say one making bread and another bricks, add value in excess of that created by independent simple firms? Formally, why should $V(1 + 2)$ exceed $V1 + V2$, where V represents firm value? Only if this condition holds does diversification add value. If the reverse is true, then diversification actually destroys value. If a complex firm existed that was less valuable than its constituent parts, an incentive would exist to break it up or unbundle it.

Asking whether extending the scope of the firm can add value, we are led to focus on the ability of the firm to achieve either higher prices or lower costs as a result of such a strategy. How might extending the scope of the firm enable it to benefit from higher prices or lower costs? There are some arguments about the possibility of firms extending the exercise of their market power in one area to another area through diversifying but these are not very convincing. Another possibility is that some firms could use a brand-name developed in one activity to charge more than an independent firm could in another activity but this also sounds dubious. It is probable, of course, that firms such as Sony or Glaxo benefit from their brand-names when introducing new products as long as they 'stick to the knitting'; that is, as long as Sony sticks to consumer electronics and Glaxo to pharmaceuticals. It seems highly unlikely, however, that Sony could charge premium prices for new products if it moved into pharmaceuticals, or Glaxo if it moved into electronics. So the benefits of brands and reputations are unlikely to operate very far from a company's core activities where its reputation was built. Thus BAT's name in the world of cigarettes seems unlikely to have counted for much when it moved into financial services. Indeed, there might even have been a negative reputation effect if people started wondering what on earth a tobacco company was doing selling insurance!

Costs and Diversification

Therefore, in order to identify what might enable firms to add value through extending scope, we need to focus on the possibility of lower costs. Economies of scope occur where a firm that is involved in two or more separable activities, such as bread and bricks, can achieve lower overall costs than would arise if two or more separate firms carried out exactly the same activities.

Looking at Figure 11.1, we see that only one heading seems appropriate to the search for a cost advantage. It is 'use of resources', formally known as the asset-utilization rationale for diversification. This refers to the possibility that the firm may have

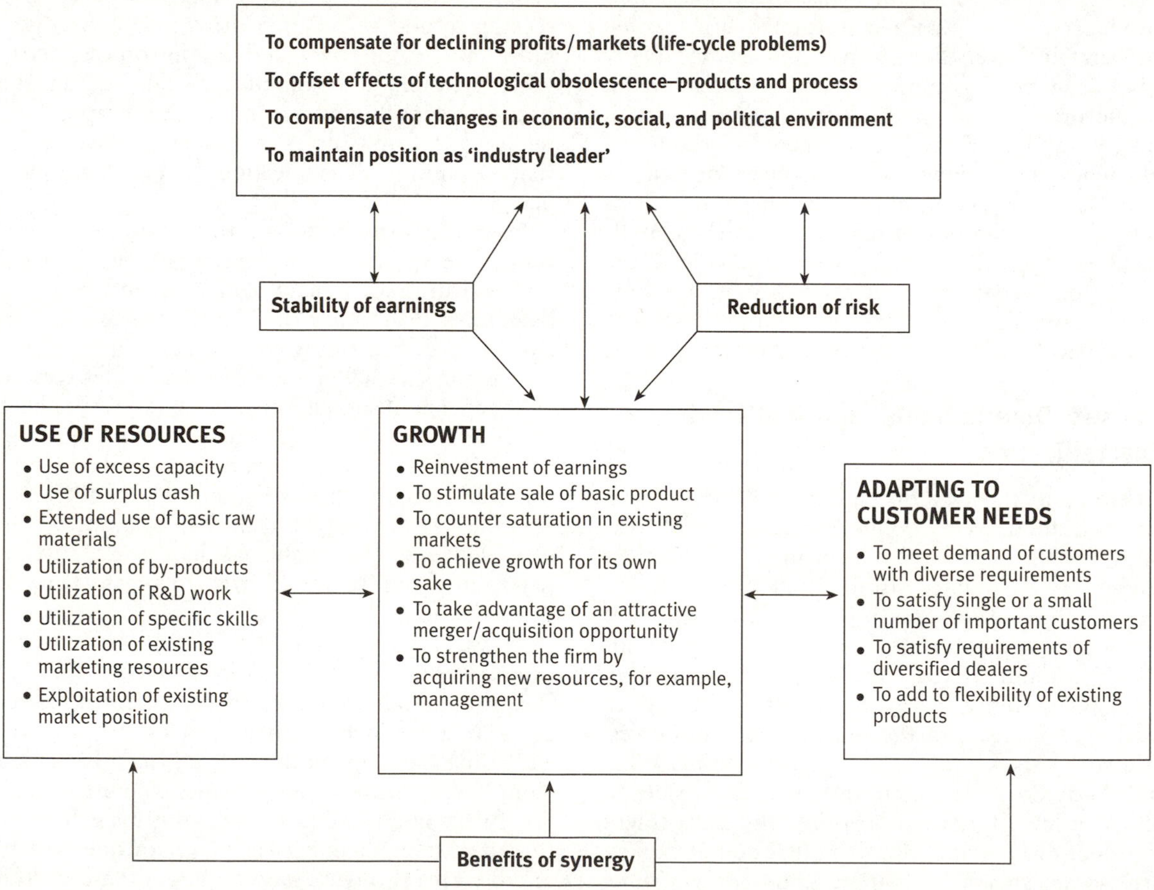

Figure 11.1 The basis for, and benefits of, diversification

Source: Based on Reed and Luffman (1986). Copyright John Wiley & Son Limited. Reproduced with permission.

some excess capacity in some area which represents a free resource to the firm. This can give the firm a cost advantage if a way can be found of utilizing this resource appropriately. One question is begged by this explanation, however. If a firm has some spare resources, in the form of excess capacity, why does it not instead choose to capitalize on them by selling those resources or hiring them out? The answer to this is that transactions costs often make this a less attractive option than using these assets to increase the scope of the firm. Transactions costs for selling or hiring out resources are likely to be particularly high in the case of intangible resources such as brand-names, managerial skills and know-how, and organizational capabilities.

Of the headings in Figure 11.1, you can see that the others are concerned with the firm's *desire* to diversify, not with its *ability* to add value from doing so. Resource utilization is also presented in the figure as a source of the desire to diversify but this misses the real significance of this heading. Using 'spare' resources is not just a motive for diversification, it is also a fundamental determinant of the firm's ability to add value from diversification. It points us in the direction of the firm's resources and its capabilities, as discussed in Chapter 10, as the basis for understanding the potential for adding value through diversification.

An important class of resources that is often under-utilized is knowledge. According to a recent report in the *Financial Times*, some observers believe that as little as 20 per cent of companies' knowledge assets are effectively utilized. A number of firms, recognizing the value of these knowledge resources, have responded with important organizational changes: Dow Chemicals, for example, has appointed a director of intellectual asset management, and several others have introduced regular knowledge audits or valuations. Management consultancies (including Coopers and Lybrand and Anderson Consulting) have developed software that allows many users to work together on the same information.

Porter's Contribution

We return now to the main issue, the use of 'spare' resources as a source of cost advantage enabling a firm to create value through diversification. Let us consider Porter's interesting empirical examination of the diversification record of thirty-three large US corporations over the period 1950 to 1986, which is summarized in Box 11.2. This is an important study because it looks at diversification strategy over time and does not, like most empirical studies of the issue, look only at the performance of currently diversified firms. (The problem with these studies is that they are based on survivors: firms which have diversified and lived to tell the story. Unsuccessful diversifiers presumably disappear somewhere along the line and are therefore not picked up in the currently diversified firm data. Furthermore, as Porter correctly emphasizes, the existence of profitable diversified firms does not in itself prove that diversification is profitable. It may simply reflect the fact that the firm's core activities are highly profitable, as with BAT's tobacco business.)

Porter's study of diversification by US firms, many of which diversified by acquisition, led him to the strong conclusion that successful, value-adding, diversification was not the norm. He found, for example, that a high proportion of companies involved in his study sooner or later divested themselves of their new activities. This in itself, of course, does not prove that diversification was a failure, but according to Porter, it certainly looks suspicious. Six of Porter's sampled firms were in fact themselves eventually taken over to be unbundled as his study was nearing completion. Some of his sample firms were very profitable but Porter argues that this was often because a profitable core activity covered up a poor diversification record.

Porter goes on to identify four approaches to diversification strategy: portfolio management, restructuring, transferring skills, and sharing activities (see Box 11.2). These are neatly summarized in his article, showing the strategic and organizational prerequisites and common pitfalls of each approach to diversification. Note, in particular, the extent to which Porter's findings are compatible with, indeed point to, a resource or capabilities approach to the firm as expounded in the previous chapter. For example, Porter rejects the portfolio management approach to diversification on the grounds that it is difficult to see how it can add value and easy to see how it can damage value. Restructuring, he believes, is a viable approach to diversification but one which is more difficult than it seems to carry out successfully. He therefore points to transferable skills and/or shared activities as the basis for successful value-adding diversification.

Box 11.2 Michael Porter on Diversification

In this box, we review some of the conclusions reached by Michael Porter in his paper 'From Competitive Advantage to Corporate Strategy', published in the *Harvard Business Review*, May–June 1987. Space dictates that we can only give a short summary here; the interested reader will benefit from reading Porter's original article in full.

Porter begins by distinguishing two types of strategy:

- competitive strategy concerns how to create competitive advantage in each of the businesses which a company operates;
- corporate strategy concerns what businesses the firm should be in and how the firm's array of businesses is managed.

Porter examined the record of thirty-three large and prestigious US companies over the period 1950–86. The overall diversification profile of these firms is given in Table 11.1. The extent of diversification can be seen to be very high: on average, each firm entered eighty new 'industries' and over twenty-seven entirely new 'fields'. (It is important to note that Porter uses the words *field* and *industry* in rather special ways. By field he means something such as insurance, which we would refer to in this book as an industry or market! Porter's meaning of the word 'industry' is much narrower than we use in this text: he has in mind a more tightly specified grouping, roughly meaning a well-defined product area.)

Table 11.2 focuses on the *acquisition* record specifically (as opposed to joint ventures and start-ups), showing the percentages subsequently divested. On average, companies divested over half of their acquisitions. In the case of unrelated acquisitions (figures not shown here) the percentage later divested was 74 per cent! If the proportion of later divestments is an indicator of diversification success, diversification in this sample seems to have performed abysmally. (We must be a little careful here, though. As Porter himself notes later, where the benefits from an acquisition come principally in the form of rapid one-off gains, there is no incentive for the acquirer to hold on to the new unit once those gains have been realized. Getting rid of the newly acquired unit is then a way of capitalizing the benefit, and not necessarily an indicator of failure.)

Table 11.1 The diversification profile of a sample of large companies

	Average over sample
Number of total entries	114.8
All entries into new 'industries' of which:	80.1
Acquisitions	70.3%
Joint ventures	7.9%
Start-ups	21.8%
Entries into new industries that represented entirely new fields of which:	27.4
Acquisitions	67.9%
Joint ventures	7.0%
Start-ups	25.9%

Source: Based on Porter (1987).

Table 11.2 The acquisition profile of sample of large companies

	Sample average
All acquisitions in new industries	61.2
Acquisitions made by 1980 and then diversified	53.4%
Acquisitions made by 1975 and then diversified	56.5%
All acquisitions in new industries in entirely new fields of which:	20.0
Acquisitions made by 1980 and then diversified	60.0%
Acquisitions made by 1975 and then diversified	61.5%

Source: Based on Porter (1987).

Porter notes that diversification is costly. So unless it provides benefits to business units which outweigh these costs, it will dissipate value. He proposes three tests which any corporate strategy must pass in order to create value:

- the attractiveness test: the industries chosen for diversification must be structurally attractive or capable of being made so (see Chapter 10);
- the cost-of-entry test: the cost of entry must not capitalize all the future profits (this is the point Peteraf makes about *ex-ante* competition that we mentioned in the previous chapter);
- the better-off test: either the new unit must gain competitive advantage from its link with the new corporation or vice versa.

Porter finds that many firms ignored the attractiveness test, or simply got it wrong, often mistaking short-term gains for long-term profit potential. He also suggests that many diversification ventures failed to satisfy the cost-of-entry test: the acquirer often had to pay not only what the object of its attention was worth, but a premium on top of that as well. Where diversification took place through start-ups, high entry costs sometimes eroded expected profits. And you will not be surprised to learn that he also suggests that it is common for managers to pay little or no attention to the better-off test!

Four Concepts of Corporate Strategy

His study led Porter to suggest four distinctive concepts of diversification strategy. The first two require no connections to be made among business units; the second two do require these connections, and it is this which gives them the best chance of success in current economic conditions.

Portfolio Management

This is the most common notion of corporate strategy. It involves building a portfolio of disparate companies and imposing strict financial control and central supervision of the autonomous units. According to Porter, it is the least likely to lead to value creation in present conditions of efficient capital markets, and it can lead to huge costs in terms of managerial complexity. Examples that Porter gives of firms that have adopted a portfolio management strategy include Gulf and Western, Consolidated Foods, and ITT.

Restructuring

This requires that an acquirer finds businesses with unrealized potential—and then actively restructures them to realize this potential and to squeeze value out. But this faces the same problem as before: the days are largely gone where these bargains existed. And even if they did, competition to grab them would push up the costs of buying them. We are back to the *ex-ante* competition point raised in the previous chapter. But some companies in the past have done this very well. For example, Hanson cut an average of 25 per cent of labour costs in acquired companies and tightened capital expenditures. Low cost and tight financial control has enabled Hanson to a recoup large proportions of its acquisition costs very quickly. It is a master of its art. Other restructurers include BTR and General Cinema.

Transferring Skills

Corporate strategy here (and in the next concept) is about finding synergy: the whole is worth more than the sum of its parts. Porter wryly notes that from reading countless annual reports 'just about anything is related to anything else! But imagined synergy is more common than real synergy'. Nevertheless, he regards the potential benefits of relatedness to be very real. One derives from the companies' ability to transfer skills or expertise among similar value chains in different business units. Value is generated by transferring proprietary *knowledge-based* skills such as production or logistical skills from one business to another. Examples of firms which have diversified using the transfer of skills strategy are 3M and Pepsico.

Sharing Activities

Porter notes that 'the ability to share activities is a potent basis for corporate strategy because sharing often enhances competitive advantage by lowering costs or raising differentiation' (see Chapter 10). Proctor and Gamble, for example, shares a common distribution system for paper towels and disposable nappies. Porter cites sharing advantages obtained by General Electric through its economies of scale and learning effects obtained over a wide variety of appliances. Other companies are built on shared R&D facilities. But not all sharing is value-enhancing; any proposal should be subject to a proper appraisal of the costs and benefits of sharing.

Porter's Three Main Conclusions

1. For most of the companies studied, diversification strategies dissipated rather than created shareholder value.
2. There is an urgent need to rethink corporate strategy: to survive, companies must understand the basis of good corporate strategy.
3. Good corporate strategy is most likely to be based on carefully thought-through approaches that involve sharing activities or transferring skills.

Both approaches are about exploiting potential interrelationships between different activities in order to reduce costs.

Transferable skills, however, only create a competitive advantage under certain conditions which he describes in full in his article. These include that the expertise or skills being transferred are both advanced and proprietary enough to go beyond the capabilities of likely competitors. His emphasis on proprietary, or firm-specific, skills is reminiscent of the capabilities approach to competitive advantage explained earlier in the previous chapter. For an example, we might consider Marks and Spencer's attempt to expand into the USA which, despite the potential assumed for transferring skills such as supply-chain management, in practice proved remarkably difficult and caused the company many problems.

According to Porter, therefore, the best basis for diversification is sharing activities. But the benefits of sharing activities, or synergy as it is often described, have to be fought for because they do not emerge spontaneously, as many superficial discussions of diversification seem to suggest. How precisely sharing activities can reduce costs and generate a competitive advantage are discussed by Porter with his usual thoroughness. A strategy based on sharing requires organizational mechanisms which actively encourage sharing. Note therefore that the Western preference for divisionalization of big firms, that is, the creation of clearly identified stand-alone divisions, is likely to be inimical to sharing, and that large Japanese firms are far less prone to this particular organizational form for precisely this reason. Japanese firms have identified the creation and sharing of capabilities and competencies as the basis of their strategy. The Japanese symbol for the enterprise is the tree and the capabilities of the firm are the soil which feeds the whole tree and its many branches. Divisionalization on Western lines would look to the Japanese like cutting the branches off from their source of nutrition.

According to Porter, successful diversifiers are those whose activities are most closely related because these offer the best opportunities for transferring skills or sharing activities. He is also quite sure that internal diversification is superior to diversification by acquisition. He develops an 'action programme' for diversification in his article which is a capabilities approach to strategy in all but name.

Evidence on Diverisfication

Several attempts have been made to study the relationship between diversification and firm performance, mainly using US data. Such studies suffer from a variety of conceptual and data problems however. For example, they are based largely on samples of diversified firms at a point of time, such as the 1980 *US Fortune* list of the 500 largest US corporations, which means they sample the survivors. The failed diversifiers have gone out of business or been taken over themselves and unbundled. Further, there are serious definitional problems with diversification. The idea sounds simple enough until you try to pin it down precisely. Researchers have had problems in distinguishing related and unrelated types of diversification and have found it impossible to develop a continuous variable to measure the degree to which each company is diversified. Finally, there is a problem of causality. If diversification is associated with good performance, it may be that successful firms are more likely to look for opportunities to diversify, not that diversification improves performance. Some studies have indeed strongly suggested that this is the more likely direction of causality. The evidence on diversification is summarized in Table 11.3.

Conclusions on Diversification

Returning to the questions raised at the start of our discussion of diversification we can now suggest some answers.

Why are there Complex Firms?

Complex firms exist in principle because they can add value over and above what would be produced by the constituent simple firms operating independently.

What is the Efficient Boundary of the Firm?

The efficient boundary of the complex firm is where increasing its complexity no longer promises to add value. Thus, a firm involved in both advertising and public relations might well make sense but extending its activities further, into say financial consulting, might be harmful to value creation. Examples of firms which developed beyond their efficient boundaries are not hard to find.

Do Diversified Firms make Sense?

If we define making sense as adding value over and above that of the individual simple firms, then the answer is that those diversified firms that add value make sense and those that do not add value do not make any sense. For reasons to be discussed in the next chapter, it is conceivable that non-value-adding diversified firms exist and persist despite the apparent contradiction of economic efficiency logic.

Why are Some Firms Diversified whilst Others are Not?

Diversification does make sense in economic terms but not for all firms, or for the same firm at all times. It depends specifically on the availability of the capabilities developed by the firm and the potential for transferring or sharing these

Table 11.3 Some evidence on the consequences of diversification

Study	Sample	Main findings
Rumelt (1974)	500 industrial companies, 1949–69	Companies which diversified around common skills and resources were most profitable. Vertically integrated companies and conglomerates were the least profitable.
Christensen and Montgomery (1981)	128 of Fortune 500 companies, 1972–77 (sub-sample of Rumelt, 1974)	Companies pursuing related, narrow-spectrum diversification were most profitable; vertically integrated firms least profitable. But performance differences primarily a consequence of industry factors.
Rumelt	273 of the Fortune 500 companies, 1955–74	Related diversification more profitable than unrelated even after adjusting for industry effects.
Varadarajan Ramanujam (1987)	225 companies, 1980–84	Related diversifiers earned higher return on equity and capital invested than unrelated diversifiers.
Markides (1992)	Sample of overdiversifiers from the 1980s	Positive returns from refocusing and reducing diversity.
Luffman and Reed (1984)	439 UK companies from the Times 1,000 1970–80	Conglomerates showed highest equity returns and growth of profits, sales, and profits.
Grant *et al.* (1988)	305 large UK manufacturing	Product diversity positively associated with profitability, but after a point relationship turns negative.

Source: Based on an original table in Grant, *Contemporary Strategy Analysis*, 2e (1995).

capabilities to exploit new opportunities for adding value. It depends essentially on the existence of economies of scope. It depends also on the fact that, because of transactional problems, it is often difficult for firms to capture the rents or profits of any under-utilized skills and other organizational assets or capabilities by selling them to someone else. The only way to capitalize fully on available resources and capabilities is then to diversify. However, not all firms with strong skills and other assets built up in their current activities will necessarily be able to identify new opportunities for exploiting these in a value-adding way. Some capabilities will be easier to exploit than others. Some firms may not even be aware of the potential value of their resources and capabilities and so fail to consider utilizing them more fully.

Why do Firms in Some Industries Diversify more Successfully than Firms in Other Industries?

This is probably because the nature of the skills, activities, capabilities, and competencies built up in some firms is easier to transfer and/or share than in other firms. In some firms, say a steel processor, the skills and capabilities developed may be substantial but too specific to steel processing to be transferred or shared. In other firms, say a chemicals processor, there may be better opportunities for exploiting capabilities more widely.

Finally, should Firms Diversify?

Yes, firms should diversify but only for the right reasons, which means adding value. The history of the diversification phenomenon suggests that diversification was not always pursued for the right reasons. There is a likelihood that some of the trend towards increasingly diversified firms was motivated by reasons other than adding value. For example, there was probably an element of fashion in the rise of diversification in the 1960s because of the attention given to certain business leaders who promoted aggressive diversification, consultants, and business school gurus who advocated diversification for all sorts of reasons (see Figure 11.1 above). Some of these people, the academic Igor Ansoff for example, placed great emphasis on synergy, and were careful to advocate diversification for the right reasons, but others failed to make clear precisely what they thought the ultimate purpose of productive enterprise was. If the enterprise had no clearly defined purpose, then of course diversification was as good a means of achieving this purpose as anything else. Other people took on board Ansoff's ideas about synergy and proceeded to oversell them. Firms need to be careful, therefore, about the attractions of diversification and clear about their ultimate purpose in pursuing it.

11.2 Mergers and Acquisitions

A crucial means by which firms pursue increasing size and/or scope is the use of mergers and acquisitions (M&As). M&As are used by firms to expand horizontally, vertically, to diversify, and to internationalize. M&As thus overlap with our previous topic but they are not synonymous and they deserve independent treatment.

M&As are certainly an important phenomenon, at least in the UK and the USA. Both countries have been characterized by high, but variable, levels of M&A activity since the 1950s, with particularly intense booms in activity in the period 1966–73 in which GEC was prominent, the mid–late 1980s in which Hanson was prominent, and in the mid-1990s also with Glaxo prominent. The industrial landscape in both countries has been radically affected by this activity. In particular, the size and the complexity of firms has grown as a result. Countries such as Japan and Germany have been less merger intensive, although contrary to what some people think, mergers do happen in both countries. What distinguishes these countries from Britain and the USA is that they do not have contested, or hostile, take-overs, that is, where one firm seeks to acquire another without the agreement of the people in effective control. In countries with an active market for corporate control, bidding firms can make an offer for a target firm directly to the shareholders and without the agreement of managers, indeed often with the hostile opposition of the target's managers. Managers and bidders then fight it out for the approval of the target's shareholders, often in a protracted and expensive battle during which it is normal for the bid price to rise well beyond its initial level. This battle is generally fought in public and with extensive press coverage.

The characteristics of M&A activity have changed over the years. Take-overs in the 1980s were in real terms bigger than before, more hostile, more hard fought, and at least in the USA, were often financed by, shall we say, more creative means, such as so-called junk bonds. In particular the more recent take-over boom seems to have involved more take-overs motivated by a desire for unbundling big complex firms, or bust-ups as some have graphically described them. It is argued by some prominent economists that what was built up in the 1960s and 1970s by M&As was partly dismantled or 'built-down' in the 1980s by the same means. This might lead us to wonder whether all that effort and expense involved in the M&A industry was socially worthwhile.

In looking at M&As, economists are seeking to understand why firms acquire and whether or not M&As make sense economically. Ultimately, we want to answer the question, should firms acquire?

Causes, Determinants, and Motives for Mergers and Acquisitions

As with diversification, it is easy to list the variety of reasons people give for firms acquiring or seeking to acquire one another. Indeed, the reasons given in Figure 11.1 for diversification is a good start to such a list for M&As: growth, earnings stability, change of direction, use of resources, and so on. We need to add to this list a few reasons for horizontal M&As specifically, that is, those between firms making the same products, such as the search for market power or economies of scale. And of course you might wish to add the bust-up or unbundling motive noted earlier. Making such a list simply demonstrates again that it is easy to think of lots of plausible reasons why firms might wish to pursue a particular action but does not explain why some firms do and others do not, nor does it take into account the question of the ability of the bidders to be successful, that is value-adding, acquirers.

Economists, you will not be surprised to learn, are sceptical about the logic of many of the explanations offered for M&As. For example, they fail to see why creating complex firms from independent simple firms makes any sense as a means of reducing risks when shareholders can create their own portfolios to suit their personal risk/return objectives. The question we need to address then is not why firms might want to acquire, but whether and to what extent firms can create value through acquiring other firms? We also recognize the possibility that the people who run firms may have other things in mind apart from creating added value, in which case they might use M&As for these purposes and in the process damage value creation. Note, however, that what is created by acquisition can be undone by acquisition. Therefore, whether it is possible to create a value-subtracting firm on a sustainable basis is open to question.

Routes to Value

From the perspective of the firm's search for value, let us consider how M&As might add value. In what way will adding together two separate entities create a more valuable combined entity? Several routes have been suggested by different authors, depending on different combinations of assumptions about firm efficiency and stock-market efficiency, as outlined in Figure 11.2, but not all of these are equally plausible, as we argue below.

Assumptions about a Firm's Efficiency

We can assume *either* a world where all firms are operated at maximum efficiency all of the time, *or* a world where some firms for some of the time are not as well run as they might be. This could be for a variety of reasons. It may be bad luck or bad judgement, it may be that the people running the firm have objectives other than adding value (see Chapter 12), or it may be simply that the people running the firm are not good managers. The precise reason need not detain us.

Assumptions about Stock Market Efficiency

It is necessary to consider the efficiency of the stock market for the following reason. The stock market places a valuation on firms reflecting the demand for its shares which in turn reflects the potential profitability and dividends of the firm. The stock market is said to be efficient if this valuation reflects the true underlying value of the firm, based on all the available information about the present and likely future performance of the firm. If the stock market is not efficient at valuing firms in this sense, then it is possible that the value of firms quoted on the market is incorrect, either too high or too low compared with the true underlying value. Whether and why this might actually happen is a controversial issue which we cannot go into here.

		Stock Market assumed to be:	
		Efficient	*Inefficient*
Firms assumed to be:	*Efficient*	synergy route	opportunistic route
	Inefficient	efficiency route	mixed

Figure 11.2 Possible routes to added value from mergers and acquisitions

Route One, the Synergy Route

Assume that the stock market is efficient at reflecting the correct underlying performance of firms and that all firms are operating to their full efficiency potential. Then to add value by M&As requires either that product prices rise or costs fall compared with the prior situation of independent firms. Either of these results is conceivable. A merger of two leading producers of cigarettes, for example, might create enough market power to let the new firm raise its prices above existing levels. This, of course, would depend on many things but in particular on being able to discourage new entrants to the industry. Moreover, the merging of two firms might make it possible to reduce costs if there are potential scale or scope economies to be realized. Formally, where C stands for costs, if $C(1 + 2)$ is less than $C1 + C2$, then economies of scale or scope exists.

Why would firms seek to achieve greater market power or lower costs by the merger route than by internal growth? The reason is that it is faster and less risky than internal growth, although this was not the case for Ferranti, the British defence electronics company, which was allegedly brought to its knees by an ill-judged acquisition. Moreover, the acquisition approach allows you to increase size or enter a new industry without creating new capacity and increasing competition in that industry. We shall return to consider this particular route again once we have looked at the other routes.

Route Two, the Efficiency Route

Assume a world in which the stock market is efficient at valuing firms but a number of firms are, for some of the time, less efficient than they might be. This could be for a variety of reasons, bad luck or bad judgement, weak management, or managers pursuing their own interests at the expense of the owners. The stock market value of these firms will reflect their underachievement relative to their perceived potential. These firms will be valued at a level below their true potential value. An opportunity exists, therefore, for another firm to buy these underachievers, shake them up, focus them on value adding, and so increase their value. We call this the efficiency route because in this case the acquisition or take-over is motivated by a desire to improve the efficiency of the acquired firm. It could also, of course, be called the Hanson route since Hanson was reputedly a master of this strategy.

But there is an interesting twist to this story. If it is possible for a bidder to improve the performance of the acquired company and so make it more valuable, why would the present shareholders sell out for less than this (enhanced) value? Once a bidder such as Hanson appears and announces its intentions, the best (most rational) strategy for any single shareholder is to hold onto his or her shares and wait for the bidder to improve the performance of the acquired firm and therefore its share value. But if all shareholders think like this, the bid cannot succeed at a price which would enable the bidder to make a profit from the take-over. Therefore take-overs of this type cannot occur if shareholders are behaving rationally, unless bidding firms are prepared to pay the true (potential) value of their intended victims. But if bidders do that, the acquisition cannot add value for the acquiring firm even if they improve the victim's performance. Therefore, rational acquirers will avoid this approach!

Route Three, the Opportunistic Route

We assume that firms are efficient but that the stock market is not perfectly efficient at reflecting the true value of firms at all points in time. (Whether the stock market is actually efficient or not at valuing firms is an empirical question over which much ink has been spilled. It may be the case, for example, that it is efficient in the weak sense that values reflect what information is currently known to shareholders, but it is not *perfectly* efficient in the sense that stock market values will always reflect the true values of firms.)

If the stock market is not *perfectly* efficient at valuing firms, then at any given time some firms must be overvalued and others undervalued relative to their real underlying value. These discrepancies are assumed to be mistakes and are not systematic or predictable. (If the mistakes were systematic and predictable, then traders would expect them and trading would eliminate them.) This means, in principle, that at any given time an overvalued firm can use its temporarily overvalued stock to purchase temporarily undervalued companies cheaply. When the true values are restored, the acquirer then sells its acquisitions at their true value and makes a profit. Of course, this assumes an awful lot, although this has not stopped people from believing it is possible. It assumes an accidentally overvalued company can recognize when it is temporarily overvalued, it assumes the firm can move quickly enough to capitalize on this good fortune before the mistake is rectified, and it assumes that the acquiring firm can make enough profit from its actions to pay for the time and the costs involved in buying and selling the victim. These costs will not be insignificant.

Note also that the M&As along routes two and three, if they happen at all, should not lead to permanent marriages. Firms acquiring other firms to improve their performance or to capitalize on a temporary valuation discrepancy have no reason to keep hold of their victims. Once they have improved the performance of the inefficient firm, they can sell it off at its true value. Opportunistic take-overs, if they exist, are by definition made only to capitalize on short-term trading opportunities. It is possible, therefore, that some of the acquisition and divestment activity noted by Porter in Box 11.3 reflects such take-overs, although it must be emphasized that Porter does not suggest this to have been the case.

Note, finally, that efficiency and opportunistically motivated M&As require certain conditions for their realization. First, some people must have a special talent for identifying undervalued assets, or valuation discrepancies. Does this seem likely? How easy is it to tell when a firm is underperforming *vis-à-vis* its potential? How easy is it to tell when the stock market is making mistakes?

Secondly, there must be a lack of competition for any particular opportunity otherwise the potential profit would be bid away. But if there is money to be made from spotting undervalued assets and value discrepancies, then resources will be attracted into this line of business. Such talents might be rare but they are not likely to be unique. Therefore competition will be the norm rather than the exception and so the potential for adding real value by these routes will be diminished and may even be eliminated.

Of course, in the real world there is room for equally talented seekers after opportunities to disagree about the value of opportunities available, so that one will make the raid and the other will hold off. But if they are equally talented, sometimes the raider will be correct in her judgements and sometimes she will not. So even differences in perception among raiders could not give rise to above-average success at raiding.

Route Four

In a world where the stock market does not value firms efficiently *and* not all firms operate to their full potential all of the time, things get a little complicated. Poorly run firms might be accidentally overvalued and thus not vulnerable to take-over. Well-run firms might be temporarily undervalued and find themselves threatened by take-over. Of course, such a firm would claim in its defence documents that it should not be taken over because it is well run, but all potential take-over victims say this as a matter of course so the claim lacks credibility. In such a world, it is likely that the take-over mechanism would do as much harm as good and indeed this is what some observers have argued.

Acquisitions and Synergy

We return now to the synergy route and the possibility that M&As can promote scale and/or scope economies. This appears to be the only serious long-run basis for creating value through M&As and it points once again to a resource or capabilities basis for understanding firm activities. Recall that Porter's study discussed above identifies four approaches to corporate strategy: portfolio, restructuring, skill transfers, and shared activities. (See Box 11.2.) Porter, you will find, is quite negative about the value-adding potential of the first two approaches, which would reflect our efficiency and opportunistic routes, although note that Porter does not use these terms. He is much more enthusiastic about the other two approaches which would involve the synergy route, that is, mergers based on a potential for exploiting an interrelationship between two firms which leads to reduced costs. Porter is therefore pointing the way to a resource or capabilities approach to strategy in general and acquisition strategy in particular.

A resource or capabilities approach to acquisition would suggest that in searching to create value through M&As, firms should seek to make acquisitions which provide an opportunity to enhance or complement their existing capabilities or exploit these capabilities more widely. Thus, a firm with a distinctive capability based on architecture, say, would make acquisitions where its organizational and human resource management skills could be applied to enhance the value of the acquired firm. Similarly, a firm with a reputation-based capability would acquire with a view to transferring its reputation to the acquired firm and enhancing its value. This, of course, by no means implies that any firm with a distinctive capability can exploit that capability in a value-adding way simply by making an acquisition. Only when the capability can reasonably be transferred to or shared with the acquired firm will the acquisition enhance value. It is far from clear, for example, that the basis of Marks and Spencer's success in British retailing (architecture plus reputation) will enable it to add value through the acquisition of Brooks Brothers in the USA. Indeed it would be surprising if it did. Marks and Spencer's reputation is very much a British phenomenon which is difficult to internationalize. Further, Marks and Spencer's architecture, that is, its staff commitment and its superbly organized local supply chain, cannot be shared with Brooks Brothers in the USA, although of course it may eventually be possible for Marks and Spencer to duplicate its approach to human resources and to supply chain management in the USA. But if it cannot, then it is difficult to see how Marks and Spencer can ever get a decent return on what it paid for Brooks Brothers, particularly in view of the fact that it is widely believed to have paid too much for it in the first place. Why then did Marks and Spencer make this particular purchase? Maybe the directors thought they could return it if it didn't fit!

Evidence on Mergers and Acquisitions

Do acquisitions create value? This is a well-researched area, although there is a lot of controversy about the results generated. Several different approaches, or methodologies, have been employed in this research and although by no means unanimous, they generally suggest that on average M&As are not value enhancing. Major studies of large samples of M&As in Britain and in the USA have suggested that, if anything, M&As on average damage value creation. This is not to deny that some acquisitions do create value for the acquirer. The problem is that many do not. If we examine the necessary conditions for an acquisition to enhance the acquiring firm's value, we shall see how this can happen. The value of the new firm, $V(1 + 2)$ created from two separate firms $V1$ (acquirer) and $V2$ (victim) is as follows:

$$V(1 + 2) = [V1 + V2 + \text{estimated merger gains}] - [V2 + \text{merger premium paid}],$$

where merger gain is the value of any synergy gain arising from the merger, and the merger premium refers to the price the acquirer pays in excess of the quoted value, $V2$, of the victim firm before the acquirer appeared. Acquirers normally have to pay well in excess of the initial market price of victims because competition between acquirers usually drives prices up, and as suggested earlier, once the victim's shareholders know that someone values their company more highly than they do themselves, they have no incentive to sell at the present valuation.

This equation means that for the value of the acquiring firm, $V1$, to increase as a result of the acquisition, the acquisition gain has to exceed the merger premium. You should be able to simplify the above equation to show this result. M&As therefore can fail to add value either because the synergy gain from the merger is poor or because any synergy gain is wiped out by paying too much for the victim. Of course, someone does nicely out of all this (apart that is from the merchant banks who organize acquisitions): the shareholders of the victim firm to be precise, who can usually count on obtaining a value well in excess of what they thought their company was worth beforehand, so perhaps victim is the wrong word to use in this context. If anyone can be described as a victim, it is the shareholders of the acquiring firm when the merger premium wipes out any potential synergy gains. Thus *even* firms with excellent capabilities who make acquisitions with good potential for synergistic gains can fail to add value if they pay too much for their victim, or cannot turn potential synergy into actual synergy. For example, the Swiss firm Nestlé paid over twice the stock market value to acquire Rowntree which was recognized as a well-run business already. Where will Nestlé find the synergy to justify such a premium?

A survey of the evidence on M&As is included as Box 11.3. This survey explains the methods used to evaluate M&As activity, the results of various studies, and the lessons to be learned. You should read this and come to your own conclusions about M&As. You may find the evidence less compelling than we do. Nevertheless, the important thing is to appreciate the scope for argument and the problems involved in coming to a conclusion.

In the light of the evidence that M&As on average are not value enhancing for acquirers, why should M&As be such a popular corporate activity in the USA and the UK? A few reasons might be suggested. First, it may be that we do not live in a value-driven world. It may be that the people running big business these days are interested in other objectives which are better served by M&As. (The next chapter considers this possibility in more detail.) For example, M&As are an easy way to get larger, so if the people running modern business prize size over value, then they will find M&As attractive for this reason.

A second reason may be that people make mistakes. The search for value is inherently experimental in nature. Firms can be expected to make mistakes. Even well-intentioned managers may make acquisitions that turn out to be mistakes. Later on they realize the mistake and divest themselves of their purchase. The high level of divestment activity identified by Porter's study may reflect some attempts to correct mistakes. There are good reasons to suspect that firms do often make mistakes over acquisitions. The evidence suggests strongly that firms fail to take enough care over acquisition policy and the problems of achieving synergistic gains. For decisions which involve such large amounts of money, acquiring firms seem to invest too little in pre-acquisition investigation and post-acquisition reorganization. To benefit from acquisitions probably requires a lot more managerial effort than many firms seem to allow for. This is certainly the belief of many people who work in the merger consulting field. Some managers may also overestimate their own capacities to make mergers value enhancing.

Conclusions on Mergers and Acquisitions

We can now provide some answers to our initial questions about M&As.

Why do Firms Acquire?

In a value-driven world firms acquire in order to enhance value, that is, firm 1 acquires firm 2 in order to create a new firm (1 + 2) which is more valuable than the sum of the existing independent firms.

Box 11.3 Evidence on Mergers and Acquisitions

In order to assess whether mergers and acquisitions (mergers for short) are successful or not, it is necessary to have a criterion of success. The criterion used by Love and Scouller (1990) is that of shareholder wealth: a merger is successful if it increases the wealth of the companies' owners. This can be measured in two ways:

- by examining the stock market value of the acquiring firm;
- by examining what happens to the profitability of the acquiring firm.

Stock Market Value Studies

The basic idea here is that if a merger proposal is *expected* to deliver increased shareholder returns, the acquirer's share prices will rise on announcement of the merger. Likewise, no change in share price or a fall in share price is indicative of no change in expected return or a fall in expected return. Statistical analysis is used to determine how an acquirer's share price behaves compared with what it would have done in the absence of merger. Typically, studies examine an average of this change in stock market value over some sample of firms.

A large number of studies of this type have examined changes in market values within a few days or weeks of a merger announcement. These broadly suggest a small positive effect on the market values. However, if a longer horizon is adopted so that the market has a chance to assess actual performance post-merger, a very different picture emerges. The initial gains in market values are lost relatively quickly and the change in share price becomes negative (and increasingly so with the passage of time).

Interestingly, share values in acquired firms (victims) tend to rise sharply on merger announcements: the acquirer often pays a significant premium to make the take-over, thereby making it less likely that shareholders in the acquiring firm will benefit overall.

Studies of Changes in Actual Shareholder Returns

Actual shareholder returns studies operate by choosing a sample of acquiring firms and a control group of other firms: this control group of non-acquirers should be as closely matched as possible to the sample of acquirers being studied. The performance over time of shareholder returns of the two groups is then compared. In this exercise, it is important to 'control for' (that is, take account of and subtract) any variations in performance due to any factors other than the factor being analysed: whether the firm was an acquirer or not.

Love and Scouller note that 'These studies show a fairly consistent pattern in which the return to the shareholders of acquiring firms are lower than those of the non-acquirers'. They quote a study undertaken in 1988 by the consultants McKinsey and Co. of a large number of US and UK acquirers. McKinsey found that in only 23 per cent of cases did the merger produce returns in excess of the costs involved in implementing the merger. Additionally, the larger the firm's acquisition programme, the larger was found to be the failure rate of the mergers. A more recent study (1997) by Mercer consultants in the USA of large-scale acquisitions found that after three years 57 per cent of the acquirers were underperforming compared with their industry average and as time passed the degree of underperformance worsened.

Profitability Studies

There has been a vast number of empirical studies of the effects of mergers on profitability. Two principal methods are used. One compares the performance pre- and post-merger of acquiring firms with the performance over the same period of a group of non-mergers. The second method examines the profit history of merging firms alone for several years prior to and after merger activity.

Findings from these studies have been rather inconclusive: some studies show weak improvement in average performance, others small average performance worsening. There is no consistently strong effect in either direction. Moreover, averages are somewhat misleading as there is typically considerable variation in performance changes between different firms in the samples. For example, a study by Meeks (G. Meeks (1977) *Disappointing Marriage: A Study of the Gains from Merger*, Cambridge University Press) found that whilst on average mergers led to a statistically significant decline in performance over the three years post-merger, it was nevertheless true that a large minority—43 per cent—experienced improved profitability!

One interesting variant is a comparison of the performances of a group of fifty merged firms with a control group of fifty pairs of companies (each pair with one bidder and one target company) where the merger attempts were abandoned. The authors of this study found that the average performance of both bidders and target firms in the three years after the merger attempt was superior to that of the merged companies. It appears that the threat of a take-over bid may be sufficient to spur performance, whilst the effects of actual take-overs were unfavourable.

Source: Love and Scouller (1990).

Do M&As Make Sense?

To the owners of an acquiring firm, an acquisition makes sense only if it adds value. Otherwise, why bother with all the time and effort involved? Of course, if the people running the business have intentions other than adding value, which is a possibility, then M&As might make sense to them even when they fail to add value for the acquirer. But would society gain from such activity? To an economist, M&As make sense only if they actually create value over and above that created by the independent firms. Acquisition activity absorbs resources: managerial time, lawyers, consultants, merchant banks, government officials, and PR specialists. If M&As fail to add value, all these resources are essentially wasted. Society is worse off because people who could be employed doing something useful and value enhancing are paid instead to do something which is basically useless to society. You might argue that at least it keeps these people in work and off the streets. But this is wrong. If the best use we can find for some of the cleverest people in the country is to organize useless activities, then we might as well admit defeat and let others move in!

Should Firms Acquire?

We hope you can fill in the answer to this one for yourself. It should be clear by now what our answer would be. The answer would involve adding value and exploiting capabilities. Of course, despite our best efforts you might believe that the value added criterion we use is too narrow a basis to judge business strategies. That is a reasonable position. You will be pleased to learn that at least you are not alone!

Conclusions

We set out in this chapter to examine the potential for adding value through extending the scope of the firm, and through mergers and acquisitions. We examined why firms diversify and acquire other firms, and whether or not these actions made economic sense. It was argued that these actions only make sense in so far as the complex firms which result are more valuable than their individual parts standing alone, that is, whether $V(1 + 2)$ exceeds $V1 + V2$. If a diversified firm is not more valuable than its parts, then its diversity makes no sense. The world would be better off with more specialized firms. If an acquirer is not worth more after an acquisition than before, what was the point of the acquisition? Was it to be bigger, to have a balanced portfolio of products, to give managers something interesting to do, to use up spare cash from your cash cow, to diversify? Is the purpose of the firm to get bigger, to diversify, to give managers something interesting to do, to have an aesthetically pleasing product portfolio? You will come across people who seem to think so. But if it is, then anything goes and studying economics and business policy is pointless. Only if business has a well-defined and difficult to achieve purpose does it make sense to study how to achieve it. If business has no clear purpose, then there is nothing to study. A degree in art appreciation would be as much use as an MBA and a lot less hard work.

How might diversification or acquisition add value to a firm? The most likely route is by achieving lower costs, such that $C(1 + 2)$ is less than $C1 + C2$. This could come about if the different parts of a complex firm can share some resources or capabilities, or if there is a possibility of transferring skills or capabilities from one firm to another. Thus, a firm with a valuable reputation can add value by diversifying if this reputation can be transferred to a different product. Or a firm with a successful approach to supply-chain management could add value by acquiring another firm if this capability could be exploited successfully in the new firm. Of course, if the successful firm can package and sell its expertise, it could create value for itself without having to bother with take-overs and merchant banks and references to the Monopolies Commission.

Further reading

Good general discussions on the issues we have covered in this chapter can be found in Kay (1993), Grant (1991), Besanko *et al.* (1996), Sadtler *et al.* (1998), and Bishop and Kay (1993). Porter's contributions are found in Porter (1985) and (1987). Issues related to diversification are discussed in Peters and Waterman (1982).

Geroski and Vlassapoulos (1990) assess the European mergers experience. Finance texts such as Brealey and Myers (1991) often give a good analysis of diversification, comparing conglomerate with portfolio diversification. The papers by Love and Scouller (1990) and Peteraf (1993), discussed in this chapter, repay reading in full.

Questions

11.1. How might a complex firm be (a) less or (b) more valuable than the sum of its constituent parts operating independently?

11.2. Why do some firms diversify and then go back to basics?

11.3. 'The existence of profitable diversified firms proves that diversification is a valuable business strategy.' Discuss.

11.4. What are the precise conditions necessary for an acquisition to add value?

11.5. If mergers and acquisitions are not value enhancing, then why are they so popular?

11.6. Outline and discuss Porter's four concepts of diversification strategy.

12 Ownership, Management, and the Search for Value

Introduction

In Chapter 4 we considered the nature, purpose, and objectives of the firm. We argued there that once the nature of the firm was properly understood, it was not possible to assume as a matter of course that the objective of the firm was the same as the objective of the entrepreneurial owner. That is, it was not possible to argue that the objective of the firm was necessarily to maximize the residual value of the coalition's efforts. We argued that the objective of the enterprise depends on the extent to which the individual coalition member's desire to create and appropriate wealth gets harnessed effectively to an overriding collective or organizational goal. This in turn was seen to depend on a variety of factors: the extent to which co-operation can be induced by forces and threats external to the firm, namely the threat of competition, and the extent to which co-operation can be induced and encouraged by appropriate incentive mechanisms, organizational designs, and governance mechanisms. The strength of the firm's desire to search for and exploit opportunities to add value thus depends on a variety of factors related to the firm's environment and the firm's organization.

We shall now examine some important aspects of modern business organization which demonstrate some of these issues whilst emphasizing that this by no means exhausts the list of issues involved. Economists have recognized that certain characteristics of the modern corporation may have compromised the desire to maximize the firm's residual value. The growing organizational complexity of the modern enterprise, and the increasing extent to which ownership appears to have been separated from management, in both the public and the private sectors, have led some economists to question the traditional assumption underlying so much economic analysis, namely the assumption of profit or value maximization. This in turn has led to a discussion of the nature and implications of alternative business objectives, and to questions about the nature and effectiveness of corporate governance mechanisms: that is, who governs the corporation, how is this government effected, how effective is the governance, and what are the implications of different forms of governance? This chapter is concerned with this discussion and with these questions.

In this chapter, we shall therefore consider the nature and significance of key aspects of modern big business organization, namely, the separation of ownership from control and the increasing size and complexity of organizations. We shall examine *inter alia* the extent of the separation of ownership from control, the nature of managerial objectives, the implications of managerial objectives, the ability of owners to detect managerial indulgence, and the ability of owners to control managerial behaviour, directly and indirectly, the market for corporate control, incentives for managers, and organizational design. Some problems we have noted before lie right at the heart of this chapter: asymmetric information, co-operation dilemmas, free-riding, opportunism, team production, and imperfect commitment. We have also already indicated in Chapter 11 that the possibility of a divergence of interest between owners and managers has implications for the development of the firm through diversification and acquisition.

12.1 Ownership, Management, and Business Motivation

The capitalist entrepreneurial enterprise as we have observed it in Chapter 4 has good motivational properties. The organization and management of a disparate group of ultimately self-interested individuals towards a common end, even one which they all share in principle, is not a simple task. By giving the entrepreneur the right to appropriate the value added by her efforts in organizing and managing the coalition of individuals, we give her a strong personal incentive to search for ways of ensuring that the enterprise produces as much added value as possible. The incentive is, if the coalition manages to produce any added value, the entrepreneur captures it. The more added value produced, the greater her personal wealth. This fact, combined with an assumption of a more or less competitive environment for products and factors of production, led economists to a general presumption of profit maximization as the force driving the behaviour of the capitalist firm. If the entrepreneur slackened in her pursuit of personal wealth, she would be pushed aside by more aggressive entrepreneurs with a stronger desire to add value.

This presumption, and the economic theory based on it, was developed in an age characterized by relatively small, entrepreneurial, competitive, and organizationally simple firms. The problem is that, according to many economists, we no longer live in such a world. The questions thus arise: to what extent have the characteristics of the modern business corporation and its environment compromised the desire to maximize added value and what have been the consequences of such a change? It has to be said at the outset that there is no consensus on these issues within economics. One group of economists, whom we might call 'managerialists', believe the changes in the nature and environment of enterprise have been of great significance for the behaviour and performance of firms. However, other economists feel that this group is making too much of some rather inconsequential details about the modern corporation. After reading this chapter, you can decide for yourself where you stand on this issue.

Consider first the characteristics of the big business corporations whose activities dominate the modern economic landscape. It is generally the case in industrial economies such as the USA or UK that a small number of very large corporations account for a large proportion of total output. It is argued that these corporations have the following characteristics.

First, they no longer operate in a highly (that is, perfectly) competitive environment which puts constant pressure on them to maximize their efforts to add value. This, of course, is a debatable proposition given the seeming intensity of international competition in modern times and the rate of technical change. However, you have to recall that economists tend to identify competitive intensity with a large number of firms producing an undifferentiated product and so by their standards all of today's big business corporations are oligopolists with varying degrees of 'market power'. However, since the evidence for this proposition is by no means clear cut, as we discussed in Chapter 10, you may prefer to think of this proposition as an assumption of the following analysis rather than an empirically established fact.

Secondly, these corporations have grown more complex organizationally, with increasing levels of hierarchy between the top and bottom of the organization reflecting the problems of co-operation and co-ordination involved in managing large numbers of people and their activities but of course never completely solving these problems. This increase in the numbers of layers of management complicates the process of decision-making and implementation involved within the enterprise and raises questions about organizational design. The increasing number of managers in the organization creates a powerful interest group whose interests will not necessarily be consonant with those of the owners, or indeed with one another. The increasing number of managers and levels of management raises questions about how coherent corporate objectives come to be formulated in practice.

Thirdly, their ownership has become separated from their management. The owners, or shareholders, no longer manage the business, and the managers no longer own any significant proportion of the business. There are, of course, exceptions to this such as Hanson Industries and Sainsbury in the UK where there has been a significant ownership presence at the top although even then not a majority presence. Ownership nowadays is widely dispersed among thousands, sometimes hundreds of thousands, of individuals and financial institutions. However, it is very much concentrated in the hands of a small number of very large financial institutions, namely pension funds, mutual funds, and insurance companies. (See Table 12.1 for some details of the extent and growth of share ownership by financial institutions in Britain.) Management nowadays is largely in the hands of professional

Table 12.1 Ownership of UK companies: percentage of total equity held by type

Type/ Year	1963	1975	1989	1993
Individuals	54	37.5	20.6	17.7
Financial institutions	30.3	48	58.5	61.6
Others	8.7	8.9	8.1	4.4
Overseas	7.0	5.6	12.8	16.3

Source: Central Statistical Office.

managers who have no significant ownership stake in the companies they run, generally a fraction of 1 per cent. They are hired, in principle, by the owners to promote their interests, which means to maximize their wealth. This wealth is now in the form of marketable shares so that what the owners are understood to want managers to maximize is the share price or the stock market value (SMV) of the enterprise. This is the modern equivalent of maximizing the entrepreneur's residual.

The combination of an arguably less fierce competitive environment, growing organizational complexity, and the separation of ownership from control, it is argued by some economists, has led to a situation where it is unlikely that the main objective of the corporation is any longer to maximize shareholder wealth, or SMV. The lack of competition means that there is an element of discretion available to those in control of the enterprise about how hard they choose to search for value. A failure to maximize value does not lead to elimination from the industry as it would do under highly competitive circumstance. The separation of ownership from control means that managers are in effective control of the enterprise and, to the extent that they can get away with it, managers will choose to ignore the wishes of the owners and pursue what they see as their own interests. In other words, they will behave opportunistically. The question then is, what might these managerial interests be and what difference will the pursuit of these interests make to the behaviour and performance of the enterprise?

Consider this question: what might managers be interested in apart from maximizing shareholders' wealth and how might this affect the behaviour of big business? The consensus among economists who have written about this issue, most famously J. K. Galbraith in his best-selling book *The New Industrial State*, is that managers place greater emphasis on the rate of growth of the business *per se*, that is, increasing the size of the business, rather than on its stock market value. There are several reasons, and some empirical support, for this view. Managerial salaries tend to be related to the size of the business they run rather than its stock market performance. A growing business provides better career prospects, that is, promotion prospects, for managers, and managers like the prestige and excitement of working for a growing business. The process by which objectives are formulated within the firm is likely to lead to an objective which those involved can think of as being in their personal interest, and growth serves this purpose well. Who is likely be against it?

Maximizing the owners' wealth, on the other hand, is perhaps not something which will automatically appeal to the average manager. Indeed, identifying the enterprise with the interests of a single group could even create a 'them and us' effect with negative consequences for the cohesion of the collective. Describing the purpose of productive activity as being to make the shareholders rich is perhaps not the best way to get everyone to give of their best. In theory, of course, matters such as individual sensitivities do not come into it. In practice, they may well do. Interestingly, the Japanese are extremely averse to describing the purpose of enterprise in these terms. Indeed, by all accounts shareholders count for very little in the average Japanese corporation.

All of this only matters, of course, to the extent that there is any real conflict between the owner's presumed desire for increasing the stock market value of the enterprise and the managers' desire for growth, or increasing the size of the enterprise. Does such a conflict actually exist and what difference would it make to the behaviour and performance of the enterprise? Under what circumstances would such a conflict arise? If such a conflict arises, what determines the extent to which managers can 'get away' with pursuing their own interests rather than those of the owners? Would owners not have an incentive to make sure managers did not 'get away' with ignoring their objectives? We shall now consider these issues.

Growth versus Stock Market Value

Consider first the likely relationship between the growth of a firm and its stock market value. Will 'growing' the business, as they say nowadays, ever conflict with the firm's stock market value? Surely if the business grows, then its stock market value will grow also. Perhaps, but not necessarily. This will depend on whether or not the investment necessary to promote business growth is worthwhile, that is, whether or not new investment in plant and equipment or advertising or R&D or skills or acquisitions adds value to the firm. How do we formally measure whether or not any particular investment is worthwhile? According to the theory of investment evaluation which we examined earlier, the formal way to evaluate an investment of any sort is to calculate its Net Present Value (NPV) defined as follows:

NPV = the discounted stream of extra income (that is, incremental annual revenue less incremental annual costs) generated by the investment over its lifetime minus the initial cost of the investment.

The discount rate used in the calculation is chosen to reflect the opportunity cost of shareholders' money. The opportunity cost of the shareholders' money depends on the alternatives available to the shareholders at the time of the investment. For example, shareholders might be able to buy a risk-free government bond with the money giving a risk-free return of 5 per cent. If this was an option, then the firm would have to produce a risk-adjusted return of at least 5 per cent to meet the shareholders' requirements.

An investment can affect the value of the firm in the following ways:

- if an investment has a positive NPV, then by definition it adds value to the firm, the shareholders will thus benefit from it as share prices rise to reflect this new value, and the firm should undertake that investment;
- If an investment does not have a positive NPV, then the shareholders will not gain from it and if they had direct control of the business, they would choose not to make it.

But of course any investment which 'grows the business' and increases its size is 'valuable' to the managers of the business, even if it does not have a positive NPV, for reasons discussed earlier. So a possible source of conflict between growth and stock market value (SMV) definitely exists. This is shown in a simple diagram of the likely relationship between growth and SMV for any particular firm (Figure 12.1).

Growth and SMV therefore only go together to the extent that the investment undertaken to produce growth has a positive NPV. To put it another way, an investment is only valuable to the shareholders if it produces a risk-adjusted return at least equal to the opportunity cost of their capital. But some investments considered by the firm, say for new plant or a new advertising campaign or extra R&D expenditure or a new computer system, will not have a positive NPV. The likely returns simply would not justify the expenditure involved. Shareholders, if they were in direct control of the business, would choose not to accept such investments because they would harm their wealth prospects. But managers might be tempted to accept them to the extent that they are more interested in growth itself than in profitable growth. So what determines whether or not managers accept investments which shareholders would find unacceptable if they were asked? This will depend first of all on the ability of owners to *detect* managerial indulgence of their own interests, and secondly on the ability of owners to *control* managerial indulgence by direct and indirect action. We shall now consider these possibilities.

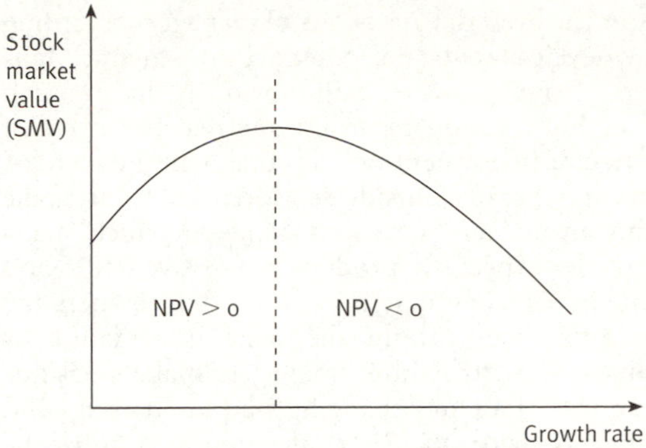

Figure 12.1 Relationship between growth of the firm and its stock market value

Detecting and Acting against Management Indulgence

Consider first the ability of owners to detect managerial decisions which adversely affect their collective wealth. Here we have a classic example of the problems caused by the phenomenon of asymmetric information and moral hazard which we discussed earlier (Chapter 4). To the extent that owners have a rather tenuous relationship with the firm, they are unlikely to be well informed about the everyday decisions of managers regarding new developments and potential investment. Managers, being insiders, will obviously have much better information regarding the real prospects of particular investment policies than will the owners, who are literally outsiders. Moreover, firms make many investment decisions some of which managers do expect to produce a positive NPV and some which they may not. How could owners tell the difference without the same information as managers? Furthermore, managers make decisions in an uncertain and changing world and even good managers with the best of intentions must be expected to make some poor investment decisions. What seems like a good investment at one point can turn out to be a bad investment when circumstances change. So the problem shareholders face is detecting when managers make poor investment decisions wilfully (or as a result of incompetence) and when they make decisions in good faith which turn out badly because of changing circumstances such as unpredictable changes in government policy or technology.

The fact is that it is impossible for owners to be perfectly informed about the actions of managers. If would be prohibitively costly for owners as a group to be perfectly, or even reasonably well-informed about each and every managerial action in order to evaluate managerial decisions. But even *if* owners as a group would find it worthwhile, that is, valuable, to invest heavily in the day-to-day monitoring of management decisions, this would not necessarily happen for the following reason.

The average firm has lots of shareholders, in many cases hundreds of thousands, although the number with significant holdings, say more than 1 per cent, may be quite small. All shareholders are likely to gain in proportion to their holdings from shareholders acting together and investing in the effective monitoring of managers because this would raise share prices. So if all shareholders contributed a fee in proportion to their holdings in order to pay for more effective shareholder monitoring of managerial actions, each would be likely to cover the costs involved. So why do we not observe shareholder coalitions doing this? Because we are back to the co-operation dilemma examined earlier (Chapter 4).

Imagine you are a shareholder asked to pay a fee for this purpose based on the small, often negligible, proportion of total shares you hold. Would you do it? Possibly, but perhaps not if you were a rational self-interest maximizer of the type economists assume us all to be. On the one hand, you gain if you pay the fee but only if most other people pay according to the plan. On the other hand, if everyone else pays according to the plan, you stand to gain more or less the same benefits even if you do not pay your share because you stand to benefit from a rise in share price even if you do not pay the fee. You cannot be effectively excluded from the benefit of rising share values just because you did not pay your fee to join the monitoring club. So why bother? Of course, everyone else works this out also and so putting together such a monitoring plan is likely to be stymied by rational individual self-interest.

Inadequate shareholder monitoring is an example of what economists refer to as the free-riding problem: the fairly common human propensity to hope that other people will pay the fare for your journey. In addition, the owners would have to consider the age-old question: *who monitors the monitors?* (‘*Quis custodiet ipsos custodes?*’, as Juvenal put it around AD 100, suggesting that the problem is not a new one.) In passing, you might now appreciate why taxation is not voluntary! Were we all asked to make a voluntary contribution to the defence of the realm or the road-building programme do you imagine for one moment we would all rush for our cheque books? Shareholder monitoring of management is a classic case of what economists call a public (as opposed to a private) good. Economists give such goods—defence is the most prominent example—a special name because they recognize that individual choices and market forces alone will fail to ensure an adequate or optimal provision of such goods. We shall be examining the issue of public goods formally in the next chapter.

Of course, shareholders do pay collectively, although indirectly, for some monitoring of managerial decisions. For a start, they are legally entitled to receive audited reports about the performance of the business on a regular basis on which they can in principle judge the performance of managers, if only *ex post facto*. But by the time they receive their annual reports the important decisions have long been made. And in any case, annual reports are an exercise in maintaining information asymmetry in favour of the managers who, it has to be remembered, usually appoint the auditors and write the annual reports. You do not find many admissions of failure in annual reports. When things are going well, managers put it down to good management. When the company is going downhill, it is due to adverse circumstances and unfair foreign competition. And the problem for shareholders is, who can say it is not? Just imagine the legal costs of arguing about this in a courtroom, as shareholders would have to do to prove conscious and intentional managerial neglect of their interests!

One possibility, of course, is comparative performance. Whilst it is difficult to evaluate the performance of any particular firm in isolation, it is possible to use standardized sets of indicators to compare the performance of similar firms. This can at least indicate cases where managerial failings might be the cause of underperformance and so put the spotlight on these managers.

Overall, however, considering the large sums at stake surprisingly little direct monitoring of management by shareholders takes place. Therefore the ability of owners to effectively *detect* undesirable managerial decisions is apparently quite limited.

Shareholder Actions

Now consider the ability of owners to control managerial behaviour by direct and indirect means. Take direct action first. Even if shareholders could detect potentially undesirable (from their point of view) management decisions, what could they do about them? In practice, it would appear not very much. Enforcing the rights of ownership can be even more costly than detecting problems in the first place and runs into the same dilemma of co-operation when meeting these costs (see above).

The British Prime Minister argued in November 1994, during the debate about the increasing salary levels of top managers in the privatized company sector, that if the shareholders of privatised companies such as British Gas felt that managers were overindulging themselves it was up to them, the shareholders, to stop it. How shareholders might stop it he did not say, for the simple reason that they would in fact find it very difficult. Of course, you might write a letter to the chairman of British Gas or National Power telling him you think he is overpaid and underworked but I would not count on a reply unless you happen to be a major institutional shareholder. Even then, the said chairman would no doubt point in reply to the ongoing difficulties in recruiting top quality managers, not to mention the even bigger salaries of the chairmen of financial institutions! The chairman paradoxically can use company money to hire the best available public relations people to put his case but the shareholders cannot! Shareholders would, and sometimes do despite free-riding problems, have to create an action group at their own expense to represent their combined interests.

So what can shareholders do next? Well, you could go to the trouble of attending the annual meeting of the shareholders when the board in principle is available for questioning, and again in principle you could demand a vote of no confidence in the board and have it removed. But it is rare for anyone to find it worthwhile to organize shareholders sufficiently to overcome the enormous odds against doing this successfully. The odds are stacked in favour of the managers who control the meeting, control the proxy votes, and more importantly control the flow of information available to shareholders in the first place. Of course, there are exceptions. In 1995, there was a well-publicized shareholder revolt against proposed payments to Maurice Saatchi, a key director of Saatchi and Saatchi, a major British advertising services company, which led to his leaving the company he had helped to create. Significantly, however, the impetus behind this revolt came from American shareholders and not from British financial institutions. American shareholders have traditionally been somewhat more active in trying to keep managers in line than is the case elsewhere (see Box 12.1 for a discussion of shareholder activism in the USA).

Of course, some shareholders are in a better position than others to obtain and analyse the information necessary to make somewhat better informed judgements about managers: the big financial institutions such as the pension funds which hold massive diversified portfolios of shares. These institutions do invest in monitoring company behaviour to some extent and do try to exert some influence on some companies some of the time to change their policies, particularly their dividend payout policies. But this monitoring is nowhere near as substantial or as effective as you might imagine and for two very good reasons. First, it would be embarrassing for the hired managers who run big financial institutions to question the pay and decisions of the hired managers who run the major industrial companies. It might raise interesting questions about their own pay levels and their own decisions. Secondly, it is far easier, less embarrassing, and considerably cheaper, to

Box 12.1 Shareholder Activism in the USA

Writing in the *Financial Times* (17 March 1993), Martin Dickson argues that in the USA the phenomenon of organized groups of shareholders acting to make underperforming management teams more accountable is becoming increasingly common. He lists nine companies facing organized shareholder pressure in March 1993: Advanced Micro Devices, Champion International, Eastman Kodak, Great Atlantic and Pacific Tea Company (A&P), General Dynamics, McDonnell Douglas, Paramount Communications, Polaroid, and Sears Roebuck.

These firms have become targets for the increasingly powerful US corporate governance movement, which is showing signs of having a big effect on the running of American firms. The corporate governance movement is a grouping of large US institutional investors, which, by making managers more accountable to shareholders, is attempting to improve corporate financial performance. Tangible evidence of its effectiveness can be found in forced resignations of CEOs at IBM, American Express, Westinghouse, and General Motors.

The ability of the movement to achieve its goals has been helped by important changes introduced by the US Securities and Exchange Commission to the way that shareholder voting battles at annual meetings are carried out. The rules, introduced in October 1992, allow investors to act in concert more easily, and to use more flexible tactics.

At the time Dickson was writing, the New York State Pension Fund, a large institutional investor, announced that because of the A&P's underperformance it would oppose re-election of existing directors at the firm's annual meeting, and urged others to follow suit. Whilst this tactic was not expected to be successful, its effect would be to increase pressure on A&P to improve performance.

Dickson argues that there were three main reasons for the recent rise of the US corporate governance movement:

- the growth of institutional investment and the decline of individual share ownership in the USA in the 1970s and 1980s, which resulted in large stakeholders having considerable leverage;
- the 1980s take-over boom encouraged managers of weak companies to erect 'poison pill' defences, often at the expense of shareholders in the companies concerned;
- the increasing use by fund managers of investment in a diversified portfolio of stocks rather than narrowly targeted investment aimed at picking winners.

Any diversified portfolio, says Dickson, contains poor performers. Investors have switched attention from selecting firms with good previous records, to investing more widely and trying to improve the performance of any 'dogs' in their portfolio by pressuring managers to run these firms better.

The ability to sort out the good from the bad performers has been greatly extended by the adoption of computerized screening programmes. One such programme set up by the New York State Pension Fund does screening in three stages:

- a statistical review of a company's performance;
- an examination of its corporate governance and executive pay;
- prediction of the group's long-term prospects under the existing management.

As screening becomes more widely used, its effectiveness will increase. Attention will become focused on the particular sets of poorly performing management, and the more widely available information will allow individual activists themselves to play an effective role in affecting corporate governance.

Dickson believes that shareholder activists have been transformed from minor irritants into groups with significant muscle. One example he gives of their success is Sears Roebuck's decision in 1992 to sell off its poorly performing financial services division after two years of co-ordinated investor pressure.

Dickson argues that the increasing trend for institutional investors to put money into troubled businesses and then to force managerial and policy changes (instead of merely withdrawing funds from their stock) is an important vehicle for improving business performance.

Source: Adapted from the article: 'Crusaders in the Capitalist Cause', by Martin Dickson, *Financial Times*, 17 March 1993.

express your disapproval of a particular company's managers by selling its shares at the going rate through the stock market rather than by taking direct action. Organizing and implementing direct action against entrenched managers is difficult and expensive. Financial institutions in most countries are not geared up to actively second-guess and control managerial behaviour. This is not generally what they see as their function. Some people think they should be more active in this area however, and there are proposals in Britain to encourage the financial institutions to become more active in corporate governance. But there are limits to this as Box 12.2 makes clear.

Box 12.2 The Influence of UK Financial Institutions on Corporate Governance

John Plender, writing in the *Financial Times* in May 1990, investigates the relationship between financial institutions and the large firms in which they purchase equity in the UK economy. How do these institutions conduct their relationships with UK business firms?

In the main, the relationship is very much an arm's-length one, with little organized, ongoing direct involvement. Nevertheless, a fair amount of 'responsible ownership' does go on, sometimes under the auspices of institutional committees, often behind closed doors. Plender points to several examples: the Prudential's decision in the 1950s to question the behaviour of Sir Bernard Docker at BSA; the assault on the perks of Marks and Spencer's board in the 1980s by the Post Office Pension Fund; rejection of the terms of British Land's corporate restructuring in 1989 by institutional investors. Yet Plender says that 'the focus of intervention has tended to be on such narrow financial matters as the dilution of existing shareholder's interests, director's incentives and the level of dividends'.

What seems most clear is that there is very little intervention by institutional investors in corporate strategy. It is far easier to cite cases of unsatisfactory management or long-term corporate decline that did *not* initiate institutional intervention in strategy—British Leyland, Distillers, Plessey, Dunlop, Chloride, for example—than cases which did. Why are British financial institutions so reluctant to intervene in corporate strategy?

Plender offers several possible explanations:

- Some firms were not susceptible to intervention for special reasons, such as protection by family and other friendly shareholdings, or by some official organization (for example, the clearing banks have been protected by the Bank of England from contested take-overs);
- dog does not eat dog: this perhaps explains why poor management at Commercial Union in the 1970s failed to initiate action from other insurers;
- in manufacturing, rising corporate profitability in the second half of the 1980s disguised weaknesses of underlying strategy;
- fear of alienating present and potential clients;
- a corporate culture centred around and averse to ownership and intervention;
- where intervention has taken place (such as by Prudential), the task is slow, painful and often unproductive, and finding alternative management is difficult;
- the financial institutions lack industry-specific expertise and information (in marked contrast to Continental European banks that play a key role in corporate strategy)

Plender looks at several cases in some detail. One of these is Lord Weinstock's GEC, which seems to have failed to break through into the international big league in electronics. It is widely thought that GEC has under-invested and has performed poorly on Nimrod and other defence contracts. Finally, the composition of GEC's board has attracted constant criticism.

Plender argues that,

> to take on GEC the institutions would have to confront a powerful, entrepreneurial personality whose mastery of the details of this complex business is legendary, even if his share stake is now dwarfed by that of the Prudential. Despite all the criticism, the financial performance has been far from poor, especially when compared with competitors in continental Europe. And the group has just embarked on a significant change of strategy, involving a number of joint ventures on which the details are none too clear, in response to the upheaval in the structure of the European market. Intervention, before the new strategy has been properly tested, might be hard to justify except in the event of an unconvincing succession to Lord Weinstock as managing director.

Source: Adapted from: 'The Limits to Institutional Power', by John Plender, *Financial Times*, 22 May 1990.

The Market for Corporate Control

So what can shareholders do when they are not satisfied with the actions of managers and the performance of 'their' company? The simplest and cheapest course of action is of course to sell their shares, which is exactly what rational shareholders do. It is better to bail out than to stay and face the costs involved in fighting managers you are not happy with. Indeed, if the bail-out option was not available, most shareholders would not find it worthwhile to be shareholders in the first place. It is the marketability of equity shares, that is, their liquidity, which makes them attractive to individuals and institutions in the first place. Does this then mean that ultimately managers can do exactly as they please because shareholders will always choose the quick and cheap option of selling out rather than monitoring managers closely and enforcing their rights? Not at all. Why not? Before we consider this, you might like to recall the discussion of M&A's in Chapter 11, in particular the discussion of the 'efficiency' route to value.

Managers cannot completely ignore the interests of shareholders for the following reasons. First, if this was likely to be the case, no one would ever choose to be a non-controlling shareholder in the first place. If minority shareholders had no fall-back protection against managers, no rational person would be a minority shareholder. The separation of ownership from control could not have happened. Secondly, it is possible that managers might at times need to raise new equity capital from the stock market, where a reputation for ignoring shareholders would make this difficult if not impossible. However, this is unlikely to be a major discipline for managers in most industrial countries because the evidence shows conclusively that most large companies most of the time make very little use of the stock market as a source of new capital. Thirdly, there is a mechanism through which the owner's dissatisfaction with managers would ultimately affect managers where it hurts. We met this mechanism in Chapter 11: it is the threat of take-over or acquisition. Economists refer to this mechanism as the market for corporate control.

The market for corporate control is exactly what its name suggests, a market for the buying and selling of the ownership rights to control the enterprise. This is where the right to control companies is traded and the usual principles of market operation apply. People seek to make money, to appropriate value, by operating in this market. They operate by identifying companies which they believe are operating below their value-adding potential as a result of management failures, or management choices which favour growth at the expense of stock market value. These companies will have a lower stock market value than they could have if they were run properly in the interests of shareholders, because the selling of shares by disaffected owners will lead to a fall in the price of these shares. This creates a valuable incentive for someone (a take-over raider) to buy the right to control such a company, change its managers, and ensure that the new managers focus more closely on maximizing shareholder value rather than growth. The incentive to do so is obvious. If you can buy an under-performing asset for £1 million, improve its performance so that it increases in value to £1.5 million, then you have potentially made an economic profit. This is called 'releasing value' by some, 'asset stripping' by others. However, there is an important qualification to this prospect of apparently easy money. Making a take-over raid is expensive and involves some risks so your potential profit has to be great enough to cover these costs and justify these risks.

The costs involved include the time and effort needed to organize the take-over, and the fees to be paid. These can be substantial: legal fees, broker's fees, merchant bank fees, consultants, PR costs, advertising costs, financing costs. Moreover, you need to consider the costs of sacking the existing managers and finding and installing new managers whose policies will be more owner friendly. Now consider the risks involved. What if you are wrong in your judgement and the victim company's performance is not the result of managerial failings? Maybe it was something beyond managerial control which affected company performance. Then your new asset is really only worth £1 million after all. Finally, do not forget that take-over bidders usually have to pay a substantial premium over market prices to acquire target companies. Why? Surely if the market values an asset at £1 million, it will be available for that price? Not necessarily. The world is never that simple.

Why might a company currently valued by the market at £1 million be more expensive than that to buy in practice? Consider the point of view of a shareholder in the company and what the appearance of a raider would tell you about the value of your company, and how you might respond to this valuable new information. The arrival of a raider on the scene tells you that someone thinks your shares are worth more than their present price. The raider represents new demand and this in itself sends prices up. Even bidding for a small percentage of a company's shares sends the price up as all dawn raiders know. But in addition, you and other shareholders know that the price offered by the raider must be below the true value of the shares in the raider's evaluation because otherwise the raider cannot hope to make a profit. So you can calculate that your best strategy is to keep your shares, hope the others sell out, wait for the raider to improve company performance to its true level, and then cash in your shares. But if you work this out, so presumably will the other shareholders, and so no one sells unless the raider offers a big enough premium on current prices to convince enough people that no further improvement is possible. But if the raider does this, how can it profit from the raid? Therefore raiding, which looks like an easy way to make money, can in fact turn into an easy way of losing it instead.

The fact that raiding is costly and potentially risky means that the market for corporate control cannot operate perfectly as a constraint on managerial behaviour. Managers can indeed get away with ignoring the interests of owners without fearing a take-over raid and the loss of their jobs. Or at least up to a point they can. That point can be expressed precisely as follows:

Actual SMV (under present management) must exceed potential SMV (under raider) less raiding costs and risks.

Managers can thus in principle indulge their own preferences for growth as long as they do not overdo it and make a raid too attractive. In general, it is impossible to say exactly how much faster such a firm will grow beyond the point desired by the owners because some managerial teams will be risk averse and not push their own preferences too hard, whilst others will be prepared to take a calculated gamble on the chances of a raid. So we can say that a growth-maximizing firm will be different from a value-maximizing firm, but just how different we cannot be sure. It will grow faster, and be less valuable, but how much faster, and with what consequences for value, we cannot say precisely. This will depend on the operation of the market for corporate control. If this market is very active, as it is in Britain and the USA, then managerial indulgence may be reasonably effectively constrained. If this market is not at all active, as is the case in Japan and Germany, then managers are effectively free from shareholder discipline.

It is precisely this comparison that has led some people in Britain and America to complain about the existence of 'short-termism' compared with what is said to be the long-termism of the Japanese and Germans. British managers, it is said, usually by themselves, work under a handicap imposed by the stock market and the financial institutions which demand large and increasing dividend payouts each year as a sign of managerial performance. If managers fail to impress the stock market and the institutions in this way, then the stock market value of the company will be pushed down and a take-over bid becomes a possibility. Managers naturally wish to avoid this and so they focus on 'short-term' earnings, so that they can maintain dividends, but at the expense of long-term investment in skills and R&D. This, it is argued, does not happen in Japan or Germany where firms are free to invest long-term without any interference from take-overs. Therefore, it is concluded that the decline of British industry is the fault of the market for corporate control. Actually, there are important flaws in this argument but these cannot be pursued in detail here. Box 12.3 provides a useful introduction to this debate.

Supply and Demand in the Market for Corporate Finance

Let us consider briefly the general economic effects of a situation where a split between ownership and control causes a number of large firms to pursue growth at the expense of shareholder value. We have so far only analysed the implications of the split for a single firm. What happens if lots of firms try to pursue such a strategy? Think about this from the point of view of supply and demand in the market for corporate finance. First, consider the supply and demand for finance in an imaginary world populated solely by owner-controlled firms which borrow money only to invest in value-creating projects. Figure 12.2 shows the equilibrium price and quantity of finance in this world. Now consider a world populated by growth maximizers constrained only by the market for corporate control. What would happen to the supply and demand for finance in this world? Take demand first. In a

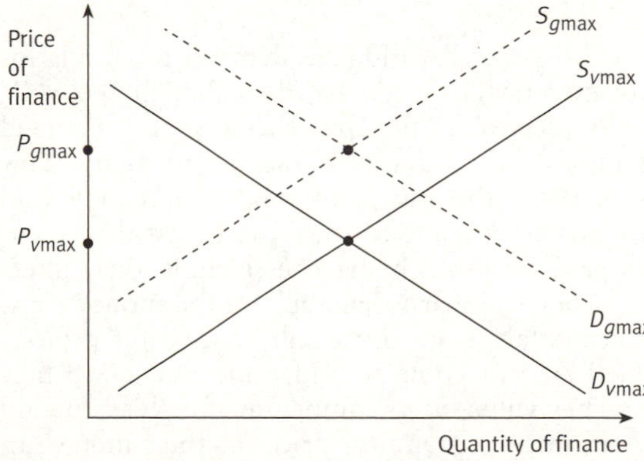

Figure 12.2 Supply and demand in the market for corporate finance

Box 12.3 Short Termism in Corporate Strategy

John Plender, writing in the *Financial Times* in 1990, investigates the criticisms of British industrialists of institutional investors in the City of London for their supposed willingness to sell shareholdings to an opportunistic bidder without giving proper consideration to the longer-term strategy of incumbent management. It is claimed that institutional fund managers are prone to behave as speculators rather than owners. This behaviour is contrasted with that of bankers in West Germany and Japan who participate in the development of corporate policy and strategy. According to this view, management is put under pressure to generate short-term performance which is inimical to capital investment and R&D.

Plender believes there is a grain of truth in this view, but argues that the conduct of institutional investors is not the explanation of short-termism. He points to fundamental problems of valuation and arbitrage as the most important causes of this phenomenon.

According to Plender, the problem is the structure of capital markets. The equity markets of the English-speaking countries differ from those of West Germany and Japan in playing host to an active market in corporate control, resulting in what is known as the dual-pricing problem. There are two bases for the valuation of a firm:

- valuation for day-to-day purposes in marginal trading;
- valuation when control of the whole firm is at stake.

The second of these values is usually the higher, with the difference being known as the premium for control. The existence of this premium creates profit opportunities through arbitrage, and facilitates changes in ownership and control. Institutional investors, operating in a competitive fund management market, are loath to turn down a contested bid for fear that the arbitrage profit will disappear if the bid fails. The continuous monitoring of fund managers' performance virtually forces them to accept the available short-term gains once a bid is under way.

Looking at matters from the point of view of incumbent management, the potential threat from take-over bids does provide a strong incentive to prudent financial control but it also provides a powerful disincentive to risk taking, which harms long-term investment in plant and machinery, research and development, and training. The structure of incentives, argues Plender, leads British managers to view the business as a portfolio of corporate acquisitions. Expansion through growth and product innovation take a distant second place.

Some firms, like the highly profitable pharmaceutical companies, with very high share prices reflecting high profits from successful past investment, are not affected by fears of hostile take-over bids. But companies with major investment programmes that have yet to pay off in higher profits are vulnerable. As the City of London earns income from dealing and advisory work concerning valuation anomalies, it is likely to identify such firms as candidates for predatory bids.

Somewhat ironically, it appears that changes taking place in Japan and West Germany are leading to capital market structures closer to those of the English-speaking countries. Decades of prosperity have led to the close ties between banks and corporations in Japan and Germany being eroded, opening up the possibility of the dual valuation problem we described above.

Source: Adapted from 'Malaise in Need of Long-Term Remedy' by John Plender, *Financial Times*, Friday 20 July 1990.

growth-oriented world, the demand for funds for investment will be greater than that in the SMV world. Represent this by a shift in the demand function to the right as shown in our figure. Now think about the supply of funds. Shareholders in this world are going to learn pretty fast that 'their' companies are not being run solely in their interests. They will learn that some of the money companies obtain from them will be used for projects which are not going to add value. What will they do? They will seek to compensate for this situation by requiring a premium price for their money. In other words, the supply curve of finance will shift to the left.

What then is the likely overall effect of a world of companies putting growth before stock market value? Our simple analysis suggests this result: The price of finance goes up, and the equilibrium quantity of finance is more or less the same as in the value-driven world. So the average company, in fact, can grow no faster than before, the economy grows no faster; all that happens is an increase in the price of finance! So the idea that Japanese companies grow faster than British companies simply because Japanese shareholders are even less powerful than those in Britain seems questionable. There must be more to Japanese dynamism than that.

Indirect Control and Incentives for Managers

Now consider some of the indirect means by which the owners might exert some control over managerial actions. If owners find it difficult to monitor managers effectively and to control them directly, then they might seek to find some way(s) of influencing managerial actions indirectly to increase the extent to which managers focus on creating shareholder value. How might they do this?

First, they could, of course, simply ask managers to make a written commitment to serve the cause of ownership wealth before making any managerial appointments. And no doubt many managers would happily make such a commitment, just as we all promise our insurers to drive carefully and to lock our windows before we go on holiday. But it is hard to see how such commitments could be made credible. Promises are cheap. It would be in everyone's interest to be able to make credible commitments of this sort, because life would be simpler, but it is difficult to see how such commitments could be monitored.

Secondly, owners could endeavour to create an effective and competitive market for managerial skills. A competitive market for managers would presumably place great emphasis on individual reputations for acting in the interests of owners and value such a reputation appropriately. Thus, to the extent that shareholders are able to influence the choice of the most senior managers, they would choose managers with a good reputation for looking after their interests and these managers would hire and promote other managers and make it worth their while to build a reputation for looking after shareholders. There are some limits to this approach however.

1. It is not clear how much influence shareholders actually exert on the choice of senior managers in the modern corporation. The fact is that senior managers tend to come from within the organization and become senior managers by pleasing their managerial predecessors. Nominally, shareholders have to approve the appointment of directors but in practice it is difficult for shareholders to organize themselves sufficiently to block the recommendations of the incumbent board of management.

2. The more senior a manager and the nearer to retirement she is, the less valuable will be her reputation as measured in discounted cash flow terms. This might appear paradoxical so you need to think about it carefully.

3. Management is a team effort and thus it is difficult to measure the contribution of individuals to its overall performance. Being a member of a successful team may be valuable, of course, but maybe not valuable enough for individual members of the team to discourage their incentive to free-ride on the efforts of the others. If the team is successful, the individual enhances her reputation anyway and if it fails, she can conveniently blame the others. How can the market properly value individual reputations effectively in such circumstances?

Thirdly, owners could encourage managers to hold shares in the company or even insist on a certain level of share ownership as a requirement for senior management. This could be called making a commitment. The proportion of total share capital held by the management team would not have to be very significant because even a very small proportion of all the shares in IBM or BT or Shell represents a lot of money. Therefore, even a small holding of the equity of such corporations would represent a big proportion of the average manager's wealth and make them more likely to act in the interests of shareholders. The difficulty with such a proposal is that individual managers are likely to be actively averse to tying up a large proportion of their personal wealth in a large complex company whose performance is beyond their personal control. The difference any single person, even a chief executive officer, can make to the long-run performance of IBM or ICI is limited. The individual is part of a large team operating in a highly uncertain environment, subject to many exogenous shocks, and as such has a limited capacity to influence overall performance. This being the case, it would simply not be rational for the individual manager to tie her wealth too closely to the performance of the enterprise. It would be rational, in fact, for managers to diversify their financial capital away from the enterprise in which they work given that the value of their human capital is by definition already closely tied to the fortunes of the business.

Finally, owners could endeavour to design performance-related compensation schemes which relate managerial income to the stock market performance of the enterprise. And indeed this does happen to some extent. Some managerial compensation contracts are explicitly related to changes in shareholder value or are related through mechanisms such as share option schemes. However, there are likely to be limits to this approach.

The first is risk avoidance. Most managers are unlikely to favour pure performance-related pay schemes. They may be attractive as an added element of a compensation package but not as the sole element. Consider this simple exercise. You are offered a job which pays £1 million if the company does well or nothing if it does badly with the chances of the company doing well believed to be fifty-fifty. Another job offers £0.5 million no matter what the company's performance is. Both jobs have exactly the same expected income therefore. Which one would you choose? Since most people tend to be risk averse when it comes to earning their daily bread, most of us are likely to choose the latter job. People who like risks are likely to be busy speculating on foreign exchange markets not looking for jobs as managers.

Performance-related compensation schemes run into another problem. One we have come across before. They require that individual contributions to overall performance are reasonably easy to evaluate. For example, could you offer a goalkeeper a compensation package related to the number of games won? This would be difficult, because the goalkeeper, whilst a vital member of a team, does not determine its performance on his own. The same is true of most executives. Of course you could offer the whole team a performance-related income, but then you run into the free-riding problem discussed earlier. If everyone's income depends on the performance of the team, then individuals have an incentive to try to free-ride on the team's efforts.

A possible solution to this is peer-group pressure, that is, to build on the individual's desire not to let the side down. This is undoubtedly a powerful force acting against free-riders. Its value is reinforced by the likelihood that peers are likely to be effective monitors of one another's performance. It might be difficult for outsiders to judge when the goalkeeper is doing his best for the team, but his team-mates are likely to find it easier. Therefore successful schemes require either that individual contributions are easily measured, or that the propensity to free-ride can be controlled by some means such as peer-group pressure. The analysis of methods for inducing one type of individual, the agents, to act in the best interest of another, the principals, is called not surprisingly principal–agent theory. Economists have in recent years investigated the design of schemes for such situations only to realize just how difficult it is to design economically efficient incentive schemes.

A final problem for the owners, of course, is that even if effective compensation schemes could be conceived, how do owners get them implemented? The problem is that in many cases the design and implementation of corporate compensation is in the hands of management anyway. Not surprisingly, therefore, we find that compensation schemes tend to reflect the interests of managers. Thus, to the extent that such schemes are tied to stock market performance, the tie is often not symmetric. If the stock value goes up, managers are rewarded but if it goes down, managers are not expected to pay some of their fixed salary back to the company. This sort of scheme could in fact be detrimental to owners for the following reason. Managers may then tend to pursue risky but high-return projects because if they succeed they stand to gain a lot but if they fail they do not bear any of the losses, although of course their reputation may suffer. A further discussion of performance-related pay is included as Box 12.4.

To sum up the discussion so far, the ability of owners to detect and act against potentially opportunistic managerial behaviour is limited by various considerations: The costs involved, co-operation dilemmas, managerial control of information, the unwillingness of financial institutions to act collectively, the costs and risks of the market for corporate control, the problems of designing effective performance-related compensation schemes. Of course, none of this *proves* that managerially controlled firms behave differently from owner-controlled firms, or if they do that it makes any difference to the general behaviour and performance of the economy. It simply suggests that such possibilities exist and that the implications for corporate governance have to be thought about.

12.2 The Internal Organization of the Firm and its Motivation

The separation of ownership from control is not the only feature of modern business organization which may compromise the firm's desire to create added value. Even if owners were still in effective

Box 12.4 Performance-Related Pay

According to *The Economist*, most large firms in the USA now use some form of performance-related pay (PRP), such as merit pay, bonuses, and share options, to reward and motivate their employees. This has been introduced for three reasons:

- to tighten employer control of wage bills;
- to increase flexibility;
- to motivate individual employees.

Some types of PRP (such as piecework and merit pay) reward individual productivity. Others (for example, profit-sharing schemes) relate pay to the performance of some larger group. But whatever the particulars of any PRP scheme, each is designed to move away from equal pay for all, regardless of contributions.

The principle of PRP has also become widely adopted outside the USA. In the UK in 1994, over three-quarters of firms used some form of financial incentives in remuneration packages. The share of PRP in total pay has steadily increased, from 10 per cent of a typical senior manager's pay in 1989 to 40 per cent five years later. PRP is being used in both public and private sectors, covering, for example, British civil servants, the BBC, and the Royal household staff.

Despite its growing use, a number of management writers and independent research groups are very sceptical about whether it actually works! Many critics claim that, far from motivating workforces, it actually has demotivating effects. According to *The Economist*, there are several kinds of objections to PRP.

- Performance is difficult to measure. Attempts to calculate individual contributions to collective performance tend to either reward routine performance (when a tangible measure such as a group's output is used) or be perceived as inconsistent or based on favouritism (where the subjective assessments of supervisor are used). It is also felt that the most senior managers rig the indicators for their own benefit.
- Money rewards do not seem a good motivator. Some critics of PRP argue that performance is primarily motivated by peer esteem and the intrinsic interest of the work. Financial incentives may have good short-term effects but do not engender long-term commitment. Even where money is a good motivator, it can have perverse consequences, such as where managers are over-zealous in their selling behaviour to the point of damaging firms' reputations.
- Management resources are allocated to devising ever more elaborate PRP schemes at the expense of more valuable management functions or thinking about other ways of bringing about better worker performance.
- PRP schemes are very costly to introduce and administer.

In Defence of PRP

It is argued that whilst accepting that these criticisms are not without force, the faults lie not with the principle of PRP but with poor administration of the schemes. It is argued that there is no real alternative to PRP, and that its critics have failed to produce anything better. With careful design, it is said, PRP is the most effective mechanism for recruiting and retaining scarce talent and sending appropriate signals to good and poor workers alike. Moreover, as reward by promotion becomes less common with the tendency for flatter organizations to replace older hierarchical structures, PRP has an important gap to fill.

New Forms of PRP

According to *The Economist*, attempts to develop PRP schemes that both motivate workers and are consistent with other organizational objectives have taken several forms:

- focusing on group rather than individual performance;
- performance measured by quality rather than by quantity;
- rewarding breadth of contribution to the business;
- remuneration related to the extent to which objectives for individual improvement have been achieved (for example, John Lewis Partnership, a British retailer);
- linking staff pay to 'know-how' and 'problem-solving' involved in jobs (for example. AT&T's Universal Card Services division in Florida).

The common thread in all these is an abandonment of general schemes and rigid formulae in favour of tailor-made schemes.

Source: Adapted from: 'Just desserts', *The Economist*, 29 January 1994, p. 77.

control of large corporations, or could find some way to impose their objectives on the top managers of the corporation, this would not in itself necessarily be sufficient to guarantee that the owner's objectives would reign supreme. This is because the sheer size and organizational complexity of big business creates a series of problems similar in nature to, although less severe than, the owner–manager split. We have in mind here the separation between top managers, middle managers, and junior managers within the typical large business organization.

Managers as a group may have similar objectives *vis-à-vis* the owners, but there is no reason to believe that managers as individuals are all equally prepared to act wholeheartedly in the interest of the management group. As we discussed in Chapter 4, people have their personal objectives and pursue their own interests much of the time and co-operate with others in the pursuit of group interests only when it suits them to do so. This being the case, or at least the case according to how economists see human nature, it is likely that top managers face the same problem with respect to middle managers, and middle managers with respect to junior managers, as owners face with respect to top managers: that is, how to ensure that the actions of subordinates match their objectives rather than those of the subordinates. As in the owner–manager case, this will depend on the ability of one group, say top managers, to detect and control the actions of the other group.

It is easy to see that the ability of managers at one level in a hierarchy to detect and control the activities of managers at the next level is likely to be greater than the ability of outside owners to control the actions of managers. All managers are insiders and, as such, senior managers are in a much stronger position *vis-à-vis* junior managers than owners *via-à-vis* managers. Top managers will have much better access to information about other managers, and the environment in which they operate, in order to judge their performance. Top managers do not face the co-operation dilemmas faced by owners which we analysed earlier. Top managers are thus, in principle, in a much better position to effectively monitor other managers. In addition, top managers can act more effectively to discipline other managers if it is felt their performance is unsatisfactory. Managers who fail to please their superiors can be sacked or refused promotion or put in charge of the branch office in Arkansas or Hokkaido. There is no need for all the rigmarole and expense which surrounds the market for corporate control. Finally, top managers are in a better position when it comes to designing and implementing performance-related compensation schemes for other managers. As we observed earlier, the design of economically efficient and workable incentive schemes is not easy, but at least top managers are in a position to experiment to find something suitable for their particular organization and circumstances.

However, the ability of one group of managers to impose itself on another is not perfect. It depends on the ability of one level of management to detect and control the activities of the next level (and to some extent also on the willingness of people at the next level to be controlled). This depends crucially on the quality and quantity of information available and the ability of the people receiving this information to process it properly in order to make the appropriate decisions. And this depends crucially on organizational design, or structure, or form, which is thus an important determinant of the extent to which individual motives are harnessed to the collective will. Let us examine this issue more closely.

The Nature and Significance of Organizational Design

Firms are organized bundles of resources with a unified administrative hierarchy. The traditional approach to the organization of the firm, and what is still the dominant approach, is called the functional or unitary or U-form. The characteristics of the U-form of organization are shown in Figure 12.3. The U-form firm is organized on functional lines with a chief executive responsible for long-term strategy and short-term operations co-ordinating and monitoring a number of functional departments headed by functional specialists. Managers are thus functionally specialized and their activities co-ordinated by the general manager or chief executive. This approach to organization is considered efficient as long as firms stay relatively simple and as long as the chief executive has the required information for effective co-ordination and monitoring of the functional managers.

As firms grow and become more complex in scope, however, problems can develop with this approach. The effort required for effective co-ordination of the separate functions increases and

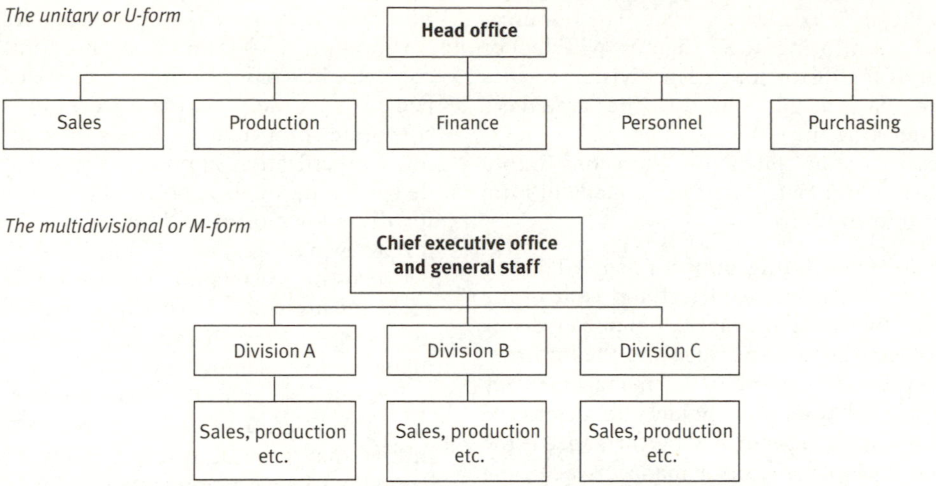

Figure 12.3 The characteristics of the two fundamental types of organizational form

impinges on the strategic functions of the chief executive. Each functional manager has to deal with an increasingly diverse range of tasks. For example, producing cosmetics and shampoos and drugs, or selling distinct products to different sorts of customers. The functional departments increasingly develop functional objectives at odds with the interests of the organization as a whole. For example, the R&D people seek more resources for R&D and the production people want the latest equipment regardless of the organization's priorities. Each functional area wants to expand its size and influence at the expense of the others and to fight off any attempts at interference by other functional managers. The potential for opportunistic behaviour increases and information can be delayed and/or distorted as it makes its way up and down the hierarchy. If things go wrong, the sales people can blame it on quality problems, the production people can blame it on poor marketing, and the accountants on everyone else. The ability of the chief executive to detect and control the actions of the functional managers diminishes as complexity grows and the information required for effective monitoring and enforcement of decisions grows beyond the capacity of the chief executive. Firms begin to suffer from what is called control loss.

It was in order to improve the ability of top managers to organize and manage the activities of increasingly complex firms and to reduce the incidence of control loss that US firms such as Du Pont and General Motors developed a new approach to organization in the 1930s. This approach to business organization proved to be very successful and subsequently spread to many large organizations in the USA and Europe. This approach is known as the multidivisional structure or M-form and its spread has been documented in a number of studies. The characteristics of the M-form are shown in Figure 12.3. In the M-form, the firm is decomposed into a series of independent operating divisions based on products, or perhaps geography, with management of each division organized on functional lines suited to short-run operations. Above the divisions is a general office headed by the chief executive officer supported by a specialist staff whose task is to plan the firm's long-term strategy, to monitor the behaviour and performance of the operating divisions, and to act as an internal capital market receiving the profits generated by the divisions and allocating these back to the divisions, or developing new divisions, according to the firm's long-term strategy.

The economic efficiency advantages of the M-form are said to be as follows.

Economizing on bounded rationality Top managers are freed from day-to-day operating responsibilities to concentrate their time and effort on planning, co-ordinating, and monitoring the activities of divisional managers. This is less demanding in terms of their capacity to store and process the relevant information needed for effective decision-making. Divisions can be run as quasi-independent firms producing monthly or quarterly financial reports to the chief executive's office. The resources devoted to monitoring these figures will reduce opportunities for distortion. Each division reports on the same basis and is judged by the same measurable criteria as the others, which makes monitoring easier and allocation decisions more rational. Better and faster use can be made of local knowledge and initiative.

Detecting and controlling opportunism The top managers are better able to detect and control the activities of divisional managers. They can determine the objectives to be pursued and the information to be provided by divisional managers. They are better placed than shareholders to determine the extent to which good or bad performance is the result of poor management, or managers behaving opportunistically, or external circumstances beyond the control of management. And they are better placed to choose managers, replace them, and provide effective incentives to ensure the pursuit of the organization's objectives.

Allocating the firm's scarce capital The chief executive's office can act as a mini capital market, collecting profits from each division and allocating these funds back to the divisions according to the potential returns available. Divisions have to bid for funds to meet their needs and these bids can be carefully examined by the office of the chief executive. This should result in an improved allocation of capital compared with a situation where each division was allowed to invest what it earned. This is because it is likely that divisional managers would prefer to reinvest in 'their' business even if the available returns were less than those available elsewhere in the organization. The same thing applies to human capital. Since good management is a scarce resource, the chief executive is in a good position to identify good management and to allocate it effectively.

Training and motivating local managers Decentralization helps to attract managerial talent which is seeking to take responsibility and it offers experience and training within the organization for more senior positions.

Of course, not everything about the M-form is necessarily positive. There are potential drawbacks. For example, it was noted in Chapter 10 that Japanese firms have been less keen on divisionalization as an approach to managing complex firms because it is believed to be potentially inimical to the creation and sharing of core competencies within the corporation. This is an important point because, of course, a key rationale for the existence of diversified firms is the potential for creating and sharing corporate competencies. If it is the case that the M-form organization approach to managing diversified firms harms this potential, then this rationale for diversification would be less powerful. Indeed, it may even suggest something about the difference between the reasons for the development of diversified businesses in Japan compared with developments in the West. It may suggest that in Japan the main motive behind diversification has been to build, nurture, and exploit corporate competencies or capabilities. In the West, however, the main motive may have been to supplement the external capital market as a control device for governing the activities of individual firms and managers with an internal capital allocation mechanism. For a further discussion of this issue see Box 12.5.

Public Ownership and its Problems

Public ownership of business enterprise was, until the privatization revolution of the 1980s, an important feature of the industrial landscape in many industrial economies. Gas, electricity, water, telecommunications, railways, coal, steel, air transport were all nationalized industries or public corporations in Britain. Most of these have been privatized completely. Many other countries have followed Britain's lead, including, of course, many formerly socialist countries in Eastern Europe. The debate about nationalization and privatization is a long and involved one and we cannot go into it here. However, we can consider why nationalization and public ownership might have failed in the light of our analysis in this chapter and Chapter 4. Public ownership of productive enterprise is, in fact, a prime example of many of the issues raised in this chapter: how to get a large number of independent factor owners, searching to maximize their own wealth, to co-operate in the pursuit of value creation or adding value in an enterprise context.

Public corporations in Britain and other countries were characterized by an extreme form of separation between ownership and control. Officially, the owners were the public and these enterprises were meant in principle to operate in the 'public interest' which presumably meant creating value for the owners. At the very least, they presumably did not exist to actively harm value

Box 12.5 Structures and Performance

The consultants McKinsey believe that 'to be successful in building world-scale businesses many UK companies will have to make significant changes in their organisational structures, processes and styles'. Some of the distinctive organizational features of UK electronic firms have been developed to meet the needs of the defence and telecommunications sectors, which has left these firms less well suited to international operation than their foreign counterparts.

McKinsey notes that many UK companies have highly decentralized structures, with divisions run as quasi-autonomous, budget-driven, profit and loss centres, and in which strategy formulation is delegated to the lowest business unit level. Examples include GEC, Ferranti, Plessey, and Racal, each having corporate centres whose role is principally that of a financial holding company. This leads to tight financial control but little in the way of policy and strategy support.

A consequence of this decentralization, says McKinsey, is that ambition is limited, planning is 'numbers driven' rather than 'issue driven', and that the tendency within UK businesses to focus on shorter-term results has been accentuated. Potential synergies and scale economies also tend to be overlooked in the absence of a strong centre. Decentralized structures have also contributed to the failure of many UK companies to develop fully global organizational structures.

Foreign Companies' more Complex Organization Supports Global Success

In contrast, the majority of foreign businesses examined by McKinsey were found to have organizational structures and processes that permitted both financial control and clear strategic vision. For example, although several Japanese companies also exhibit considerable decentralization, this tends to be balanced by corporate centres playing a major role in defining and managing new initiatives, giving financial support to the massive investments these often require, and by forging clear and consistent company vision. Philips and IBM have very different matrix structures but have been successful in attaining scale and scope economies across diverse activities. Both Japanese companies and large matrix companies are willing to allocate senior management resources to strategy and the search for synergy.

Whilst some US defence firms and a number of Korean companies have until recently had decentralized organisation structures similar to the UK model, these are now moving to build centres which play key roles in group strategy.

A major lesson from this analysis is that companies should recognize, and act on, the need for organizational evolution as circumstances change. Of pressing contemporary importance is the need to develop the appropriate organizational approach to international operations. Many successful foreign companies have progressed through several modes of international organization. Many UK companies seem not to have done so, often remaining wedded to a traditional 'exporter' approach to international operations.

We conclude this summary by returning to an issue noted earlier. The important role played by defence and telecommunications in shaping UK organizational structures created an engineering orientation and a focus on tailor-made and highly specific projects agreed with a particular customer. This has proved to be inimical to the development of skills in new product innovation, the creation of new markets, the marketing and selling approaches appropriate for success in competitive markets, and the management of risks (except those associated with portfolio management). It has also detracted attention from the control of cost drivers and the promotion of production volumes, so important to modern consumer electronics.

McKinsey's conclusion is:

> To suceed in globally competitive markets, UK companies will therefore need to develop new organisational structures, processes and capabilities, and to break out of the cycle by which they have focused 'successfully' on defence. In doing so, the development of new leadership styles may be as important as the necessary changes in the formal structure.

Source: Adapted from NEDC (1988) *Performance and Competitive Success: Strengthening UK Electronics*, McKinsey and Company, London: HMSO.

creation. In practice, the owners were represented by the government of the day (actually, of course, the civil servants) which was responsible for operating these enterprises on behalf of the 'people'. In practice, however, this meant appointing the chairman and approving key directorial appointments, laying down some vague and not always internally consistent ground rules concerning the financial, economic, and social obligations of these companies, and keeping an eye on their performance. The board of directors then determined the company's policies and appointed the senior managers who were actually responsible for running these companies.

Consider the difficulties involved in actually getting such 'public' enterprises to operate in the interests of the owners. First, many public corporations in Britain and elsewhere were statutory monopoly suppliers so external competitive pressures, which might have induced co-operative behaviour, was lacking (see Chapter 7 for a formal analysis of monopoly). Secondly, it was not really clear exactly what the owners wanted. As nominal owner-shareholders of British Electric plc, they would have benefited from profit-maximizing behaviour; in other guises, however, the 'owners' also wanted cheaper electricity, environmentally friendly power stations, secure well-paid jobs, and the use of expensive British coal to protect jobs in the mining industry. Thirdly, even if the public had been able to agree on a clear overriding objective for these enterprises, it lacked the means to impose it on them. The public's control over the government is very weak. The government in turn had little day-to-day influence over the board of directors, and the board of directors had less than full control of the operating managers, and the operating managers faced powerful worker's unions which could often appeal over their heads to the government of the day. Finally, even if it had been clear what the public wanted and the means had been available to impose this on the enterprises, there was no one involved who had a powerful enough personal incentive to make sure this happened. In other words, no individual or small group of people existed who stood to gain personally by organizing and managing the enterprise in such a way as to focus it clearly on value creation, and indeed there were individuals who stood to gain by making sure that it did not.

Of course, in some ways the difficulties faced by the owners were actually less severe than in the private enterprise case discussed earlier. The government, for example, as the sole representative of the 'public' shareholders, certainly had the resources available to invest in adequate monitoring of these companies had it chosen to do so and did not face any co-operation dilemmas of the sort faced by individual small shareholders or financial institutions. Moreover, the government could act to change the chairman and the board of directors if it so wished, which is not something the shareholders in private companies can easily do. And finally, the government controlled the borrowing capacity of these companies and could have cut off their supply of funds had it so wished.

In other ways, however, the 'owners' were in a more difficult position. They could not sell their shares in these companies as a way of expressing their dissatisfaction with them, at least not until Mrs Thatcher came along and changed the rules. And even if the public had shares it could actually sell, this would not have mattered because these companies could not be taken over. There was no market for corporate control for publicly owned companies because that would have meant the possibility of returning these companies to the private sector when parliament—the people—had decided to put them in the public sector.

Public sector corporations such as Britain's nationalized industries were thus a classic case of the difficulty of getting right the fundamental problems of business organization referred to earlier: the governance mechanisms, the incentive mechanisms, and organizational designs, which determine the extent to which an enterprise actively pursues a coherent objective such as the maximum possible residual, or added value. Those economists who advocated nationalization as a means to improving economic performance failed to appreciate the organizational and incentive difficulties involved, partly of course because their training had failed to alert them to the nature and significance of these difficulties. As explained before, economists until quite recently have generally *assumed* that firms existed to maximize something or other so avoiding any need to confront the fundamental organizational and managerial problems involved in getting large numbers of individuals to co-operate towards any particular objective.

Conclusions

We set out in this chapter to extend our earlier analysis of the nature of business objectives. We have considered in particular the nature and implications of two particular aspects of business organization: the apparent separation of ownership from management control, and the increasing size and complexity of firms. We have examined the nature and implications of specifically managerial-type objectives, the ability of owners to detect managerial indulgence, the ability of owners to control managerial indulgence, the nature and significance of the market for corporate control, incentives for managers, and the nature and significance of organizational design. We have observed the real significance of problems arising from asymmetric information, co-operation dilemmas, opportunism, free-riding, and team production. We have looked specifically at the problematic nature of owner-management relations in the context of public ownership or nationalized corporations.

We have concluded that there is a potential conflict between the objectives of owners and managers which could compromise the firm's desire to search for value, although we have made clear that this proposition is open to debate. We have argued that the mechanisms by which owners endeavour to govern the corporation are imperfect. There seems to be great dependence in some countries on one particular mechanism, the market for corporate control, which is expensive and risky to use and which may have an undesirable side-effect, namely short-termism. We have suggested that some corporations for some of the time may thus be pursuing objectives other than maximizing economic profits. We have concluded, however, that the ability of top managers within the organization to impose their objectives on the organization is enhanced by organizational design which gives those at the top more control over the rest of the organization. It is possible that the superior monitoring and control capacity of large diversified corporations is one way in which these organizations add value for shareholders, although whether owners will ultimately benefit from this depends on the actions of top managers.

Futher reading

D. A. Hay and D. J. Morris (1991), *Industrial Economics and Organisation*, Oxford: Oxford University Press. Chapter 9 of this book is an excellent survey of the issues dealt with in this chapter but at considerably greater length and at a somewhat more advanced level of analysis.

M. Ricketts (1994), *The Economics of Business Enterprise*, London: Harvester Wheatsheaf. Chapters 8 and 9 of this book are also excellent, but again the treatment is quite advanced.

For an excellent discussion of the market for corporate control and its effects on companies and the economy see A. Peacock and G. Bannock (1989), *Take-overs and the Public Interest*, Aberdeen: Aberdeen University Press.

For discussion of the varied approaches to corporate governance in five major economies, see J. Charkham (1994), *Keeping Good Company*, Oxford: Oxford University Press. On the problems of public sector corporations, see NEDO (National Economic Development Office) (1976), *A Study of UK Nationalised Industries*. London: HMSO.

Questions

12.1. Outline the nature and discuss the possible significance of the main characteristics of the modern business corporation.

12.2. Does it matter that the owners do not manage and the managers do not own?

12.3. Is there a conflict between maximizing the stock market value of the firm and maximizing the growth of the firm?

12.4. Why do shareholders not invest more in the monitoring of managers?

12.5. What lies behind the rise of the 'corporate governance movement' described by Dickson in Box 12.1 and what is the likely outcome of the rise of this movement?

12.6. What are the 'limits to institutional power' discussed by Plender in Box 12.2?

12.7. Explain the nature and discuss the significance of the market for corporate control.

12.8. Why is it likely to be difficult for shareholders to get managers to focus on the creation of shareholder value by indirect methods?

12.9. Outline and evaluate the presumed benefits of the multidivisional form of organization. Are there any disadvantages arising from the multidivisional form?

12.10. Examine the case for public ownership of industries such as electricity and telecoms in the light of the discussion in this chapter.

Part IV

The Search for Value and the Wider Environment of the Firm

Many components of the environment in which the firm operates are exogenous from the point of view of the firm, or at least approximately so. These aspects of its environment affect the value-generating potential of the firm, but are beyond its control or influence. The firm has therefore to take them as given; it is this which defines what we call exogenous.

What are the principal exogenous elements of the business environment? The first is the structure of regulatory institutions, from the local level, up to national and international levels. Regulations cover a huge range of business-relevant activities, including the competitive (or anti-competitive) practices of firms, the environmental impacts of business activity, disclosure of information, and the general propriety of its conduct. Whilst it can be the case that the business community as a whole may have a powerful impact on the evolution and shaping of regulatory policy, this is rarely possible for an individual firm (although this can happen when regulators develop close working relationships with regulated parties, and the phenomenon of regulatory capture takes place).

The second principal set of exogenous forces acting on the firm are general macroeconomic conditions, operating at both national and international levels. Firms are strongly affected by changes in the rate of interest, rates of tax, the level of aggregate demand in the economy, and the like. But the firm cannot affect these variables—it has to take them as given.

The fact of exogeneity does not imply, however, that the firm need passively accept whatever buffeting it receives—for better or worse—from these elements of its environment. It can—and should—try to anticipate what will happen, think through how these events will affect its ability to generate value, and develop an appropriate strategic posture that will allow it to do the best it can under those circumstances.

A precondition for developing effective responses is the ability to understand your environment. To some extent, this involves putting yourself in other's shoes and seeing why they act as they do. Thus, in Chapter 13, where we consider the legislative, regulatory, and institutional environment in which businesses operate and by which they are constrained, we have attempted not only to describe what the regulatory structure currently consists of but also to explain why regulation occurs. Understanding this will put you in a better position to anticipate future changes in regulation.

The 'why' of regulation arises from the fact that the social consequences of the private search for value are not always those that are deemed acceptable to the public or its political institutions. This underpins much of competition policy and anti-trust legislation, and also policy concerning the natural-environmental and public health impacts of economic activity.

The most significant effects on business profit potential are likely to arise from domestic and international macroeconomic conditions which are largely outside the control of individual firms. At the time of writing (1998), many businesses are being buffeted by the effects of the Asian economic crisis. Some countries have found that their currencies have devalued by more than 50 per cent, with dramatic implications for business prosperity (both in Asia and in the rest of the world). Chapter 14 uses a simple supply and demand framework to explain the basic mechanisms of the macroeconomy in the short, medium, and long-term time horizons.

But understanding is not necessarily enough to make the most of the available opportunities and to minimize the damage caused by threats. It is also desirable to predict or forecast future trends and changes. Chapter 15 introduces you to some simple forecasting techniques. This area can quickly lead into difficult statistical and mathematical complexities. We avoid these by focusing only on some simple, but nevertheless very powerful techniques, and by providing the reader with a way forward if he or she wishes to become more fully acquainted with forecasting techniques.

The final chapter of the book examines the international dimensions of business activity. What we hope to show in our discussion is that international economic relationships are not necessarily exogenous forces. The firm can, at least partially, determine what kind of international relationships it enters by its strategic choices. It is often said that we now live and work in a global economy. If this is true, it is because firms (and consumers) have chosen to do so, as we shall demonstrate below.

13 The Search for Value and the Legislative and Regulatory Environment

Introduction

In this chapter, we consider some important aspects of the statutory and regulatory environments which impinge on business behaviour. We investigate why and in what ways government develops laws and regulations to control business behaviour.

Our focus is on two areas of regulation, competition policy and safeguarding of the natural environment. Underlying each of these areas of policy is the following question: is the search for value by businesses always consistent with the good of the economy or nation as a whole? From the time when Adam Smith wrote *The Wealth of Nations*, a widely held view sees individual value-maximizing behaviour, in conjunction with exchange through free markets, as consistent with socially optimal outcomes. The notion that there is no necessary conflict between private self-interest and the common good is deeply rooted in economic theory, and finds much support in the worlds of business and politics.

Nevertheless, intuition leads one to be cautious about this belief. In many aspects of human life we do not expect unbridled self-interest to lead to the best outcomes from society's point of view. This is presumably why most societies have criminal codes to prohibit certain kinds of behaviour.

Of more relevance to this text is the fact that business behaviour may well involve one group trying to benefit at the expense of another. One firm's search for a competitive advantage over its rivals could be seen in this light, as could an attempt to gain monopoly power. It is by no means obvious that *all* forms of business behaviour are in the common interest. Regulatory policy aims to restrict behaviour which is not in the collective interest.

The main theme of this chapter is to identify situations in which the free operation of supply and demand through markets might result in outcomes that, from society's point of view, are less good than is possible. The phrase 'market failure' is used by economists to describe these situations. An understanding of these arguments should help managers to anticipate the directions in which public regulation may develop in the future.

The Criterion of Economic Efficiency

In this section, we define a criterion of what is 'socially good' that can be used to rank different outcomes. The criterion is based on two premises: first, the value of a good is the value which the consumer of the good places on it; secondly, social value is the sum of the values that all individuals derive from it.[1] This criterion means that anything which increases value in the aggregate is a good thing.

It will also be convenient to introduce another term, economic efficiency. A pattern of resource use is economically efficient if it maximizes the *net social value* that can be derived from the use of those resources.

13.1 Competition Policy

A central proposition in economic analysis is that resource allocation through (perfectly) competitive markets leads to an economically efficient alloca-

[1] In order to justify the second of these premises, one has to presume either that income and wealth are distributed equitably, or that the *mechanisms* by which wealth and income are distributed are legitimate and fair.

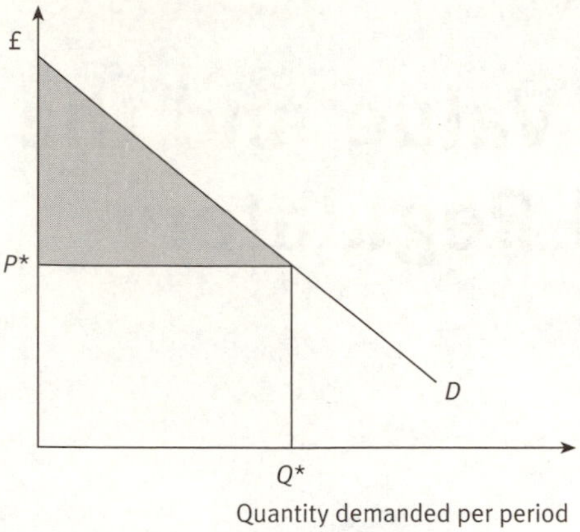

Figure 13.1 A market demand curve and consumers' surplus at price P^*

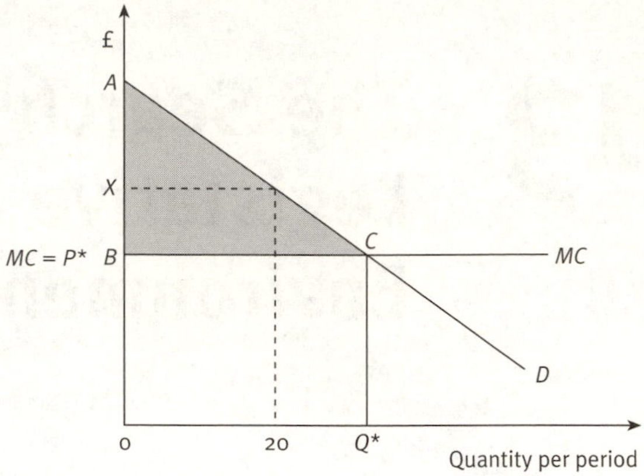

Figure 13.2 The efficient level of output

tion of resources. Individual preferences for goods are embodied in market demands. Firms obtain added value by producing commodities at lower cost than the market price. Individuals gain added value (or consumer surplus) if the price they pay is less than the subjective value they derive from the consumption of a good. The consumers' surplus at a particular price P^* and for the market demand shown is given by the shaded area in Figure 13.1. Total social added value is the sum of the added value obtained by firms (economic profit) and the added value obtained by consumers (consumer surplus). These ideas were explained in Chapter 1, and you might like to go back there to refresh your understanding of them.

In a competitive market new entry continually drives economic profits down to zero. Firms can only survive in the long run by producing efficiently, and by producing what consumers demand. The private pursuit of profit is consistent with the social good because production is dictated by the strength of consumer preferences, and because competitive markets drive out less than fully efficient producers.

One other piece of terminology will be introduced before we begin our analysis. The best use of a set of resources is the one that attains the largest amount of net social value. This net value is simply the gross benefits—the total amount of well-being derived from the use of the resources—less the total costs incurred in using the resources.

Consider the market shown in Figure 13.2. The market demand curve, *D*, shows how much consumers value additional goods, and so tells us the marginal benefit to society of the good. The marginal cost curve, *MC*, shows the marginal cost to society of making available additional units of the good. For simplicity, we illustrate the case where marginal costs are constant.

Which output level maximizes net value? Consider, for example, whether it is beneficial to produce the twentieth unit. The marginal benefit of this to society would be x; its marginal cost to society is P^*. Since marginal benefit exceeds marginal cost, from a social point of view this unit is worth producing. Indeed, by doing so, society's net value rises by an amount $(x - P^*)$. More generally, whenever the marginal benefit of producing an additional good exceeds its marginal cost, that additional good should be produced. Using this reasoning, it should be clear that all units up to and including Q^* should be produced.

The *output* level which maximizes social net benefit is the one where the demand curve (representing marginal gross benefit to society) intersects the marginal cost curve. What price is consistent with this level of output? Only at price P^* will consumers willingly purchase the level of output, Q^*. Note that at this efficient price/quantity combination, price equals marginal cost. This result is the 'marginal cost pricing' principle. Resources will be allocated efficiently only when price is equal to marginal cost.

An additional piece of information can be extracted from Figure 13.2. The shaded triangle *ABC* is the total net social value derived from producing and consuming Q^* units of this particular good. It is the excess of the total value consumers derive from the good (the area underneath the demand curve *D*) over the total cost of producing the good (the area beneath the marginal cost curve, *MC*). No other output level is capable of yielding a net social benefit as large as this, and so Q^* is the socially efficient output level of this good.

Efficiency and Market Structure: A Comparision of Competitive and Monopolistic Markets

Let us compare two forms of market structure, the perfectly competitive market and a pure monopolistic market, from the standpoint of the economy as a whole. In Figure 13.3, *S* is the industry long-run supply curve.

What would be the industry output in (*a*) a competitive market and (*b*) a monopolistic market? Assuming profit maximization, each firm sets output at a level which equates marginal cost (*MC*) and marginal revenue (*MR*). In perfect competition, the market demand curve shows the marginal revenue of each firm. So at any market equilibrium price, the firm's average and marginal revenue equal that price. The *industry output* in a competitive market is thus given by Q_c.

But the monopolist's marginal revenue curve, shown in Figure 13.3 by the curve labelled MR_M, lies below the market demand curve. Equating its marginal cost and marginal revenue, the monopolist produces output Q_m.

The efficiency rule that price equals marginal cost is satisfied in a competitive market, but not in a monopolistic market. From society's point of view, the competitive industry is efficient, but monopoly produces a smaller, inefficient output level. This can be shown diagrammatically. The efficiency loss due to monopoly is shown by the shaded triangle *ABC* in Figure 13.3. If the monopolist were to expand output from Q_m to Q_c, total net value would be increased by the amount *ABC*. In a monopoly market there *is* a difference between what is privately and what is socially optimal. The monopolist obtains more profit at Q_m than Q_c, but the economy gains more net value at Q_c than Q_m.

Scale Economies and Efficiency

The comparison we have just made assumes that long-run average cost is constant, and so does not depend on the size of the firm. But if scale economies are present, a monopolist is likely to have lower average costs than a competitive firm. We illustrate this in Figure 13.4 by drawing the monopolist's average cost curve below the average cost curve for a competitive market. Consider the two shaded areas indicated by the triangle *ABC* and the rectangle *BDEF.* The area *ABC* represents an efficiency loss arising from the monopoly producing a lower output than a competitive industry (that is, Q_m as compared with Q_c). However, by producing the output Q_m at a lower average cost, there is also an efficiency gain to take into account, represented by the area of the rectangle *BDEF.* The net efficiency difference is therefore given by *ABC* − *BDEF.* If this difference is positive (that is, *ABC* is larger than *BDEF*), a competitive market is more efficient; if the difference is negative (that is, *ABC* is smaller than *BDEF*), a monopolistic market is the

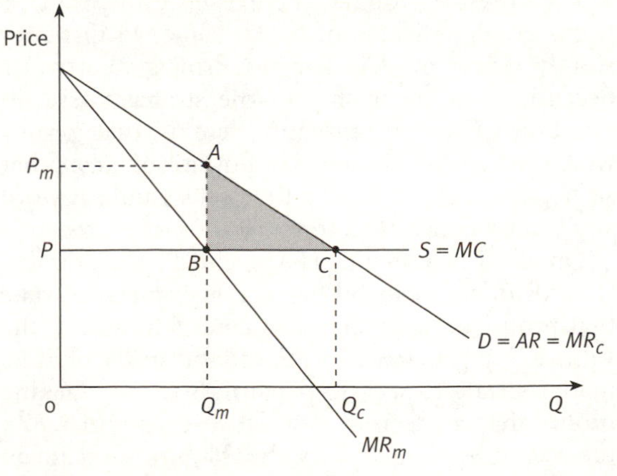

Figure 13.3 A comparison of output levels in competitive and monopolistic markets

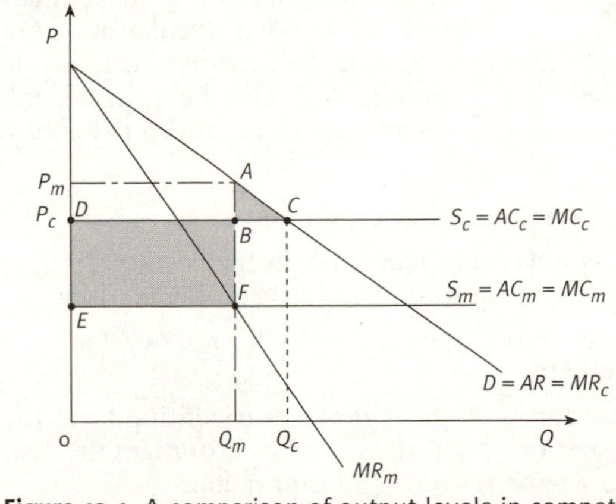

Figure 13.4 A comparison of output levels in competitive and monopolistic markets where average costs are lower in the monopolistic market

more efficient. In the case we have drawn, monopolistic production is the more efficient overall.

So where cost savings arise from a greater scale of output, there can be no general presumption in favour of either type of market. The gains from exploiting scale advantages benefit not only the individual firm but also the economy as a whole. On the other hand, competitive markets, by equating price with marginal cost, avoid the efficiency loss which arises when goods for which the consumers' valuation exceeds the marginal cost of production are not produced. To know which of these two effects is more important can only be ascertained by analysing each case on its own merits.

Static and Dynamic Efficiency

Our comparison has used the criterion of static efficiency. What we did was to compare monopoly with competition at a particular point in time and to address the question:

> If other things were equal, would monopoly result in a less efficient allocation of resources than competitive markets?

However, it is also important to compare market structures in terms of their *performance over time*. We could describe this as dynamic efficiency. Two important dimensions of dynamic efficiency are:

1. innovation in production processes;
2. new product innovation.

Two plausible stories can be told here. On the other hand, competitive markets have a superior innovative performance because the force of competition encourages firms to innovate to protect their profits, and indeed to survive. Insulation from competition implies that the incentive to innovate is lower for a monopolist. On the other hand, monopolistic firms are superior innovators because of:

- superior access to capital resources;
- less uncertainty and risk in the market, leading to a climate more conducive to innovation;
- scale economies in research and development activity;
- the ability to prevent others benefiting from the firm's own new ideas, which encourages the firm to devote resources to innovation.

The available empirical evidence is not conclusive about which type of market has a superior dynamic performance. It is sometimes claimed that the success of the Japanese and West German manufacturing industries in the 1960s and 1970s was a consequence of competitive industrial structures. But close scrutiny makes it clear that these economies are far from perfectly competitive in the textbook senses, and it is at least as likely that the key to their performances lies in particular (and unique) configurations of cultural, institutional, and historical circumstances. Once dynamic efficiency is brought into consideration, the relative merits of competitive and monopolistic markets become very difficult to assess. Moreover, the best market type (from an efficiency viewpoint) may not be perfectly competitive nor pure monopoly, but rather some intermediate form, such as oligopoly.

Generating and Appropriating Added Value

Next let us suppose that firms in the same industry are not all equal. Some possess distinctive capabilities, allowing them to produce more cheaply, to respond to market opportunities more quickly, or to command price premia relative to their rivals. The nature and sources of distinctive capabilities were explained in Chapter 10, as were the ways in which firms can appropriate and sustain the added-value opportunities generated by distinctive capabilities. This suggests an entirely different attitude towards the social worth of business profitability, depending on whether the source of profits is the exploitation of a strategic asset or whether the profits arise from distinctive capabilities.

Where profitability arises from exploiting strategic assets, such as monopoly power or exclusive rights to sell a product, the existence of profits is not a good indicator of social value. Profits may simply reflect the leverage the firm is able to use because of its ownership of the strategic asset in question. The central point here is that profits which arise from monopoly power (or any other strategic asset) are not in themselves indicative of any value being added for society by the firm.

On the other hand, where added value derives from distinctive capabilities, it is legitimate to argue that profits do correspond to a net addition to the value being generated in the economy. It would be inappropriate to seek to penalize firms for making profits that arise from distinctive capabilities. On the contrary, public policy should aim to create an environment in which firms have incentives to develop and sustain distinctive capabilities.

This means that the implementation of competition policy faces formidable practical questions. Suppose a merger is proposed between two major banks, such as Barclays and Nat West in the UK. Should it be allowed? If the dominant effect of the merger would be to secure efficiency gains—perhaps by exploiting economies of scale or scope—the answer might be yes. But if the merger merely creates a more powerful market player, the answer might be no. Whether a particular merger would be socially desirable depends on the relative size of the social costs and social benefits.

The Regulation of Market Power and the Firm's Search for Value

As the exercise of monopoly power may generate efficiency losses, government regulation may secure efficiency gains by controlling the exercise of monopoly power, or by preventing its emergence. There are several ways in which this can be done. One approach seeks to prevent the emergence of that power in the first place, through controls on take-overs and mergers. If monopoly power already exists, policy may be directed towards breaking that power by division of a firm's assets, or by encouraging the creation of rivals. Liberalization of international trade can be a very powerful tool in reducing local or national monopoly power. A third option is to regulate business behaviour through establishing price or profit ceilings and the like. Fourthly, the monopolist could be nationalized and operated in the public interest. Finally, an important component of competition policy relates to the control or prohibition of restrictive and anti-competitive practices—activities by one or more firms which restrict competition.

In the UK, control has concentrated on large firms where there have been grounds for believing that unreasonable prices have been charged and profits extracted, on merger proposals where substantial market power is expected to result, and on the control of restrictive practices. The European Union has also developed an extensive competition policy programme. At the time of writing, competition legislation in the UK is about to be radically changed, to bring it more into line with European legislation and practice, and to improve its effectiveness in controlling anti-competitive agreements. A brief survey of the proposed new regime in the UK and the existing EU competition policy legislation is provided in Box 13.1.

13.2 Protection of the Natural Environment

The market is a powerful mechanism for achieving efficient resource allocation but, as we have seen, it does not necessarily lead to socially desirable outcomes. In this part of the chapter, we will investigate circumstances in which the unhindered play of market forces, through effects on the natural environment, fails to produce efficient outcomes.

Externalities

An externality occurs when an action generates unintended effects upon others for which no payment (or compensation) is made. Externalities can arise either in production or consumption. The externality may be beneficial or harmful. Let us focus attention on a harmful (negative) production externality. Suppose it takes the form of toxic emissions into rivers arising from chemical industry activities. In the discussion that follows, we shall assume for simplicity that the industry is competitive. The consequences of this externality are shown in Figure 13.5. Chemicals output is measured on the horizontal axis.

The curve labelled *SMB* is the social marginal benefit from the use of the chemicals. This can also be thought of as society's demand curve for the chemicals. *PMC* (private marginal costs) denotes

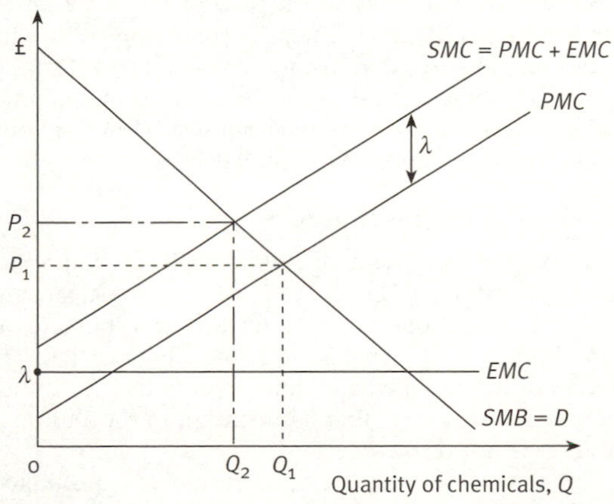

Figure 13.5 A negative externality

Box 13.1 Competition Policy in th European Union and the UK

European Union Legislation

Merger Policy

In order to qualify for investigation, the merger must have an EU dimension, defined in terms of the scale of world and EU turnover. However, if each of the firms has more than two-thirds of its aggregate EU turnover in the same member state, jurisdiction of the merger investigation passes to that country. Emphasis is on maintaining effective competition: any merger posing a threat to competition is prohibited. It is the responsibility of the European Commission to show detriment rather than of the firms to demonstrate benefit.

Merger agreements must be referred to the European Commission, which decides whether a threat is posed to competition and then issues a clearance or prohibition decision. This decision is subject to appeal in the European Court of Justice. If a merger proceeds without notification and subsequent investigation leads to a finding of incompatibility, the Commission may order separation and divestiture. Substantial fines are payable by company directors and officers, and by firms (up to 10 per cent of aggregate turnover) for non-compliance.

Of all the merger cases investigated, less than 10 per cent have been the subject of a full-scale investigation and only one merger proposal has been rejected out of hand (*Aérospatiale-Alenia/De Havilland*).

Abuse of a Dominant Position

EU monopoly policy aims to control the conduct of firms with market power rather than to shape market structure *per se*. Article 86 of the Treaty of Rome states that 'any abuse by one or more undertakings of a dominant position within the Common Market or in a substantial part of it shall be prohibited as incompatible with the Common Market in so far as it may affect trade between Member States'. There is scope for a wide interpretation of what counts as abuse: any form of behaviour which could not have occurred in a competitive market may be deemed abusive. However, only gross forms of abuse have been attacked.

Anti-competitive Practices

Article 85 of the Treaty of Rome (1957) gives the European Commission extensive powers to investigate and order the cessation of anti-competitive practices. It can also impose stiff penalties on offending parties. The Treaty of Rome stated a commitment to the 'institution of a system ensuring that competition in the Common Market is not distorted'.

In general, restrictive agreements are prohibited, although there are exemptions where it is shown that the agreement has a beneficial effects. Article 85 states that 'agreements . . . and concerted practices which may affect trade between Member States and which have as their object the prevention, restriction or distortion of competition within the Common Market shall be prohibited as incompatible within the Common Market'.

There are several grounds for exemption from the general prohibitions stated in Article 85. These are given where it is felt that the wider economic benefits of the agreements outweigh their anti-competitive effects. For example, improving production or distribution and contributing to technical or economic progress are acceptable arguments for maintaining an agreement. Agreements may be permitted when they have an insignificant effect on competition between Member States. 'Block exemptions' exclude whole categories from prohibition, such as in areas of R&D and patent licensing. The Commission has looked understandingly upon agreements aimed at reducing an industry overcapacity problem. There has also been a favourable outlook on agreements aimed at encouraging research and the development of key industries of the future. However, no agreement is allowed, irrespective of beneficial effects, if the firms are able to eliminate a substantial part of the competition for the product. The Commission typically prohibits price-fixing, quantity restrictions, parallel pricing (that is, prices moving up or down together), information agreements, and market-sharing.

The Commission pays special attention to small and medium-sized firms, recognizing that these firms may be unable to take advantage of economies of scale and may be the victims of predatory pricing. Competitive restrictions by small firms are exempt from Article 85 on the grounds of insignificance.

The EU can terminate anti-competitive agreements and substantial fines may be imposed on the firms involved (up to 1 million ECUs or 10 per cent of turnover on each party). Both firms and Member States can appeal to the European Court of Justice against decisions taken by the Commission.

Vertical Agreements

Vertical relationships are allowed as long as effective competition is preserved. There is great emphasis on breaking down any barriers to parallel imports. EU policy examines market structure when assessing the likely effects of vertical restraints. Exclusive dealing is prohibited by the Commission on the grounds that it prohibits imports, thus giving dealers complete protection from intra-brand competition. The Commission is willing to grant temporary territorial protection to firms with a smaller market share if the protection aids them in establishing a market. With regard to selective distribution, the EU line is that the requirements that a supplier makes of his retailers must be laid down uniformly and must not be applied in a discriminatory fashion. Selective distribution systems are not to be used as a means to restrict or distort competition.

The Proposed UK Competition Law

General Principles

The new UK competition law is designed to be complementary to and consistent with European competition law. It has been designed so that firms do not face two different bodies of case law within the EU and the UK. Unless there are very good reasons to do otherwise, the proposed UK legislation fits in the frameworks laid down by Articles 85 and 86 of the Treaty of Rome. It is felt that this will maximize the effectiveness of the regulatory framework and minimize the burdens imposed on business.

The legislation is intended to prohibit anti-competitive behaviour. Prohibitions will be enforced primarily by the Director-General of Fair Trading (DGFT), aided by a system of sector regulators. Companies breaching prohibitions will be subject to fines, and third parties damaged by anti-competitive behaviour will be entitled to seek compensation. Decisions of the DGFT are subject to appeal to a newly created Competition Commission.

Merger Policy

The new legislation will not significantly change the merger provisions operating under the 1973 Fair Trading Act. Merger proposals qualify for investigation if the value of the assets taken over exceeds a designated threshold (currently £70 million) or where a position of market power is created (currently set at 25 per cent of market share). If the Secretary of State decides that a merger merits investigation, then the case is referred to the Monopolies and Mergers Commission (MMC), which investigates the proposal and reports to the Secretary of State. This regime will remain unchanged, with the MMC becoming a part of the new Competition Commission.

The burden of proof is on the MMC to show that a merger is against the public interest, in which case the Secretary of State can prohibit the merger. In considering whether a proposed merger is against the public interest, the emphasis is increasingly being placed upon maintaining and promoting effective competition. This has tended to divert attention away from conglomerate mergers where there are no issues of competition since there are no common products.

Abuse of a Dominant Position

The general principle of the new framework is that abuse by a firm of a dominant position in any market in the UK is prohibited. It is modelled closely on Article 86 of the EC Treaty. The regulations will strengthen the regime operating currently under the Fair Trading Act. The DGFT decides whether a prohibition is infringed, and if so, determines the fines or other response.

Previous provisions relating to complex monopoly and scale monopoly under the 1973 Fair Trading Act will be retained. These allow the MMC to investigate cases where at least two firms together supply at least 25 per cent of a particular good or service in the UK and conduct their business in a way that might distort competition (complex monopoly) and to investigate a 'scale monopoly situation', defined as existing when one firm supplies 25 per cent or more of any good or service in the UK. In both cases, the MMC rules whether the actual or potential restriction on competition is against the public interest.

Prohibition of Anti-competitive Agreements

The Restrictive Trade Practices Act (1976) and the Resale Prices Act (1976) are to be repealed, with a concomitant winding down of the Restrictive Practices Court. The regime created by this legislation is widely believed to be ineffective, with excessive time spent monitoring agreements of little concern, and inadequate powers to tackle cartel behaviour.

In its place there will be a general prohibition of agreements and cartels which have the object or effect of preventing, restricting, or distorting competition in the UK. The term *agreement* is to be interpreted broadly, including, for example, decisions by associations of companies and concerted practices. Provision is made to exempt from prohibition agreements where their wider economic benefits more than offset their anti-competitive effects. This part of the new competition law is based closely on Article 85 of the EC Treaty. Most vertical agreements will be exempt from the scope of the prohibition, an important departure from the European practice.

the marginal costs met by chemical producers. The industry *PMC* curve is also the industry supply curve. Industry profit is maximized at an output of Q_1 and price P_1, at which each firm is equating its marginal cost and marginal revenue. Note that industry output, Q_1, is the sum of the output of each firm.

Where there are no external costs, private and social marginal costs are identical, and Q_1 is also the socially efficient level of output. However, in our example there are external costs arising from pollution damage. These costs are described by the curve *EMC* (external marginal cost). Social marginal costs (*SMC*) are the sum of private and external marginal costs. The output which maximizes social net benefits is Q_2, where social marginal costs and marginal benefits are equal.

Note that if output is below Q_2, the benefit society derives from an additional unit is greater than the cost incurred in producing it. By producing another unit, the economy gains a positive *net* benefit. Production should therefore be increased. Conversely, when output is greater than Q_2, the benefit society derives from the marginal unit is less than the cost incurred in producing it. The economy will gain if less is produced. Only at the point where social marginal benefit equals social marginal cost will it not be possible to make society better off by changing the output level. Therefore, in this example, market forces would lead to an inefficient outcome, producing too much output at too low a price.

Bargaining and the Work of Ronald Coase

Ronald Coase (1960) showed that external effects may not lead to inefficient outcomes if affected parties are able to bargain with each other. To illustrate this argument, it will be helpful to follow a hypothetical example. Consider two neighbours, one who plays a trumpet for his own enjoyment, the other who finds the noise disturbing. Figure 13.6 shows these two aspects of the situation. The curve MB_T denotes the marginal benefits to the musician from playing his trumpet, MC_N denotes the marginal cost of the noise to the disturbed neighbour. The horizontal axis is measured in units of noise, labelled Ψ.

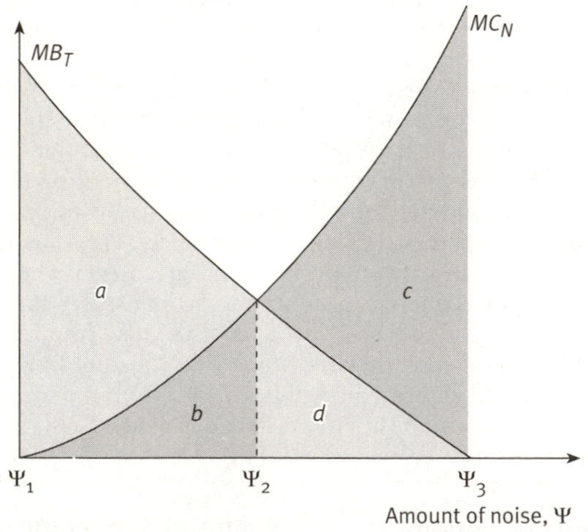

Figure 13.6 Bargaining possibilities in the case of a negative externality

Notes: MB_T = Marginal benefit of music to the trumpeter.
MC_N = Marginal cost of music to the neighbour.

If the musician behaved without any regard for his neighbour, and were not subject to any external control, he would maximize his private benefit at the output Ψ_3, where all additional benefits to him from trumpet playing have been exhausted. This would not be an efficient outcome. That is found at the output level Ψ_2 where the marginal benefit of music playing is equated with its marginal cost. How might such an outcome be achieved?

One method is via bargaining between the two neighbours. Suppose the musician agrees to reduce noise from Ψ_3 to Ψ_2. The gains to the disturbed neighbour would be shown by the area $c + d$. The loss to the musician is represented by the area d. Provided the neighbour compensated the musician by some payment greater than d but less than $c + d$, both individuals would be in a superior position than was the case initially. In effect, trade between the interested parties would have led to a *mutual* improvement. Furthermore, the post-bargaining outcome is in this case efficient.

Potentially inefficient outcomes can be avoided if the affected parties are able to bargain with one another. But bargains are not always possible. Let us now see why.

Limitations of Bargaining Solutions to Externalities and Implications for Public Policy

Bargaining solutions to externality problems are unlikely to take place when the number of affected parties is large. Where many people are involved, the costs of bargaining may be so large as to prevent it taking place. Bargaining also requires that the affected parties can be identified. It is easy to think of circumstances where this is either difficult or impossible. What we have here, in essence, is a problem of transaction costs, a matter discussed earlier in Chapter 4.

These conditions suggest that bargaining is not likely to be an effective means of dealing with external effects where the natural environment is concerned. Typically, environmental pollution affects a large number of people, and it is often difficult to identify all the affected parties. An additional difficulty arises from the fact that the adverse impacts on the natural environment of many types of economic activity persist over long periods of time. Economic activity today does not only affect those living today, but also imposes external costs on future generations. If people living in the future 'matter', then bargaining solutions require that the interests of future generations be included in the bargaining process. It is difficult to see how this can take place.

Bargaining is also unlikely to lead to efficient outcomes where the externalities are also public goods. A public good has a very important property: consumption of the good by one person does not prevent another person also consuming it. Examples include national defence, the services of lighthouses, radio and television transmissions, and public health programmes. In each of these cases, consumption is non-rivalrous in the sense just described.

Public goods often have a second property, that of non-excludability. Once the good is made available to one person, others cannot easily be excluded from using it. This is true for national defence, lighthouse services, and public health schemes. Non-excludability poses severe difficulties for bargaining solutions. The reason for this is the 'free-rider' problem. If someone cannot be prevented from consuming a public good and believes that others will pay for its provision, there is an incentive for others to 'free-ride' on its provision. In a bargaining process, the individual has an incentive to understate his or her willingness to pay. So the true social valuation of a public good will not be revealed in a bargaining process, and as a consequence it is likely to be underprovided.

Many environmental goods and services (such as clean air, ground and water, wilderness areas, and ecosystems with extensive biodiversity) are public goods. Environmental protection measures also often fall within the class of public goods. Bargaining is unlikely to lead to optimal amounts of environmental resources or environmental protection. Public goods will be examined in more detail later in this chapter.

Public Policy and the Environment

Our discussion has led to two conclusions:

- unregulated market behaviour may fail to produce socially efficient outcomes in the presence of externalities;
- direct bargaining can lead to efficient outcomes, but is unlikely to be feasible where externalities take the form of significant effects on the natural environment.

Can public policy provide a framework within which efficiency gains are achievable? An affirmative answer can be given to this question. In order to achieve efficiency gains, public policy should be directed so that either

- firms are *prohibited* from doing things where their social costs exceed their social benefits, or
- firms should be given *incentives* to not do things for which the social costs exceed the social benefits.

Quantitative Regulations

Quantitative regulations, often labelled as 'command-and-control' measures, operate by establishing standards or limits that producers or consumers must comply with. They typically lay down maximum amounts of specified pollutants that can be emitted in given periods of time, or require that some index of pollution-concentration be kept below a prescribed limit. In extreme cases, regulations prohibit the use highly damaging inputs, or require that a pollutant emission be zero.

Alternatively, regulations may require the use of particular 'clean' technologies in some production processes. In motor vehicle production, mandatory technology regulations are used widely. These include emissions standards for engine units of given sizes and for particulate emissions from diesel engines, and requirements that manufacturers install catalytic converters to produce engines that are operable using unleaded fuel. Standards-based approaches to pollution control have been (and remain) the main component of control programmes in the USA and Europe.

Incentive Schemes: Taxes, Subsidies, Marketable Permits, and Pollution Taxes

Incentive schemes operate by providing monetary inducements to firms or consumers to behave in ways that are thought to be socially desirable. The most straightforward example is a pollution tax. Recall the example of a chemical industry producing a harmful pollutant. What happens if a pollution tax, equal to the monetary value of the damage done by an additional unit of the pollutant, is levied on producers for each unit of emissions?

To deduce the consequences of this pollution tax, refer back to Figure 13.5. For simplicity, we suppose that the output to pollution ratio is constant. The horizontal axis can then be read either in units of pollution or in units of chemicals output. The tax is levied at λ per unit of pollution, the monetary value of a marginal unit of pollution. This increases post-tax production costs; the marginal cost schedule is raised from *PMC* to *SMC*. The externality has been 'internalized' into the firms' cost schedules.

Two consequences follow:

- the firms in the industry will now choose to produce Q_2, the socially efficient output;
- as producers bear pollution costs, they have a continuous incentive to reduce the pollution. Firms will invest in pollution abatement as long as the cost involved is less than the tax avoided. This is exactly what economic efficiency requires.

Pollution Abatement Subsidies

Pollution targets can also be attained using pollution abatement subsidies. A subsidy is a negative tax, so the incentive effects on firms already in the industry will be the same whether a subsidy of λ is given for each unit of pollution abated or a tax at the rate λ is levied on each unit of pollution emitted. The short-term effects on emissions levels are identical.

The long-run effects of taxes and subsidies are likely to be very different, however. This is because their *income* effects are different (see Chapter 3). Pollution taxes reduce the profitability of the affected industry, whereas subsidies increase profitability. Subsidies might, therefore, encourage entry into the industry, decreasing the effectiveness of the control programme. The opposite effect will follow from tax schemes.

Marketable Emissions Permits

A third type of incentive-based pollution control scheme involves the use of marketable emissions permits. In order to implement a system of pollution control using marketable permits the control authority must

1. decide how much of the relevant type of pollution is to be allowed;
2. print sufficient emissions permits so firms may pollute up to the total allowable limit;
3. sell, or distribute in some other way, the emissions permits to potential polluters;
4. guarantee that emission permits can be traded between firms;
5. subject any firm to a prohibitively expensive fine for any pollution it generates in excess of the amount allowed by the permits it possesses;
6. monitor the operation of the scheme, periodically changing the total allowable amount of pollution as conditions change.

At first sight this system might appear to be no different from the use of simple quantitative controls. But there is one major difference: the permits can be exchanged between firms. The consequences of this are very important, as we shall see in a moment.

How are the permits initially allocated? One method involves giving them to firms, either in proportion to firm size or to the level of their current emissions. A second method involves the auctioning of permits. Whatever method is chosen, the total quantity of permits issued is identical. So the impact on pollution is unaffected by how this *initial* allocation is made.

What makes this scheme so interesting is what happens next. A market will develop in the transferable permits. Some firms are willing to pay large amounts for permits, others only small sums. In the course of trading, a single market price will emerge. The firms which *purchase* permits are those willing to pay at least the market price. For them, pollution abatement is expensive and they prefer to buy permits rather than to pay large sums to reduce pollution. On the other hand, those firms which *sell* permits are those for whom the value of using a permit is less than the market price; these will be firms for whom pollution abatement is relatively cheap, and who will therefore prefer to pay to abate pollution, and more than cover these costs by the proceeds from selling permits.

It is this process of trading that leads to the efficiency property of a transferable permit system. The pollution abatement effort becomes concentrated in the hands of those firms which can do it most cheaply. Permits to pollute become concentrated in the hands of firms which have the highest pollution abatement costs. In this way, the total cost of achieving any pollution reduction target is minimized.

A Comparison of the Different Methods of Pollution Control

Taxes, subsidies, and marketable permits are each cost-effective: they achieve any chosen pollution target at the lowest possible cost. We have already explained why this is so for marketable permits. The reason why it is also true for taxes (and subsidies) is very simple. For any given tax (or subsidy) rate, firms will reduce pollution whenever the cost of doing so is less than the tax they would have to pay (or the subsidy they would lose) on additional units of pollution. The end result is that most pollution abatement is done by firms for whom it is cheap to abate, and least is done by those for whom abatement costs are the highest. Transferable permits, pollution taxes, and pollution abatement subsidy are equivalent ways of achieving the same goal, and each attains the goal at the lowest cost. Furthermore, each of these three instruments has desirable incentives. Reducing pollution increases a firm's income, and so an ever-present incentive exists to develop low-cost methods of reducing pollution.

Economists therefore have two main criticisms of command-and-control instruments. First, they fail to create appropriate incentives. Once a target has been achieved, no incentive exists to search for low-cost ways of reducing pollution further. Secondly, they are not cost-effective. Typically, the same degree of control is placed on firms irrespective of how costly it is to reach that target. Cost-efficiency is squandered by not focusing control where the costs of doing so are lowest.

In assessing the performance of the marketable emissions permit schemes in the USA in comparison with the older command-and-control approaches, Tietenberg has written:

> The [marketable emissions permits] programme has unquestionably and substantially reduced the costs of complying with the Clean Air Act. Most estimates place the accumulated capital savings for all components of the programme at over $10 billion. This does not include the recurrent savings in operating costs. (Tietenberg, 1990)

These cost savings accrue to polluting firms and to the economy as a whole. If firms are to be controlled, it is clearly desirable that the cost is as low as possible. Many kinds of command-and-control regulation give firms little or no flexibility in how they are to achieve targets. This lack of flexibility tends to result in high costs. Incentive schemes are inherently more flexible. They allow firms to choose how to reach targets and, through trade, how the overall control effort should be allocated.

A consensus is emerging that the degree of environmental regulation will increase in the medium and longer term, and that control will rely increasingly on pollution taxes and marketable permits. The following statement by two eminent American environmental economists, Cropper and Oates, illustrates this expectation:

> effluent charges and marketable permit programs are few in number and often bear only a modest resemblance to the pure programs of economic incentives supported by economists . . . As we move into the 1990's, the general political and policy setting is one that is genuinely receptive to market approaches to solving our social problems. Not only in the United States but in other countries as well, the prevailing atmosphere is a conservative one with a strong predisposition towards the use of market incentives wherever possible, for the attainment of our social objectives. (Cropper and Oates, 1992, pp. 729 and 730)

Open Access Resources

Markets often fail to deliver socially efficient outcomes where a natural resource is characterized by conditions of open access. A resource is described as an open access resource when it is not possible to prevent anyone who wishes to use it from doing so, or where the cost of imposing such restrictions is prohibitively high. Examples of open access resources include:

- marine fisheries;
- wilderness areas;
- natural forest areas, including tropical moist forests;
- acquifers (that is, surface and underground freshwater stocks);
- the earth's atmosphere;
- river systems.

To illustrate why open access conditions often lead to inefficient outcomes, let us consider the case of a marine fishery. As we shall see, marine fisheries are prone to being overfished. In an extreme case, the stock of a particular species may be driven to a level at which it cannot recover, and the species becomes extinct.

There are two reasons why excessive harvesting is likely to occur in these circumstances. First, the actions of each fishing boat imposes external costs on all others. When one boat withdraws fish from the sea, the total stock is reduced, and so it becomes more difficult for others to catch fish. Each fishing vessel incurs private or internal costs, but also imposes external costs on others by increasing the amount of effort that is required to catch a given quantity of fish. The excessive harvesting arises because the owner of each vessel takes account of *only* private revenues and costs in deciding upon the amount of fishing to be undertaken. For a socially efficient outcome, all costs—private and external—should be included in this decision.

In conditions of open access, whenever private profits can be obtained, more vessels will tend to be attracted to fish in these waters. Where the number of boats is large, individualistic, unco-operative behaviour is likely to prevail. Even though each fisherman realizes the effects of his actions on others, he is likely to proceed in a self-interested way, grabbing whatever he can on the assumption that everyone else is doing the same (this is a Prisoner's Dilemma, discussed earlier in Chapters 4 and 8).

The second cause of inefficiency arises from the lack of incentives to 'invest' in future stocks. When fish stocks are low, rational behaviour suggests that boat owners reduce their catch today to allow stocks to recover and grow. Investing in the future in this way offers the prospect of larger returns in the future for small costs today. But the open access regime implies that this action is very unlikely; any individual who invests in this way is unlikely to be able to appropriate the returns on his investment. The returns ultimately become available to the whole industry, not to the individual 'investor'. Moreover, a free-rider problem exists here. Any one individual can benefit by others agreeing to reduce their catches, but by increasing his own catch (compare this with the cartel model we discussed earlier).

Market forces alone will not generate efficient collective outcomes because each fisherman will equate his *private* marginal costs and marginal benefits. The two kinds of externalities we have just described will drive a wedge between what is privately and what is collectively optimal. Clearly it will often be in the interests of fishermen collectively to agree to an optimum overall catch, together with quotas for individual fishing vessels, provided all parties to the agreement can be relied upon to maintain the agreement. This is most unlikely in open access conditions with large numbers of players in the industry; even if newcomers could somehow or other be prevented from gaining access, the transactions costs of creating and policing agreements will tend to be high, reducing the likelihood of efficient bargaining outcomes being attained.

It is common for governments, or supranational institutions such as the European Union, to intervene in and regulate the fishing industry. One common approach is to establish limited rights of access through territorial restrictions on fishing activity. However, at best this can be only a partial solution to overfishing, as it does not alter the open access to domestic fishermen. If fewer non-British boats fish in British waters, for example, this may just encourage British vessel owners to step up their own efforts. Regulation might also consist of attempts to impose limits on the size of the fishing fleet, and on the amount of fishing effort that is permitted. Some recent European regulatory policy has been directed at fishing effort, placing restrictions on the seasons in which designated species may be harvested and the number of days on which vessels may put out to sea.

Other regulatory approaches tried include quotas on permissible catches (this is currently the major type of regulation in European waters) and controls relating to the type of equipment (boats, types of net, mesh sizes, and so on) used in marine fishing. There seems to be little to suggest that any of these schemes have met with much success in terms of reducing overfishing. Moreover, the costs to fishermen of these types of control are immense. This is not surprising when one realizes that they all share the characteristic of being command-and-control instruments, and do not provide appropriate patterns of incentives to vessel owners that address the root causes of overfishing.

One method that has been successful in New Zealand fisheries—and could be more widely adopted in the future—is the use of transferable fishing quotas. These work in very similar ways to the transferable permit schemes we discussed earlier, and have similar advantages over more conventional forms of command-and-control.

Public Goods

It has not been the intention of this chapter to provide an exhaustive account of all forms of market failure (nor of possible government responses to these failures). We conclude our discussion of this issue by looking a little further at the important issue of public goods.

As we explained earlier, where goods are public rather than private, resources will tend to be inefficiently allocated. The inefficiencies we have in mind manifest themselves in two principal ways:

- under-provision of public good;
- under-protection of public goods.

Under-provision follows from the non-excludability property and the attendant free-rider problem. It is difficult for a producer to extract a financial return from the provision of a public good, so many public goods will either not be provided at all by free markets, or will be under-provided. Even if a firm could extract enough revenue to make market provision worthwhile, many people will tend to understate the extent of their willingness-to-pay and so market demand will be a systematically downwardly biased representation of the true social value of the good. Under-protection of public goods tends to follow for similar reasons. Why would a profit-oriented owner of a public good (such as a tropical forest) bother to protect that asset for others to enjoy if no revenues can be extracted from the action?

A final problem concerns the efficient price of a public good. If the use of the good does not impose costs on others (which it will not do if it is a public good, because of the non-rivalry property), the socially efficient price for use should be zero! Recall that the efficient price is equal to the marginal cost of producing of output, which in this case is zero (once the good exists). So even if, somehow or other, a price could be extracted, any price other than zero would be socially inefficient!

The implication of these arguments seems to be that only the public sector is in a position to create or maintain pure public goods in socially efficient ways. We have already noted applications of this idea to environmental problems. Another important application is to knowledge, and the processes which generate it: research, development, and invention. Knowledge is close to being a pure public good. Think, for example, of the case of knowledge about a new drug formula. Once available, consumption of it is non-rivalrous. Also, as a matter of practice, it is difficult and costly to exclude others from using it. Will knowledge be generated in socially efficient quantities in a pure market economy? Our analysis of public goods suggests the answer is probably no, and explains why the state plays such a large role, in most countries, in the generation of knowledge.

The Costs of State Intervention

Market failure occurs when resource allocation through market processes results in inefficient outcomes. We have suggested that state intervention can result in superior outcomes in these circumstances. But it is important to remember that intervention has costs as well as benefits. Market failure provides a prima-facie case for intervention, but intervention is not of positive net benefit unless the *social costs* of intervention are lower than the *social efficiency gains* arising from intervention.

Intervention can be very costly, both in financial terms and in broader measures of social cost. The costs of subsidizing European agriculture, for example, are immense. What can be said in conclusion is that intervention is likely to be desirable in some circumstances, but we must always be careful to estimate the relevant gains and costs of intervention.

13.3 The Firm and its Regulatory Environment

The Impact of Competition and Environmental Control Policy on Firms

In this final part of the chapter, we investigate the impact of regulation on business and consider how firms might respond to the prospect of future regulations. It would be a mistake to believe that competition and environmental controls will not impose costs on the business sector as a whole—costs no less real than those associated with capital, labour, or any other cost.

The main objectives of competition policy are to prevent the emergence of market power and to minimize the extent to which existing market power is exercised in anti-competitive ways. It limits the extent to which firms can accumulate strategic assets based on market power, or reduces the value of those assets (by restricting the ways in which the asset can be used). Clearly, the value which can be appropriated by firms which are targeted by competition policy will be reduced, and so competition policy is costly to those firms.

But this does not imply that competition policy is costly to the business sector as a whole. A well-designed and administered programme should benefit business as a whole. First, those firms which would have suffered (in profitability) as a result of the anti-competitive practices of others will benefit. To some extent, therefore, competition policy merely alters the pattern of value appropriation within the business community.

But there may be net benefits to business from competition policy. Value creation based on distinctive capabilities is potentially sustainable over time as it is not targeted by competition policy regulations. In contrast, value appropriation based purely on market power is constantly under threat from regulation. The framework of regulation thus creates a strong incentive for firms to search for and exploit distinctive capabilities. To the extent that this search is successful, competitive advantage is gained by firms. This offers the prospect of further benefits to one country's business sector by giving it a competitive edge in world markets.

It is interesting to study the business strategy of the software giant Microsoft in this light. The commanding position that Microsoft has in personal and business computing through its ownership and control of the Windows operating interface and related products has allowed Microsoft to generate huge profits built largely upon a set of distinctive capabilities. But having obtained dominance in its chosen markets, it now possesses important strategic assets. A variety of stand-alone and network software packages for business and personal use have been designed to run as part of one integrated system. Once customers have invested heavily in components of this system, the costs of transferring to alternatives can be immense. Moreover, with the market penetration of Microsoft products being so high, these products have become industry standard, and customers become locked into Microsoft operating systems, interfaces, and software.

In these circumstances, Microsoft has a powerful and difficult-to-challenge strategic asset, based on what are known as network externalities. In recent years, the company has become concerned that this will lead to competition policy regulation, and its current business strategy contains elements which appear to be aimed at heading off the likelihood of regulation. Microsoft appears, for example, to be unwilling to allow the demise of the Apple corporation, one of its rivals, and is currently writing software for use by its business rival. At the time of writing, a number of computer hardware and software firms are constructing an alliance to produce a network computer product which is designed to challenge the dominance of stand-alone PCs with sophisticated internal software. Microsoft is considerably less sanguine about this form of rivalry than the rather less threatening form from Apple.

Let us now consider the impact on firms of environmental controls. We have seen that environmental regulation falls into two classes: first, command-and-control regulation, which restricts what a firm is allowed to do or requires that certain things be done; secondly, incentive programmes, using taxes, subsidies, or marketable pollution permits.

Command-and-control regulations are clearly costly for the regulated firms. The magnitude of these costs will rise as the strictness of controls is increased. There is also reason to believe that these costs will increase at an increasing rate as the level of control increases—so that a doubling of the strictness of required standards more than doubles the cost of meeting the standards. This is easy to see. Imagine a filtering system that captures 20 per cent of any particle emissions flowing through a chimney stack. If the cost of each filter is $1,000 and the uncontrolled flow of particles is 100 per second, $1,000 will purchase an emission reduction of 20 per second (20 per cent of 100). However, with two filters—the second filter installed above the first—$2,000 will buy an emissions reduction of 36 (20 per cent of 100, plus 20 per cent of 80 per cent of 100). The average and marginal costs of control will rise with increasing levels of control.

Where incentive programmes are used, the costs are less evident. If tax incentives are used to achieve pollution reductions, firms are not required to do anything but they will be financially penalized if they do not reduce pollution. If they do reduce pollution to avoid paying taxes, they will instead incur abatement costs. Either way, the business sector bears additional costs. Costs cannot be avoided but they can be minimized if economically efficient control programmes are pursued. Very similar comments apply to marketable permit schemes. As we explained previously, subsidy schemes will, in the first instance, increase business profitability. However, the ultimate effects on the business sector will depend upon what steps the government takes to fund subsidy payments. If it does this by higher corporate taxes, then the initial positive effects on business profitability will be negated.

As we saw earlier, although incentive-based approaches to environmental improvement do impose costs on the affected business sectors, these costs will be considerably lower than would be the case if command-and-control regulations were used. For example, the United States Environmental Protection Agency has recently calculated that its emission reduction programme—based on transferable emissions reduction credits—has cost US industry \$2.5 billion by early 1996, but that it would have cost twice that amount under a traditional command-and-control programme.

Can firms avoid regulatory costs by shifting them onto the consumers of their goods or services? This is a difficult question to answer, and requires that the incidence of the tax be analysed. To do this, the tools of supply and demand analysis first presented in Chapter 2 can be used. Let us look at this in the case of a competitive market where all firms are required to pay additional taxes on each unit of output. Figure 13.7 illustrates the case. D and S_1 denote the pre-tax market supply and demand schedules, and so P_1 and Q_1 are the initial price and quantity equilibria. A tax of λ per unit output is now imposed on each firm in the industry, as a result of which the industry supply curve shifts from S_1 to S_2. The post-tax equilibrium price is P_2. Note that although the industry supply curve has shifted upwards by the full extent of the tax, showing that firms seek to raise their prices by the amount necessary to pass on the tax to the consumer, firms have only succeeded in passing on to consumers some of the tax in higher prices.

We can take this analysis a little further. At the new equilibrium quantity traded, Q_2, the total amount of tax paid to government is represented by the rectangle P_3P_2AC (that is, a tax rate λ on each of the Q_2 units sold). But the final incidence of the tax is as follows: consumers pay the amount P_1P_2AB whilst firms pay P_3P_1BC. Business profitability also suffers because fewer units are sold after the tax has been levied. The impact of taxes on business profitability is thus quite subtle, with the actual incidence of the tax depending on the relative shapes of the market demand and supply curves for the product in position. (Check for yourself that by varying the slopes of either curve, the pattern of incidence of the tax will alter).

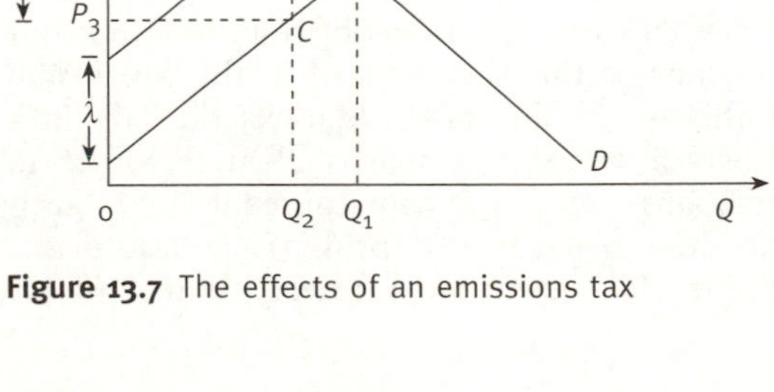

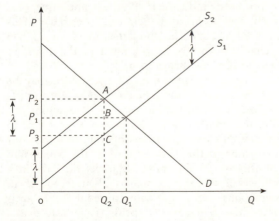

Figure 13.7 The effects of an emissions tax

Two further points deserve attention before we finish our discussion of the impact on firms of regulations. First, there may be ramifications operating through international competitiveness. In particular, if one country introduced controls to a significantly higher standard than elsewhere, domestic firms will experience a fall in the extent to which their products are price-competitive in world markets. This may be offset to some extent by a depreciating exchange rate, but currency depreciation also imposes costs by requiring that greater quantities of exports are needed to pay for given quantities of imports. So if one country imposes controls to an unusually high level, it risks incurring costs of these types.

Secondly, even though regulation does impose control costs on the economy, this does not imply that all firms suffer. There are several good reasons why some firms, at least, can be net beneficiaries, particularly as environmental standards tighten. We discuss some reasons for this in the following paragraphs.

How should Firms Respond to Regulations and the Prospect of Future Regulations?

In developing business strategy, a firm should pay attention to the potential benefits of being 'environmentally friendly'. One such benefit might derive from reputation effects. An often-remarked phenomenon in the last couple of decades has been the development of a number of markets in which consumers appear to be willing to pay price premia for goods or services that are perceived to satisfy certain environmental criteria. The magnitudes and growth rates of these markets are rather uncertain, but it seems safe to forecast that they will develop relatively quickly, particularly in the high income economies. Such reputation effects may be valuable assets to acquire, particularly in resource-based industries such as oil refining and timber production, where the links with environmental degradation are most evident. As consumer awareness of environmental linkages develops, so the range of products for which value can be gained from environmentally responsible behaviour increases. Detergent manufacturers now routinely promote brands using assertions about the low impacts of their products, and some large food retailing chains are now committed to selling food grown without the use of inorganic fertilizers and pesticides.

First-mover advantages may also accrue to those firms who most quickly identify and respond to emerging market opportunities. In the short to medium term, environmental controls will have their greatest impact on firms that can offer waste management and emission reduction technologies. Legislation is moving in the direction of creating product life-cycle liability for environmental damages, and this will add to value-creation opportunities in these sectors. In some industries, it has been common for firms whose goods are positioned towards the top of the product ranges to incorporate environmentally friendly materials into their goods (such as BMW and Mercedes in the car industry), but the trend appears to be for this to spread down the product range through time.

It should be clear from earlier discussions that so-called ecological tax schemes will be an important component of any future environmental protection programme. An important recent report from the DIW economic research institute in Berlin has investigated the effects of a tax on energy derived from fossil fuels, to rise at 7 per cent annually over a ten-year period. Tax proceeds would be used to reduce taxes elsewhere, in the German case by financing cuts in employers' contributions to health, unemployment, and pension funds. Whilst the package would be neutral in its overall fiscal impact, very substantial relative price changes would occur. For example, after ten years, iron and steel prices would rise by nearly 20 per cent, whilst government service prices would fall by 3 per cent. Relative price changes of these magnitudes are bound to have large impacts upon the relative size and profit opportunities of different sectors of the economy.

Finally, substantial cost advantages are likely to accrue to firms which anticipate controls rather than respond to controls *ex post.* These come about for two reasons. First, anticipation allows adjustments to be planned carefully and implemented gradually. Slow adjustment is invariably less costly than rapid, enforced adjustment. Secondly, in the learning processes that accompany accommodation to stricter environmental regulations, innovation will take place. Those in a position to build organizational strengths that are suitable for exploiting and sustaining these emerging techniques will be in the best positions to benefit from controls.

Conclusions

We began this chapter by asking whether it is always the case that the outcome of a private search for value by firms is consistent with a socially 'desirable' outcome. The answer has to be that these are not always compatible with one another.

If one interprets the word 'desirable' to mean ethically good outcomes, there is little that need be said. There is no good reason to believe that the outcomes of market economies are ethically good, nor is there any good reason to believe that they will be ethically bad. Ultimately, ethical questions of this kind cannot be addressed, let alone resolved, by economic analysis, so in our capacity as economists we must remain agnostic on this. It is worth noting that several attempts have been made to argue that the processes of market economies—as opposed to outcomes—are morally desirable. Arguments of this kind are usually made by asserting that market mechanisms tend to promote individual liberties and freedoms which are taken to be ethically desirable. This appeared to underlie the attachment to market mechanisms that became known in the 1980s as Thatcherism and Reaganism.

A second interpretation of desirability may be in terms of economic efficiency. Here economists have much to say. We have shown throughout this book that market processes have the potential to generate efficient allocations of resources. But our discussions in this chapter lead to the conclusion that this is not inevitable. Markets do 'fail' in a number of ways, particularly when it comes to interactions with the environment and anti-competitive behaviour. A prima-facie case exists, therefore, for government intervention. But we also noted that government intervention in the economy can result in efficiency failures. Whether such intervention is warranted in any particular instance is something that has to be decided by an analysis of the relative advantages of intervention in that case.

Further reading

General Reading on Competition Policy

John Kay (1993), particularly in chapter 20, gives an interesting discussion of competition policy as it relates to business strategy. Rigorous (but somewhat theory-oriented) analyses of the welfare economics basis of economics are found in articles by Bator and Chipman, reprinted in Townsend (1971). Beauchamp and Bowie (1988) contains a good selection of readings on matters related to business ethics. Parkin and King (1995) contains a comprehensive and very readable account of market failure and public choice (chapter 19) and industry policy (chapter 20).

Contestability

An important recent development in the analysis of business economics has been the theory of *contestable markets*, developed by W. J. Baumol, an American business economist and consultant. A market is contestable if firms are able to enter or leave the market freely. Baumol (1982) argues that this condition alone is sufficient to bring about all the desirable properties of perfectly competitive markets. The importance of this claim is clear; whereas it is virtually impossible to achieve all the conditions of perfect competition except in very unusual circumstances, making market entry or exit free is a more easily achieved goal. If this theory is correct, policy should concentrate on increasing the *mobility* of firms across markets, rather than attempting to control the pricing (and other) behaviour of firms.

Environmental Regulation

A more extensive analysis of all aspects of environmental economics, firmly grounded in economic theory, can be found in Perman *et al.* (1996). Pollution control policy is analysed in chapters 8 and 9 of that reference. A briefer account is found in the survey article by Cropper and Oates (1992). Coase's classic article (1960) on bargaining repays careful reading.

Questions

13.1. In what circumstances might government increase social well-being by intervention in the operations of markets?

13.2. What is meant by 'regulatory capture' and how can this affect the outcomes of regulation?

13.3. 'It will always pay a firm in the long run to behave in an environmentally friendly manner.' Discuss.

13.4. What are the relative implications for business profitability of the following pollution control instruments:

(a) pollution taxes;

(b) pollution abatement subsidies;

(c) marketable emissions permits?

13.5. What problems does the regulator face in attempting to obtain an operational definition of anti-competitive behaviour?

13.6. Given the discussions in this chapter, why was deregulation such a central component of the political programmes of many European countries during the 1980s and early 1990s?

14 The Firm and the Macroeconomic Environment

Introduction

One component of the firm's environment over which it has little or no control is the macroeconomic climate of the country (or countries) in which the business is located. Yet this climate affects a firm's ability to create value in a variety of ways. For example, the strength of demand for a firm's products can be significantly affected by the level of aggregate activity in the economy as a whole. The prices which a firm must pay for its inputs will at least partially be determined by demand and supply conditions in input markets; these in turn are shaped in important ways by the prevailing patterns of taxes and subsidies. And as we saw in Chapter 9, business investment decisions are influenced by the market rate of interest, which reflects general macroeconomic conditions.

Our objective in this chapter is to show how a simple economic modelling framework—principally built around supply and demand tools—can be of use in understanding the workings of the macroeconomy. This will help the manager to anticipate how the economy is likely to evolve in the short and medium-term future, and so to impart valuable information about changes in the firm's business environment.

14.1 Macroeconomic Conditions in the Short and Medium Term and the Firm's Search for Value

We begin this chapter by examining a set of economic indicators which provide summary information about key aspects of the macroeconomy. The following chapter will show how some of these—the cyclical indicators—can be used for forecasting purposes. Perhaps the most fundamental indicator is gross domestic product (GDP).

The Gross Domestic Product (GDP) of an economy is the total value of all goods and services produced in a country over some period of time.

GDP is a measure of the total value of output produced *within* one country. But we may also be interested in a measure of the total output produced by productive resources *belonging* to one country. One such measure is gross national product (GNP).

The Gross National Product (GNP) of an economy is the total value of all goods and services produced by the productive resources of that country over some period of time.

These two measures of aggregate output will differ when countries produce abroad as well as in the domestic economy, or when residents own assets abroad. For example, some of the output produced in the UK is attributable to productive resources owned by foreign citizens. This will be included in the UK's GDP but not in her GNP. Similarly, the value added overseas by assets owned by UK citizens will be excluded from her GDP but included in her GNP. Expressing this in different terms, GNP will differ from GDP by the amount of net wage and property income from abroad, as shown by the following accounting identity:

GDP + Net wage and property income from abroad = GNP.

For illustrative purposes, we show in Table 14.1 some national accounts statistics for the year 1994. You can see that net property income from abroad was £10,519 million in that year. Wage and property income received from UK-owned productive resources located overseas exceeded wage and property income paid overseas for the use of foreign-owned resources located in the UK by that amount, and so GNP exceeded GDP by £10,519 million.

Gross national product can be broken down into various components. The following accounting identity decomposes GNP into a domestic demand component and a net overseas trade component. We shall use this identity extensively in later parts of this chapter to help in understanding the workings of the macroeconomy. The GNP identity can be written as:

$$\text{GNP} = \underset{\text{(Domestic demand)}}{(C + I + G)} + \underset{\text{\{Net overseas trade\}}}{\{X - M\}}$$

In this expression, C denotes total consumers' expenditure, I is investment expenditure (including stock building), and G denotes government expenditure. X denotes exports and property income inflows, whilst M denotes imports and property income outflows. All terms in the expression are flows over a particular interval of time, expressed in monetary terms.

We have defined GNP as an *output* measure. But it can also be interpreted in two other ways. First, UK GNP is also a measure of the value of all *incomes* received by UK citizens. And secondly, it is a measure of net *expenditure* on goods and services produced by resources owned by UK citizens.

Table 14.1 National income statistics, 1994 (expressed in £ million at 1994 prices)

Consumers' expenditure	428,084
General government consumption	144,084
Gross domestic fixed capital formation	100,075
Value of physical increase in stocks	3,303
Total domestic expenditure	675,546
Export of goods and services	173,925
Total final expenditure	849,471
less imports	−180,605
Gross domestic product at market prices	668,866
less taxes on expenditure	−96,950
plus subsidies	7,224
GDP at factor cost	579,140
Net property income from abroad	10,519
GNP at factor cost	589,659

Note: In the original source, there is a separate item labelled 'Statistical Discrepancy', amounting to £124 m. This has been included in the imports row in this table. This does not affect the values of GDP and GNP.

Source: United Kingdom National Accounts, 1995 (The Blue Book), Table 1.2.

The reason why we can interpret GNP in these three ways is that output, income, and expenditure are in essence the same thing looked at in different ways (and because the conventions of national accounting define them so that these equivalences hold).

It will be helpful to look at Table 14.1 This shows GNP broken down into various components. There is one complication here that we have not yet mentioned. If you look at the last line, you will see that GNP is measured at *factor cost.* This means that the GNP total shown has had expenditure taxes netted out, and subsidies (from government) added back in. However, all rows up to and including the one labelled *gross domestic product at market prices* have not had taxes and subsidies netted out—they are measured at market prices, in other words. Note how taxes and subsidies are used to convert GDP from market price terms into factor cost terms towards the bottom of the table.[1]

The sum of C, G, and I (the first three rows in the table) is often called domestic demand: expenditures on these items generates incomes. But if a country trades internationally, some of those incomes will be remitted abroad. This is why, in the eighth row, the value of imports is subtracted in the process of arriving at GNP. Similarly, domestic income will be augmented by export receipts, which explains why export receipts are shown as an addition in the table. Finally, as we saw earlier, GNP includes the net property income from abroad, and so it is added to the figures in the penultimate row.

In Box 14.1, we show how the various categories in Table 14.1 relate to the fundamental GNP identity that was presented earlier. You should read the contents of this box to convince yourself of the various relationships.

Net Measures of Output and Income

In addition to GDP and GNP, two other measures of the overall level of economic activity are available. These are net domestic product (NDP) and net national product (NNP). The latter pair differ

[1] The terms exports and imports in Table 14.1 do not include any property income inflows or outflows. As you can see, these flows are accounted for seperately in the table. However, in the accounting identity given earlier, GNP = $C + I + G + (X - M)$, the terms X and M were being used differently, and do include property income inflows ands outflows respectively.

Box 14.1 The GNP Indentity (1994)

C	= Consumers' expenditure *less* taxes on expenditure *plus* subsidies
	= 428,084 − 96, 950 + 7,224 = 338,358
I	= Gross domestic fixed capital formation *plus* value of physical increase in stocks
	= 100,075 + 3,303 = 103,378
G	= 144,084
$(X - M)$	= Exports *less* imports *plus* net property income from abroad
	173,925 − 180,605 + 10,519 = 3,839

Thus the identity is:

GNP	$= C + I + G + (X - M)$
589,659	= 338,358 + 103,378 + 144,084 + 3,839

from the former by taking account of the consumption of capital. By definition

GDP − value of capital consumption = NDP

GNP − value of capital consumption = NNP

NDP and NNP are alternative measures of an economy's net income. The word *net* signifies that all relevant costs have been subtracted from the gross value of output. In the process of producing output, some part of the capital stock will be consumed. In arriving at a measure of the economy's net income, capital consumption should be regarded as a cost of production, and deducted from the gross income measures. By convention, net national product is also known as national income.

Other Aggregate Economic Indicators

It is useful to have indicators not only of the overall level of activity of an economy, but also of conditions in particular sectors of the economy. Table 14.2 lists a number of variables that have important implications for business decision-making, and some indicators that are available for these variables. Statistics are available in most economies for output levels in these subsectors. Many of these indicators are published at monthly frequency, although some are only available at longer time intervals.

Their usefulness depends very much on the needs of the user. For example, operators in financial markets attach great importance to information on inflation rates and interest rates, as these dominate returns on financial assets. Firms with substantial export trade, or using large quantities of imported components, will pay particular attention to exchange rates. And as we will see in the next chapter, many of these sectoral indicators are useful for forecasting purposes.

Table 14.2 Some important economic indicators

Consumers' expenditure:	
	Retail sales
	Auto sales
	Consumer credit
	Consumer confidence
	Durable goods orders
Investment expenditure:	
	Housing starts
	Business inventories
	Construction output
Inflation:	
	Retail price index
	Tax and price index
Labour market conditions:	
	Earnings
	Unemployment
Cost and availability of credit:	
	Short and long rates of interest
Government economic stance:	
	Budget deficit
	PSBR
External position:	
	Exchange rate
	Trade balance
	Balance of payments on current account
	Balance of payments on capital account

Salient Characteristics of the Macroeconomy

The evolution of GNP through time exhibits several common features in most market economies. In particular, a time series of observations on GNP seems to contain three components:[2]

GNP = trend component + cyclical component + random component.

These three components of GDP—the long-term trend, the medium-term cycle, and the short-term random element—are portrayed schematically in Figure 14.1.

Figure 14.2 shows the actual values of Australian, Japanese, UK, and US GNP over the period 1960 to 1993. In order to facilitate comparison of the relative performance of these four economies over the period, the GNP levels have been standardized so that each is given the value 100 in 1960. The series are also given in constant price (otherwise known as real) terms. This means that general changes in the price level are not reflected in the figures, which therefore measure changes only in the quantity of output over time.

The long-run trend component is evident in each of the four curves. But it is also clear that there has been a markedly greater rate of trend increase for Japan than for the other three economies. Figure 14.3 plots the natural logarithm of GDP for the UK. A useful property of the logarithm of a series is that its slope represents the growth rate of the series. A constant slope implies a constant growth rate. The straight line in the figure is a line of statistical best fit to the series. From the slope of this line, we can deduce that average growth rate has been 2.25 per cent per year.[3] It seems reasonable to argue that the UK trend growth rate has been approximately constant over the years 1960–1995, although there has been much greater variation around this trend in the latter part of that period.

The other two components—cyclical and random—are less obvious, but can be identified with careful scrutiny. In Figure 14.3 they comprise the deviations of actual GDP from its trend level. The cyclical component can be seen by noting that for lengthy periods GDP is above trend, whilst for others it is below trend.

The Macroeconomy in the Short Term and the Circular Flow of Income

A simple, but very useful, way of visualizing the basic operation of the macroeconomy is by considering the circular flow of income. Stripped down to its essence, the idea is represented in Figure 14.4.

Imagine an economy consisting of just two 'sectors', households (*H*), and firms (*F*). Households own productive assets—labour, land, capital—and rent these out to firms. Firms use these productive assets to produce goods and services, which are sold to households. There are two types of flow in this model. First, 'real' flows of productive assets from households to firms, and produced goods and services from firms to households. These are represented by the vertical lines in the centre of the figure, Secondly, monetary-income flows are represented by the outside semi-circular loops.

The total level of 'national income' in this economy can be measured as the sum of these monetary flows over a given period of time (say a year), on either the 'income' side or the 'expenditure' side. If an economy's aggregate income is in equilibrium, it will have no tendency to diverge from its present level. In this case, household income (the sum of wages, rent, interest, and profits earned in one year) will be equal to the value of households' expenditure on goods and service in that year. These flows are then mutually sustaining. Households' incomes and expenditures are equal, as are firms' incomes and expenditures.

Although simplicity is an attractive characteristic, this scheme is too simple for understanding the workings of the economy. In particular, it omits three important sets of relationships, and three associated sectors:

1. households and businesses borrow and save; these saving/borrowing relationships are mediated by the *financial sector* of the economy;

---

[2] When GNP figures are measured at higher frequencies than annually, a fourth component can often be observed, consisting of within-year seasonal variations. We ignore seasonality in this chapter, and all graphs use data which have been adjusted to remove seasonality.

[3] The trendline was obtained using the regression package, PCGIVE version 8, by estimating the following equation by Ordinary Least Squares over the sample period 1960 Q1 to 1993 Q4:

$$\text{Ln(UK GDP)}_t = \alpha + \beta \text{ TIME}_t + u_t.$$

The estimated regression equation is

$$\text{Ln}(\widehat{\text{UK GDP}}) = 4.63 + 0.0056 \text{ TIME}.$$

This is the equation of the line of best fit; its slope (0.0056) implies that GDP grew at just over 0.5 per cent per quarter, equivalent to an *annual* trend growth rate of about 2.25 per cent.

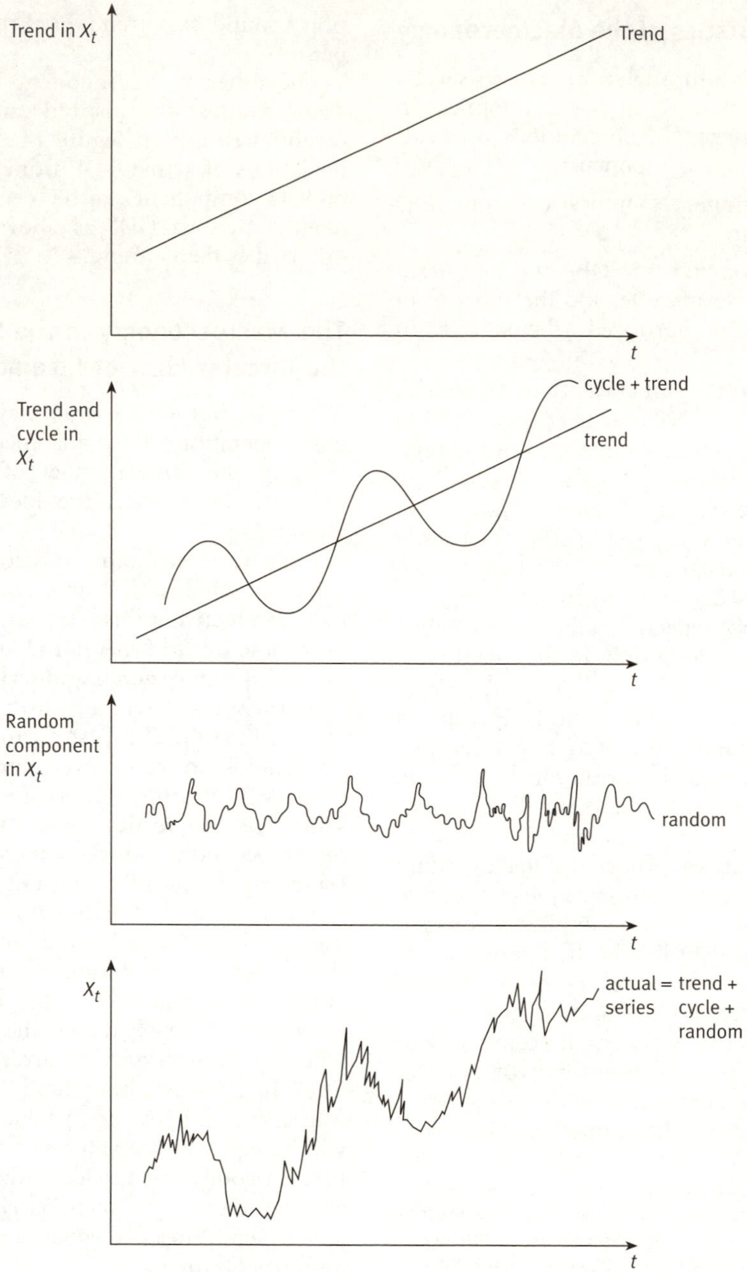

Figure 14.1 Components of economic time series

2. household and business incomes and expenditures are subject to a variety of taxes, and are augmented by transfer payments and other expenditures by the *government sector*;
3. incomes and expenditures are transferred to and received from abroad, in the forms of trade and capital flows. In other words, the national (or domestic) economy interacts with an *overseas sector*.

Figure 14.5(a) includes these three sectors. To keep the diagram uncluttered, only monetary flows are illustrated. It is helpful to interpret the diagram in

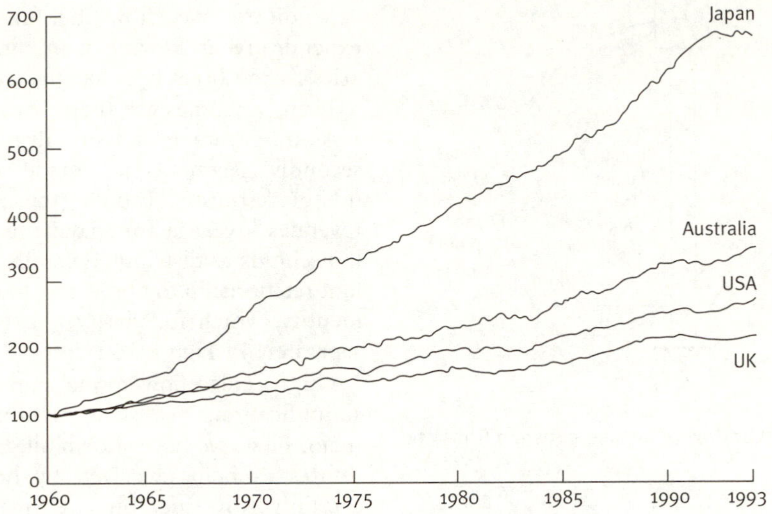

Figure 14.2 GDP: Japan, Australia, USA, UK, (1960–1993)

the following way. The basic circular flow of income between households and firms has been augmented by a series of inflows and outflows. Alternatively, we could call these *injections* into and *withdrawals* from the circular flow of income:

INJECTIONS (J) = investment (I)
+ government expenditure and transfer payments (G)
+ export revenues and overseas income receipts (X).

WITHDRAWALS (W) = Savings (S)
+ government taxation (T)
+ import expenditure and other payments of income to overseas (M).

Let us follow the various flows shown in Figure 14.5(a). Households receive incomes in two ways: from firms, after the payment of taxes (labelled here *disposable income*) and from government transfers. Household income is then either

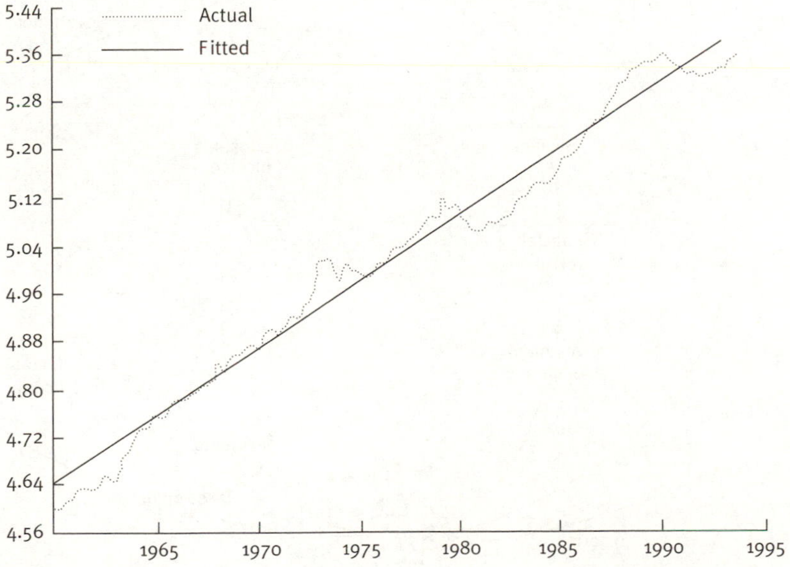

Figure 14.3 The growth trend for the UK economy

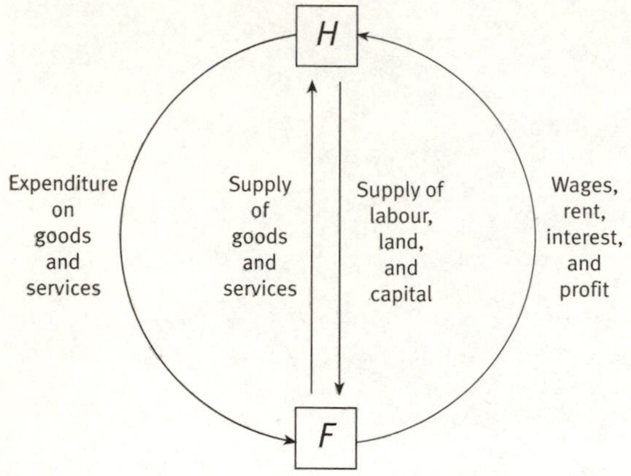

Figure 14.4 The circular flow of income between firms and households

consumed (C) or saved (S) with financial intermediaries. Of this consumers' expenditure, a part is spent on UK-produced goods (C^*) and so remains within the circular flow of income, and the remainder purchases imported goods and services. Import expenditures are a withdrawal from the UK's circular flow of income.

The income of firms arises from three sources: consumption expenditure on UK-produced goods (C^*), export receipts from overseas, and investment expenditure. We show the funds for investment expenditure as flowing from financial intermediaries (using household savings).

Firms' incomes are then dispersed in two ways. First, taxes are levied on business incomes, and secondly, payments are made to factors for the use of resources. Profits (the excess of business revenues over factor payments) also return to households as distributed profits. The most important relationship to observe in the figure is the GNP identity, which for clarity is extracted and shown separately in Figure 14.5(b).

Our circular flow model contains a number of simplifications; we shall mention only a few of them. First, we have shown all government expenditures as being received by households; this is certainly not true, but we treat all government expenditures as if they were received by households. A second simplification arises from our treatment of savings and investment. The sources and uses of savings and investment are more complex than are shown here. Thirdly, government tax revenues show no recognition (in Figure 14.5(a)) of such things as taxes on expenditure and on imports. It turns out to be the case, however, that no harm is done by representing flows as we have done. If all possible linkages were shown, the figure

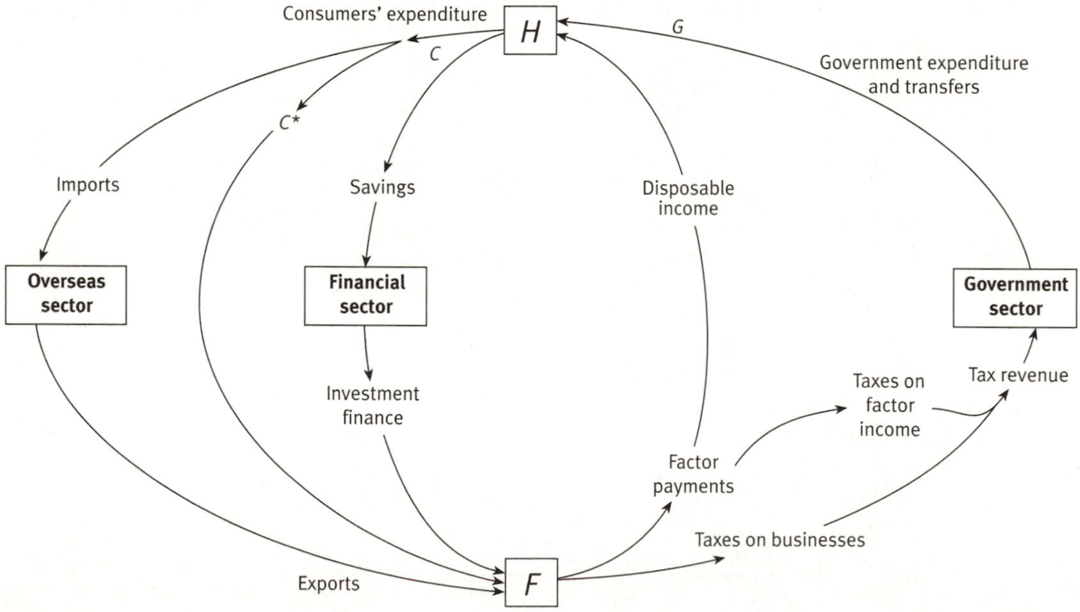

Figure 14.5a The augmented circular flow of income

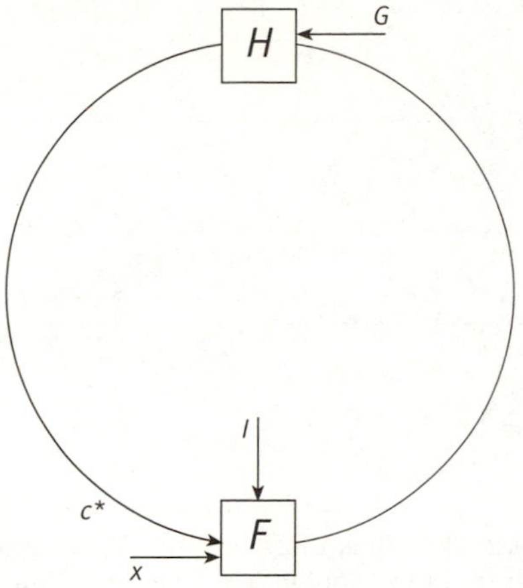

Figure 14.5b The basic circular flow of income

would be considerably more difficult to read, but with little additional benefit.

Equilibrium Income

National income equilibrium requires that the flows of income and expenditures between firms and households must be equal and constant through time. This requires withdrawals to be equal to injections, or algebraically.

$$W = J$$
$$S + T + M = I + G + X.$$

However, not all possible levels of national income are consistent with an *equilibrium* level of income. Figure 14.6 shows how the *planned* levels of W and J vary with the level of national income.

The total planned level of withdrawals increases as national income rises. A moment's thought should convince you that each of the components of W—savings, taxation, and import expenditure—is likely to increase as the level of national income becomes higher.

On the other hand, the level of injections, J, is shown as being unaffected by the level of national income. This would be the case if

- export receipts are determined by the levels of income in other countries, not by domestic income;
- government expenditure is largely set each year at planned levels, and does not vary with the level of national income;
- investment expenditure is influenced by the rate of returns available on capital projects, which is largely unaffected by short-term variations in income.

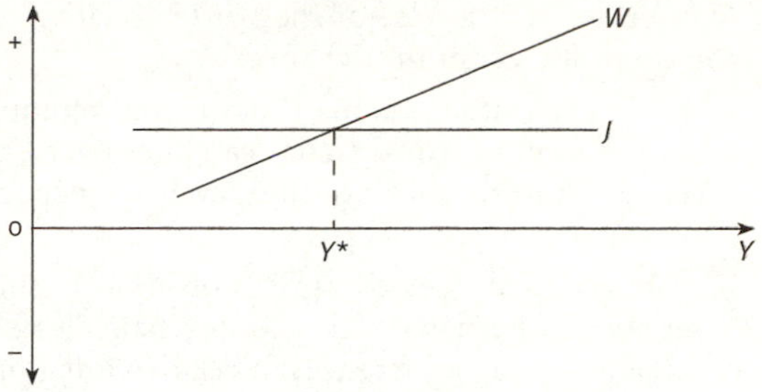

Figure 14.6 The relationship of withdrawals and injections to the level of national income

Under these assumptions, each component of J will be independent of the level of income, at least in the short term.[4] The level of national income can only be in equilibrium when planned injections equal planned withdrawals. For the W and J functions shown in Figure 14.6, this occurs at one and only one level of income, Y^*.

The Macroeconomy in the Short Term: Changes in the Equilibrium Level of National Income

Our analysis has shown that the equilibrium level of national income is determined by the intersection of two functions, one showing planned withdrawals from the circular flow of income and the other planned injections into that flow. This implies that any change in planned withdrawals or injections will change the equilibrium level of national income.

Withdrawals or injections change for three reasons.

1. Conditions in the domestic economy alter:
   - business confidence can change, altering the planned level of investment.
   - consumer confidence can change, with consequent impacts on the proportions of disposable income saved and consumed.

[4] These assertions are, of course, questionable. However, it turns out to be the case that we do not need them to hold exactly. What *is* important about the 'model' is that *withdrawals increase at a faster rate than injections* as the level of income rises (and from a lower initial value). There is little doubt that this is correct, and the conclusions we draw below remain valid provided those conditions are met.

2. Conditions in the rest of the world (relative to the domestic economy) change:
   - trade cycle fluctuations (booms and slumps in the level of world trade) can alter overseas expenditures, altering the level of export receipts earned;
   - changes in the relative prices of imports and exports (perhaps due to exchange rate changes, or to differences in relative inflation rates) can affect the monetary values of import and export flows.
3. The government sector alters its mix of fiscal policies (taxation and government expenditures) or changes the cost and availability of credit:
   - the public sector can alter its net withdrawal of income from the circular flow;
   - changes in credit availability or cost can alter any component of W and J, especially savings and investment flows.

Let us illustrate one of these changes, using Figure 14.7 to visualize the problem. Suppose that the government chooses to increase the level of expenditure without altering its tax revenues. Increased government expenditure shifts the injection function upwards (from J_1 to J_2).[5] At the original income level, Y^*_1, injections now exceed withdrawals, causing a cumulative rise in income until it reaches Y^*_2. At the new level of income, planned injections once again equal planned withdrawals (but with both now being at a higher level than before), and so Y^*_2 is a new equilibrium level of income.

The Multiplier Effect

An increase in injections, such as the rise in government expenditure that we have just investigated, may lead to an increase in equilibrium national income of a greater magnitude. The *government expenditure multiplier*, k_G, is the ratio of the increase in national income to the increase in government expenditure that brought it about. Thus,

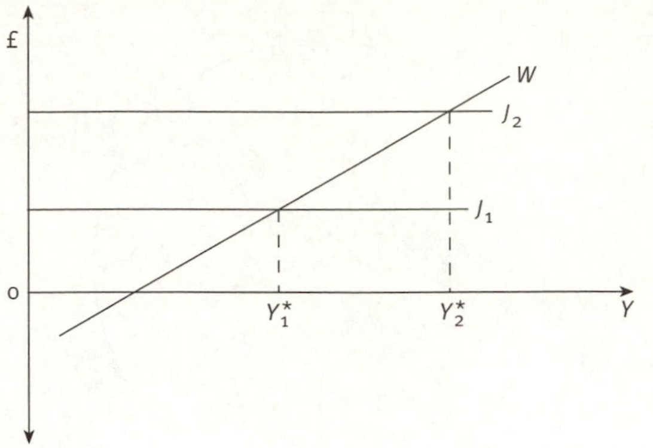

Figure 14.7 The effect of an increase in government expenditure on the equilibrium level of national income

$$k_G = \frac{\Delta Y}{\Delta G} = \frac{Y_2 - Y_1}{G_2 - G_1}\ .$$

suppose that ΔY were £20 million, whilst ΔG were £10 million. Then the government expenditure multiplier would have a value of two.

In general, the government expenditure multiplier will have a value greater than one. Why should this be the case? Imagine an increase of £10 million in G; this would raise incomes received in the economy by £10 million, and so k_G must be at least equal to one. But this is not the whole picture. As these incomes of £10 million are received, some proportion of that will be spent, causing additional (second-round) income increases. These will be partly spent, causing third-round income increases, and so on. If the proportion of any additional income spent in the domestic economy were one-half, then the sequence of initial and subsequent income increments (ΔY) would be + 10 + 5 + 2.5 + 1.25 + . . . This is a geometric sequence, and the sum of all individual components will go to 20 as the length of the sequence becomes indefinitely large. Note that, because the multiplier is two, the final increase in income is twice as large as the initial injection that caused the income rise.

Other Multipliers

Government expenditure is not alone in having multiplier effects. A change in any component of W or J will have a multiplier effect (although the multiplier would be negative for increases in a withdrawal component). In general, if we let X denote any component of either W or J, then we can define a multiplier coefficient for X as:

[5] It is important to note that the increase in G shifts the injection function upwards, and does not cause a movement along the original J function. If income were to increase, G might well rise; if it did, that would already be incorporated in the original injection function. But we are here talking about a planned increase in G *irrespective* of the level of income. The whole curve therefore shifts upwards, by an amount equal in magnitude to ΔG.

$$k_x = \frac{\Delta Y}{\Delta X}.$$

So for example, an investment multiplier, k_I, would be defined as $\Delta Y/\Delta I$ and a taxation multiplier, k_T as $\Delta Y/\Delta T$. These different multipliers will usually be different in magnitude.

Expenditure, Output, and the Price Level

Changes in the level of expenditure (operating through changes in one or more components of either *W* or *J*) will change the level of equilibrium national income. But what effect will changes in expenditure have on the volume of *output* and on *prices*? First, note that the value of national income, *Y*, can be broken down into a volume (or quantity) component and a price component, that is:

$Y = Q \times P$.

Changes in income may thus consist of changes in the quantity of output, *Q*, or changes in the price level, *P*, or a combination of the two.

A Simple Keynesian Model of the Income, Output, and Price Relationship

Consider the following simple macro model. The economy has a production capacity ceiling that determines a maximum volume of output. Output will be at its maximum when all productive resources are employed, and are used at full efficiency. Figure 14.8 illustrates how one might expect output and prices to respond as income increases through a succession of rises in aggregate expenditure.[6]

Imagine an economy operating with a large amount of spare capacity. As aggregate expenditure increases, higher spending induces a greater volume of output, sold at unchanged prices. The increase in aggregate expenditure has raised national income, but with all the increase being accounted for by the *Q* component of *Y*. If this process of expansion continues far enough, supply will eventually be constrained by the capacity ceiling of the economy. Beyond this point, further expenditure increases cannot bring forth more real output but will instead result in price level increases. When the economy is operating beyond its capacity constraint, the output curve shown in the top part of the figure becomes horizontal (as *Q* can rise no further) whilst the price level curve (shown in the central part of the figure) becomes upward sloping.

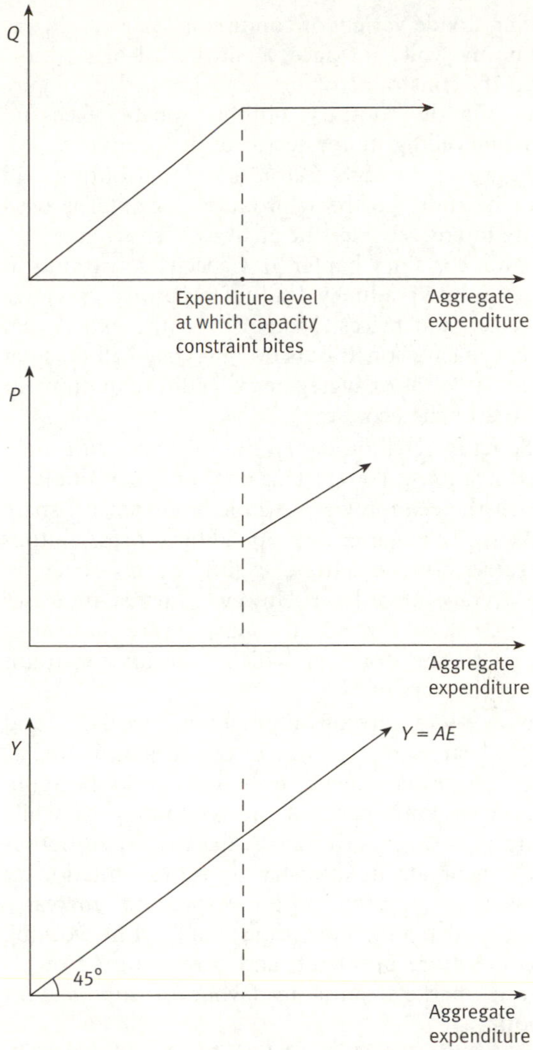

Figure 14.8 A simple Keynesian model of the relationships between aggregate expenditure, output, and the price level

A Modified Model of the Relationship between Expenditure, Output, and the Price Level

Clearly, the relationships we have just described are too simplistic. The business sector of any economy consists of a diverse set of industries operating

[6] The term aggregate demand is sometimes used instead of aggregate expenditure. We shall use the latter, but will from time to time refer to the level of demand in the economy; this should also be taken to refer to the level of aggregate expenditure.

under a wide variety of conditions. As a result, the economy will not face a single 'all-or-nothing' capacity constraint of the kind implied by Figure 14.8. On the contrary, output probably faces no *absolute* ceiling in any sector of the economy.

However, in each sector, additional output will become more costly to produce as capital is used more intensively (see the analysis of short-run production costs in Chapter 5). Capacity constraints in practice bite gradually, leading to upward pressures on costs and prices. Moreover, to the extent that such capacity constraints do bite, they will do so at different levels of aggregate expenditure in different sectors of the economy.

So let us retell our story, but this time with some modifications. We start again from a position in which the economy as a whole has extensive spare capacity. As aggregate expenditure rises, output increases. Initially, there is little or no effect on the average price level. However, further increases in aggregate expenditure push more industries closer to the point at which capacity constraint pressures start to bite.

Now the ability of output to rise weakens, and prices bear a greater share of the burden of adjustment to rising expenditure. Bottlenecks begin to appear in some parts of the economy even while there is still general excess capacity. These bottlenecks generate inflationary pressures. Inflationary pressures intensify as the expansion increases labour demand, overtime and shift-working become more prevalent, and bargaining power in labour markets shifts in favour of suppliers of labour.

We represent these relationships in Figure 14.9. For ease of comparison, the simple predictions of the previous section are reproduced as dotted lines. There are two main differences between this story and the earlier version portrayed in Figure 14.8.

1. There is no longer an absolute upper limit on real output, Q. Instead, the responsiveness of output to expenditure becomes lower as the level of aggregate expenditure increases.
2. Inflationary pressures begin even while the economy has some spare capacity, but they intensify quite markedly as that capacity diminishes. At very high levels of aggregate expenditure, further demand pressures are almost entirely reflected in price level changes.

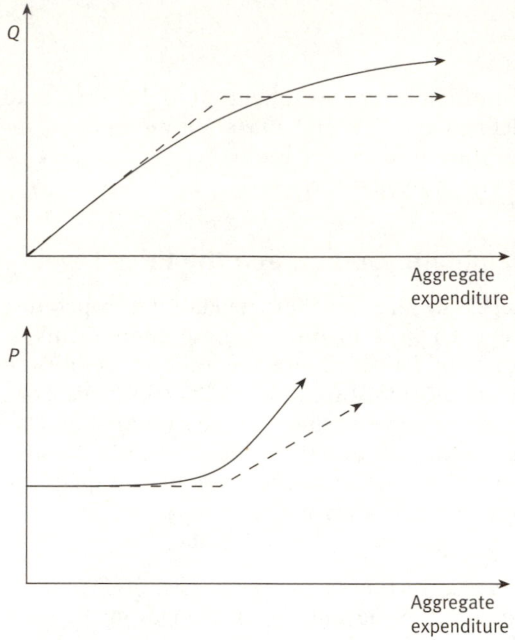

Figure 14.9 A modified account of the relationships between expenditure, output, and the average price level

The Aggregate Demand/Aggregate Supply Model of the Macroeconomy

We can further enrich our insights into the workings of the macroeconomy by using a simple supply and demand model. More specifically, it is *aggregate demand* and *aggregate supply* that we wish to investigate. Aggregate demand is simply another name for what we have been calling aggregate expenditure so far in our presentation. Aggregate supply will be defined and explained shortly.

Possible shapes for the aggregate demand (AD) and aggregate supply (AS) curves of an economy are shown in Figure 14.10. Each curve shows a relationship between the average price level (P) and the quantity of aggregate output (Q). The *aggregate demand* curve shows the economy's price–quantity relationship for a particular level of aggregate expenditure (Y). It shows all the quantities of output that could be purchased at each possible price for any particular total level of expenditure. For example, suppose that national income, Y, is £100. Then Q would be 5 if P were 20; Q would be 10 if P were 10; and Q would be 25 if P were 4. The AD curve simply shows the quantity of goods that would be purchased at each average price level, for a given level of national income.

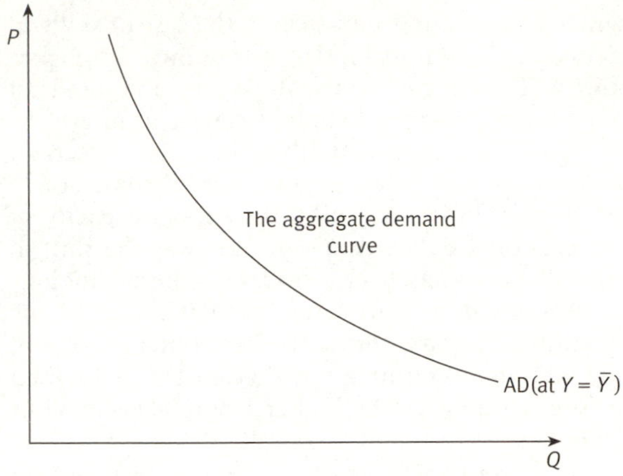

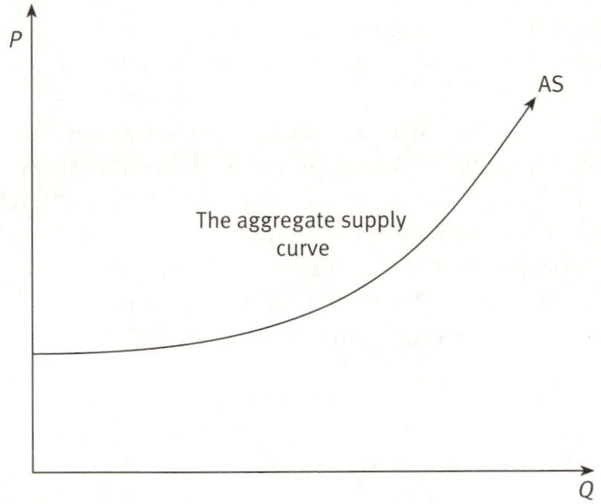

Figure 14.10 The aggregate demand and aggregate supply curves

Now turn to the *aggregate supply* curve. This shows the relationship between the average price level of an economy and the amount of output that firms intend to supply. Why should the AS curve have the shape indicated in Figure 14.10? Look again at Figure 14.9. For each level of aggregate expenditure (or aggregate demand, as we are now calling it), one could read off the corresponding price and output levels. When all such combinations of prices and quantities are calculated and then plotted together, the result is the aggregate supply curve. It shows the quantity of real output that suppliers intend to bring to the market at various price levels.

Using the AD/AS Model to Predict Short-Term Economic Changes

The aggregate expenditure and supply market model is a useful way of understanding the consequences of a variety of changes affecting the economy. These changes can be classified into demand-side and supply-side changes. We begin by looking at changes which impact on the demand side of the economy. An *increase* in aggregate demand could be caused by any of the following:

- an increase in the ratio of consumption to disposable income;
- an increase in government expenditure;
- a decrease in direct taxation;
- an increase in planned investment expenditure;
- a rise in the value of exports or a fall in the value of imports.

An increase in aggregate demand shifts the AD curve to the right. The consequences of this will depend on the shape of the AS curve at the point where the AS and AD curves initially intersected. Three possible outcomes are illustrated in Figure 14.11. In the top panel, the increase in aggregate demand (from AD_1 to AD_2) results in both higher real output and a higher average price level. The intuition behind this is straightforward. At the initial position, the economy is operating with some spare capacity, but at a point where capacity pressures are beginning to bite in parts of the economy. Higher demand (and so higher expenditure) results in more orders, and so output expands. But cost and price increases also occur at points in the economy where it is difficult to raise supply quickly.

Now suppose an aggregate demand increase takes place at a time when the economy has large amounts of spare capacity, such as at the deepest point of a recession. The results are illustrated in the central panel. Here, the additional expenditure generates no inflationary pressure, and its full effect is felt in output changes. This is the case that the economist John Maynard Keynes appears to have had in mind when he advocated expansionary demand-side policy in Britain in the interwar years.

The third panel shows another possibility. The economy is here operating at an 'overheated' point. Very little scope exists in the short run for output expansion; attempts to raise output will result in

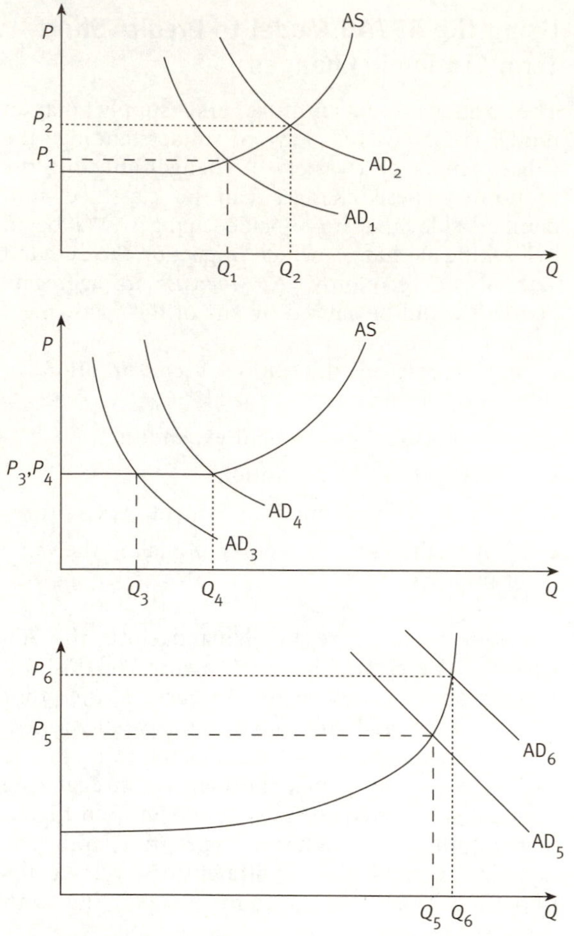

Figure 14.11 The possible effects of an increase in aggregate demand

substantial price increases. This is clearly not a good state in which to have an increase in aggregate expenditure!

An Increase in Aggregate Supply

An increase in aggregate supply could be caused by many things, including:

- technological progress;
- innovations in processes of production;
- measures that increase the geographical and occupational mobility of labour;
- reductions in cost-push wage pressure.

An increase in aggregate supply shifts the AS curve to the right. However, the way in which the curve shifts is more important than in the case of shifts in demand. Two possibilities are shown in Figure 14.12. The upper panel illustrates the kind of supply-side change one might expect from a technological improvement that has the effect of augmenting the 'effective' quantity of some scarce productive inputs. It shifts the supply capacity of the economy outwards. Notice the way the shift in the AS curve has been portrayed: the technology improvement is represented as if it increases the quantity of inputs, and so the horizontal portion of the AS curve continues further to the right than before. Output will be higher before capacity constraints start to bite.

The lower panel corresponds to improvements in the ability of the economy to bring forth additional output when the economy is operating close to full capacity. It is what one might expect if resources become more mobile, in an occupational or geographical sense. Another cause might be altered relative bargaining strengths in the labour market, so that upward pressures on wages are ameliorated at high levels of labour demand.

A supply-side improvement leads to higher real output and a lower average price level. Contrast this with the case of a demand-side increase which

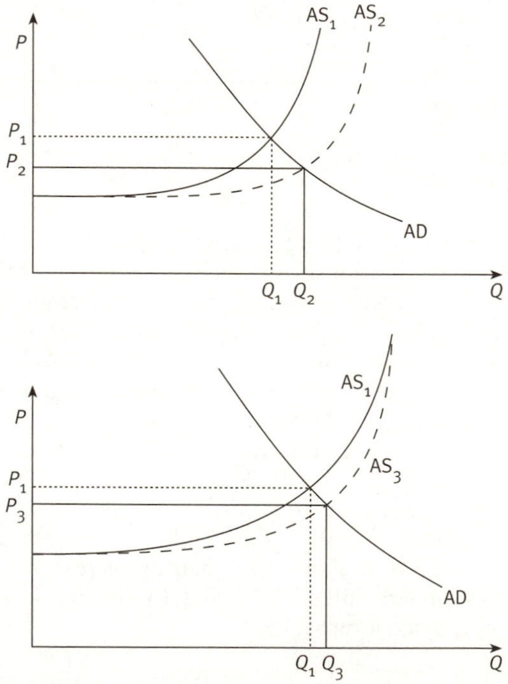

Figure 14.12 Possible consequences of an increase in aggregate supply

generally leads to higher real output and a *higher* average price level. This suggests that government policy might be better directed at seeking supply-side improvements, rather than at demand-side policy, particularly where the economy is operating near 'full employment' of productive inputs. Unfortunately, supply-side improvements are particularly difficult for government to bring about, particularly if they are sought quickly.

Changes in the Price Level and Inflation

Our earlier discussions have concentrated upon the relationship between expenditure, output, and the *price level*. However, a change in the average level of prices can sometimes initiate inflation. Inflation is a process in which the average level of prices is continually changing. Whilst inflation usually involves increasing prices, it can also consist of falling prices (in which case we might call it disinflation).

One-off changes in the price level are most likely to spark off periods of inflation when conditions in labour and product markets are conducive to cost and price rises. Suppose that workers aim to maintain the real value of their wages, and so seek wage increases to compensate for an increase in average prices. Moreover, suppose that product market conditions are such that firms can succeed in passing on higher input costs in the form of higher prices. These conditions can *initiate* a wage–price spiral (or an inflationary spiral). They are most likely to exist when the economy is operating at high levels of demand and has little spare capacity.

But a wage–price spiral can only be *sustained* if the government allows the money supply to expand in an accommodating manner. That is, an inflationary process in which prices and wages rise at say 5 per cent per year can only be sustained over time if the money supply is allowed to expand at no less than 5 per cent per year. The monetary policy of a government is, therefore, important in determining whether inflation can persist through time. There are reasons to believe that the rate of inflation is related to an economy's unemployment rate. Let us now turn our attention to consider this matter.

Is there a Relationship between Inflation and Unemployment?

In 1958, Professor Phillips wrote a famous paper in which he argued that the rate of wage inflation was negatively related to the level of unemployment of labour (and had been over a long period of time). Figure 14.13 shows the general form of the relationship suggested by Phillips. Two other points deserve attention in the Phillips curve relationship.

- There is one level of unemployment at which inflation is zero (and so the price level remains constant). We provide some estimates from one recent study of what this level of unemployment is for various countries in Table 14.3.
- At very high levels of unemployment, inflation will become negative, and so the average price level will be falling.

Phillips's paper also offered an explanation of this relationship. Suppose that government chooses to maintain a high level of aggregate demand, perhaps in order to keep output high and unemployment low. This results in a 'tight' labour market with upward pressures on the price level. These pressures lead to wage-led *inflation*, in which prices rise continuously. So high levels of aggregate demand tend to be associated with high levels of output, low levels of unemployment, and inflation. On the other hand, reductions in aggregate demand reduce inflation, but at the cost of increasing unemployment. Hence a Phillips curve, such as the one illustrated in Figure 14.13, is generated.

The Phillips curve implies the existence of a trade-off between inflation and unemployment. Government can choose the combination of unemployment and inflation it wants from the possibilities shown along the Phillips curve; but reducing unemployment can only be obtained at the cost of increasing inflation. The nature and existence of the

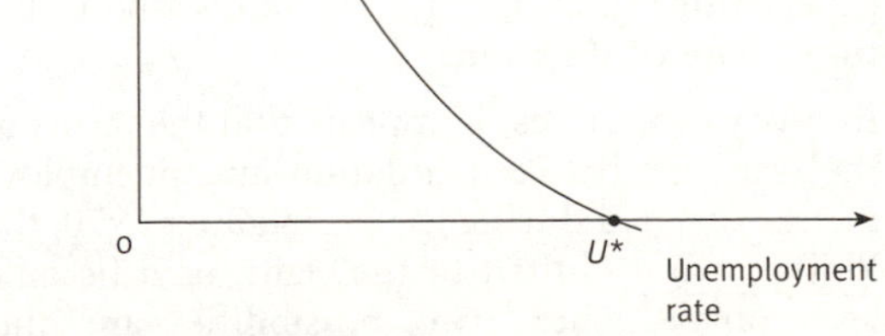

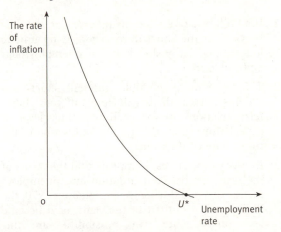

Figure 14.13 The Phillips curve relationship between inflation and unemployment

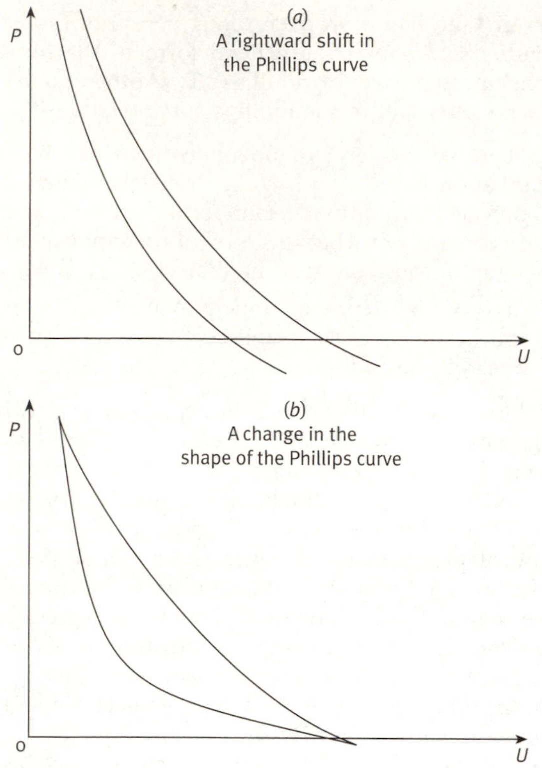

Figure 14.14 The shifting Phillips curve

Phillips curve relationship is controversial, however. What seems certain is that if such a relationship does exist, it is far more complex than our account suggests. But a number of points are widely agreed.

1. If a Phillips curve relationship exists, it will only be valid in the short term. There is no unique long-term relationship between unemployment and inflation.
2. There are many possible different short-term Phillips curves; there will be a different short-term relationship for each particular level of expectations that the public holds about the future rate of inflation.
3. In many economies, it appears that the terms of the trade-off between inflation and unemployment worsened during the period after 1970; the Phillips curve shifted to the right, or it became less convex. These two possibilities are illustrated in Figure 14.14. As a consequence of this, the level of unemployment that is consistent in the long term with stable prices—what is sometimes called the 'natural rate of unemployment'—has become larger.

Each of these three points is discussed a little further in Box 14.2.

Supply-Side Policy

Economic policy of the 1980s and 1990s has tried to increase the output potential and output-responsiveness of the economy, in the process reducing its inflationary tendencies. This is often described as 'supply-side' policy. Any action which aims to improve the efficiency or dynamic responsiveness of a market can be called a supply-side policy. The term covers a variety of actions. These can be loosely classified into:

- those targeted at labour markets;
- those targeted at product markets;
- those directed at money and financial markets.

Interventions in labour markets aim to make labour more flexible and more mobile (both in geographical and occupational terms). They are also intended to make labour markets more competitive, by reducing monopolistic buying or selling power. Measures which have been used to seek these goals include trade union and industrial relations reforms, abolition of statutory wage or price controls, changes in housing tenure regulations, reductions in the cost of movement of location or type of employment, and the development of education and training programmes that provide transferable skills.

Many of the changes we have just listed will improve product market efficiency too. Additional measures that have been used or proposed include a wide variety of deregulation programmes, alterations to the tax and benefit systems to create appropriate patterns of incentives, and changes that reduce the cost or ease of entry into markets. In financial markets, deregulation has been seen as a way of increasing market efficiency, which will then reduce the costs of funds and attain a better match between the use of scarce funds and the expected return on the use of those funds.

Supply-side policy can be represented in terms of the various frameworks that we introduced previously. In Figure 14.16, panel (*a*) illustrates supply-side policy using the modified Keynesian model. Seen in this light, supply-side policy aims

Box 14.2 Phillips Curves and the Natural Rate of Unemployment

Since the time when Phillips wrote his classic paper, a consensus has emerged that an economy does not have one unique Phillips curve relationship. Rather, there is one separate relationship for each different level of expectations that the public holds about what the inflation rate will be in the immediate future. This notion is portrayed in Figure 14.15.

The following notation is used. The symbol $\dot{p}$ denotes the rate of inflation. $E(\dot{p})$ is the expected rate of inflation in the immediate future. Four Phillips curves are shown, corresponding to expected inflation rates of 10 per cent, 5 per cent, 0 per cent and −5 per cent respectively. We might regard 'the Phillips curve' referred to above as the one with zero expected inflation ($E(\dot{p}) = 0$). Notice that at an unemployment level of U^*, actual inflation is zero. But expected inflation is also zero, because the curve is constructed on that assumption. The unemployment level U^* is known as the natural rate of unemployment (NRU). This unemployment is regarded by economists as a long-term equilibrium rate for two reasons:

- the actual inflation rate is zero, and so there is no reason to implement macroeconomic policies to eliminate rising (or falling) prices;

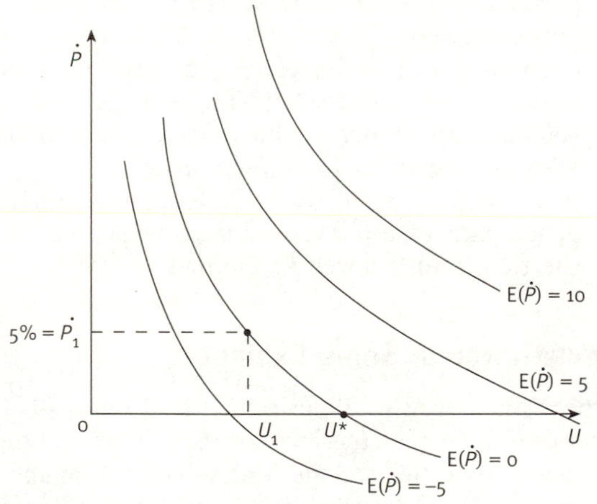

Figure 14.15 Expectations-augmented Phillips curves and the natural rate of unemployment

- the expected rate of inflation is equal to the actual rate of inflation (both zero) and so people's expectations are correct. There is no reason why expectations should be changed, therefore.

Many attempts have been made to estimate the NRU for various countries. One study (Cross *et al.*, 1996) estimates NRUs for 1990 as shown in Table 14.3.

Suppose that the government decided that the unemployment rate U^* is unacceptably high, and succeeds in reducing it to U_1. At this level of unemployment, the actual level of inflation will be, say, 5 per cent. The economy can no longer be on the Phillips curve labelled $E(\dot{p}) = 0$, as agents will revise their expectations into line with the actual level of inflation. The economy therefore moves onto the Phillips curve for which $E(\dot{p}) = 5$. Notice that on this curve, unemployment has to be much higher to bring about zero inflation.

It is often thought that the 1970s decade was one in which many economies were going through an inflationary process in which the relevant Phillips curve was 'moving to the right', as inflationary expectations were being continually revised upwards. Economic policy in the 1980s can be interpreted as attempting to force inflationary expectations downwards, in an attempt to get back on the Phillips curve at which $E(\dot{p}) = 0$, and to set an unemployment target at the NRU level, U^*.

Table 14.3 The NRU for a selection of countries

	NRU
USA	6.21
Japan	2.31
Germany	4.98
France	7.53
Great Britain	6.47
Italy	10.57

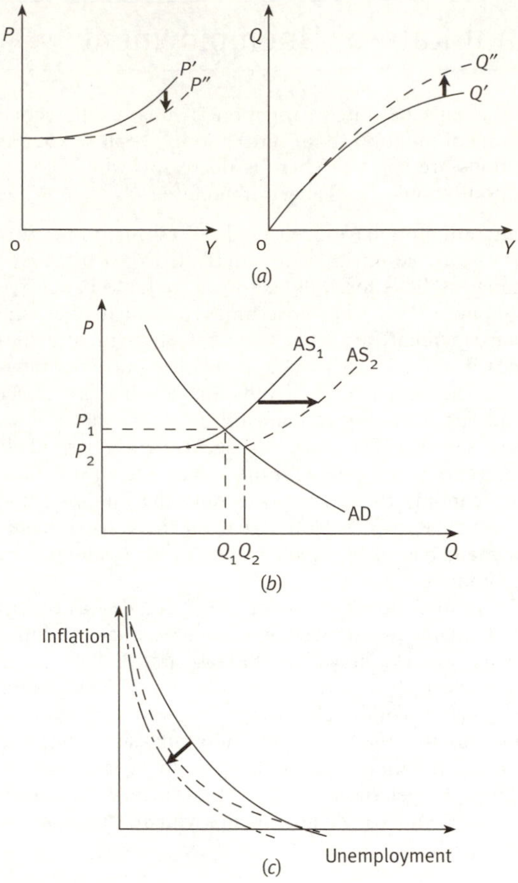

Figure 14.16 Supply-side macroeconomic policy

to increase the *Q/P* ratio at any level of aggregate expenditure. A similar interpretation can be put on supply-side policy when viewed in terms of AD and AS (see panel (*b*)). By shifting AS to the right, for any level of AD, *P* will be lower and *Q* higher. When viewed in terms of the Phillips curve (see panel (*c*)), the goal is to shift the Phillips curve to the left, or to increase its degree of convexity, so obtaining a better inflation/unemployment trade-off.

14.2 The Economy in the Long Term: Economic Growth

At the start of this chapter, we argued that the output of an economy typically shows an upward trend, even after the value of output has been adjusted to eliminate the effect of changes in the average level of prices over time. These rising trends constitute long-term economic growth. In this section, we shall examine in a more systematic way the recent growth experience of several economies, and consider the possible causes of economic growth.

Salient Features of Economic Growth

We begin by noting some of the dominant features of growth in the postwar years.

- Growth rates are typically positive, usually in the range 2–4 per cent per year.
- A 'Golden Age' of growth occurred in the period 1950–73. For many countries, this was a time of remarkably high growth.
- There have been some very rapid growth episodes in particular countries. This is particularly evident in Japan in the Golden Age, and Pacific Asia during the period after 1980.
- Some evidence suggests the existence of convergence or catching-up processes. Many individual examples can be cited. The Japanese economy was catching up to advanced industrial GDP per head levels through the period 1950–73. In 1957, income per head in Japan was only 13 per cent of the US level; by 1992 it had become approximately equal. More recently, many economies in the rest of Pacific Asia (including Malaysia, South Korea, and Taiwan) appear to be catching up to per capita output levels of the USA and Japan). China, now growing at over 9 per cent p.a., is clearly embarked on a convergence path to the levels of income per head of the rich industrialized economies.

Growth Rates: Some Examples

One simple way of describing the growth of an economy is to plot the level of its GDP over time. We have done this for the Malaysian and Japanese economies over the period 1970 to 1993 in Figure 14.17. It is important to ensure that changes in the value of GDP which arise purely from price level changes are not confused with economic growth. This is why we have used *constant price* (rather than current price) GDP data in all figures in this chapter. A constant price series for GDP values each component of output in each period in terms of the price levels that prevailed in one particular year—usually known as the base year.

To facilitate comparison of growth performance

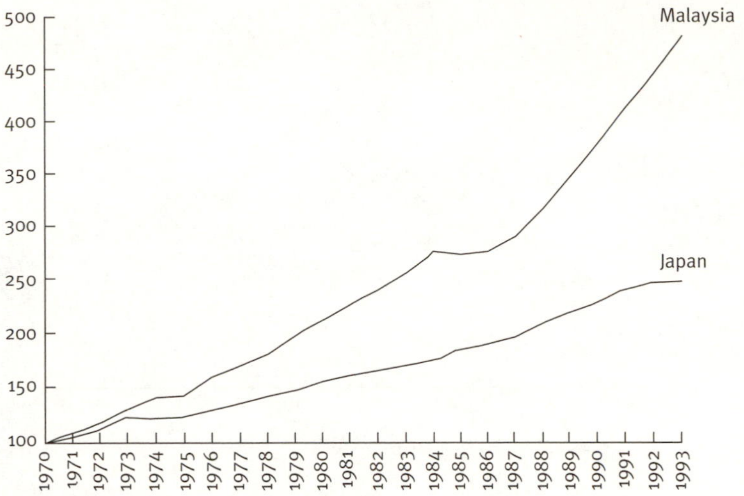

Figure 14.17 GDP: Malaysia and Japan, 1970–1993

of the two economies, it is useful to standardize GDP levels so that they are all equal to some given number at the start of the period in question. It was on this basis that we claimed earlier that Japan's growth was strongest from the group that included Australia, Japan, the UK, and the USA. However, Figure 14.17 shows that the trend increase of GDP in Malaysia has been even more impressive than that of Japan. The total 'amounts' of growth over the twenty-four years are easily compared in the figure. Japan's GDP increased by about 150 per cent over this period (from 100 to 250), whilst Malaysia's rose by nearly 400 per cent.

The UK has been one of the more slowly growing economies in recent years. We reproduce in Figure 14.18 a graph which shows the natural logarithm of GDP in the UK (rather than the level of GDP itself). You may recall from an earlier comment that the graph of the logarithm of a series has the useful property that its slope can be used directly to make inferences about the growth rate.[7] In particular,

- if the logarithm of the GDP series rises along a linear path, then the growth rate is constant. Moreover, the slope of the path is a measure of that growth rate, g;
- in contrast, if the logarithm of the series does not rise at a constant rate, then the growth is not constant. For example, if its rate of increase slows down over time, the growth rate is slowing down (and will be reflected in a smaller slope as one moves along the curve from left to right).

We suggested earlier that a straight line seems to be provide a reasonably good fit to the actual series. This suggests that the UK experienced constant growth over the period. But looking at Figure 14.18, we can find another plausible interpretation. This suggests that there was one more-or-less constant growth rate in the UK up to about 1980, but the growth rate has been rather slower since then.

It is not clear which of these interpretations is the better one, and we shall not attempt to draw any conclusion about which is more accurate. However, it is important to note that growth rates can, and probably do, change over time. It may be desirable not only to look at growth rates over long periods, but also over shorter periods (such as one decade) in order to try and identify any changes in the underlying trends. Figure 14.19 shows the average growth rates of the UK economy over three consecutive decades together with the period 1990 to 1993.

Growth rates do appear to have fallen over the period as a whole, albeit to a very small degree. The last four-year period may also be rather atypical,

[7] Let X be some variable of interest. Suppose that X_t denotes the value taken by the variable at time t, whilst X_{t-1} denotes its value one period earlier. The growth rate of X between periods t and $t-1$ can be measured by:

$$g_X = \frac{X_t - X_{t-1}}{X_{t-1}}.$$

For example, if X increased from 100 in 1990 to 110 in 1991, the growth rate of X between 1990 and 1991 would be:

$$\frac{110 - 100}{100} = 0.1.$$

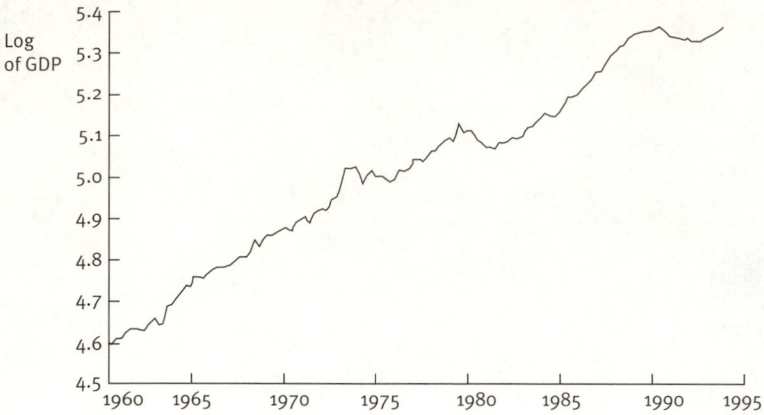

Figure 14.18 UK natural logarithm of constant price GDP

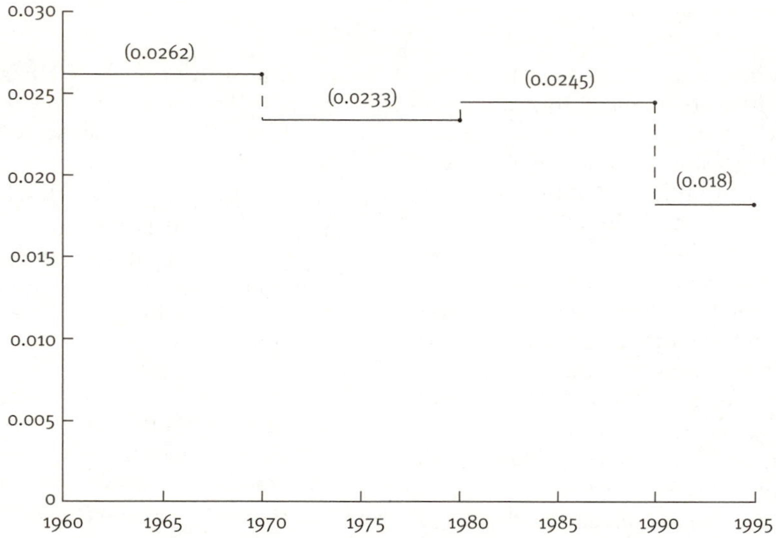

Figure 14.19 Average growth rates for the UK economy by decade

dominated as it was by years of a business cycle downturn. The UK growth rate has accelerated in the years after 1993 (not shown in the diagram).

The Forces Contributing to Economic Growth

There are two ways in which one might try and explain the process of economic growth. First, we might think about growth at the level of the individual firm. Much of this book has been concerned with the ways in which firms create value. If the firm adds increasingly large amounts of value through time, that firm is a growing firm. This suggests that an analysis of growth could be conducted by analysing how firms can add growing amounts of value through time.

But one can also approach the analysis of growth at the level of the economy as a whole—it can be regarded as a macroeconomic issue. This second approach is the one we shall concentrate upon in this chapter. However, it will become apparent that good explanations of growth need to take account of both macroeconomic conditions and also the motivations, capabilities, opportunities, and organization of individual firms.

A simple accounting identity is useful in understanding economic growth. The output of any economy can be decomposed in the following way:

output = productivity × hours × employment rate × participation rate × population.

Using symbols to express this decomposition, we have:

$$Q = \frac{Q}{H \times L} \times H \times \frac{L}{LF} \times \frac{LF}{POP} \times POP$$

where Q is total output, H is an average worker's hours, L is total employment, LF is the total labour force (those seeking employment or in employment), and POP is the population size.

This expression is useful by pointing to a number of possible sources of output growth. Output can grow if any term on the right-hand side of this expression grows. So output growth can arise from the following sources:

1. an increase in productivity, Q/HL. As HL is the total number of hours worked during some period of time by all employed persons, Q/HL is the average output per hour worked, a measure of the productivity of labour. We shall return in a moment to consider how labour productivity might grow;
2. an increase in the hours of employment of an average worker, H;
3. an increase in the employment rate, L/LF;
4. an increase in the participation rate of the population in the labour force, LF/POP;
5. an increase in population size, POP.

Some of these factors contribute to sustained economic growth more than others. Consider first the employment rate, L/LF. Output can increase if the employment rate rises. However, as L/LF is a proportion which cannot exceed one, it is not possible for increases in the employment rate to be a source of *sustained* economic growth.

The participation rate LF/POP is also a proportion which cannot exceed one. But it is quite possible that this proportion may initially be much lower than one, but become gradually higher over a very long period of time. Indeed, for many countries, the process of economic development has been associated with an increase in the proportion of the population who seek paid employment. The participation of women in labour markets has shown an increasing trend in many countries, and so may well be a contributory factor to growth over quite long periods. Nevertheless, there are bounds to how far this can proceed. Much the same is true of average hours worked. Although hours of employment do exhibit marked variation over time, hours worked per day cannot exceed twenty-four, and so cannot contribute to indefinite output growth.

We are left, therefore, with two components that contribute to sustained economic growth. First, population growth can continually augment the productive capacity of an economy. Population growth has accounted for a substantial part of the output growth in many economies. The second component is productivity improvements—that is, increases in the ratio Q/HL.

Increases in labour productivity can come about in a number of ways:

- as a result of innovation and technical progress. These open up new output and investment opportunities, and increase the economic efficiency of the conversion of inputs into outputs, thereby reducing average costs of production. They are therefore major contributors to productivity growth;
- capital accumulation. Additions to a firm's physical capital stock increase the amount of machinery per worker, thereby raising labour productivity. There may be limits to the extent to which capital accumulation can raise labour productivity. Our discussion of the law of diminishing marginal returns in Chapter 5 suggests that the increments to labour productivity arising from the use of more capital will, other things being equal, eventually fall to zero. But in practice other things will not remain constant. As new capital is built and installed, it will embody technical progress and incorporate recent innovations. Technical progress, innovation, and the accumulation of capital often go hand in hand, with the latter being the means by which innovations and new techniques become adopted. Two other beneficial effects of capital accumulation also warrant mention. First, if production is characterized by economies of scale, these may be achieved through the accumulation of capital. Secondly, the use of machinery releases labour for growth elsewhere in the economy;
- human capital growth: human capital refers to the quality of labour, its acquired expertise, developed through the processes of training and education;

- superior organisation of production, improving efficiency in the use of productive resources.

Empirical Estimates of the Causes of Growth

Many attempts have been made to estimate the contributions to economic growth arising from population growth, capital accumulation, and technical change. The most ambitious and comprehensive attempt is that of Maddison (1991). Let us examine briefly how he set about this. Suppose the economy's output, Q, is produced through the production function:

$$Q = Q(K, L, \Omega).$$

where K denotes the physical capital stock, L is the employed labour force, and Ω is an index denoting the state of technology. Output can change if any of these variables change. An expression for the change in output in terms of changes in one or more of these determinants is:

$$\Delta Q = \frac{\Delta Q}{\Delta K} \times \Delta K + \frac{\Delta Q}{\Delta L} \times \Delta L + \frac{\Delta Q}{\Delta \Omega} \times \Delta \Omega.$$

The *growth rate* of Q is not the change in Q (i.e. ΔQ) but the change in Q as a proportion of its original level (that is, $\Delta Q/Q$). So to obtain an expression for the growth rate of Q, we need to divide the previous equation by Q. This gives:

$$\frac{\Delta Q}{Q} = \frac{\frac{\Delta Q}{\Delta K} \times \Delta K}{Q} + \frac{\frac{\Delta Q}{\Delta L} \times \Delta L}{Q} + \frac{\frac{\Delta Q}{\Delta \Omega} \times \Delta \Omega}{Q}.$$

This states that the growth in output is equal to the sum of

1. the growth in output due to increased capital;
2. the growth in output due to increased labour;
3. the growth in output due to increased technology.

The left-hand side of this equation, the output growth rate, is empirically observable. Also the first two components on the right-hand side of the equation are (indirectly) observable. With measures of these three magnitudes, Maddison is able to identify the contributions of increases in capital and increases in labour to the observed growth of output. It is not possible to measure technology increases in any straightforward way, and so the contribution of technology to growth cannot be directly identified. However, if growth can only arise from more capital, more labour, or more technology, then the 'unexplained' part of growth can be attributed to technical change. The residual or unexplained component is obtained as follows:

the growth in output *less* the sum of the growth in output due to increased capital and the growth in output due to increased labour

and is interpreted as the growth in output due to increased technology. We present some of Maddison's results obtained in this way for the periods 1950–1973 and 1973–1987 in Table 14.4. What is striking about these results is the large contribution that appears to have been made by technical progress, particularly in the earlier of the two periods. Technical progress contributes up to 70 per cent of measured output growth. However, in many respects this is an unsatisfactory result. The part of growth attributed to technical change is best seen as a measure of our ignorance—it incorporates all those things that affect growth except increased uses of labour and capital.

Even if we were to regard technical progress as a distinctive entity, it is treated as being exogenous in this approach; technical progress just 'happens' and can be taken advantage of when it does. A better approach would treat technology as endogenous, that is dependent on the choices and behaviour of managers and other individuals. Modern theories of growth see technical change

Table 14.4 Sources of economic growth

	Capital	Labour	Technical progress	GDP growth
	(1)	(2)	(3)	(1)+(2)+(3)
1950–1973				
FRANCE	1.84	0.18	3.02	5.04
GERMANY	2.27	0.15	3.50	5.92
JAPAN	2.93	2.51	3.83	9.27
UK	1.75	0.01	1.27	3.03
USA	1.37	1.17	1.11	3.65
1973–1987				
FRANCE	1.48	−0.24	0.92	2.16
GERMANY	1.28	−0.49	1.01	1.80
JAPAN	2.29	0.66	0.78	3.73
UK	1.12	−0.19	0.82	1.75
USA	1.24	1.31	−0.04	2.51

Source: Derived from Maddison (1991).

as endogenous, dependent on the rates of investment in physical and human capital. This suggests another weakness of the findings reported in Table 14.4. Part of the contribution that is labelled 'technical progress' should be attributed to investment in human capital.

The factors we have looked at can 'account for' growth, but they do not necessarily represent an *explanation* of growth. In particular, we need more fundamental explanations of why some economies grow more quickly than others, and why growth is more rapid at some times than others.

The factors that might be included in a more fundamental explanation of growth include:

- the availability of funds for investment purposes (which will depend upon the nature of the economy's financial institutions, among other things);
- the extent to which an economy is involved in foreign trade, allowing it to overcome domestic resource shortages and open up new markets;
- the degree of competitiveness of an economy (which will reflect its productivity, price level, output quality, and its exchange rate);
- the institutional and economic structures that emerge after episodes of war and changes of political regime;
- the nature of the education and training structures of an economy;
- the extent of labour mobility;
- the proportions of labour working in the agricultural sector relative to that in manufacturing;
- general cultural, social and institutional characteristics of particular countries, and historically specific legacies.

The role of government can also be very important, particularly in so far as it provides supporting conditions for economic growth. Government can affect growth by the stance it takes towards maintaining buoyant demand conditions, so that firms can expect reasonable returns on investments. Its economic and social policies will shape the ways in which a country's health and educational systems evolve. And the patterns of incentives facing owners, workers, and managers will depend upon tax and social security regimes.

Growth at the Level of the Firm

Conventional economic theory places great emphasis on the role of competition in driving out inefficiency. In many models of the economy, it is assumed, either implicitly or explicitly, that all firms operate at full economic efficiency. In these circumstances, growth can only arise from greater quantities of inputs, or pure technical progress.

But suppose that many (or even most) firms do not operate at their theoretical optima at all points in time, or that newly developed techniques do not become uniformly and completely adopted immediately. This opens up possibilities for growth of a completely different kind. Moreover, these possibilities will be most widespread in a period of rapidly changing techniques.

This suggests that it is also fruitful to analyse growth in the framework that has been adopted through most of this book. Business activity is concerned with adding value. Economic growth depends on the desire and ability of those who manage firms to seize, exploit, and protect opportunities to add value. Growth is thus intrinsically about change, and about recognizing one's capacities and advantages, and seizing opportunities to add value as they arise. Seen in this light, the relevant questions that need to be addressed by analysts of growth are:

- what drives people and organizations to do these things;
- why are some organizations (and some countries) better at them?

Answers to these questions are, of course, extremely difficult to find. But in addition to the conditions we listed above, the following seem to be of importance:

- the economy's institutional structure and the incentive structures it generates;
- co-operation: the willingness of firms to co-operate and the inducements which exist to co-operate;
- the patterns of relationships of the business sector (and of individual firms) with government and the public sector.

Conclusions

Conditions of aggregate demand and aggregate supply determine the levels of a number of key economic variables—including the price level, national income, and unemployment—in the short term and medium term. These conditions are influenced by forces operating within a country, and also by external forces. Government may use its policy instruments—particularly fiscal and monetary policy—to influence these short and long-term economic conditions.

It is much less clear what determines the long-term growth of an economy. The accumulation of capital and the rate of technical progress seem to play important roles, but it also appears that more general structural conditions of the economy and the socio-cultural contexts within which economic activity takes place are of considerable importance. Of greatest importance, ultimately, may well be the patterns of incentives affecting economic behaviour, and the attitudes that individuals have towards working collectively to achieve common goals.

Further reading

There is a huge number of texts available giving extensive coverage of macroeconomic issues, at various levels of rigour and comprehensiveness. It is often the case that the best sources are to be found in general economics texts designed for first-year economics undergraduate programmes. Each of the following texts is excellent, being both comprehensive and relatively easy to follow:

Chrystal and Lipsey (1997), especially part II;

Parkin and King (1995), parts 6, 7, and 8 (each part of which is written by a leading authority in the field and contains a wealth of empirical illustration);

Mankiw (1992): a superb book, at a level which is a little more advanced than the previous two.

Central bank reports, such as the *Bank of England Quarterly Bulletin*, present up to date information and analyses of current issues relating to money and inflation. One can also get a good feel for macroeconomic issues, from a business perspective, by reading the *Financial Times* newspaper or *The Economist* or *Fortune* magazines.

Questions

14.1. Using Figure 14.6, use comparative static analysis (assuming *ceteris paribus*) to deduce the likely effects of:

(a) an increase in intended capital spending by firms;

(b) an increase in the savings ratio (out of disposable income);

(c) an increase in taxation on household incomes;

(d) an increase in the proportion of consumer goods bought from overseas.

14.2. In what circumstances would you expect there to be a large difference between an economy's GDP and its GNP?

14.3. Obtain a reasonably long data series for some economic indicator (such as unemployment or car sales). Try and identify the long-term and cyclical trends in the series. Does the series you have chosen contain a seasonal component as well?

14.4. Figure 14.4 portrays the circular flow of income and expenditure for an economy as a whole. Is there a counterpart for this at the level of an individual firm?

14.5. Explain what is meant by a multiplier effect. Can a multiplier effect occur when government spending increases in an economy operating at or near full employment?

14.6. Use the AD/AS model to predict the consequences on the price level and on output of

(i) an increase in wage rates;

(ii) an increase in labour productivity.

14.7. What is the difference between supply-side and demand-side economic policy? Why is it often claimed that supply-side policy is the better of the two?

14.8. How can the 'natural rate of unemployment' (NRU) be reduced? Is it possible to interpret any policies that are being pursued by the government at the moment as attempts to reduce the NRU?

14.9. Why do some countries grow faster than others over long periods of time?

15 Economic Forecasting

Introduction

Firms strive to create value in a business environment. Within this environment, variables such as consumers' disposable income, income growth rates, and wage rates have significant effects on the search for value. If managers were able to make or obtain good forecasts of these variables, this would be of considerable value to firms. Is it possible to make good forecasts? If it is possible, how can managers obtain them? These are the questions that we try to answer in this chapter. Our approach will be non-technical. Managers will not in general find it appropriate to undertake forecasting themselves; specialists will be better suited to that activity. But it is important that the users of forecasts—business managers—should know

- from where forecasts can be obtained;
- how economic forecasts are generated;
- how much trust can be placed in them.

We shall concentrate our discussion on forecasting aggregate level variables, such as the level or growth of gross domestic product (GDP) and consumers' income. Aggregate level variables are particularly important, reflecting as they do the 'state of health' of the economy as a whole. However, there is no reason why the techniques we discuss cannot be applied much more broadly. They can be used for forecasting almost any economic or business variable.

It will be useful to distinguish between three time horizons for forecasting: the short term, the medium term, and the long term. At the level of the economy as a whole, short-term changes arise predominantly from random shocks, which are largely unforecastable. Our discussion of forecasting concentrates on the medium and longer-term horizons where systematic patterns are more likely to be evident. Identifying these patterns and extrapolating them forward in time is one of the main methods by which forecasts are made. However, as we shall see, it is by no means the only method that can be used.

No 'golden rules' of forecasting will be presented. Prediction of any form of human activity is inherently uncertain, and economic activity is no exception. However, forecasting has become an industry, and can claim a reasonably good track record. We aim to acquaint you with the techniques available, paying attention to methods which are relatively simple. Suggestions for reading at the end of the chapter point you to sources of additional information.

15.1 Econometric and Time Series Forecasting Techniques

Approaches to Forecasting

Let us start by reviewing the main approaches available to the economic forecaster. The basic menu of techniques is shown in Figure 15.1. Three general classes of technique are available:

- econometric (behavioural) models;

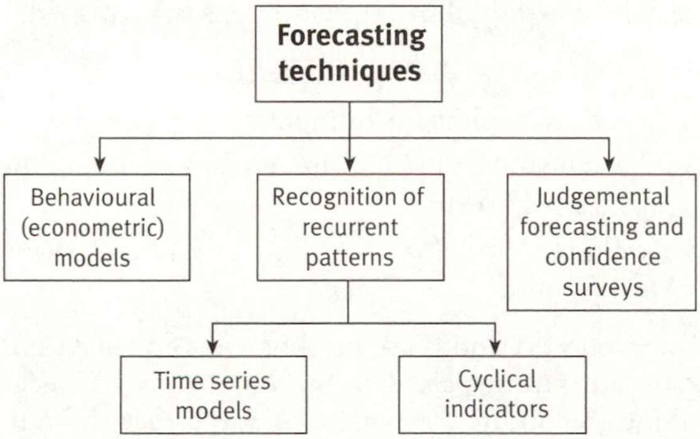

Figure 15.1 Forecasting techniques

- recognition of repeating patterns;
- judgemental forecasting.

Econometric Models

An econometric model is a statistical representation of one or more economic relationships among a set of variables. These relationships derive from economic theory which posits that a variable of interest is determined by (or 'caused by') one or more other variables. More complex models consist of systems of multiple relationships among sets of variables. We restrict attention to the case of a single relationship.

Suppose that the inflation rate, *INF*, is determined by the rate of growth of the money supply, ΔM. This could be written as

$$INF = f(\Delta M)$$

which just asserts that inflation depends in some way upon money growth. If the relationship is linear, the function can be written as

$$INF = \alpha + \beta \Delta M.$$

This is a determinist relationship among the two variables *INF* and ΔM. For any given value of ΔM, there will be a unique value that *INF* will take with certainty. An econometric model, however, also includes a second component. This component derives from the recognition that variables of interest are partly determined by random processes. Thus, if u denotes a random variable (a variable whose outcome is determined by a chance process), then we might write the econometric model as:

$$INF_t = \alpha + \beta \Delta M_t + u_t$$

where the subscript t denotes a particular time period.

One could forecast future values of INF with certainty if the following conditions are satisfied:

1. the economic theory is correct;
2. α and β are known numbers;
3. the value taken by u in the relevant period in the future is known;
4. we know the value of ΔM in the relevant period in the future.

In practice, α and β are not known, and have to be estimated from past data by some statistical technique. Secondly, the particular value that the random variable u will take in any future period is not known—the best one can do is to assign probabilities to particular outcomes (or ranges of outcomes). Thirdly, it will rarely be true that we know the value that the explanatory variable will take in the forecast period. To proceed, it will be necessary to make some assumptions about what it will be, or to deduce its value in some other way.

Finally, there is no guarantee that the economic theory we use as the basis of the econometric model is actually correct. In many areas of activity, economics provides a variety of explanations, some of which may be contradictions of others. In the profession of economics, as well as in business life, nothing is certain!

Despite all these difficulties, econometric models can be used for forecasting. Techniques exist that allow α and β to be estimated with calculable degrees of precision; we can assign probabilities to particular outcomes taken by the random variable; and it is often possible to make good inferences about future values of the explanatory variables. All of this implies that econometric forecasting can, *in certain circumstances*, yield useful forecasts that can be reasonably accurate, and whose margins of error can be established. Moreover, in situations where government intervenes, or some major change of 'regime' occurs (such as moving from fixed to floating exchange rates, or entering into a monetary union), an econometric model may be the *only* way in which predictions can be made. In such situations, past behaviour will be a poor indicator of the future, and a basis in terms of economic theory is needed for any reasonable forecast.

Econometric models are the most technically difficult method of forecasting and require the largest amount of information. A serious limitation of simple econometric models is that they typically require knowledge of the future values of some explanatory variables; these values are often obtained from time series modelling techniques (see below).

In most countries, the central bank, the treasury, and other government departments use econometric models on a regular basis. Some of these forecasting models are huge and complex. The UK Treasury macroeconomic forecasting model, for example, contains several hundred equations and requires a large staff to operate it. Econometric models are also widely used for forecasting by the academic community and many large commercial organizations, particularly those involved in financial markets.

Much of the output of this forecasting industry finds its way into the public domain, or is available relatively cheaply. The fruits of this econometric forecasting should, therefore, be included in the portfolio of forecasting information and techniques exploited by firms. Box 15.1 lists the major institutions undertaking regular macroeconomic forecasting in the UK.

Because of the extensive statistical techniques used in econometrics, we do not attempt to show the reader how to do econometric modelling and forecasting. The suggestions for Further Reading at the end of this chapter offer a number of references that you might wish to pursue.

Recognition of Repeating Patterns

A different approach to forecasting is possible whenever a variable exhibits a repeating pattern. In this case, it does not matter whether we know what causes the variable to change. All that matters is whether the pattern can be identified. If it can, then extrapolation techniques can generate forecasts of the variable. We can separate this class into two sub-categories:

- time series models;
- leading indicators.

Time series models are built upon the premise that the variable we seek to forecast contains identifiable patterns. Time series analysis does not try to 'explain' how a variable is determined: it is agnostic about cause and effect. All that matters is whether the past history of the variable of interest contains regularities that can be exploited for forecasting purposes.

We saw in Chapter 14 that these patterns or regularities might consist of three components: a trend, a cycle, and a short-term component. These can be represented by a mathematical model, the parameters of which can be estimated by statistical methods. Time series models have impressive fore-

Box 15.1 Macroeconomic Forecasting in the United Kingdom

Government or Official Forecasting

Bank of England
UK Treasury

International Organizations

OECD
EU
IMF
United Nations
World Bank

The Academic Community

Cambridge Econometrics
Cambridge Economic Policy Group
City University Business School
Liverpool University
London Business School
National Institute for Economic and Social Research
Warwick University Macro-Econometric Modelling Bureau

Treasury Model Users

The ITEM group (an independent group producing forecasts using the Treasury model)

Commercal Forecasting

Henley Centre
Oxford Economic Forecasting

The City

Consensus Economics Incorporated: for a wide variety of indicators on an international basis
CSFB
Goldman Sachs
Shearson Lehman
UBS Phillips and Drew
Most major financial institutions
Many large companies

Pressure Groups

Confederation of British Industry
Trades Union Congress

Regional Forecasts

Scottish, Welsh, and Northern Ireland Offices
Fraser of Allander Institute, University of Strathclyde

casting records, but can be daunting in their mathematical complexity. Once again, it is beyond our scope to describe and explain how time series models can be constructed and estimated. We shall restrict attention to one simple time series technique that can be used for forecasting long-term trends. For the reader who is interested in learning about and perhaps mastering time series techniques, a number of references are provided in the Further Reading section.

Leading indicators also exploit pattern recognition, and have the advantages of simplicity and ease of comprehension. They are widely used for forecasting, particularly in financial markets. As we shall concentrate on this technique in Section 15.2, an explanation of leading indicators is deferred until then.

Judgemental Forecasting

Forecasting is often done less rigorously than we have outlined so far. Just consider how people make informal predictions. We tend to use mixtures of hunches, intuition, general knowledge of market conditions and market expectations, liberally spiced with other 'outside' prognostications. Sources of information we might use for this come from the financial press, radio and television commentary, surveys of employers' intentions, and forecasts emanating from governmental agencies and independent organizations.

Forecasts formed in this way may not always be expressed in precise numerical forms. They are essentially eclectic (drawing on a variety of sources in ad hoc ways), and accord a large role to personal judgement. Hence our use of the description 'judgemental forecasting'. Such forecasts are often good ones, however. And they are likely to be better when predictions from professional forecasting organizations are explicitly incorporated. If something approaching a consensus of opinion can be extracted from professional forecasts, a judgemental forecaster would be well advised to give great weight to that consensus.

Forecasting Long-Term Trends using a Spreadsheet

Let us begin by investigating how a simple time series technique can be used to forecast a long-run trend. We show you how to do this using the spreadsheet package EXCEL, part of the Microsoft Office suite of programmes. Several other commonly available spreadsheet programmes could do this just as well.

The data in Appendix 15.1 consists of quarterly observations for the period 1960 Q1 to 1997 Q1 on United States GDP, measured in billions of US dollars. The series is in 'constant 1990 prices' form. This means that variations in GDP simply due to changes in the average price level have been extracted out of the series: each figure in the time series shows the level that US GDP would have taken in the quarter in question if the average price level had always been at its 1990 level.

Suppose that we wish to predict future values of US GDP. One way of doing this would be to plot the level of US GDP over time, look for the underlying trend, and then project that trend forwards in time. Clearly, this will only work if there *is* an underlying trend in the series. Figure 15.2 shows a plot of US GDP obtained using the Chart command in EXCEL.

Is there an underlying long-run trend in United States GDP? There does appear to be one. So let us proceed to see what it is. At this point, it is useful to remember a few elementary results from mathematics. If a variable grows over time at a *constant* rate, its level rises *exponentially*. This is what you would expect, for example, if a sum of money were saved in a fixed interest rate account, with interest being continuously compounded. However, if the variable grows at a constant rate, the *natural logarithm* of that variable rises *linearly* over time. This is illustrated and explained in Box 15.2.

Armed with this information, we can now calculate the trend in US GDP and use that estimated trend for forecasting. Box 15.3 takes you through the necessary steps to do this in EXCEL.

Figures 15.4 and 15.5 show the two charts obtained in this way. The first of these shows the plot of US GDP and the fitted exponential trend. The goodness of fit seems fairly high, with the trendline never drifting too far from the actual values of Y. It seems reasonable to argue, therefore, that there is a constant underlying trend. The growth rate parameter is 0.0068. The term x on the output corresponds to t in equation (15.1) in Box 15.2. So this equation tells us that US GDP was equal to $2,496.8 billion in 1960 Q1, and grew at a proportionate rate of 0.0068 per period (ie 0.68 per cent per period). As each period is one quarter of a year, this corresponds (roughly) to an annual growth rate of 4×0.68 per cent or 2.7 per cent.

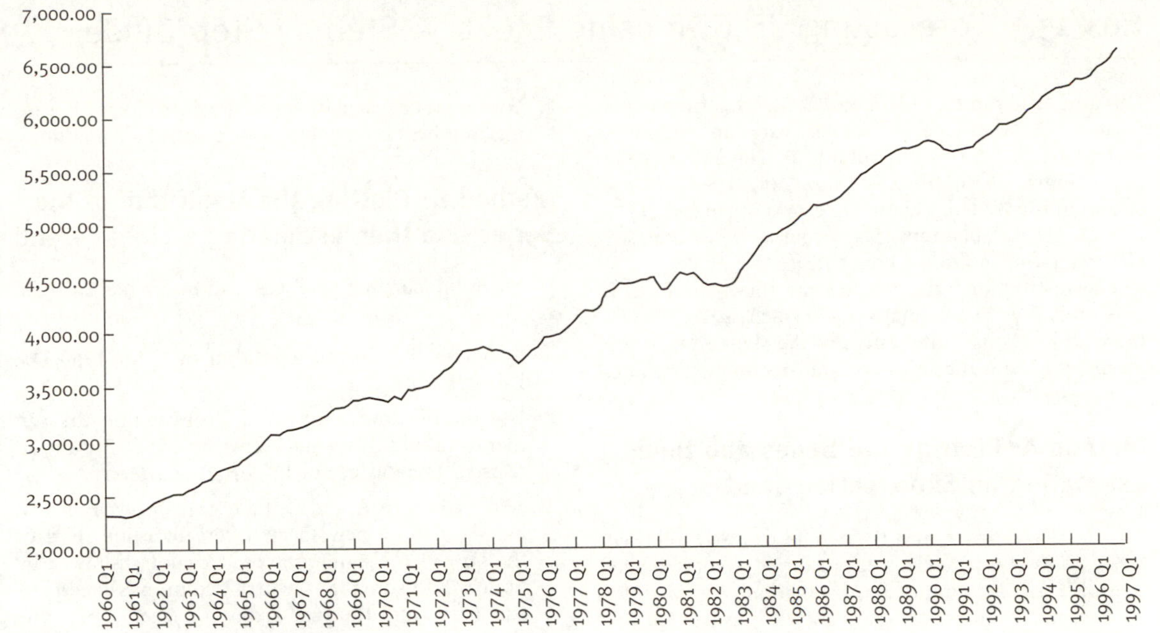

Figure 15.2 US GDP in \$1990 (billions)

Knowing that in the long run (ignoring trade cycle and seasonal effects and short-term fluctuations), US GDP gets 2.7 per cent larger per year, it is a simple matter to predict how large it will be at any point in the future.

Equation (15.1), you will remember, is:

$$Y_t = Y_0 e^{gt}. \qquad (15.1)$$

We have estimated this as

$$Y_t = 2496.8e^{0.0068t}$$

In this expression, t stands for the number of quarters after the initial period of 1960 Q1. 1997 Q1, the last period for which we know the value of US GDP, is 149 quarters after that initial period. So

Box 15.2 Constant Growth

Suppose a variable Y grows through time at a constant rate g. Then if Y_0 represents the initial value of Y (its value at some reference point in time) then its value t periods later is given by:

$$Y_t = Y_0 e^{gt}. \qquad (15.1)$$

If the value of Y_t is plotted for successively larger values of t, we obtain a graph similar to that shown in the left-hand panel of Figure 15.3. The magnitude of Y increases exponentially.

However, if we take natural logarithms of both sides of (15.1) we obtain:

$$\ln(Y_t) = \ln(Y_0 e^{gt}) = A + g_t \qquad (15.2)$$

where $A = \ln(Y_0)$ and $\ln(Y)$ denotes the natural logarithm of Y.

It is clear from equation (15.2) that the log of Y_t increases linearly with time, as shown in the right-hand panel of Figure 15.3.

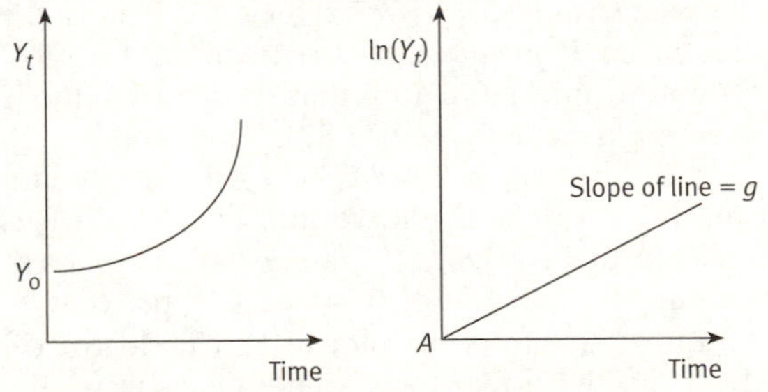

Figure 15.3 Representations of a constant growth rate

Box 15.3 Forecasting US GDP using EXCEL: A Step-by-Step Guide

I assume that you have data on US GDP loaded already in an EXCEL worksheet. Dates are listed in column A and values of US GDP in column B. The labels of the two columns of numbers—'Dates' and 'US GDP' are shown in row 1. This is how the data is organized in the EXCEL file in Appendix 15.1. Begin by relabelling US GDP as Y for notational convenience.

The instructions given below are those for EXCEL Version 5. If you use a later version (such as EXCEL 97), there will be small differences in the steps from those given below, but the steps are fundamentally the same.

Method A: Plotting the Series and then Estimating an Exponential Trend

1. Select columns A and B, then go to *insert* followed by *chart* (on a new sheet) to create a chart of the series Y. Use the *line chart* option, followed by option 2 in the chart types shown. Ensure that the 'first 1 column' is used for x axis labels and the 'first 1 row' is used for legend text. The plot will now appear on a new worksheet page.
2. Move the pointer to anywhere on the plotted line, and click the left mouse button. Then choose *insert*, followed by *trendline*, choosing the *exponential* trend type. Go into *options* and tick the box for *display equation on chart*. Also, choose the option to project the line 20 periods forward.
3. The resulting output shows the original plot, the exponential trendline, the equation of that trendline (which should be $y = 2496.8e^{0.0068x}$) and the 20–period forecast line.
4. You can then calculate forecast values either by reading numbers off the graph or using the equation.

Method B: Plotting the Logarithm of the Series and then Estimating a Linear Trend

1. Move the cursor to cell C2, and insert the formula: =ln(B2)
   to obtain the natural logarithm of Y for 1960 Q1. Label column C as 'LY'.
2. Use the fill-down command (from within the *edit* menu) to fill this formula down to cell D150, and so construct the values of LY for all quarters.
3. Select columns A and C, then go to *insert* followed by *Chart* (on a new sheet) to create a line chart of the series LY. Use the *line chart* option, followed by option 2. Ensure that the first 1 column is used for x axis labels and the first 1 row for legend text. The plot will now appear.
4. Move the pointer to anywhere on the plotted line, and click the left mouse button. Then choose *insert*, followed by *trendline*, choosing the linear trend type. Go into *options* and tick the box for *display equation on chart*. Also, choose the option to project the line 20 periods forward.
5. The resulting output shows the original plot, the linear trendline, the equation of that trendline (which should be: $y = 7.8227 + 0.0068x$) and the 20–period forecast line.
6. You can then calculate forecast values either by reading numbers off the graph or using the equation.

plugging t = 149 into this equation and solving, we obtain the value of $6,877.2 billion. (This is the value of GDP *predicted* by the trendline for 1997 Q1: note from Figure 15.4 that the actual value is lower—it is actually $6,635.87). After another 20 quarters (that is, in 2002 Q1), t will be 169 and using the formula again, we find that US GDP is predicted to be $7,879.10, larger than its current value by a proportion of 0.146 or 14.6 per cent.[1]

Figure 15.5 shows the plot of LY (the log of US GDP) and the fitted linear trend. Once again, the goodness of fit seems fairly good, with the trendline never drifting too far from the actual values of LY. The slope of the linear trend is 0.0068. This means that the series grows proportionately by 0.0068 per period, or by 0.68 per cent. Compounding this growth rate over 20 quarters, we find that US GDP will have risen by a proportion of 0.146 (14.6 per cent), the same value we obtained previously. It should not be surprising to find that the two estimates are identical. They are exactly equivalent ways of doing the same calculation. You can use whichever method you prefer.

One final point must be borne in mind. The GDP figures we have used were all expressed in 1990 price level terms. Any price level increase between 1990 and our forecast period is not taken into consideration in arriving at the forecast. Very

[1] Another way of finding out this proportionate increase is to calculate the value of $e^{(169 - 149)} = e^{20} = 1.146$. That is, US GDP increases by a factor of 1.146. This is another way of saying it has got larger by a proportion of 0.146 or 14.6 per cent.

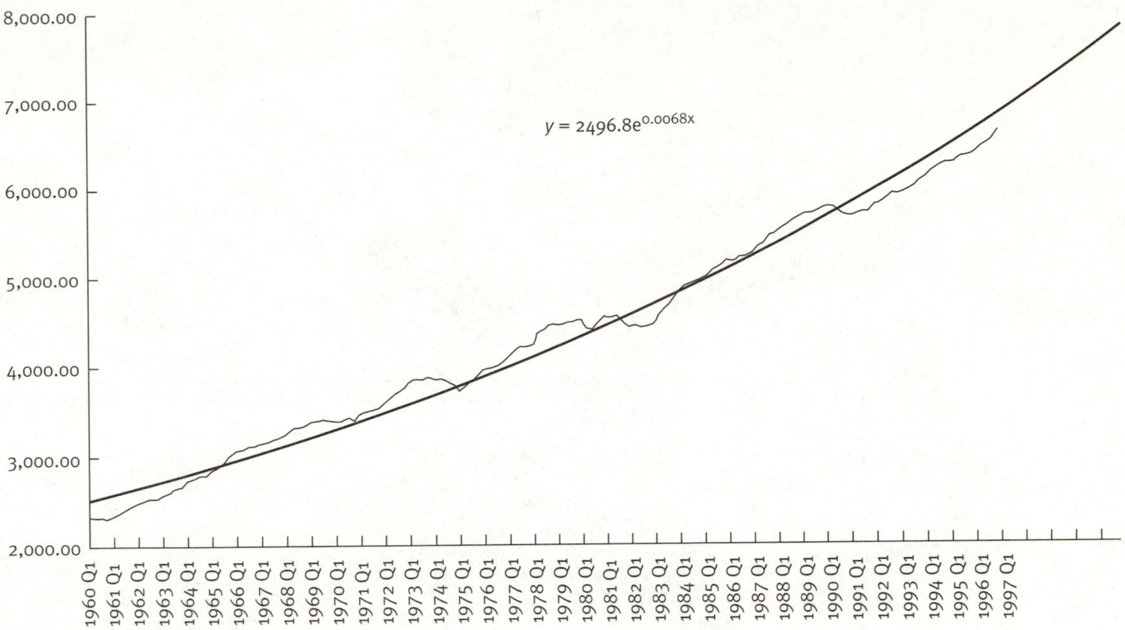

Figure 15.4 US GDP: a fitted exponential trend

often, this is the basis on which we do wish to get a forecast. Inflation could be taken into account, of course. One way would be to use a US GDP series in current prices, rather than constant 1990 prices. But that assumes that the inflation rate remains the same in the future as it has on average over the recent past, a rather bold assumption. A second method would be to obtain a separate forecast of inflation. But that is, of course, another story!

The example we have just been through was one in which the graph of the logarithm of GDP suggested a constant, underlying rate. But this will not always be true. Look, for example, at the graph of the logarithm of Japanese GDP over the period 1960–1997 in Figure 15.6(*a*). It would be quite wrong to claim that there is a constant GDP growth rate in Japan for the whole of this period. A more plausible inference would be the following: Japanese GDP grew at one underlying rate over the period from 1960 to 1973. Thereafter, it grew at a slower rate. This interpretation is shown in Figure 15.6(*b*). The graphical techniques we have examined in this section can still be used. However, the projection line used for forecasting should be based only on the period since 1973.

Some Concluding Comments on Forecasting using Time Trends

We have illustrated two methods of forecasting which operate by extrapolating a simple linear trend. These techniques can be used for predicting future values of trending variables, but should be used with caution. They assume that there is a constant growth trend over the whole period (or at least over some reasonably long period back into the past) and that this rate will continue into the future.

But matters may be more complicated than this. If the trend changes over time, then the appropriate trend to use in forecasting should be the current one. If we knew when the trend changed, then the average growth rate since that change could be calculated, and then used to extrapolate forwards in time. However, this begs the question of how such a change could be detected. At the very least, this is going to be very difficult. Moreover, if the trend is not constant, it casts doubts on whether any historically observed growth rate is appropriate for forecasting. Finally, if the trend rate of growth is constantly evolving, or the trend is non-linear, then the simple model we have illustrated here would not be an appropriate one to use.

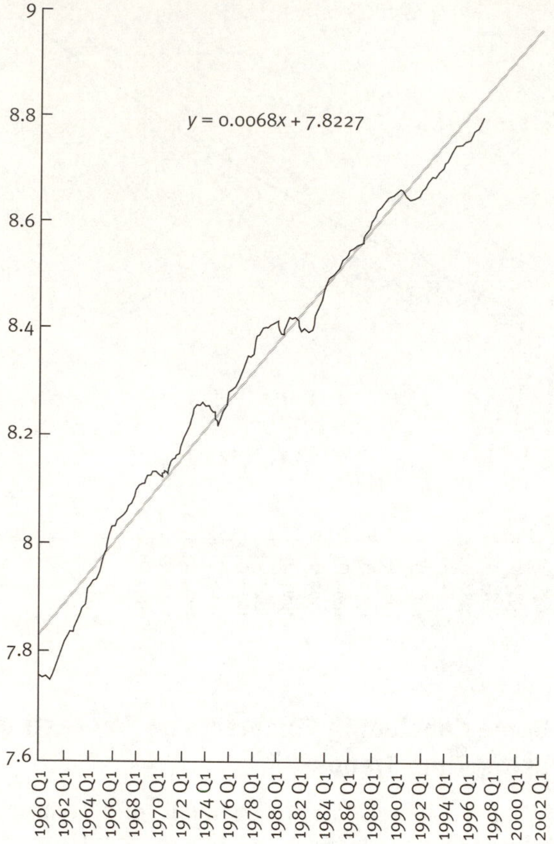

Figure 15.5 Logarithm of US GDP (1990 prices)

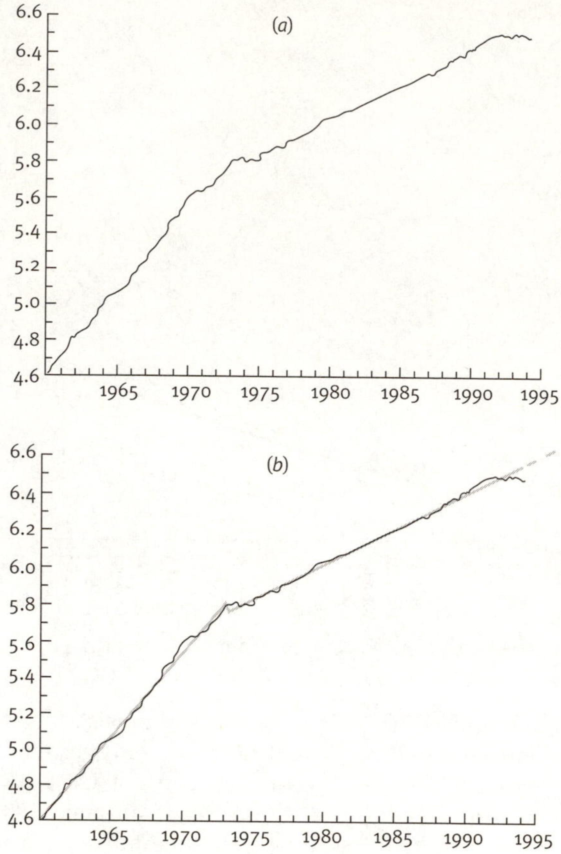

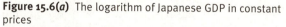

Figure 15.6(*a*) The logarithm of Japanese GDP in constant prices
(*b*) The logarithm of Japanese GDP in constant prices: actual and fitted values, assuming a change in the underlying growth rate during 1973

15.2 Forecasting Business Cycles

In most industrialized economies, aggregate economic activity tends to exhibit repeated medium-term fluctuations. These fluctuations are generally known as business cycles. A very early, but still useful statement of the nature of business cycles was given by Arthur Burns and Wesley Mitchell (1938):

> Business cycles are a type of fluctuation found in the aggregate economic activity of nations that organise their work mainly in business enterprises: a cycle consists of expansions occurring at about the same time in many economic activities, followed by similarly general recessions, contractions and revivals which merge into the expansion path of the next cycle; this sequence of changes is recurrent but not periodic; in duration business cycles vary from more than one year to ten or twelve years; they are not divisible into shorter cycles of similar characteristics with amplitudes approximating their own.

A stylized representation of the cyclical behaviour of GDP is shown in Figure 15.7. The smooth line labelled *trend output* denotes the underlying long-term path of GDP. For simplicity, we have assumed a constant underlying growth rate, and so the level of GDP rises along an exponential path.

Leaving aside short-term random fluctuations and the effects of government interventions, the actual path of output over time tends to exhibit cyclical behaviour about its long-term trend, with the economy passing through a series of phases. Let us begin by looking at the point labelled *A*, an

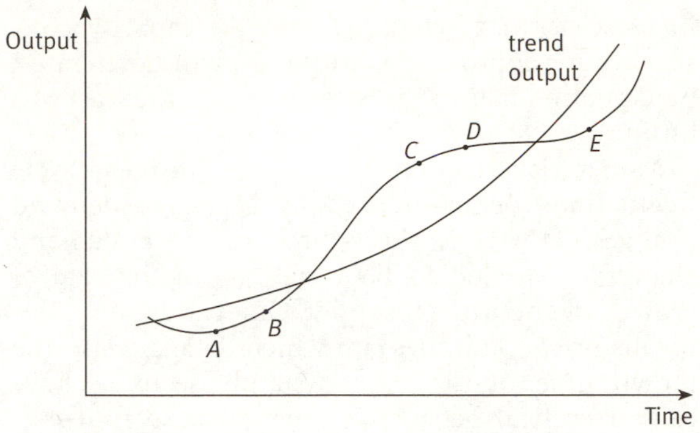

Figure 15.7 The business cycle

economic *slump* or *trough*. Here output is substantially below its trend level. With the passage of time, the economy enters a recovery phase or upswing (going through a point such as *B*) during which output rises towards and then passes beyond its trend level. The economic boom or peak is characterized by output attaining its greatest distance above the trend, after which the economy enters a downturn or recession phase.[2] Point *D* lies in such a downturn; the recession then deepens until another slump is reached at *E*.

This description is rather stylized, and it would be hard to find any economy passing through a cycle of such simplicity. One reason for the difficulty in identifying business cycles is that they are imposed on top of long-term growth processes. As a result, the downswing part of the cycle may not be associated with any absolute fall in output; instead, it will often only be apparent as a reduced rate of short-term increase in GDP. Another reason for this difficulty lies in the difficulty of separating short-term irregular movements—what economists call shocks—from the regular cyclical behaviour. Nevertheless, we can detect something approximating this form of business cycle in most market economies. Indeed, if you look back to Figure 15.4, it will be evident in the behaviour of US GDP.

But what is of paramount importance is that business cycles are repetitive: output evolves through time along a continuous cyclical path. It is precisely this repetitive behaviour of the business cycle that offers the possibility of forecasting medium-term changes in the economy. What makes forecasting such a hazardous and uncertain business (and potentially so very profitable to good forecasters) is the fact that the pattern does not repeat itself *precisely*. The lengths of time between successive peaks and troughs vary from cycle to cycle, as do the amplitudes of the divergences between cyclical output and trend output.

The existence of business cycles is detectable in many market economies. Figure 15.8 shows the variations of GDP about its long-run trend for the UK, USA, and Japanese economies.[3] In the UK, trade cycle peaks occurred in 1973 Q1, 1979 Q1, and 1988 Q3; the deepest points of recessions occurred in 1975 Q2, 1982 Q3, and 1992 Q3. Other, less pronounced, peaks and troughs are also evident for the UK. Cyclical behaviour of output is also clearly evident in the US GDP.

Why do Business Cycles Occur?

There is no consensus explanation of business cycles. Economists have proposed a variety of explanations, each of which is plausible and consistent with some of the observed characteristics of business cycles. It is not appropriate in this text to take you through these alternative theories in depth. It will suffice to outline some of them. Suggestions for further reading are provided at the end of this chapter.

Keynesian economists have conventionally given explanations centred around the behaviour of aggregate demand. They focus on the ways in which the multiplier and accelerator mechanisms generate cyclical fluctuations in aggregate demand. What is important in this explanation is the accelerator mechanism, which links investment decisions to output changes. For investment to remain at constant positive levels, output has to

[2] The term 'recession' is used in a variety of ways. In the UK, for example, it is conventional to define an economy as being in recession when there have been at least two successive quarterly declines in real GDP. Another usage is illustrated by the following description: '[A *recession is*] a persistent and pervasive contraction in overall economic activity' (National Bureau of Economic Research). In this book, we use the term recession to mean a particular stage of a business cycle. It does not necessarily imply either of the previous two meanings.

[3] We obtained these graphs in the following ways. Time trends for the logarithm of GDP were obtained (using the method of Ordinary Least Squares). These time trends were then subtracted from the actual values. The residuals left (actual minus fitted values) are what are shown in the three diagrams. They show, therefore, variations about the (estimated) long-term trends.

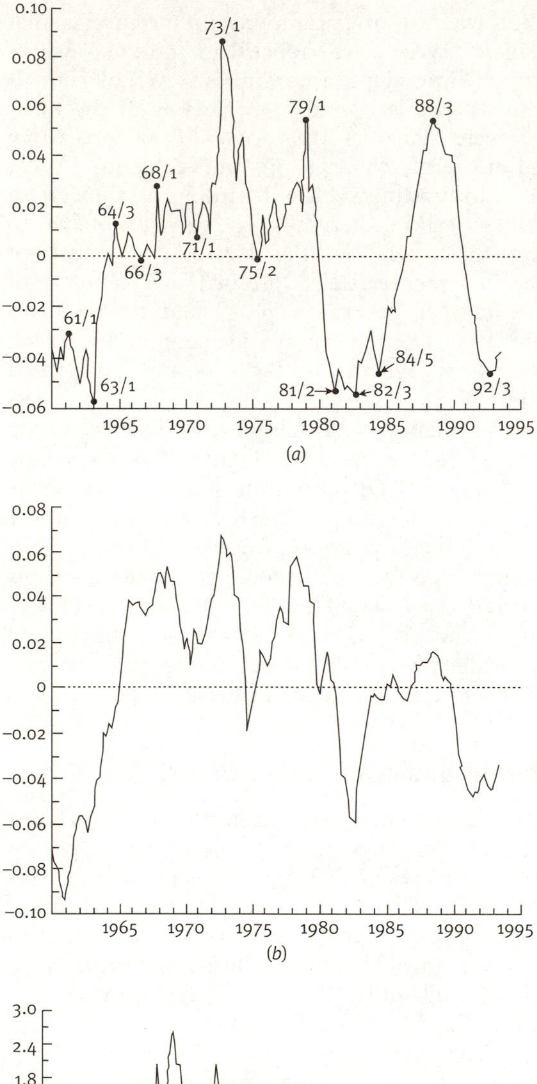

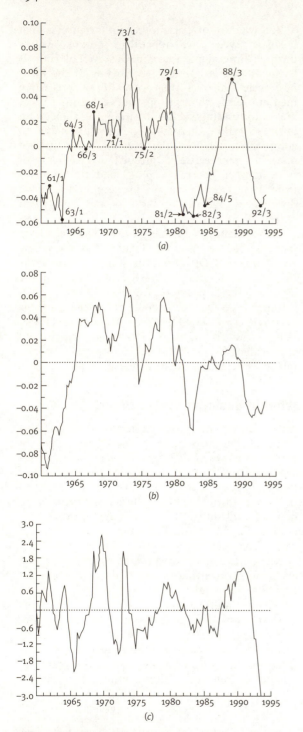

Figure 15.8 The business cycle: UK, USA, and Japan
(a) The UK business cycle
(b) The US business cycle
(c) De-trended Japanese GDP

increase at an accelerating rate. As capacity constraints are approached, output growth decelerates, precipitating falls in investment and so the start of a business cycle downturn.

Monetarist economists also see business cycle fluctuations being induced by aggregate demand changes. However, the source of these demand changes is argued to be variations in the rate of growth of the money supply. One can easily point to historical episodes in which changes in the growth rate of the money supply seem to have caused cyclical behaviour. One can also find evidence consistent with the view that turning-points in the business cycle have been precipitated by sudden money supply changes. For example, the start of the Great Depression in the USA is sometimes attributed to excessive monetary contraction. What is more difficult is giving a convincing account of the repetitive nature of trade cycles in this way.

The equilibrium theory of the business cycle sees cycles as reflecting short-term variations in potential output. These variations are due to expectational errors. Economic actors use indicators to form expectations about the future. From time to time, the indicators provide misleading information; agents then form inappropriate expectations, which in turn change potential output levels. In contrast to Keynesian theory, there is no rationale for aggregate demand-based stabilization policy by government. Policy should be based on clearly stated and strictly followed rules, to minimize the prospects of expectational errors being made.

Real business cycle theory points to the role played by random shocks on the demand and supply sides of the economy. These can initiate sequences of adjustments that lead to sustained upswings and downswings in activity. More importantly, real business cycle theory maintains that random shocks have permanent effects, changing the trend rate of growth itself. If this is correct, it undermines one of the major assumptions used in this chapter—namely, that there is a smoothly evolving long-term trend, unaffected by the cyclical variation of the economy around it.

Finally, some recent explanations centre on the idea of political business cycles. Suppose that government policy is not motivated by the goal of maximizing social welfare, but rather is designed to maximize the political advantage of whichever party happens to enjoy current political

Table 15.1 Business cycle theories

Cause	Appropriate government policy
Keynesian theory Fluctuations in aggregate demand	Demand management policy, maintaining demand at appropriate levels using tax, spending, and monetary changes
Monetary theory Erratic monetary growth	Constant, stable, and predictable growth of the money supply
Equilibrium theory Short-term variations in potential output and expectational errors	No action necessary or desirable, other than firm adherence to announced rules
Real business cycle Random shocks on the demand or supply side of the economy	Stable and predictable economic policy
Political business cycle Partisan self-interest	Reduce scope for partisan behaviour to be electorally rewarded

power.[4] Without setting out the arguments, suffice it to say that the assumption of partisan self-interest in economies with elected governments is sufficient to generate business cycles of the kind we have been discussing in this chapter.

Is the business cycle disappearing? There are some reasons for believing that the magnitude of cyclical movements, and particularly the severity of recessions, have decreased in the period since the end of the Second World War. Furthermore, the duration of recessions may have declined as well. For example, post-1945 US recessions comprise only 20 per cent of the average cycle, compared with 48 per cent in previous years.

There are several reasons why we should expect these changes. First, in almost all economies, there has been an increase in the relative share of the service sector in the whole economy. Services appear to be less susceptible to business cycle movements. Secondly, government policy has explicitly been directed at 'smoothing out' the variability of output around its long-term trend. This has been done largely through demand-management policy, as we explained in Chapter 14.

[4] Perish the thought, some might say. Others may wonder why there is any doubt about the veracity of this supposition! Whatever its merits might be, economists have given this view relatively little attention. This reflects how deeply rooted is the assumption in economic theory that the public sector attempts (not always successfully) to maximize social well-being.

The world economy has also had a more stable financial system in the years after the Second World War. The volume of trade has grown enormously, and business management techniques (such as inventory control) have improved. Each of these may also have contributed to less volatility in economic activity levels.

But it is far from certain that business cycles are of declining importance. Fluctuations in the Western industrialized economies have been greater in the period since the early 1970s than in the 1950s and 1960s. The recession of the early 1980s was the most severe since 1945 in the UK. It is clearly prudent to expect that cyclical behaviour will continue to characterize economic activity for the foreseeable future.

Cyclical Indicators

A cyclical indicator is a statistic, the movements of which bear some stable relationship with the fluctuations in the business cycle. In this section, we deal with indicators that predict movements in the overall level of activity of the economy, as measured by its GDP. From now on this will be denoted as *the economy*. However, it should be noted that cyclical indicators can be used for predicting many variables of interest to business managers, not only the level of GDP itself.

The essence of cyclical indicators lies in the following two points:

1. the movements of the economy through time follow a repeated cyclical path (usually around a rising long-term trend);
2. some other variables share the same cyclical pattern, even though they may be out of phase with the business cycle itself.

Cyclical indicators are conventionally classified into three groups:

Leading indicators: whose phases *precede* those of the economy (the peak of a leading indicator comes before that of an economy's peak);

Coincident indicators: phases *coincide* with those of the economy (the peak of a leading indicator comes at the same time as that of an economy's peak);

Lagging indicators: phases *succeed* those of the economy (the peak of a leading indicator comes after that of an economy's peak).

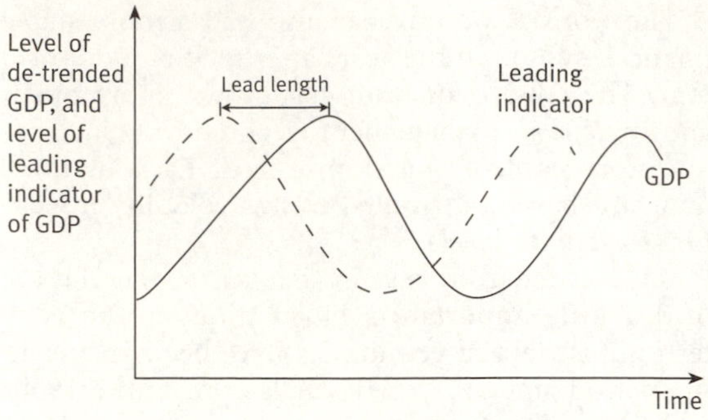

Figure 15.9 A leading indicator for GDP

We restrict attention to the case of leading indicators, as these are of most use for prediction. The nature of a leading indicator is illustrated in Figure 15.9 (in which the growth trend of GDP has been removed).

There are very many variables that could be used as cyclical indicators. Which of these will serve as good indicators of economic activity? The answer depends on how easy the variable is to obtain, and how reliable it is in its timing characteristics. An ideal indicator would satisfy a variety of conditions, such as those listed in Table 15.2. Those variables that are best at meeting these criteria are the ones selected as cyclical indicators.

Table 15.2 Criteria for selection of leading indicators

Relevance

- Economic significance: there should be an economic rationale for the observed relationship between the indicator and the reference series
- Breadth of coverage: indicators which cover a wide range of activities are preferred to more narrowly defined ones

Cyclical Behaviour

- Length and consistency of the lead of the indicator over the reference series at turning-points
- Cyclical conformity: a high degree of correlation between the indicator and the reference series is desirable
- Absence of extra or missing cycles in relation to reference series
- Smoothness: how promptly a cyclical turning-point can be distinguished from irregular movements

Practical Considerations

- Frequency of publication: high frequency of publication is preferred to low frequency
- Absence of excissive revisions after initial publication
- Timeliness of publication and accessibility
- Availability of long series with no breaks

Composite Indicators

Usually several variables can act as leading indicators. Rather than using one of these, a set of them can be amalgamated to form a composite indicator. This composite indicator will tend to have superior properties to any of its individual components for the following reasons:

- an individual indicator may sometimes give false signals due to its own irregular behaviour;
- all indicators will contain some individual idiosyncrasies and random variability. This implies that the use of an indicator for forecasting involves an element of risk or uncertainty. The reader will probably be aware of the principle that a diversified portfolio of individually risky assets will be less risky than a non-diversified portfolio. Similarly, the variance of a composite indicator (a measure of its riskiness as a predictor) will usually be lower than the variance of its individual components.

Forecasting Using Cyclical Indicators

If a good cyclical indicator can be found, its behaviour through time will closely match the cyclical behaviour of the whole economy. Furthermore, if that indicator is a leading indicator, its movements will precede in time the equivalent movements of the whole economy. This creates a basis for economic forecasting. Once we have identified the length of the lead time in question—on the basis of past experience—then observations of the current state of the leading indicator will serve as forecasts of the state of the economy that lead time ahead. In other words, current movements in the leading indicator predict the emerging stages of the business cycle.

As we noted earlier, whilst business cycles are inherently repetitive, they are not necessarily periodic. That is, the length of time between successive peaks and troughs is not constant over time. This makes forecasting hazardous because there is no guarantee that changes in time between peaks and troughs will apply equally to GDP and its leading indicators. Furthermore, the amplitudes of cyclical variations—the magnitudes of the individual peaks and troughs—vary from cycle to cycle, and will not necessarily be matched by equal proportional changes in the values of indicators. As a result, it is too much to expect that leading indicators can

Table 15.3 UK cyclical indicators

Indicator	Indicator name	Median	Earliest	Latest
LONGER LEADING				
Composite longer leading indicator index, comprising:	DKBR	−13	−24	−6
Financial surplus/deficit of industrial and commercial companies, divided by the GDP deflator	DKDJ	−17	−33	12
CBI survey: change in optimism (% balance)	DKDK	−12	−37	−4
Three-month interest rate on prime bank bills (inverted)	DKDH	−14	−29	1
Total dwellings started, Great Britain	DKBW	−12	−43	5
Yield curve (inverted)	DKOD	−15	−33	2
SHORTER LEADING				
Composite shorter leading indicator, comprising:	DKBS	−5	−14	4
Change in consumer credit, divided by GDP deflator	DKHK	−6	−33	6
New car registrations	DKBY	−7	−26	7
CBI survey: new orders over past four months	DKDM	−7	−31	5
EC/Gallop survey: consumer confidence index	DKOF	−6	−25	4
FT Non-financials share index	DKDI	−8	−22	8

Notes: Last three columns refer to the median, earliest, and latest timing, in months of the indicator, relative to GDP; (−) denotes leads, (+) denotes lags.

give predictions about *magnitudes* of imminent GDP changes, nor about the precise *timing* of forthcoming stages in the business cycle. We have to be content with more modest objectives, or at least to recognize the large amounts of uncertainty in any leading-indicator prediction.

Conventionally, the use of leading indicators has leaned towards identifying turning-points in the business cycle—the points at which peaks turn into recessions, or at which recoveries begin. This type of information is extremely valuable in business planning, particularly with regard to investment and financial planning.

UK Leading Indicators

Most countries now publish cyclical indicators on a regular basis. In this section, we focus on the UK system of cyclical indicators. Table 15.3 lists the two categories of composite leading indicator compiled for the UK economy, and their component parts. The second column in the table gives the name attributed to each indicator by the UK Central Statistical Office. If you wish to find values of these indicators in official government publications, they will be listed under those names.

The three columns on the right-hand-side of the table show the timing properties of the respective indicators. For forecasting purposes, the median time of lead is used. It is obtained by calculating the lead time (in months) between each indicator peak and the following GDP peak. The lead times calculated in this way are then ordered in ascending order of lead time; the median lead is the central value of lead time.

The composite longer leading indicator precedes GDP peaks by thirteen months, with all of its five component parts leading by between twelve and seventeen months. However, the final two columns show that there are large variations from cycle to cycle in the lead time of any particular indicator. For example, changes in the CBI quarterly survey of changes in business optimism typically precede changes in GDP by one year. But in at least one case, the delay between a peak in this measure of business confidence and the following peak in GDP was over three years. By contrast, the smallest lead time was merely four months.

As business managers will usually want as much advance warning of changes as possible, the longer leading indicators are of great value, particularly when one realizes that there are often substantial delays between the time at which an indicator changes and the time when that information becomes published. The shorter leading indicators have median leads of around six months. Their usefulness lies in reinforcement of messages. If one forms an expectation of an imminent GDP fall on the basis of the behaviour of a longer leading indicator, and that expectation is subsequently reinforced by the behaviour of some shorter leading indicator, the expectation can be held with greater confidence.

Despite these rather encouraging assertions, one should be wary of placing too much reliance on leading indicators. Their performance in predicting the next boom or slump will inevitably be poorer than their ability to 'track' previous cycles. The reason for this lies in the fact that indicators have been selected precisely for their ability to mirror past (and so known) GDP movements; if they did not do this well they would not have been selected! It is much less likely that they will mirror as yet unknown changes so well. A second reason for caution lies in a point made several times above—cycles may be regular but they are not periodic (that is, they do not repeat at fixed, constant intervals of time. Finally, indicators can tell us little or nothing about the magnitude of the forthcoming peaks and troughs. It would be useful to know this, but leading indicators cannot give us this information.

Conclusions

Predicting future values of business and economic variables can be immensely valuable to businesses for tactical and strategic planning. There are a number of approaches available, differing in terms of their technical complexity. Some simple techniques are available that can be implemented easily using commonly available spreadsheet programmes, such as Microsoft EXCEL. Provided that historical patterns are broadly repeated in the future, these techniques can provide good forecasts of the future levels of variables of interest.

Forecasting is far more problematic where the future does not consist simply of an extrapolation of the past and present. In these cases, forecasting requires a behavioural or explanatory model, rather than merely time series techniques. In some senses, any good manager will have a more or less well-articulated, but usually informal, explanatory model of the relevant system in his or her mind. Econometric models formalize and codify this way of structuring the world around us, and so providing a strong foundation for prediction. But, unfortunately, they are very difficult to construct and operationalize. The best a manager can probably hope to do is to understand what econometric models are, and to use forecasts produced by specialist organizations.

Further reading

Good general accounts of economic and business forecasting are available in Holden *et al.* (1990), *Economic Forecasting: An Introduction*, and Keating (1985); *The Production and Use of Economic Forecasts.*

More advanced sources, discussing the techniques of econometric forecasting, include Hall (1994), *Applied Econometric Forecasting Techniques*, and Dicks and Burrell (1994), *Forecasting In Practice.*

An excellent account of time series forecasting is given in Enders (1995), *Applied Econometric Time Series.* Forecasting with cyclical indicators is discussed in Britton and Pain (1992), 'Economic Forecasting in Britain' (chapter 4), CSO (1993), Central Statistical Office, *Cyclical Indicators*, Central Statistical Office (1995), *Leading Indicators*, Stutely (1994), *The Economist Guide to Economic Indicators*, and Moore (1993), 'Review of CSO Cyclical Indicators'.

The political business cycle is analysed by Hibbs (1987), *The American Political Economy*, Minford and Peel (1982), 'The Political Theory of the Business Cycle', Nordhaus (1975), *The Political Business Cycle*, and Rogoff and Sibert (1988) 'Elections and Macroeconomic Policy Cycles'.

Questions

15.1. What factors are likely to affect the price of
(i) houses, and
(ii) air travel demand,
(*a*) in the short term and (*b*) in the long term?

15.2. Suppose you were asked to forecast UK gross domestic product for the next five years. How would you go about obtaining such a forecast?

15.3. What are the strengths and weaknesses of using cyclical indicators as a forecasting technique?

15.4. Why is it difficult to make good predictions of
(*a*) exchange rates,
(*b*) financial asset prices?

Appendix 15.1 Time series data for United States GDP

Date	US GDP
1960 Q1	2329.09
1960 Q2	2324.03
1960 Q3	2327.21
1960 Q4	2314.14
1961 Q1	2331.33
1961 Q2	2365.60
1961 Q3	2398.22
1961 Q4	2446.38
1962 Q1	2479.83
1962 Q2	2505.38
1962 Q3	2524.69
1962 Q4	2522.57
1963 Q1	2559.55
1963 Q2	2594.41
1963 Q3	2636.69
1963 Q4	2657.18
1964 Q1	2726.18
1964 Q2	2747.62
1964 Q3	2778.94
1964 Q4	2785.18
1965 Q1	2838.53
1965 Q2	2877.98
1965 Q3	2930.03
1965 Q4	3004.57
1966 Q1	3063.93
1966 Q2	3069.70
1966 Q3	3102.67
1966 Q4	3116.09
1967 Q1	3134.94
1967 Q2	3148.60
1967 Q3	3185.34
1967 Q4	3203.83
1968 Q1	3247.87
1968 Q2	3299.92
1968 Q3	3319.82
1968 Q4	3326.53
1969 Q1	3376.70
1969 Q2	3382.71
1969 Q3	3400.84
1969 Q4	3392.25
1970 Q1	3382.35
1970 Q2	3367.28
1970 Q3	3410.97
1970 Q4	3386.00
1971 Q1	3470.56
1971 Q2	3478.45
1971 Q3	3500.82
1971 Q4	3517.07
1972 Q1	3580.08
1972 Q2	3638.84
1972 Q3	3679.58
1972 Q4	3737.29
1973 Q1	3829.85
1973 Q2	3847.87
1973 Q3	3844.80
1973 Q4	3874.01
1974 Q1	3838.33
1974 Q2	3847.98
1974 Q3	3814.42
1974 Q4	3799.47
1975 Q1	3714.21
1975 Q2	3757.07
1975 Q3	3827.14
1975 Q4	3877.31
1976 Q1	3952.91
1976 Q2	3967.63
1976 Q3	3981.52
1976 Q4	4023.09
1977 Q1	4082.09
1977 Q2	4151.10
1977 Q3	4209.28
1977 Q4	4200.80
1978 Q1	4229.77
1978 Q2	4365.43
1978 Q3	4399.11
1978 Q4	4450.92
1979 Q1	4452.34
1979 Q2	4456.46
1979 Q3	4483.78
1979 Q4	4492.14
1980 Q1	4511.22
1980 Q2	4395.58
1980 Q3	4396.64
1980 Q4	4484.96
1981 Q1	4546.19
1981 Q2	4527.23
1981 Q3	4550.90
1981 Q4	4478.60
1982 Q1	4423.25
1982 Q2	4440.91
1982 Q3	4421.25
1982 Q4	4427.37
1983 Q1	4455.52
1983 Q2	4576.81
1983 Q3	4644.99
1983 Q4	4724.72
1984 Q1	4815.87
1984 Q2	4880.05
1984 Q3	4906.43
1984 Q4	4939.16
1985 Q1	4971.67
1985 Q2	5010.53
1985 Q3	5074.35
1985 Q4	5103.21
1986 Q1	5170.33
1986 Q2	5167.03
1986 Q3	5196.36
1986 Q4	5213.43
1987 Q1	5252.17
1987 Q2	5317.30
1987 Q3	5369.11
1987 Q4	5447.07
1988 Q1	5482.16
1988 Q2	5540.45
1988 Q3	5575.43
1988 Q4	5628.66
1989 Q1	5673.29
1989 Q2	5698.49
1989 Q3	5698.49
1989 Q4	5719.34
1990 Q1	5758.21
1990 Q2	5777.20
1990 Q3	5749.88
1990 Q4	5689.81
1991 Q1	5658.84
1991 Q2	5683.36
1991 Q3	5697.58
1991 Q4	5711.71
1992 Q1	5778.05
1992 Q2	5814.44
1992 Q3	5858.14
1992 Q4	5920.27
1993 Q1	5919.43
1993 Q2	5947.59
1993 Q3	5982.12
1993 Q4	6052.95
1994 Q1	6089.81
1994 Q2	6163.82
1994 Q3	6217.44
1994 Q4	6263.28
1995 Q1	6269.93
1995 Q2	6281.62
1995 Q3	6340.48
1995 Q4	6344.50
1996 Q1	6375.47
1996 Q2	6448.73
1996 Q3	6482.42
1996 Q4	6543.42
1997 Q1	6635.87

16 The Search for Value, International Trade, and Economic Performance

Introduction

National economies are highly interdependent. There are two principal ways in which this interdependence is manifested. First, economies are strongly affected by what happens elsewhere. This is evident in stock markets: collapses of confidence on Wall Street are quickly transmitted to other financial centres across the world. It can also be seen in interest rate behaviour: when interest rates rise in Germany, other European countries find it difficult to resist pressures to raise their own rates. Interdependence is perhaps most marked in the medium-term fluctuations of national income, the so-called business cycles. Changes in business circumstances in one part of the world spill over to other parts, leading to situations of recession or boom happening more or less simultaneously in many parts of the world economy.

The second way in which interdependence manifests itself is through the consequences of national economic decisions. Policy effectiveness is strongly conditioned by how policy impacts on other countries, and how they respond to those impacts. A clear example of this can be seen in the areas of monetary and fiscal policy: the room for manoeuvre available to one country is circumscribed by conditions elsewhere, and the ability of a government to reach its goals by the use of fiscal and monetary instruments is dependent on what others are doing at the same time. Exchange rate determination also shows this interdependence. If international money and foreign exchange markets do not find some country's target level for its exchange rate credible, there is little prospect of it being maintained. In this respect, the world economy is similar to an oligopolistic market: as we showed in Chapter 8, the pay-off to any one player's strategy depends on the strategies pursued by all other players in the game. When countries agonize about giving up their 'sovereignty' by becoming members of supra-national institutions (such as the European Union economic and monetary union), it is as well to recognize that genuine economic independence is not being given up; it did not exist in the first place!

But it is clear that economic interdependence does not only concern national economies: it also shows itself at the level of markets for particular goods or services. For most tradable goods and services, the prices of similar commodities are closely linked between countries. In such markets, firms in one country court disaster if they attempt to price their goods without taking account of international prices. Interdependence does not only limit price-setting autonomy. Knowledge and techniques tend to diffuse rather quickly, and consumer tastes and preferences are more closely integrated than they have been hitherto.

What is it that brings about this interdependence? To a large extent, it is the consequence of international trade and exchange—in goods, services, financial assets, and productive resources. Our first objective in this chapter is to describe the nature, extent, and significance of international trade and production. This will be the theme of the next section.

Section 16.1 elaborates on the theory of international trade and exchange that we first looked at in Chapter 1. International trade occurs because it brings about net benefits; that is, it adds value. In using economic theory to identify the source of this value, we make use of two principles that were introduced in the first chapter: opportunity costs and comparative advantage.

Because international trade takes place between different countries, it (usually) involves more than one currency. The rate of exchange of one currency for another is, of course, a price. And like all prices, an exchange rate can change, even in a world where exchange rates are supposedly fixed (as they were said to be for much of the period after the Second World War). Like all prices, they cannot be predicted with certainty. Most trade and exchange involves certain kinds of risk. But exchange rate uncertainty means that international trade has an additional risk, and so an additional cost, compared with domestic trade. Currency conversion and the administrative procedures that tend to be associated with movements of goods and services across borders generate transactions costs (see Chapter 4) that reduce the volume of trade. So there are potential benefits from reducing exchange rate variability, perhaps by increasing the degree of economic integration between economies. We investigate the potential benefits (and the potential costs) of international economic integration in Section 16.2.

Our orientation in Section 16.3 is rather different. We focus on the individual firm and the markets in which it operates. Then we discuss international production, the phenomenon of multinational companies, and the firm's search for value in an international market environment. The trend towards internationalization of firms' productive activity is the second principal cause of the economic interdependence that we noted at the start of this introduction. Our previous discussions of diversification, mergers and acquisitions, and transactional difficulties prove to be fruitful ways of understanding international production. We also consider some other phenomena that have attracted much recent interest in business management writing: networks and alliances, and the globalization of economic activity.

16.1 International Trade and the Creation of value

Let us consider the following characteristics—what might be called the 'stylised facts'—of international trade.

- The volume of world trade, measured both in absolute terms and relative to world output levels, has been growing, and continues to do so.
- For most individual economies, the volume of trade with the rest of the world has been rising over time and continues to do so, both in absolute and relative terms.
- An increasing proportion of total trade flows between countries involves manufactured goods, as opposed to trade in primary products such as food and commodities.
- Although much trade in earlier periods was between countries with very different patterns of resources, the most intense and rapidly expanding trade is now among countries with similar patterns of endowment of productive resources.
- Large quantities of similar products are exchanged between national economies. Trading in similar goods is becoming of greater importance than trading in dissimilar goods. For example, a substantial proportion of trade between European Union (EU) countries involves exchange of motor vehicles.

Figure 16.1 shows the value of merchandise (goods and commodities, but not services) exports as a proportion of gross domestic product (GDP) for nine countries over the period since 1870. This statistic is often regarded as an index of the degree of openness of an economy to international trade. Three phases are evident in the behaviour of this index over time. The years after 1870 until the outbreak of the First World War (1914) were generally characterized by high and growing international trade. There were exceptions of course: in our sample of countries, for instance, Argentina and Brazil both had trade falling as a proportion of GDP.

During the interwar years, through the Second World War, and up to 1950, the intensity of world trade slumped dramatically in most countries. Between the two world wars, a collapse of the world economy took place, with trade taking place largely within (but not between) closed regional blocs. The major economies became much less open, many introducing restrictive barriers to the import of goods. Figure 16.1 suggests that Japan was an exception to this general picture. However, if another index of openness is constructed, defined as the ratio of the sum of exports and imports to

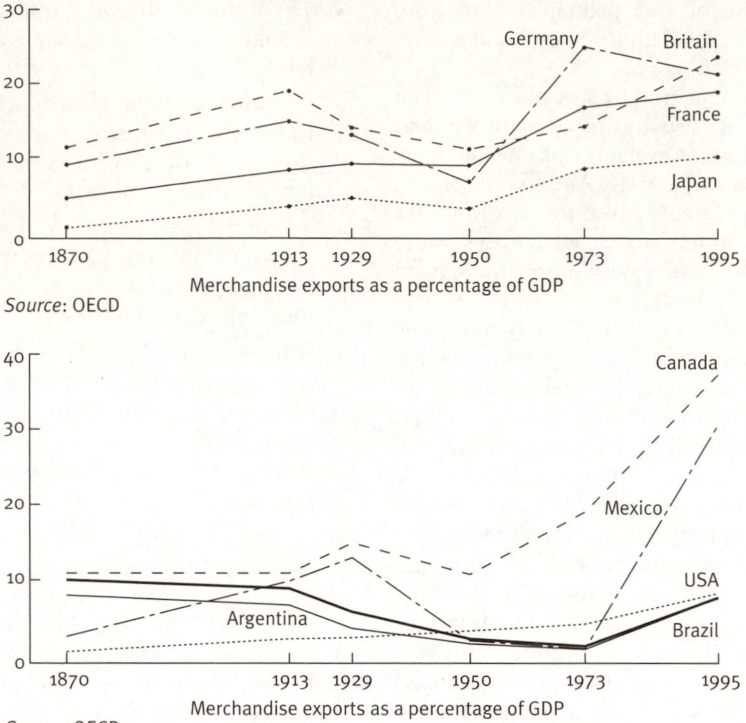

Source: OECD

Figure 16.1 Merchandise exports as a percentage of GDP

GDP, we see that Japan also exhibited falling trade intensity over that period. The collapse of the Mexican trade to output ratio began later than others but once started was very pronounced.

The third phase begins after 1950, typified by rapid growth in trade intensity as formal and informal barriers to trade were steadily dismantled. The rise in export values as a proportion of total output for the world economy as a whole in the phase after 1950 is clearly shown in Figure 16.2. Indeed, the final four-year period (in which large parts of the world economy were in recession) had strong export growth despite there being little change in world output.

Table 16.1, giving data for each OECD member country, shows the importance of manufactured goods in international trade. Columns *B* and *E* show manufactured goods as proportions of exports and imports in 1992. The first seven countries listed are the G7 group of leading industrial nations. For the European Union countries (final row), these proportions were 83.2 per cent and 76.5 per cent respectively. Table 16.1 also shows that manufactured goods are taking a rising share of foreign trade; in each of the OECD countries, manufacturing imports grew more quickly than total imports over the decade 1982–92. Manufacturing exports grew faster than total exports in all OECD economies except Iceland and Japan.

Evidence illustrating the last two of our five stylized facts will be presented later in the chapter.

The Theory of Comparative Advantage

Why does international trade occur? Because trade is a voluntary activity, it will take place only if it confers net benefits on the parties concerned. International trade takes place because it adds value. However this does not mean that all will benefit *equally* from it. Nor does it mean that those affected by trade, but not party to it, necessarily benefit.

The potential benefits of trade were clearly articulated by Adam Smith, as is clear from this excerpt from *The Wealth of Nations*, first published in 1776:

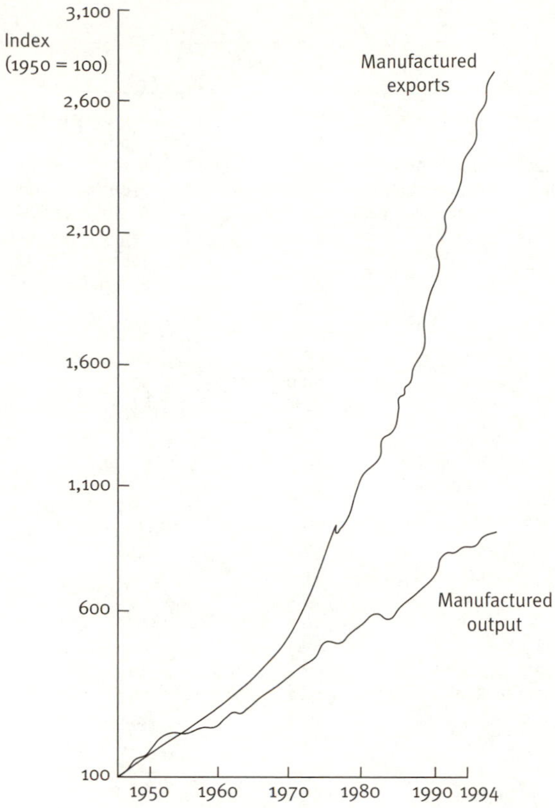

Figure 16.2 The growth of world output and exports of manufactured goods

> It is the maxim of every prudent master of a family, never to attempt to make at home what it will cost him more to make than to buy. The taylor does not attempt to make his own shoes, but buys them of the shoemaker. The shoemaker does not attempt to make his own clothes, but employs a taylor . . .
>
> What is prudence in the conduct of every private family, can scarce be folly in that of a great kingdom. If a foreign country can supply us with a commodity cheaper than we can make it ourselves, better buy it of them with some part of the produce of our own industry, employed in a way in which we have some advantage. (Adam Smith, *The Wealth of Nations*, 1776, book iv, chapter 2).

Smith recognised that countries trade with one another because mutual benefits can be obtained. He suggested that the source of these gains were productivity advantages held by different countries. Fifty years or so later David Ricardo spelled this out more completely.

We outlined Ricardo's theory of trade in Chapter 1 (but without attributing the ideas to him). Let us now take that analysis a stage further. Ricardo dealt with two countries—England and Portugal—trading two goods, cloth and wine. Suppose that each of these goods is produced using labour alone. Suppose that the quantities of cloth *or* wine that can be produced by one worker employed in some period of time in each country are as shown in Table 16.2.

Here each country has an *absolute* advantage in the production of one good: it can produce that good with a lower quantity of input than the other country. England's advantage lies in cloth and Portugal's in wine. In such circumstances, mutual gains are possible from specialization and exchange. We will not go through the arithmetic here, as that was done in Chapter 1. But convince yourself that mutual gains are possible before reading further.

Ricardo sees trade arising from differences in labour efficiencies. These efficiency differences are reflected in price differences for the same good across countries. Price differences then stimulate trade. But how do these variations in labour efficiency come about? Climate is one source of such variation. For example, it is likely that in Mediterranean countries labour efficiency will be relatively high in the production of citrus fruits, but low in the production of beaver pelts. A second source arises from differences in the state of technological knowledge between nations. In the Silicon Valley district in California, the general level of knowledge about computer technology is sufficiently advanced to confer efficiency advantages on its workforce. More generally, productivity variations will tend to arise through different amounts of learning acquired by the labour force. Labour productivity differences may also come about because stocks and qualities of other inputs will not be the same everywhere, but Ricardo's one-input model does not permit us to tell such a story.

The example that we used to introduce Ricardo's theory of trade is of limited interest. It does not deal with circumstances where one country has an absolute advantage in *both* goods. Such a case is illustrated in Table 16.3.

Here Portugal has an absolute advantage in the production of both cloth and wine. But there are still potential gains to be had from specialization and trade. To see why, we need to consider *opportunity costs* and *comparative advantage*. In England, one worker can produce two rolls of cloth in the same time taken to produce one gallon of wine. The opportunity cost of one gallon of wine is two rolls of cloth. In Portugal, one worker can produce

Table 16.1 Imports and exports in the OECD economies

	IMPORTS			EXPORTS		
	Total imports	Manufacturing imports		Total exports		Manufacturing exports only
	Imports by value: Average annual change, per cent, 1982–1992	Manufacturing imports as per cent of total imports	Imports by value: Average annual change, per cent, 1982–1992	Exports by value: Average annual change, per cent, 1982–1992	Manufacturing exports as per cent of total exports	Manufacturing exports by value: Average annual change, per cent, 1982–1992
	A	*B*	*C*	*D*	*E*	*F*
Country						
Canada	8.4	86.2	9.6	6.5	66.8	8.1
France	7.5	77.4	10.7	9.6	80.0	10.2
Germany	10.2	78.2	13.6	9.4	91.5	9.7
Italy	7.2	70.3	12.2	8.4	89.8	9.1
Japan	5.9	49.1	14.0	9.4	98.3	9.4
UK	8.4	79.8	10.3	7.0	83.8	8.9
USA	8.1	80.9	11.1	7.4	81.5	8.9
Australia	4.8	86.4	5.8	5.6	43.2	12.0
Austria	10.7	85.7	12.9	11.0	91.7	11.5
Belgium	8.1	77.1	10.7	9.0	83.5	9.8
Denmark	7.2	76.9	9.7	10.3	66.7	12.0
Finland	4.5	73.7	6.7	6.0	85.5	6.8
Greece	8.9	73.0	12.4	8.6	57.0	9.4
Iceland	6.0	77.2	7.3	8.4	15.9	5.5
Ireland	8.8	81.0	10.4	13.4	72.2	14.6
Luxembourg	8.1	77.1	10.7	9.0	83.5	9.8
Netherlands	8.0	73.7	11.5	7.8	64.4	10.5
New Zealand	8.4	86.2	9.6	6.5	66.8	8.1
Norway	5.3	83.2	6.5	7.2	39.4	7.5
Portugal	12.3	76.4	16.5	16.1	83.1	17.3
Spain	12.3	73.6	19.3	12.3	79.6	13.2
Sweden	6.1	80.3	8.4	7.7	86.8	8.4
Switzerland	8.7	86.6	10.1	9.9	95.8	10.0
Turkey	10.0	69.6	13.9	9.9	72.3	15.5
EU	8.7	76.5	12.1	9.0	83.2	10.0

Source: OECD (1994).

Table 16.2 Absolute advantage

	Cloth	Wine
England	2	1
Portugal	1	2

Table 16.3 Comparative advantage

	Cloth	Wine
England	2	1
Portugal	3	2

three rolls of cloth in the same time taken to produce two gallons of wine. The opportunity cost of one gallon of wine in Portugal is, therefore, one and a half rolls of cloth.

Portugal has a lower opportunity cost of producing wine than England, and is said to have a comparative advantage in wine production. You should now calculate the opportunity costs of cloth production in each country. If you do this correctly, you will find that England has a lower opportunity cost (and so has a comparative advantage) in cloth production. This is so in spite of the fact that England is less good in absolute terms than Portugal in producing cloth.

It is worth noting that if you apply the reasoning

of comparative advantage to the data we looked at in our first example, the conclusion we reached then remains the same. You will find that England has a comparative advantage in clothing, whilst Portugal has a comparative advantage in wine. Therefore, England should produce clothing and Portugal wine.

What matters as far as trade is concerned is always comparative advantage, not absolute advantage. It is specialization and trade on the basis of comparative advantage that creates the potential for exchange to add value. You may be much better than another person in both research and management. But if your advantage is greatest in management, it is better that you manage and have the other person do research. This pattern of specialization will also be better for the other person.

Specialization creates potential benefits. These benefits are realized through trade. This is best illustrated with a diagram. In Figure 16.3, the solid lines represent the production possibilities of the two countries. In constructing the figure, we have taken England to have 150 workers and Portugal to have 100 workers. Thus, given the production data in our second example, England can produce 150 gallons of wine, or 300 units of cloth, or any combination of cloth and wine on the straight line

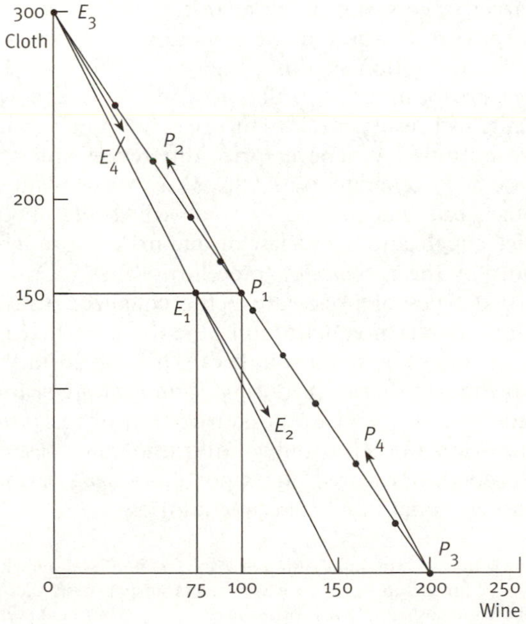

Figure 16.3 The gains from international trade

connecting those points. Portugal can produce 200 gallons of wine, or 300 units of cloth, or any combination of cloth and wine on the straight line connecting those points. Suppose, for the sake of simplicity, that we choose as reference point a situation in which each country uses half of its workforce in the production of each good, but does not trade with the other. Then England and Portugal would be at the points denoted by E_1 and P_1 on their respective production possibility frontiers.

Imagine that the two countries agreed to exchange at a rate of 4 gallons of wine for 7 rolls of cloth. Portugal sells wine to England in exchange for cloth, and so moves along the ray from P_1. England moves from the point E_1. If 40 gallons of wine were exchanged for 70 rolls of cloth, Portugal and England would reach the points P_2 and E_2 respectively. Both countries have gained from trade, as they have reached consumption combinations that were not feasible before trade.

P_2 and E_2 may not, of course, be the consumption bundles regarded by consumers as the best ones attainable. After all, choosing points E_1 and P_1 to start from was completely arbitrary. Different starting-points allow for different after-trade bundles of consumption goods. One case warrants special attention. Suppose that each country specializes completely according to its comparative advantage. Portugal specializes completely in wine (point P_3) whilst England specializes completely in cloth (point E_3). Trade allows Portugal to move from P_3 in the direction of P_4, whilst trade allows England to move from E_3 in the direction of E_4. How much trade takes place is determined by consumer preferences for the goods in the two countries. Complete specialization followed by trade turns out to be the way in which the *maximum* gains are obtained; the post-trade consumption possibilities are the greatest.

How would the exchange rate between the two goods be determined? The *potential* gains from trade will only be converted into *actual* gains when the countries agree an exchange rate that allows each of them to get a good more cheaply than by making it at home. This means that the exchange rate must allow the countries to acquire a good through trade at a better rate than its domestic opportunity cost. The exchange rate of 7 rolls of cloth for 4 gallons of wine permits this. England does better trading 7 rolls of cloth to obtain 4 gallons of wine than by using her own workers to make 4 gallons of wine. She would have to give up 8 rolls of cloth to get an additional 4 gallons of wine from domestic production.

The actual exchange rate will depend in part on the relative bargaining strengths of the two countries. We can predict, however, that the exchange rate will lie somewhere between the two opportunity cost ratios. If it lay outside these limits, one country would do worse by trading, and so would not trade. These two opportunity cost ratios are known as the 'limits to the terms of trade'. In our numerical example, the 7: 4 rate was chosen simply because it happened to lie half-way between these two limits.

The Heckscher–Ohlin Theory of Trade

In the 1920s, two Swedish economists—Eli Heckscher and Bertil Ohlin—gave a more fully articulated account of how international trade generates gains (Ohlin, 1933). The Heckscher and Ohlin (HO) model is based on comparative advantage. But it deals with two or more productive resources rather than the single (labour) input of the Ricardian theory, and so is more general than Ricardo's model.

Suppose that each country has two inputs, capital and labour, and that two goods can be produced. One of these we call the 'capital-intensive good', a good which, for technical reasons, is best produced using a high ratio of capital to labour. The other is the 'labour-intensive good', best produced using a high ratio of labour to capital.

The central propositions of the HO theory are as follows.

- Goods differ in their input requirements. Some require a high ratio of labour to capital. Others require a high ratio of capital to labour. Goods can be ranked in terms of their input requirements.
- Countries differ in their endowments of inputs. Some are relatively capital abundant, others are labour abundant.
- A capital-abundant country will tend to specialize in and export goods which are best produced in a capital-intensive manner. In exchange, it will import labour-intensive goods.

The key to all this comes from differences in relative stocks of resources. Capital is relatively scarce in one country, whilst labour is relatively scarce in the other. Differences in factor supplies mean that the costs of producing goods vary between countries. A capital-rich country has a low relative price of capital (that is, a low price of capital in terms of labour). So the relative price of the capital-intensive *good* will be low, and it has a comparative advantage in goods that are best produced using capital-intensive methods.

Conversely, the country well endowed with labour has a low relative price of labour, and so a low relative price of the labour-intensive good. It has a comparative advantage in goods best produced using labour-intensive methods.

The essence of the HO theorem is that these differences in relative prices precipitate trade flows. More generally, it asserts that each country tends to specialize its production in, and then export, those goods that are intensive in its abundant factor. The USA, rich in terms of skilled labour and R&D capacity, is predicted to specialize in and export products which use those inputs intensively.

Factor and Product Price Equalization

But there seems to be a paradox here. The HO theorem states that trade flows result from price differences. Yet, in the absence of barriers to trade, we can regard different national markets as parts of one single international market. And in a single market, a good must sell at one price: the *law of one price* must apply, as we showed in Chapter 6.[1]

The resolution of this paradox is as follows. In the *absence* of trade, differences in factor endowments will result in different prices (of both inputs and outputs). Whenever price differences emerge, these will generate trade flows, as we explained above. But this process of trade will bring about price equalization. The law of one price is brought about by the *presence* of trade flows.

Two types of prices are being equalized. Trade brings about an equalization of real *factor* (that is, input) prices between countries. This conclusion is known as the *factor price equalization theorem.* But trade will also lead to an equalization of real *product* prices in each country. After trade the price of any good, measured in opportunity cost terms, must be equal in all trading countries.

[1] Matters are not quite as simple as the text implies. Even with no impediments to trade, the existence of transport costs and/or transaction costs imply that prices need not be identical at every place or point in time in a single market. At best, therefore, one would only expect the law of one price to hold approximately.

How exactly are these price equalizations brought about? Consider factor prices first. Prior to trade, labour is relatively cheap in the country with a high labour endowment. This country then sells the labour-intensive good abroad. The effect of this is to increase labour demand and so its price rises. Trade has an equivalent effect in the country that is well endowed with capital, increasing the price of capital. In equilibrium, the relative price of labour to capital will be equal in the two countries. Equalization of the real *product* prices is brought about in a similar way: trade alters the patterns of demand and supply for each good in the two countries until relative prices are equalized in all trading countries.

The Gains from Trade

We must not lose sight of the gains that trade generates. It permits countries to increase their consumption possibilities. Trade enables the capital-scarce country to lessen the adverse consequences of capital shortage, by importing goods made where capital is abundant. In the same way, the relative scarcity of labour in the other country can be mitigated by importing such goods from sources of plentiful labour. Trade thus relaxes resource constraints on each country. Consider trade between the petroleum-rich countries of the Middle East and the capital-intensive countries of Western Europe. The exchange of petroleum and petroleum derivatives for manufactured goods relieves resource constraints that each group of countries would otherwise face, thereby raising living standards.

The Product Cycle Theory of Trade

One interesting application of the HO theorem is the product cycle theory of trade. Human skills, acquired through education, training, and learning in employment, have similar properties to physical capital, and are known as human capital. The acquisition of these skills requires investment in people (as opposed to investment in physical capital). Once acquired, these skills yield flows of services over time. Within the general category of human capital, research and development skills have become of particular importance, especially in creating and bringing new manufactured products to the market.

Product cycle theory suggests that manufactured products are initially produced by countries richly endowed in research and development capacity. Such countries—the USA being one example—have a comparative advantage in goods intensive in these inputs, and so will export new manufactured products. This is a direct consequence of the HO theorem.

As the product matures through its life cycle, its production (and subsequent differentiation) becomes more routinized. The contribution played by research and development skills diminishes, and efficient production comes to depend more heavily on the use of capital and less skilled labour. Comparative advantage thus shifts to economies richly endowed in these inputs, which therefore take over as the major exporters of the established products. The patterns of production and international exchange evolve over the life cycle of the product. We do not expect countries that develop advantages in the initial sale of new manufactures to retain these advantages as the product becomes mature. Personal computers and motor vehicles each illustrate the product cycle theory.

Trade in Manufactures

The HO theory of trade provides a powerful basis for international trade theory, but it does not explain two of the stylized facts we noted earlier:

- the existence of intense and rapidly expanding trade between countries with *similar* factor endowments;
- the fact that large quantities of similar products, particularly manufactured goods, are exchanged between national economies.

These facts appear to be inconsistent with the HO theorem, which suggests that trade takes place between countries with *different* factor endowments. HO implies that trade will take place to the greatest extent where such differences are the greatest. And the logic of the HO theorem also implies that trade should be primarily in *dissimilar* goods.

Much trade is of this form, particularly trade in primary commodities (minerals, fuels, other extracted resources, and foodstuffs). British, Russian, and Saudi Arabian exports of oil and gas can be accounted for in this way, as can Brazilian timber and American cinema exports. But manufactured goods have taken an increasing proportion

Table 16.4 United States international trade in manufactured goods, 1988

Category	Exports	Imports
Motor vehicle engines	1,194	3,107
Gas turbines	2,250	1,142
Harvesting machinery	731	510
Metal-cutting tools	455	1,588
Air-conditioning machinery	954	795
Lifting and loading machinery	970	773
Ball and roller bearings	413	962
Line telephone equipment	1,522	3,442
Electronic micro-circuits	4,114	8,778
Film	1,430	1,285
Books	922	832
Sound recording, disks, tapes	2,050	1,683

Source: Adapted from Kenen (1994), and originally from United Nations, *Yearbook of International Trade Statistics*, 1988.

of total trade flows between countries. Moreover, many countries export and import considerable quantities of the same type of good, often in roughly equal amounts. Trade in manufactured goods—also known as 'intra-industry trade'—involves the importing of goods which are broadly similar to and compete with those produced in the domestic economy. This kind of trade is not based on resource differences between trading partners.

The growth of intra-industry trade is evident within the European Union. Most of the rapid trade growth within the EU is in manufactured goods. The phenomenon of intra-industry trade can also be seen in Table 16.4, which shows US exports and imports of selected manufactured goods in 1988. If HO comparative advantage theory cannot explain intra-industry trade and its growth, how can we explain it? Two main answers have been suggested, one based on economies of scale, the other on product differentiation and consumer desires for diversity.

Trade in Manufactured Goods and Scale Economies

Economies of scale can provide a benefit from reciprocal trade in manufactures. In the absence of international trade, a typical manufacturing firm may be too small to fully exploit all potential scale economies, or it may have an insufficient *accumulated* amount of output to exploit all scope and learning economies. Firms will then seek additional markets to realize these economies.

Scale, scope, accumulated output, and learning economies are often very substantial in manufacturing industry. Moreover, as the technological sophistication of products increases, development costs take up an increasing proportion of overall costs and the pressures to produce large output volumes intensify. Looking at the list of product categories in Table 16.4, we see that all are characterized by these forms of economies. This is particularly evident in the cases of microelectronic circuitry and the production of motor engines. The existence of scale, scope, and learning effects creates an incentive for the firm to expand its output. Selling in foreign markets as well as domestic markets is an obvious route to this end. Furthermore, with domestic markets constantly being targeted by foreign producers, the pressure on each producer to grab a share of the international market is intensified.

Product Differentiation and Consumer Desires for Diversity

In many markets the goods being traded are not homogeneous. Consumer preferences for diversity and quality tend to encourage product differentiation. Typical manufactured goods markets are neither perfectly competitive nor monopolistic but rather imperfectly competitive. Oligopolistic rivalry and monopolistic competition are the norm rather than the exception.

There are many ways in which the existence of imperfect competition helps to explain the prevalence and growth of intra-industry trade. We shall look at two of these. The Swedish economist Staffan Linder has developed an explanation of trade in manufactures based upon the structure of consumer demands (Linder, 1961). Suppliers respond to preferences for diversity by differentiating products. A typical firm produces goods in a range of qualities and types. The increasing desire for diversity will tend to increase the magnitude of a country's *range* of output over time.

For any type of product, a consumer faces a range of domestically and externally produced differentiated goods. The consumer makes choices from overlapping sets of products produced in different countries. Cultural differences, national preferences, and the existence of transactions and transport costs will give domestic producers an advantage over foreign firms when consumers make their choices. But the importance of each of these tends to fall over time. Linder's model demonstrates that the greatest amount of trade takes place between countries with similar income levels, not between those with very different income levels as the HO theory implies.

A second explanation is based on the existence of economies of scale. Where scale economies are very large, a firm will find it advantageous to produce a single good in large volume, targeted at some point along the range of consumer preferences, rather than producing a diversified range of outputs as suggested by Linder. A simple example will be useful for illustrating the argument. Suppose that consumers have preferences concerning the colour of a product, and that in the market as a whole, these preferences are distributed evenly along the colour spectrum. In any interval on the spectrum, there are as many consumers preferring such goods as there are preferring goods from any other equal-sized interval. We represent these ideas in Figure 16.4.

Consider first the situation in which there is no trade. How will firms choose the colour for their good? Suppose there are four equal-sized firms in a country. With consumer preferences evenly distributed along the colour spectrum, game theory analysis suggests that, in equilibrium, firms will spread themselves evenly across the range of colours. In so doing, each gains a quarter share of the total market. What happens when trade is allowed? Again, for simplicity, we assume conditions in the foreign markets are identical to those in the home market (so there are four foreign firms of equal size, and consumer preferences are spread evenly over the same colour spectrum).

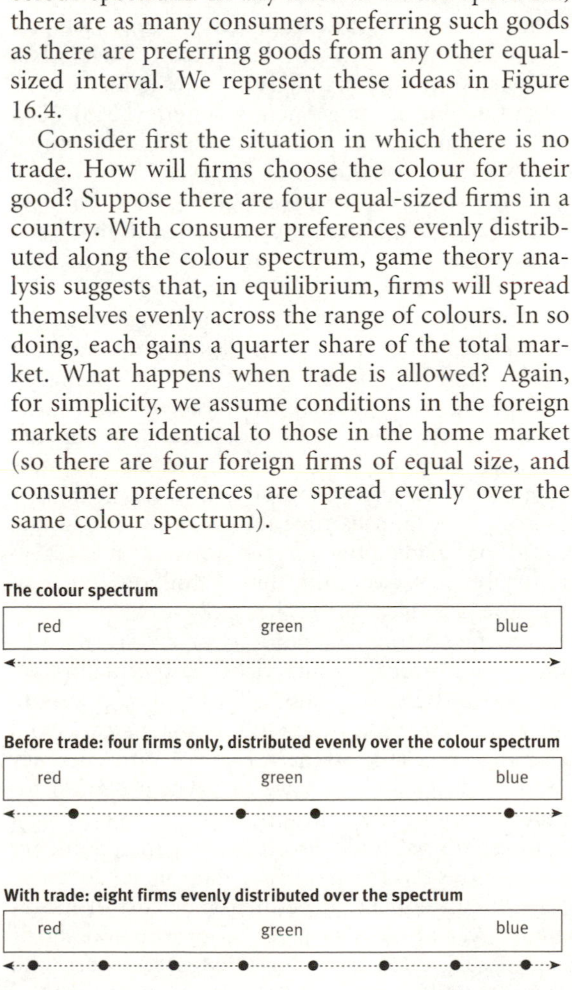

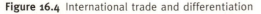

Figure 16.4 International trade and differentiation

It is easy to show that the eight firms will now distribute themselves evenly over the spectrum. The 'gap' between firms will diminish, as twice as many firms are now positioned evenly along the colour range. Each domestic firm will sell only half of what it was previously selling to domestic consumers, but will be compensated by sales in the foreign market. Even though there are no differences in costs, preferences, or resource endowments, international trade opens up. It does so simply as a consequence of the diversity of consumer preferences in an imperfectly competitive market. Where do the gains from trade come from in this case? They do not arise from comparative advantage. Instead, the gains come from greater diversity of output and so increased product choice.

16.2 Trade Policy and Economic Integration

Free Trade: Winners and Losers

Since trade brings benefits to buyers and sellers it may be sensible for governments to adopt 'free trade'. Under these circumstances there are no tariffs or other official barriers to trade, and government does not use financial measures to deter imports or promote exports. Free trade maximizes the opportunities for specialization and exchange. Moreover, as prices reflect conditions of supply and demand, the transactions that take place will reflect comparative advantage. Productive inputs will be used in the most efficient ways.

However, free trade is not necessarily beneficial for everyone. There are both winners and losers within any trading country. Consider the case of a country richly endowed with capital but with a relative scarcity of labour. The HO theorem implies that this country will export capital-intensive goods and import labour-intensive goods. As a result of this, the relative price of capital rises and the relative price of labour falls in that county. In purchasing power terms, wages will fall, whilst the real return to capital will rise. From the point of view of labour, trade has adverse effects.

It follows from this that trade restrictions can benefit some *sections* within an economy, even though the aggregate prosperity of the economy would fall. Specifically, protection of domestic industry (by using import tariffs, for example) increases the real income of owners of the resource used intensively in the protected good. For example, if the USA introduced tariffs against goods made using unskilled labour, this would make US unskilled workers better off.

This is a rather important conclusion, and helps to explain why liberalisation of world trade can be politically difficult. In the period of trade liberalization at the end of the eighteenth and the start of the nineteenth century, liberalization met with strong resistance from many quarters, as, for example, in the conflicts associated with the abolition of the Corn Laws in England. At the present time it is by no means uncommon for workers in labour-intensive industries in the affluent industrialized economies to press for protection against imports from 'low-wage' developing economies. It is not difficult to observe particular groups fighting for their interests (such as French farmers, British coal-miners, and US steel workers) and pressing for continued or additional protection. Our analysis suggests that such demands are well founded, even though it would be disadvantageous to the economy as a whole to accede to them.

Despite these episodes, trade liberalization in the period since 1945 has proceeded with relatively little conflict. European unification, for example, has proceeded quite smoothly. One reason for this may lie in the growing importance of intra-industry trade; it is much less likely that large, easily identifiable sectors will suffer from trade in this case.

A second reason why opposition has been relatively muted may be that those who suffered directly were compensated in other ways. The efficiency gains and increased competition arising from the dismantling of tariff barriers can stimulate growth, thereby providing compensations. Note also that as trade should raise the total real income of participating nations, it is possible for the gainers to compensate the losers, so that all are better-off post trade and compensation.

The Costs and Risks of International Trade

There are three important differences between international and domestic trade:

- international trade carries additional risks compared with domestic trade;
- international trade usually involves higher transactions costs;
- information is likely to be poorer when trading across national boundaries.

Additional risk arises largely from the possibility of exchange rate variation. A champagne producer is able to know the price received for each bottle sold to a French consumer. But when the champagne is exported to an American consumer, this is no longer necessarily true. If the contract is denominated in dollars, then the number of francs received by the seller will depend on the dollar–franc exchange rate that prevails at the time of currency exchange. The champagne seller could insist that the payment be made in francs, but this merely transfers the risk to the American buyer. As risk is costly, the American purchaser is likely to require a lower contract price for bearing that risk.

Such risk is most acute under floating exchange rates determined by market forces. Even when exchange rates are 'fixed', as is the case for currencies in the European Monetary System (EMS), risks still exist, as currencies can move within permitted bands around some fixed target level. In the case of the EMS, the permitted variability was until 1992 2.25 per cent; speculative pressure led to that band being widened to 15 per cent! Moreover, the possibility always exists that the fixed target will itself be changed in a realignment of exchange rates, or that a country will choose to leave the system, as the UK and Italy did in 1992.

Exchange rate risk can be transferred in another way. Traders can make contracts on *forward* exchange rate markets. Returning to our example, suppose the American importer must pay 1 million francs in six months time for the wine. A contract could be made now on the forward market to purchase in six months time 1 million francs at an agreed dollar price, irrespective of whatever the exchange rate happens to be in six months time. This process shifts risks to speculators on the forward market who will charge a premium for taking that risk. International traders can avoid exchange rate risk by the use of forward currency markets, but they will have to pay a premium for unloading that risk onto others.

International trade also tends to generate higher transactions costs than the equivalent domestic trade because of the time or money cost of movements over borders. Sources of information shortcomings include geographical distance, cultural and linguistic differences, and the lower stock of relevant knowledge acquired through experience and learning. All of these suggest that search costs will often be higher in international trade, particularly when this involves new products or new markets. Higher costs, poorer information, and greater risks all diminish the quantity of trade taking place. Not surprisingly, the last four decades have seen national and international institutions seeking to reduce these impediments to trade.

The Search to Reduce Impediments to Trade and the Promotion of International Economic Integration

In the early period of recovery after the Second World War, trade policy was primarily concerned with dismantling tariff barriers and other formal impediments to trade. The General Agreement on Trade and Tariffs (GATT) was established to administer and oversee this process. It encouraged bilateral and multilateral tariff reductions. Progress was slow yet extensive, and GATT played an important role in the opening up of the world economy to trade.

Of great importance in some parts of the world was the creation of customs unions. A customs union is an agreement between a set of nations to abolish tariff barriers to trade within the union, whilst maintaining common levels of tariff on trade with the outside world. The European Economic Community was for many years essentially such a union. Other customs unions—often called free trade areas—were developed in North America and Northern Europe. The COMECON group of socialist countries also instituted a customs union (but one in which trade was centrally administered).

Tariffs, quotas, and other formal impediments to trade are not the only obstacles, however. The existence of national boundaries creates a variety of formal and informal obstacles. As tariffs and quotas became dismantled within the European Community, the importance of these informal barriers became increasingly apparent. This led the European Commission to propose the establishment of a 'single market' within Europe.

The term single market refers to a customs union supplemented by the abolition of all non-tariff barriers to trade, harmonization of national standards and administrative procedures applying to the movements of goods and services, and the abolition of restrictions on the movement of labour and capital. Creating a single market has become a central objective of the European Union, but one which has not yet been fully achieved in practice.

Until exchange rate variability is eliminated, there will necessarily be limits to the extent to which a genuine single market can be achieved, and so to attaining the potential gains from trade. Exchange rate management has been a central objective of the European Union. The primary vehicle for this within Europe has been the European Monetary System. This requires that central banks in each Member State use reserves of foreign currencies to intervene in foreign exchange markets to counterbalance market pressures that would otherwise cause relative currency values to change. This practice requires that the underlying performances of Member States do not differ too much, and that members adopt broadly similar monetary and fiscal policies. In this way, real interest rates and other key economic variables will not diverge too much between economies, thereby keeping the size of required central bank interventions manageable.

Achieving consistency of economic performance has proved elusive. Moreover, the scale of financial asset flows on international markets has grown so large relative to the sizes of official reserves that central banks have at times found it impossible to maintain exchange rate stability. This has contributed to the calls from some quarters within Europe for economic (fiscal) and monetary union, and the creation of a single currency.

16.3 Multinational Corporations and Business Co-operation

Suppose that a firm believes it has an opportunity to add value by selling some product in a foreign market. How might it go about exploiting this opportunity? The firm could work through the market, producing the good in the domestic economy for export sales. Alternatively, it might find a foreign firm to produce and sell the product under licence. If the licensing outcomes are attractive to each party, this could develop into a third arrangement, long-term partnership. Here market transactions and formal contracts are being augmented with non-market, co-operative structures. Another option would be to engage in a joint venture with a foreign firm. In this case, the use of the market has been more completely replaced by administrative structures. Clearly there are many other more or less similar institutional arrangements that could be used. Their common feature is the existence of co-operative behaviour and the establishment of appropriate formal and informal structures to support that co-operation and determine the division of the value generated between the parties.

International economic activity may also be undertaken by means of foreign direct investment. Foreign investment flows can be classified as follows:

- indirect (portfolio) investment: one party makes a loan of funds abroad or acquires title to a financial asset in another country;
- direct investment: one party builds or acquires ownership of productive capacity in a subsidiary in another country.

The essential difference concerns the type of control over the use of the invested funds. In the former case, the lender does not exercise direct control over the use of the funds, whilst in the latter case it does. Instead of one firm dealing with another through a mixture of market transactions and co-operative arrangements, a single firm—the 'multinational enterprise'—owns and manages productive assets in two or more economies.

The growth of multinational enterprises has been one of the most important economic phenomena in recent decades. Although not all of these companies are large, many are strikingly so. The three largest—Exxon, Ford, and General Motors—have sales larger than the GNP of all but a handful of national economies. Moreover, with annual growth rates of over 10 per cent, they are expanding more quickly than the world economy as a whole.

Why do some firms become multinational companies? The British economist Dunning (1981, 1988, 1993) has developed a theory of the multinational enterprise (MNE) based around the concepts of ownership-specific advantages, location-specific advantages, and international internalization of production. We provide a brief summary of Dunning's theory of the MNE in Box 16.1.

Choosing the Appropriate Mode of International Activity

How do firms choose from the menu of alternative institutional arrangements to carry out their international economic activity? What makes some firms produce at home for export sales (as Japanese companies did so successfully until the mid-1980s)? Why do others (such as Unilever, ICI, Philips, United Biscuits, and British American Tobacco) choose the option of direct foreign investment, becoming multinational firms. And why do some prefer to operate by collaborative agreements and alliances (such as Microsoft)?

A full answer to these questions is beyond the scope of this text. We have given (in Box 16.1) one explanation of why firms might choose the multinational enterprise route. However, some further insights can be gained by using a few principles with which you are now familiar. The firm will search for the arrangement which generates the highest sustainable value over time. Which option does so depends on the particular circumstances and transactional problems involved.

Using markets to sell goods for export offers a number of advantages, particularly in terms of simplicity and flexibility. Where a firm envisages making only a limited commitment to foreign markets, it may be the only sensible option. Moreover, this arrangement does not require the firm to give up control of any part of its managerial functions. But it does have weaknesses, particularly when large-scale, continuous foreign sales are envisaged. Other arrangements may economize on transactions costs, or may be more effective as learning and information-transferring mechanisms. Moreover, governments may favour domestic producers over foreign firms, and there might then be significant strategic benefits from acquiring an organized presence in a foreign market.

Multinationality may also confer advantages as compared with home production and exporting. We have seen that international trade is often more risky and more costly than within-country trade. By maintaining productive capacity in a variety of countries, and by having the ability to transfer goods and services between subsidiaries in different countries at administered (rather than market) prices, some of these risks can be reduced or more effectively hedged (balanced off against one another in an offsetting manner) by a multinational firm than by a domestic exporter. Multi-

Box 16.1 Dunning's Theory of the Multinational Enterprise

Dunning begins from the premise that firms are motivated to add value by growth. Growth could be achieved within the firm's home country or by external expansion. Expansion abroad is beset by a variety of difficulties, uncertainties, and so costs, as we explained earlier. Other things being equal, one would expect firms to choose the option of growing within the home market.

Ownership Advantages

The existence of expansion into foreign markets is explained by other advantages which more than compensate for the costs of foreign market growth. In particular, a firm contemplating investing abroad must believe it has some form of competitive advantage over domestic firms already operating in foreign markets. Dunning calls these *ownership advantages*—they explain *why* multinational enterprise exists. There are several possible advantages that a multinational firm may have over domestic rivals:

- ownership or control of strategic assets, such as patents, or access to raw materials not available to local firms;
- size advantages: economies of scale and scope;
- access advantages: superior access to capital, R&D resources, and developing markets;
- possession of distinctive capabilities in architecture, innovation, or reputation (see Chapter 11).

Location Advantages

These ownership advantages explain foreign market involvement but do not explain why a firm should pursue the route of production abroad rather than produce and export to foreign markets. For firms to choose multinationality rather than export-led expansion, it must be the case that there are cost or revenue advantages in locating production abroad rather than producing at home for export. Dunning calls these *location advantages*: they explain *where* production takes place. Location advantages include:

- lower labour costs or financial incentives to attract inward investment;
- evasion of tariff or other barriers to international trade;
- resource immobility: some resources must be used in the place where they are located;
- establishment of specialized knowledge of local market conditions and consumer wishes.

Internalization Advantages

We now come to the final step in Dunning's argument. Even where ownership advantages and location advantages exist, a firm may choose to work with other firms abroad under licensing arrangements, joint ventures, or other collaborative schemes. The option of becoming an MNE, says Dunning, is chosen whenever it is advantageous to *internalize* resource allocation decisions within the boundaries of the firm. Internalization is principally a way of reducing transactions costs by eliminating, or mitigating the consequences of, various forms of uncertainty. For example, multinationality can:

- reduce transaction costs;
- ensure control in the supply chain of the business;
- reduce the risks of losing control of technical know-how and protect property rights;
- lessen price uncertainty;
- reduce the risks of political interference.

nationality may also make sound strategic sense for a firm faced with a high probability of finding its export markets subject to tariff barriers or other forms of protection.

The multinational form offers some advantages compared with licensing arrangements, partnerships, and joint ventures. These derive from its ability to protect distinctive capabilities. Firms often derive value from the exploitation of what Williamson (1983) calls intangible property assets—patents, recipes, copyrights, trade marks, and the like. When these are harnessed as distinctive capabilities, they allow the firm to sustain supernormal profits. The multinational firm's control over its use of these resources implies it can limit the extent to which these assets are copied or acquired by others. Host governments, of course, are unlikely to be willing to allow multinational firms to operate without transferring technology or other intangible assets to the domestic economy. An illustration of this is discussed in Box 16.2.

Box 16.2 Motorcycle Manufacture in Vietnam

Economic growth in Vietnam is changing the way in which people travel. In particular, travel by bicycles is being replaced by motorized transport. Demand for motorcycles is growing at over 10 per cent annually, a fact which not surprisingly has attracted the attention of foreign producers. Those who have shown interest in constructing motorcycles in Vietnam, rather than just exporting to it, include the Japanese manufactures Honda and Yamaha, VMEP of Taiwan, and Piaggio, an Italian scooter firm.

The attractions of producing within Vietnam derive not only from the fast growth of the local market and low labour costs, but also from the existence of a 60 per cent import surcharge that would thereby be avoided. Whichever firm breaks into production in Vietnam will get the lion's share of the market. The preferred mode of entry by Honda and its rivals appears to be by establishing 100 per cent foreign-owned subsidiaries—the classical multinational corporation form. In addition, the subsidiary plants in Vietnam would be assembly-oriented, with little or no research or development capacity, thereby minimizing the extent of technology transfer. Multinational firms, in other words, have often sought to guard their competitive advantage by minimizing technology transfer.

This is not, of course, what the Vietnamese authorities (or other host governments) prefer. They seek arrangements in which a large part of the assets are domestically owned, and production is not merely for domestic consumption but is partially destined for export markets. In addition, host governments attempt to source components locally (in Vietnem's case, it requires at least 60 per cent domestic sourcing) and to attain technology transfer as rapidly as possible. The extent to which these goals can be obtained depends upon the respective bargaining powers of host countries and multinational firms. In the past, the strongest positions were usually held by the multinational producers; these were able to extract bargains which were very favourable to themselves from governments desperate to bring prestigious manufacturing capacity into their economies. In recent years, increased competition among manufacturers combined with greater resolve and bargaining acumen on the past of host country governments has switched the balance of advantages.

The rivals for one of the few licences to produce in Vietnam are being forced to make major concessions in an attempt to capture a prize. VMEP has gifted 120 new machines to Vietnam's traffic police, and has boosted considerably local production of parts that supply models it produces at two plants licensed in 1992. Honda, the front-runner in the competition, has chosen the Vietnamese Ministry of Heavy Industry as a joint-venture partner, and has undertaken a feasibility study for a plant able to produce 350,000 units in its first five years. Honda appears willing to allow at least 30 per cent Vietnamese ownership of the assets it installs. It has proposed bringing its own component suppliers into Vietnam to create local capacity. Piaggio has promised that it will deliver technology transfer through the development of new models, rather than just assembling its traditional Vespa scooter.

Source: Adapted from the *Financial Times*, 21 February 1995.

Unless it received due compensation, a firm would be sensible to prevent others from learning from it or appropriating some of its distinctive capabilities or strategic assets. But very often there is something to be gained, and so a policy of minimizing transfers of knowledge to others can be short-sighted. In some circumstances, co-operation which involves mutual sharing of knowledge and resources can lead to the value generated by the co-operating venture being greater than the sum of the values of its parts. A number of business management writers have recently suggested that the internalization which multinational enterprises offer is becoming costly rather than beneficial, and that international production will increasingly take place using long term co-operative arrangements between firms rather than through the more traditional multinational enterprise mode. It is to this possibility that we now turn.

International Competition, Networks, and the Global Economy

The progressive dismantling of trade barriers since 1945, improvements in information technologies, lower transport costs, and the huge scale of foreign direct investment have contributed to a rapid growth of international trade and an unprecedented openness of the world economy. Together with the diffusion of production technologies, these have intensified the degree of competition in most markets. National boundaries are of diminishing importance to economic activity. Two recent developments are of considerable importance: the so-called globalization of economic activity, and the growth of informal networks linking firms within and between countries.

The phrase 'globalization of economic activity' is sometimes used to describe a world economy that is rather more international—in the sense of the number of national economies participating, and the extent of their trade—than it has been before. But if the term is to have any substance, it must refer to a *qualitatively* distinct set of arrangements. What might these be? Economic activity is global when sellers and buyers regard the world economy as a single market, or more precisely, as a set of single markets in particular products. In its complete form, production location, input sourcing, and sales decisions are made without reference to political boundaries. Stephen Kobrin, writing in the *Financial Times* in 1995, argues that three interrelated phenomena sharply differentiate the emerging twenty-first century global economy from its predecessors.

- Dramatic increases in the cost, risk and complexity of technology have rendered even the largest national market too small to be a meaningful economic unit. For example, high technology sectors such as pharmaceuticals and telecommunications have experienced escalating research and development costs and shortening product life cycles. Firms must expand internationally to enable value to be added in the face of these twin pressures.
- There has been a significant change in the mode of organization of international economic transactions; strategic alliances between firms are replacing trade and the multinational firm as the dominant mode.
- The global economy is integrated not through administrative hierarchies (as in multinational companies, investing directly overseas and managing trade internally within the firm) but through information systems and information technology. These developments have increasingly rendered national markets irrelevant as economic units.

The growth of networks and alliances is evident in many sectors. In aircraft manufacture, Boeing (USA) and Airbus (Europe) are jointly exploring the concept of a super jumbo jet. The computing firms IBM, Siemens, and Toshiba are co-operatively developing a new generation of high performance chips. A new photographic film and camera system—the Advanced Photographic System—has been developed by Kodak, Canon, Nikon, and others. And several computing software and hardware firms are committed to introducing a network-based computer system to challenge Microsoft's dominance in operating systems and software.

Alliances such as these are sometimes the only way to justify massively expensive development costs when the market is dominated by one seller, outcomes are uncertain, or any single national market size is relatively small. The growth of collaborative arrangements is also related to changes in technology, particularly its greater complexity and more rapid pace. Individual firms are no longer able to master techniques as they emerge, nor to identify and develop more than a small proportion of potential applications. In the face of stagnant sales in a mature market, the new format of camera and camera film we mentioned above was developed by a consortium, none of whose members was willing individually to take the huge risks involved. Alliances are also a response to increased competition. Intensified competition in world car markets has led to unprecedented changes in the business strategies of car manufactures and in the relationships between assemblers and component manufactures (see Box 16.3).

Networks are essentially informal, co-operative relationships forged between firms. One could even regard a network as a single 'firm' consisting of a number of entities which, although legally distinct, are organizationally related through co-operative structures. They are based on medium and long-term commitments of each party to the other, and involve transfers and exchange of technology and information. It is interesting to observe that the growth of these *co-operative* arrangements is a response to the increasing *competitiveness* of the world economy. This interchange of knowledge is contrary to the rationale and mode of operation of multinational firms, which are organized in ways that internalize information flows and minimize transfers to the outside. Information technology developments have played an important role in stimulating these changes. Whilst the speed of information exchange and processing has increased, its cost has fallen. Networking no longer requires

Box 16.3 Recent Development in World Car Markets

Intensifying competition between multinational car manufacturers has put greater pressure on profit margins, with a higher priority being given to cost reductions. The consequences have included substantial changes in the relationships between car assemblers and the suppliers of components. Until recently the major multinational car makers did not co-ordinate components purchases; purchasing was typically carried out independently by each production division or subsidiary. In the case of General Motors (GM), for example, its total annual parts purchases of $70 billion were until 1992 split between twenty-six separate operations.

Separation of purchasing made sense when component requirements differed widely between branches and when manufacturers had made little attempt to co-ordinate their vehicle programmes over different regional markets. But the cost-reduction pressures have led most car assemblers to introduce programmes to rationalize production. Among the more ambitious are the 'Ford 2000' programme, Volkswagen's 'platform strategy', and GM's network of alliances. Common features of these include

- vertical disintegration: component manufacture no longer to be done in-house;
- co-ordination between product development teams in subsidiaries in different countries leading to new models being conceived on a global basis;
- common basic structures and components of vehicles for different markets, with heterogeneity being limited to styling and bodywork.

To implement these strategies, the manufacturers of cars require:

- components to be available in very large volumes;
- components produced to a high and uniform quality but still at low prices;
- flexibility in component supply: very fast response and the ability to respond to changing specifications. Car assemblers now seek much shorter lines of communication with the components suppliers, and the establishment of long-term co-operative relationships with particular suppliers.

These requirements have led to the following processes in components manufacturing.

1. The need to more fully exploit economies of scale. The greater use of common parts allows far larger production runs to be undertaken, and so economies of scale to be realized in their manufacture. Attaining these potential economies, though, has necessitated structural changes in the components industry, and in the relationships between suppliers and purchasers of components. The most evident change has been consolidation of component firms. Estimates by the Union Bank of Switzerland suggest that in 1995 there were 157 mergers or take-overs involving at least one European firm. Of these, 73 were cross-border deals between different European countries, and 39 involved a non-European parent firm. The main acquisitions of European components manufactures by European and other firms during 1995 are listed in Table 16.5. Industry analysts expect that within ten years this continuing process will have reduced the number of firms from several hundred to about fifteen to twenty global groups.
2. The ability of component makers to offer global coverage. A successful firm will have to be able to readily supply a standard quality component in large quantities to car manufacturers anywhere in the world. This need for global coverage has already led to consolidation in seat-making, in which there are now only six major producers after international acquisitions by Johnson Controls and Lear Seating, the two largest US suppliers. Similar consolidation has also taken place in braking, lighting, and fluid handling systems.
3. An increasing tendency for components suppliers to enter into long-term co-operative arrangements with assemblers. Provided trust can be built, collaboration of this type is likely to mean that components firms will increasingly produce whole sub-assemblies without exposing themselves to the risks that they would otherwise incur. The assemblers gain in a number of ways, particularly through the outsourcing of components construction to suppliers with distinctive capabilities in that field, allowing the assemblers to focus effort in areas in which their strengths lie.

Whilst co-operative arrangements can be valuable to each partner, they do not guarantee success. Collaborators are exposed to exploitative, strategic behaviour by their partners, particularly in the initial phases whilst trust is gradually being built up. Moreover, shocks or disturbances can have more serious repercussions when firms have become locked into reciprocal collaboration, and the option of turning to other parties is precluded.

Source: *Financial Times*, 21 May 1996.

Table 16.5 Main acquisitions of European components companies announced in 1995

Target	Country	Acquirer	Country	Sector
Acts	UK	Tsuchiya Manufacturing	Japan	air-induction parts
Altissimo	Italy	Amiclas	Italy/France	lighting
Automotive Products	UK	Automotive Products[1]	UK	brakes and clutches
Becker	Germany	Harman International	USA	interior parts
Bellino	Germany	UPF group	UK	pressings
CEAc	France	Exide	USA	batteries
Ebyl Durmont	Austria	Magna	Canada	interior parts
Empe	Germany	MBO[2]	Germany	interior parts
Euroval Motorenkomponenten	Germany	Mahle	Germany	valves
FSO Clutches	Poland	Valeo	France	clutches
GKN axles	UK	Dana	USA	axles
Hammerverken	Sweden	Autoliv	Sweden	seat sub-systems
Harman SA (50 per cent)	France	Magneti Marelli	Italy	mirrors
Hohe	Germany	Donnelly Mirrors	USA	mirrors
Isodelta (49 per cent + options)	France	Autoliv	Sweden	steering wheels
Mannesmann Fahrzeugtelle	Germany	Lunke & Sohn	Germany	pressings
Manufacuras Fonos	Spain	Tenneco	USA	exhausts
Melfin	UK	Trimcom Automotive	UK	seating
Mercedes-Benz plastics, Woerth	Germany	SAI	France	plastic parts
Plastifol	Germany	Automotive Industries	USA	interior parts
Reydel	France	Plastic Omnium	France	plastic parts
Roth Freres	France	Johnson Controls	USA	seating
Safiplast	Italy	Ergom	Italy	fuel tanks
Safiplast	Italy	Solvay	Belgium	fuel tanks
SEIM	France	MGI Coutier	France	wiper pumps
Sommer Alibert[3]		Masland	USA	interior parts
Stry-Daimler-Puch	Austria	Daewoo	Korea	engines & drivetrain
Thermal-Werke	Germany	Valeo	France	heaters
Vaisala Technologies	Finland	Breed Technologies	USA	sensors
VDT	Netherlands	Bosch	Germany	gearboxes
Viktor Achter	Germany	Milliken	USA	textiles

Notes:

[1] Management buy-out.

[2] CVC and Goldman Sachs.

[3] Fifty per cent of UK subsidiary.

Source: *Financial Times*, 21 May 1996.

the presence in the same place of co-operating parties. A corollary of the expansion of networks between firms has been the reduced importance of multinational organization *per se*. Moreover networking, by allowing greater specialization of tasks among sets of collaborating partners, has allowed firms to focus their activities more tightly and so has been a contributory factor to vertical disintegration in some sectors (see again the example in Box 16.2).

Francis Bidault and Thomas Cummings (1996) have summarized the potential benefits of alliances to the collaborating partners:

- alliances offer access to new technology, to additional manufacturing capacity, to new markets and distribution channels, and to service capabilities;
- alliances are effective vehicles for mutual learning: the associated transfer of knowledge can be a potent source of innovation;
- by placing their resources, capabilities, and expertise in new contexts, partners can identify their own (and the others') weaknesses and unexploited strengths;
- an alliance can improve management processes;
- alliances expose the organization—and each of its components—to additional threats as well as additional opportunities; the challenges posed by

additional threats can bring about superior working practices.

A good illustration of the mutual benefits that can be derived from co-operative alliances is given by Bidault and Cummings. In the late 1960s, Bakaert, a Belgian steel-wire manufacturing firm, realized it could not enter the rapidly growing Japanese economy without a local partner. The partner it found was Bridgestone, the largest Japanese tyre manufacturer. A joint venture was built through which Bakaert exclusively supplied steel-tyre cord to Bridgestone. Whilst Bakaert's goal was to gain access to a growing market, Bridgestone sought access to state of the art technology for an important component of its product. The technology transfer was rapidly completed, and within five years, productivity at the new Japanese plant had reached the levels of Bakaert's Belgian operation. The gains to Bridgestone were clear; those to Bakaert were enhanced by its learning from Bridgestone of superior production organization techniques which eventually enabled it to double productivity at its Belgian plant. The mutual benefits were obtained only because each side was willing to make a commitment to the other, and so to build a long-term trust relationship.

Conclusions

We began this chapter by giving a systematic account of the comparative advantage theory of trade, introduced first by Ricardo and later developed by Heckscher and Ohlin. In Section 16.1, we outlined a number of other theories of trade. These should not be seen as rivals, but rather as being complementary to one another. The HO approach is successful at explaining much trade, particularly inter-industry trade such as trade in primary products and foodstuffs, but it does not explain all trade. The existence of what we have called intra-industry trade seems to depend on the existence of imperfect competition in goods markets, or on the existence of economies of scale.

We then looked at a variety of institutional arrangements that have been adopted to promote the benefits of international trade. Within Europe, the imminent adoption of an economic and monetary union is likely to push these gains to their furthest limit.

Our emphasis then shifted to the firm and its role in international economic behaviour. A mode of international business organization known as the multinational corporation was examined. Recent trends, however, are pointing to a move away from multinationality towards a looser form of co-operative business organization, exploiting networks and alliances.

Further reading

The classic early texts that developed the theory of international trade are David Ricardo (1817), *On the Principles of Political Economy and Taxation* and Adam Smith (1776), *An Inquiry into the Nature and Causes of the Wealth of Nations.* A highly readable and extensive modern account of trade theory can be found in the Open University text, *Economics and Changing Economies* (1995) by Mackintosh *et al.*, particularly part 7 (chapters 12, 13, and 14). An excellent, but more advanced, account of the economic theory of international trade and international economic relationships is Kenen (1994), *The International Economy.*

The phenomenon of multinational firms is examined at length in Dunning (1988), *Explaining International Production*, Dunning (1993), *The Globalisation of Business*, and in Young *et al.* (1988), *Foreign Multinationals and the British Economy.*

Kobrin (1991) contains a very good discussion of globalization of economic activity. A good discussion of the recent economic developments in the European Union can be found in Ceccini (1989), *The European Challenge 1992—The Benefits of a Single Market.*

An influential book linking trade theory to business strategy is Michael Porter (1990), *The Competitive Advantage of Nations.*

Questions

16.1. What are the sources of a nation's comparative advantage?

16.2. Is it meaningful to argue that a country can have a 'sustainable competitive advantage' over others in the same way that one firm can have a sustainable competitive advantage over other firms producing similar products?

16.3. What are the advantages and disadvantages of enlarging membership of the European Union to include some former countries of the East European Soviet bloc?

16.4. What factors might interfere with the ability of France and the UK to trade?

16.5. What benefits can be derived from multinational enterprise (MNE) for (*a*) the host country and (*b*) the home (or parent) country of the MNE?

16.6. What advantages should be obtained by countries engaging in multilateral trade liberalization negotiations, such as the Uruguay Round?

16.7. What limits, if any, exist on the extent to which business activity can be globalized?

Bibliography

Alberts, W. W. (1989), 'The Experience Curve Doctrine Revisited', *Journal of Marketing*, 52/3: 36–49.

Arthur, W. Brian (1996), 'Increasing Returns and the New World of Business', *Harvard Business Review*, 74, July–Aug., 100–9.

Bator, F. M. (1957), 'The Simple Analytics of Welfare Maximisation', *American Economic Review*, 47, 22–59, reprinted in H. Townsend (ed.) (1971).

Baumol, W. J. (1977), *Economic Theory and Operations Analysis*, 4th edn., London: Prentice-Hall.

—— (1982), 'Contestable Markets: An Uprising in the Theory of Industry Structure', *American Economic Review*, 72, 1–15.

—— (ed.) (1986), *Micro theory: Applications and Origins*, Brighton: Wheatsheaf.

—— and Blinder, A. S. (1991), *Economics*, New York: Harcourt-Brace-Janovitch.

—— Panzar, J., and Willig, R. (1982), *Contestable Markets and the Theory of Industrial Structure*, New York: Harcourt-Brace-Janovitch.

Beauchamp, T., and Bowie, N. (eds.) (1988), *Ethical Theory and Business*, Englefield Cliffs, NJ: Prentice-Hall.

Besanko, D., Dranove, D., and Shanley, M. (1996), *Economics of Strategy*, New York: John Wiley.

Bidault, Francis, and Cummings, Thomas (1996), *Mastering Management, Part 19*, London: The *Financial Times*.

Bishop, M., and Kay, J. A. (eds.), *European Mergers and Merger Policy*, Oxford: Oxford University Press.

Boston Consulting Group (1972), *Perspectives on Experience*, Boston: Boston Consulting Group.

—— (1981), *Les mecanismes fondamentaux de la competitivité, Hommes et Techniques*, Paris: Boston Consulting Group.

Brealey, R., and Myers, S. (1991), *Principles of Corporate Finance*, New York: McGraw Hill.

Britton, A., and Pain, N. (1992), 'Economic Forecasting in Britain', *National Institute of Economic and Social Research*, Report No. 4, Chapter 4.

Burns, A. F., and Mitchell, W. C. (1938), *Statistical Indicators of Cyclical Revivals*, New York: NBER.

Ceccini, P. (1989), *The European Challenge 1992—The Benefits of a Single Market*, Wildwood House Edition, Aldershot: Gower.

Central Statistical Office (1993), 'CSO Cyclical Indicators', *Economic Trends*, July, London: HMSO.

—— (1995), 'Leading Indicators', *Economic Trends*, Oct., London: HMSO.

Chamberlin, E. H. (1933), *The Theory of Monopolistic Competition*, Harvard University Press.

Chandler, A. D. (1990), 'The Enduring Logic of Industrial Success', *Harvard Business Review*, Mar.

Charkham, J. (1994), *Keeping Good Company*, Oxford: Oxford University Press.

Chipman, J. S. (1965), 'The Nature and Meaning of Equilibrium in Economic Theory', in Townsend (1971).

Chrystal, K. A., and Lipsey, R. G. (1997), *Economics for Business and Management*, Oxford: Oxford University Press.

Coase, R. H. (1937), 'The Nature of the Firm', *Economica* NS, 4: 386–405, reprinted as chapter 2 in O. E. Williamson and S. G. Winter (eds.) (1993), *The Nature of the Firm*, Oxford: Oxford University Press.

—— (1960), 'The Problem of Social Cost', *Journal of Law and Economics*, 3: 1–44.

Cobb, Charles W., and Douglas, Paul H. (1928), 'A Theory of Production'. *American Economic Review*, 18 (1, suppl.), 139–65.

Cropper, M. L., and Oates, W. E. (1992) 'Environmental Economics: A Survey', *Journal of Economic Literature*, 30: 675–740.

Cross, R., Darby, J., and Ireland, J. (1996), 'Hysteresis and Ranges or Intervals for Equilibrium Unemployment', paper presented for Conference on European Unemployment, Florence, 21–22 Nov.

Dicks, G., and Burrell, A. (1994), 'Forecasting in Practice', in Hall (1994).

Dixit, A. K., and Nalebuff, B. J. (1991), *Thinking Strategically: The Competitive Edge in Business, Politics, and Everyday Life*, New York: W. .W. Norton and Co.

—— and Pindyck, R. S. (1994), *Investment under Uncertainty*, Princeton: Princeton University Press.

Dunning, J. H. (1988), *Explaining International Production*, London: Unwin Hyman.

—— (1993), *The Globalisation of Business*, London: Routledge.

Elliot, R. F. (1991), *Labour Economics*, London: McGraw-Hill.

Emerson, M. *et al.* (1988), *The Economics of 1992: The EC Commission Assessment and the Economic Effects of Completing the Internal Market*, London: Oxford University Press, for the Commission of the European Communities.

Enders, W. (1995), *Applied Econometric Time Series*, New York: Wiley.

'The Economics of 1992', *European Economy* (1988), No.

35, Mar., Luxembourg: Commission of the European Communities.

Galbraith, J. K. (1967), *The New Industrial State*, London: Hamish Hamilton.

Geroski, P., and Vlassapoulos, A. (1990), 'European Merger Activity: A Response to 1992', in *Continental Mergers are Different*, Centre for Business Strategy, London Business School.

Grant, R. M. (1991), *Contemporary Strategy Analysis*, Oxford: Blackwell.

Hall, R. E., and Jorgenson, D. W. (1967), 'Tax Policy and Investment Behaviour', *American Economic Review*, 57, June, 391–414.

Hall, S. (ed.) (1994), *Applied Econometric Forecasting Techniques*, Hemel Hempstead: Harvester Wheatsheaf.

Hay, D. A., and Morris, D. J. (1991), *Industrial Economics and Organization*, Oxford: Oxford University Press.

Henderson, B. D. (1973), *The Experience Curve Reviewed*, Boston: Boston Consulting Group.

Hibbs Jnr., D. A. (1987), *The American Political Economy*, Cambridge, Mass.: Harvard University Press.

Hirschman, W. B. (1964), 'Profits from the Learning Curve', *Harvard Business Review*, 42: 125–39.

HMSO (1978), *A Review of Monopolies and Mergers Policy: Consultative Document*, London: HMSO.

Holden, K., Peel, D. A., and Thompson, J. L. (1990), *Economic Forecasting: An Introduction*, Cambridge: Cambridge University Press.

Jackson, T. (1997), *Inside Intel*, New York: HarperCollins.

Katz, M. L., and Rosen, H. S. (1991), *Microeconomics*, Boston: Irwin.

Kay, J. (1993), *Foundations of Corporate Success*, Oxford: Oxford University Press.

Keating, G. (1985), *The Production and Use of Economic Forecasts*, London: Methuen.

Kenen, P. B. (1994), *The International Economy*, 2nd edn., Cambridge: Cambridge University Press.

Knight, F. H. (1921), *Risk, Uncertainty and Profit*, New York: Houghton Mifflin Company.

Kobrin, S. J. (1991), 'An Empirical Analysis of the Determinants of Global Integration', *Strategic Management Journal*, 12: 17–31.

Lieberman, M. B. (1984), 'The Learning Curve and Pricing in the Chemical Processing Industries', *RAND Journal of Economics*, summer, 213–28.

Linder, S. B. (1961), *An Essay on Trade and Transformation*, New York: John Wiley.

Lipsey, R. G., and Chrystal, K. A. (1999), *Principles of Economics* 9/e, Oxford: Oxford University Press.

Love, J. H., and Scouller, J. (1990), 'Growth by Acquisition: The Lessons of Experience', *Journal of General Management*, spring.

Lumby, S. (1988), *Investment Appraisal and Financing Decisions*, 3rd edn., Wokingham: Van Nostrand Reinhold.

Mackintosh, M., Brown, V., Costello, N., Dawson, G., Thompson, G., and Trigg, A. (1995), *Economics and Changing Economies*, Milton Keynes: International Thomson Business Press, for the Open University.

Maddison, A. (1991), *Dynamic Forces in Capitalist Development*, Oxford: Oxford University Press.

Mankiw, N. G. (1992), *Macroeconomics*, New York: Worth Publishers.

Markandya, A., and Richardson, J. (eds.) (1991), *The Earthscan Reader in Environmental Economics*, London: Earthscan.

Marris, R. (1964), *The Economic Theory of 'Managerial' Capitalism*, London: Macmillan.

Mercer Consultants (1997), *Survey of Large Mergers between 1987 and 1997*, New York.

Miller, G. J. (1994), *Managerial Dilemmas*, Cambridge: Cambridge University Press.

Minford, P., and Peel, D. (1982), 'The Political Theory of the Business Cycle', *European Economic Review*.

Monopolies and Mergers Commission (1976), *Indirect Elecrostatic Reprographic Equipment*, London: HMSO.

Moore, B. (1993), 'A Review of CSO Cyclical Indicators', *Economic Trends*, No. 477, July.

Myers, G. (1993), 'Barriers to Entry', *Economics and Business Education*.

Nelson, C. R. (1989) *The Investor's Guide to Economic Indicators*, New York: Wiley.

Nilson, R. 'OECD Leading Indicators', *Economic Studies*, No. 9, Paris: OECD.

Nordhaus, W. D. (1975), 'The Political Business Cycle', *Review of Economic Studies*.

OECD (1987), 'Leading Indicators and Business Cycles in Member Countries; 1965–1985', *OECD Main Economic Indicators—Sources and Methods*, No. 39, Jan., Paris: OECD.

Office of Fair Trading (1994), *Barriers to Entry and Exit in UK Competition Policy*, Research paper, London: Office of Fair Trading.

Ohlin, B. (1933), *International and Interregional Trade*, Cambridge, Mass.: Harvard University Press.

Parkin, M. and King, D. (1995), *Economics*, Wokingham: Addison-Wesley.

—— Powell, M. and Matthews, K. (1997), *Economics*, Wokingham: Addison-Wesley.

Peacock, A. and Bannock, G. (1989), *Take-overs and the Public Interest*, Aberdeen: Aberdeen University Press.

Perman, R., Ma, Y., and McGilvray, J. (1996), *Natural Resource and Environmental Economics*, Harlow: Longman.

Peteraf, M. A. (1993), 'The Cornerstones of Competitive Advantage: A Resource Based View', *Strategic Management Journal*, 14.

Peters, T. J., and Waterman Jr., R. H. (1982), *In Search of Excellence*, New York: Harper & Row.

Phillips, A. W. (1958), 'The Relation between Unemployment and the Rate of Change of Money Wage Rates in the UK 1861–1957', *Economica*, Nov.

Pike, R., and Neale, W. (1994), *Corporate Finance and*

Investment: Decisions and Strategies, Hemel Hempstead: Prentice-Hall.

Porter, M. (1980), *Competitive Strategy: Techniques for Analysing Industries and Competition*, New York: Free Press.

—— (1985), *Competitive Advantage: Creating and Sustaining Superior Performance*, New York: Free Press.

—— (1987), 'From Competitive Advantage to Corporate Strategy, *Harvard Business Review*, May–June.

—— (1990), *The Competitive Advantage of Nations*, London: Macmillan.

Prahalad, C. K., and Hamel, G. (1990), 'The Core Competence of the Corporation', *Harvard Business Review*, May.

Pratten, C. F. (1987), 'A Survey of the Economies of Scale', Report prepared for the EC Commission, Brussels.

Rappaport, A. (1992), 'CEOs and Strategists: Forging a Common Framework', *Harvard Business Review*, May–June, 84–91.

Reed, R., and Luffman, G. A. (1986), 'Diversification', *Strategic Management Journal*.

Rhys, G. (1993), 'Competition in the Car Industry', *Developments in Economics*, 9, Ormskirk: Causeway Press.

Ricardo, D. (1817), *On the Principles of Political Economy and Taxation*, 1971 edn., Harmondsworth: Penguin.

Ricketts, M. (1994), *The Economics of Business Enterprise*, 2nd edn., Hemel Hempstead: Harvester-Wheatsheaf.

Rogoff, K., and Sibert, A. (1988), 'Elections and Macroeconomic Policy Cycles', *Review of Economic Studies*, 55.

Ross, S. A., Westerfield, R. and Jordan, B. (1992), *Fundamentals of Corporate Finance*, 2nd edn., Boston: Richard D. Irwin.

Sadtler, D., Campbell, A., and Koch, R. (1998), *'Breakup!' When Large Companies are Worth more Dead than Alive*, Capstone.

Sangster, A. (1993), 'Capital Investment Appraisal Techniques: A Survey of Current Usage', *Journal of Business Finance and Accounting*, 20/3, Apr.

Scherer, F. M., and Ross, D. (1990), *Industrial Market Structure and Economic Performance*, 3rd edn., Boston: Houghton Mifflin.

Schmalensee, R., and Willig, R. D. (eds.) (1989), *Handbook of Industrial Organisation*, Amsterdam: North-Holland.

Schumpeter, J. (1943), *Capitalism, Socialism and Democracy*, London: Allen and Unwin.

Shank, J. K., and Govindarajan V. J. (1989), *Strategic Cost Analysis: The Evolution from Managerial to Strategic Accounting*, Homewood, Il.: Irwin.

Shepherd, W. G. (1990), *The Economics of Industrial Organisation*, New Jersey: Prentice-Hall.

Smith, A. (1776), *An Inquiry into the Nature and Causes of the Wealth of Nations*, London: Everyman edition, David Campbell Publishers, 1991.

Stalk, G., Evans, P., and Shulman, L. E. (1992), 'Competing on Capabilities: The New Rules of Corporate Strategy', *Harvard Business Review*, Mar.

Stutely, R. (1994), *The Economist Guide to Economic Indicators*, London: Penguin Books.

Tietenberg, T. H. (1990), 'Economic Instruments for Environmental Regulation', *Oxford Review of Economic Policy*, 6/1: 17–34.

Tirole, J. (1989), *The Theory of Industrial Organisation*, Cambridge, Mass.: MIT Press.

Townsend, H. (ed.) (1971), *Price Theory*, Harmondsworth: Penguin.

UN World Drug Report (1997), Oxford University Press for the UN Drugs Control Programme.

Varian, H. (1990), *Intermediate Microeconomics*, New York: Norton.

Vernon, R. (1966), 'International Investment and International Trade in the Product Cycle', *Quarterly Journal of Economics*, May.

Williamson, J. (1983), *The Open Economy and the World Economy*, New York: Basic Books.

Williamson, O. E. (1985), *The Economic Institutions of Capitalism*, New York: The Free Press.

Young, S., Hood, N., and Hamill, J. (1988), *Foreign Multinationals and the British Economy*, London: Croom Helm.

Index